ENCYCLOPEDIA OF UNION GENERALS

Encyclopedia of UNION GENERALS

Samuel W. Mitcham, Jr.

REGNERY
HISTORY

Copyright © 2025 by Samuel W. Mitcham, Jr.

All rights reserved. No part of this book may be reproduced in any manner without the express written consent of the publisher, except in the case of brief excerpts in critical reviews or articles. All inquiries should be addressed to Regnery History, 307 West 36th Street, 11th Floor, New York, NY 10018.

Regnery History books may be purchased in bulk at special discounts for sales promotion, corporate gifts, fund-raising, or educational purposes. Special editions can also be created to specifications. For details, contact the Special Sales Department, Regnery History, 307 West 36th Street, 11th Floor, New York, NY 10018 or info@skyhorsepublishing.com.

Regnery History® is an imprint of Skyhorse Publishing, Inc.®, a Delaware corporation.

Visit our website at www.regneryhistory.com.
Please follow our publisher Tony Lyons on Instagram @tonylyonsisuncertain.

10 9 8 7 6 5 4 3 2 1

Library of Congress Cataloging-in-Publication Data is available on file.

Cover design by David Ter-Avanesyan
Cover Painting by Ole Peter Hansen Balling

Print ISBN: 978-1-5107-8286-0
eBook ISBN: 978-1-5107-8525-0

Printed in the United States of America

Contents

INTRODUCTION		VII
A	ABERCROMBIE – AYERS	1
B	BAILEY – BUTTERFIELD	21
C	CADWALADER – CUTLER	97
D	DANA – DYER	165
E	EATON – EWING	203
F	FAIRCHILD – FULLER	219
G	GAMBLE – GROVER	245
H	HACKLEMAN – HURLBUT	287
I	INGALLS	359
J	JACKSON – JUDAH	363
K	KANE – KRZYZANOWSKI	377
L	LANDER – LYTLE	403
M	MACKENZIE – MOWER	427
N	NAGLE – NICKERSON	499
O	OGLESBY – OWEN	511
P	PAINE – PRINCE	523
Q	QUINBY	573
R	RAMSAY – RUTHERFORD	577
S	SALOMON – SYKES	617
T	TAYLOR – TYNDALE	723
U	ULLMAN – UPTON	753
V	VAN ALEN – VOGDES	759
W	WADE – WRIGHT	773
Z	ZOOK	831

APPENDIX I: BRIEF CHRONOLOGY OF THE CIVIL WAR — 835

APPENDIX II: BRIEF CHRONOLOGY OF THE MEXICAN WAR — 845

BIBLIOGRAPHY — 849

INTRODUCTION

INTRODUCTION

Who were the Union generals? Simply put, they were the men who won the war for the United States. I know this is an oversimplication, but on the battlefield—"where the rubber met the road"—to use a twenty-first-century expression, they won the war for the North.

The purpose of this book is to provide a short biography of each of the 588 Union generals. When they finish this book, I want the readers to feel that they know something about each Union general—at least glancingly. I would like them to feel they at least have an idea about how well each general did his job.

Occasionally, I will provide my evaluation of a general's ability or character, or how well he handled a particular event or situation. I am a graduate of Command and General Staff College and am qualified through the rank of major general. I also have a PhD, was a professor for twenty years, and am the author of more than forty books on military history, so I am perhaps not completely without qualifications to make an assessment. In the final analysis, however, the readers must draw their own conclusions. They may take my opinion on a particular matter as a pearl of wisdom or a piece of garbage, however they choose.

Space does not allow me to provide an in-depth anaylsis of the Union's upper military echelon—generals like Grant, Sherman, Sheridan, McClellan, etc. An essay on these are included, but they have been covered in many books. The reader may find the biographical essays of people like Martin Curtis, Emory Upton, William Francis Bartlett, or George L. Hartsuff more edifying. They were heroes of the first order, but many people know little or nothing about them. Not all 588 Union generals were heroes, of course. A few were quite the opposite and some were somewhere in between. But the Union generals were human beings, after all, and therefore imperfect. My purpose is to describe them "warts and all." This will no doubt offend some people. Many people offend so easily these days, mainly because they enjoy it so much. My advice to these people is: grow up!

Another question which needs to be asked is: "Who was a Union general?" This question only surprises the novice because there were, in a sense, four Union armies: the United States Army (hereafter cited as the Regular Army); the Regular Army officers who were brevet (i.e., honorary)

INTRODUCTION

general officers; the United States Volunteer general officers; and the volunteer officers who were generals by brevet only.

Because the antebellum U.S. Army did not pass out medals like it does today, it rewarded people by giving them "brevets" or honorary promotions. They were addressed by their brevet rank but paid at their Regular Army or substantive rank, which was always lower. This system also saved the parsimonious antebellum army of that day some money.

The United States Army (Regular Army) officers were the professional, career soldiers. They often had two ranks: their volunteer rank and their U.S.A. or Regular Army rank. A good example is George Armstrong Custer. He was commissioned second lieutenant on June 24, 1861. He was promoted to first lieutenant three weeks later and to captain, staff rank, on June 5, 1862. He was promoted to brigadier general of volunteers on June 29, 1863, and later earned Regular Army brevets to lieutenant colonel, colonel, brigadier, and major general. He was appointed major general of volunteers on April 24, 1865, to rank from April 15. He was, however, still only a captain in the Regular Army. He was mustered out of the volunteer service on February 1, 1866, and reverted to his Regular Army rank of captain. In the reorganization following the end of the Civil War, he was given the permanent (Regular Army) rank of lieutenant colonel in the 7th Cavalry, effective July 28, 1866. This was the rank he held when he died. To avoid confusion, most Civil War brevets will not be mentioned in this book because they are generally, for practical purposes, irrelevant. In the summer of 1863, for example, Custer was a brigadier general commanding a brigade of cavalry on the Eastern Front. He was also brevetted major, Regular Army, for his services at Gettysburg. I am sure he considered this a good thing, but it really didn't mean very much—and Custer knew it.

Incidentally, the term "Regular Army" was not regularly used in the 1860s; they commonly used the term "U.S.A." (United States Army) for career officers. Regular Army is used in this book to avoid confusion and to conform to modern usage.

There were also 1,367 men who were Union generals by brevet only. They will not be covered in this book. This is not to imply they were not worthy—almost all of them were. Some of them commanded brigades or even divisions and materially contributed to the ultimate Northern victory.

ix

Others held substantive ranks as low as captain, and their brevets were honorary in the extreme. To include them all, however, would bring the total number of Union generals to 1,955 and would require at least three volumes (see below). I hope someday someone does write a book or a dissertation about the Union brevet brigadier generals. But it won't be me! I do, however, wish them the very best in this endeavor.

Another issue which needs to be clarified is the date of promotion, which is frequently mistaken for the date of rank (DOR). Often they are the same date, but by no means always. Usually, they only differ by a day or so, but sometimes they are months apart. Many historians—including at least two of the very best—use the date of rank as the date of promotion. This is incorrect. The appropriate date, in my view, is the date of appointment, usually by President Lincoln. A good example is the case of John Buford. He was a brigadier general commanding a cavalry division on July 1, 1863, when he so capably and heroically staved off a Union disaster at Gettysburg by preventing the Confederates from seizing the high ground south of the town. Some authors cite July 1 as the date he became a major general. But it wasn't. He was still a brigadier general on July 2 and on November 21, for that matter. He was severely ill that day with typhoid fever and was taken to Washington, D.C., to the home of his good friend, Major General George Stoneman, so he could receive the best medical care. He was also suffering from severe rheumatism, general exhaustion, and depression caused by the recent death of his six-year-old daughter. At first, Buford improved, but then he contracted pneumonia, and on the morning of December 16, it was clear he would not survive.

Stoneman ignored several layers of the chain of command, went directly to the White House, and asked Abraham Lincoln to promote Buford to major general immediately. Lincoln referred the matter to Secretary of War Edwin Stanton, who (for reasons I never understood) distrusted the capable Buford and did not want to promote him. But when he was assured that Buford was, in fact, dying, Stanton relented and agreed to the promotion. Lincoln promulgated the appointment immediately,

INTRODUCTION

citing Buford's "distinguished and meritorious service at the Battle of Gettysburg." He listed the date of rank as July 1.

When he learned that he was being promoted, Buford rose up from his deathbed and asked, "Does he mean it?" He then lay back on his pillows and muttered: "It is too late. Now I wish I could live." He passed away at 2 p.m. that same day. His promotion was dated December 16, 1863, with a date of rank of July 1.

I believe there are three books which are indispensable in researching Union generals: *Civil War High Commands* by John H. Eicher and David J. Eicher; George W. Cullem's *Biographical Register of the Officers and Graduates of the United States Military Academy*; and Ezra Warner's *Generals in Blue*. All books on Union and Confederate generals must forever be measured against Warner's *Generals in Blue* and *Generals in Gray*. He averred that there were 583 Union generals, excluding brevets. His source was the *Memorandum Relative to the General Officers in the Armies of the United States during the Civil War*, which the U.S. War Department published in 1906. It is perhaps ironic that this listing was compiled by Marcus J. Wright, formerly major general, Confederate States Army (Warner, *Generals in Blue*, p. xx). I disagree with Wright (and therefore Warner) on a couple of minor points and have not included four of his generals in my essays. For example, Warner lists David Henry Williams as a brigadier general as of November 29, 1862, but the *Official Records* (Vol. XXI, p. 60 and XXV, Part 2, p. 26) state that he was a colonel commanding the 82nd Pennsylvania Infantry Regiment during the Battle of Fredericksburg (December 11 to 15). The *Official Records* do not list Williams as a brigadier general or ever commanding a brigade.

On the other hand, I believe seven men—John M. Chivington, James Henry Lane, William Warren Lowe, Thomas Lawson Price, Adolf von Steinwehr, Roy Stone, and Robert Williams—qualify as Union generals but were not listed as such by General Wright. I have included essays on them. Three men are questionable: James Lawlor Kiernan, Edmund Kirby, and William W. Lowe. Kiernan is not listed as generals in the *Official Records* or Eicher, but is included in Warner. William W. Lowe is not included in

Introduction

Warner but is included in Eicher. Edmund Kirby was a first lieutenant who was mortally wounded at Chancellorsville. Lincoln appointed him brigadier general on May 28, 1863—the day he died. Warner lists him as a general. I have erred on the side of caution and included essays on all three. I have not included James Oakes, who was listed in Eicher but not in Warner. He was appointed brigadier general on August 7, 1861 but declined to serve as such. He spent the entire war as a field grade Regular Army officer.[1] I have also included Friend Smith Rutherford, who was not listed in Warner. A colonel, he submitted his resignation on June 15, 1864. He died of chronic diarrhea five days later. Meanwhile, Lincoln nominated him for brigadier general on June 18, but Rutherford never knew it. All of this brings the total number of Union generals to 588.

The Civil War was essentially fought by the volunteer. Regular Army troops constituted only three percent of Union troops—and more than half of those joined the "Regulars" during the war. When the South seceded, only 16,367 Regular Army troops were on the rolls, of which 14,657 were present for duty. Of these, 1,108 were officers (about 75 percent of whom were West Point graduates). Two hundred seventy of the 1,108 "went South." During the war, 2,898,304 men served in the Union Army, which formed 2,125 volunteer regiments during the conflict. Only nineteen Regular Army regiments existed when the war began. There were simply not enough trained officers to go around.

According to Clayton R. Newell in his excellent little book, *The Regular Army Before the Civil War* (pp. 51–52), there were 750 West Point graduates available in December 1860. Of these, 168 joined the Confederacy, while 556 remained loyal to the Union. Twenty-six took no active part in the war at all. These numbers were somewhat balanced by the 194 West Pointers who had left the army. Of these, 102 returned to the colors, while 92 joined the South.

The West Pointers had a disproportionate impact on the war, but that was not always good. As Napoleon said, "In war, as in prostitution, the

---

1 Field grade officers are majors, lieutenant colonels, and colonels.

amateur sometimes outperforms the professional." The reader should keep in mind that the United States Military Academy at West Point, then as now, produces second lieutenants. There were a handful of army schools operating in 1861, such as the Cavalry School for Practice at Carlilse Barracks, Pennsylvania, but not many more. Today, an American officer who spends twenty years in the service can expect to spend eight of them in various schools. Mr. Lincoln's army (like Mr. Davis's) had only a rudimentary training infrastructure by today's standards. They had no Infantry Officer Basic Course, Engineer Officer Advanced Course, Ranger School, Command and General Staff College, Industrial War College, etc. Certainly they had nothing that even approached the Prussian War Academy.

There were only five generals in the 1860 U.S. Army and one of them joined the boys in gray. Similar deficiencies are seen at every level in both the Union and Confederate armies. OJT (On-the-job) training might be fine in the civilian economy under certain circumstances, but the battlefield is no place for it; however, the Northern and Southern armies had no other choice. This is one of the primary reasons we lost so many young Americans in the Civil War. Thousands of men fell "training" their officers—or weeding out the incompetents. The discerning reader will pick up on that in *Encyclopedia of Union Generals*, as well as in *Encyclopedia of Confederate Generals*.

ORGANIZATION OF THE ARMY

Company: The smallest traditional military unit, it was usually recruited and organized locally. In 1861, it typically consisted of sixty to one hundred men, although some might be higher or lower. Naturally, this number decreased as the war wore on, for obvious reasons. It was normally commanded by a captain. Cavalry companies were sometimes called **Troops**. Companies were often divided into smaller formations, such as platoons, sections, and squads.

Battery: The artillery equivalent of a company, it normally included four to six artillery pieces and eighty to one hundred men and was commanded by a captain. Two guns were generally commanded by a lieutenant and were called a **section**. Single guns were commanded by sergeants.

Battalion: normally two per regiment, consisting of two to five companies each. (There is no rule of thumb here.) Some independent battalions were not under a regimental headquarters. Quite a few had only eight companies. Battalions were usually commanded by a lieutenant colonel or a major. Some regiments did not have subordinate battalions. Cavalry battalions were sometimes designated **squadrons** and were usually smaller than infantry battalions; they frequently consisted of only two companies. An artillery battalion might consist of two to eight batteries.

Regiment: the fundamental combat unit of the Union Army, it consisted of a regimental staff and ten companies, or six hundred to one thousand men. Cavalry regiments tended to be smaller and contained two to six squadrons. Normally a colonel commanded them, although it was not unusual for lieutenant colonels, majors, and even captains to direct a regiment. Artillery regiments often totalled 1,800 men, although heavy artillery regiments were smaller (about 1,200 men). There were always exceptions in the infantry, cavalry, and artillery.

Brigades: usually consisted of four regiments, plus a brigade staff and support units, but might include two to ten regiments. It was normally commanded by a colonel or brigadier general.

Divisions: consisted of two to six brigades, a divisional staff, and supporting units, including artillery, and a major general or brigadier general usually led them, although sometimes the commander was a colonel.

Corps: two to six divisions, a staff, and supporting units.

Armies: two to eight corps, although some had only divisions and did not have intermediate corps headquarters.

Military Division (called army groups today): controlled one or more armies and/or more than one department (i.e., territorial) command.

All units had supply trains or at least supply wagons. Higher units also controlled medical units, hospitals, quartermaster, ordnance, mess hall, labor battalions, provost marshal troops, and other support and service support formations. There were so many varieties of situations in the Civil War that Union formations had to adjust to, that practically any organizational structure the reader can imagine did occur, at one time and place or another.

Union Rank Structure (lowest to highest): private; corporal; sergeant; first sergeant; sergeant major; third lieutenant (which was rare); second lieutenant; first lieutenant; captain; major; lieutenant colonel; colonel; brigadier general; major general; lieutenant general; and general (established 1866). There were a few special ranks, such as quartermaster sergeant (equivalent to a sergeant major) or ordnance sergeant (equivalent to a first sergeant).

HOUSEKEEPING DETAILS

One flaw the Union Army failed to correct until 1864 was that it only had two grades of general officer: brigadier ("one star") general and major ("two star") general. It did have one lieutenant general—Winfield Scott—but he held this rank by brevet only. It only had one lieutenant general (full rank) during the entire war. Ulysses S. Grant was promoted to lieutenant general on March 4, 1864, to rank from March 2. Grant did not become a full general (i.e., four star general) until January 25, 1866—several months after the South surrendered. William T. Sherman also became a lieutenant general several months after Grant. And—remarkably enough—there the list ends.

The Confederacy also began the war with two grades of generals but quickly realized it needed more. In August 1861, it created the rank of "general," (i.e., full general). The following year, it created the rank of lieutenant general, which was intermediate between general and major general. It fought its war with four grades of general officer, while the much larger U.S. Army essentially had only two. This created problems for the North, which it could have avoided, as the more astute reader will discern. A great many colonels commanded brigades and should have been promoted to brigadier general but never were. (Many of these were brevetted to that rank in the omnibus promotions after the war.) The Union army did retain the "general-in-chief," a *de facto* third rank, held at different times by Scott, McClellan, Halleck, and Grant, which partially alleviated the problem, but only at the highest level. The South did not appoint a general-in-chief until February 1865, when it was too late to do any good.

INTRODUCTION

All West Point cadets were commissioned on July 1 of their graduation year unless otherwise indicated. This happened very rarely except in 1861, when the entire class graduated a few weeks early because of the outbreak of the Civil War, and the United States needed every trained officer it could get.

Pre-war, many West Point cadets graduated as "brevet second lieutenants." They were, in effect, third lieutenants. They were normally promoted to second lieutenant within a year.

Although the term "Chief of Staff" was extensively used in the Civil War, it was not as widely used then as it is today. In the 1860s, the Assistant Adjutant General often served as the *de facto* chief of staff. This was more likely to take place in the Confederate Army, but it occurred in the Union Army as well.

The North (and South) also had territorial commands. The largest was the department, followed by the district and the subdistrict. Occupied cities and major towns were controlled by commandants. Many departments, districts, etc., controlled combat units. They had to. It was not enough for the Union legions to conquer a particular territory. It had to control it, or the Rebels would cut their supply lines. Confederate guerillas and raiders such as Bedford Forrest and John Hunt Morgan were famous for raising havoc in the Union rear. Ulysses S. Grant, for example, abandoned his Mississippi Central offensive in December 1862 and retreated back to the Tennessee border, despite the fact that he outnumbered the Confederate Army of Mississippi more than two to one. He was not defeated in the field. But Confederate General Earl Van Dorn destroyed his main supply depot at Holly Springs and Nathan Bedford Forrest destroyed his rail lines in western Tennessee so thoroughly that they could not be used again until after the war. Grant had no choice but to retreat, because he did not have enough food or ammunition to sustain his offensive.

The starting point for any book on Union generals is Ezra Warner's *Generals in Blue*. Nothing I have written above should be intrepretated as criticism of Warner; to the contrary, I have nothing but respect for his work and admiration for him as a historian. His work was published in 1964, and it is hard to conceive how he did it without the internet, which has made the life of a Civil War historian so much easier. Much has been written on the Civil War in the past half-century, however, and new information has been unearthed, so I felt it was time for another look at the generals in blue.

One book often overlooked by historians is *Civil War High Commands* by John H. and David J. Eicher. It is huge (+1,000 pages) and pricey, but worth every penny and is cheap at twice the price. If I had to list any Civil War reference books as indispensable, this would make the short list. Also indispensable is *The War of the Rebellion: A Compilation of the Official Records of the Union and Confederate Armies* (Washington, D.C.: 1880–1901).

Another valuable resource is *Medical Histories of Union Generals* by Dr. Jack D. Welsh, M.D. I consider it the definitive source on the medical histories of the Federal generals.

All ranks mentioned in the period 1861 to 1866 are volunteer ranks, unless otherwise indicated.

The North and South disagreed about many things. One of them was what to name certain battles. The North tended to name them after the nearest stream. The South usually named them after the nearest place. What the Confederates called the Battle of Sharpsburg, for example, was (is) called the Battle of Antietam in the North. Since this is a book on Union generals, Union place names will take precedence here.

Finally, a word about footnotes. Essentially, there aren't any—just a handful of informational notes. Some readers will wish there were more. So do I. But the typical book is sixty thousand to seventy thousand words long and this book exceeds 250,000 words with almost six hundred photographs and is approaching multi-volume territory. Multi-volume books generally lose money, which publishers understandably loathe to do, so the choice is simple: cut the footnotes, cut the information, cut the photographs, or scrap the project altogether. I chose the first alternative. Now I get to listen to the critics whine about the lack of footnotes. But that's okay, let them have their fun, for as Finnish composer and poet Jean Sibelius said, "No one ever erected a statue to a critic."

A

· ABERCROMBIE – AYERS ·

JOHN JOSEPH ABERCROMBIE was born in Baltimore, Maryland, on March 4, 1798. He entered the United States Military Academy at West Point in 1817 and graduated in 1822 (37/40)[2] and spent the next forty-three years in the army, mainly in infantry regiments. Between tours of garrison duty, he fought in the Black Hawk War in 1832 and against the Seminoles in Florida (1837). Meanwhile, he was promoted to first lieutenant (1828) and captain (1836) and was brevetted major for his conduct in the Battle of Lake Okeechobee, Florida.

Abercrombie fought in the Mexican War and was wounded at Monterrey on September 23, 1846, after which he was brevetted lieutenant colonel. He received substantive promotions to major (1847) and lieutenant colonel (1852); and did more garrison duty in the Northwest. He founded Fort Abercrombie in Dakota (now North Dakota) in 1857. On February 25, 1861, he was promoted to colonel, Regular Army, and was named commander of the 7th Infantry Regiment then stationed in Minnesota.

When the Civil War began, Abercrombie was one of the oldest field officers in either army. He nevertheless commanded a brigade in the Department of Pennsylvania. Under the overall command of his father-in-law, General Robert Patterson, he fought against Stonewall Jackson in the minor Union victory in the Battle of Falling Waters on July 2, 1861. He was promoted to brigadier general on August 31, 1861.[3]

After commanding a brigade in Maryland and in the Shenandoah Valley, he led a mixed brigade of New York and Pennsylvania troops in the Virginia Peninsula and was slightly wounded in the head during the Battle of Seven Pines (Fair Oaks) on May 31, 1862.[4] General Abercrombie distinguished himself by repelling a Confederate attack in the Battle of Malvern

---

2 For West Point graduates, this abbreviation indicates the general's class rank and the size of the class. In this case, Abercrombie finished 37th in a class of forty. All West Point graduation dates (and commissioning dates) are July 1, unless otherwise indicated. All generals completed the course in four years, unless otherwise stated.

3 All Civil War ranks cited hereafter are volunteer (U.S.V.) ranks unless otherwise stated.

4 Appendix 1 provides a brief chronology of the Civil War, including the dates of the major battles and campaigns.

Hill (July 1). His brigade suffered 624 casualties, including 124 killed and 67 missing, during the Seven Days fighting.

Abercrombie briefly commanded a division in the IV Corps of the Army of the Potomac in July and August 1862 but did not see any major fighting. Considered competent but too old for active campaigning, he spent the rest of the war commanding depots in Washington, D.C., and Virginia. Unemployed from June 1864 to March 1865, he was commander of Fort Schuyler, New York, at the end of the war.

John Abercrombie retired on June 12, 1865. He nevertheless spent 1866–1869 on court-martial duty.

General Abercrombie retired to Roslyn, Long Island, New York, where he died on January 3, 1877, at age seventy-eight. He is buried in The Woodlands Cemetery, Philadelphia.

ROBERT ALLEN was born in West Point, Ohio, on March 15, 1811, and was educated in local public schools. He graduated from the U.S. Military Academy at West Point in 1836 (33/49), and was commissioned brevet second lieutenant in the artillery. Promotions to second lieutenant (1836), first lieutenant (1838), captain, staff (1846) and major (May 17, 1861) followed. After ten years' garrison duty, mostly on the U.S.–Canadian border, he first saw action with Winfield Scott's army during the Mexican War and was brevetted major for his gallant conduct in the Battle of Cerro Gordo (April 18, 1847).

His real talent, however, lay in the field of logistics. He transferred to the quartermaster branch, where he became known for his incredible efficiency. He was chief quartermaster for the Department of the Pacific when the Civil War began.

Allen served as chief quartermaster of the Department of Missouri (1861–1863) and the Military Division of the Mississippi (1863–1865). He was responsible for transporting and supplying Union forces in several major campaigns, including Vicksburg and Atlanta. His sterling performance kept the Union divisions on the Western and Trans–Mississippi fronts well supplied and resulted in Allen's promotions to colonel, staff

(February 19, 1862), and brigadier general (May 23, 1863). He was brevetted major general in 1866.

After the war, Allen reverted to the rank of colonel, staff. He served as assistant quartermaster general of the army from 1866 until his retirement in 1878. He died while traveling in Europe on August 5, 1886, at age seventy-five, and is buried at the Cimetiere de Chene-Bougeries in Geneva, Switzerland.

BENJAMIN ALVORD was born in Rutland, Vermont, on August 18, 1813. He entered West Point in 1829 and graduated in 1833 (22/43). Commissioned brevet second lieutenant, he was assigned to the 4th Infantry and spent twenty-one years of his career with that regiment, mostly in Indian Territory (now Oklahoma) and in the Pacific Northwest. He also briefly served as an assistant professor of mathematics at West Point. He was promoted to second lieutenant in 1835 and to first lieutenant in 1836.

Alvord fought in the Seminole Wars and was on garrison duty on the frontier when the Mexican War began. He took part in the military occupation of Texas and fought at Palo Alto and Resaca de la Palma, for which he was brevetted captain.[5] He was chief of staff to General Riley during the drive from Vera Cruz to Mexico City and earned a brevet to major and a substantive promotion to captain, staff (1847).

After Mexico, Alvord joined the Paymaster branch, although he did return to the 4th Infantry for a tour of duty in California and Oregon. He was promoted to major in 1854 and was chief paymaster in Oregon from 1854 to 1862. On April 16, 1862, he was promoted to brigadier general of volunteers and was named commander of the Department of Oregon, which included the present-day states of Washington and Idaho. He remained in this backwater post until March 23, 1865, when he resigned his volunteer rank and became paymaster for units in and around New York City. In the meantime, he became a noted mathematician and wrote extensively on natural history and winter grazing in the Rocky Mountains.

---

5 Appendix 2 gives a brief chronology of the major battles and events of the Mexican War.

Benjamin Alvord emerged from the war as a lieutenant colonel in the Regular Army. He was promoted to colonel in the Paymaster branch in 1872. Later that year, he became Paymaster General of the Army. He was promoted to brigadier general in 1876 and retired in 1880.

General Alvord died in Washington, D.C., on October 16, 1884, at age seventy-one. He is buried in Rutland, Vermont. One of his six children, Benjamin Alvord, Jr., became a brigadier general and was adjutant of the American Expeditionary Force in Europe during World War I.

ADELBERT AMES was born on October 31, 1835, in East Thomaston (now Rockland), Maine, the son of a sea captain. Adelbert was a sailor aboard a chipper ship before he entered West Point in 1856. He graduated on May 6, 1861 (5/45) and was commissioned into the artillery. He was promoted to first lieutenant eight days later.

As a battery commander in the 5th U.S. Artillery,[6] Ames fought in the 1st Battle of Bull Run, where he was seriously wounded in the right thigh but refused to leave his guns. He was brevetted major and, in 1893, was awarded the Congressional Medal of Honor for his actions on July 21, 1861. He was on wounded leave until September. Uncommonly brave, he commanded a battery in the Peninsula and Seven Days Campaigns, where he was brevetted lieutenant colonel for his actions at Malvern Hill.

Realizing that the infantry offered better prospects for promotion, Ames returned home, where he secured command of the 20th Maine Infantry Regiment, along with a promotion to colonel, on August 20, 1862. He led the 20th at Antietam and Fredericksburg. During the Chancellorsville Campaign, he served as aide to General Meade, the commander of the V Corps. Probably due to Meade's influence, he was promoted to brigadier general on May 20 and was given command of a brigade.

Part of the XI Corps, Ames's brigade performed well at Gettysburg. When Francis C. Barlow was wounded and captured, Ames assumed

---

[6] All units mentioned in this book are regiments, unless otherwise indicated.

command of his division and held East Cemetery Hill, where he fought the Rebels hand-to-hand. He reverted to brigade command after Gettysburg. Sent to South Carolina, he took part in a series of unsuccessful operations against Charleston. In April 1864, he was transferred to Benjamin Butler's Army of the James and, as a division commander, was part of its failed attempts to capture Richmond. Bottled up in the Bermuda Hundred peninsula, he briefly commanded the X Corps in November 1864. He and his men were transferred to North Carolina that winter, and Ames led the successful assault on Fort Fisher on January 15, 1865. He was brevetted major general on January 23.

Ames reverted to the Regular Army rank of captain after the war but was promoted to lieutenant colonel in 1866 and became commander of the District of Raleigh, North Carolina. When the governor of Mississippi was deposed by the Federal Army in June 1868, Ames was named provisional governor of the state.

John F. Kennedy later wrote: "No state suffered more from carpetbag rule than Mississippi." Whether Ames was personally corrupt is a matter of historical debate, but many of the people he appointed definitely were. "Taxes increased to a level fourteen times as high as normal in order to support the extravagances of the reconstruction government . . ." Kennedy noted. Ames held office until March 10, 1870. A radical Republican, he was elected to the U.S. Senate, where he served from February 24, 1870 to January 10, 1874. He was elected governor of Mississippi on January 4, 1874. Ex-Confederates were not allowed to vote in this election.

During his second term, Governor Ames was unable to maintain order. His reign was characterized by widespread racial unrest and violence, riots, lynchings, voter fraud, corruption, and voter intimidation. To suppress the white supremacists, Ames called out the state militia and asked for federal military intervention, but President Grant refused to send in the troops. The Democrats won the election of 1875, and it was obvious they had the votes to impeach Ames and his African American lieutenant governor. Ames made a deal: He would resign if all articles of impeachment against him were dropped. They were. He stepped down on March 29, 1876.

After leaving office, Ames engaged in the flour-milling business and lived in Northfield, Minnesota; New York City; and Tewksbury,

Massachusetts. He rejoined the army as a brigadier general in 1898 and served in Cuba during the Spanish-American War. He was mustered out as a division commander.

Ames died at his winter home in Ormond Beach, Florida, on April 13, 1933, at age ninety-seven—the last of the Civil War generals who had substantive rank to pass away. (Brigadier General Aaron Daggett died in 1938 at age 100, but he held brevet rank only.) Ames is buried in Hildreth Cemetery, Lowell, Massachusetts.

General Ames married Blanche Butler, the daughter of Benjamin Butler, in 1870. They had six children.

JACOB "JAKE" AMMEN was born in Fincastle, Virginia, on January 7, 1806, but his parents moved to Georgetown, Ohio, when he was a small child. Educated in local schools, he graduated from West Point in 1831 (12/33). Commissioned second lieutenant, he was an assistant professor of mathematics at West Point until the autumn of 1832, when he was stationed in Charleston, South Carolina, as part of the 1st Artillery Regiment during the Nullification Crisis of 1832–33. He was sent back to West Point in 1834 as an assistant professor and was promoted to first lieutenant in 1836 but resigned his commission the following year and pursued a career in education. He taught at Bacon College (now Transylvania University) (1838–40), Jefferson College (1840–43), and Indiana University (1843–55), where he became chair of the Department of Mathematics. He left academia in 1855, became a civil engineer, and lived in Ripley, Ohio. Meanwhile, he used his family connections to help his friend, Ulysses S. Grant, garner an appointment to West Point.

Ammen joined the army immediately after the Rebels fired on Fort Sumter. Initially a captain in the 12th Ohio,[7] he helped build Camps Dennison and Chase, and was promoted to lieutenant colonel on May 2.

---

7   All Union formations are volunteer infantry regiments unless otherwise stated.

Ammen was named colonel of the 24th Ohio on June 22, 1861. The regiment served in western Virginia and fought in the Union victory at Cheat Mountain. Transferred to the Western Front, Ammen led a brigade at Shiloh and during the Siege of Corinth. Although a stern disciplinarian who occasionally hung offenders up by their thumbs, he was well respected by his men, who called him "Uncle Jake." He was promoted to brigadier general on July 19, 1862.

Jacob Ammen's health failed him in the fall of 1862, and he spent the next year in rear area or backwater assignments, including commandant of the prison facility of Camp Douglas, the Department of Middle Tennessee (late 1863), and the District of Kentucky (December 1863–February 1864). In February 1864, Ammen was named commander of the 4th Division of the XXIII Corps, which headquartered in Knoxville. He was simultaneously commander of the District of East Tennessee, and effectively exercised a territorial, rather than combat, command, although some of his units occasionally skirmished with small bands of Rebels. Ammen commanded East Tennessee until January 4, 1865, when he resigned his commission and returned home.

Post-war, General Ammen worked as a farmer, surveyor, and civil engineer. He also served on a survey commission which selected routes for the Panama Canal. Blind by 1891, he lived with a son in Lockland, Ohio, until his death on February 6, 1894, at age eighty-seven. He is buried in Spring Grove Cemetery, Cincinnati.

ROBERT ANDERSON was born on June 14, 1805, at "Soldier's Retreat," the family's estate near Louisville, Kentucky. His father, Lieutenant Colonel Richard C. Anderson, Sr., crossed the Delaware with Washington and was an aide to Lafayette at Yorktown. Robert graduated from West Point in 1825 (15/37) and was commissioned second lieutenant in the 3rd Artillery Regiment. In 1832, after a tour with the U.S. envoy to the Republic of Columbia, Anderson served in the Black Hawk War as the colonel, staff, of Illinois volunteers. After the Sauk Indians surrendered, he was selected as one of the two officers to escort Chief Black Hawk to Jefferson Barracks. The other was Second Lieutenant Jefferson Davis.

Anderson was promoted to first lieutenant in 1833 and served as an assistant instructor at West Point and on the staff of Winfield Scott during the Second Seminole War, where he captured forty-five Indians near Fort Lauderdale. He was promoted to captain in 1841 and took part in the Mexican War, fighting in the Siege of Vera Cruz, the Battle of Cerro Gordo, and the Battle of Molino del Rey (September 8, 1847) where he was severely wounded in the shoulder. He did not recover until 1848, after which he was on relatively light duty until 1859 due to poor health. He spent most of this period writing field manuals and inspecting iron beams used in Federal construction projects. He was promoted to major in 1857.

In November 1860, Anderson was assigned to command U.S. forces in the Charleston, South Carolina area. After the Palmetto State seceded, he moved most of his forces from Fort Moultrie to the more easily defended Fort Sumter, which created a furor. Despite his Southern sympathies, he remained in command throughout the crisis leading up to outbreak of the war. Ironically, his Confederate opponent was G. T. Beauregard, his former student at West Point. Cadet Beauregard rated Anderson as his favorite instructor at the Academy. He even sent Anderson cigars and brandy during the stalemate, but Anderson declined them.

Rebel guns opened up on Fort Sumter on April 12, 1861, and after a thirty-four-hour bombardment, Anderson raised the white flag on April 13. He was hailed throughout the North as a national hero and went on a highly successful recruiting campaign. He was seen throughout the United States as a symbol of the loyal Union officer. Lincoln promoted him to brigadier general, Regular Army, on June 17, 1861, and gave him command of the Department of Kentucky, which was later designated the Department of the Cumberland. He performed ineffectively in this position.

Until late 1860, Anderson had a solid but undistinguished career. After Fort Sumter, his nerves were shot, and he was not fit for higher command. He quietly stepped down on October 7, 1861, at Lincoln's request. He was replaced by William T. Sherman. Anderson was unemployed until August 1863, when he briefly commanded Fort Adams, Rhode Island. He retired on October 27, 1863, as a brigadier general. He was brevetted major general,

Regular Army, on February 3, 1865. He returned to Charleston and raised the flag over Fort Sumter on April 14, 1865—four years after its surrender.

Anderson struggled financially after the war and, in 1869, moved to Europe, where the cost of living was lower. In poor health for years, he died on October 26, 1871, in Nice, France. He was buried in the West Point Cemetery. His brother Charles commanded the 93rd Ohio during the war and later was governor of Ohio (1865–66).

CHRISTOPHER COLUMBUS ANDREWS, son of a farmer, was born in Hillsborough, New Hampshire, on October 27, 1829. He attended school during the winter months until 1843, when he moved to Boston to continue his education. He studied law at Harvard, was admitted to the bar in 1850, moved to Kansas Territory where he became an advocate for the Free Soil cause, and settled in St. Cloud, Minnesota, in 1856. He was elected to the state senate as a Democrat in 1859. He supported Stephen Douglas in the election of 1860.

Andrews enlisted in the Union Army as a private in 1861 but was promoted to captain and company commander in the 3rd Minnesota in November. He served on the Western Front and was captured when Confederate General Forrest overran Murfreesboro in July 1862, but was exchanged in October. He was promoted to lieutenant colonel in December, became commander of the regiment, and was promoted to colonel on August 9, 1863. Meanwhile, he took part in Grant's various campaigns against Vicksburg.

After the fall of the Confederate Gibraltar, Andrews was sent to Arkansas as a brigade commander and participated in the capture of Little Rock in September 1863. He remained there as post commandant and helped recruit Unionists and organize Arkansas as a free state. He was promoted to brigadier general on April 10, 1864. He also commanded a division in the VII Corps until the end of the year. Sent to Pensacola, Florida, he was given command of a division in the XIII Corps and took part in the Siege of Mobile and the capture of Fort Blakeley (April 2–9, 1865). He was brevetted major general on March 9.

General Andrews briefly commanded the District of Mobile, but was soon sent to Texas, where he commanded the Subdistrict of Houston. He was discharged in January 1866. His post-war career was also distinguished and included tours as ambassador to Denmark (1869–71), minister to Sweden and Norway (1869–77), and consul-general to Brazil (1882–85). He later became Minnesota forestry commissioner and devoted the rest of his life to Minnesota forestry, where his progressive ideas were gradually adopted. He was also a prolific writer. One of his books was a *History of the Campaigns of Mobile* (1867 and 1889).

C. C. Andrews died on September 21, 1922, at the age of ninety-two. He was buried in Oakland Cemetery, Saint Paul.

GEORGE LEONARD ANDREWS was born on August 31, 1828, in Bridgewater, Massachusetts. He attended West Point and graduated at the head of his class in 1851 (1/42). He was commissioned brevet second lieutenant of engineers and was promoted to second lieutenant in 1854. Andrews was assistant construction engineer at Fort Warren in Boston Harbor (1851–54) and assistant professor of engineering at West Point from 1854 to 1855, when he resigned his commission. He engaged in civil engineering until the outbreak of the Civil War.

Andrews was appointed lieutenant colonel of the 2nd Massachusetts in May 1861. Sent to the Department of the Shenandoah, the regiment took part in minor operations in the lower valley until the spring of 1862, when (as part of General Banks's army) it was attacked and defeated by Stonewall Jackson during his famous Valley Campaign. Meanwhile, Andrews succeeded to regimental command and was promoted to colonel on June 13. Still operating under Banks, Andrews fought in the Union defeats at Cedar Mountain and took part in the Second Manassas Campaign, although he did not participate in the Second Battle of Bull Run.

During the Battle of Antietam (September 17, 1862), Andrews's regiment fought in the infamous cornfield, where its attacks were checked, and it suffered thirteen killed, fifty-three wounded, and two missing. Andrews received high praise from his brigade commander, which led to his being given command of a brigade the following month. He was promoted to brigadier general on November 10.

In early 1863, Andrews and his men sailed from New York City to New Orleans. In March, Andrews was named chief of staff of the Department of the Gulf and simultaneously chief of staff of the Army of the Gulf. He took part in the Siege of Port Hudson and personally accepted the Confederate commander's sword when he surrendered on July 9. He was then named commander of the District of Baton Rouge and Port Hudson. He often praised the bravery of the "colored" troops and was deeply involved in the recruitment of African Americans into the *Corps d'Afrique*. By August 1863, he raised nineteen thousand men in nineteen regiments of infantry and two regiments of engineers—all African American. He was relieved of his command on February 27, 1865, and named provost marshal of the Department of the Gulf—a bit of a demotion. This was probably due to his long association with General Banks. He served on General Canby's staff during the operations against Mobile, did a good job, redeemed his reputation, and was praised by the general. After the city surrendered, he became Canby's chief of staff. Andrews resigned his commission on August 24, 1865, but was nevertheless brevetted major general in 1866.

General Andrews spent the first two years after the war as a planter in Mississippi. He was U.S. marshal for Massachusetts from 1867 to 1871, when he became a professor of French at West Point. He continued to teach modern languages at the Academy until his retirement in 1892. He died in Brookline, Massachusetts, on April 4, 1899, at age seventy. He is buried in Mount Auburn Cemetery, Cambridge, Massachusetts.

LEWIS GOLDING ARNOLD was born in Perth Amboy, New Jersey, on January 15, 1817. He entered West Point in 1833, graduated in 1837 (10/50), and was commissioned second lieutenant in the 2nd Artillery Regiment. He was promoted to first lieutenant in 1838 and remained in that grade for nine years. Meanwhile, he participated in transferring the Cherokee to the West, served on the Canadian border, and fought in the Second Seminole and the Mexican Wars. He was brevetted captain for his actions at Contreras and Churubusco, where he was wounded. He nevertheless returned to duty in time to fight at Chapultepec, where he was severely wounded. Brevetted major, he received a substantive promotion to captain in October 1847. He was sent back to Florida in the 1850s and led a detachment against the Seminoles in the Battle of Big Cypress (April 1856). He also performed routine garrison duty at Fort Monroe, Virginia (1848–53).

Arnold was at Fort Independence, Massachusetts, when South Carolina seceded. He was transferred to Dry Tortugas in the Florida Keys the following month and was promoted to major in May. Sent to Santa Rosa Island in Pensacola Bay, he heroically defended the island and Fort Pickens against Confederate ground attacks and artillery bombardments. They remained in Union hands throughout the war. He was promoted to brigadier general on January 28, 1862. He remained in Florida as commander of the Department of Florida, the Western District of the Department of the South, and the District of Pensacola. In September 1862, he was transferred to New Orleans where he directed the defenses of the city. Tragically, while inspecting the troops on November 10, 1862, he suffered a paralyzing stroke. Arnold was on medical leave for more than a year because the army hoped his condition would improve. When it became obvious that it would not, General Arnold retired on February 8, 1864. The North lost a valuable commander.

Lewis G. Arnold died in Boston on September 22, 1871, at the age of fifty-four. He left behind a wife and at least seven children. General Arnold was buried in St. Mary's Episcopal Church Cemetery, Newton Lower Falls, Massachusetts.

RICHARD ARNOLD was born on April 12, 1828, in Providence, Rhode Island, the son of a U.S. Congressman and governor of Rhode Island. He graduated from West Point in 1850 (13/44) as a brevet second lieutenant. He was assigned to the 1st Artillery and spent his antebellum career at various posts, including Key West, Florida; San Francisco; and the Pacific Northwest, and was aide to General John E. Wool (1855–1861). He was

promoted to second lieutenant (1851), first lieutenant (1854), and captain (May 14, 1861).

Initially, Arnold commanded a battery in the 2nd U.S. Artillery and fought in the First Battle of Bull Run, where he lost all his guns in the Union rout. He later directed the artillery for Franklin's division of the I Corps. After a tour of duty as assistant inspector general of the VI Corps, he served as corps chief of staff from May to November 1862 and was brevetted major for his conduct in the Battle of Savage Station (June 29). Arnold was promoted to brigadier general on April 4, 1863, and was transferred to Louisiana as chief of artillery for the Department of the Gulf. He directed the army's guns in the Siege of Port Hudson and in the Red River Campaign. Late in the campaign, General Banks relieved General Albert L. Lee of his command and named Arnold chief of cavalry for the Army of the Gulf. This move must have astonished Arnold, who had little background in the mounted branch. In this post he performed adequately but certainly did not distinguish himself. He returned to the artillery two months later, after the Red River Campaign ended, and—back in his own element—excelled as commander of the Union guns in the Siege of Mobile. One of the better artillery officers in the Civil War, he was brevetted major general in 1866.

After Appomattox, Arnold reverted to his Regular Army rank of captain. He commanded a battery at Little Rock, Arkansas, served in several posts with the 5th and 1st Artillery Regiments, and was promoted to major in 1875. His last post was on Governor's Island in New York City. Here he died on November 8, 1882, at age fifty-four, five days after he was promoted to lieutenant colonel. He was buried in the Swan Point Cemetery in the city of his birth. The infamous traitor, Benedict Arnold, was one of Richard's ancestors.

ALEXANDER SANDOR ASBOTH (called "Sandor") was born in Keszthely, Hungary, on December 18, 1811, the son of a highly regarded agricultural expert. His family moved to what is now Serbia when he was eight. Although he wanted to be a soldier, he yielded to his family's wishes and studied engineering at the Mining Academy of Seimechbanya and the *Institutum Geometricum* in Pest (now part of Budapest). He graduated and became a civil engineer, regulating the flow of the Lower Danube.

In 1848, Asboth joined the Hungarian revolutionary Lajos Kossuth in an unsuccessful revolt against the Habsburg dynasty. A captain at the end of the year, Asboth fought in the battles of Kápolna and Nagysalló in 1849 and was promoted to major. He became Kossuth's adjutant and was promoted to lieutenant colonel before the revolution was crushed. He fled to the Ottoman Empire with Kossuth and, in 1851, emigrated to the United States, where he worked as an engineer.

In the 1850s, he befriended John C. Fremont and in July 1861 became an engineer officer in General Fremont's Department of the West. Fremont named him chief of staff and promoted him to brigadier general on September 3, even though he lacked the authority to do so. The U.S. Senate later negated Fremont's illegal promotions. Meanwhile, Asboth assumed command of the 4th Division of Fremont's Department of the Missouri. It was transferred to Samuel Curtis's Army of the Southwest in November 1861.

Asboth helped push the Confederates out of Missouri and fought in the Battle of Pea Ridge, where on March 7, 1862, his right arm was broken by a Rebel minié ball. Disregarding his wound, he was back in action the next day. He was promoted to brigadier general on March 22. After he recovered, Asboth led a brigade in the Army of the Mississippi during the Siege of Corinth. Subsequently, he was given rear area and territorial commands in Kentucky and Ohio and commanded the prisoner of war camp at Alton, Illinois.

In August 1863, General Asboth was appointed commander of the District of West Florida. Florida historian William W. Davis noted that, when he was not engaged in pillaging, "Asboth was an urbane and pleasant follow" who loved flowers, dogs, and fine horses. With seven hundred men, he led a significant cavalry raid into the Florida panhandle and smashed the Confederate forces there during the Battle of Marianna on September

27, 1864. Asboth himself was among the casualties. He was shot twice while leading a charge. His left cheekbone was broken, and his left arm was fractured in two places. He saw no further field duty and, in 1865, went to Paris, where a famous surgeon removed the bullet from his cheek. He never fully recovered from his wounds, however.

Asboth returned to Florida where he briefly exercised district command after the war. He was discharged from volunteer service on August 24, 1865 and was brevetted major general in 1866.

Sandor Asboth became U.S. ambassador to Argentina in 1866. The following year, he became ambassador to Argentina and Uruguay. He held both posts until January 21, 1868, when he died from the effects of his Marianna wounds at the age of fifty-six. He was initially buried in Buenos Aires. In 1990, in accordance with his last will and testament, his remains were reinterred in Arlington National Cemetery. He was buried with full military honors.

CHRISTOPHER COLUMBUS AUGUR was born on July 10, 1821, in Kendall, New York. His family moved to Michigan later that year. Augur entered West Point in 1839 and graduated in 1843 (16/39) as a brevet second lieutenant in the infantry. He was promoted to second lieutenant in 1845, first lieutenant in 1847, and captain in 1852, which was rapid advancement for that day. Augur served as an aide-de-camp to Generals Hopping and Cushing during the Mexican War. He also fought the Yakima and Rogue River Indians in Washington and Oregon in the 1850s. He was promoted to major in the 13th Infantry on May 14, 1861.

Christopher Augur was named commandant of cadets at West Point in August 1861. He was promoted to brigadier general of volunteers on November 12 and, in December, assumed command of a brigade in McDowell's corps. He was given command of Sigel's old division under Nathaniel P. Banks in July and was severely wounded at Cedar Mountain on August 9, 1862, by a bullet in his right hip. On November 14, Lincoln promoted him to major general.

When Banks succeeded Benjamin F. Butler as the commander of the Army of the Gulf on December 14, Augur accompanied him to Louisiana as a division commander. His division formed Banks's left wing during the Siege of Hudson from April 27 to July 9, 1863. Here he demonstrated a Regular Army officer's disdain for volunteer troops. When one of his attacks failed, he refused to call for a truce, declaring that, if the volunteers could not force the Confederates out of their positions, they could stink them out as their bodies decayed in the hot Louisiana sun.

After Port Hudson surrendered, Augur commanded the XXII Corps and the Department of Washington [DC] from October 1863 until after the end of the war. Although his efforts against Confederate guerrilla John Singleton Mosby were not successful, Secretary of War Stanton was pleased with his performance. When Grant reorganized the army in early 1864, he wanted Augur as one of his corps commanders, but Stanton refused to release him, stating he was too important to replace. In April 1865, his men tracked down and killed John Wilkes Booth.

Augur reverted to his Regular Army rank of lieutenant colonel in 1866. Promoted to colonel and commander of the 12th U.S. Infantry Regiment in 1866, he became commander of the Department of the Platte (1867–71); the Department of Texas (1871–75); the Department of the Gulf (1875–78); the Department of the South (1878–80); the Department of Texas again (1881–83); and Military Division of the Missouri (1883–85). He retired as a brigadier general in 1885.

General Augur was known for his courtly manner, calmness, and commanding presence. He was also highly active in the Episcopal Church. His Civil War record was solid but not spectacular. Mrs. Augur had at least ten children. One of them, Jacob Arnold Augur, became a brigadier general. Meanwhile, Christopher Columbus Augur died in Georgetown, District of Columbia, on January 15, 1898, at age seventy-six. He is buried in Arlington National Cemetery.

WILLIAM WOODS AVERELL was born on November 5, 1832, in Cameron, New York. His name is sometimes misspelled "Averill." He received a local education and worked as a drugstore clerk before gaining admission to West Point in 1851. He graduated in 1855 (26/34) and was commissioned brevet second lieutenant in the Mounted Rifles Regiment. Sent to the Western frontier, he was promoted to second lieutenant in 1856. In New Mexico Territory in October 1858, he was severely wounded in the left thigh while fighting the Kiowa. He was disabled until April 1861, when he took a risky trip across the country to New Mexico with a message summoning his old regiment to Virginia.

Averell was promoted to first lieutenant on May 14, 1861. He initially served as an aide to Andrew Porter and as an assistant adjutant general to a division in northeastern Virginia. On August 23, he became colonel of the 3rd Pennsylvania Cavalry. After fighting in the Peninsular Campaign and in the Seven Days battles, he was given command of the 1st Cavalry Brigade of the Army of the Potomac on July 6, 1862. He contracted malaria in Virginia and missed the Maryland Campaign because of illness; nevertheless, he was promoted to brigadier general on September 26, 1862. Because of his youth, Lincoln had to appoint him three times before the Senate finally confirmed his nomination on March 11, 1863.

William Averell fought at Fredericksburg, and on February 12, 1863, assumed command of the 2nd Division of the Cavalry Corps. He led his unit in the Battle of Kelly's Ford on March 17. The action was inconclusive, but it was the first time the Union cavalry stood toe to toe with the Rebel cavalry on the Eastern Front.

General Averell took part in Stoneman's Raid during the Chancellorsville Campaign and performed so poorly that General Hooker relieved him of his command on May 8 and replaced him with General Pleasonton. Later that month, Averell secured command of a cavalry brigade in West Virginia, where he fought in several small engagements. He was the only Union cavalryman to achieve even small victories against General Early's horsemen before the arrival of General Sheridan. Meanwhile, his men were equipped with six-shot revolvers and 7-shot repeating rifles. On August 7, 1864, Averell surprised and smashed General James McCausland's cavalry in the Battle of Moorefield, West Virginia, and captured four hundred prisoners and four guns, at a cost of forty-two casualties.

Phil Sheridan, the Union commander of the Army of the Shenandoah, was not happy with Averell's operations in the Battle of Fisher's Hill (September 21–22). He relieved Averell of his command on September 23.

He was unemployed for the rest of the war and resigned both his Regular Army and volunteer commissions on May 18, 1865. He was nevertheless brevetted major general in 1866.

William Averell's performance during the Civil War was mixed. In civilian life, he served as U.S. consul general to British North America (1866–69). He then became an entrepreneur and inventor and became wealthy. He was a pioneer in the field of laying asphalt pavement and in the manufacture of steel castings and insulated electrical cables, among other inventions.

Meanwhile, many people became convinced that Sheridan treated Averell badly. In 1888, by an Act of Congress, Averell was reinstated into the army and placed on the retired list as a captain (his last Regular Army rank), without back pay.

General William W. Averell died in Bath, New York, on February 3, 1900, at age sixty-seven.

ROMEYN BECK AYRES was born at East Creek, New York, near the Mohawk River. His father, a country doctor, taught him Latin. When he attended West Point (1843–47), his prowess in that language was legendary among the cadets. He graduated in 1847 (22/38) and was commissioned brevet second lieutenant in the 4th Artillery. He was sent to Mexico City, but the fighting was over when he arrived.

Ayres was promoted to second lieutenant in 1847, first lieutenant in 1852, and captain on May 14, 1861. He spent his antebellum career alternating between frontier duty and garrison duty in Rhode Island, New York, and California. He was at the Artillery School at Fort Monroe, Virginia, when the war began.

Romeyn Ayres spent the entire war in the Army of the Potomac, where he fought at Bull Run, the Peninsula Campaign, the Seven Days battles, Antietam, and Fredericksburg. Meanwhile, he moved up rapidly and excelled at every level: battery commander, divisional chief of artillery, and chief of artillery of the VI Corps. He was promoted to brigadier general on

April 4, 1863. An ambitious officer, he realized further promotion opportunities in the artillery were limited. In April 1863, he arranged a transfer to the infantry. He commanded a brigade of the V Corps at Chancellorsville, where his performance was adequate but hardly distinguished. He was, nevertheless, promoted to divisional command just before the Battle of Gettysburg. He fought in the Wheatfield, where his unit suffered heavy casualties. Again, his performance was adequate. After the battle, he was sent to New York City to help suppress the draft riots. Afterward, he took part in the Rapidan and Mine Run campaigns.

In March 1864, the Army of the Potomac was reorganized, and Ayres was demoted from division to brigade commander. His unit suffered heavy casualties in the Wilderness but continued to fight at Spotsylvania, Cold Harbor, and in the Siege of Petersburg, where he was slightly wounded. Given another division (this one of Regulars) on June 6, 1864, he was brevetted to major general in December. He did well in the Weldon Railroad fighting and was highly commended for his actions at Five Forks (April 1, 1865). He was present at Appomattox.

After the war, Ayres commanded the District of the Shenandoah Valley (1865–66). He was mustered out of volunteer service and returned to his Regular Army rank of lieutenant colonel on April 30. His subsequent career consisted mainly of garrison duty in the South, including postings to Little Rock; Jackson Barracks, Louisiana; and Key West, Florida. He was promoted to colonel of the 2nd Artillery in 1879.

General Ayres outlived two wives. They had several children, one of whom retired as a lieutenant colonel in the 8th Cavalry. His second mother-in-law was Juliet Hopkins, who was famous for establishing hospitals for Confederate soldiers.

Romeyn Beck Ayres died at Fort Hamilton, Brooklyn, New York, on December 4, 1888. He was sixty-two years old. He is buried in Arlington National Cemetery.

B
· BAILEY – BUTTERFIELD ·

JOSEPH BAILEY was born on May 6, 1825, in Morgan County, Ohio. He earned a degree in civil engineering from the University of Illinois at Urbana-Champaign, after which he moved to Wisconsin, where he was employed in the lumber industry. He successfully constructed a log dam on the Wisconsin River, which was used by lumber raftsmen.

Despite being a Democrat, Bailey joined the Union Army at the start of the war. Initially, he was a captain and company commander in the 4th Wisconsin Infantry Regiment. Assigned to the Army of the Gulf, he was named acting chief engineer for New Orleans shortly after the city was occupied in April 1862. Taking part in the Siege of Port Hudson, he was promoted to major of the 4th Wisconsin on May 30, 1863, and to lieutenant colonel on July 15. The following month, his regiment was converted into a cavalry unit.

When the Red River Campaign of 1864 began in March, Bailey was named chief engineer of the XIX Corps. He was wounded in the head during the disastrous Union defeat at Mansfield on April 8, but it was not serious. Shortly after, the Union inland fleet was trapped near Alexandria, Louisiana, because the level of the Red River was too low for it to negotiate the rapids near the town. Bailey met with Admiral Porter, the naval commander, and suggested building dams to force the river to rise.

Joseph Bailey was a calm, quiet, unassuming man, and at first, Porter did not take him seriously. "If you can dam better than I can, you must be a good hand at it, for I've been damning all night!" the admiral joked. Soon after, however, Bailey, Porter, General Banks, and Major General David Hunter (Grant's representative) met and adopted Bailey's proposal, largely because no one had any better ideas. None of the senior officers were convinced it would work.

In the Civil War, the military engineers on both sides were frequently better at their jobs than the commanders—often by a wide margin. Such was the case in Alexandria. Bailey's plan worked, and the Union fleet escaped. Admiral Porter hailed him as the savior of the inland flotilla and presented him with a sword. Lincoln promoted him to brigadier general on November 10. He skipped the rank of colonel. Meanwhile, Bailey constructed a floating bridge over the Atchafalaya River, which allowed the battered Army of the Gulf to escape.

Bailey's appointment expired on March 4, 1865. He was reappointed on April 16. Meanwhile, he commanded the District of Baton Rouge, a cavalry division, the District of North Louisiana (February 9–March 11, 1865) and an engineer brigade in the Mobile Campaign of 1865.

Joseph Bailey moved to Vernon County, Missouri, in October 1865 and was promptly elected sheriff. Apparently, he intended to run for Congress in 1868 and would likely have been elected. On March 21, 1867, however, near Nevada, Missouri, he arrested two men for stealing a hog but failed to disarm them. They shot him to death. The killers escaped justice, but a third man involved in the crime was lynched. General Bailey is buried in the Evergreen Cemetery, Fort Scott, Kansas. He was forty-one years old when he died. President Johnson brevetted him major general posthumously on March 28.

ABSALOM BAIRD was born on August 20, 1824, in Washington, Pennsylvania. He graduated from Washington College (now Washington & Jefferson College) in 1841, at age sixteen. He entered West Point in 1845 and graduated in 1849 (9/43) as a brevet second lieutenant in the 2nd Artillery. He served in Texas and Virginia, and from 1852 to 1859, he was an assistant professor of mathematics at West Point. He was promoted to second lieutenant in 1850 and first lieutenant in 1853.

Baird was promoted to brevet captain, staff, when the war began. He fought at Bull Run, which began a long and successful combat career. Later, he fought in the Siege of Yorktown, Cumberland Gap, Thompson's Station, Chickamauga, Chattanooga, the Atlanta Campaign, the March to the Sea, and the Carolinas Campaign. Meanwhile, he was successively chief of staff of IV Corps, commander of a brigade, and commander of a division from November 1862 until the end of the war. He proved to be highly competent at every level. He was promoted to brigadier general on April 30, 1862. He led a brilliant charge at Jonesborough (Jonesboro), Georgia, on September 1, 1864, which led to President Lincoln nominating him for promotion to major general on January 23, 1865.

Post-war, Baird served as commander of the Department of Louisiana. He was mustered out of volunteer service on September 1, 1866, and was promoted to lieutenant colonel, Regular Army, in 1867. He spent the rest of his career in the inspector general's branch. He became a full colonel in 1885.

President Cleveland appointed Baird inspector general of the army in March 1885. He was confirmed in September and served until August 20, 1888, when he reached the mandatory retirement age of sixty-four. Meanwhile, he was promoted to brigadier general on September 22, 1885.

In 1896, General Baird was awarded the Congressional Medal of Honor for a charge he led at Jonesboro in 1864. He died on June 14, 1905, in Relay, Maryland, near Baltimore, at the age of eighty. He was buried in Arlington National Cemetery. His son, William Baird, served with the 6th Cavalry and retired as a lieutenant colonel in 1916. His grandson, Colonel John Absalom Baird (1890–1951), is also buried at Arlington.

EDWARD DICKINSON BAKER was born in London, England, on February 24, 1811, the son of a poor Quaker school teacher. The family moved to Philadelphia in 1816, where his father established a school. Later, he moved the family to Indiana and then Illinois.

Edward operated a drayage business and became a part-time Disciples of Christ preacher, where he honed his oratory skills. He served briefly in the Black Hawk War but did not see combat. Baker, who now lived in Springfield, became involved in local politics and was elected to the Illinois House of Representatives in 1837. He served in the Illinois Senate from 1840 to 1844.

Baker ran for Congress as a Whig in 1844. One of his opponents was Abraham Lincoln, who was also a Whig. Even though Baker defeated Lincoln, the two became close personal friends. Baker served in Congress from March 4, 1845, until he resigned in late

1846 because he joined the army and serving in both the military and Congress was of questionable legality at that time. He was colonel of the 4th Illinois Infantry Regiment during the Siege of Vera Cruz and the Battle of Cerro Gordo until James Shields, his brigade commander, was badly wounded. Baker assumed command of the brigade and earned a high commendation from General Winfield Scott for his performance. Shortly after, the enlistments for the men of the 4th Illinois ran out, and they returned to the United States and were discharged.

Rather than run against his friend Lincoln for Congress, Baker moved to Galena, where he was again elected to the U.S. House of Representatives. He served from 1849–1851 but was not a candidate for re-election in 1850. Lincoln, meanwhile, named his second son "Edward Baker Lincoln."

Baker moved to San Francisco, where he established a lucrative law practice but lost a race for Congress in 1859. He then relocated to Oregon, which sent him to the Senate as a Republican in 1860. Lincoln would almost certainly have appointed him to his cabinet in 1861, but the Democratic governor of Oregon would have appointed a Democrat to succeed him, and Lincoln needed every vote he could get in the Senate.

As a lawyer, a businessman, a politician, and a military officer, Baker was known for his lack of attention to details and his tendency to spend money as fast as it came in. He was also known as a brilliant orator.

When the war broke out, Baker volunteered immediately. On April 20, 1861, Secretary of War Simon Cameron authorized Baker to form a California regiment with himself as colonel. His regiment—the 1st California Infantry—was eventually accredited to Pennsylvania and became the 71st Pennsylvania, even though most of its men had never seen the state. Eventually, Baker was involved in forming a brigade. He became a brigadier general on August 6, 1861, and, on September 21, Abraham Lincoln appointed him major general. His brigade included the 1st, 2nd, 3rd, and 5th California Infantry Regiments.

On October 21, acting on a false report that the Confederate camp at Ball's Bluff (on the south bank of the Potomac and forty miles northwest of Washington) was unguarded, Baker's commander (Charles P. Stone) ordered an attack. Baker's brigade was supposed to reinforce the initial assault wave but was delayed because Baker had failed to ensure that there were enough boats to accomplish this task. By 4 p.m., the Rebels brought up their full strength and crushed the Yankees. About this time, they fired a volley, and Baker was struck in the chest and the head by four bullets. He died instantly. He was fifty years old. When Lincoln heard the news, tears poured down his cheeks and he was so grief-stricken that he almost fell.

General Baker was buried in the San Francisco National Cemetery. He is the only sitting member of the U.S. Senate to be killed in action.

LAFAYETTE CURRY BAKER (sometimes spelled La Fayette) was born on October 13, 1826, in Stafford, New York. A poorly educated drifter, he worked as a mechanic and lived in various locations antebellum, including Michigan, New York, San Francisco, and the District of Columbia. He was a shady and duplicitous character who initially served as a spy for General Winfield Scott in 1861. The information he provided was considered valuable enough for Scott to promote him to captain. He became an ally of Secretary of War Edwin Stanton, who arranged for him to be named provost marshal of Washington, D.C., from September 12, 1862. Promoted to colonel of cavalry on May 5, 1863, he became head of the National Detective Police Bureau on November 7, 1863.

Baker had little respect for the law or the Constitution and used torture and brutal interrogation techniques on "disloyal" suspects who fell into his hands. He also apprehended smugglers, draft dodgers, and others. He was not above taking a bribe and became known as "the Czar of the Underworld." After Lincoln was assassinated, he pursued and played a major role in the apprehension of John Wilkes Booth, who was captured after he was shot. Booth died that same day. As a reward, Baker received a hefty payment and a promotion to brigadier general from President Andrew Johnson. It was dated April 26, 1865, but it was never confirmed by the Senate.

Baker later fell out with Stanton and accused him of being involved in the Lincoln assassination. He was mustered out of volunteer service on January 15, 1866. He wrote a controversial and largely fabricated *History of the United States Secret Service*, published in 1867. He survived a couple of assassination attempts but was found dead in his home on July 3, 1868, reportedly from meningitis or typhoid fever. Certain historians have speculated that he was murdered via arsenic poisoning. This seems likely, but the evidence is difficult to evaluate.

Baker was forty-one years old when he died. He is buried in Forest Hills Cemetery, Philadelphia.

NATHANIEL PRENTISS BANKS was born in the factory town of Waltham, Massachusetts, on January 30, 1816. From a family of modest means (his father was a mill worker), Banks was educated in a one-room schoolhouse. He dropped out (against his will) to go to work as a bobbin boy for two dollars a week. Dissatisfied with his lot in life, Banks resolved to rise above his working-class origins. He became a voracious reader and turned himself into a fine orator.

In 1847, Banks married Theodosia Palmer. They were happily married for forty-seven years and had four children. Like her husband, Mrs. Banks loved expensive clothes, fine food, and glittering parties. They both tended to overspend.

Banks ran for the legislature in 1844 but lost. He was elected as a Democrat in 1848 and was re-elected in 1850. He was elected speaker of the Massachusetts House of Representatives in 1851 and was narrowly elected to Congress in 1852. Re-elected in 1854, he switched to the Republican Party and became Speaker of the House in 1856. He was a compromise candidate who was elected on the 133rd ballot. Banks was the first Republican to win national office.

Although he opposed both slavery and the radical abolitionists, Nathaniel Banks was an accomplished compromiser and was well liked by almost everyone, including the Southern fire-eaters. He was ambitious to become president of the United States. After the Democrats won the election of 1856, Banks lost his speakership. Undeterred, he ran for governor of Massachusetts in November 1857. He was elected and twice re-elected, serving from January 7, 1858 to January 3, 1861.

ENCYCLOPEDIA OF UNION GENERALS

A highly successful and popular politician, Banks made the biggest mistake of his life on June 3, 1861, when he accepted Abraham Lincoln's offer to become a major general. Despite having no military experience whatsoever, he instantly became the fourth highest-ranking officer in the Union Army, outranked only by Winfield Scott, John C. Fremont, and George McClellan. Perhaps even more seriously, as a general, Banks was unteachable.

Banks was crushed by Stonewall Jackson in the Shenandoah Valley in 1862. He was nicknamed "Commissary Banks" because the Southerners captured so many of his wagons and supplies that he indirectly supplied the Confederate Army for months. Jackson smashed him again at Cedar Mountain on August 9. On November 9, Lincoln ordered him to replace Benjamin Butler as commander of the Department of the Gulf. He was not prepared for the level of corruption he found in New Orleans, and he proved unable to deal with it.

In 1863, General Banks captured Alexandria, Louisiana, from Confederate General Taylor, whom he outnumbered five to one. He also captured Port Hudson after a siege of forty-seven days, by starving the fortress into surrender. He launched two all-out but poorly coordinated assaults on the place, and both were disasters.

In 1864, Banks attempted to overrun Confederate Louisiana and capture Shreveport. He outnumbered General Taylor 32,000 to 8,800, but his Army of the Gulf was routed at Mansfield on April 8. Taylor pursued Banks for two hundred miles, all the way across Louisiana, and surrounded him twice. The badly led Union army only barely managed to escape.

When he heard about Mansfield, General Grant demanded that Banks be replaced. Abraham Lincoln resisted the idea but finally caved on May 7. General Edward R. S. Canby arrived to replace him on May 18. Banks remained in command of the Department of the Gulf but not the army. He resigned his volunteer commission effective September 6, 1865.

Nathaniel Banks was a political chameleon. At various times, he was a Democrat, Republican, Radical Republican, Conservative Republican, an Independent, Radical Republican again, pro-business, pro-labor, pro-reconciliation, anti-reconciliation, pro-universal suffrage, anti-universal suffrage, and pro-women's suffrage. In the end, this destroyed his credibility. His presidential ambitions died at Mansfield, and he began to take bribes to finance his lavish lifestyle. These included one from Russia, whereby he would support the sale of Alaska to the United States. He was re-elected to Congress in late 1865 and served until 1873, but he was defeated in the election of 1872. He was re-elected in 1874 and served until 1879. He lost again in 1878. He served as U.S. marshal for the Boston district but, after an investigation of corruption led to his being found guilty of dereliction of duty, he was not reappointed when his term expired in 1887. His last hurrah was in 1888 when he was again elected to Congress, but he was suffering from dementia. His mental decline was apparent to all, and he was defeated for re-election in 1890. Even so, Congress voted him an annual pension of $1,200.

Nathaniel P. Banks was confined to the McLean Asylum for the Insane in 1893. He died there on September 1, 1894, at the age of seventy-eight. He is buried in the Grove Hill Cemetery in Waltham.

FRANCIS CHANNING BARLOW was the son of a Unitarian minister. He was born in Brooklyn, New York, on October 19, 1834, but was raised in Brookline, Massachusetts. He studied law at Harvard, where he was valedictorian in 1855. He was a lawyer on the staff of the *New York Tribune* when the war began.

Barlow enlisted in the 12th New York Militia Regiment as a private on April 19, 1861. He was promoted to first lieutenant on May 1. The 12th was a 90-day unit and was mustered out on August 1, having never left New York. Barlow soon joined the 61st New York Infantry and became its lieutenant colonel on November 9. He was promoted to colonel in early 1862 and first saw action in the Peninsula Campaign. He fought in the Battle of Seven Pines and in the Seven Days battles, where his regiment held part of Malvern Hill against several enemy attacks. His brigade commander praised Barlow for his "intelligence, coolness, and readiness."

After Malvern Hill, Barlow was given command of a brigade. He led it into the thickest fighting on the Sunken Road (a.k.a. the Bloody Lane) at

Antietam (September 17) until an artillery shell threw shrapnel into his face and groin. He captured three hundred prisoners before he went down and earned the highest praise from his superiors. He was promoted to brigadier general on September 19, 1862, while in the hospital. It took him months to recover.

Barlow had a very youthful appearance and certainly did not look like a general. He was known for his informal dress and usually wore a checkered, flannel shirt. He was also noted for his confidence and his hatred of straggling. His columns were followed by a detachment of men with fixed bayonets, who were ordered to move stragglers along.

Barlow's brigade fought at Chancellorsville and was one of the few XI Corps brigades not routed. After the battle, General Howard named Barlow commander of the 1st Division, XI Corps, replacing the wounded General Devens, and ordered him to restore the fighting spirit of the division. He promptly sacked Colonel Leopold von Gilsa, a popular brigade commander. Many of the men of the division thought him unnecessarily harsh.

On July 1, General Barlow committed a serious tactical error at Gettysburg by moving to higher ground on Blocher's Knoll and exposing both of his flanks. The Rebels under General Early overwhelmed his division and smashed the XI Corps. Barlow was wounded on the left side and a minié ball passed through his body near the spine and left him temporarily paralyzed. His men left him for dead, and he was captured by the Confederates. They left him behind on July 5, when General Lee retreated. He did not return to duty until late March 1864, when he was given command of a division in Hancock's II Corps. His health was still bad, and he was forced to take frequent convalescent leaves. He nevertheless fought in the Wilderness and distinguished himself at Spotsylvania, after which he was brevetted major general. He also fought at Cold Harbor and in the early stages of the Siege of Petersburg. His health collapsed in July, and he was on leave until just before Appomattox. He was given command of William Hays 2nd Division of II Corps on April 6, 1865, and led it in the battles of Sayler's Creek and High Bridge. He was promoted to major general on May 26 and resigned his commission on November 16, 1865.

Although he definitely misfired at Gettysburg, Francis Barlow was one of the best division commanders in the Union Army. His wife was noted for her intelligence and charm. She served as an army nurse until 1864, when she contracted typhus and died. She had no children. After the war, Barlow married the sister of Colonel Robert Gould Shaw, who was killed leading the famous 54th Massachusetts at Battery Wagner. She bore Barlow three children.

Post-war, Barlow served as a U.S. marshal and as attorney general and secretary of state for New York. He was a founder of the American Bar Association.

Francis C. Barlow died of Bright's disease in New York City on January 11, 1896, at age sixty-one. He was buried in the Walnut Street Cemetery, Brookline, Massachusetts.

JOHN GROSS BARNARD was born on May 19, 1815, in Sheffield, Massachusetts. He entered West Point in 1829 and graduated in 1833 as an eighteen-year-old brevet second lieutenant of engineers (2/43). He had a forty-eight-year career as an army engineer, beginning with the construction of Fort Adams in Newport, Rhode Island. He worked on many important coastal defense and fortification projects in his career, including tours of duty at Fort Hamilton, New York City; New Orleans; Pensacola; Mobile; Fort Livingston, Fort Jackson, and Fort St. Philip, Louisiana; San Francisco; and as chief engineer for a projected railroad in Mexico. He succeeded Robert E. Lee as superintendent of West Point (1855–56) and later studied construction projects in Europe. He also distinguished himself by strengthening American supply lines during the Mexican War, for which he was brevetted major. Meanwhile, he was promoted to first lieutenant (1833), captain (1838), and major (1858).

Barnard was present at Bull Run and served on the Blockade Strategy Board. He became chief engineer of the Military District of Washington, D.C. and supervised the construction of its fortifications. Lincoln appointed him brigadier general on September 23, 1861. He was chief engineer of the Army of the Potomac during the Peninsula Campaign and selected the Union positions for the Battle of Gaines Mill and Malvern Hill.

He returned to his Washington duties in August 1862 and remained there until June 1864, when he joined Grant's staff, a post he held until after Lee surrendered. Meanwhile, he was brevetted major general on July 4, 1864. He was a premier U.S. engineer officer, despite a heredity deafness which grew worse as he grew older.

General Barnard was mustered out of volunteer service on January 15, 1866, and reverted to colonel, Regular Army. He was president of the Board of Engineers for Fortifications and River and Harbor Improvements until he retired on January 2, 1881. Despite all of his accomplishments and great intellectual and scientific prowess, he was modest and retiring by nature. He died in Detroit on May 14, 1882, at age sixty-six, and is buried in Center Cemetery, Sheffield, Massachusetts.

JAMES BARNES was born in Boston, Massachusetts, on December 28, 1801. He attended the Boston Latin School and then West Point, from which he graduated in 1829 (5/46). He was commissioned second lieutenant in the 4th Artillery, served in the Black Hawk War without seeing combat, was posted in Charleston, South Carolina, during the Nullification Crisis, and was an instructor of tactics and French at West Point. He was promoted to first lieutenant in 1836 but resigned his commission later that year and became a railroad civil engineer. He was named superintendent of the Western Railroad in 1839 and directed other railroads until the Civil War began.

On July 26, 1861, Barnes was commissioned colonel of the 18th Massachusetts Infantry. He took part in the Peninsula and Seven Days Campaign, but his regiment was engaged in rear area activities and saw no combat. His brigade commander, John Martindale, was relieved of his command after Malvern Hill, and was replaced by Barnes, who did not see action until after the Battle of Antietam, when he successfully attacked Lee's rearguard and killed or captured three hundred Rebels.

James Barnes again distinguished himself in the Battle of Fredericksburg, which led to his promotion to brigadier general on April

4, 1863. He also fought at Chancellorsville, where his division commander, Charles Griffin, fell ill, and Barnes replaced him on May 5.

On July 2, during the Battle of Gettysburg, Barnes effectively ruined his career by withdrawing two of his brigades from the Wheatfield without permission. He lost control of his troops, was wounded in the leg by a shell fragment, and lost consciousness, and there were rumors that he was intoxicated. Although he eventually recovered, General Barnes was never given another combat command. He spent the rest of the war on court-martial or garrison duty and spent a year as commandant of the infamous Point Lookout POW camp. He was brevetted major general on January 13, 1866, and was mustered out on January 15.

Barnes returned to railroading after the war and helped supervise the construction of the Union Pacific. He died in Springfield, Massachusetts, on February 12, 1869, at age sixty-seven. He is buried in the Springfield Cemetery. His son, John Sanford Barnes, was an Annapolis graduate, the fleet captain of the Atlantic Squadron during the Civil War, and founding president of the Naval History Society.

JOSEPH K BARNES was born in Philadelphia on July 21, 1817, the son of a federal judge. He had no middle name, only the initial "K." He studied at Harvard and the University of Pennsylvania, from which he received his medical degree in 1838. He was commissioned an assistant surgeon in 1840 and assigned to West Point for a few months. Sent to Florida in 1841, he took part in the Second Seminole War.

Barnes was stationed at Fort Jessup, Louisiana, from 1842 to 1846. He served with Zachary Taylor in Texas and northern Mexico and was chief surgeon of a cavalry brigade with Winfield Scott during the drive on Mexico City. He was present at Cerro Gordo, Contreras, Churubusco, Molina del Rey, Chapultepec, and the capture of Mexico City.

From 1848 to 1861, Dr. Barnes served at a variety of posts and locations, including Fort Croghan, Texas; Fort Scott and Fort Leavenworth, Kansas; San Francisco; Fort McHenry, Baltimore, Maryland; Philadelphia; and West Point, among others. He was promoted to surgeon (major) in 1856.

Barnes was stationed in the Cascades, at Fort Vancouver, Washington Territory, when the war broke out. He was named medical director of the Western Department and medical director of the Department of Kansas in June 1861. In May of the following year, he was ordered to Washington as surgeon general of the city. He was promoted to lieutenant colonel on February 9, 1863 and to colonel on August 10.

Dr. Barnes was a friend of Secretary of War Edwin Stanton since before the war. Stanton clashed with surgeon general William H. Hammond and wanted to replace him with a less controversial figure. He promoted Barnes to acting surgeon general on September 3, 1863, and to surgeon general on August 22, 1864. He was promoted to brigadier general that same day. He was brevetted major general in 1866. During the war, his office controlled dozens of military hospitals and transports. General Barnes spent twenty-two years as surgeon general and stood at the deathbeds of Abraham Lincoln and James A. Garfield. He retired in 1882.

After suffering for years, Joseph Barnes died of nephritis (an inflammation of the kidneys) on April 5, 1883. He was sixty-five years old. He was interred in the Oak Hill Cemetery, Washington, D.C.

HENRY ALANSON BARNUM was born in Jamesville, New York, on September 24, 1833. He was educated in local schools and the Syracuse Institute, from which he graduated in 1856. He read law and passed the bar exam in 1860.

In April 1861, Barnum joined the army as a private in the 12th New York but was promoted to captain and company commander on May 13. He advanced to major on October 16. He served in the Peninsula Campaign and in the Seven Days battles. On July 1, 1862, during the Battle of Malvern Hill, he was shot through the hip and dangerously wounded. Thinking the wound was mortal, the Federals reported him as killed in action and left him behind. He fell into Confederate hands, was incarcerated in Libby Prison in Richmond, and was subsequently exchanged in August. He helped raise the 149th New York in Syracuse and became its colonel on

October 4, 1862. He took part in the Gettysburg Campaign, but he had returned to duty too soon and was forced to step down for medical reasons. He rejoined his regiment in Tennessee on November 10, 1863.

Colonel Barnum distinguished himself in the Battle of Lookout Mountain on November 24, 1863. Here, he was severely wounded in the right forearm but continued to push his attack forward. For his courage in this battle, he was awarded the Congressional Medal of Honor in 1889.

Although he was forced to take another medical leave, Barnum rejoined the 149th in time to fight at Kennesaw Mountain, Georgia, on June 26, 1864. On July 20, he was wounded again, this time by a shell fragment at Peach Tree Creek. On September 10, after the fall of Atlanta, Barnum was given command of a brigade, which he led for the rest of the war. He took part in Sherman's March to the Sea and the Carolinas Campaign. He was promoted to brigadier general on May 31, 1865, and was brevetted major general in 1866. General Barnum resigned from the army on January 9, 1866. He became a major general in the New York Militia in January 1867.

After the war, General Barnum was an inspector of New York prisons and harbormaster of New York City in 1872. He was elected to the legislature as a Republican in 1865 but was defeated for re-election in 1868. He returned to the General Assembly in the 1880s. He also served as president of the *New York Post*.

Barnum named his second son Malvern Hill Barnum. In 1898, "Mal" was seriously wounded on San Juan Hill on exactly the same date as his father was wounded at Malvern Hill, Virginia. Mal fought in France in World War I and retired as a major general.

Henry A. Barnum died on influenza in New York City on January 29, 1892. He was fifty-eight. He was interred in Oakwood Cemetery, Syracuse.

WILLIAM FARQUHAR BARRY first saw the light of day in New York City on August 18, 1818. He entered West Point as a cadet in 1834 and graduated as a second lieutenant of artillery in 1838 (17/45). He was initially stationed on Northern Frontier during the New York-Canadian border disputes. He served in the Mexican War, the Seminole War, and the Bleeding Kansas border war. He was promoted to first lieutenant in 1842 and to captain in 1852. Along with future Union Generals William H. French and Henry J. Hunt, he co-authored *Instruction for Field Artillery*, which was published in 1860.

General Cullen recalled that Barry "was one of the most genial of men, possessed inexhaustible buoyancy of spirit, carried sunshine into the gloomiest recesses of society . . ." He was stationed at Fort Pickens, Florida, when the war began. He was promoted to major on May 14, 1861, and was transferred to the Department of Northeast Virginia, which was later named the Army of the Potomac. He was its chief of artillery at Bull Run. Despite this defeat, he was promoted to brigadier general on August 26, and remained chief of artillery of the Army of the Potomac until August 27, 1862. He fought in the Peninsula Campaign (including the Siege of Yorktown) and the Seven Days battles.

Barry was transferred to Washington, D.C., in the fall of 1862, where he supervised the artillery and ordnance of the forces defending the nation's capital and served on several ordnance boards. On March 15, 1864, he was placed in charge of artillery for William T. Sherman's Military Division of the Mississippi, a post he held for the rest of the war. He served with Sherman in the Atlanta Campaign, the March to the Sea, and the Carolinas Campaign. He was brevetted major general on January 23, 1865, and was mustered out of the volunteer service on January 15, 1866.

Post-war, Barry was colonel of the 2nd Artillery on the Canadian frontier. From 1867 to 1877, he commanded the Artillery School for Practice at Fort Monroe, Virginia. He became commander of Fort McHenry in Baltimore Harbor, Maryland, in 1877 and helped suppress the Great Railroad Strike later that year. General Barry died in Baltimore on July 18, 1879. He was sixty years old. He was buried in Forest Lawn Cemetery, Buffalo.

JOSEPH JACKSON BARTLETT was born on November 21, 1834, in Binghamton, New York. His father was a gunmaker. He was educated locally and read law in Utica. He was admitted to the bar in 1858 and established a practice in Elmira shortly before the war began.

Bartlett joined the army as a major in the 27th New York on May 21, 1861. His colonel was Henry W. Slocum. The regiment fought at the First

Bull Run, and Bartlett assumed command of the regiment after Slocum was wounded. He maintained order during the retreat and was rewarded with a promotion to colonel on September 21, after Slocum was promoted to brigadier general.

Joseph Bartlett fought in the Peninsula Campaign, at Seven Days, and in the Maryland Campaign, where he distinguished himself in the September 14 attack on Crampton's Gap. His brigade was lightly engaged in the East Woods sector at Antietam, and he was promoted to brigadier general on October 4, 1862. His appointment expired on March 4, 1863 but he was reappointed on March 30. This time it was approved by the Senate.

During the Chancellorsville Campaign, Bartlett's brigade lost more than a third of its 1,500 men in the Battle of Salem Church, but again Bartlett maintained order. The brigade was lightly engaged at Gettysburg. Bartlett was acting commander of Charles Griffin's division during the Mine Run Campaign. Here, he suffered his most embarrassing moment of the war. Jeb Stuart raided his camp and Bartlett was forced to escape by fleeing only in his underwear.

He reverted to brigade command for the Overland Campaign and was wounded in the Wilderness. He fought at Spotsylvania, Cold Harbor, and in the Siege of Petersburg. He briefly commanded a division during the Appomattox Campaign and was brevetted major general in December 1864. He was mustered out of the service on January 15, 1866. He came down with rheumatism during the war and suffered from it for the rest of his life.

After the war, Joseph Bartlett resumed his legal career. He was U.S. minister to Norway and Sweden from 1867 to 1869. He was deputy commissioner of pensions from 1885 to 1889 during Grover Cleveland's first administration.

General Bartlett died on January 14, 1893, in Baltimore, Maryland. He was fifty-eight years old. He is buried in Arlington National Cemetery.

WILLIAM FRANCIS BARTLETT was born in Haverhill, Massachusetts, on June 6, 1840. He was a student at Harvard when the war began but

dropped out to join the 4th Massachusetts Infantry Battalion, a militia unit, as a sergeant on April 17, 1861. He so impressed his commander that he promoted Bartlett to captain on July 10. The 4th was a 90-day unit which never left the state.

On August 8, Bartlett joined the 20th Massachusetts Infantry, which was then forming, as a captain and a company commander. Known as "the Harvard regiment," it was sent to Virginia in September and fought in the disaster at Ball's Bluff on October 21. In 1862, it participated in the Siege of Yorktown, where Bartlett was shot in the left knee on April 24 and physicians were forced to amputate his leg. After he recovered, he returned to Harvard and finished his degree. He resigned his commission on November 12, 1862. Shortly thereafter, he accepted the colonelcy of the 49th Massachusetts, which was then forming. It was a nine-month regiment.

Bartlett and the 49th were sent to Louisiana and took part in the Siege of Port Hudson. Because of his missing leg, he had to ride a horse, making him an easy target for the Confederates. During the assault of May 27, 1863, he was shot twice—in the left wrist and the right leg. He was still recovering when the enlistments of his men expired, so Bartlett resigned his commission for a second time on September 1.

William Bartlett was an officer known for his zeal, inexhaustible energy, Christian faith, and courage. He returned to Massachusetts in the autumn of 1863 and organized the 57th Massachusetts, a "Veterans' regiment," made up of men who had previously served. They were sent to Virginia. Bartlett was recommissioned a colonel on April 9, 1864. Less than a month later, on May 6, he was wounded in the head during the Battle of the Wilderness. He returned to Massachusetts and was there when, at age twenty-five, he was promoted to brigadier general on June 22, 1864. He rejoined the Army of the Potomac as a brigade commander in July.

On July 30, Bartlett fought in the Battle of the Crater, where his prosthetic leg was blown off. Unable to walk, he was captured when the Yankees retreated, and was incarcerated in Richmond's notorious Libby Prison. He was racked with disease (including dysentery) when he was exchanged on September 24. It took him months to recover.

Bartlett returned to active duty in June 1865. Even though the South had surrendered, there were still many men under arms, and Bartlett commanded a division in the IX Corps, then in the Washington, D.C. area, in June and July. He was mustered out on July 18, 1866.

After the war, Bartlett was manager of the Tredegar Iron Works in Richmond and became nationally famous as an advocate of national unity and a mild Reconstruction. Later he managed the Pomeroy Iron Works and the Powhatan Iron Company. He eventually settled in Pittsfield, Massachusetts, where he died of tuberculosis on December 17, 1876. He was thirty-six years old. Herman Melville later wrote a poem about him.

HENRY BAXTER was born in Sidney Plains, New York, on September 8, 1821, but his family moved to Jonesville, Michigan, when he was a child. He was a 49er; with a party of thirty men, he went to California to search for gold, but he returned empty handed in 1852. He then became a miller and joined a local military unit, the Jonesville Light Guards. It became Company C, 7th Michigan Infantry, after the war began.

Captain Baxter fought in the Peninsula Campaign and was seriously wounded in the abdomen in the Seven Days Battle. He was nevertheless promoted to lieutenant colonel on July 1, 1862. He was with Sedgwick's division when it marched into an ambush at Antietam and was decimated. Baxter was severely wounded in the right leg and returned to Michigan to recover. (One source stated that he was also hit in the chest by a spent ball.) He became commander of the regiment and was advanced to full colonel before the Battle of Fredericksburg, where he was ordered to make an amphibious assault across the Rappahannock against Mississippi sharpshooters. He was successful, but not before one of them shot Baxter through his left shoulder. He was given command of a brigade when he returned to duty and was promoted to brigadier general on April 9, 1863. He took part in the Battle of Chancellorsville that May.

Gettysburg was the high point of Baxter's Civil War career. On July 1, Confederate General Robert Rodes's division attacked piecemeal and Baxter's men slaughtered Edward O'Neal's brigade. Then Baxter took a position behind a stone wall. Confederate General Iverson ordered an advance without conducting a reconnaissance, and Baxter ambushed him. The North Carolina brigade lost 900 of its 1,300 men in less than ten minutes. Baxter continued to fight Ewell's II Corps until his men were virtually out of ammunition. He fell back to the north end of Cemetery Ridge. About half the brigade was killed or wounded, including Baxter's entire staff.

Henry Baxter was rightly hailed as one of the heroes of Gettysburg. In 1864, he fought in the Battle of the Wilderness, where he was shot in the left leg. The same bullet killed his horse, which then fell on him. After recovering from his latest injury, he served in the Siege of Petersburg and the Appomattox Campaign. He was mustered out of the service on August 24, 1865, and was brevetted major general in 1866.

After the war, Baxter was U.S. minister to Honduras from 1869 to 1872. He then returned home and went into the lumber business, but died of pneumonia in Jonesville, Michigan, on December 30, 1873. He was fifty-two. He was buried in Sunset View Cemetery, Jonesville.

GEORGE DASHIELL BAYARD was born in Seneca Falls, New York, on December 18, 1835. His grandfather was John B. Bayard, a colonel in the Continental Army and later a member of Congress. George's family moved to Iowa Territory when he was young. He was admitted to West Point in 1852, graduated in 1856 (11/49), and was commissioned second lieutenant in the 1st Cavalry. For the next five years he fought Indians on the frontier of Kansas, Colorado, Utah, and Nebraska, fighting Cheyenne and Mormons. In 1860, a Kiowa shot him in the face with a poisonous arrow. He was in pain for months.

Bayard was promoted to first lieutenant in March 1861 and to captain, Regular Army, on August 20, 1861. Seven days later, he became colonel of the 1st Pennsylvania Cavalry.

Bayard was named chief of cavalry of the III Corps and was promoted to brigadier general on April 28, 1862. He fought in the Union defeats at battles of Port Republic, Cedar Mountain, and the Second Battle of Bull Run.

Still bothered by his old wound, Bayard took a leave of absence in September and missed the Battle of Antietam. When he returned, he was named chief of cavalry of the Left Grand Division. On December 13, 1862, he was in the front yard of General Franklin's headquarters, the Bernard house, when a Confederate artillery round bounced up and struck him in the upper leg, mangled his hip and legs, partially cutting his inguinal artery. He died the following afternoon. Had he lived another four days, he would have celebrated his twenty-seventh birthday. He planned to marry Mary Eleanor Bowman, the daughter of the superintendent of West Point, on his birthday.

General Bayard was buried in Princeton Cemetery, Princeton, New Jersey.

GEORGE LAFAYETTE BEAL was born in Norway, Maine, on May 21, 1825, the son of one of the founders of the town. He studied at Westbrook Seminary, became an agent for the Canadian Express Company, and joined the local militia, the Norway Light Infantry. He became its captain in 1855 and was still its commander when the war began.

The Norway Light became Company G of the 1st Maine on May 21, 1861. This 90-day unit was stationed in Washington, D.C. and mustered out in early August. Beal became colonel of the 10th Maine on October 26. He fought in the Valley Campaign of 1862 and at Cedar Mountain, the Second Bull Run, and Antietam, where his horse was killed, and he was severely wounded in both legs. Beal and his regiment were mustered out of the service on May 8, 1863.

Beal returned to the colors on December 17, 1863, as colonel of the newly formed 29th Maine Infantry Regiment. Organized in Augusta, it left for Louisiana on January 31, 1864 and arrived on February 16. Beal was given command of a brigade on April 19. He led it in the Red River Campaign, including the Battles of Mansfield and Pleasant Hill. Beal's brigade was sent to Virginia in July and participated in Sheridan's Shenandoah Valley Campaign. He was brevetted brigadier general on August 22 and led an attack that broke the Rebel lines at Cedar Creek on October 19. This led to his promotion to brigadier general on November 30, 1864. He was in western North Carolina when the war ended. Early in the Reconstruction era, he commanded the Eastern District of South Carolina. He was mustered out on January 15, 1866, and brevetted major general the following month.

Post-war, General Beal was active in the Maine Republican Party. He was a presidential elector for Grant in 1872 and was appointed pension agent at Portland, Maine, that same year. In 1880, he became adjutant general of the Maine Militia, a post he held until 1885. He was state treasurer from 1888 to 1894.

George L. Beal died suddenly of heart disease in the town of his birth on December 11, 1896. He was seventy-one years old. He is buried in the Norway Pine Grove Cemetery.

JOHN BEATTY was born on December 16, 1828, in Sandusky, Ohio. Educated in local schools, he went into the banking business, starting as a clerk. He and his brother established the Beatty Brothers Bank (later the First National Bank) in Cardington, Ohio. He also dabbled in politics. He joined the Republican Party and was a presidential elector for Abraham Lincoln in 1860.

In April 1861, he volunteered for military service as a private in the 3rd Ohio. He became its lieutenant colonel on April 27. He took part in McClellan's Western Virginia Campaign and was promoted to colonel and regimental commander on February 12, 1862. Sent to Kentucky, he was part of Ormsby Mitchell's raid into Tennessee and northern Alabama. He returned to Kentucky and fought in the Battle of Perryville on October 8. He was promoted to brigadier general on November 29.

Beatty fought in the Battle of Stones River, where he had two horses shot out from under him. He took part in the Tullahoma Campaign and was given command of an infantry brigade on November 5. He led it at Chickamauga and Chattanooga, and Sherman's drive on Knoxville. He resigned his commission on January 28, 1864, and returned home so that his brother could join the army. The North lost a fine brigade commander.

General Beatty was elected to Congress and was twice re-elected, serving from February 5, 1868 to March 3, 1873. After he left Congress, Beatty moved to Columbus, Ohio, where he opened another bank and served as its president until 1903. He also held a number of posts in the Ohio Republican Party and was an unsuccessful gubernatorial candidate in 1884. He published his Civil War diary, *The Citizen Soldier*, in 1879. Beatty also authored several novels and financial articles.

John Beatty married in 1854 and fathered at least six children. He died of heart disease on December 21, 1914, in Columbus, Ohio. He was eighty-six years old. He was buried in the Oakland Cemetery, Sandusky, Ohio.

SAMUEL BEATTY was born in Mifflin County, Pennsylvania, on December 16, 1820. His family moved to Stark County, Ohio, when he was nine, and established a family farm in Jackson Township. Beatty spent his entire life on this farm except for the years he served in the U.S. Army.

Beatty had little formal education. He enlisted in the 3rd Ohio Infantry at the start of the Mexican War and rose to the rank of lieutenant. Discharged in 1847, he returned to the family farm. He was elected sheriff of Stark County in 1857 and was re-elected in 1859.

When the Civil War began, Beatty organized an infantry company, the Canton Light Guards, which was incorporated into the 19th Ohio on April 27, 1861, with Beatty as captain. He was elected colonel of the regiment on May 29. After training at Camp Chase in Columbia, the regiment fought in McClellan's Western Virginia Campaign, including the Battle of Rich Mountain (July 11). Sent west, it fought at Shiloh. On May 27, 1862, Beatty was given command of a brigade in the Army of the Ohio. He fought in the Battle of Perryville as part of the Army of the Cumberland and directed Horatio Van Cleve's division during the Battle of Stones River after that officer was wounded. He was pushed back by Breckinridge's attack of January 2, 1863, but was saved by the Union artillery.

Beatty was promoted to brigadier general on April 15, 1863. He reverted to brigade commander and served in the Tullahoma Campaign and at Chickamauga, where he was officially commended for his bravery. He also fought in the Atlanta Campaign, the Battle of Franklin, and the Battle of Nashville, where he commanded Thomas J. Wood's division. (Wood was acting commander of the IV Corps at Nashville.) He was mustered out on January 15, 1866, and was brevetted major general the following March.

After the war, General Beatty returned to his farm and worked the soil for the rest of his life. He died on his farm in Jackson Township, Stark County, Ohio, on May 26, 1885. He was sixty-four years old. He was interred in the Massillon City Cemetery, Massillon, Ohio.

WILLIAM WORTH BELKNAP was born in Newburgh, New York, on September 22, 1829, the son of a career soldier. He graduated from Princeton University in 1848, studied law at Georgetown, and passed the bar exam in 1851. He moved to Keokuk, Iowa, and set up a legal practice. In 1856, he ran for the Iowa legislature as a Democrat and was elected, serving from 1857 to 1858. He also joined a local militia company, the City Rifles, and became its captain.

Belknap was a ruggedly handsome, charismatic man who was six feet tall and weighed two hundred pounds. The average man at that time was just over 5'7" and weighed 143 pounds. He also had a booming voice and seemed to be a natural commander. He joined the army on December 7, 1861, as a major in the 15th Iowa Infantry. He first saw action at Shiloh, where he was slightly wounded when his horse was shot out from under him on April 6, 1862. He was acting commander of his regiment during the Siege of Corinth, where he again earned the praise of his superiors. He was promoted to lieutenant colonel on August 20 and to full colonel and regimental commander on June 3, 1863. He continued to serve on the Mississippi Valley front and was present when Vicksburg surrendered.

Belknap and his men were transferred to Georgia and joined Sherman on his drive to Atlanta in the summer of 1864. Belknap distinguished himself by repulsing two Confederate attacks in the Battle of Atlanta on July 22. The last one involved hand-to-hand fighting. He also excelled in the Battle of Ezra Church. This led to his promotion to brigadier general on July 30, 1864. He was given command of a brigade the next day, and on September 10 assumed temporary command of a division in the XVII Corps, Army of the Tennessee. He reverted to brigade command on October 20.

William Belknap took part in the March to the Sea and the Carolinas Campaign. He was brevetted major general at the end of the war and was offered a Regular Army commission but declined it. He was mustered out on August 24, 1865.

Following the war, Belknap (now a Republican) was a collector of internal revenue (1865–69). On the recommendation of General Sherman, he was appointed Secretary of War on October 25, 1869, and served until March 2, 1876. He was a popular secretary, but his regime was marked by corruption and incompetence. His salary was $8,000 a year ($187,365 in 2021 money), which was not enough for Carita, Belknap's socially ambitious first wife. They held lavish parties which were partially financed by basically selling "tradership" positions at Western forts. All sutlers had to be approved by the secretary of war, who accepted kickbacks or bribes. One group reportedly paid Carita $6,000 per year in quarterly installments. After her death in December 1870, the payments went to her sister Amanda, whom Belknap married in 1873. Belknap also equipped his soldiers with inferior equipment. The Indians purchased repeating rifles and high-quality single-shot breech-load rifles, as opposed to the inferior single-shot breech-loaders provided by the War Department. They were also prone to jamming. This was a factor in the Battle of Little Big Horn, where Crazy Horse's braves were better equipped than the men of Custer's 7th Cavalry.

In early 1876, the Democrat-controlled House of Representatives launched an investigation and found that Belknap had accepted $24,000 in bribes ($562,094 in 2021 money) from just one post trader. Secretary Belknap resigned on March 2. The House nevertheless indicted him, and he was tried by the Senate, which voted 36 to 25 to impeach him, with 13 not voting; however, a two-thirds majority (40 votes) was needed to convict. (Some senators felt the point was moot since he had already resigned.) Belknap was also indicted by a Federal grand jury and was actually arrested by the U.S. Attorney General, but President Grant used his influence and got the charges dismissed.

After his resignation, Belknap returned to the practice of law. He resided in Philadelphia and Keokuk, Iowa, although he maintained an office in Washington. Meanwhile, his second wife died and he remarried. On October 12, 1890, he died suddenly of a massive heart attack. He was sixty-one years of age. He was buried in Arlington National Cemetery. His son, Hugh R. Belknap, became a U.S. Congressman.

HENRY WASHINGTON BENHAM was born in Connecticut (probably in the town of Meriden) on April 17, 1813. He attended Yale for a year but entered West Point in 1833. He graduated at the top of the Class of 1837 (1/50) and was commissioned second lieutenant of engineers—the most coveted branch of all. He was promoted to first lieutenant in 1837, captain in 1848, and major on August 6, 1861. He also earned a brevet to captain in 1847 for his bravery at Buena Vista, where he was slightly wounded.

Benham spent his entire antebellum career in the engineers. He mainly constructed coastal defenses and built the sea wall for the protection of Great Brewster Island in Boston Harbor.

Benham was named chief engineer of the Department of the Ohio when the war broke out. During McClellan's Western Virginia Campaign, he distinguished himself by leading a vanguard and pursuing Robert S. Garrett's troops from Laurel Hill to Carrick's Ford, where the Rebel general was killed. This earned Benham a brevet to colonel (Regular Army) and a promotion to brigadier general of volunteers on August 13, 1861. He was given command of an infantry brigade, but he handled it poorly. His commander, William S. Rosecrans, officially reprimanded him for failing to follow orders which were given to him several times, and for allowing a small Confederate army under John B. Floyd to escape. As a result, he was transferred to South Carolina. There, in June 1862, he botched an attack on Secessionville. General Hunter relieved him of his command and had him court-martialed. Clearly unfit to command an infantry brigade, his commission as brigadier general was revoked, but the revocation was cancelled on February 6, 1863, and he returned to the engineers.

Now back in his proper domain, Benham distinguished himself once more as an engineer. He was named commander of the Engineer Brigade of the Army of the Potomac and earned commendation from General Hooker for his part in the Chancellorsville Campaign. He was primarily concerned with bridging operations, and Benham was especially adept in the construction of pontoon bridges. His 2,200-foot pontoon bridge across the James River in June 1864 was the longest ever constructed on the North American continent. At the end of the war, General Meade praised his "earnest and faithful" discharge of all duties assigned to him. He was brevetted major general and mustered out of volunteer service in January 1866.

Post-war, he was a lieutenant colonel of engineers and engaged in improving Boston Harbor and New York Harbor and their defenses. He was promoted to colonel, Regular Army, in 1867 and retired on June 30, 1882. Henry W. Benham died in New York City on June 1, 1884, at age seventy-one. He was interred in the Oak Hill Cemetery, Washington, D.C.

WILLIAM PLUMMER BENTON was born in New Market, Maryland, on December 25, 1828. He sometimes went by his middle name. His father died when he was four months old, and his mother moved the family to Richmond, Indiana, in 1836. As a teenager, he spent two or three years as a chairmaker. In 1846, at age eighteen, he enlisted in the Mounted Rifles Regiment and fought in the Mexican War, including the Battles of Contreras, Churubusco, and Chapultepec, as well as the capture of

Mexico City. After the war, he read law and was admitted to the bar in 1851. He was elected district attorney for Wayne County as a Whig in 1852 and judge of the Common Pleas Court in 1856, but he was defeated for re-election in 1858.

Benton returned to the colors on April 27, 1861, as a captain and company commander in the 8th Indiana Militia Regiment. It was redesignated 8th Indiana Volunteer Infantry and Benton was elected its colonel. He led it during McClellan's Western Virginia Campaign. After this, the 8th was ordered to Missouri, where Benton was given command of a brigade and was promoted to brigadier general on April 30, 1862.

General Benton played a prominent role in the minor Union victory at Cotton Plant, Arkansas, in July 1862. Sent across the Mississippi with Grant in 1863, he fought at Port Gibson, Champion Hill, Big Black River, and the Siege of Vicksburg. He was slightly wounded in the First Battle of Jackson.

Benton commanded a division in the XIII Corps, Department of the Gulf, in 1863 and early 1864, and was briefly commander of the corps in May and June 1864. He exercised district command at Baton Rouge and Port Hudson later that year. In 1865, he commanded the Reserve Division of the Department of the Gulf, was a division commander in the XIII Corps during the Mobile Campaign, and fought in the Battle of Spanish Fort. He was mustered out of the service on July 24, 1865, and brevetted major general in 1866.

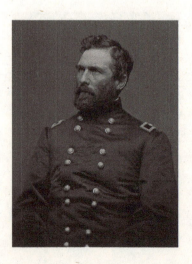

Benton remained in Louisiana after the war and President Johnson appointed him collector of internal revenue for the city of New Orleans. Unfortunately, he caught yellow fever and died there on March 14, 1867, at age thirty-eight. He was buried in Greenwood Cemetery, New Orleans.

HIRAM GREGORY BERRY was born in Thomaston (now part of Rockland), Maine, on August 27, 1824. He was employed as a carpenter, a contractor, and a banker. He ran for the legislature in 1852 and, at age twenty-eight, was elected. He ran for mayor of Rockland as a Democrat in 1856 and became the town's second mayor, but he was defeated for re-election in 1857. Berry was also chief engineer of the local fire department and captain of the Rockland City Guards, the local militia unit. In 1852, he established his own door, sash, and blinds company, but it was destroyed by a fire in 1855. He became president of the Lime Rock National Bank in Rockland in 1857, but resigned when he entered the army on June 5, 1861.

A prominent citizen who was considered a natural leader, Berry was ordered to recruit a regiment. He did so and became colonel of the 4th Maine Infantry on June 15. He fought in the First Bull Run and performed so well that he was given his own brigade (March 13, 1862) and was promoted to brigadier general seven days later, although one source listed his promotion date as April 28. In any case, he commanded a brigade in the Peninsula and Seven Days campaigns and was wounded in the stomach at Malvern Hill (July 1). His performance was impressive. On February 8, 1863, he was given command of Daniel Sickles's former division in the III Corps and was promoted to major general on March 10, 1863.

General Berry fought in the Battle of Chancellorsville and was shot by a North Carolina sharpshooter firing from a tree at 7 a.m. on May 3. A minié ball struck him in the arm close to the shoulder, passed downward through his body, and lodged in his hip. He died at 7:26 a.m. General Hooker rode up a few minutes later and, seeing Berry's body, dismounted, kissed his forehead, and broke down in tears. The Union lost one of its most promising young generals.

Hiram Berry was thirty-eight years old when he died. He was buried in the Achorn Cemetery, Rockland, Maine.

DANIEL DAVIDSON BIDWELL was born in Buffalo, New York, on August 12, 1819. His father was a wealthy ship builder and businessman. One of twelve children, Daniel was educated in local schools. A prosperous and influential civic leader, he was instrumental in organizing the city's first police force and was police justice of the city when the war broke out. He was also captain of a company in the Buffalo City Guards.

Bidwell enlisted in the 65th New York Infantry as a private in April 1861 but was soon promoted to captain. As such, he helped organize the 74th New York Militia Regiment. He was named colonel of the 49th New York Infantry on October 21.

Colonel Bidwell led his regiment in the Peninsula Campaign but was not present at South Mountain or Antietam. Bidwell led the 49th at Fredericksburg and at Salem Church during the Chancellorsville Campaign (May 4, 1863), where he captured two hundred prisoners at a loss of only thirty-five men. He also fought at Gettysburg and in the Overland Campaign. When his division commander, General Getty, was wounded in the Wilderness on May 5, 1864, Bidwell's brigade commander, General Neill, replaced him, and Bidwell temporarily replaced Neill. He distinguished himself the next day by checking an attack from Confederate General Gordon, who had already routed the brigades of Union Brigadier Generals Truman Seymour and Alexander Shaler.

The physically imposing Bidwell fought "like a man of iron," according to General Sedgwick. Known for his courage and his coolness in combat, he took part in the Battles of Spotsylvania and Cold Harbor, at Fort Stevens in the defense of Washington (July 12), and in the early stages of the Siege of Petersburg. He was given command of a brigade on August 6, 1864, and was promoted to brigadier general on August 11.

Transferred to the Army of the Shenandoah, Bidwell participated in the Third Battle of Winchester (Opequon) and Fisher's Hill. His luck ran out during the Battle of Cedar Creek on October 19, 1864, when he was

mortally wounded by a Confederate shell. He suffered intense pain for several hours before he passed away. Among his last words were: "Tell them I died doing my duty." He was forty-five years old. He was buried in Forest Lawn Cemetery, Buffalo, New York.

HENRY WARNER BIRGE was born on August 25, 1825, in Hartford, Connecticut. He became a merchant and was living in Norwich, Connecticut, when the war began. He immediately joined the staff of Governor W. A. Buckingham and enrolled in the 4th Connecticut Infantry as a major on May 23, 1861. He resigned his commission in November to organize the 13th Connecticut Infantry at

New Haven. He became its colonel on February 18, 1862. It left for Ship Island off the Mississippi coast on March 17 and arrived on April 13. It was sent to Louisiana and was involved in the operations against Forts St. Phillip and Jackson (April 15–28), which resulted in the fall of New Orleans, the Confederacy's largest city. Later that year, it was involved in minor operations in the La Fourche and Thibodeaux sectors of south Louisiana.

Henry Birge was given command of a brigade in the XIX Corps in January 1863 and took part in the Teche Campaign, the capture of Alexandria, and the Siege of Port Hudson. After two major attempts to storm the fortress failed, Birge was selected to lead an elite force designed to spearhead the third assault; fortunately, the garrison surrendered before the attack was launched. He was promoted to brigadier general on September 19, 1863.

General Birge took part in the Red River Campaign, including the Battles of Mansfield, Pleasant Hill, and Monett's Ferry. General Banks reported that he "deserved and received the highest commendation." Following this Union disaster, Birge briefly commanded the District of Baton Rouge, was then sent to the Shenandoah with the XIX Corps and took part in the defeat of the Confederate Army of the Valley. He was transferred to Sherman's command in late 1864 and commanded the District of Savannah. In March 1865, he was given command of a division in the X Corps (part of the Department of North Carolina), which he led until the end of the war. He was brevetted major general on February 25, 1865, and resigned his commission on October 18.

After the war, General Birge lived in Georgia for a time and worked as a cotton planter and a lumberman. Later, he moved to New York City, where he died on June 1, 1888. He was sixty-two years old. He was buried in Yantic Cemetery in Norwich, Connecticut.

DAVID BELL BIRNEY, the son of noted abolitionist and anti-slavery activist James G. Birney, brother of Union General William Birney, and cousin of Confederate General Humphrey Marshall, was born on May 29, 1825, in Huntsville, Alabama. His father freed the family's

ENCYCLOPEDIA OF UNION GENERALS

B ·

slaves, became an abolitionist, moved to Cincinnati and later to Michigan, and finally to Philadelphia in 1848. David graduated from the Phillips Academy in Andover, Massachusetts. He read law, was admitted to the bar, and practiced in Philadelphia from 1856 until the outbreak of the war. Foreseeing the coming conflict, he spent a great deal of time studying military books.

Birney entered the service on April 21, 1861, nine days after Fort Sumter was fired on, as lieutenant colonel of the 23rd Pennsylvania Militia Regiment, which he raised largely at his own expense. Using his father's well-connected political influence, he was promoted to colonel on August 31, 1861, and to brigadier general on February 6, 1862. He commanded a brigade in Philip Kearny's division of Samuel P. Heintzelman's III Corps, which he led in the Peninsula Campaign. Heintzelman had Birney court-martialed for disobeying orders, but Kearny testified on his behalf and he was acquitted.

General Birney fought in the Seven Days battles, the Second Bull Run, and in the Battle of Chantilly (September 1), where General Kearny was killed. Birney assumed command of the division after Kearny died. It remained in the Washington, D.C., fortifications and missed the Battle of Antietam. He fought at Fredericksburg and landed in trouble for allegedly refusing to support Meade's division, but the III Corps commander officially commended him for his performance, and he did not have to face another court-martial.

Birney fought hard at Chancellorsville and his brigade suffered heavy casualties. He was promoted to major general on May 20, 1863. At Gettysburg, the III Corps commander, Daniel Sickles, made an unauthorized movement and created a salient in Union lines. The Confederates crushed it and Birney's division was slaughtered. The general himself was wounded twice, but both injuries were minor. As he watched the survivors of his division stream past, Birney wished aloud that he was already dead.

David Birney assumed command of the remnants of the III Corps after Sickles's leg was shattered by a Rebel shell. He was soon replaced by an outsider, William H. French, but III Corps had suffered so many casualties that it had to be disbanded. Birney was transferred to the II Corps. He led his new division at the Wilderness (where he was wounded by a shell fragment), Spotsylvania, and Cold Harbor, and so impressed General Grant that he elevated Birney to the command of the X Corps of the Army of the James on July 23, 1864.

As the siege wore on, Birney developed diarrhea, which grew progressively worse. He was forced to step down on October 7. He was sent home in an ambulance, where doctors discovered that he had typhoid fever. He died on October 18, 1864, in Philadelphia, at age thirty-nine. He was buried in the Woodlands Cemetery, Philadelphia.

David Birney was known as a cold, Puritanical man and, according to Colonel Lyman of Meade's staff, was not popular with the troops. He was, however, tactically proficient and one of the more successful "political generals" of the Union Army.

WILLIAM BIRNEY, the older brother of Union General David B. Birney, was born on May 28, 1819, in Huntsville, Alabama. Like his father, he became a fervent abolitionist. He grew up on his father's plantation in Danville, Kentucky. He was educated at Centre College and Yale and set up a law practice in Cincinnati, Ohio. Independently wealthy, he spent five years in Europe before becoming a university professor for two years, teaching English literature at Bourges College in France. He also took part in the French Revolution of 1848. Birney returned to the United States in 1853 and established a daily newspaper, the *Philadelphia Register*.

Birney joined the Union Army on May 22, 1861, as a captain in the 1st New Jersey Infantry and fought in the First Bull Run. He was promoted to major in the 4th New Jersey on September 27 and took part in the Peninsula Campaign and the Seven Days Battles. On June 27, he was captured at Alexander's Bridge. Exchanged on August 15, he participated in the Second Manassas Campaign, including the battles of the Second Bull Run and Chantilly, as well as the Maryland Campaign, including the battles of South Mountain and Antietam. He was wounded in the hip and left foot at Fredericksburg on December 13. He became a colonel on January 13, 1863, and led the 4th New Jersey at Chancellorsville.

Birney was an early advocate of using "colored" troops (United States Colored Troops or USCT) in combat. He became commander of the 2nd USCT Infantry Regiment on May 22, 1863, and was promoted to brigadier general on June 6. His primary mission was to enlist and train USCT. He organized seven such regiments, formed them into a brigade, and led them in South Carolina. They did not perform well in the Palmetto State but fared much better in Florida, including the Battle of Olustee (February 20, 1864), where they formed the rearguard in the Federal retreat, and may have saved the defeated white troops.

In late August 1864, Birney's brigade was transferred to Virginia as part of Butler's Army of the James. It was soundly defeated at the Battle of Chaffin's Farm. In December, it joined the all-black XXV Corps, and took part in the Siege of Petersburg and the Appomattox Campaign. Birney was mustered out of the service on August 24, 1865, and was brevetted major general in 1866.

General Birney lived in Florida for several years after the war but moved to Washington, D.C., in 1874 and set up a law practice. He was the U.S. Attorney for the District of Columbia for several years and penned a biography of his father. He also wrote prolifically on religion and history. He died at his home in Forest Glen, Maryland, on August 14, 1907, at age eighty-eight.

FRANCIS PRESTON "FRANK" BLAIR, JR., the brother of Lincoln's first Postmaster General, Montgomery Blair, was born in Lexington, Kentucky, on February 19, 1821, into a prominent political family. His father was known as the founder of the Republican Party.

Francis, Jr., was educated in schools in Washington, D.C., at Yale, and at the University of North Carolina. He graduated from the University of New Jersey (now Princeton) in 1841. He studied law at Transylvania University in Kentucky and was admitted to the bar. He set up a practice in St. Louis in 1842.

Blair went west in 1845 and hunted buffalo. After the Mexican War broke out, he joined Stephen W. Kearny's command in Santa Fe. Kearny appointed Blair attorney general of New Mexico Territory. He later became judge of the circuit court. He returned to St. Louis in 1847 and became known as a passionate free-soil advocate, even though he was a slave holder. He advocated freeing the slaves and sending them to South and Central America. He served in the Missouri legislature from 1852 to 1856, when he was elected to Congress. He served there from 1857 to 1859 and from 1861 to 1864. He was defeated for re-election in 1858, but he successfully challenged the results. Blair was apparently re-elected in 1863, but his opponent contested that election, and Blair was ousted in 1864. Meanwhile, Francis Blair fought in the Civil War.

As soon as South Carolina seceded, he helped organize a home guard called the Wide Awakes, to prevent Missouri secessionists from taking the state out of the Union. He was named colonel and commander of the 1st Missouri Infantry on April 26, and took charge of the 1st Missouri Artillery on June 12. For political reasons, he declined an appointment as brigadier general of volunteers. Later, he and Fremont became rivals for power. As one point, Fremont had Blair arrested, but he was released by order of Abraham Lincoln. Blair's opposition, along with Fremont's waste, corruption, and mismanagement, led to Fremont's downfall on November 2, 1861. Fremont's issuing of an unauthorized Emancipation Proclamation was also a major contributing factor.

Through clever political maneuvering, Blair became chairman of the Military Affairs Committee in 1861. Congress voted for compensated emancipation in the District of Columbia in April 1862, and Blair was largely responsible for that; however, he spoke against emancipating the slaves, because he believed it would weaken sympathy for the main objective, which was preserving the Union. He declared that it would make Rebels out of the whole non-slaveholding South and alienate many working men in the North, "who," he said, "are not ready to see their brethren in the South put on equality with manumitted negroes."

Blair was promoted to brigadier general on August 7, 1862, and to major general on March 13, 1863. He commanded in Missouri and in the Vicksburg Campaign, where he proved to be a competent brigade and division commander. He became commander of the XV Corps on October 29 and led it at Chattanooga, Missionary Ridge, and in the drive to relieve

Burnside at Knoxville. At Lincoln's request, he gave up command on December 11 and returned to Congress. The following spring, Lincoln allowed him to return to active duty, and he assumed command of the XVII Corps on April 23, 1864, and (with some minor breaks) led it until the end of the war. He took part in the Atlanta and Carolinas campaigns, as well as the March to the Sea. After the surrender, he briefly served as chief of cavalry in the Department of Missouri. He resigned his commission on November 1, 1865. General Sherman said of him: "I always regarded him as one of the truest patriots, most honest and honorable of men, and one of the most courageous soldiers this country ever produced." Grant said, "There was no man braver than he." He was, however, also known for his irascibility.

The war ruined Blair financially. He opposed Radical Reconstruction and broke with the Republican Party. In 1868, he was the Democratic Party's nominee for vice president but was defeated. In 1871, the Missouri legislature selected him to fill a vacancy in the U.S. Senate, but he suffered a stroke which paralyzed his right side in 1872 and was defeated for re-election. He later became insurance superintendent for the state, which was basically a no-show job, given to him by a political friend. He died from head injuries suffered in a fall in St. Louis on July 8, 1875, at age fifty-four. He is interred in Bellefontaine Cemetery, St. Louis, Missouri.

LOUIS BLENKER was born in Worms, Germany, on July 31, 1812. He was named **Ludwig Blenker** at birth but changed his name after arriving in America. He was initially trained as a goldsmith, attended a technical school in Munich, and enlisted in an Uhlan (lancer) regiment which accompanied Prince Otto of Bavaria to Greece in 1832. (Otto was King of Greece from the establishment of the monarchy until he was deposed in 1862.) Blenker became an officer under Otto but left his service in 1837. He studied medicine in Munich and went into the wine business. A colonel in the Worms militia, he joined the anti-monarchy Revolution of 1848, even though he knew its chances of success were grim. He commanded the Free

Corps that took Ludwigshafen (May 10, 1849) and occupied Worms but was unable to capture Landau. When the Prussian Army entered the Palatinate, he fought them in several engagements and was noted for his fearlessness. When the revolt collapsed, he sought refuge in Switzerland and immigrated to New York, where he became a farmer.

When the Civil War began, he organized the 8th New York Infantry with himself as colonel. Most of his men were German immigrants. He was accused of selling licenses to sutlers at $100 per license, but it was never proven. The allegations continued to hound him throughout his career, however, and some members of his staff were convicted of war profiteering.

The 8th New York was in reserve at Centreville during the First Battle of Bull Run. He helped cover the retreat of the shattered army on July 21 and 22 and did a good job. This led to his promotion to brigadier general on August 9, 1861. Eight days later, he was given command of a division in the Washington defenses. Blenker loved pomp and circumstance. He was a fine organizer and a good tactician but poor at logistics. His brigade was earmarked to join McClellan's army in the Peninsula but was instead sent to the Mountain Department in northern Virginia. Blenker was injured near Warrenton on April 6, 1862, when his horse fell on him, and he was permanently incapacitated.

The general was unemployed for some time. He submitted his resignation and was mustered out of the service on March 31, 1863. He died as a result of his injuries at Rockland County, New York, on October 31, 1863, and left his wife and three daughters in poverty. General Blenker was buried in the Rockland Cemetery. He was fifty-one years old.

JAMES GILLPATRICK BLUNT was born on July 21, 1826, in Trenton, Maine. He grew up on the family farm and ran away to sea at age fifteen. After spending five years as a sailor on merchant ships, he moved to Ohio in 1845, attended the Starling Medical College, graduated in 1849, and became a physician and a fanatical abolitionist. He left his practice at New Madison, Ohio, moved to "Bleeding Kansas" in 1856, and became a colonel in the Kansas

Militia. He was a Jayhawker, and his associates included abolitionist Jim Lane, the commander of the "Free State Army," and John Brown. Blunt was active in the Underground Railroad, was a Kansas legislator, and a member of the Wyandotte Constitutional Convention (1859), where he served as chairman of the militia committee.

Blunt became lieutenant colonel of the 3rd Kansas Infantry Regiment of Lane's Kansas Brigade and commanded Fort Scott. The 3rd Kansas was an irregular and undisciplined partisan force which was not accepted into the Union Army until April 1862. Blunt was appointed brigadier general of volunteers on April 14 and was named commander of the Department and Army of Kansas on August 16. It was redesignated Kansas Division of the Army of the Border on September 19. He fought in the First Battle of Newtonia, Missouri (a Confederate victory), on September 30, 1862, where his vanguard panicked. The following month, Blunt advanced with his full division (which included three regiments of Native Americans) and smashed Confederate General Douglas Cooper's brigade in the Battle of Old Fort Wayne. He lost fourteen men as opposed to Cooper's 150 and forced him to abandon Missouri. Blunt also played a key role in the Union victory at Prairie Grove, Arkansas, on December 7.

James Blunt distinguished himself in a number of battles in the Trans-Mississippi, including Honey Springs (July 17, 1863), which brought much of the Indian Territory under Union control. His promotion to major general was dated March 13, 1863. He was the highest-ranking officer from Kansas in the Civil War.

The low point in Blunt's career was the Battle of Baxter Springs on October 6. William Quantrill's pro-Confederate raiders attacked his escort. More than eighty of his 100 men were killed (no prisoners were taken), among them his adjutant, Major Henry Curtis, the son of Samuel Curtis, the senior Union general in the sector. Blunt (who barely escaped) was removed from command of the District of the Frontier for this disaster. His constant quarreling with his superiors played a role in this decision. Later, he was given command of a cavalry division in the Army of the Border and redeemed himself when he defeated Sterling Price's rearguard in the Second Battle of Newtonia on October 28, 1864. Following this defeat, the Rebels retreated to Texas.

Blunt ended the war as commander of the District of South Kansas. He was mustered out of the service on July 29, 1865, and returned to Fort Leavenworth, where he practiced medicine and read law. He was admitted to the Kansas bar and moved to Washington, D.C., in 1869, to practice. In 1873, he was accused of charging Indian tribes exorbitant lobbying fees. Blunt charged up to 50 percent of the amount he recovered. He was never convicted of a crime, however.

As the years progressed, General Blunt became mentally unbalanced. In February 1879, he was committed to an insane asylum in Washington, D.C., where he died on July 27, 1881, at the age of fifty-five. He was interred in the Mount Muncie Cemetery, Leavenworth, Kansas.

WILLIAM HENRY CHARLES BOHLEN was born in Bremen, Germany, on October 22, 1810, while his parents were on a vacation trip. He was called Henry. His father was born a German but became a naturalized American citizen and lived in Philadelphia. His mother was also of German descent. When he was a young child, Henry's father put him in the military academy at Delft, the Netherlands. He returned to the United States in 1832, became a dealer in European wines and liquors, and grew wealthy.

When the Mexican War began, Bohlen became an aide-de-camp to Major General William J. Worth, a good friend. He participated in the Siege of Vera Cruz and the battles of Cerro Gordo, Contreras, Churubusco, and Chapultepec, among others. After the fall of Mexico City, he returned to his business in Philadelphia. Later, he was travelling in Europe when the Crimean War broke out. He joined the staff of the French army and took part in the storming of Sevastopol. After the war, he lived in the Netherlands until the Civil War began.

In 1861, Bohlen asked for and received permission to form a regiment in Philadelphia. Dubbed the 75th Pennsylvania, it consisted mainly of German immigrants. Bohlen was commissioned colonel on September 30. He was initially part of General Blenker's division. In December, he was given command of a brigade in Carl Schurz's division. On April 30, 1862, he was promoted to brigadier general.

Bohlen fought against Stonewall Jackson in the Valley, including the Battle of Cross Keys, where he performed well and covered the army's retreat. He took part in the Second Bull Run Campaign, and on August 22, 1862, on the orders of General Sigel, he led his brigade on a pointless reconnaissance across the Rappahannock River. In the Battle of Freeman's Ford, his brigade suffered heavy losses and retreated in disorder. General Bohlen was shot through the head by a Rebel infantryman while he was trying to recross the river. He was fifty-one years old. His body was returned to Union lines on September 10, and he was buried in the Laurel Hill Cemetery, Philadelphia. He left behind a widow and two daughters. One of his grandsons was the German industrialist Gustav Krupp von Bohlen und Halbach.

JAMES BOWEN was born on February 25, 1808, in New York City. His father was a wealthy merchant who saw to it that his son was well educated. Independently wealthy, he was socially prominent and acquired a large rural estate in Westchester County. He became a director, vice president and treasurer, and then president of the New York and Erie Railroad. In 1857, the governor appointed him one of the members of the Board of Police Commissioners, which elected him chairman of the board. In this post, he helped reform the troubled New York City Police Department.

Bowen was a superb organizer and, during the Civil War, organized six infantry regiments. He was appointed to lead them and was promoted to brigadier general on October 11, 1862. He was sent to New Orleans with his men but was considered too old for field duty. He was named provost of the Department of the Gulf. After months in this unfamiliar environment, his health broke, and he was forced to resign from the army on July 27, 1864. He was nevertheless brevetted major general in 1866.

Back in New York City, he was appointed a Commissioner of Charity and Correction for New York City. The politically motivated legislature increased the commissioners' salaries from $5,000 to $10,000 a year. Bowen was outraged and refused to accept the increase. His staunch opposition forced the legislature to revoke the pay raise. Meanwhile, he introduced the ambulance system into hospital service. He also materially improved the care of patients and the training and schooling of physicians.

James Bowen was a good, quiet man of refinement, breeding, and culture. He died at his summer home near Hastings-on-Hudson, New York, on September 29, 1886, at age seventy-eight. He was interred in the Presbyterian Cemetery at Dobbs Ferry, New York.

JEREMIAH TILFORD "JERRY" BOYLE was born on May 22, 1818, in Mercer (now Boyle) County, Kentucky. He was the son of the chief justice of the state supreme court, for whom the county was later named. Young Boyle was educated at Centre College, the College of New Jersey (now Princeton) and at Transylvania University in Lexington, Kentucky, where he studied law. He was admitted to the bar and set up a successful legal practice in Harrodsburg and Danville, Kentucky. A Whig, he favored the gradual emancipation of the slaves, even though he was a slave owner himself.

Boyle adhered to the Union in 1861 and raised a brigade of infantry for the Union Army. He was commissioned brigadier general on November 29, 1861. After spending the winter in Kentucky and Tennessee, Boyle and his men joined Buell's Army of the Ohio. He arrived at Shiloh during the night of April 6/7 and performed well. His division commander, General T. L. Crittenden, reported, "Boyle behaved with conspicuous gallantry, sharing every danger of his command, inspiring his troops with a confidence and courage like his own." Boyle's losses were 29 killed, 138 wounded, and 11 missing (263 total).

On May 27, Edwin Stanton, the secretary of war, named Boyle military governor of Kentucky. His rule was harsh, and he proved to be tactically inept. Rebel cavalry galloped through the state almost at will, while he did little except sit in his headquarters in Louisville and signal for reinforcements. His high-handed civil policies alienated moderates and included using troops to control elections, impressing slaves into railroad work gangs, and arbitrarily leveling large fines on Southern sympathizers. He was summarily relieved in December 1863 and was given command of a division in the Army of the Ohio, but he was unhappy in his new assignment and resigned his commission on January 26, 1864.

After he left the army, Boyle was president of the Louisville City Railroad (1865–66) and the Evansville, Henderson & Nashville Railroad (1866–71). He also engaged in land speculation. General Boyle died in Louisville on July 28, 1871, at age fifty-three. He was buried in the Bellevue Cemetery, Danville, Kentucky.

Boyle was married and had at least nine children. One of them, William O. Boyle, was the youngest lieutenant colonel in the Union Army. He was killed in action in Virginia in December 1864 at age nineteen. His father never got over the loss of his son.

LUTHER PRENTICE BRADLEY was born on December 8, 1822, in New Haven, Connecticut. He worked as a bookkeeper and a salesman while simultaneously obtaining a commission in the militia. He moved to Chicago in 1855 and went into the book business. He became a captain in the 1st Illinois Militia and by 1861 was a lieutenant colonel in the Chicago Legion. On November 6, 1861, he became lieutenant colonel of the 51st Illinois.

Bradley fought in the Battle of Island Number 10 on the Mississippi and was with Buell's army when it occupied Nashville, Tennessee. He missed the Battle of Perryville but was nevertheless promoted to colonel on October 15, 1862. He commanded his regiment at Stones River (December 31, 1862–January 2, 1863) and rose to brigade command on January 9, 1863. After the Tullahoma campaign, he fought in the Battle of Chickamauga, where he was wounded in the right arm and hip on September 19. It took him months to recover. He rejoined the army on June 27, 1864, and was promoted to brigadier general on July 30. He fought in the Atlanta Campaign as part of the Army of the Cumberland and in the Tennessee Campaign until November 29, when he was severely wounded in the left shoulder in the Battle of Spring Hill. He did not return to duty until June 3, 1865.

Bradley decided to make the army his career, and on July 28, 1866, was appointed lieutenant colonel of the newly formed 27th Infantry Regiment. He was stationed at various points in the American West, mainly in Nebraska and Wyoming. He fought in the Indian wars and was in charge of the troops who killed Chief Crazy Horse in 1877. He became colonel of the 3rd Infantry Regiment in 1879 and the 13th Infantry Regiment from June 1879 to 1884, which he led in Georgia, Louisiana, and New Mexico. He commanded the District of New Mexico from 1884 to 1886, when he reached the mandatory retirement age of sixty-four. General Bradley settled in Tacoma, Washington, and died on March 13, 1910, at age eighty-seven. He is buried in Arlington National Cemetery. According to his obituary, his "agreeable manner won him many friends."

EDWARD STUYVESANT BRAGG was born on February 20, 1827, in Unadilla, New York. He was educated in local schools and at Geneva College (now Hobart College) but dropped out in order to read law. He was admitted to the bar in 1848. Two years later he moved to Fond du Lac, Wisconsin, and set up a law practice. A Douglas Democrat, he was elected district attorney of Fond du Lac County in 1853.

As soon as he learned that the Confederates fired on Fort Sumter, Bragg recruited a company of 90-day volunteers. Later asked if he fought to end slavery, Bragg replied: "I fought for the Constitution." Shortly after, he recruited a second company of three-year volunteers called "Bragg's Rifles," with himself as captain. It became part of the 6th Wisconsin Infantry and was sent to Virginia, where it became part of the Iron Brigade. It was on the Rappahannock during the Peninsula Campaign and was lightly engaged, but it was heavily engaged in the Second Bull Run Campaign. The commander of the 6th Wisconsin was severely wounded at Groveton on August

28 and was replaced by Edward Bragg. He commanded the rearguard of the army when it retreated on August 30.

Except for Gettysburg, Bragg fought in all of the major battles of the Army of the Potomac, including South Mountain, Antietam (where he was wounded in the left arm and his regiment suffered 50 percent casualties), Fredericksburg, Chancellorsville (where he was wounded again), the Bristoe Campaign, the Mine Run Campaign, the Overland Campaign, including the Wilderness, Spotsylvania Court House, North Anna, Cold Harbor, and the Siege of Petersburg. He was reported as killed in action at Antietam and missed the entire Gettysburg Campaign after he was kicked by a horse.

Meanwhile, Bragg was promoted to major (September 17, 1861), lieutenant colonel (June 21, 1862), colonel (March 24, 1863), and brigadier general (July 1, 1864). He assumed command of a Pennsylvania brigade on May 6, 1864. The brigade had performed poorly under its previous, often intoxicated commander, but did very well under Bragg's leadership. On June 6, 1864, he assumed command of the Iron Brigade and led it until February 14, 1865. He was on detached duty in Baltimore at the end of the war and missed the Appomattox Campaign. He was mustered out of the service on October 9, 1865.

Edward Bragg proved to be a superb combat leader. He recalled that many of his men did not like him because he was a strict disciplinarian, "but once they were under fire, they would do anything for me." The feeling was mutual. Bragg's right arm was shattered at Antietam. As he was being carried to the rear on a litter, he saw a critically wounded enlisted man lying along a fence row. He ordered the litter bearers to take him off the stretcher and carry the private instead. When they refused to obey, Bragg summoned all of his energy, rolled off the litter, and rested in the shade of a tree. When the medics found Bragg, he was unconscious. The wounded enlisted man survived and outlived the general by many years.

After the war, Bragg resumed his law practice and relaunched his political career. He became postmaster of Fond du Lac in 1866 and a member of the Wisconsin State Senate, 1868–70. He ran for attorney general of Wisconsin in 1871 but went down to defeat, along with the entire Democratic ticket. He also lost a Congressional election in 1874 but was elected in 1876. He served as a Congressman from Wisconsin from 1877 to 1883 and 1885 to 1887. He failed to win renomination in 1884, mainly because he was arrested for fraud. The charges were dubious and eventually were dropped, but they killed Bragg's candidacy in 1884. He lost a renomination bid in 1886 and temporarily retired from elective office. He declined the Democratic nomination for governor in 1894.

Bragg served as U.S. minister to Mexico under Grover Cleveland (1888–89) and consul-general to Cuba and British Hong Kong under President Theodore Roosevelt (1902 and 1902–06, respectively).

After a long illness, General Bragg suffered a paralytic stroke on June 19, 1912, and died the next day at age eighty-five in his home in Fond du Lac. He is buried there in the Rienzi Cemetery. He was a cousin of Confederate General Braxton Bragg.

JOHN MILTON BRANNAN was born on July 1, 1819, in Washington, D.C., although his family later moved to Indiana. At age eighteen, he was a messenger in the U.S. House of Representatives and so impressed the Congressmen that his application to West Point was supported by 114 of them. He entered the Academy in 1837 and graduated in 1841 (23/52). He was commissioned brevet second lieutenant in the 1st Artillery. Promotions to first lieutenant (1842) and captain (1854) followed. Meanwhile, he served in upstate New York during the border dispute with Canada and in the Mexican War, where he fought at Vera Cruz, Cerro Gordo, Contreras, and Churubusco. Brannan was brevetted captain and was severely wounded just before the fall of Mexico City. He also fought in the Third Seminole War, which lasted from 1855 to 1858. In between, he did routine garrison duty for a number of posts, mainly in the southeast United States.

Brannan's life was touched by scandal in 1858 when his first wife, Eliza Crane Brannan, mysteriously disappeared after taking a ferry from Staten Island to Lower Manhattan. It was assumed that she either committed suicide or was murdered by Brannan. Later, it was discovered that she had secretly fled to Europe with another army officer and married him, without divorcing Brannan. In any case, he was at Fort Taylor, Florida, when the Civil War began.

On September 28, 1861, Brannan was named commander of the Department of Key West and was promoted from captain to brigadier general of volunteers. He assumed command of a brigade the following month. He commanded 1,573 Union troops in the Battle of Saint John's Bluff (October 1–3, 1862) and occupied Jacksonville, Florida, on October 3.

Ormsby Mitchel, the commander of the Department of the South, died on October 31. Brannan temporarily replaced him and held the command of the X Corps until January 20, 1863. He was given command of a division in the Army of the Cumberland on April 13 and led it in the Tullahoma Campaign and at Chickamauga where, against repeated Confederate attacks, he stood firm with George Thomas, "the Rock of Chickamauga." His division suffered 38 percent casualties—an astonishingly high number.

From October 1863 until the end of the war, Brannan was chief of artillery of the Army (and District) of the Cumberland. He fought at Chattanooga, Missionary Ridge, and the Atlanta Campaign. He was involved on the periphery of the Tennessee Campaign of 1864, where his job was to defend Chattanooga. He was brevetted major general on January 23, 1865. He commanded the artillery of the Military Division of the Tennessee from June to December 1865, and was commander of the District of Georgia from then until May 31, 1866, when he was mustered out of volunteer service and reverted to his Regular Army rank of major.

Brannan served in the 1st Artillery Regiment after the war and was stationed at Fort Trumbull, Connecticut; Fort Wadsworth, New York; and Ogdensburg, New York. He was promoted to lieutenant colonel in 1877 and helped suppress the railroad riots in Philadelphia later that year. He was promoted to colonel in 1881 and commanded the 4th Artillery Regiment until his retirement in 1882.

General Brannan resided in New York City until his death on December 16, 1892, at age seventy-three. He was initially buried in Woodlawn Cemetery in Brooklyn but was later reinterred at the West Point Cemetery.

MASON BRAYMAN was born in Buffalo, New York, on May 23, 1813. He was apprenticed to a printer at age seventeen and five years later became the editor of a local newspaper. He also read law and was admitted to the bar in 1836. Antebellum, Brayman was a lawyer in Michigan, a newspaper editor in Kentucky and Ohio, and a lawyer in Springfield, Illinois, where he knew Abraham Lincoln and Stephen A. Douglas.

Brayman was raised as a Calvinist and grew up hating liquor. He was a leader in the temperance movement and in the Baptist Church. He was employed by the Illinois Central Railroad and the Cairo and Fulton Railroad in the 1850s. He campaigned for Lincoln in the famous Senate race against Douglas in 1858.

Mason Brayman joined the army as a major in the 29th Illinois Infantry in August 1861. He fought at Fort Donelson, where he had two horses shot out from under him and distinguished himself at Shiloh by rallying his troops in the face of Rebel fire. He assumed command of his regiment on April 15, 1862, and was promoted to colonel on April 19. He was promoted to brigadier general on September 24 and commanded the District of Jackson, Tennessee, from October 1862 to March 1863. Here he did not perform well against Nathan Bedford Forrest. He was nevertheless given command of an infantry brigade in the XVI Corps of Grant's army in March 1863.

Brayman's brigade took part in the Siege of Vicksburg, where he suffered a heat stroke. After this, he was physically unfit for field service and was given a series of territorial or district commands in Camp Dennison, Ohio; Cairo, Illinois; Natchez, Mississippi; Vicksburg; and Vidalia, Louisiana. He was mustered out of the service on August 24, 1865, and was brevetted major general in 1866.

After the war, Brayman again became a newspaper editor in Springfield and Quincy, Illinois. He was in semi-retirement and living in Ripon, Wisconsin, by 1873. The Panic of 1873, however, destroyed his savings, and he turned to President Grant for a patronage job. Grant named him territorial governor of Idaho in 1876. He mishandled the complicated political situation in that state and was dumped by President Hayes in 1880. He returned to Wisconsin and later moved to Kansas City, Missouri, where he died of Bright's Disease on February 27, 1895, at age eighty-one. He was interred in the Hillside Cemetery, Ripon, Wisconsin.

HENRY SHAW BRIGGS was born in Lanesborough, Massachusetts, on August 1, 1824. His father was George Nixon Briggs, who was governor of Massachusetts from 1844 to 1851. Henry attended Williams College and graduated with the Class of 1844. He was admitted to the bar in 1848.

Briggs established a law practice in Pittsfield and dabbled in politics. He was a member of the Massachusetts House of Representatives from January to June 1856 and was Police Justice of the town of Pittsfield for part of 1857. He also took an interest in the state militia and was commander of the "Allen Guards," as the local militia company was called. It was incorporated into the 8th Massachusetts after Fort Sumter.

Briggs's company was part of the Fort McHenry garrison near Baltimore in 1861. On June 21, Briggs was named commander of the 10th Massachusetts, which served as part of the Washington garrison during the winter of 1861–62. Sent to the Peninsula, Briggs distinguished himself in the Battle of Seven Pines (Fair Oaks), where he was wounded in both legs on May 31, 1862. He was promoted to brigadier general on July 19.

Briggs's wounds were serious. He was sent back to Massachusetts and later to Camp Chase, just outside Washington, but he was still unfit for field duty. Later, in February 1863, he commanded the Middle Department, which headquartered in Baltimore. He briefly commanded a brigade in the I Corps in the latter part of July 1863, but did not see any significant fighting. He was commander of Camp Rendezvous (for Draftees) in Alexandria, Virginia, by August 1863. He held this post until July 1864. After that, he served on court-martial boards until he resigned from the service on December 4, 1865.

Henry Briggs returned to Massachusetts and was auditor for the state of Massachusetts from 1866 to 1870. He also served as Justice of the Central Berkshire District Court (1869–1873), after which he resumed his law practice.

General Briggs suffered from heart disease in his last years. He died on September 23, 1887, in Pittsfield, Massachusetts, at age sixty-three. He is buried in the Pittsfield Cemetery.

JAMES SANKS BRISBIN was born on May 23, 1837, in Boalsburg, Pennsylvania. He graduated from the local academy and became a teacher. Later, he purchased the *Centre Democrat* newspaper in Bellefonte, Pennsylvania, and served as its editor. He also read law and was admitted to the bar. Brisbin achieved prominence as an anti-slavery orator.

In April 1861, just after Fort Sumter, Brisban enlisted in the Pennsylvania Militia as a private. He transferred to the 2nd U.S. Dragoons on April 26 with a rank of second lieutenant and fought in the First Bull Run, where he was wounded in the side and the arm. On August 5, he was promoted to captain and transferred to the 5th Cavalry and fought in the Peninsula Campaign and the Seven Days battles. He was sent to northern Virginia in the autumn of 1862 and took part in the Maryland, Fredericksburg, and Chancellorsville Campaigns. He was injured when he fell off his horse at Beverly Ford, Virginia, on June 9, 1863. In late June, he briefly commanded the Cavalry Department of the Susquehanna during the Gettysburg Campaign. He took part in the subsequent pursuit of Lee's army and was wounded in the leg at Greenbrier, Virginia, on July 26.

Meanwhile, Lincoln decided to recruit African Americans. Seeing that his scope for advancement was better with the USCT (United States Colored Troops), Brisbin received permission to organize a black cavalry regiment with himself as colonel. His date of promotion was March 1, 1864.

Although the 5th USCT Cavalry Regiment was not officially accepted into Federal service until October 24, 1864, its nucleus was formed before that. Meanwhile, Brisbin took part in the Red River Campaign in Louisiana. Apparently, he was attached to the staff of Albert Lee, the cavalry commander of the Army of the Gulf, so that he could gain experience with the horse soldiers; in any case, he was wounded in the right foot during the Battle of Mansfield on April 8. He was back in Kentucky that fall and led the 5th USCT Cavalry in several small battles. The regiment performed well under his leadership. He was engaged in recruiting in the spring of 1865 and was promoted to brigadier general on May 1, 1865. He was mustered out of the volunteer service in January 1866. He was brevetted major general the following month.

After the war, he accepted a Regular Army commission as a lieutenant colonel in the 9th Cavalry. He was sent to the Pacific Northwest, where he served in several different campaigns. He participated in the Little Big Horn Campaign and offered George Custer four companies, but "Yellow Hair" said he could defeat the Indians without them. Brisbin never forgave Custer for this and later called him "an insufferable ass."

Brisbin was a prolific writer. He authored several books (including a biography of James Garfield) and had one bestseller, *Beef Bonanza*, about how to make money on the Great Plains. He was promoted to colonel and named commander of the 1st Cavalry near in 1869. He died in Philadelphia on January 14, 1892, at age fifty-four. He was buried in Oakwood Cemetery in Red Wing, Minnesota, the hometown of his second wife.

JOHN RUTTER BROOKE was born on July 21, 1838, in Pottstown, Pennsylvania and was educated in nearby schools. He joined the army on April 20, 1861, as a captain in the 4th Pennsylvania Infantry. The regiment's enlistments expired on July 20. As the bulk of the Union Army advanced on Confederate positions at Bull Run on July 21, most of the 4th Pennsylvania went the other way, and no one could stop them. Captain Brooke was discharged on July 26 (after the battle). His purpose was not to avoid combat, however, but to recruit the 53rd Pennsylvania. He was successful and was commissioned its colonel on November 7.

Colonel Brooke fought in the Peninsula Campaign of 1862 until June 1, when part of his right index finger was shot off at Seven Pines. When he returned to duty twenty days later, it was as an acting brigade commander. He fought in the Seven Days battles (including Gaines Mill, Peach Orchard, Savage Station, White Oak Swamp, and Malvern Hill). In August, Brooke reverted to regimental commander. He was sent to Maryland and fought at Antietam. At Fredericksburg, Colonel Brooke pushed to within sixty yards of the Rebel front lines at the Stone Wall, but the 53rd Pennsylvania was slaughtered by Lee's artillery and infantry. It lost 39 killed and 119 wounded out of 283 men engaged. Brooke held his command together despite appalling casualties.

By the end of the year, John Brooke was again a brigade commander. He fought at Chancellorsville and Gettysburg, where he battled Longstreet's men in the Wheatfield on July 2. He prevented a Southern breakthrough but was seriously wounded in the left ankle. He did not return to limited active duty until after Christmas. After commanding the Convalescent Camp at Harrisburg, Pennsylvania, he joined Grant's army at the end of March 1864. He fought in the Overland Campaign and received his belated promotion to brigadier general on June 7, 1864.

Brooke was wounded again at Cold Harbor on June 3—this time critically. He received a brevet promotion to major general while in the hospital. He returned to light (court-martial) duty in September but could not return to the field until March 1865, when he assumed command of a division in western Virginia.

After Appomattox, Brooke accepted a lieutenant colonelcy in the 37th Infantry Regiment (Regular Army). He was later promoted to colonel (1879); brigadier general (1888), and major general (1897). Meanwhile, he served in several posts on the frontier. He commanded the I Corps in Puerto Rico during the Spanish-American War and was military governor of the island after the Spanish surrender. He later held the same position in Cuba. His last command was the Department of the East (1900–02).

General Brooke reached the statutory retirement age of sixty-four on July 21, 1902. He settled in Philadelphia, where he wrote his autobiography. His death occurred there on September 5, 1926. He was buried in Arlington National Cemetery. Brooks was the next to last Union general to pass away.

WILLIAM THOMAS HARBAUGH BROOKS was born in New Lisbon (now Lisbon), Ohio, on January 26, 1821. He entered West Point in 1837 at age sixteen and graduated in 1841 (46/52). He was commissioned brevet second lieutenant in the 3rd Infantry. Promotions to second lieutenant (1842), first lieutenant (1846), captain (1851), and major (March 12, 1862) followed. Meanwhile, Brooks served on the frontier and in various garrisons. He saw action in the Second Seminole War and the Mexican War, where he earned a brevet at Monterrey. He also fought in the Siege of Vera Cruz, the Battles of Cerro Gordo, Contreras, and Churubusco, earning a brevet to major in the process. He ended the war on the staff of General David E. Twiggs. Later, Brooks fought the Navajos in New Mexico Territory in the 1850s. When the Civil War began, he was on garrison duty at Fort Hamilton, Brooklyn, New York.

Brooks was appointed brigadier general of volunteers on September 28, 1861, and commanded a brigade during the Peninsula Campaign and Seven Days battles. He was wounded in the leg by a bullet at Savage Station on June 29, 1862. He was back in command during the Maryland Campaign, where he fought at Crampton's Gap (September 14) and Antietam, where he was wounded in the face by a musket ball (September 17). General Newton Curtis recalled he was a modest man, devoid of any self-seeking characteristics, who was "conspicuous for skill and personal bravery." He proved to be a brave and capable commander.

He was given command of a division in the VI Corps when he returned to duty in October. Brooks fought at Fredericksburg and Chancellorsville. He was promoted to major general on June 10, 1863, but it was revoked on April 6, 1864, allegedly because he was a leader in the conspiracy to remove General Burnside from command of the Army of the Potomac after the Fredericksburg disaster. Meanwhile, Brooks commanded the Department of the Monongahela during the Gettysburg Campaign and prepared Pittsburgh for defense, although this proved unnecessary. He later returned to field duty and led a division at Cold Harbor and the Siege of Petersburg. His health failed him, however, and he resigned on July 14, 1864.

Post-war, Brooks settled on a farm near Huntsville, Alabama, which seems a strange place for a Union general to retire. His neighbors, however, treated him with respect and even affection. He died on July 19, 1870, at age forty-nine. He was buried in Maple Hill Cemetery, Huntsville. His wife continued to live in Huntsville until her death in 1921.

EGBERT BENSON BROWN was born in Brownsville, New York. He signed on to a whaling ship and sailed halfway around the world before settling in Toledo, Ohio, around 1841. He became a successful grain dealer and was city clerk, city councilman, and eventually mayor of Toledo. He moved to St. Louis in 1852 and went into the railroad business.

At the start of the Civil War, Brown actively sought to keep Missouri in the Union. He was commissioned lieutenant colonel in the 7th Missouri Infantry on August 21, 1861. He resigned this position on May 1, 1862, to become a brigadier general in the Missouri State Militia (Union), and assumed command of the District of Southwest Missouri, Department of the Mississippi, on June 5.

Brown's primary mission was to suppress pro-Southern guerrillas and defeat raids from Confederates operating out of the Indian Territory and Arkansas. He experienced several successes, most notably defeating General Jo Shelby in the Second Battle of Springfield (January 8, 1863). Here, he was wounded in the hip and the left shoulder and permanently lost the use of his left arm.

Returning to duty in June, he was named commander of the District of Central Missouri, a post he held until November 1863, when he assumed command of a brigade in the Army of the Frontier. Meanwhile, he was promoted to brigadier general, U.S. volunteers, on April 4, 1863.

Despite his victories, Brown was sometimes criticized for his lack of vigor. In the Battle of Westport on October 23, 1864, during Confederate General Sterling Price's Missouri Raid, Union commander Alfred Pleasonton relieved Brown of his command and arrested him for not obeying an order promptly enough. General Brown was tried by a military court for disobeying orders but was acquitted. Even so, Brown was unemployed until January 1865, when he assumed command of the District of Rolla, a post he held at the end of the war. He resigned his commission on November 10, 1865. He was not brevetted major general in the post-war honorary promotions.

Brown served as a pension agent in St. Louis from 1866 to 1868. He resigned and took up farming in Illinois. He died at a granddaughter's home in West Plains, Missouri, on February 11, 1902, at age eighty-five. He was interred in Kinder Cemetery, Cuba, Missouri.

ROBERT CHRISTIE "BUCK" BUCHANAN was born in Baltimore on March 1, 1811. He was the nephew by marriage of President John Quincy Adams. His grandfather Andrew served as a brigadier general in the American Revolution.

Robert Buchanan was appointed to West Point in 1826, during John Quincy Adams's administration. He graduated in 1830 (31/42) and was commissioned second lieutenant in the 4th Infantry Regiment. He served in the Black Hawk War (where he commanded gunboats during the Battle of Bad Axe) and against the Seminoles. He was also involved in the removal of the Cherokees to Indian Territory. He was with Taylor and Scott in the Mexican War, where he commanded Maryland Volunteers, fighting at Palo Alto, Resaca de la Palma, Molino del Rey, Chapultepec, and the capture of Mexico City. He was promoted to first lieutenant (1836) and captain (1838) and was brevetted to major and lieutenant colonel for "gallant and meritorious conduct" in Mexico. He was promoted to major in 1855.

In the mid and late 1850s, Buchanan commanded the District of Southern Oregon and Northern California. He headquartered at Fort Humboldt and fought the Rogue River Indians in Oregon. He was stationed in San Francisco when the Civil War began. He was ordered to Washington, D.C., where on September 9 he was given command of a brigade of "Regulars" in the capital defenses. He fought in the Peninsula and the Seven Days battles as part of V Corps, as well as at the Second Bull Run, Antietam, and Fredericksburg.

Buchanan was a good commander who was commended for his actions at the Second Bull Run and Fredericksburg. He was appointed brigadier general on November 29, 1862. His appointment expired on March 4, 1863, and he reverted to his Regular Army rank, which was now lieutenant colonel. His close association with General Fitz John Porter, the scapegoat for the Union defeat at the Second Bull Run, was a factor in the Senate's failure to act on

Buchanan's nomination. Also, he and Ulysses S. Grant had clashed before the war (Buchanan was a bit of a martinet) and hated each other. Buchanan, in fact, was a factor in Grant's resignation from the army in 1854. This certainly did not help Buchanan. In any case, he was given a backwater assignment as commander of Fort Delaware—a definite demotion. He was assistant provost marshal in Trenton, New Jersey from late April 1863 to November 1864. He was promoted to colonel, Regular Army, on February 8, 1864—a rank he gained via seniority. He was brevetted major general in 1866.

After the war, Robert Buchanan commanded the 1st Infantry Regiment at New Orleans from December 1864 to August 1865. He later commanded the District of Louisiana and forced upon the state a carpetbagger governor and legislature. His promotion to brigadier general, Regular Army, failed in the Senate. His last command was Fort Porter, New York, where he retired on December 31, 1870.

Robert C. Buchanan died of apoplexy in Washington, D.C., on November 29, 1878, at age sixty-seven. His remains are buried in the Rock Creek Cemetery, Washington.

CATHARINUS PUTNAM BUCKINGHAM was born in Zanesville, Ohio, on March 14, 1808. He was the grandson of Rufus Putnam, the Revolutionary War general who played a major role in the colonization of Ohio and who was nicknamed "the Father of the Northwest Territory." Catharinus became a West Point cadet in 1825 and graduated in 1829 (6/46). He was close personal friends with Cadet Robert E. Lee (2/46). Buckingham was commissioned second lieutenant in the 3rd Artillery.

Initially on topographical duty, young Buckingham was assistant professor of Natural and Experimental Philosophy at West Point from October 1830 until he resigned his commission on September 30, 1831. He then became a professor of mathematics and natural philosophy at Kenyon College, Ohio (1833 to 1836), was principal of a private school in Gambier, Ohio (1836–38), and later was a merchant and owner of the Kokosing Iron Works in Knox County, Ohio.

On May 3, 1861, Buckingham returned to the colors as assistant adjutant general (and de facto chief of staff) of the Ohio Commissary with the rank of major general of militia. He was promoted to adjutant general in July. On July 19, 1862, he became a brigadier general of volunteers and AAG to Edwin M. Stanton, the secretary of war. Buckingham carried the dispatch to George B. McClellan, relieving him of command of the Army of the Potomac.

Buckingham quickly tired of the Washington political circus and resigned his commission on February 11, 1863. He moved to New York and became a grain elevator constructor. He moved to Illinois in 1868 and built the Illinois Central grain elevators with his brothers—an ultimately unsuccessful business. He then became president of Chicago Steel Works. He also wrote a textbook, *Elements of the Differential and Integral Calculus*, which was published in 1875.

General Buckingham died in Chicago on August 30, 1888, at age eighty. He was buried in Woodlawn Cemetery in the town of his birth. He was married three times (outliving the first two) and had at least eight children.

RALPH POMEROY BUCKLAND was born on January 20, 1812, in Leyden, Massachusetts. His grandfather was a Revolutionary War artillery captain who died aboard a British prison ship. His parents moved to Ravenna, Ohio, in 1813. His father died when he was young, and he acquired a rudimentary education while working on an uncle's farm. He went down the Mississippi River on a flatboat at age eighteen and lived in New Orleans for three years. Meanwhile, he was educated in local schools, the Tallmadge (Ohio) Academy and Kenyon College. He was admitted to the bar in 1837 and set up a practice in Fremont, Ohio. He was mayor of the town (1843–45) and served two terms in the Ohio State Senate from 1855 to 1859. He was also a delegate to the Whig National Convention of 1848, which nominated Zachary Taylor for president. After the Whig Party collapsed, he became a Republican.

Buckland joined the Union Army on January 10, 1862, as colonel of the 72nd Ohio Infantry. He became a brigade commander in Sherman's division on March 1, 1862, and fought in the Battle of Shiloh, after which he was praised by General Sherman as "a cool, judicious, intelligent gentleman." He was largely responsible for saving Sherman's division from complete destruction on April 6.

Ralph Buckland remained with Sherman's XV Corps during Grant's Vicksburg campaigns and in the subsequent siege. Buckland was promoted to brigadier general on April 15, 1863.

On September 25, 1863, Buckland was severely injured when his horse fell on him. Both his right hip and right arm were damaged. When he returned to duty on January 26, 1864, he was commander of the Department of Memphis. He remained in the river city until January 6, 1865, when he resigned his commission. He was brevetted major general in 1866.

General Buckland returned to Ohio, ran for Congress, and was elected. He served from March 4, 1865 to March 4, 1869. He was not a candidate for re-election in 1868. He resumed practicing law in Fremont and became a prominent Episcopalian. From 1877 to 1880, he was the government director of the Union Pacific Railroad.

General Buckland was a semi-invalid during his last years. He died in Fremont on May 27, 1892. He was eighty years old. He was buried in Oakwood Cemetery, Fremont, Ohio.

DON CARLOS BUELL was born on March 23, 1818, in Lowell, Ohio, the oldest of nine children. His first cousin was George P. Buell, who became a brevet brigadier general. Don Carlos's father died in a cholera epidemic when he was eight, and he grew up in Lawrenceburg, Indiana. His uncle took him in and finished raising him. He was an introverted child but believed discipline could overcome any obstacle. He was educated in a Presbyterian school, which had similar values, and he excelled in mathematics and horsemanship.

In 1837, Buell's uncle obtained an appointment to West Point for him. He graduated with the Class of 1841 (32/52) and was commissioned second lieutenant in the 3rd Infantry. He was almost immediately sent to Florida to fight the

Seminoles but did not see any action. Eventually, the regiment was sent to Illinois, where Buell beat an enlisted man over the head with the blunt end of his sword. He was court-martialed but was found not guilty. Winfield Scott, the general-in-chief, felt he should be punished, but the court declined to reconsider the case.

Buell served with Taylor in Texas and northern Mexico and with Scott from Vera Cruz to Mexico City. He earned three brevets and was wounded in the shoulder at Churubusco (August 20, 1847). After the Mexican surrender, Buell served in the adjutant general's branch in Washington, D.C., and California. Meanwhile, he was promoted to first lieutenant (1846) and captain (1851). He married Elizabeth Margaret Hunter, the widow of General Richard B. Mason, in 1851. They had no children.

When the war began, Buell was promoted to lieutenant colonel, Regular Army (May 11, 1861), and brigadier general of volunteers (August 7), but he was sent to California—probably by General Scott. After the Union debacle at Bull Run, George McClellan replaced Scott as general-in-chief and gave his friend Buell command of the newly formed Army of the Ohio, which was basically an unruly horde. Buell quickly imposed discipline and established order. This was a major contribution to the Union war effort. Meanwhile, the Lincoln administration tried to pressure him into advancing into East Tennessee, but Buell would not consent. He proposed taking Nashville via a coordinated effort with Grant's Army of the Tennessee. Nashville was much more strategically important, so Henry Halleck, the department chief, agreed. He was pushed along by Ulysses Grant's capture of Forts Henry and Donelson, which doomed the Tennessee capital anyway. Buell occupied Nashville on February 25.

At the beginning of April, Buell was ordered to reinforce Grant's Army of the Tennessee then camped near Pittsburg Landing on the Tennessee River. As fate would have it, the Confederates launched a surprise attack at Shiloh (just south of the landing) on April 6. Buell's reinforcements (twenty thousand men) arrived that night, just in time to save Grant's army. Meanwhile, Buell was promoted to major general on March 22, 1862.

Buell's main weakness as a military commander was his lack of speed. Under Halleck's command, he slowly pursued the Rebels after Shiloh and it took him a month to reach Corinth, Mississippi. That summer, Buell was outmarched and outflanked by Confederate General Braxton Bragg, who invaded Kentucky. Buell was forced to move most of his army into the Blue Grass State to meet Bragg. The two armies clashed in a meeting engagement at Perryville on October 8. Although the Northerners badly outnumbered the Rebels and won a tactical victory, the fighting was inconclusive, and Bragg's army lived to fight another day. Lincoln lost patience with Buell's slow pursuit and sacked him on October 24. He relinquished command to Rosecrans on October 30. Lincoln also did not like the fact that Buell was a friend of McClellan, had a pro-Southern wife, and had no problem with slavery (he owned eight slaves in his lifetime) or the Southern way of life. Buell's conduct during the Perryville Campaign was the subject of an investigation by a military committee, which was mildly critical of his performance.

Although Buell and Grant were professional rivals, Grant considered Buell "a brave, intelligent officer" and a loyal one. He asked Secretary of War Stanton that Buell be restored to active duty, but his request was never acted on. After he became general-in-chief in March 1864, Grant offered Buell a possible assignment but he refused to serve under George Thomas or William T. Sherman because he was senior to both of them.

Pride goeth before a fall. Buell's volunteer commission expired on May 23, 1864, and he reverted to his regular army rank of colonel. Humiliated by this demotion, Don Carlos Buell resigned his commission on June 1, 1864.

After he resigned, Buell lived in Indiana and then Kentucky, where he was the president of the Green River Iron Company. His wife died in 1881, and this sent him into a depression. His final years were characterized by illness, declining health, and poverty.

Don Carlos Buell died on November 19, 1898, in Rockport, Kentucky, at age eighty. He is buried in Bellefontaine Cemetery, St. Louis, Missouri.

JOHN BUFORD, JR., was born at "Rose Hill" plantation in Woodford County, Kentucky, on March 4, 1826. His older half-brother was Napoleon Bonaparte Buford, who

ENCYCLOPEDIA OF UNION GENERALS

also became a Union general. His cousin, Abe Buford, was a Confederate general who rode with Nathan Bedford Forrest.

The Buford family moved to Rock Island, Illinois, when John was eight. His father, Colonel John Buford, was a prominent Democrat and an opponent of Abraham Lincoln. John, Jr. opted for a military career. He was admitted to West Point in 1844 and graduated in 1848 (16/38). He was commissioned brevet second lieutenant in the 1st Dragoons. Buford was promoted to second lieutenant (1849), first lieutenant (1853), and captain (1859). Meanwhile, he fought the Sioux on the Western frontier, served in Bleeding Kansas, and in the "Utah War" against the Mormons (1857–58). He was stationed at Fort Crittenden, Utah, when the war began.

Buford joined the U.S. Volunteers as a major and an assistant inspector general in November 1861. Initially part of the Department of the Ohio, he was then stationed in the Washington defenses, where he was commissioned brigadier general on July 27, 1862. Given a brigade of cavalry, he first saw Civil War combat as part of John Pope's Army of Virginia. He distinguished himself in the Second Battle of Bull Run, where he was wounded in the knee by a spent bullet. The wound was painful but not serious.

John Buford continued to command cavalry in the Maryland Campaign (including the battles of South Mountain and Antietam) and in the battles of Fredericksburg and Chancellorsville. He was elevated to division command on May 22, 1863.

When Joe Hooker assumed command of the Army of the Potomac, he considered appointing John Buford commander of the Cavalry Corps but chose Alfred Pleasonton instead. Later, he opined that Buford would have been a better choice.

General Buford led his division (2,700 men) at Brandy Station and Upperville. He will, however, forever be associated with the Battle of Gettysburg. On July 1, 1863, he recognized the importance of the high ground south of the town and essentially selected the battlefield for which Lee and Meade struggled for three days. Although his division was severely battered on July 1, his leadership, courage, coolness, and brilliance on that critical day is hard to overstate. He seriously delayed the Confederate advance, gave the infantry of Reynolds's I Corps time to arrive and deploy, and was undoubtedly one of the heroes of the battle now considered by most historians to be the turning point of the war.

Buford took part in the pursuit of the Army of Northern Virginia and in the Bristoe Campaign (October 1863). Unfortunately, he was stricken with typhoid fever and died on December 16. He was promoted to major general on his deathbed (see the Introduction to this volume.) He passed away in the arms of his aide, Captain Myles Keogh, who would be killed at Little Big Horn. General Buford was thirty-seven years old. He was buried in West Point Cemetery.

NAPOLEON BONAPARTE BUFORD, the half-brother of General John Buford, was born in "Rose Hill," his father's plantation in Woodford County, Kentucky, on January 13, 1807. He entered West Point in 1823 at age sixteen, graduated in 1827 (6/38), and was commissioned second lieutenant in the 3rd Artillery Regiment. Of him, classmate and future Confederate General Leonidas Polk wrote: Buford "is as good a fellow as ever lived . . . a true Christian, a true soldier, and a gentleman, every inch of him."

Buford was stationed at Fort Monroe, Virginia, and Fort Sullivan, Maine, before returning to West Point as an assistant professor of National and Experimental Philosophy (1834–35). He resigned his commission on December 31, 1835, and settled in Rock Island, Illinois, where he engaged in iron manufacturing and banking. He became president of the Rock Island and Peoria Railroad and was president of the Bank of the Federal Union, also in Rock Island. It went bankrupt at the start of the Civil War when major Southern bondholders defaulted. He assigned his property to his creditors and began his Civil War career on August 10, 1861, as colonel of the 27th Illinois Infantry, which he led in the Battle of Belmont, Missouri.

On March 4, 1862, Colonel Buford was promoted to the command of the "Flotilla Brigade" of the Army of the Mississippi. It was an infantry brigade on board gunboats. It fought in the Union victory at Island No. 10. On April 15, 1862, Lincoln promoted Buford to brigadier general.

Napoleon Buford commanded a conventional infantry brigade in the Siege of Corinth, where his performance left much to be desired. Ulysses S. Grant declared that he would barely make a respectable hospital nurse and "is just unfit for any other military position." Recalled to Washington, he was part of the court-martial of General Fitz John Porter, who was convicted of cowardice and disobedience by secret ballot. It is now generally conceded that the charges were false and the trial unjust. In any case, Buford was unemployed until June 1863, when he assumed command of the post of Cairo, Illinois, which consisted of a single infantry regiment. On September 12, he was named commander of the District of Eastern Arkansas, headquartered in Helena, a post he occupied until March 9, 1865, when he was removed from command on the direct order of General Grant. He was sent home and was unemployed for the rest of the war. He was mustered out of the service on August 24, 1865. He was brevetted major general in 1867.

From 1867 to 1869, General Buford was a special commissioner of Indian Affairs and government inspector of the Union Pacific Railroad. He then returned to civilian life and resided in Chicago, where he died on March 28, 1883, at age seventy-six. He was interred in the Chippiannock Cemetery, Rock Island, Illinois.

STEPHEN GANO BURBRIDGE was born on August 19, 1831, in Georgetown, Kentucky. He came from a military family. His grandfather was a captain in the American Revolution, and his father held the same rank in the War of 1812. Stephen was educated at Georgetown College and the Kentucky Military Institute in Frankfort. He later read law and was admitted to the bar but never practiced. When the Civil War began, he was managing his large plantation in Logan County.

He joined the Union Army on August 27, 1861, as colonel of the 26th Kentucky Infantry Regiment. He led it in the Battle of Shiloh. A. J. Smith and William T. Sherman were complimentary of his performance and had a high opinion of him. (Generals Grant and Schofield did not.) He commanded a brigade in the XIII Corps during the various Vicksburg campaigns, including the smashing Union victory at Fort Hindman (Arkansas Post) in January 1863. He also took part in the Siege of Vicksburg. He was promoted to brigadier general on June 12, 1862.

On February 15, 1864, Grant named Burbridge commander of the District of Kentucky. In this capacity, he became known as the "Butcher of Kentucky." He was certainly hard on the civilians and banished many from the state. He also suppressed newspapers, impressed blacks (both slave and free) as laborers, arrested many prominent citizens (including the chief justice of the Kentucky Supreme Court), ordered that one candidate be taken off the ballot, issued fines and levees to suspected "disloyal" persons, used the army to intimidate voters, and summarily executed several suspected guerrillas. During the election of 1864, he also suppressed the supporters of Democratic candidates. He even arrested and deported the lieutenant governor. Governor Thomas E. Bramlette called him an "imbecile" whose actions were nothing but the "blundering of a weak intellect and an overwhelming vanity."

The Kentucky Militia was considered incompetent when Burbridge assumed command and grew worse under his leadership. He did, however, successfully recruit former slaves into the army and play a role in the defeat of John Hunt Morgan in the summer of 1864. Burbridge was brevetted major general on July 4, 1864, for "the repulse of John Morgan's recent invasion." His negatives far outweighed his positives, however, and his efforts to suppress the guerrillas failed. On February 22, 1865, after Lincoln met with a legislative delegation from Kentucky, Burbridge was relieved of his command. Major General John M. Palmer succeeded him. He was unemployed for the rest of the war and resigned his commission on December 1, 1865.

Probably the most hated man in Kentucky, Burbridge moved to Brooklyn, New York. He died there on December 2, 1894. He was sixty-three years of age. He is buried in Arlington National Cemetery.

HIRAM "GRIZZLY" BURNHAM was born in Narraguagus (now Cherryfield), Maine, in 1814. He worked as a lumberman, owned a small sawmill, and grew into a bear of a man who knew how to command respect. During the "Aroostook War," he formed a militia company and served as its captain. Fortunately, this border conflict with Canada was resolved without an actual war. He later served as coroner and was elected county commissioner as a Republican.

Burnham entered the army as lieutenant colonel of the 6th Maine Infantry on July 15, 1861. He was promoted to colonel on December 12. He fought in the Peninsula Campaign; in Maryland, including the battles of Crampton's Gap and Antietam; and at Fredericksburg, where his regiment was lightly engaged.

In the spring of 1863, the Union high command formed the "Light Division" of the VI Corps. It was designed to move quickly and featured the use of mules instead of wagons to carry supplies. Burnham was given command of one of its brigades, but when its commander, General Pratt, resigned, Burnham became division commander and led it from May 3 to 11.

During the Battle of Chancellorsville, the VI Corps formed the Union left flank at Fredericksburg. The Light Division attacked Marye's Heights on May 3 and suffered 30 percent casualties. Burnham was wounded but not seriously. He also fought at Salem Church the next day. The division was dissolved after the Chancellorsville debacle and Burnham reverted to brigade command. Burnham's men were in reserve behind Little Round Top during the Battle of Gettysburg.

Hiram Burnham was promoted to brigadier general on April 30, 1864, and was given command of a brigade in the XVIII Corps of the Army of the James. He led it from April 28 until his death, except for the period July 31 to August 3, when he commanded a division. During the Battle of Chaffin's Farm on September 29, 1864, he was leading his men in an attack on Fort Harrison, when a Rebel bullet hit him in the intestines. He died soon after. "Say to my family and friends, that I have tried to do my duty," were his last words. General Burnham was forty-nine or fifty years old. He is buried in the Pine Grove Cemetery, Cherryfield, Maine.

WILLIAM WALLACE BURNS was born in Coshocton, Ohio, on September 3, 1825, the son of a locally prominent political figure and a major general in the Ohio Militia. William was also related to George Washington via his mother's line. The well-connected Burns secured an appointment to West Point in 1842 and graduated with the Class of 1847 (28/38). He was set back a year because he failed English as a plebe. Commissioned brevet second lieutenant in the 3rd Infantry, he was promoted to second lieutenant (1847), first lieutenant (1850), and captain (1858).

Burns was sent to Mexico in 1847 but the fighting ended by the time he arrived. He spent the next several years on garrison duty in the West and Southwest, was on recruiting duty in Philadelphia (1854–56), served as regimental quartermaster in the Third Seminole War (1856–57), and was chief commissary officer for Albert Sidney Johnston during the Utah War against the Mormons (1857–58). He was stationed at Fort Smith, Arkansas, when the Civil War began, and narrowly avoided being captured by Arkansas militiamen when they took the place on April 23, 1861.

Burns was General McClellan's Chief Commissary Officer during his Western Virginia Campaign of 1861. His success here led to his being promoted to major, Regular Army, on August 3. Burns, however, wanted a combat command—and got it. He assumed leadership of the Philadelphia Brigade on October 22, after Edward Baker was killed at Ball's Bluff. Meanwhile, Burns was promoted to brigadier general of volunteers on September 28, 1861.

General Burns served in the Peninsula Campaign and saved a Union artillery battery at Seven Pines. Ironically, shortly after this battery fired the shot that critically wounded Confederate General Joseph E. Johnston. He was replaced by Robert E. Lee, who gave the Union Army all sorts of problems over the next three years.

Burns was wounded in action at Savage Station on June 29, 1862. His brigade was split by a Rebel attack, and Burns was hit in the face by a minié ball, but he ignored his wounds, rallied his troops, and repulsed the attack. The next day, at Frayser's Farm (Glendale), he checked a Confederate attack that had already routed one Union division. He thus helped save the Army of the Potomac. Meanwhile, his horse fell, and he sustained more injuries. In addition, he contracted malaria and his facial wound became infected. He was sent to the rear to recuperate and was on sick leave until mid-November.

General Burns commanded a division in the Battle of Fredericksburg in December 1862. He then went to the Western Front under the belief that he was about to be promoted to major general and given command of a corps. He should have been, frankly, but his promotion was blocked by Secretary of War Stanton as punishment for Burns's strong support for George McClellan—or at least that is what Burns believed. He tried to force the issue by resigning his volunteer commission, under the assumption that Lincoln would refuse his resignation and give him his promotion. Lincoln, however, accepted it. Burns returned to the Commissary Department as a major, and politics cost the North another fine commander. He spent the rest of the war as chief commissary officer of the Department of the Northwest. In the fall of 1865, he became chief commissary officer of the Department of the South, headquartered in Charleston, South Carolina. He was military commandant of the city for nineteen days in 1868. Significantly, he was never brevetted major general.

Burns became lieutenant colonel, Regular Army, and assistant commissary for general subsistence in 1874. Stationed in Washington, D.C., he was promoted to colonel in 1884. He retired on September 3, 1889, and settled in Beaumont, South Carolina, where he died on April 12, 1892, at age sixty-six. He is buried in Arlington National Cemetery.

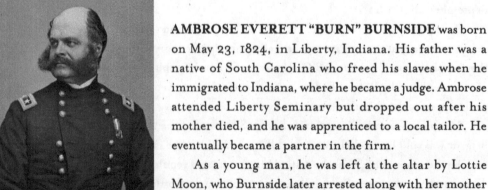

AMBROSE EVERETT "BURN" BURNSIDE was born on May 23, 1824, in Liberty, Indiana. His father was a native of South Carolina who freed his slaves when he immigrated to Indiana, where he became a judge. Ambrose attended Liberty Seminary but dropped out after his mother died, and he was apprenticed to a local tailor. He eventually became a partner in the firm.

As a young man, he was left at the altar by Lottie Moon, who Burnside later arrested along with her mother and sister as Confederate spies. They were, and Burnside kept them under house arrest for months, but he never charged them with espionage. Meanwhile, he married Mary Bishop in 1852. They had no children.

Burnside graduated from West Point in 1847 (18/38) and was commissioned second lieutenant in the 2nd Artillery. He was sent to Mexico but arrived too late to see any fighting. He was on occupation duty in Mexico City until 1848. He then spent two years on the frontier, protecting Western mail routes, where his commander was Captain Braxton Bragg. He was wounded in the neck by an Apache arrow during a skirmish in New Mexico in 1849.

"Burn" was promoted to first lieutenant in 1851 but resigned in 1853. He devoted his attention to manufacturing an invention of his: the Burnside breechloading carbine. This business venture failed because of a factory fire and because the government broke its $100,000 contract with Burnside. (Apparently, another gun manufacturer bribed Secretary of War John Floyd to do this.)

Burnside was an outgoing, likeable, friendly man who had a talent for remembering everyone's name. A Democrat, he ran for Congress in 1858 but was crushed. Financially ruined, he assigned his remaining assets to creditors and took a position as treasurer of the Illinois Central Railroad. His boss was a former West Point classmate, George C. McClellan.

When the Civil War began, Burnside was a brigadier general in the Rhode Island Militia. He became colonel of the 1st Rhode Island Infantry on May 2 and became a brigade commander in June. He fought credibly at Bull Run but without particular distinction; he was nevertheless promoted to brigadier general on August 9.

Ambrose Burnside commanded the North Carolina Expeditionary Force from September 1861 to July 1862. Here he was highly successful, especially in the victories at Elizabeth City, Roanoke Island, and New Bern, and he closed 80 percent of the North Carolina coast to Confederate shipping. He was promoted to major general on March 19 and his task force was upgraded to IX Corps.

The corps was transferred to the Army of the Potomac during the Maryland Campaign and fought at Antietam. Here, Burnside forced a crossing of the creek over the famous Burnside Bridge. It was a flawed

ENCYCLOPEDIA OF UNION GENERALS

battle, however, because Burnside moved slowly and failed to conduct a reconnaissance. Had he done so, he would have discovered several sites which were easily fordable. As a result, Robert E. Lee was able to bring up reinforcements and save his army, if only barely.

Lincoln sacked McClellan on November 5 and replaced him with Ambrose Burnside as commander of the Army of the Potomac. Burnside did not want the appointment and felt himself inadequate to the task. He proceeded to prove it. He caved to pressure from Abraham Lincoln, who wanted immediate, aggressive action. He launched a series of frontal assaults and was soundly defeated at Fredericksburg on December 13. He suffered 13,000 casualties, as opposed to fewer than 5,500 for the South.

In January 1863, he tried again, but because of heavy winter rains, his army bogged down, and he was checked without a battle. This campaign was called "the Mud March." By now, his soldiers had lost faith in him, and he was sacked on January 26. He was replaced by Joseph Hooker, who Burnside despised.

Burnside offered to resign his commission, but Lincoln returned him to the command of the IX Corps and made him commander of the Department of the Ohio. Here, he suppressed popular dissent, shut down unfriendly newspapers, tried civilians via military tribunals, and arrested Ohio Congressman Clement L. Vallandigham. Meanwhile, he successfully met Confederate raider John Hunt Morgan, captured him, and destroyed most of his command. He also invaded East Tennessee, took Knoxville, and captured the Cumberland Gap after bluffing the garrison into surrender. Confederate General Longstreet tried to recapture Knoxville but was defeated by Burnside at Fort Sanders on November 29. He had partially redeemed his reputation.

The IX Corps was part of Grant's Overland Campaign of 1864 and in the Siege of Petersburg. On July 30, 1864, in the Battle of the Crater, Burnside blasted a fifty-yard hole in Lee's lines. Largely because of interference from George G. Meade, but partially because of his own mismanagement, he suffered a humiliating defeat when the Rebels rallied. He was relieved of his command on August 17. Later, the U.S. Congress Joint Committee on the Conduct of the War exonerated Burnside and placed the blame for the Federal defeat on Meade and with considerable justification. Burnside was nevertheless unemployed for the rest of the war. He resigned his commission on April 15, 1865—the day Abraham Lincoln died.

Pulitzer Prize–winning author Bruce Catton concluded that Burnside "was a simple, honest, loyal soldier, doing his best even if that best was not very good." He noted Burnside never schemed or engaged in backbiting and "in an army many of whose generals were insufferable prima donnas, Burnside never mistook himself for Napoleon."

Burnside returned to the railroad business and was president of the Cincinnati and Martinsville Railroad, the Martinsville Railroad, the Indianapolis and Vincennes Railroad, and the Rhode Island Locomotive Works. He became a Republican and was three times elected governor of Rhode Island, serving from 1866 to 1869. He was also commander-in-chief of the Grand Army of the Republic veterans' organization (1871–73) and the first president of the National Rifle Association. He was elected to the U.S. Senate in 1874 and re-elected in 1880. He died suddenly of an angina pectoris on September 13, 1881 in Bristol, Rhode Island. He was fifty-seven years of age. He was buried in Swan Point Cemetery, Providence, Rhode Island.

His unusual beard was called "burnsides." Later, the syllables were reversed and called "sideburns."

CYRUS BUSSEY was born in Hubbard, Ohio, on October 15, 1833, the son of a Methodist minister. The family moved to Indiana when he was four. At age fourteen, Cyrus worked as a clerk in a dry goods store. He started his own mercantile business the next year. In 1855, he moved to Davis County, Iowa, started another business, read law, and was admitted to the bar. He also went into politics and in 1859 was elected to the Iowa State Senate. A Democrat, he was a delegate to the Baltimore convention which nominated Stephen Douglas for president in 1860.

In April 1861, right after Fort Sumter, he became the aide to Samuel J. Kirkwood, the governor of Iowa, with the rank of lieutenant colonel of militia. In August, he was promoted to colonel and commander of the 3rd Iowa Cavalry Regiment. He fought at Pea Ridge, where his regiment faced several hundred Confederate Indians on March 7. It lost twenty-four killed (of which eight were scalped), seventeen wounded, and nine missing out of 235 engaged.

Bussey assumed command of a cavalry brigade in eastern Arkansas on November 2 and became part of the XIII Corps. He took part in Grant's Vicksburg campaigns and led a cavalry division during General Sherman's second drive on Jackson, Mississippi, in July 1863. Afterward, he returned to the west side of the Mississippi and was promoted to brigadier general on April 10, 1864.

General Bussey directed a cavalry brigade during the Camden Expedition as part of Steele's VII Corps in Arkansas, where he did not win any special praise. In February 1865—after the fighting was over—he was given command of an infantry division. He was mustered out of volunteer service on August 24, 1865, and brevetted major general in 1866.

Post-war, Cyrus Bussey worked in the commission business in St. Louis and New Orleans. He was assistant secretary of the interior from 1889 to 1893, after which he practiced law in Washington, D.C. He died of pneumonia at his home on March 2, 1915, at age eighty-one. His remains lie in Arlington National Cemetery.

RICHARD BUSTEED was born on February 15, 1822, in County Cavan, Ireland. He emigrated to the island of St. Lucia; returned to Ireland; and then moved to Canada. He finally emigrated to the United States, residing in Ohio, Connecticut, Illinois, and New York. Meanwhile, he read law, was admitted to the bar in 1846, and was in private practice until 1856. He was corporation counsel for New York City from 1856 to 1859. He also worked as a newspaper writer and a Methodist preacher.

Busteed joined the army on October 1, 1861, as a captain in the Chicago Light Artillery. The regiment was sent to Cairo, Illinois, fought at Forts Henry and Donelson, the Battle of Shiloh, and Grant's unsuccessful Central Mississippi Campaign. Busteed was promoted to brigadier general on August 7, 1862, and commanded a brigade in the VII Corps, which was basically destroyed by Stonewall Jackson at Harpers Ferry in September. Busteed was away on temporary duty in New York City and Washington and was not among the prisoners. Later, he commanded a brigade and was on garrison duty in Yorktown, Virginia. The Senate, however, did not act upon his appointment, which expired on March 4, 1863. He resigned his commission six days later.

Lincoln graced Busteed with a recess appointment to the U.S. District Court for the Middle District of Alabama, the Northern District of Alabama, and the Southern District of Alabama. He was renominated for the same position in January 1864. In late 1867, in Mobile, Alabama, he was shot in the chest and leg by a political enemy, but he recovered. He held office until 1874, when he resigned because the Judiciary Committee of the U.S. House of Representatives recommended his impeachment for using his position for his personal interest.

After he left the Federal bench, Busteed resumed private practice in New York City. He practiced until his death on September 14, 1898, at age seventy-six. He was buried in Woodlawn Cemetery, The Bronx, New York.

BENJAMIN FRANKLIN BUTLER was born on November 5, 1818, in Deerfield, New Hampshire, the son of a privateer. After his father died of yellow fever in the West Indies, Butler's mother moved the family to Lowell, Massachusetts, where she operated a boarding house. His application for West Point was rejected, so he attended Waterville (now Colby) College, from which he graduated in 1838. He was admitted to the bar and set up a practice in Lowell. He was a combative attorney who specialized in bankruptcy law.

Antebellum, Butler was a Democrat and frequently spoke against abolishing slavery. In the deadlocked Charleston convention of 1860, Butler cast his vote for Jefferson Davis for president of the United States on fifty-seven consecutive ballots. He ended up supporting future Confederate General John C. Breckinridge in the election of 1860.

Despite a lack of military experience, Butler secured an appointment as brigadier general of militia in 1855. During the riots following Fort

Sumter, he reestablished railroad connections between Baltimore and Washington and secured Annapolis for the Union. Lincoln appointed him major general of volunteers on May 16, 1861. He was one of the most senior Union generals for most of the war.

Sent to Fort Monroe, Virginia, Butler suffered his first defeat at Big Bethel on the Virginia Peninsula. He successfully attacked Forts Hatteras and Clark in North Carolina in August and became a hero in the North, which was starved for victories. After a recruiting tour in New England, he took part in the occupation of New Orleans and became military governor. President Lincoln intended for Louisiana to be the showcase for presidential reconstruction. But the women of New Orleans did not like Yankees—especially Butler, whom they considered common white trash and a corrupt thief. He became known as "Beast" or "Spoons" Butler because he changed headquarters frequently, and when the rightful owner returned, all the silverware was gone. Jewish women were quite prominent in the Crescent City in those days, and Butler was a notorious anti-Semite, which did not help him at all. In May 1862, a woman from an upper story dumped the contents of a chamber pot on Admiral David Farragut. In retaliation, Butler issued a general order stating that any woman who insulted or showed contempt for a Union soldier should be treated as a prostitute. He also issued orders commanding preachers and priests to pray for Abraham Lincoln, or they would be arrested. He confiscated cotton and purchased it at rigged auctions, making himself rich. He also shut down newspapers and recruited USCT (United States Colored Troops), which outraged even some Northern officers, although they later did well in combat. Facing the potential of a popular revolt within a Rebellion, Lincoln sacked him on December 17, 1862. He was succeeded by Nathaniel P. Banks, who was much more successful in winning the "hearts and minds" of the people. (Banks defeated Butler in the Massachusetts gubernatorial election of 1859.)

Butler was still popular in Radical circles, so Lincoln gave him command of the Department of Virginia and North Carolina in November 1863. Headquartered in Norfolk, it was upgraded to the Army of the James and was directed to land south of Richmond and seize the railroad center of Petersburg. The center was virtually undefended on May 5, 1864, but by the time Butler advanced, General Beauregard had received significant reinforcements. Although still badly outnumbered, he defeated Butler at Drewry's Bluff on May 16 and isolated his army in the Bermuda Hundred peninsula, where it remained for most of the rest of the war.

In December 1864, Butler's troops were ordered to take Fort Fisher, North Carolina. His plan failed and Grant sacked him on January 8, 1865. (With the election of 1864 over, Lincoln felt he could allow this.) He was unemployed for the rest of the war and resigned his commission on November 30, 1865.

Butler was a political chameleon. In late 1865, he called for a second war against the South and was one of the most radical of Republicans. Meanwhile, he was elected to Congress, serving from 1867 to 1875 and 1877 to 1879. He made four gubernatorial runs but only won a single one-year term (1883–84). He was, however, a rich man and lived well.

Benjamin F. Butler was a poor tactical commander and perhaps the most corrupt of the Union generals. He died in Washington, D.C., on January 11, 1893, at age seventy-four. He was buried in the Hildreth Cemetery in Lowell, Massachusetts.

DANIEL BUTTERFIELD was born on Halloween, 1831, in Utica, New York. His father was the founder of the Overland Mail Company and co-founder of what became American Express. Daniel graduated from Union College in Schenectady, New York, in 1849, and he worked for his father's companies, mostly in the South. Butterfield was indicted for arson upon the testimony of a co-conspirator in 1851. One person died in the fire. The co-conspirator was eventually hanged but charges against Butterfield were dropped in 1853. He eventually became superintendent of the Eastern Division of American Express, headquartered in New York City. He joined the 71st New York Militia Regiment as a captain and was elected colonel of the 12th Militia in 1859.

Butterfield led the 12th to Washington a week after Fort Sumter surrendered. His regiment was the first Union formation to cross into Virginia. He became a brigade commander on July 10 and served in the First Bull Run Campaign. He was promoted to brigadier general on

September 7 and assumed command of a brigade in Fitz John Porter's V Corps. The following year, he wrote *Camp and Outpost Duty for Infantry*, an army training manual.

Butterfield served in the Peninsula Campaign and the Seven Days battles, where he distinguished himself. He was wounded at Gaines' Mill on June 27, 1862. He led his brigade at the Second Bull Run but came down with camp fever and missed Antietam. He became a division commander on November 1. Meanwhile, he wrote the bugle call "Taps." He also designed distinctive divisional patches which are a characteristic of U.S. Army uniforms to this day. (General Philip Kearny apparently originated the idea, but Butterfield popularized it.) He succeeded Porter as commander of the V Corps and led it in the Battle of Fredericksburg, after which he became chief of staff of the Army of the Potomac (January 1863), now under Hooker. He was promoted to major general on November 29, 1862.

Generals Butterfield and Hooker developed a close personal relationship, and their headquarters was characterized by wild, drunken parties, complete with prostitutes and whores. It was said the HQ was a place no gentleman would care to go and no lady could go. Butterfield was disliked by most of his colleagues.

Following Hooker's defeat at Chancellorsville, he was replaced by George G. Meade. The Headquarters of the Army of the Potomac was always characterized by political intrigue. Meade did not trust Butterfield but retained him until after Gettysburg. Butterfield and Sickles (another Hooker crony) conspired against Meade before the battle. On July 3, 1863, the third day of the battle, as Confederate artillery pounded the U.S. line in preparation for Pickett's charge, Butterfield was wounded. In his absence, Meade officially replaced him on July 14.

That fall, after he recovered, Butterfield rejoined Hooker as chief of staff of the XI and XII Corps of the Army of the Cumberland at Chattanooga. The two corps were later consolidated in the XX Corps. Butterfield was given command of a division on April 14, 1864, which he led in the Atlanta Campaign until June 29, when he fell ill. (He was apparently still suffering from his Gettysburg wound.) Due to his poor health, he was sent to Vicksburg on light duty. Later, he was involved in recruiting duty. He also commanded the forces in New York harbor. He was mustered out on August

14, 1865, although he remained in the Regular Army until 1870—often unemployed.

Post-war, Ulysses S. Grant named Daniel Butterfield assistant treasurer of the United States. He accepted a $10,000 payment from currency speculator Jay Gould in exchange for Butterfield telling Gould when the government was planning to sell gold. This cost him his job in October 1869. He worked for American Express after that. He also married well. His first wife died in 1884 and he married a widow who was worth $3,000,000 ($75,000,000 in 2023 money.) He was awarded the Congressional Medal of Honor in 1892 for his actions at Gaines' Mill thirty years before.

General Butterfield died at his summer residence in Cold Spring, New York, on July 17, 1901. He was sixty-nine years of age. He is buried just across the Hudson River in the West Point Cemetery, even though he had no association with the Academy. "Taps" was played at his funeral.

C
· CADWALADER – CUTLER ·

GEORGE CADWALADER was born in Philadelphia on May 16, 1806. His grandfather was Pennsylvania Militia Brigadier General John Cadwalader. George read law, was admitted to the bar, and joined the Pennsylvania Militia in 1824. He was elected brigadier general in 1832. He did little to suppress the anti-Catholic, anti-Irish riots of May 1844, for which he was criticized. In July, however, he ordered his troops to fire into a mob which was trying to destroy St. Philip Neri Church. Twelve rioters and two militiamen were killed. He obtained a U.S. Volunteer commission as a brigadier general in 1847, fought in Mexico, and was brevetted major general for his courage in the Battle of Chapultepec. He was discharged in 1848.

Cadwalader was a successful businessman in the 1850s. When the Civil War began, he was appointed major general of Pennsylvania Volunteers on April 19, 1861. On May 15, he was named military commander in Maryland and obeyed Lincoln's order suspending writs of habeas corpus, even though this involved ignoring an order from the chief justice of the U.S. Supreme Court. He later commanded a division in Robert Patterson's Army of the Shenandoah. He held state rank only until April 26, 1862, when he was commissioned major general of U.S. volunteers. He briefly commanded the post of Corinth, Mississippi, in August 1862 and otherwise served on court-martials, boards of inquiry, and the like. He returned to Philadelphia in the fall of 1862 as commandant of the city, where he spent the rest of the war. He resigned his volunteer commission on July 6, 1865.

After the war, he helped establish the Military Order of the Loyal Legion of the United States (MOLLUS), a veterans' organization of former Union officers. He was commander-in-chief of the group from its founding until his death, which occurred in Philadelphia on February 3, 1879. He was seventy-two. General Cadwalader was buried in the Christ Church Burial Ground, Philadelphia.

JOHN CURTIS CALDWELL was born on April 17, 1833, in Lowell, Vermont. After graduating from Amherst College, he moved to Maine and became principal of the Washington Academy in East Machias.

Caldwell entered the Union Army and was elected colonel of the 11th Maine on November 12, 1861, despite having no military training. He took part in the Peninsula Campaign and was promoted to brigadier general on April 30, 1862. He distinguished himself at Seven Pines (Fair Oaks), after which General Kearny praised his "personal gallantry." Caldwell's brigade continued to perform well at Antietam, where it captured more than three hundred Confederates. General McClellan reported that it maneuvered under enemy fire "as steadily as [if] on drill." Caldwell was, however, criticized for handling his brigade poorly during his assault on the sunken road. Caldwell was wounded in this action. During the Battle of Fredericksburg, one of his regiments broke and ran during the assault on Marye's Heights, reflecting poorly upon Caldwell, who was wounded twice (in the left shoulder and side) but not seriously.

During the Battle of Chancellorsville, General Caldwell again performed well, covering the retreat of the army from the Chancellorsville crossroads. On May 22, he was given command of a division in Hancock's II Corps.

Gettysburg was Caldwell's worst day of the Civil War. During the afternoon of July 2, he was ordered to reinforce III Corps in the wheatfield but was caught in the right flank by McLaws's division. General Sykes, the commander of the V Corps, criticized Caldwell, which led to an investigation. Caldwell was exonerated, but his reputation was marred.

Caldwell briefly commanded II Corps on July 3, and on three other occasions, but Gettysburg effectively ruined his military career. When the Army of the Potomac was reorganized on March 23, 1864, several units consolidated, and Caldwell was left without a command. He was unemployed for the rest of the war. He was brevetted major general on January 13, 1866, and was mustered out two days later.

Post-war, John Caldwell held several government posts, including adjutant general of the Maine Militia (1867–69), U.S. consul to Valparaiso,

Chile (1869–74), U.S. minister to Uruguay and Paraguay (1874–82), and U.S. Consul to San Jose, Costa Rica (1897–1909). He suffered from dementia in his sunset years and died in Calais, Maine, at the home of a daughter, on August 31, 1912, at age seventy-nine. He was buried in the St. Stephen Rural Cemetery, St. Stephen, New Brunswick, Canada, just across the river from Calais.

ROBERT ALEXANDER CAMERON was born on February 22, 1828, in Brooklyn, New York. He moved to Indiana in 1842 and attended Indiana Medical College and the Rush Medical College in Chicago. His interest in medicine waned, however, and in 1857, he bought and published the *Valparaiso Republican*, a newspaper. He was elected to the Indiana House of Representatives and was a Lincoln delegate to the 1860 Republican National Convention.

Cameron enlisted in the 9th Indiana Infantry Regiment when the war began and on April 23, 1861, was elected captain. He fought in the Western Virginia Campaign, and when the enlistments in his 90-day regiment expired, he was appointed lieutenant colonel of the 19th Indiana. In early 1862, he was transferred to the 34th Indiana because he could not get along with his regimental commander.

The 34th fought at New Madrid and Island No. 10 in Missouri and took part in the capture of Memphis on June 6, 1862. He was promoted to colonel and assumed command of the 34th on June 15.

Colonel Cameron took part in the various Vicksburg campaigns and was wounded in the eyes at the Battle of Port Gibson on May 1, 1863. He was promoted to brigadier general on August 11, 1863, and was given command of a brigade in the XIII Corps, Army of the Gulf. He became a division commander on March 3, 1864, and fought in the Red River Campaign, where his division was routed at Mansfield on April 8. Cameron nevertheless succeeded to corps detachment command after Thomas E. G. Ransom was wounded at Mansfield. He led the XIII Corps troops in Louisiana until April 27. He then reverted to divisional command.

After Red River, Cameron was given a backwater assignment as commander of the District of La Fourche. He was there when the war ended. He resigned his volunteer commission on June 22, 1865, and was brevetted major general in 1866.

General Cameron moved to Colorado after the war and devoted most of the rest of his life to developing that state. He was one of the founders of Greeley, Colorado Springs, and Fort Collins. He lived in San Francisco for a few years before returning to Colorado as a postal clerk in Denver. He was warden of the Colorado State Penitentiary at Canon City from 1885 to 1887. He was also a farmer, rancher, and real estate developer.

General Cameron died on March 15, 1894, in Canon City. He was sixty-six. He was interred in Greenwood Cemetery, Canon City.

CHARLES THOMAS CAMPBELL was born in Franklin County, Pennsylvania, on August 10, 1823. He attended Marshall College in Lancaster but apparently never graduated. He joined the 8th U.S. Infantry Regiment as a second lieutenant when the Mexican War began and rose to the rank of captain before being discharged in 1848. He did not see combat.

Campbell was elected to the Pennsylvania legislature in 1852. He rejoined the army on May 29, 1861, as a captain and battery commander in the Pennsylvania Light Artillery. He was promoted to lieutenant colonel in the 1st Pennsylvania Artillery (state troops) on August 5 and became its colonel on September 13. He fought in the Battle of Dranesville on December 20. He resigned his state commission on February 1, 1862, and joined the Union Army as commander of the 57th Pennsylvania Infantry. He fought in the Peninsula Campaign including the Battle of Seven Pines, where he was wounded three times (in the right arm, left leg and pelvis), had his horse shot out from under him, and was captured by the Rebels. Despite his injuries, he managed to escape that same day.

It took Charles Campbell months to recover from Seven Pines. Still suffering from his wounds, he was appointed brigadier general on November

29, 1862. He led a brigade in the Battle of Fredericksburg on December 13, where he was again seriously wounded in the abdomen and right arm. A bullet went through his liver, and he was not expected to live, but he did.

Campbell's initial appointment as brigadier general expired on March 4, 1863. He reverted to the rank of colonel but was reappointed March 13. This time, he was confirmed, but it was November 7, 1864, before he returned to active duty as commander of the District of Wisconsin in the Department of the Northwest. He commanded the district until the end of the war. He was discharged from Federal service in January 1866.

After the war, Campbell moved to the Dakota Territory as an inspector of Indian agencies. Later, he ran a stagecoach line and a hotel. His stagecoach station grew into the town of Scotland, South Dakota, of which he was mayor. General Campbell fell down the straits of his hotel and died in Scotland on April 15, 1895, at age seventy-one. He was buried in the Yankton City Cemetery, Yankton, South Dakota.

WILLIAM BOWEN CAMPBELL was born on February 1, 1807, in Sumner County, Tennessee. He studied law in Abingdon, Virginia, under his uncle, Governor David Campbell. He returned to Tennessee in 1829, was admitted to the bar in 1830, and established a law practice in Carthage, Tennessee, but was practicing at the state circuit court in Sparta, Smith County, in 1831. He moved back to Carthage in 1835. The following year, he joined the army as the captain of a mounted rifle company and fought in the Creek and Second Seminole Wars.

Late in 1836, Campbell ran for the U.S. House Representatives as a Whig. He was elected and served from 1837 to 1843. He did not seek re-election in 1842. He was appointed major general of the Tennessee Militia in 1843. When the Mexican War began, he was elected commander of the 1st Tennessee Infantry and fought in the Battle of Monterrey, where his regiment suffered one-third casualties. He later joined Scott's army in the Siege of Vera Cruz and the Battle of Cerro Gordo.

After the fall of Mexico City, Campbell was named circuit court judge by the Tennessee legislature. Campbell was elected governor in 1851 by a vote of 63,333 to 61,673. He was a strong opponent of secession. Serving from October 16, 1851 to October 17, 1853, he was the last Whig governor from Tennessee. He did not run for re-election; instead, he became president of the Bank of Middle Tennessee in Lebanon. He was succeeded as governor by Andrew Johnson. He became a circuit judge again in 1859 and supported the Constitutional Union candidate John Bell for president in 1860.

Campbell canvassed Tennessee in opposition to secession in early 1861 but was not successful. After the Volunteer State left the Union, he was offered a command in the Confederate Army. Instead, after middle Tennessee fell into Union hands, he accepted Abraham Lincoln's offer for the post of brigadier general on July 3, 1862. He resigned on January 26, 1863, because of declining health and because he did not want to fight his fellow Tennesseans.

In 1864, Campbell supported George McClellan for president of the United States. After Lincoln was assassinated, he backed Andrew Johnson's presidency. In 1866, he was elected to the U.S. House of Representatives. He died in office in Lebanon, Tennessee, August 19, 1867, at age sixty. He was buried in Cedar Grove Cemetery, Lebanon. Fort Campbell, Kentucky, was named in his honor.

EDWARD RICHARD SPRIGG "ED" CANBY, the brother-in-law of Brigadier General John Parker Hawkins, was born on November 9, 1817, in Piatt's Landing, Kentucky. He initially attended Walsh College but dropped out to enroll in West Point in 1835. He graduated in 1839 (30/31) and was commissioned second lieutenant in the 2nd Infantry Regiment. Between tours of garrison duty, mostly in the West, he fought in the Second Seminole War; in Mexico, where he was brevetted three times during Scott's drive on Mexico City; and in the Utah War. He was stationed at Fort Defiance, New Mexico Territory, when the Civil War began. He was promoted to colonel, Regular Army, and commander of the 19th Infantry on May 14, 1861. In June, he was placed in charge of the Department (later District) of New Mexico.

ENCYCLOPEDIA OF UNION GENERALS

In early 1862, the Confederates invaded New Mexico. Led by Canby's former subordinate, Henry H. Sibley, they defeated Canby in the Battle of Valverde on February 20–21. Canby, however, executed a brilliant defensive strategy. He got into Sibley's rear at Glorieta Pass (March 26–28), and burned the Confederate wagons and destroyed most of their horses and mules. Their supply line collapsed, and the starving Rebels were forced to retreat to Texas.

Canby became a brigadier general of volunteers on April 11, 1862. In August, he was transferred to Washington, D.C., on administrative duty. He was sent to New York City at the end of the draft riots, during which about 1,200 people were killed, as commander of both the city and the harbor. On November 9, he returned to Washington as assistant adjutant general to Secretary of War Edwin Stanton.

E. R. S. Canby was a tall, taciturn man with none of the social graces of a Nathaniel Banks, but he was a modest, highly capable administrator. Some of his cousins were Confederates, but after they were captured, he played no favorites and would not release them early.

On May 7, 1864, Ed Canby was promoted to major general and replaced Banks as commander of the Army of the Gulf and the Military Division of Western Mississippi. On November 8, while aboard the gunboat *USS Cricket*, on the White River of Arkansas, General Canby was wounded in the hip by a Confederate sniper. He recovered quickly and commanded the Union forces operating against Mobile in the spring of 1865. He captured Fort Blakeley on April 9, 1865, and Mobile fell on April 12. He accepted the surrender of Richard Taylor at Citronelle on May 4 and the Trans-Mississippi Department (represented by Simon Boliver Buckner) on May 26. These were the last major Southern forces to lay down their arms.

Appointed brigadier general in the Regular Army in 1866, Canby commanded various departments during Reconstruction, where he impressed even his opponents with his fairness and honesty, although sometimes he irritated Southerners, other times Carpetbaggers, and some-times both. He was given command of the Pacific Northwest in August 1872. On Good Friday, April 11, 1873, near Tule Lake, California, he was attempting to negotiate peace with the Modoc Indians when Captain Jack, the Modoc leader, shot the unarmed general twice in the head. Canby's throat was also cut. The Indians killed one of the peace commissioners and wounded others. General Canby was fifty-five years old. He was buried in Crown Hill Cemetery, Indianapolis. He was reportedly the only U.S. general killed in the Indian Wars. Captain Jack was hunted down and executed for murder before the year was out.

General Grant believed Canby lacked aggression and considered him more of an administrator than a leader but admired his knowledge of regulations and constitutional law. He called Canby an officer of "great merit" and said: "His character was as pure as his talent was great." He heatedly objected when Stanton transferred Canby out of the capital during Reconstruction.

JAMES HENRY CARLETON was born in Lubec, Maine, on December 27, 1814. Little is known of his childhood. He was a lieutenant in the Maine Militia during the bloodless Aroostook War (a boundary dispute between Great Britain and the United States) and so impressed the American officers that they granted him a second lieutenant's commission in the 1st Dragoons. Here he trained under Edwin V. Sumner at the Cavalry School for Practice (Carlilse Barracks, Pennsylvania) for a year and a half. Then he was posted to Indian Territory. He later served in the American West and was promoted to first lieutenant (1845) and captain (1847). He fought in the Mexican War, where he distinguished himself at Buena Vista and was brevetted major.

Carleton also took part in expeditions into Pawnee and Oto territory. He fought Jicarilla Apaches in New Mexico in 1856 and, in 1859, investigated a September 1857 massacre at Mountain Meadows, where Mormons killed dozens of settlers. The following year, Carleton led the Bitter Spring Expedition and killed several suspected Paiute raiders along the Los Angeles-Salt Lake Road.

When the Civil War started, Carleton was in California. He initially commanded Camp Tajon, but on August 3, 1861, assumed command of the 1st California Infantry. He was promoted to colonel on August 19. He became commander of the District of Southern California in October, suppressed Southern sympathizers there, and led the so-called California

Column against Confederate forces in Arizona. (Carleton, incidentally, was not anti-Southern or even anti-slavery. He owned at least one slave himself.) He won the Battle of Picacho Pass (also known as Picacho Peak) on April 15, 1862, and captured Tucson, Arizona, in early June. Meanwhile, he was promoted to brigadier general on April 30. He then continued to march east, joined Canby, and helped push the Confederates out of New Mexico. Although he was a tough disciplinarian, Carleton was popular with his men and was a fine tactician.

Once the Rebels left, Carleton (who succeeded Canby as commander of the Department of New Mexico) turned his attention to the Mescalero Apache and the Navajo. He employed brutality, torture, and scorched earth tactics. Several hundred Native Americans died on a forced march across the desert. From Carleton's point of view, his efforts against the Comanche and Kiowa in northern Texas were less successful. He suffered a repulse in the First Battle of Adobe Walls (November 25, 1864) but managed to successfully withdraw, despite being heavily outnumbered. It would be a decade before their power was broken.

Carleton was brevetted major general in 1866. He was discharged from volunteer service on April 30, 1866. On July 31, he was promoted to lieutenant colonel, 4th U.S. Cavalry, and became military governor of New Mexico. Post-war, he wrote several books on military history, including one on Buena Vista. James H. Carleton died from pneumonia on January 7, 1873, in San Antonio, at age fifty-eight. He is buried in the Mount Auburn Cemetery, Cambridge, Massachusetts.

WILLIAM PASSMORE CARLIN was born on November 23, 1829, in Rich Woods, Illinois. Educated in local schools, he received an appointment to West Point in 1846, possibly because his uncle was a former governor of Illinois. In any case, he graduated in 1850 (20/44) and was commissioned brevet second lieutenant in the 6th Infantry. He was promoted to second lieutenant in 1851, first lieutenant in 1855, and captain in March 1861. Meanwhile, he was stationed at Fort Snelling, Minnesota; fought several campaigns against the Plains Indians, including the Sioux and Cheyenne; and served in the Utah War (1858). He commanded Fort Bragg, California, for almost a year.

As soon as the Civil War began, Carlin was appointed colonel of the 38th Illinois Infantry and helped rout the Missouri State Guard troops at Fredericktown on October 21, 1861. He was placed in charge of the District of Southeastern Missouri, after which, he was given a brigade of infantry in the spring of 1862. He took part in the Siege of Corinth; fought in the Battle of Perryville; and at Stones River (December 31, 1862, to January 2, 1863). Despite a lack of tact when dealing with superiors, he was promoted to brigadier general on April 15, 1863.

Carlin continued to serve on the Western Front in the Tullahoma Campaign, the Battle of Chickamauga (where he was slightly wounded), the Siege of Chattanooga (including Lookout Mountain and Missionary Ridge), and the Atlanta Campaign. He took a month's furlough to get married, but returned on August 17, 1864, when he assumed command of a division in the Army of the Cumberland. He was with Sherman during the March to the Sea and the Carolinas Campaign. He was mustered out of volunteer service on August 24, 1865, and was brevetted major general in 1866. He joined the 34th Infantry as a major postwar.

After 1865, William Carlin served mainly on the frontier and at various times was in Dakota Territory, Wyoming Territory, Nebraska, and Idaho Territory. He was promoted to lieutenant colonel in 1872 and full colonel and commander of the 4th Infantry Regiment in 1882. He was advanced to brigadier general in 1893. He retired later that year after forty-three years' service and bought a ranch in Montana Territory.

While riding on a train near Whitehall, Montana, General Carlin died suddenly on October 4, 1903. He was seventy-three. He is buried in the Carrollton City Cemetery, Carrollton, Illinois.

EUGENE ASA CARR was born on March 20, 1830, in Hamburg, Erie County, New York. He graduated from West Point in 1850 (19/44). Commissioned brevet second lieutenant in the Mounted Rifles, he was promoted to second lieutenant in 1851, to first lieutenant in the 1st Cavalry in 1855, captain in 1858, and major on July 17, 1862. Meanwhile, he fought

Indians (especially Lipan Apaches) on the frontier and became known as "the Black Bearded Cossack." He also helped quell disturbances in Utah and "Bleeding Kansas." He was severely wounded in a skirmish against the Lipans in 1854. The start of the Civil War found him in command of Fort Washita, Indian Territory.

Carr's first Civil War battle was Wilson's Creek (August 10, 1861), where the Union forces were routed. He was nevertheless brevetted lieutenant colonel (Regular Army) for his conduct. Six days later he was given command of the 3rd Illinois Cavalry. After briefly commanding a brigade, he assumed command of a division in the Army of the Southwest on February 9, 1862. On March 7, during the Battle of Pea Ridge, he distinguished himself but was wounded in the neck, arm, and ankle in the process. On April 30, President Lincoln promoted him to brigadier general.

Hors d'combat until June, he resumed divisional command, and from October 7 to November 12, he was acting commander of the Army of the Southwest. He resumed command of a division in southeastern Missouri until being transferred to the Army of the Tennessee for Grant's final drive on Vicksburg. He fought at Port Gibson, Champion Hill, Big Black River, and the Siege of Vicksburg. After the fall of the city, Carr was transferred back to Arkansas, where he led a cavalry division in the Camden Expedition. After that failure, he briefly directed the District of Little Rock. His superior, General Joseph Reynolds, relieved him of his command for being drunk at a dinner party on June 30.

Carr's last action in the Civil War was as a division commander in the campaign against Mobile, Alabama, which fell on April 12, 1865. He was brevetted major general on March 11, 1865, and was mustered out of volunteer service on July 15, 1866.

After the war, Carr reverted to the rank of major, returned to the frontier, and fought Cheyenne and Sioux, among others. He won a noteworthy victory against a combined force of Arapaho, Cheyenne Dog Soldiers, and Sioux at Summit Springs on July 11, 1869. With 294 men (fifty of them scouts) he defeated Chief Tall Bull, overran his village, and killed thirty-five Native Americans, including two women and two children. Tall Bull was among the dead. Carr's carefully prepared surprise attack was so successful that his forces suffered only one casualty, and he was only wounded.

Eugene Carr was promoted to lieutenant colonel (4th Cavalry) in 1873 and colonel (6th Cavalry) in 1879. He became a brigadier general, Regular Army, in 1892 and retired in 1893. In 1894, he finally received his Congressional Medal of Honor for his actions at Pea Ridge in 1862.

General Carr died in Washington, D.C. on December 2, 1910, at the age of eighty. He was buried in the West Point Cemetery.

JOSEPH BRADFORD CARR was born in Albany, New York, on August 16, 1828. The son of Irish immigrants, he moved to Troy and worked as a tobacconist. He joined the New York Militia as a private in 1849 and received a commission in 1850. By 1859, he was a colonel commanding the 24th New York Militia Regiment.

Carr was involved in recruiting the 2nd New York Infantry at Troy, New York, when the Civil War began. He was elected colonel on May 10. His regiment was sent to Fort Monroe, at the tip of the Virginia Peninsula, and fought in the Battle of Big Bethel (June 10), which was an embarrassing defeat for the North. Carr also fought in the Peninsula Campaign and the Seven Days battles, where he commanded a brigade. He was promoted to brigadier general on September 7, 1862, but the Senate did not act on his appointment, which expired on March 4, 1863, and Carr reverted back to colonel. He was reappointed brigadier on March 30, 1863, but this appointment was returned to the president on April 7, and once again he became a colonel. He was appointed a third time on April 9, 1864, and was finally confirmed. In the meantime, he fought at Bristoe Station, Fredericksburg, and Chancellorsville, where he became an acting division commander when Hiram Berry was killed. He distinguished himself at Gettysburg, holding his ground near the Peach Orchard despite heavy Confederate attacks. He was injured in this battle when his horse was shot from under him, but he did not leave the field.

On May 2, 1864, Grant reassigned Carr to command a USCT division in the Army of the James. He served with the XVIII Corps at Cold Harbor and in the Bermuda Hundred and briefly was commandant of Yorktown. From October 1864 to June 1865, he was again a brigade commander in the Army of the James. He was brevetted major general on June 1 and mustered out on August 24, 1865.

Postwar, Carr was a manufacturer and a major general in the New York Militia. He also became a Republican politician and served three terms as New York secretary of state (1879–1885). He ran for lieutenant governor in 1885 but lost. General Carr returned to Troy where he died on February 24, 1895. He was sixty-six. He was buried in Oakwood Cemetery, Troy, New York.

HENRY BEEBEE CARRINGTON was born in Wallingford, Connecticut, on March 2, 1824. He was a passionate abolitionist from his youth. He attended Yale University, graduated in 1845, spent a year as a professor of Greek and natural science at the Irving Institute in Tarrytown, New York (1846–47), and returned to Yale as a student in the Law School and a teacher at a nearby women's institute. In 1848, he moved to Columbus, Ohio, where he formed a law partnership with William Dennison, Jr., who was later governor of the state (1860–62) and postmaster general under Lincoln and Johnson (1864–66). Carrington became an elder in the Second Presbyterian Church in Columbus and fathered eight children.

Carrington helped organize the Republican Party in 1854. He was a close friend of Salmon Chase, who appointed him judge advocate in 1857 and adjutant general of the Ohio Militia in 1858. When the Civil War broke out, Carrington established Camp Thomas four miles north of Columbus, where he mustered ten militia regiments into service and organized 26 more. He was commissioned colonel of the 18th U.S. Infantry Regiment on May 14, 1861, and engaged in organizing and training until December 16, when he left to join General Buell at Louisville, Kentucky, where he helped organize the Army of the Ohio. Organizing new volunteers was one of his fortes. By the end of the war, he had organized 139,000 of them.

In August 1862, at the request of Indiana Governor Oliver P. Morton, Secretary of War Stanton sent Carrington to Indianapolis to help organize thousands of new recruits for Morton. He also helped infiltrate the Knights of the Golden Circle (Copperheads), who were encouraging desertion. Morton found Carrington indispensable and arranged for him to be named commander of the District of Indiana and promoted to brigadier general on March 20, 1863.

Henry Carrington was a natural spymaster whose main task was to infiltrate groups which were considered disloyal. People who fell into that category were arrested and tried by military courts for infringing on the war effort. Carrington thought they should be tried by Federal civil courts but was overruled by Morton, Stanton, and Lincoln.

Carrington stayed in Indiana throughout the war. He was mustered out on August 24, 1865, and reverted to the rank of colonel in 1865. He was sent west with his regiment (the 18th Infantry) after the war. Carrington was assigned to protect the Bozeman Trail in Colorado. In December 1866, about 1,500 Indians attacked a detachment of eighty troopers under Captain William J. Fetterman and killed them all.

Fetterman was part of an anti-Carrington faction and had disobeyed his colonel's orders not to pursue the Indians too far from the fort. A court of inquiry exonerated Carrington, but his military career was essentially ruined. He retired from active duty in 1870 and became professor of military science at Wabash College, Indiana. His first wife died in 1870. The following year, he married the widow of a Fetterman Massacre victim.

Henry Carrington wrote several books in his career and earned an LL.D. degree from Wabash College in 1873. He died in Boston on October 26, 1912, at age eighty-eight. He is buried in Fairview Cemetery, Hyde Park, Massachusetts.

SAMUEL SPRIGG "RED" CARROLL was born near what is now Takoma Park, Maryland, on September 21, 1831. (Takoma Park is now a suburb of Washington, D.C.) He entered West Point in 1852 and graduated in 1856 (44/49), with a commission as a brevet second lieutenant in the 9th Infantry Regiment. He was promoted to second lieutenant in the 10th

infantry in 1856. His antebellum service was in Minnesota and Utah and as quartermaster at West Point, where he was when the war began.

Carroll was promoted to first lieutenant in September 1861 and to captain in November. On December 7, he became colonel of the 8th Ohio Infantry, a three-year regiment which he led early in the Valley Campaign. He was promoted to command a brigade in General Shields's division on May 10, 1862, and led it in the battles of First Winchester (May 25), Cross Keys (June 8), and Port Republic (June 9), where his horse was wounded, fell on him, and dislocated his right shoulder. He fought with Banks at Cedar Mountain (August 9). Five days later, while skirmishing near the Rapidan, he was shot in the chest. After he recovered, he led a brigade in the III Corps at Fredericksburg and was with II Corps at Chancellorsville and Gettysburg. Carroll's command was the famous "Gibraltar Brigade," which played a vital role in defending Cemetery Hill on July 2, 1863, and in repulsing Pickett's Charge on July 3.

Carroll was wounded at Bristoe Station on October 14. He reported back for duty on March 25, 1864, as a brigade commander. He again distinguished himself in the Wilderness, where he received a flesh wound in the right arm on May 5. He was wounded again on May 10 but not seriously. His promotion to brigadier general occurred on May 23.

While on a reconnaissance near Spotsylvania Court House on May 13, General Carroll was wounded again, and this time it was serious. His left elbow was shattered by a Confederate bullet and it took him months to recover. He was not able to return to light (court-martial) duty until December. It was April 1865 before he could assume another command, and it was a provisional division in the Shenandoah. He was mustered out of volunteer service on January 15, 1866, and became the lieutenant colonel of the 21st Infantry Regiment in 1867. He never fully recovered from his wounds, however, and was forced to retire on June 9, 1869.

Carroll was popular with his men, who called him "Old Bricktop." He was less popular with his wife. They were married in 1856, and she bore him three children, but after he retired—according to her divorce petition—he was unfaithful to her with two women, one of whom was of "notorious character." She also charged him with drunkenness, cruelty, and using such vile language toward her that it made her ill. The divorce was granted in the early 1880s. Mrs. Carroll later remarried the general for a year but divorced him again in 1886 when he failed to reform.

Samuel S. Carroll died of pneumonia on his country estate near Takoma Park, Maryland, on January 28, 1893. He was sixty years of age. He was interred in the Oak Hill Cemetery, Washington, D.C.

SAMUEL PERRY "POWHATAN" CARTER was reportedly the only United States naval officer to be both an admiral and a general. He was born on August 6, 1819, in Elizabethton, Carter County, Tennessee. The county of his birth was named for his ancestors. He attended the local Duffield Academy, Washington College in Limestone, and what is now Princeton.

Carter enlisted in the navy in February 1840 and spent five years as a midshipman. He enrolled in the U.S. Naval Academy at Annapolis in 1845 and graduated the following year. He served in the Siege of Vera Cruz in March 1847. He sailed the seven seas during his antebellum career, including service with the Pacific and Brazilian squadrons. After Mexico, he was stationed at the U.S. Naval Observatory for some years and was a professor of mathematics at the Naval Academy (1850–53). He was commissioned lieutenant in 1855 and was aboard the screw frigate USS San Jacinto in 1856 when it bombarded Chinese fortifications near Canton at the request of the American consulate. He was back at Annapolis when the Civil War began.

At the request of U.S. Senator Andrew Johnson, Carter was detached to the Federal Army to recruit Unionists in East Tennessee. The Confederate occupation of the region prevented this, but Carter was able to raise a brigade of infantry from Tennesseans fleeing to Kentucky. It became part of the Army of the Ohio in December 1861.

Carter was commissioned colonel in July 1861 and was promoted to brigadier general on May 2, 1862. He was given special permission to hold both army and navy commissions simultaneously. He commanded a brigade in the Battle of Mill Springs (January 19, 1862), in the occupation of the Cumberland Gap (June 1862), and in the Perryville Campaign. He launched a successful cavalry raid into eastern Tennessee in late 1862. Meanwhile, he was promoted to lieutenant commander, USN, in July 1862.

General Carter fought in several small but successful battles in eastern Tennessee, as well as in the Knoxville Campaign. He was provost marshal of the Army of the Ohio from October 1863 to January 1865. He was leading a division in the XXIII Corps when General Joseph E. Johnston surrendered and briefly commanded XXIII Corps in June and July 1865. Carter was mustered out of volunteer service on January 15, 1866.

Promoted to commander in 1865, Carter resumed his naval career. He joined the Pacific Fleet and commanded the *USS Monocacy*, a sidewheel gunboat. He was promoted to captain (1870), commodore (1878), and retired in 1881. He was promoted to rear admiral on the retired list in 1882. He lived quietly in Washington, D.C., until he passed away on May 26, 1891, at age seventy-one. He is buried in the Oak Hill Cemetery, Washington.

During his operations in East Tennessee, he often used the code name "Powhatan." This became a nickname and is sometimes mistaken for his legal name.

SILAS CASEY was born in East Greenwich, Rhode Island, on July 12, 1807. He enrolled in the U.S. Military Academy in 1822 and graduated four years later (39/41). Commissioned second lieutenant in the infantry, he was promoted to first lieutenant (1836), captain (1839), major (1847), and lieutenant colonel (1855). Meanwhile, he fought the Creeks, the Seminoles, and the Mexicans. He was brevetted to major for courage at Contreras and Churubusco, and to lieutenant colonel for his conduct at Chapultepec, where he was severely wounded while leading an attack on September 13, 1847. In between wars, Casey served on the frontier in Michigan, California, and Oregon Territory, escorted topographical parties, and did garrison duty. He was on San Juan Island, Washington

Territory, when the United States and the British Empire almost came to blows in the "Pig War" of 1859.

Lieutenant Colonel Casey was stationed at Fort Steilacoom, Washington Territory, when the Civil War began and was almost immediately summoned to the east coast. He was promoted to colonel, R.A., and commander of the 4th Infantry Regiment on October 9, 1861, although the advancement was moot because Casey became a brigadier of volunteers on August 31, 1861. He commanded a brigade for two weeks before being given a divisional command on October 23. Part of IV Corps, Casey fought in the Peninsula Campaign and at Seven Pines (May 31–June 1, 1862), where some of his troops fled the field in panic. General McClellan, the commander of the Army of the Potomac, blamed Casey for their behavior and relieved him of his command on May 31, effectively ruining his career. Later, when McClellan conducted a review of his former division, the soldiers turned their backs on him and would not cheer him, as was the custom.

Silas Casey commanded a provisional brigade in the Washington fortifications, performed staff duties and was involved in judging court-martials for the rest of the war. He was also president of the Board for the Examination of Candidates for Officers of Colored Troops. Perhaps as a slap at McClellan, he was promoted to major general, Regular Army, on March 10, 1863, with a date of rank of May 31—the day McClellan relieved him. He wrote a three-volume *System of Infantry Tactics* (1862) and *Infantry Tactics for Colored Troops* (1863). *System of Infantry Tactics* was popular on both sides of the line.

General Casey was discharged from volunteer service on August 24, 1865, reverted to the rank of colonel, and resumed command of the 4th Infantry. He retired on July 8, 1868, after more than forty years on active duty. He died of a failure of his digestive system in Brooklyn, New York, on January 22, 1882, at age seventy-four. He was eulogized as "a reserved, unassuming gentleman, a gallant soldier . . . and a proficient scholar in higher mathematics." He was buried on the Casey farm in North Kingstown, Rhode Island.

His sons included Rear Admiral Silas Casey, who commanded the Pacific Squadron (1901–03); Brigadier General Thomas L. Casey, the chief engineer of the U.S. Army; and Lieutenant Edward W. Casey, who commanded the Cheyenne Scouts of the 8th Cavalry and was killed in action against the Sioux in 1891.

ROBERT FRANCIS CATTERSON was born on March 22, 1835, in Marion County, Indiana. He attended Adrian College, Michigan, and the Cincinnati Medical College (now part of the University of Cincinnati) to become a physician. He set up a practice in Rockville, Indiana.

When the war began, Catterson gave up his medical practice and enlisted in the 14th Indiana Infantry as a private on April 23, 1861. He was promoted to first sergeant in June and elected second lieutenant in July. He became a first lieutenant in March 1862.

Catterson first saw action in the Battle of Kernstown on March 23, 1862. He was promoted to captain on May 4 and fought against Stonewall Jackson in the Valley Campaign. He also served in the Maryland Campaign, including the Battle of Antietam, where he suffered four wounds in the right knee, left thumb, left foot, and the right buttocks. He returned to duty on October 18 as lieutenant colonel of the recently activated 97th Indiana Infantry. He became the regiment's colonel on November 25. Sent west, he was given command of a brigade in the Army of the Tennessee and fought in the various Vicksburg Campaigns and the subsequent siege. He was involved in the Tullahoma Campaign, as well as the Siege of Chattanooga, the Atlanta Campaign, the March to the Sea, and the Carolinas Campaign, where he briefly served as chief of staff to John A. Logan's XV Corps at the end of March 1865. He returned to his brigade on April 4 and was promoted to brigadier general on May 31.

After the war, Catterson relocated to Arkansas where he engaged in cotton speculation but without much success. He then became a carpetbagger and commanded the state's African American militia under Governor Powell Clayton. He also served as a U.S. marshal but was relieved by Clayton. He was elected to the Arkansas House of Representatives for one term in 1868 and became the Republican mayor of Little Rock from November 13, 1871 to November 10, 1873. After the collapse of

Reconstruction in Arkansas in 1874, Catterson moved to Chicago and then to Minnesota, where he failed as both a farmer and a merchant. He moved to San Antonio around 1910 and spent his last days at the Veterans' Hospital there, suffering from a stroke. He died on March 30, 1914, at age seventy-nine, and is buried in the San Antonio National Cemetery.

JOSHUA LAWRENCE CHAMBERLAIN, one of the great heroes of the Civil War, was born on September 8, 1828, in Brewer, Maine. His grandfather was a colonel in the War of 1812 and his father was a lieutenant colonel in the Aroostook War. Joshua was a fervent member of the Congregational Church and was educated in a private military academy. He taught himself Greek so he could gain admission to Bowdoin College, with which he was associated for much of his life. He graduated in 1852 and spent three years as a student in the Bangor Theological Seminary. He reportedly mastered Greek, Latin, German, French, Arabic, Hebrew, and Syriac. He married Fanny Adams in 1855. She bore him five children.

Chamberlain began his educational career in 1855 as an instructor in logic and natural theology at Bowdoin. He became a professor of rhetoric and oratory and eventually a professor of modern languages. He received a two-year leave of absence in 1862, supposedly to study foreign languages, but instead he accepted a lieutenant colonelcy in the 20th Maine on August 8, 1862. (He was offered the colonelcy of the regiment but preferred to learn more about his new profession first.) He fought at Fredericksburg, where a musket ball nicked his right ear. The 20th Maine missed Chancellorsville due to an outbreak of smallpox, and it was under quarantine. Chamberlain begged General Butterfield to commit the regiment anyway, saying, "If we couldn't do anything else we would give the Rebels smallpox!" but Butterfield refused to allow it. Chamberlain joined the fighting anyway and had his horse shot out from under him.

Promoted to colonel and regimental commander on May 20, his most famous battle was Gettysburg, where on July 2, 1863, he saved the Union position on Little Round Top against repeated Rebel attacks. When he ran

ENCYCLOPEDIA OF UNION GENERALS

out of ammunition, he launched a desperate bayonet charge which saved the Union flank. In 1893, he was awarded the Congressional Medal of Honor for this attack. Colonel Chamberlain was twice slightly wounded in the process when a minié ball smashed against his sword scabbard and drove it into his left leg, and a piece of shell or a rock splinter penetrated his right instep. The regiment lost 130 men out of 358 engaged.

Chamberlain became a brigade commander on August 20 and held this position for most of the rest of the war. On June 18, 1864, a minié ball struck him in the hip and severed arteries, fractured his pelvis, and exited through his left hip. He was not expected to live, so his corps commander, Gouverneur K. Warren, asked General Grant to promote him (Chamberlain) immediately, so that he could die as a general. Grant did so on June 19. It was one of two such battlefield promotions he granted during the war.

Chamberlain returned to duty on February 27, 1865, and was again severely wounded in the chest and left arm on March 29, but he remained in command. After General Lee surrendered, Grant detailed Chamberlain to preside over the surrender parade of the Army of Northern Virginia, April 12, 1865. He saluted the defeated Confederates—a move which was criticized by some in the North, but Chamberlain refused to apologize. He commented that he never saw the Confederate Battle Flag without thinking of the immense bravery of the men who fought under it.

Joshua Chamberlain fought in twenty battles and multiple skirmishes. He had six horses shot from under him and was wounded six times. He was in more or less constant pain for the rest of his life.

Chamberlain was brevetted major general on January 13, 1866, and was mustered out two days later. He declined a regular army commission, returned home, and was elected governor of Maine later that year. He was re-elected in 1867, 1868, and 1869, serving from January 2, 1867 to January 4, 1871, as a Republican. He then returned to Bowdoin as president of the college from 1871 to 1883. He resigned to move to New York City and practice law.

General Chamberlain died on February 24, 1914, in Portland, Maine, from complications of the wound he received at Petersburg in 1864. One author declared that he was the last casualty of the Civil War. He was eighty-five years old. General Chamberlain is buried in Pine Grove Cemetery, Brunswick, Maine.

ALEXANDER CHAMBERS was born in Great Valley, Cattaraugus County, New York, on August 23, 1832. He was appointed to the U.S. Military Academy in 1849, graduated in 1853 (43/52), and was commissioned brevet second lieutenant in the 5th Infantry Regiment. He was promoted to second lieutenant in 1855, first lieutenant in 1859, and captain on May 14, 1861. In the interim, he fought in the Third Seminole War, served on the frontier in Utah, Texas, and New Mexico, fought the Navajo in the southwest, and performed garrison duty. When the Civil War began, he was sent to Iowa on recruiting duty. He became colonel of the 16th Iowa Infantry in March 1862.

Chambers's first Civil War battle was Shiloh, where he was shot in the arm. A spent bullet also struck him in the hip and caused him a great deal of pain. He was also wounded at Iuka (September 19, 1862), this time in the neck and right shoulder, and was captured. The Confederates released him during their subsequent retreat. He recovered and returned to field duty on May 30, 1863, when he was given command of a brigade during the Siege of Vicksburg.

Chambers was promoted to brigadier general on August 11, 1863, and he was given command of a division in the XX Corps, but his appointment was cancelled by the Senate on April 6, 1864, ostensibly because he was not a legal resident of Iowa. Meanwhile, he fought at Chattanooga and in the Meridian expedition. After losing his generalship, Chambers went on Veterans' Furlough in Iowa with his brigade, was Mustering and Disbursing Officer at Davenport, Iowa, from May 12 to November 25, 1864, and commanded the 18th Infantry Battalion, a Regular Army unit, at Lookout Mountain, near Chattanooga, until August 25, 1865.

He was brevetted brigadier general in 1868. His post-war career was uneventful, and he was promoted to major (1867), lieutenant colonel (1867), and colonel and commander of the 17th Infantry Regiment on March 1, 1886.

He was stationed at Nashville, Tennessee; Louisville, Kentucky; Fort Kearny, Nebraska; Fort Randall, Dakota Territory; Fort Fetterman, Wyoming; Lexington, Kentucky; Little Rock, Arkansas; Camp Sheridan, Nebraska; Fort Columbus, New York; Fort Townsend and Vancouver Barracks, Washington; and Fort Lapwai, Idaho, among others. He also took part in the Big Horn and Yellowstone Expeditions and was military attaché to the U.S. Legation in Constantinople, Turkey. After a lengthy illness, General Chambers died at age fifty-five on February 2, 1888, in San Antonio, Texas. He was buried in Forest Hill Cemetery, Owatonna, Minnesota.

STEPHEN GARDNER CHAMPLIN was born in Kingston, New York, on July 1, 1827. He was educated in local schools and in the Rhinebeck Academy in Dutchess County. He began studying medicine in 1842 and by 1845 had established a medical practice in Wawarsing.

Champlin gave up medicine in 1848 or 1849 and began reading law. He attended the State and National Law School and was admitted to the bar in 1850. He moved to Grand Rapids, Michigan, in 1853 and was elected judge of the Recorder's Court in 1856. He was also active in the Michigan Militia and was elected captain of the Grand Rapids Light Artillery. He was elected major of the Grand River [militia] Battalion in 1858. That same year, he was elected Prosecuting Attorney for Kent County.

Champlin joined the Union Army on June 10, 1861, as major of the 3rd Michigan Infantry, then at Grand Rapids. It left the city for Virginia on June 13. On August 30, near Bailey's Corner in Virginia, he won a minor action which was observed by General McClellan. The army commander was lavish in his praise. Champlin was promoted to colonel and regimental commander on October 22.

Colonel Champlin led his regiment in the Peninsula Campaign and was wounded in the hip at Seven Pines on May 31, 1862. Although only partially recovered, he fought in the Second Bull Run, where he overextended himself. His wound broke open, and he was in the hospital on November 29, when his promotion to brigadier general came through. He was given command of the post of Grand Rapids on September 24, 1863, but he resigned his commission on November 8 because he could not effectively do his duty.

General Champlin died in Grand Rapids, Michigan, on January 24, 1864, of complications from his Seven Pines wound. He was thirty-six years old. He was buried in the Fulton Street Cemetery, Grand Rapids, Michigan.

EDWARD PAYSON CHAPIN was born in Waterloo, New York, on August 16, 1831, the son of a Presbyterian minister. Educated locally, he read law and was admitted to the bar in 1852. He set up a practice in Buffalo and was the shortstop for the city's first semi-pro baseball team. He was active in the militia and joined the Federal Army on September 6, 1861, as a captain in the 44th New York Infantry. He was sent to Virginia, where he was promoted to major on January 2, 1862. He fought in the Peninsula Campaign and was seriously wounded in the Battle of Hanover Court House (May 27), after which he was highly praised by his superiors.

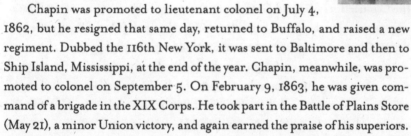

Chapin was promoted to lieutenant colonel on July 4, 1862, but he resigned that same day, returned to Buffalo, and raised a new regiment. Dubbed the 116th New York, it was sent to Baltimore and then to Ship Island, Mississippi, at the end of the year. Chapin, meanwhile, was promoted to colonel on September 5. On February 9, 1863, he was given command of a brigade in the XIX Corps. He took part in the Battle of Plains Store (May 21), a minor Union victory, and again earned the praise of his superiors.

On May 27, General Banks's Army of the Gulf launched its first unsuccessful and poorly coordinated assault on the Confederate fortress of Port Hudson. Chapin was wounded in the knee by Confederate shrapnel but continued to push forward until he was within a few yards of the Rebel trenches, when a Confederate infantryman shot him in the head. He was probably dead before he hit the ground. Four months later, Lincoln promoted him to brigadier general, effective May 27.

Edward Chapin was thirty-one years old when he was killed. His remains were buried in Maple Grove Cemetery in the town of his birth.

GEORGE HENRY CHAPMAN was born in Holland, Massachusetts, on November 22, 1832. His family moved to Indiana when he was six. Here his father and uncle published pro-Democrat newspapers in Terre Haute and Indianapolis. Young Chapman studied at the Marion County Seminary.

In 1847, Chapman secured an appointment as a midshipman in the U.S. Navy. He served aboard frigates until 1850, when his uncle died, and he was forced to return home. He published the *Indiana Republican* and studied law part-time. Admitted to the bar in 1857, he became an assistant clerk in the U.S. House of Representatives in 1860.

Chapman joined the Union Army as the major of the 3rd Indiana Cavalry on November 2, 1861. He served in the Army of the Ohio that winter and then transferred to the infantry in Virginia, where he briefly commanded a brigade in the Seven Days battles, despite his low rank. He fought in the Second Bull Run and at Antietam and was promoted to lieutenant colonel on October 25, 1862. He was promoted to colonel on March 12, 1863, and led his former regiment (the 3rd Indiana Cavalry) in the Chancellorsville and Gettysburg campaigns. He was one of the first to engage the advancing Confederates at Gettysburg on July 1. Shortly after the battle, Chapman was named commander of a cavalry brigade.

George Chapman fought in the Valley Campaign of 1864 and was promoted to brigadier general on July 21. He led his brigade until September 19, when he was wounded in the Third Battle of Winchester. He resumed command of his brigade on November 1. He assumed command of a cavalry division on January 1, 1865. After the Battle of Waynesboro (March 2), he was ordered to hold the Shenandoah Valley with three small regiments and a handful of guns. The war ended shortly after. On January 7, 1866, he resigned his commission. He was brevetted major general later that year.

Postbellum, Chapman was a judge of the Criminal Court of Marion County, Indiana. He also served as the receiver for two bankrupt railroads and served in the Indiana State Senate, beginning in 1880. General Chapman died near Indianapolis on June 16, 1882, at age forty-nine. He is buried in the Crown Hill Cemetery, Indianapolis.

AUGUSTUS LOUIS CHETLAIN was born on December 26, 1824, in St. Louis, Missouri. His parents were Swiss immigrants who moved to Galena, Illinois, when he was an infant. He was educated in local schools and entered the business world as a clerk in 1852. By 1859, he was wealthy enough to retire. He sold his business interests and traveled in Europe until it appeared the Union was going to break up. He returned home and is said to have been the first man from Illinois to volunteer. He and Ulysses S. Grant formed an infantry company, and Grant suggested Chetlain command it. It was initially a three-month unit and was part of the 12th Illinois when its enlistments expired. It re-mustered into the Federal service on August 1. Meanwhile, Chetlain entered the U.S. Army as a captain on May 2 and was elected lieutenant colonel of the 12th the next day.

The 12th Illinois was posted to Cairo, Illinois, and occupied Paducah, Kentucky, on September 6. As acting regimental commander, Chetlain first saw action at Forts Henry and Donelson in February 1862. He distinguished himself at Shiloh, where he was slightly wounded on April 6, 1862. He was promoted to colonel on April 17. He again distinguished himself in the Siege of Corinth and the Second Battle of Corinth (October 3–4).

After the battle, Chetlain was commandant of Corinth and was given the task of organizing and training African Americans (USCT) for Union service. He was then sent to Memphis and (at Grant's suggestion) was tasked with training USCT in Tennessee and Kentucky. He excelled in this job and, by October 1864, produced seventeen thousand well-armed, trained, and disciplined soldiers. He was promoted to brigadier general on December 18, 1863. He was brevetted major general on January 18, 1866, and mustered out on January 26.

Chetlain was an assessor for the Internal Revenue Service from 1867 to 1869. He became U.S. consult in Brussels, Belgium, from 1869 to 1872, after which he returned to Chicago and became a highly successful banker. A brilliant administrator, he served as president of the Home National Bank, an organizer of the Industrial Bank of Chicago, and a director of the Chicago

Stock Exchange. He was also an active philanthropist. He published his autobiography, *Recollections of Seventy Years* in 1899.

General Chetlain died in Chicago on March 15, 1914, at age eighty-nine. He is buried in the Greenwood Cemetery, Galena, Illinois.

JOHN MILTON CHIVINGTON was born in Lebanon, Ohio, on January 27, 1821. He became a Methodist minister and a fervent abolitionist. He moved to Kansas as a young man, but his outspoken abolitionist views put his life in danger, so he fled to Nebraska Territory. He moved to Denver, Colorado Territory, in 1860. Within the Methodist Church, Chivington was not considered stable. When the Civil War began, he declined a chaplaincy and was commissioned major in the 1st Colorado Infantry.

Chivington distinguished himself fighting the Rebels in eastern Arizona and western New Mexico territories. On March 26, 1862, he led a four-hundred-man detachment in a surprise attack at Johnson's Ranch. He captured a major Confederate supply train and killed four men, wounded twenty, and took seventy-five prisoners. Chivington lost five killed and fourteen wounded. Meanwhile, the Federal and Confederate forces fought a tactically indecisive battle at Glorieta Pass, but the Rebels did not have enough supplies to remain in New Mexico and were forced to retreat to Texas. Chivington was promoted to colonel and commander of the 1st Colorado Cavalry Regiment in April 1862. On November 28, 1862, he was named commander of the District of Colorado and was promoted to brigadier general, but the appointment was returned to the President on February 12, 1863, and subsequently withdrawn. Chivington reverted to the rank of colonel but retained his district command until early 1865.

John Chivington hated Native Americans with a passion and became infamous for the Sand Creek Massacre. On November 29, 1864, he led roughly nine hundred volunteers, mostly from the 3rd Colorado Cavalry, in an attack on peaceful village of around seven hundred Cheyenne and Arapaho, about two-thirds of whom were women, children, and infants. The chief raised the white flag but was ignored. Some 150 to four hundred

Indians were killed (sources vary widely), most of their bodies mutilated, and a great many were scalped. Other body parts, including genitalia, were taken as trophies. About fifteen whites were killed and fifty wounded—several from "friendly fire"—because a great many of the attackers were drunk.

Chivington's membership in the Freemasons was suspended after Sand Creek, and he lost his position as Grand Master of Masons for Colorado, but other than that he was not punished. The Joint Committee on the Conduct of the War investigated the matter and condemned Chivington and his followers in strong terms, but no court-martial charges were ever preferred. He resigned his commission on January 4, 1865, and returned to Nebraska to administer the estate of a son who had drowned. He seduced and then married his daughter-in-law, but she divorced him for non-support in 1871. Unsuccessful in business, Chivington lived in Canada, Nebraska, Washington, D.C., California, and Ohio, where he announced his candidacy for the state legislature, but withdrew when he realized that the Sand Creek Massacre ended any hope he had of being elected. He spent his time attempting to gain money without labor, according to his ex-wife. He eventually became a deputy sheriff in Denver.

John M. Chivington died of cancer in Denver on October 4, 1894, at age seventy-three. He was buried in Fairmount Cemetery, Denver. He stood by his actions at Sand Creek until the day he died.

MORGAN HENRY CHRYSLER was born in Ghent, New York, on September 30, 1822. Educated locally, he was a farmer most of his adult life. He joined the 30th New York Infantry as a private in April 1861. He was promoted to captain on June 1, major on March 11, 1862, and lieutenant colonel on August 30, 1863. Meanwhile, he fought in the Peninsula Campaign, the Second Bull Run, Antietam, and Chancellorsville, where the 30th New York lost 653 of its 1,050 men. The regiment was discharged from the service on June 18, 1863, after their enlistments expired. Chrysler asked for permission to form a new cavalry regiment, which was instantly granted. In less than sixty days, his 2nd New York Veteran Volunteer Cavalry

Regiment (a.k.a. the Empire Light Cavalry) mustered 1,176 men. It was stationed in the Washington, D.C. defenses during the winter of 1863–64.

Chrysler was promoted to colonel on December 13, 1863, and his regiment was transferred to New Orleans. They took part in the Red River Campaign, including the disastrous Battle of Mansfield (April 8, 1864). Chrysler helped cover the Union retreat. He was wounded in the shoulder skirmishing on the Atchafalaya River on July 28, 1864. On August 6, after he partially recovered, he was elevated to brigade commander. He led a cavalry brigade consisting of the 1st Louisiana (Union) Cavalry Regiment, the 31st Massachusetts Mounted Infantry, and the 2nd New York Veteran Cavalry Regiment in the final campaign against Mobile in 1865.

On November 11, 1865, Chrysler was finally promoted to brigadier general—the next to last wartime appointment. (Joel L. Dewey was the last, nine days later.) Chrysler briefly served as military governor of North Alabama before being mustered out on January 15, 1866. He was brevetted major general on March 16, 1866.

Postbellum, General Chrysler returned to his farm. He died at Kinderhook, New York, on August 24, 1890, at age sixty-seven. He was interred in the Prospect Hill Cemetery, Valatie, New York.

WILLIAM THOMAS CLARK was born on June 29, 1831, in Norwalk, Connecticut. He was a schoolteacher before he moved to New York City, read law, and was admitted to the bar in 1854. In 1856, he moved to Davenport, Iowa, and established a law practice. He helped recruit the 13th Iowa Infantry Regiment and was mustered into Federal service on November 2, 1861, as a first lieutenant.

Clark initially served as adjutant of his regiment but became an assistant adjutant general and was promoted to captain on March 6, 1862. He fought at Shiloh, in the Siege of Corinth, and in the various attempts to take Vicksburg. He was assistant adjutant general of James McPherson's XVII Corps during the battles of Raymond, Jackson,

Champion Hill, and Big Black River as well as the Siege of Vicksburg. He became assistant adjutant general of the Army of the Tennessee in January 1864 under William T. Sherman. Shifted east, he took part in all of General Sherman's campaigns from Chattanooga to the sea and into the Carolinas. He was promoted to major (November 24, 1862). lieutenant colonel (February 10, 1863) and was brevetted brigadier general for his part in the Battle of Atlanta (July 22, 1864). Clark was finally rewarded for his years as an excellent staff officer by being given command of a brigade in the Army of the Tennessee, which he led from January 26, 1865, until after the Confederate surrender in North Carolina. He was finally promoted to brigadier general on May 31, 1865. Transferred to Texas that summer, he commanded a predominantly African American division of the XXV Corps from August 1, 1865. Its mission was to help the Union Army oust Napoleon III's forces from Mexico, if necessary. It wasn't. Faced with the American military threat, the French withdrew voluntarily, and the XXV Corps was disbanded in January 1866. Clark was brevetted major general on January 13, 1866, and mustered out on February 1.

William Clark settled in Galveston, Texas, and founded the First National Bank. He also organized the first African American school in the area. As a Republican and a Carpetbagger, he was elected to Congress in 1869 and took office on March 31, 1870. He was deeply involved in a scheme to sell west Texas lands to the Federal government for $40,000,000—the proceeds of which would be used to subsidize the construction of railroads in which he reportedly had an interest. The plan failed, as did an intrigue he was involved in with Mexican General Jose Antonio Mexia, who promised to turn over Matamoros to the United States for $200,000. The scheme was favored by Generals Grant and Sheridan, but was rejected by President Andrew Johnson and Secretary of State William H. Seward.

Clark was re-elected to the House of Representatives in 1871 but only because of serious voting irregularities. The Republican governor threw out more than three thousand Democratic votes. Clark was unanimously expelled from Congress on May 13, 1872, when it was determined that he actually lost by 135 votes.

Clark was postmaster of Galveston from 1872 to 1874, when he accepted a position with the Bureau of Revenue in New York City, a job he held until his death in Manhattan on October 12, 1905. He was 74. He was buried in Arlington National Cemetery.

CASSIUS MARCELLUS CLAY was born on October 19, 1810, in Madison County, Kentucky. His father was one of the wealthiest planters and slave owners in the state. He was a cousin of Henry Clay and a member of one of the most powerful political families in the nation. Cassius attended Transylvania University and Yale, from which he graduated in 1832. While there, he became an abolitionist, although he (like Lincoln) favored an incremental, gradual solution to the problem rather than immediate, uncompensated emancipation.

Cassius married Mary Jane Warfield in 1833. She bore him ten children, six of whom lived into adulthood

Meanwhile, Cassius Clay was elected to three terms in the Kentucky House of Representatives, serving from 1835 to 1841. He began publishing an anti-slavery newspaper, *True American*, in Lexington in 1845. He had a turbulent relationship with almost everyone, and his anti-slavery agitation earned him death threats and two assassination attempts, but he never backed down from an argument or a fight. In 1847, an angry mob attacked him and cut his hand severely. One of the ruffians pointed a pistol at Clay's head and pulled the trigger. Fortunately for him, it misfired.

Even though he opposed the annexation of Texas, Clay joined the 1st Kentucky Cavalry during the Mexican War and fought in the Battle of Buena Vista. He was captured by the Mexicans on January 23, 1847, but was exchanged. He was mustered out on June 7. He returned home and resumed his anti-slavery crusade and was almost assassinated in 1849 when he was beaten and stabbed. He beat off six assailants and killed one of them.

Clay was a founder of the Republican Party and became a friend of Abraham Lincoln, whom he supported in the election of 1860. Clay briefly ran for the vice-presidential nomination but was defeated by Hannibal Hamlin. After the election, Lincoln named him minister to Russia on May

1, but he resigned a month later. Lincoln appointed Clay major general on April 15, 1862, and he acted as Lincoln's emissary to the Kentucky legislators. Clay rejected the appointment and resigned on March 11, 1863, because the cause of abolition did not have enough support in Kentucky. He served as U.S. minister to Russia from 1863 to 1869.

After the war, Clay divorced his wife after forty-five years of marriage. She charged him with abandonment when, in fact, she could no longer tolerate his many infidelities. In 1894, at age eighty-four, he married the orphaned sister of one of his sharecroppers. She was fifteen years old. She later divorced him and two other husbands as well. (Divorce, of course, was rare in those days—unlike today.) In 1900, a group of the first Mrs. Clay's friends gave Cassius M. Clay a serious beating for his adultery.

Postbellum, Clay enlisted in the cause of Cuban independence and called for the nationalization of the railroads. He left the G.O.P. in 1869 and became a Liberal Republican and eventually a Democrat. He was president of the Kentucky Constitutional Convention in 1890. The ninety-two-year-old Cassius Marcellus Clay died of "general exhaustion" on July 22, 1903, at his home, "White Hall," in Madison County. He was buried in Richmond Cemetery, Madison County, Kentucky.

POWELL CLAYTON was born on August 7, 1833, in Bethel Township, Pennsylvania. His middle name was "Foulk," but he dropped it later. He was of Quaker ancestry. He attended the Forwood School in Wilmington, Delaware, and the Pennsylvania Literary, Scientific and Military Academy in Bristol. He studied civil engineering and moved to Kansas in 1855, where he worked as a surveyor and engaged in land speculation. He was elected city engineer of Leavenworth shortly before the outbreak of the war.

Clayton became a captain in the Kansas Militia in April 1861 and entered Federal service as a captain and company commander in the 1st Kansas Infantry. He fought at Wilson's Creek (August 10), where he was commended for his leadership. This led to his promotion to lieutenant colonel of the 5th Kansas Cavalry on December 28 and to colonel and regimental commander on March 7, 1862.

Clayton spent the entire war west of the Mississippi and mostly in Arkansas. He fought in the battles of Helena, Little Rock, and Pine Bluff (October 25, 1863) and in the Camden Expedition, among others. Highly competent, he was loved by his men and respected by his foes. He was generally considered the best Union cavalry commander in the Trans-Mississippi. This led to his promotion to brigadier general on August 1, 1864. He was mustered out of the service on August 24, 1865, but without the usual brevet of major general. He was also not above enriching himself by speculating in cotton while still in command of Pine Bluff. Additionally, he also leased confiscated plantations, received kickbacks, and made himself rich. After the war, he became the Carpetbagger governor of Arkansas and purchased a large plantation not far from Pine Bluff in Jefferson County.

As governor, Clayton issued state bonds to finance the construction of railroads. He tried to suppress the Ku Klux Klan but with limited success. On the positive side, his administration established the first free public school system in the state's history as well as the Arkansas Industrial University and the Arkansas School for the Deaf. He survived an impeachment attempt and served as governor from July 2, 1868 to March 4, 1871, when he was elected to the U.S. Senate. By 1876, home rule was re-established in Arkansas, and Clayton was defeated for re-election. He left office on March 3, 1877.

Clayton continued to dominate the Arkansas Republican Party and control a considerable amount of patronage. He was president of the Eureka Springs Railroad from 1883 to 1899 and was U.S. ambassador to Mexico from 1897 to 1905. After that, he resided in Washington, D.C., where he died on August 25, 1914, at age eighty-one. He is buried in Arlington National Cemetery. His brother John was a colonel in the Union Army. He won a disputed election to Congress in 1888, but was assassinated before he could take office.

GUSTAVE PAUL CLUSERET (pronounced Kloo-zuh-ray) was born in Suresnes, France, on June 13, 1823. He attended Saint Cyr military academy

(France's West Point) and received a commission in 1843. He was a captain in the 23rd Mobile Guard Battalion in 1848 and helped suppress the Socialist uprisings of that year. He supported an anti-Bonapartist demonstration in January 1849, which resulted in a demotion. He fled France for London after Louis Napoleon Bonaparte (later styled Napoleon III) launched his successful coup in December 1851.

Cluseret achieved reinstatement in the French Army in 1853 but only as a lieutenant. He fought in Algeria and in the Crimean War, where he was wounded in the Siege of Sevastopol. He was nicknamed "Captain Tin Can" because he hoarded canned meat and bread rations for himself at the expense of his soldiers. He resigned from the army in 1858 and became a mercenary.

Cluseret was in Algeria and New York City in the late 1850s but emerged as a colonel in the War of Italian Unification in 1860. He led the De Flotte Legion (a French formation) for a time, but it was incorporated into the Piedmontese Army, and he lost his colonelship.

His next war was the American Civil War. He emigrated to New York in 1862 and was commissioned colonel in the Union Army on March 10. He initially served as an aide to General McClellan but then "hitched his wagon" to John C. Fremont in May 1862. He led a brigade in the Union defeat at Cross Keys but was praised for fighting tenaciously. He was promoted to brigadier general on October 14. He was, however, arrested on unspecified charges in January 1863. He resigned his commission on March 2, 1863. He later edited *New Nation*, a New York City–based newspaper associated with Fremont. It adopted a Radical Republican viewpoint, supported Fremont for president, and criticized Lincoln's gradualist approach to the abolition of slavery. He and Fremont later fell out.

Cluseret returned to Europe in 1866 and was involved in the Fenian Brotherhood, which attempted to undermine British influence in the Mediterranean. London sentenced him to death *in absentia* in 1867. He joined the cause of Socialism after, and briefly returned to America to avoid arrest in France. He returned to his homeland in 1871 but, during the civil unrest of that year, was forced to flee to Switzerland disguised as a priest. He lived well, suggesting to some that he was a spy, in the pay of Prussia. He eventually emigrated to the Ottoman Empire and apparently fought in the Russo-Turkish War of 1877–1878, although little is known of this part of his life.

Taking advantage of an amnesty, Cluseret returned to France in 1880 but had to flee again after writing an article critical of General Ernest Courtot de Cissey. He lived in Constantinople until 1886, earning a living as an artist. He returned to France and settled in Hyeres, a town near Toulon, where he ran for public office. In this Socialist region, he was three times elected to the Chamber of Deputies, serving from 1888 to 1890. He eventually abandoned Socialism for nationalism and became increasingly anti-Semitic. General Cluseret died in Toulon on August 22, 1900, at age seventy-seven. He is buried in the Suresnes Old Cemetery, Suresnes, France.

JOHN COCHRANE was born in Palatine, New York, on August 27, 1813. He was the grandson of John Cochran, the surgeon general of the Continental Army. He attended Union College and then Hamilton College, from which he graduated in 1831. He was admitted to the bar and, after practicing at Oswego and Schenectady, moved to New York City. He campaigned for Franklin Pierce when he ran for president in 1852 and was rewarded with an appointment as surveyor of the port of New York.

Cochrane was elected to Congress as a Democrat and served from 1857 to 1861. He focused on land reform. Perhaps foreseeing the sectional conflict, he did not run for re-election in 1860. He recruited the 65th New York Infantry (which was also known as the 1st U.S. Chasseurs), became its colonel, and was mustered into Federal service on June 11, 1861. He led his regiment in the Peninsula Campaign and was promoted to brigadier general on July 19, 1862. He directed a mixed New York and Pennsylvania brigade of six regiments at Antietam and also fought at Fredericksburg. He resigned his commission, ostensibly for reasons of health, on February 25, 1863. The real reasons were probably political. He was among those who actively conspired to have General Burnside, the commander of the Army of the Potomac, sacked. In any case, he returned to the political realm. In

1864, the Radical Democratic Party nominated him for vice president and running mate of John C. Fremont, but Fremont soon withdrew.

Cochrane served as New York State Attorney General from 1864 to 1865 and was a delegate to the Republican National Convention in 1868. He became a Democrat again in 1872. He was president of the Common Council of New York in 1872 and 1873 and served as acting mayor when Mayor A. Oakley Hall had to temporarily step aside during the Tweed investigation.

General Cochrane died on February 7, 1898, at his home in Manhattan, New York City. He was eighty-four years old. He was buried in Albany Rural Cemetery, Menands, New York.

PATRICK EDWARD CONNOR was born in a rural part of County Kerry, western Ireland, on March 17, 1820. His family emigrated to New York City when he was a child, and he was educated there. He enlisted in the U.S. Army in 1839 (listing his last name as "O'Connor") and fought in the Seminole War. Later, he was a dragoon stationed at Forts Leavenworth, Atkinson, Sandford, and Des Moines. He was discharged as a private in 1844. After living in New York, he moved to Texas and became a nationalized citizen.

When the Mexican War began, he joined the Texas volunteers as a private but was soon promoted to first lieutenant. Later advanced to captain, he fought at Palo Alto, Resaca de la Palma, and Buena Vista, where he was wounded in the left hand by a musket ball. He resigned on May 24, 1847, near Monterey, Mexico, due to rheumatism. A 49er, he moved to California in January 1850. He joined the California State Rangers and helped hunt down and kill Joaquin Murrieta, a Mexican outlaw, and three of his men. He collected a nice reward.

When the Civil War began, Connor was commander of the Stockton Blues, a militia company. He expanded the unit into a regiment, the 3rd California Infantry. It was initially sent to Utah to protect the wagon train routes from Indians to guard against a Mormon uprising, and to protect non-Mormons from Latter Day Saints. Connor became commander of the District of Utah on August 6, 1862. He and his men wanted to be transferred to Virginia, but he was unable to arrange it. Meanwhile, he established Camp (later Fort) Douglas, Utah.

Connor was named commander of the District of the Plains on March 28, 1863. It included Nevada and the territories of Utah, Nebraska, Colorado, and parts of Dakota and New Mexico territories. He was promoted to brigadier general two days later. Meanwhile, in a dispute between miners and the Shoshone, two miners were killed. On January 29, 1863, Connor attacked and slaughtered a large Northwestern Shoshone encampment at Bear River (a.k.a. the Bear Creek Massacre). About 250 Native Americans were killed; only 160 women and children survived. Connor lost 21 killed and 46 wounded.

In August 1865, he led 2,000 cavalrymen in the Battle of Tongue River, where he killed 63 Sioux and Arapaho, destroyed their village, and captured 600 horses.

Patrick Connor was mustered out on April 30, 1866, and brevetted major general on May 4. After the war, he engaged in mining, established a newspaper and a silver mine, and founded the town of Stockton. General Connor died in Salt Lake City, Utah, on December 17, 1891, at age seventy-one. He was buried in the Fort Douglas Cemetery, Salt Lake City.

SELDEN CONNOR was born on January 25, 1839, in Fairfield, Maine. He graduated from Tufts College in 1859 and then moved to Vermont, where he studied law. When the war began, he enlisted as a private in the 1st Vermont on May 2, 1861. He was commissioned lieutenant colonel in the 7th Maine Infantry on August 22. Initially, it was part of the Washington, D.C. garrison but was sent to the Peninsula in April 1862. It fought in the Siege of Yorktown, the Battle of Williamsburg, and the Seven Days battles, including Savage Station, Glendale (Frayser's Farm), and Malvern Hill. Sent north, it took part in the Battles of Crampton's Gap, Antietam, and Fredericksburg, where Colonel Connor was slightly wounded.

The 7th Maine was sent home after Fredericksburg but was back in Virginia in time for the Chancellorsville Campaign, where Connor was slightly wounded on May 4, 1863. It fought at Gettysburg, the victory at Rappahannock Station (November 7), and the Mine Run Campaign. Connor became commander of the 19th Maine on January 11, 1864. He led his regiment in the Battle of the Wilderness, where his left thigh bone was shattered by a Confederate bullet on May 6. Physicians had to remove 3½ inches of his femur.

President Lincoln appointed Seldon Connor brigadier general on June 11, 1864. The promotion was largely honorary. Because of his wound, he was never able to return to the field. His weight was two hundred pounds when he was wounded. He lost one hundred pounds. General Connor was in the Douglas Hospital until August 1865. He was mustered out of the service on April 7, 1866.

Shortly after he returned home, he suffered a fall and reinjured his leg. He was not able to leave his house for two years. In 1868, he was appointed an assessor for the Bureau of Revenue Service. He became a regional collector in 1874. The following year, he was elected governor of Maine as a Republican. He was re-elected twice and served from January 5, 1876 to January 8, 1879. In 1878, he won a plurality with 44.8 percent of the vote. Without a majority, the election was thrown into the legislature, where the Democrats and Greenback-Labor candidates united to elect the Democrat, who had received only 22.4 percent of the popular vote. During his time as governor, he successfully advanced the public school system.

Connor was a U.S. pension agent from 1882 to 1886 and from 1897 to 1912. He became adjutant general of Maine in 1893. He was also president of the Society of the Army of the Potomac and was vice commander-in-chief of the Military Order of the Loyal Legion of the United States.

General Connor died on July 9, 1917, at the age of seventy-eight. He was buried in the Forest Grove Cemetery, Augusta, Maine.

JOHN POPE COOK was born on June 12, 1825, in Belleville, Illinois, into a prominent political family. His father was a congressman, and his grandfather, Ninian Edwards, was a U.S. senator and former governor of Illinois. John was related by marriage to Abraham Lincoln. Orphaned at

an early age, he was well educated at Jacksonville College and by his grandfather, who taught him law. Admitted to the bar, he was elected mayor of Springfield in 1855, county sheriff in 1856, and commander of the local militia company. He became colonel of the 7th Illinois Infantry on April 25, 1861—only two weeks after Fort Sumter.

Cook became a brigade commander in October and distinguished himself at Fort Donelson in February 1862, his only significant battle in the Civil War. As a reward, he was promoted to brigadier general on March 22. He briefly commanded the 6th Division of the Army of the Tennessee. His division was turned over to Benjamin Prentiss and was destroyed at Shiloh. Cook, meanwhile, was transferred to the Washington, D.C. area, where a commanded a brigade in the capital defenses. That autumn, he was sent to the Northwest, where he fought the Sioux in Iowa and in the Dakota Territory. In November 1864, he was named commander of the District of Illinois, which was headquartered in Springfield. He remained here until the end of the war. He was mustered out on August 24, 1865, and brevetted major general in 1866.

General Cook was elected to the Illinois House of Representatives in 1868 as a Republican. In 1879, he was placed in charge of Rosebud, the Sioux agency in South Dakota. He eventually retired to Ransom, Michigan, where he died on October 13, 1910, at age eighty-five. He was buried in the Oak Ridge Cemetery, Springfield, Illinois.

PHILIP ST. GEORGE COOKE was born in Leesburg, Virginia, on June 13, 1809. He entered West Point in 1823, graduated in 1827 (23/38), and was commissioned second lieutenant in the 6th Infantry. He became regimental adjutant, served on the Western Frontier, fought Sac Indians, took part in the Black Hawk War, fought Comanches, and transferred to the newly formed 1st Dragoons Regiment in 1833—the same year he was promoted to first lieutenant.

Cooke had a long and distinguished career in the Old Army, exploring the Far West and fighting outlaws, Mormons, Mexicans, Jicarilla Apache, and the Sioux. He also served in "Bleeding Kansas" and as an observer for the U.S. Army during the Crimean War. He was promoted to captain (1835), major (1847), lieutenant colonel (1853), and colonel (1858). When the Civil War began, he was commander of the Department of Utah. His two-volume manual on cavalry tactics, written in 1858 and published in 1862, was highly controversial. Cooke emphasized the value of cavalry charges, because he did not realize that the rifled musket made such charges obsolete. Others believed that the future of the mounted branch lay in reconnaissance and screening. Sensibly, the U.S. War Department did not adopt it as official doctrine.

Cooke was given command of the 2nd Cavalry (formerly 2nd Dragoons) in August 1861 and was promoted to brigadier general, Regular Army, on November 21, 1861. He initially commanded a cavalry brigade in the Washington defenses but was then transferred to the Peninsula, where McClellan gave him command of the Cavalry Reserve—essentially a cavalry division. His forces were bested by the Rebels almost every time they met, and his son-in-law, Confederate General Jeb Stuart, humiliated him by riding completely around the Army of the Potomac and only losing one man.

Cooke fought in the Battle of Williamsburg and the Seven Days battles. At Gaines' Mill, he ordered the 5th Cavalry to assault Confederate infantry. It was slaughtered. General Cooke was not employed in active field service after Seven Days. For the rest of the war, he served on court-martial duty, recruiting duty, and as commander of the District of Baton Rouge. He was brevetted major general, Regular Army, in 1866.

Postbellum, Philip St. George Cooke commanded the Department of the Platte (1866–67), the Department of the Cumberland (1869–70), and the Department of the Lakes (1871–73). He retired in 1873 after more than half a century of service. He wrote several books of an autobiographical nature about service on the antebellum frontier. He retired to Detroit, Michigan, where he died on March 20, 1895, at age eighty-five. He is buried there in Elmwood Cemetery. He was the father of Brigadier General John Rogers Cooke, CSA, and father-in-law of Brevet Brigadier General Jacob Sharpe, USV.

JAMES COOPER was born on May 8, 1810, in Frederick County, Maryland. He was educated at Mount St. Mary's College in Emmitsburg, Maryland, and Washington College (now Washington and Jefferson), Pennsylvania. He graduated in 1832 and studied law under Thaddeus Stevens in Gettysburg, where Cooper made his home. He was admitted to the bar in 1834. Attracted to politics, he served in Congress as a Whig (1839–43), in the Pennsylvania House of Representatives (1844–45, 1847, and 1849), and in the U.S. Senate (1849–1855). He also spent six months in 1848 as attorney general for the state of Pennsylvania and was speaker of the Pennsylvania House of Representatives for a year (1847). After he left the Senate, he moved back to Maryland.

Totally without military qualifications, Abraham Lincoln nevertheless appointed him brigadier general of U.S. volunteers on August 12, 1861, for political reasons. He served as a recruiter in his home state of Maryland and commanded a brigade against Stonewall Jackson in the Shenandoah Valley Campaign of 1862, with predicable results. His health could not stand the strain of active campaigning, so he was named commandant of Camp Chase, the paroled prisoner-of-war camp in Columbus, Ohio. He died there of congestion of the lungs on March 28, 1863, at age fifty-two. He was buried in Mount Olivet Cemetery in Frederick, Maryland. His son, Captain James Cooper, was a company commander in the 2nd Maryland Infantry until he was seriously wounded near Petersburg on June 16, 1864. Discharged in August, he died the following year.

JOSEPH ALEXANDER COOPER was born on a farm near Cumberland Falls, Kentucky, on November 25, 1823. His family moved to Campbell County, Tennessee, in 1824, where they worked another farm near Jacksboro. Cooper volunteered for the Mexican War and spent several months on occupation duty in Mexico City with the 4th Tennessee Infantry. He supported John Bell and the Constitutional Union Party in the election of 1860 and sought to create a new, pro-Union state of East Tennessee in the run-up to the Civil War. Meanwhile, he attempted to recruit pro-Unionist Tennesseans into the Federal cause. He had more than five hundred men by the time the Confederates approached Jacksboro. Cooper and his men fled to Kentucky. Initially a captain in the 1st Tennessee (Union) Infantry, he became colonel of the 6th Tennessee Infantry on August 8, 1861. As part of the Army of the Ohio, he participated in the operations around the Cumberland Gap and in the Battle of Mill Springs on January 19, 1862.

Colonel Cooper was a Baptist deacon. He hated alcohol and was a strict disciplinarian, but was nevertheless popular with his men because he always put their needs first. His regiment took part in the Kentucky (Heartland) Campaign of 1862 and the Stones River Campaign, during which he repulsed an attempt by Confederate General Joe Wheeler to capture a major wagon train. He was part of the Tullahoma Campaign, the Battle of Chickamauga, and the Knoxville Campaign of late 1863. He was given command of a brigade on March 7, 1864, and led it in the Atlanta Campaign. Cooper performed well, but his command suffered 30 percent casualties in the Battle of Resaca. He was promoted to brigadier general on July 30, 1864. He fought in the Battle of Jonesboro (Jonesborough) (August 31–September 1) and temporarily commanded a division. During Hood's disastrous Tennessee Campaign of 1864–65, Cooper alternated between brigade and division command. Sent to North Carolina, he fought in the Battle of Bentonville. He was brevetted major general on January 13, 1866, and was mustered out of the service on January 15.

Post-war, General Cooper worked for Carpetbagger Governor William "Parson" Brownlow. He and Cooper wanted civil rights (including voting rights) extended to former slaves, while ex-Confederates were disenfranchised. To enforce his policy, Brownlow appointed Cooper commander of the Tennessee State Guard with the rank of brigadier general. His attempts to suppress the Ku Klux Klan were ultimately not successful and he resigned his command in May 1869. Meanwhile, he fell out with Andrew Johnson and lost bids for election to the U.S. House of Representatives and the U.S. Senate. In 1869, President Grant appointed him internal revenue collector for the Knoxville District, a post he held until 1879.

General Cooper moved to Kansas in 1880 and returned to farming. He died there in his home near St. John in Whitley County on May 20, 1910, at age eighty-six. He was buried in the Knoxville National Cemetery.

JOSEPH TARR COPELAND was born in New Castle, Maine, on May 6, 1813, into a family of modest means. His grandfather left him $500, which Joseph used to attend Harvard. After he graduated, he read law under Daniel Webster. He returned to Maine and enlisted in the 3rd Militia Regiment during the bloodless Aroostook War of 1839. Cooper rose to the rank of colonel before moving to St. Clair, Michigan, in the early 1840s. He served in a variety of local offices, including a term in the Michigan State Senate (1850–51). He was elected circuit judge in 1851, a position which automatically made him a member of the Michigan Supreme Court. He also built a sawmill in Bay City, Michigan, and bought an estate in Pontiac. His mansion on the shore of Orchard Lake was called "the castle."

When the 1st Michigan Cavalry Regiment formed on August 14, 1861, Copeland was its lieutenant colonel. He fought with Banks's army in the Shenandoah Valley Campaign of 1862, after which he returned to Michigan and became the commander and colonel of the newly formed 5th Michigan Cavalry Regiment on August 30, 1862. One of the first officers to appreciate the significance of the Spencer Repeating Rifle, he saw to it that his men were equipped with this state-of-the-art weapon. He was promoted to brigadier general on November 29, 1862, and became commander of the Michigan Cavalry Brigade (the Wolverines). Sent back to the Eastern Front, his performance apparently left something to be desired, or perhaps at age fifty, he was just considered too old for cavalry leadership in the field. He was relieved of his command on June 29, 1863, and replaced with George Armstrong Custer. Copeland protested his removal but to no avail. He spent the rest of the war commanding the draft depots at Annapolis and Pittsburgh, and the prison camp at Alton, Illinois. He resigned his commission on November 8, 1865.

After the war, Joseph Copeland converted his Pontiac estate into a resort hotel and managed it until 1878, when he moved to Orange Park,

Florida. He became the town's postmaster in 1879 and was appointed judge of Clay County in 1881. He was reappointed in 1885 and 1887.

General Copeland died on his eightieth birthday (May 6, 1893) in Orange Park, Florida. He was buried in Magnolia Cemetery, Orange Park, but was later re-interred in the Oak Hill Cemetery, Pontiac, Michigan.

MICHAEL "MICK" CORCORAN, the son of a British Army officer, was born in Carrowkeel, County Sligo, Ireland, on September 21, 1827. In 1846, he joined the Revenue Police, searching for moonshiners in County Donegal. He also joined the Ribbonmen, a Catholic rebel guerrilla force. He emigrated to New York City in 1849, arrived penniless, and secured work in a tavern. He joined the 69th New York Militia Regiment as a private in 1851 and was promoted to captain three years later. He became associated with the corrupt Tammany Hall political machine because he could deliver Irish votes and obtained a clerkship at the post office and later at the city register's office.

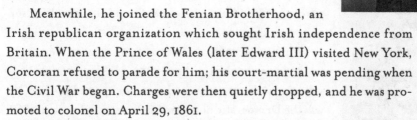

Meanwhile, he joined the Fenian Brotherhood, an Irish republican organization which sought Irish independence from Britain. When the Prince of Wales (later Edward III) visited New York, Corcoran refused to parade for him; his court-martial was pending when the Civil War began. Charges were then quietly dropped, and he was promoted to colonel on April 29, 1861.

Corcoran led the "Fighting 69th" to Washington, D.C. and commanded his regiment at the First Bull Run (July 21), where he was shot in the leg and captured. He was not exchanged until August 15, 1862, and was promoted to brigadier general four days later. He was then given command of a brigade at Yorktown and fought in the Suffolk Campaign. Simultaneously, he engaged in recruiting Irishmen for the Union. He was quite successful; his eight regiments later formed the 155th, 164th, 170th, 175th, and 182nd New York Infantry Regiments.

On April 12, 1863, he had an altercation with Lieutenant Colonel Edgar A. Kimball of the 9th New York Infantry. Corcoran tried to pass through the 9th's area without giving the required password and was stopped by a sentry. When Kimball sided with the sentry, an argument ensued, during which Kimball called Corcoran an "Irish son of a bitch," whereupon Corcoran shot and killed him. He was never arrested or tried for murder but was held censurable and remanded for trial at some future date. Even so, he was placed in command of a division in the VII Corps. Later, he was given command of a division of the XXII Corps in the Washington defenses. He visited Abraham Lincoln and asked for combat duty but was blocked because of his pending court-martial.

On December 22, 1863, while returning from inspecting railroad defenses and riding alone near Fairfax, Virginia, he was thrown by a runaway horse and his skull was fractured. He died the same day at age thirty-six. He is buried in Calvary Cemetery, Woodside, New York. His book, *The Captivity of General Corcoran*, was published posthumously.

JOHN MURRAY CORSE was born on April 27, 1835, in Pittsburgh, Pennsylvania. His family moved to Burlington, Iowa Territory, when he was seven. Here, his father served as mayor for six terms and established a prosperous book and stationery business. He later took his son in as a partner.

Young Corse obtained an appointment to West Point in 1853 but resigned in April 1855. He then attended law school in Albany, returned home, and passed the bar. He was the Democratic nominee for secretary of state in 1860 but was defeated in the general election. He joined the Federal Army on July 13, 1861, as major of the 6th Iowa Infantry. He initially served in Missouri and was on the staff of General John Pope in the Battle of Island Number 10. He was assistant inspector general and judge advocate of the Army of the Mississippi from February to May 1862. Promoted to lieutenant colonel on May 21, he rejoined his regiment and fought at Farmington and in the Siege of Corinth (1862) and the various Vicksburg Campaigns, where he showed considerable ability. He became colonel and regimental commander on March 29, 1863, and distinguished himself in the Siege of Vicksburg. He was promoted to brigadier general on August 11, 1863, and led a brigade in the Army of the Tennessee in the Chattanooga Campaign. He was wounded in the leg at Missionary Ridge (November 25). After he recuperated, he served as commander of draft depots in Indianapolis and Springfield and as an inspector general on General Sherman's staff until July 1864, when he was given command of a division in the XVI Corps.

Corse is best known for his conduct in the Battle of Allatoona Pass (October 5, 1864), which he successfully defended with 2,100 men against at least 3,300 Rebels. One source estimated the Confederate strength at 7,000. In any case, Corse's defense was heroic. He lost a third of his men, part of his ear, and was wounded in the cheekbone, but remained in command and held his fortified position.

After he recovered, Corse took part in the March to the Sea and the Carolinas Campaign. He was brevetted major general for Allatoona Pass on January 23, 1865, and discharged from the service on April 30, 1866.

Postbellum, John Corse turned down a lieutenant colonelcy in the regular army and returned to Iowa, where he engaged in bridge and railroad construction. He also worked as Collector of Internal Revenue for the Chicago region and as postmaster of Boston under President Cleveland. He was also chairman of the Massachusetts State Democratic Committee. He died on his fifty-eighth birthday, April 27, 1893, in Winchester, Massachusetts. He was interred in an impressive mausoleum in the Aspen Grove Cemetery, Burlington, Iowa.

DARIUS NASH COUCH (pronounced "Coach") was born on a farm in Putnam County, New York, on July 23, 1822. He was educated in local schools, enrolled in West Point in 1842, and graduated in 1846 (13/59). Commissioned brevet second lieutenant in the 4th Artillery, he was promoted to second lieutenant (February 1847), and first lieutenant (December 1847). Meanwhile, he earned a brevet to first lieutenant for his gallant conduct in the Battle of Buena Vista (February 23, 1847). Always very thin, his health was frail after Mexico. He served in a variety of posts over the next eight years, including Fort

Monroe, Virginia; Fort Pickens, Florida; Fort Columbus, New York harbor; Jefferson Barracks, Missouri; Fort Johnston, North Carolina; and Fort Mifflin, Philadelphia. He also fought in the Third Seminole War (1849–50). From 1853 to 1854, he took a leave of absence and worked for the Smithsonian Institution in northern Mexico, where he discovered four new species: Couch's Kingbird and Couch's Spadefoot Toad, as well as two species of reptiles.

Lieutenant Couch resigned from the army in 1855. He was a merchant in New York City (1855–57) and settled in Taunton, Massachusetts, where he was a copper fabricator in a company owned by his wife's family. When the Civil War began, he became colonel of the 7th Massachusetts Infantry Regiment on June 15, 1861. He assumed command of a brigade on August 4 and was promoted to brigadier general five days later. Part of the Army of the Potomac, he was named divisional commander in September and was promoted to major general on July 25, 1862. Meanwhile, he fought in the Peninsula Campaign, including the Siege of Yorktown and the Battle of Williamsburg. He distinguished himself at Seven Pines and fought in the Seven Days battles. By July, his health failed him, and he submitted his resignation, but General McClellan, the army commander, refused to forward it to the War Department.

Couch took part in the Maryland Campaign of 1862, including the Battle of Antietam, where his division was kept in reserve. On November 14, he was named commander of the II Corps, which he led at Fredericksburg. Here, his corps suffered four thousand casualties. He led seventeen thousand men in the Battle of Chancellorsville, where he was commander of the Army of the Potomac for a few hours on May 3, after General Hooker was stunned by flying debris from a house hit by a Rebel shell. Couch himself was slightly wounded. After this battle, Lincoln offered Couch command of the Army of the Potomac, but he declined for reasons of health. He quarreled with Hooker and asked to be transferred. Lincoln placed him in command of the newly created Department of the Susquehanna on June 11, and he directed militia in skirmishes against Lee's army. He took part in the pursuit after Gettysburg.

General Couch returned to the field in December 1864, commanding a division in the Army of the Ohio, which he led in the Battle of Nashville and in the Carolinas Campaign. He resigned his commission on May 26, 1865, and returned to Taunton.

Couch was a fine division and corps commander; however, he was noted for his temper and impatience. He frequently clashed with both superiors and subordinates. His ill health prevented him from going down in history as one of the great Union generals, although he was very good.

Post-war, Darius Couch ran for governor of Massachusetts on the Democratic ticket in 1865 but was defeated. Later, he was president of a mining company in West Virginia. He moved to Connecticut in 1871, where he was quartermaster general and then adjutant general of the state militia (1883–1885). General Couch died in Norwalk, Connecticut, on February 12, 1897, at age seventy-four. He was buried in Mount Pleasant Cemetery, Taunton, Massachusetts.

ROBERT COWDIN (sometimes misspelled "Coudin" or "Cowden") was born in Jamaica, Vermont, on September 18, 1805. He moved to Boston in 1825 and found employment in the lumber business. He joined the militia in 1838, spent eight years on the Common Council of Boston, and held a variety of minor offices in the city's correctional system.

By 1861, he was a colonel and commander of the 2nd Massachusetts Militia Regiment. He first saw action at Blackburn's Ford (July 18, 1861) and fought in the First Battle of Bull Run three days later, where his horse was killed. He fought in the Peninsula Campaign, including the Battles of Williamsburg and Seven Pines, and in the Seven Days battles, including Frayser's Farm (Glendale) and Malvern Hill. He arrived in time to fight in the Battle of Chantilly in the Second Bull Run Campaign.

General Hooker recommended him for promotion, and on September 26, 1862, he was appointed brigadier general. He was given command of a brigade in the Washington defenses, but Congress adjourned on March 4, 1863, without acting on his promotion. Perhaps this was because of his age. In any case, his appointment expired, he was relieved of his command, and he was mustered out on March 30, 1863.

Robert Cowdin returned to Boston in 1863 and spent ten years on the city's Common Council and Board of Aldermen. He died in Boston on July 9, 1874, at age sixty-eight. He is buried in the Mount Auburn Cemetery, Cambridge, Massachusetts.

JACOB DOLSON COX was born on October 27, 1828, in Montreal, Lower Canada (now Quebec). His parents were from New York, and his father was in Montreal superintending the construction of the roof of the church of Notre Dame when he was born. After studying law for two years in New York, Cox moved to Ohio and became a bookkeeper for a brokerage firm. He eventually studied at Oberlin College (1846–50), where he obtained a degree in theology. He then became superintendent of the Warren County School System, resumed his legal studies, and was admitted to the bar in 1853.

Cox was an abolitionist and helped organize the Ohio Republican Party when the Whig Party collapsed in 1854. He was an Ohio state senator from 1860 to January 1862, privately studied military science, and accepted a commission as brigadier general in the Ohio Militia on April 23, 1861, despite a lack of military training.

Cox initially commanded Camp Jackson, the recruiting center at Columbus. He assumed command of the Kanawha Brigade in May 1861 and led it successfully in McClellan's Kanawha Valley Campaign. He remained in western Virginia until the Maryland Campaign, where his brigade was expanded into a division. It was part of the IX Corps at South Mountain (September 14, 1862). After its acting commander, Jesse L. Reno, was killed, Cox directed the corps under the general supervision of Ambrose Burnside, who was commander of a two-corps "wing." Cox nearly overwhelmed the Rebel right at Antietam, but was caught in the flank by A. P. Hill's division, which forced him to fall back.

Cox was appointed major general on October 6, 1862, but the Senate failed to confirm the appointment, which expired on March 4, 1863. Meanwhile, Cox was assigned to command the District of Ohio in October 1862. He later directed the District of Michigan. In December 1863, he returned to the field as commander of the XXIII Corps, which he led in the Atlanta, Tennessee, and Carolinas campaigns. He saved the Union center in the battle of Franklin (November 30, 1864) and was promoted to major general on February 18, 1865. This time his appointment was confirmed by the Senate. He was mustered out on January 1, 1866.

Cox was elected governor of Ohio in November 1865 and served from 1866 to 1868. He sided with Johnson's Reconstruction plan against the Radical Republicans. He advocated segregation and opposed African American suffrage and even suggested that they be put on reservations.

Cox did not seek re-election in 1867. President Grant nominated Cox for Secretary of the Interior and he took office on March 5, 1869. Unfortunately for Cox, he was a civil service reformer and Grant was not. Cox resigned on October 31, 1870.

For the rest of his life, Cox held a laundry list of impressive jobs, including president of the Wabash Railroad, Congressman (1877–79), president of the Toledo & Wabash Railroad, professor and dean of the Cincinnati Law School (1881–97), and president of the University of Cincinnati (1885–89). He also wrote several books on the Civil War and was a noted microscopist. He was also a highly capable tactical commander, although he could have moved more rapidly at Antietam.

Jacob Dolson Cox died on August 4, 1900, while on vacation in Gloucester, Massachusetts. He was seventy-one years old. He is buried in the Spring Grove Cemetery, Cincinnati, Ohio.

JAMES CRAIG was born on February 28, 1817, in Washington County, Pennsylvania. His parents moved to Mansfield, Ohio, and then to New Philadelphia, Ohio, where Craig studied law. He was admitted to the bar in 1839 and settled in St. Joseph, Missouri. He served in the Missouri Mounted Rifles during the Mexican War. Mustered out in 1848, he became the state attorney for his district (1852–56) and was elected to the state senate. In 1856, he was elected to the U.S. Congress as a Democrat and served from 1857 to 1861. He was defeated for re-nomination in 1860. Lincoln appointed him brigadier general on March

22, 1862. The move was political: the president wanted Missouri Democrats to support the Union. Craig's mission was to guard the overland mail routes in Kansas and Nebraska. On November 2, 1862, he was named commander of the District of Nebraska, a post he held until he resigned his commission on May 5, 1863. He "returned to the colors" as a brigadier general of Missouri State Militia in May 1864 but resigned again on January 2, 1865.

General Craig was president of the Hannibal and St. Joseph Railroad from 1861 to 1872 and was the first president of the St. Joseph & Denver Railroad, which is now part of the Union Pacific system. He also served as president of other, smaller railroads and served as comptroller for the city of St. Joseph near the end of his life. He died at St. Joseph on October 12, 1888, at age seventy-one. He was buried in the Mount Mora Cemetery, St. Joseph, Missouri.

SAMUEL WYLIE CRAWFORD was born in Bedford, Indiana, on November 8, 1829. He graduated from the University of Pennsylvania in 1846 and from the University of Pennsylvania School of Medicine in 1850. He joined the U.S. Army as an assistant surgeon on March 10, 1851.

Crawford served at various posts on the Western frontier and Newport, Rhode Island, until September 1860, when he was ordered to Fort Moultrie, South Carolina, as post surgeon. His predecessor had recently died in a yellow fever epidemic. Crawford moved to Fort Sumter with the garrison on December 26, 1860. Despite his purely medical training, he helped man cannons during the Confederate bombardment of April 12–13, 1861. Afterward, he radically changed careers and became an infantryman, initially as major of the 13th U.S. Infantry Regiment. He became assistant inspector general of the Department of the Ohio in September and was wounded in a skirmish in February 1862. On April 25, he was promoted to brigadier general and led a brigade in Banks's Shenandoah Valley Campaign of 1862. At Cedar Mountain (August 9), his brigade attacked and initially routed the Confederates but was not supported by other units. The Rebels rallied, counterattacked, and defeated Crawford's command, which suffered 50 percent casualties.

On September 15, Crawford assumed command of a division when Alpheus S. Williams was given command of the XII Corps. Two days later, at Antietam, he was wounded in the right thigh but continued to fight until he almost fainted from loss of blood. Taken to the rear, it took him eight months to recover. In May 1863, he returned to duty as commander of the Pennsylvania Reserve Division in the Washington defenses.

Crawford commanded the Pennsylvania Reserve for the rest of the war and distinguished himself in the defense of the Little Round Top at Gettysburg. He also did well in the Overland Campaign and was brevetted major general on August 1, 1864. Meanwhile, he was injured in the Battle of Spotsylvania Court House when he was struck by a large tree limb that was shattered by a cannon ball. He was also wounded in the chest on August 18 near the Weldon Railroad. Only at the Battle of Five Forks (April 1, 1865) was his performance substandard, when his division wandered into heavy woods away from the main Union attack. He was present at Appomattox and was one of the few men to be on hand at both the beginning and the effective end of the war.

Crawford reverted to the rank of lieutenant colonel when he was mustered out of volunteer service on June 15, 1866. He became colonel of the 16th Infantry Regiment in 1869 and retired in 1873. He was promoted to brigadier general, regular army, in 1875. Crawford authored a book, *The Genesis of the Civil War*, which was published in 1887. He died in Philadelphia on November 3, 1892, at age sixty-two. He was buried in the Laurel Hill Cemetery, Philadelphia.

THOMAS LEONIDAS CRITTENDEN was born in Russellville, Kentucky, on May 15, 1819, into a prominent Kentucky family. He was the son of U.S. Senator John Jordan Crittenden; the brother of General George B. Crittenden, CSA; and the cousin of Thomas T. Crittenden, USV. Thomas L. Crittenden read law, was admitted to the bar in 1840, and was elected district commonwealth attorney in 1842. When the Mexican War began, he joined the army and served as an aide to General Zachary Taylor. He

became lieutenant colonel of the 3rd Kentucky Infantry in 1847 and was mustered out the following year. After he became president, Taylor appointed Crittenden U.S. consul to Liverpool in 1849. He returned to Kentucky in 1853 and labored as a merchant until the Civil War began.

Thomas L. Crittenden became a major general in the Kentucky Militia in 1860. He adhered to the Union and became a brigadier general of volunteers on September 27, 1861. He became a division commander in the Army of the Ohio, which helped save Grant's forces at Shiloh on April 7, 1862. He was promoted to major general on July 17 and assumed command of the II Corps of the Army of the Ohio on September 29. His corps participated in the Kentucky (Heartland) Campaign and was lightly engaged at Perryville.

Crittenden commanded the Left Wing of the Army of the Cumberland at Stones River, where the fighting was heavy. When the army was reorganized in 1863, Crittenden's command was redesignated XXI Corps. He led it in the Tullahoma Campaign and at Chickamauga, where he and General Alexander McCook were blamed for the disaster and relieved of their commands. A subsequent exhaustive investigation led to their complete exoneration. Crittenden was given command of Thomas G. Stevenson's division in the Army of the Potomac on May 12, 1864, after that officer was killed in action. Crittenden led it at Spotsylvania and at Cold Harbor. He was relieved of his command at his own request on June 9 and was unemployed until December 13, when he resigned his commission.

Thomas L. Crittenden was an average to mediocre commander but not a poor one. Certainly he was overshadowed by some of his more dynamic peers, such as General Thomas, but his career seems to have been ruined by his long association with William Rosecrans, rather than anything he did.

Crittenden was appointed state treasurer for Kentucky in January 1866. President Johnson later offered him a colonelcy in the post-war army, which he accepted. He commanded the 32nd and later the 17th Infantry Regiments. He retired in 1881. General Crittenden died in Annadale, Staten Island, New York, on October 23, 1893. He was seventy-four years old. He was buried in Frankfort.

Crittenden married Catherine "Kitty" Todd, the daughter of his father's second wife and thus his stepsister. Their son, Second Lieutenant John Jordan

Crittenden, III, was with the U.S. 7th Cavalry at Little Big Horn and was killed there. He was twenty-two years old. At his father's instructions, John was buried with his men. Thomas and Kitty Crittenden also had two daughters.

THOMAS TURPIN CRITTENDEN was born in Huntsville, Alabama, on October 16, 1825, but his family moved to Texas shortly afterward. He was a nephew of U.S. Senator John J. Crittenden and a first cousin of Union General Thomas Leonidas Crittenden and Confederate General George B. Crittenden. He is sometimes confused with another cousin, Thomas Theodore Crittenden of Missouri. He grew up in Texas but attended Transylvania College in Lexington, Kentucky, became an attorney, and practiced law in Hannibal, Missouri. When the war with Mexico began in 1846, he enlisted in the army and became a second lieutenant in the Missouri Mounted Battalion. After the war, he settled in Madison, Indiana.

The Confederates fired on Fort Sumter on April 12, 1861. Five days later, Crittenden joined the Union Army and was commissioned captain in the 6th Indiana Militia (later Infantry), a three-month regiment. He became its colonel on April 27. He led it with considerable success in the Western Virginia Campaign of 1861. When the regiment's enlistments expired, Crittenden reorganized it as a three-year command. He led it into Kentucky in September and spent the winter near Bowling Green. He fought at Shiloh during the second day of the battle (April 7, 1862) and was promoted to brigadier general on April 30.

Crittenden arrived in Murfreesboro, Tennessee, on July 12. He was slated to assume command of the post on July 13, but he and his entire command were captured by Nathan Bedford Forrest on July 13. He was exchanged in October and was given another brigade in March 1863, but only for a month. Murfreesboro ruined his military career, and he resigned on May 5. He saw no further service, and it is hard not to conclude that he was treated unjustly.

After the war, Crittenden practiced law in Washington, D.C. He moved to San Diego, California, in 1885 and became a real estate developer. He died on September 5, 1905, during a visit to East Gloucester, Massachusetts. He was seventy-nine years old. He is buried in Arlington National Cemetery.

MARCELLUS MONROE CROCKER was born in Franklin, Indiana, on February 6, 1830. He was admitted to West Point in 1847 but resigned in February 1848, to study law. He was admitted to the bar and practiced in Des Moines, Iowa.

Crocker joined the Union Army as a captain in the 2nd Iowa Infantry on May 27, 1861. He was promoted to major four days later; to lieutenant colonel on September 6; and to colonel of the 13th Iowa Infantry on December 30. He distinguished himself on the first day of the Battle of Shiloh (April 6, 1862) and took command of his brigade after its commander, Colonel Abraham M. Hare, was wounded. Following the battle, General John McClernand, his divisional commander, officially commended him as "an able and enterprising officer" and recommended him for promotion. During the Siege of Corinth, he was given command of the "Iowa Brigade," which became known as "Crocker's Greyhounds." He distinguished himself again in the Second Battle of Corinth (October 3), by delaying the Confederate advance long enough for General Rosecrans to organize a defense. The North won the battle the next day. Crocker was promoted to brigadier general on April 4, 1863.

General Crocker took part in the final Vicksburg Campaign as an acting division commander and fought at Raymond (May 12) and Champion Hill (May 16). He became so sick during the final days of the Siege of Vicksburg that General Grant personally ordered him to the rear. After recovering somewhat, he was given another division and launched a small but highly successful raid into Louisiana, capturing Fort Beauregard and a significant amount of artillery at no loss to himself. General Grant later remarked that "I have never seen but three or four division commanders his equal." Unfortunately, Crocker suffered from tuberculosis, which was called consumption in those days. As his division was en route to join Sherman for the drive on Atlanta, Crocker became very ill. He submitted his resignation for reasons of health on May 14, 1864, but Secretary of War Stanton refused to accept it, stating that the country could ill afford to lose an officer of his caliber. Instead, General Crocker was transferred to New Mexico, where it was thought his health might improve. Apparently, it did so, although he was dissatisfied in New Mexico, commanding a post of six companies which, he said, would be better commanded by a captain. By December, he felt well enough to ask for active field service.

Marcellus Crocker's political views changed over time. He was a War Democrat when the war began but became a Republican. Near the end of the war, he came out in favor of giving African Americans the vote. It was also suggested that he run for governor of Iowa, but he declined, saying he could do the most good in the field.

On March 1, 1865, Crocker was relieved of duty in Santa Fe and ordered to report to General Thomas in Nashville. But his health collapsed en route, and he never joined the Army of the Cumberland. He was instructed to personally report to the War Department as soon as his health allowed.

Crocker made it to Washington but died of consumption in the Willard's Hotel on August 26, 1865. He was thirty-five. He was buried in Woodland Cemetery, Des Moines, Iowa.

GEORGE CROOK was born on September 8, 1828, on a farm near Taylorsville, Ohio. He entered the United States Military Academy in 1848 and graduated in 1852 (38/43). He was commissioned brevet second lieutenant in the 4th Infantry and was promoted to second lieutenant in 1853, first lieutenant in 1856, and captain on May 14, 1861. In the meantime, he fought Indians in Oregon and northern California and was severely wounded by an arrow in the Pit River (California) Expedition of 1857.

Crook was the prime Indian fighter of his era. He learned wilderness and survival skills and was fluent in several Native American languages. When the Civil War began, he was recalled to the East and named commander of the 36th Ohio Infantry Regiment.

George Crook led the 36th in the Western Virginia Campaign and subsequent operations in the mountains of what became West Virginia. He was given command of a brigade in the Kanawha District in March 1862. He was wounded in a skirmish near Lewisburg on May 23. He returned to the command of his regiment, which formed the headquarters guard for John Pope during the Second Battle of Bull Run (August 29-30). When Crook's brigade commander, Colonel Augustus Moor, was captured on September 12, Crook took charge of the brigade. He was promoted to brigadier general on September 7.

General Crook led his brigade at South Mountain and Antietam, and was transferred to the Army of the Cumberland and fought at Hoover's Gap, Tennessee (June 24, 1862). In July, he was elevated to the command of a cavalry division, which he led at Chickamauga and Chattanooga. He returned to the command of the Kanawha Division in West Virginia in February 1864.

Crook crushed a mixed Confederate infantry/cavalry force at Cloyd's Mountain on May 9 and destroyed much of the Virginia and Tennessee Railroad. He then joined Sheridan for the Shenandoah Valley Campaign of 1864, where he fought in the Third Battle of Winchester, Fisher's Hill, and Cedar Creek. He was promoted to major general on October 21, 1864. His force was officially designated the Army of the Kanawha on July 2 and became the Army of West Virginia on August 8. General Crook was captured by Confederate raiders on February 21, 1865, at Cumberland, Maryland. He was exchanged the following month and led a cavalry division of the Army of the Potomac in the Appomattox Campaign. He was mustered out of volunteer service on January 15, 1866.

Despite his far above average performance, George Crook reverted back to his regular army rank of major after the war. He was promoted to lieutenant colonel in July 1866. He was sent to the Pacific Northwest, where he arguably became the greatest Indian fighter in American history. He defeated the Snake Indians, then the Paiute, Pit River, and Modoc tribes before being transferred to Arizona. Here, he smashed the Yavapai and Tonto Apache in 1872 and 1873. For his many successes, Crook was promoted to brigadier general, Regular Army, on October 29, 1873. He was named commander of the Department of the Platte (1875-82 and 1886-88), during which he defeated the Sioux, the Lakota Sioux, and the Northern Cheyenne. He commanded the Department of Arizona (1882–86), where he defeated but could not capture Geronimo. He commanded the Department of Missouri from 1888 to 1890.

George Crook was promoted to major general, Regular Army, in 1888. In his last years, he was a vocal proponent of treating his former adversaries justly. Indian chiefs always praised Crook's honesty. He died suddenly on March 21, 1890, in Chicago. He was sixty-one years old. He was buried in Arlington National Cemetery.

JOHN THOMAS CROXTON was born in Paris, Kentucky, on November 20, 1836, the son of a wealthy planter and slave owner. Tall and handsome, he graduated from Yale (with honors) in 1857, read law, and taught in Mississippi for a time. He returned to Kentucky in 1859, opened a prosperous practice in Paris, and engaged in agriculture. He also became a strong pro-emancipation advocate and spent money buying Sharps rifles for free-soil men in "Bleeding Kansas," although he denied being an abolitionist; instead, he favored gradual emancipation.

On October 9, 1861, after Kentucky's neutrality collapsed, Croxton became lieutenant colonel of the 4th Kentucky Mounted Rifles. He proved to be a natural soldier and leader. He fought at Mill Springs (January 19, 1862), where General Thomas secured eastern Kentucky for the Union. He was promoted to colonel and regimental commander that March (at age twenty-four) and became an acting brigade commander in August.

Croxton's command took part in the Kentucky Campaign and was present but not engaged at Perryville. During the Stones River Campaign, his brigade guarded the wagon trains against Rebel cavalry attacks. He participated in the Tullahoma Campaign and fought at Chickamauga, where his brigade was part of Thomas's XIV Corps. They saved the Union Army, but Croxton was painfully wounded in the left leg on September 20. His division commander, John M. Brannan, praised his performance.

Croxton reverted to regimental commander during the Siege of Chattanooga. He led his men up Missionary Ridge on November 25, until a Rebel cannon ball blew up a hut he was passing by. He was buried and pinned under the debris, which reopened his wound from Chickamauga.

Colonel Croxton was known for his courage, calmness, tactical acumen, and self-confidence. He commanded a cavalry brigade in the Atlanta Campaign and was promoted to brigadier general on July 30, 1864, at age twenty-seven. As Sherman engaged in his famous March to the Sea, Croxton joined Thomas's forces in Tennessee and distinguished himself in the rout of Hood's army at Nashville on December 16, 1864. He seized Tuscaloosa, Alabama, a major Southern supply center, on April 4, 1865, and burned the University of Alabama. He was named commander of the District of Southwest Georgia at the end of the war. He was brevetted major general in January 1866.

General Croxton resigned his commission on December 26, 1865, and returned to Paris and the practice of law. He also helped establish the *Louisville Commercial*, a pro-Republican newspaper. President Grant appointed him U.S. minister to Bolivia in 1872. He died in La Paz, Bolivia, on April 16, 1874. He was thirty-seven. General Croxton's remains were transported to the town of his birth, where he is interred in the Paris Cemetery in Paris, Kentucky.

CHARLES CRUFT was born in Terre Haute, Indiana, on January 12, 1826. He graduated from Wabash College, Indiana, in 1842 and worked as a bank clerk, read law, was admitted to the bar, and was president of the Alton & Terre Haute Railroad from 1855 to 1858. He became publisher of the *Wabash Express* newspaper in 1861.

When the Civil War broke out, Cruft went to Virginia and watched the First Battle of Bull Run as a spectator. He returned home and raised the 31st Indiana Infantry. He joined the Federal Army as the regiment's colonel on September 20, 1861, and was elevated to brigade command at the end of November.

Fort Donelson was Colonel Cruft's first major battle. He performed with the same marked ability and competence which would characterize all his battles. General McClernand praised him as an "officer of courage and good conduct." He was wounded on February 15, but details are not recorded. In any case, he was present at the Battle of Shiloh, where he fought in the Hornet's Nest sector and was severely wounded in the left leg, shoulder, and head. He still had not returned to duty on July 16, 1862, when he was promoted to brigadier general. He took part in the Heartland Campaign of 1862 and was again wounded in the Battle of Richmond, Kentucky. His brigade was present at Perryville but was not decisively engaged.

Cruft continued to serve on the Western Front, fighting in the Stones River, Tullahoma, Chickamauga, Chattanooga, and Atlanta Campaigns and occasionally functioned as a division commander. He commanded a Provisional Division at the Battle of Nashville. He was brevetted major general on March 7, 1865, and mustered out on August 24, 1865.

After the war, General Cruft returned to his law practice and rose high in the Masonic Order, becoming part of the Supreme Commandery, Knights Templar of the United States. He died March 23, 1883, in the town of his birth. He was fifty-seven years old. He is buried in Woodlawn Cemetery, Terre Haute, Indiana.

GEORGE WASHINGTON CULLUM was born on February 25, 1809, in New York City. His parents moved the family to Meadville, Pennsylvania, when he was a child. He entered West Point in 1829, graduated in 1833 (3/43), and was commissioned brevet second lieutenant in the engineers. He was promoted to second lieutenant (1836) and captain (1838). He alternated between erecting defensive works on the Atlantic coast and teaching at West Point. He was still just a captain with twenty-three years' time in grade when the war began.

On April 9, 1861, Cullum was promoted to lieutenant colonel, Regular Army, and named aide-de-camp to the general-in-chief, Winfield Scott. He was promoted to brigadier general of volunteers on November 12, 1861. He served brief stints as chief of staff and chief engineer of the Department of the Missouri and chief of staff and chief engineer of the Department of the Mississippi. When

Henry W. Halleck became general-in-chief, Cullum returned to Washington and became his chief of staff. He was Halleck's chief until September 8, 1864, when he became superintendent of the U.S. Military Academy at West Point. He held this position until August 1866. He was mustered out of volunteer service on September 1, 1866, and reverted to the rank of lieutenant colonel. He was brevetted major general in March 1866.

Cullum continued to perform engineer duties at various locations until 1874, when he retired as a colonel. He married General Halleck's widow in 1875. It was his only marriage. She died in 1884, leaving him a considerable fortune. He had no descendants, so he bequeathed his money to various relatives (including Halleck's), West Point, the American Geographical Society, and several museums, churches, hospitals, and libraries.

General Cullum died of pneumonia in New York City on February 28, 1892, at age eighty-three. He was buried in the Green-Wood Cemetery, Brooklyn, New York. His *Biographical Register of the Officers and Graduates of the United States Military Academy*, which was published in three volumes, is still a valuable source for historians and researchers.

NEWTON MARTIN CURTIS was born in De Peyster, New York, on May 21, 1835. He grew into an impressive figure: 6'7" tall and weighing 225 pounds. (The average Union soldier was a little over 5'7" and weighed 143 pounds.) He attended Gouverneur Wesleyan Seminary and became a teacher, an attorney, and the postmaster of De Peyster, which is in far upstate New York, near the Canadian border.

Curtis entered the Union Army on May 15, 1861, as a captain and company commander in the 16th New York Infantry and first saw action in the First Battle of Bull Run, where the 16th was lightly engaged. Curtis took part in the Peninsula Campaign in April and May 1862. An easy target because of his size, he was shot in the chest in a skirmish near West Point, Virginia (May 7). The 16th also fought in the Maryland Campaign, including the Battles of Crampton's Gap and Antietam. In October, Curtis transferred to the 142nd New York (which was forming at Ogdensburg) as its lieutenant colonel. It was initially part of the Washington defenses and remained there until April 1863, when it was sent to Suffolk, Virginia. Here the North successfully checked Longstreet's corps in a siege that lasted from April 20 to May 4. Sent back to Washington, it was part of the pursuit of Lee's army after Gettysburg.

In 1864, the regiment became part of the X Corps, Army of the James, and fought at Cold Harbor, the Bermuda Hundred, and in the Siege of Petersburg. Curtis assumed command of a brigade on June 21, 1864, and on October 28, was brevetted brigadier general for his courage in the Battle of Chaffin's Farm (a.k.a. New Market Heights) (September 29–30).

Curtis's brigade took part in the assault on Fort Fisher, North Carolina, on January 15, 1865. He was awarded the Congressional Medal of Honor in 1891 for his courage and leadership in this battle. In the process, he was wounded four times, most seriously when he was struck just above the left eye by a fragment from a Confederate shell and permanently lost his vision in that eye. He was promoted to brigadier (full rank) on January 15.

Curtis returned to duty in April as chief of staff of the Department of Virginia. He was brevetted major general on January 13, 1866, and was mustered out on January 15.

After the war, he was a collector of customs in upstate New York, then a Special Agent for the Treasury Department (1867–1880). He later worked for the Department of Justice and was elected to the New York State Assembly, serving from 1883 to 1891. He was elected to Congress as a Republican in 1891, serving from 1891 to 1897, where he was known as a fervent opponent of the death penalty. He was not a candidate for re-election. He wrote a book, *Bull Run to Chancellorsville*, which was published in 1906.

A war hero of the first order, General Curtis died in New York City on January 8, 1910, at age seventy-four. He was buried in Ogdensburg Cemetery, Ogdensburg, New York.

SAMUEL RYAN CURTIS was born on February 3, 1805, near Champlain, New York. He attended West Point, graduated in 1831 (27/33), and was commissioned brevet second lieutenant in the 7th Infantry. He was stationed at Fort Gibson, Indian Territory (now Oklahoma) but resigned

in 1832. He relocated to Ohio, where he worked as a civil engineer and was a colonel in the Ohio Militia. During the Mexican War, he served as colonel of the 3rd Ohio, and held the large depot at Carongo, northern Mexico, against attacks from numerically superior forces.

Curtis moved to Iowa in the 1850s and worked on river improvements and on the American Central Railroad. He became mayor of Keokuk in 1856 and was elected to Congress as a Republican, serving from 1857 to 1861. An abolitionist and supporter of Lincoln, he was considered for a cabinet position, but instead, he accepted the colonelcy of the 2nd Iowa Infantry. He resigned his seat in Congress on August 4, 1861, and was promoted to brigadier general on August 7. On December 25, General Halleck appointed him commander of the Army of the Southwest. On March 7 and 8, 1862, he defeated Earl Van Dorn's Army of the West at Pea Ridge, Arkansas, which effectively secured Missouri for the Union until 1864. It was one of the few major battles in the Civil War in which Union forces were outnumbered and much of the credit for the victory should go to the highly competent Curtis. As a reward, he was promoted to major general on March 23, 1862.

General Curtis later invaded northeastern Arkansas and captured Helena in July. He fell out, however, with William Gamble, governor of Missouri, when he (Curtis) expressed his abolitionist views too strongly. Lincoln transferred Curtis to the command of the Department of Kansas and Indian Territory in early 1864. He was sent back to the state when Confederate General Sterling Price invaded Missouri. Curtis dubbed his force "the Army of the Border" and decisively defeated Price in the Battle of Westport on October 23.

In the last phase of the war, Curtis was placed in command of the Department of the Northwest, where he put down Indian uprisings in Minnesota and the Dakota Territory. He was mustered out on April 30, 1866.

Samuel Curtis returned to Iowa post-war, where he helped negotiate Indian treaties, and worked for the Union Pacific Railroad. He died on December 26, 1866, at Council Bluffs, Iowa, at age sixty-one. He is buried in the Oakland Cemetery in Keokuk. One of his sons, Major Henry Zarah Curtis, was killed by Quantrill's Raiders in 1863. Another, Samuel S. Curtis, was lieutenant colonel of the 3rd Colorado Infantry.

GEORGE ARMSTRONG CUSTER was born in New Rumley, Ohio, on December 5, 1839, the son of a farmer and blacksmith. The family moved to Michigan when he was young. George attended West Point, where he was nicknamed "Autie," "Fanny," and "Curley." Like his brothers, he was known for his practical jokes. He was not a good student and finished dead last in the Class of 1861 (34/34). He also raked up an incredible 726 demerits—one of the worst records in the history of the academy. He was nevertheless commissioned second lieutenant, joined the 2nd (later 5th) Cavalry, and served as the messenger between Generals McDowell and Winfield Scott during the First Battle of Manassas.

As a young West Point graduate, Custer was well connected within the army. He served as an aide to General McClellan during the Peninsula Campaign and was promoted to captain, Regular Army, on June 5, 1862, but was demoted to first lieutenant twelve days later. He took part in the Maryland Campaign, including the battles of South Mountain and Antietam. In 1863, he served as an aide to General Alfred Pleasanton, the commander of the Cavalry Corps.

Pleasanton reformed the cavalry, dismissed political generals, and replaced them with young officers who were ready to fight aggressively. One of these was Custer, who was promoted to brigadier general and brigade commander on June 29. He was twenty-three years old. The rest of Custer's life was a constant pursuit of glory and publicity. It was also characterized by aggressiveness, fearlessness, and an absolute belief in his own destiny. He distinguished himself in the Gettysburg Campaign, where his horse was shot out from under him, and he narrowly avoided capture. He performed so well, however, that he was elevated to division command on July 15.

For the rest of the war, Custer was generally successful, although not always so. He played a major role in the conquest of the Shenandoah Valley.

On April 9, 1865, he approached Confederate General Longstreet under a flag of truce and demanded he unconditionally surrender the Army of Northern Virginia to himself and General Sheridan. Longstreet replied that he was not in command of the army, but if he was, he would not surrender to Sheridan. He ordered the deployment of units which no longer existed to meet the threatened attack, and Custer withdrew in confusion. Lee surrendered to Grant later that day. Shortly after, Custer seized a prized racehorse. The owner approached General Grant and demanded that the stolen horse be returned. Grant ordered Custer to return the horse, but he did not.

George Custer was promoted to major general on April 24, 1865, making him the youngest major general in the army. He was posted to Texas, where he was mustered out of volunteer service on February 1, 1866, and reverted to his regular army rank, which was now lieutenant colonel. He was assigned to the 7th Cavalry on July 28.

Custer's post-war career was rocky, to say the least. He was court-martialed for being AWOL (away without leave) while he paid a visit to his wife. He was suspended from duty without pay for a year. At Sheridan's request, he was allowed to return after ten months to help in a campaign against the Cheyenne. On November 27, 1868, he attacked Chief Black Kettle's camp, killed about a hundred warriors, and ruthlessly slaughtered dozens of women and children, as well as 875 Indian horses and ponies. He was assigned to the Dakota Territory in 1873, to protect railroad survey parties from the Lakota Sioux.

Custer returned to Washington in early 1876 to testify in the impeachment trial of William W. Belknap. Custer's sensational testimony against Grant's secretary of war included a number of unfounded accusations and attacks on the president's brother. This led to a permanent split between Grant and Custer, who at one point was arrested on Grant's orders. Grant refused to allow Custer to command an upcoming expedition against the Sioux. Only an appeal from Brigadier General Alfred Terry, Custer's immediate superior, caused Grant to relent and allow Custer to command his regiment in the operation, but the president ordered that Terry—not Custer—command the expedition. (The permanent commander of the 7th Cavalry, Samuel Sturgis, was on detached duty.) Restored to duty,

Custer decided to "cut loose" from Terry and operate on his own. The result was the Battle of Little Big Horn. Custer pressed forward with part of his command—five companies, which totaled 208 officers and men. On June 25, 1876, they were attacked by 1,800 to 3,500 Indians, depending on one's source. In any case, Custer's command was totally wiped out within an hour. He was thirty-six years old. His body was initially buried in a shallow grave on the battlefield, along with his brother, Tom, who was one of the few figures in American History to earn the Congressional Medal of Honor twice. Another brother, a nephew, and a brother-in-law were also killed. George Armstrong Custer was re-interred in the West Point Cemetery in 1877. He remains one of the most controversial figures in U.S. history.

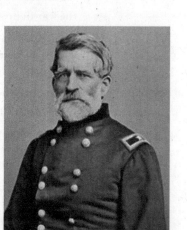

LYSANDER CUTLER was born on February 16, 1807, on a farm in Royalston, Massachusetts. He was educated at local schools, became a surveyor, and eventually a schoolmaster at Dexter, Maine, at age twenty-one. The previous several teachers were beaten, flogged, and run off by the unruly students. Cutler spent his first day thrashing every bully in the school.

Cutler engaged in a variety of business activities before the war, including owning a woolen mill, a foundry, a flour mill, and a sawmill. He became wealthy and even served in the Maine State Senate in the early 1840s. Additionally, he became a colonel in the Maine Militia and skirmished with Indians in the 1830s. He was financially wiped out by the Panic of 1857 and the subsequent economic depression. He moved to Wisconsin in 1857 and worked as an iron ore and grain broker.

Cutler was commissioned colonel of the 6th Wisconsin Infantry Regiment on July 16, 1861. He imposed discipline and was unpopular with the troops, many of whom were immigrants; he was nevertheless promoted to brigade commander on March 13, 1862. His first Civil War battle was the Second Bull Run, where he proved himself to be a fierce warrior. He was also shot in the thigh and missed the Maryland Campaign. He was placed in temporary command of the Iron Brigade during the Battle of

Fredericksburg, where he again performed well. He was promoted to brigadier general on April 15, 1863.

Cutler's brigade was lightly engaged at Chancellorsville and heavily engaged at Gettysburg, where it lost half its men on the first day (July 1, 1863). Cutler had two horses shot out from under him. The next two days, he helped defend Culp's Hill.

Assigned to the V Corps in the reorganization of 1864, Cutler fought in the Battle of the Wilderness, where he assumed command of a division after General Wadsworth was mortally wounded. He served in the Overland Campaign and the subsequent Siege of Petersburg. On August 21, 1864, during the Battle of Globe Tavern, he was struck in the face by a piece of Confederate shrapnel. Disfigured and badly wounded, he spent the rest of the war in hospitals or commanding the draft center in Jackson, Michigan (i.e., on light duty). Lincoln appointed him brevet major general on August 19, 1864. He resigned from the army on June 30, 1865.

Lysander Cutler never really recovered from his wounds. He died of a stroke in Milwaukee, Wisconsin on July 30, 1866. He was fifty-nine years old. Doctors attributed his death to complications from his Globe Tavern wound. He was buried in the Forest Home Cemetery, Milwaukee, Wisconsin.

D

DANA – DYER

NAPOLEON JACKSON TECUMSEH DANA was born on April 15, 1822, in Fort Sullivan, in Eastport, Maine, the son of an officer in the 1st Artillery and a West Point graduate. His father died when he was eleven years old. Napoleon followed in his footsteps, however, and entered West Point in 1838, at age sixteen. He graduated in 1842 (29/56) and was commissioned second lieutenant in the 7th Infantry Regiment. He was stationed at Fort Pike, Louisiana (1842–43 and 1843–45), and Pass Christian, Mississippi (1843), before taking part in the occupation of Texas. He was promoted to first lieutenant in early 1847.

Dana distinguished himself in the Mexican War, fighting at Fort Brown, Monterrey, Vera Cruz, and Cerro Gordo, where he was shot in the hip and left for dead. A brutal detail found him thirty-six hours later. He was brevetted captain after Cerro Gordo. After he recovered, he was sent to Boston, Minnesota, and Washington, D.C. on recruiting, quartermaster, and construction assignments. He resigned his commission in 1855. He settled in St. Paul, Minnesota, and became a banker and brigadier general in the state militia.

Dana formally joined the Union cause on October 2, 1861, as colonel of the 1st Minnesota Infantry. He was given command of a brigade in the Army of the Potomac on October 20 and fought at Ball's Bluff the next day. He was promoted to brigadier general on February 6, 1862, and took part in the Siege of Yorktown, the Peninsula Campaign, the Battle of Seven Pines, and the Seven Days battles (including Frayser's Farm and Malvern Hill). He was seriously wounded in the left leg at Antietam, where his brigade fell victim to a surprise Rebel attack on its left flank and lost nine hundred men. He was appointed major general on November 29, 1862, but was not confirmed by the Senate. His appointment expired on March 4, 1863, but Lincoln reappointed him on March 6, and the Senate confirmed him three days later. He commanded the Philadelphia defenses during the Gettysburg Campaign.

After he recovered, Dana was given command of a division in the XIII Corps, Department of the Gulf, and served in Louisiana and Texas. He directed the corps from October 25, 1863 to January 3, 1864, and commanded Union forces in the Battle of Stirling's Plantation (September 29,

1863), in which he was defeated by Confederate General Tom Green and lost more than five hundred men, including 450 captured. Dana reverted to division command in 1864 and then commanded the District of Vicksburg and the Department of Mississippi, where he was when the war ended. He resigned from the army on May 27, 1865, and became a miner in California and Alaska.

Napoleon J. T. Dana went into the railroad business in 1872 and worked as superintendent of the Chicago, Burlington & Quincy Railroad, among others. He later worked in the U.S. Pension Department until he was fired by President McKinley for being a Democrat. By a special act of Congress in 1894, he was placed on the retired list as a captain, enabling him to collect a pension. He retired in Washington, D.C. General Dana died of apoplexy while on a trip to Portsmouth, New Hampshire on July 15, 1905. He was eighty-three. He was interred in the Harmony Grove Cemetery, Portsmouth, New Hampshire.

JOHN WYNN "BLACK JACK" DAVIDSON was born on August 14, 1825, in Fairfax County, Virginia, the son of an artillery officer who died of disease while serving in the Second Seminole War in Florida. "Black Jack" became a West Point cadet in 1841 and graduated four years later (27/41) as a brevet second lieutenant in the 1st Dragoons. He was promoted to second lieutenant in 1846, first lieutenant in 1848, captain in 1855, and major, Regular Army, on November 14, 1861. Initially assigned to Fort Leavenworth, Kansas, he took part in the conquest of  California during the Mexican War. He later fought Indians and was involved in massacring the Pomo tribe on the island of Bo-No-Po-Ti in northern California in 1850, in retaliation for killing two ranches. Antebellum, he served mainly on the Western Frontier and was defeated and seriously wounded by Jicarilla Apaches in the Battle of Cieneguilla (March 30, 1854).

In January 1861, Davidson was stationed at Fort Tejon, California but was quickly sent to the east as the sectional crisis deepened, and assumed command of a brigade in the Army of the Potomac in October 1861. A native-born Virginia, he was offered a commission in the Confederate Army but declined it. He was promoted to brigadier general on February 6, 1862. He fought in the Peninsula Campaign, including Yorktown and Williamsburg. After taking part in the Seven Days battles, he was transferred to Missouri, where he commanded the District of St. Louis (August–November 1862) and the Army of Southeast Missouri from November 1862 to February 1863. Most of his forces were then transferred to General Grant, but Davidson remained in the Trans-Mississippi and directed a division in Frederick Steele's Army of Arkansas. He took part in several minor operations and played a major role in the capture of Little Rock in September 1863.

After leading a cavalry division in Arkansas in 1864, Davidson took charge of the District of Natchez in November. He led an unsuccessful raid into Confederate Mississippi in late 1864. It was his last Civil War operation. Mustered out of the service on January 15, 1866, he was brevetted major general on March 12.

After the war, Davidson reverted to the rank of lieutenant colonel and joined the 10th Cavalry, a Buffalo soldiers' unit. He became the first professor of military science at Kansas State Agricultural College in 1868 and served until 1871. He also taught French and Spanish. After serving in Indian Territory and Texas, he commanded Fort Richardson, Texas, for two years. He was colonel of the 2nd Cavalry at Fort Custer, Montana Territory, in 1881. After being injured when his horse fell, General Davidson went to St. Paul, Minnesota, where he died on June 26, 1881, at age fifty-five. He is buried in Arlington National Cemetery.

HENRY EUGENE DAVIES, the nephew of Union Brigadier General Thomas Alfred Davies, was born on July 2, 1836, in New York City, the son of a judge. He was educated at Harvard, Williams College, and Columbia College, and was admitted to the bar in 1857.

He entered Union service as a captain in the 5th New York Infantry on May 9, 1861. He became a major in the 2nd New York Cavalry on August 1; lieutenant colonel,

December 6, 1862; colonel, June 16, 1863; and brigadier general on September 16, 1863. In the meantime, he fought at Big Bethel, Virginia (June 10, 1861), skirmished on the Rappahannock Line during the Peninsula Campaign, and was heavily engaged in the Second Bull Run Campaign. His regiment took severe losses in the Battle of Brandy Station (June 9, 1863) and Aldie (June 17) and guarded the army supply base at Westminster, Maryland, during the Gettysburg Campaign.

Davies participated in the indecisive Bristoe Campaign and Sheridan's unsuccessful Richmond Raid (May 1864). He was in the thick of the action in the Battle of Haw's Shop (May 28), where a Southern minié ball cut his saber in half and his horse's tail was shot off. He fought in numerous engagements in 1864, including the defeat at Trevilian Station (June 11–12), the battles around Petersburg, and the raids on the Weldon Railroad. On February 6, 1865, he was wounded in the Battle of Hatcher's Run when a Confederate bullet went through his right breast. He was out of action for two weeks. Davies was acting division commander on three occasions and temporarily commanded the Cavalry Corps of the Army of the Potomac from February 24 to March 25, 1865. He then reverted to divisional command. He was promoted to major general (full rank) on June 7. His last assignment was as commander of the Middle District of Alabama. He resigned from the army on January 1, 1866, after amassing a solid record of achievement as a federal general.

Postbellum, Davies became a prominent New York attorney and served a term as assistant district attorney for the Southern District of New York (1870–73). He moved to Beacon, New York, and wrote a biography of General Sheridan. He died suddenly of a hemorrhage of the lungs while visiting friends in Middleborough, Massachusetts, on September 7, 1894. He was fifty-eight. He was buried in St. Luke's Churchyard, Beacon, New York.

THOMAS ALFRED DAVIES was born on his father's farm on December 3, 1809, near Black Lake, New York, in the far north of the state, near the St. Lawrence River.

He was the uncle of Union General Henry Eugene Davies. Thomas entered West Point in 1825 and graduated in 1829 (25/46) as a brevet second lieutenant in the 1st Infantry Regiment. After doing frontier duty in Wisconsin and garrison duty at West Point, he resigned in 1831 and became a civil engineer and merchant in New York City.

Davies returned to the colors when the Civil War erupted and was elected colonel of the 16th New York Infantry on May 15, 1861. He became a brigade commander on July 8 and fought in the First Battle of Bull Run. Thereafter, his brigade was part of the Washington defenses. Davies was promoted to brigadier general on March 11, 1862, and was transferred to the Army of the Tennessee, where he commanded a division. He arrived too late to fight at Shiloh but took part in the Siege of Corinth and the Second Battle of Corinth (October 3–4). He was named commander of the District of Columbus, Kentucky (1862–63), where he showed great timidity in the face of Nathan Bedford Forrest's raiders. He ordered all reserve ammunition in his sector destroyed, the gun carriages burned, and the cannons dumped into the Mississippi River, even though Forrest was nowhere near the place and had fewer men than did Davies. One military investigator found his orders so ridiculous that he recommended Davies be dismissed from the service for the good of the treasury. Indeed, he was transferred and named commander of the District of Rolla, Missouri (1863–64), and the District of North Kansas (1864–65). He was mustered out on August 24, 1865, and brevetted major general in 1866. His performance as a Union general was below mediocre.

After the war, Davies returned to New York and made a fortune in real estate. He published a number of books of a theological and philosophical nature. He also wrote *How to Make Money and How to Keep It*, which was later revised and republished by Henry Ford.

General Davies died in Ogdensburg, New York, on August 19, 1899, and was buried in the family cemetery in nearby Oswegatchie, New York. He was eighty-nine.

EDMUND JACKSON DAVIS was born on October 2, 1827, in St. Augustine, Florida, the son of a lawyer and land developer. He moved to Galveston, Texas, with his widowed mother in 1848. He was admitted to the bar the next year and moved to Corpus Christi, where he successively served as a lawyer, collector of customs, a district attorney, and district judge. He also had a ranch in Webb County.

Davis was a supporter of Sam Houston, who strongly opposed secession. He also urged Colonel Robert E. Lee to remain faithful to the Union. He stood for election as a delegate to the Texas Secession Convention but was defeated. After secession came, he refused to take the oath of allegiance to the Confederacy and was stripped of his judgeship. He then fled to Washington, D.C., where Lincoln gave him a commission to recruit the 1st (U.S.) Texas Cavalry Regiment. He did so from disaffected Texans who fled to Louisiana. It was activated in New Orleans in November 1862 and spent almost a year in the defenses around the city. It was part of the failed Sabine Pass Expedition (September 1863), the Teche Campaign (October), and the more successful Rio Grande/Brownsville Expedition (October–June 1864). At this point, Edmund Davis was placed in command of a cavalry brigade in the XIX Corps and took part in minor operations around Morganza and Baton Rouge and on the Atchafalaya River. He was promoted to brigadier general on November 10, 1864. Later, he directed the Districts of Morganza and Baton Rouge. He ended the war in a minor administrative post. He was mustered out August 24, 1865.

Davis, who was a Radical Republican, was elected governor of Texas in 1869 (with the help of the military) and served from 1870 to 1874. He pushed for civil rights for African Americans but was crushed when he ran for re-election in 1873 and was the last Republican governor of Texas until 1978—105 years later. In 1873, with the Democratic Party on the assent, he asked President Grant to send troops to keep him in office, but the president refused, and he was forced to vacate the capitol. He ran for re-election in 1880 and was crushed again.

Governor Davis died on February 7, 1883, at age fifty-five. He is buried in the Texas State Cemetery, Austin.

JEFFERSON COLUMBUS DAVIS, the oldest of eight children, was born on his father's farm on March 2, 1828, in Clark County, Indiana, near

present-day Memphis, Indiana. He wanted to be a soldier from childhood. Physically, he grew into a somewhat tall man for his day (5'9") but weighed only 125 pounds. In June 1847, he joined the 3rd Indiana to fight in the Mexican War. He became a sergeant, distinguished himself at Buena Vista, and received a commission as a second lieutenant, Regular Army, in the 1st Artillery (June 1848) and was stationed at Fort McHenry, Maryland. Later, he was posted to Fort Washington, Maryland (just outside the capital); Fort Monroe, Virginia; Fort McHenry again; Florida; and Fort Moultrie, South Carolina. He was at Fort Sumter when the Civil War began. He was promoted to first lieutenant (February 1852) and captain, R.A., May 14, 1861.

Davis's first assignment was to raise a regiment in Indiana. He organized the 22nd Indiana Infantry and was promoted to colonel on August 1. After General Nathaniel Lyon was killed in the Union disaster at Wilson's Creek (August 10), Davis was sent to Missouri, where he became a brigade commander and then commander of the District of Central Missouri. Meanwhile, hundreds of pro-Union recruits flocked to the colors and he soon commanded eighteen thousand to twenty thousand men. He was promoted to brigadier general on April 30, 1862. Meanwhile, he assumed command of a division in Samuel Curtis's Army of the Southwest. He took part in the campaign to eject Confederates from Missouri and fought in the Battle of Pea Ridge, where he played a prominent part in the Union victory.

Davis and his men were ordered to cross the Mississippi and took part in the Siege of Corinth. He fell ill and took a furlough to Indiana to recuperate, but rushed to Kentucky when the Confederates invaded that state. He was placed in charge of organizing Louisville for defense. On September 22, General "Bull" Nelson (who was in command of this sector) asked him how many men he mustered, Davis was unable to give him an estimate—or perhaps was just unwilling to. Davis informed Nelson that he was a Regular Army officer, and Nelson (a volunteer officer) had no authority to give him orders. Nelson became angry and expelled Davis from Louisville. General Horatio Wright, who was in command in Cincinnati, sent Davis back to Louisville. On September 29, another altercation occurred. Davis, who was noted for his quick temper, borrowed a pistol, found Nelson, and murdered him. General Buell, the commander of the Army of the Ohio, demanded that Davis be court-martialed, and General William Terrill wanted Davis hanged. He escaped retribution, however, because the Union desperately needed capable and experienced officers, which he was. His only punishment was that he never achieved full promotion beyond that of brigadier general. (He was brevetted major general for Kennesaw Mountain in 1864.)

Davis continued to command a division on the Western Front at Stone River, Chickamauga, Chattanooga, and the Atlanta Campaign. He was named commander of the XIV Corps (fourteen thousand men) on August 24, 1864, and led it in Sherman's March to the Sea. Here, at Ebenezer Creek on December 9, he deliberately removed a pontoon bridge, which meant that six hundred former slaves, who were following his corps, fell into the hands of Joseph Wheeler's Confederate cavalry. Many of the African Americans tried to escape by swimming but drowned in the icy water. The rest were captured and returned to slavery. Later, Secretary of War Stanton brought up the incident, but General Sherman fully supported his corps commander, and Stanton dropped the matter.

Davis led XIV Corps in the Carolinas Campaign and until the end of the war. In 1866, he was the commander of the Department of Kentucky, and was mustered out on volunteer service on September 1. He reverted to his Regular Army rank of colonel on July 23, 1866.

Postbellum, Davis commanded the 23rd Infantry Regiment and was the first commander of the Department of Alaska (1867–1870). He expelled Russian residents from their homes on the grounds that they were needed by Americans. After General Canby was murdered, Davis led U.S. forces in the Modoc War, 1872–73, and forced the Indians to surrender. He was in St. Louis during the general strike of 1877 and was urged to fire on strikers with his Gatling guns, but he refused to do so.

A controversial figure to say the least, General Davis was still on active duty when he died in Chicago on November 30, 1879, at age fifty-one. He was buried in Crown Hill Cemetery, Indianapolis, Indiana.

GEORGE WASHINGTON DEITZLER was born on November 30, 1826, in Pine Grove, Pennsylvania, the child of German immigrants. He lived

in Illinois and California before settling in Kansas in 1855. He farmed, worked in real estate, started a sawmill, and enrolled in the abolitionist cause, which—for him—included running guns into the state. He was arrested for treason by territorial authorities but was released after four months incarceration.

A tireless anti-slavery advocate, he was elected to the territorial legislature and subsequently re-elected, serving from 1857 to 1860. He served a term as speaker of the Kansas House of Representatives and was a member of the Topeka Constitutional Convention, under which he became a state senator. He was elected mayor of Lawrence in 1860 and also served as treasurer of the Lawrence University of Kansas, an Episcopal institution which was later absorbed by the University of Kansas.

When the war began, Deitzler raised the 1st Kansas Infantry and became its colonel on June 5, 1861. He became a brigade commander on July 24 and fought in the Battle of Wilson's Creek, where he was wounded in the right leg. He never fully recovered from this wound. He spent most of the next year commanding a brigade in the District of Kansas but was sent east to join the Army of the Tennessee in November 1862. On April 4, 1863, he was appointed brigadier general. He fought in the Vicksburg campaign, but the Mississippi heat and his earlier wound proved too much for him. After the city fell, he resigned for reasons of health effective August 12, 1863, and returned to Kansas. His resignation was accepted on August 22. He was already home by that date, when the Confederate guerrilla leader Quantrill raided Lawrence. He narrowly escaped by hiding in a gulch.

In 1864, Deitzler became a major general in the Kansas Militia and commanded ten thousand men against Confederate Major General Sterling Price's Missouri Expedition. He joined Samuel Curtis's Army of the Border in the Battle of Westport, and the numbers made a difference. Outnumbered more than two to one, Price was decisively defeated.

George W. Deitzler was an effective commander. After the war, he was involved in promoting railroads. He also owned a hotel in Lawrence. Deitzler moved to San Francisco in 1872. He was in Tucson, Arizona in the spring of 1884, when he was thrown from a buggy by a runaway team and broke his neck. General Deitzler died of his injuries on April 11, 1884, at age fifty-seven. He is buried in Oak Hill Cemetery, Lawrence, Kansas.

RICHARD DELAFIELD was born in New York City on September 1, 1798. He was one of fourteen children, but fortunately his father (an English immigrant) was a wealthy merchant. Richard attended West Point from 1814 and graduated at the head of the Class of 1818 (1/23). He was also the first cadet to become an acting assistant professor at the Academy. (He taught mathematics.) Delafield was commissioned second lieutenant in the Corps of Engineers. He was subsequently promoted to first lieutenant (1820), captain (1828), major (1838), lieutenant colonel (August 6, 1861), and colonel (June 1, 1863). His career was highly varied and included constructing fortifications at the Hampton Roads and on the Mississippi River delta, designing and building the first cast-iron 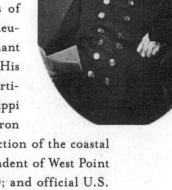 tubular-arch bridge in the United States; construction of the coastal defenses of New York City; two tours as superintendent of West Point (1838–1845 and 1856–1861, a total of twelve years); and official U.S. observer of the Crimean War. He also led the delegation to study the armed forces of Europe, including Great Britain, France, Belgium, Germany, the Austro-Hungarian Empire, and Russia.

Considered too old for active field service in 1861, he was an advisor to the New York governor on the creation of volunteer forces. He was in charge of the defenses of New York City from 1861 to 1864.

Brigadier General Joseph G. Totten, the chief of engineers, died on April 22, 1864. Delafield was chosen to replace him. He was promoted to brigadier general on May 19. Brevetted major general, Regular Army, in March 1866, he retired on August 8, 1866, after forty-five years' service.

In retirement, General Delafield served as a regent of the Smithsonian Institution and a Lighthouse Board member. He died in Washington, D.C., on November 5, 1873, at age seventy-five. He was buried in the Green-Wood Cemetery, Brooklyn, New York.

ELIAS SMITH DENNIS was born on December 4, 1812, in Newburgh, New York. He grew up on Long Island and moved to Carlyle, Illinois, in 1836, where he married the widow of Congressman Charles Slade in 1838 and thus acquired a gristmill. Locally popular, he was a Democratic member of the Illinois House of Representatives (1842–44) and Senate (1846–48). He was appointed U.S. Marshal for the Leavenworth, Kansas, district by President Buchanan in 1857.

Dennis was mustered into Federal service as lieutenant colonel of the 30th Illinois Infantry on August 6, 1861. He was an excellent commander and was commended for his performance at Fort Donelson. He became colonel of the 30th on May 1. He was given an infantry brigade shortly after and was advanced to brigadier general on March 16, 1863. He took part in the various campaigns against Vicksburg and fought at Port Gibson, Raymond, and Big Black River. In May 1863, he was placed in charge of the District of Northeast Louisiana. He commanded the Federal troops at Milliken's Bend (June 7), which was a marginal Union victory. After the Texas Greyhound Division left the area, he was involved in leasing abandoned plantations to Carpetbaggers and was accused of selling two hundred barrels of flour, as well as other provisions, to the Rebels, while his own men were on half rations, but this was never proven.

Dennis led a division of the Army of the Tennessee (July 1863–September 1864) in the Chattanooga and Atlanta campaigns, and part of his division participated in Sherman's Meridian Expedition. For reasons not made clear by the records, he was demoted to the command of a reserve brigade in the Military Division of Western Mississippi—a backwater sector—in November 1864. He nevertheless distinguished himself again in the reduction and capture of Mobile in April 1865.

During Reconstruction, Dennis returned to Madison Parish, which he had conquered during the war. At first, the native Southerners did not trust him, but they soon determined that he was a fervent Democrat and not a Carpetbagger, and he made many friends. Considered fair and impartial, he was elected parish judge and then sheriff, an office he held for several years. Popular with local widows, he divorced his first wife in 1871 and married a Madison Parish woman who owned a 757-acre plantation. He moved back to Illinois in 1887 and lived on a small farm near Carlyle. He died of pneumonia in Carlyle on December 17, 1894, at age eighty-two. One of his stepsons, Jack Slade, was a famous gunfighter who was hanged by Montana vigilantes in 1864.

FREDERICK TRACY DENT, the brother-in-law of Ulysses S. Grant and cousin of James Longstreet, was born in White Haven (his father's plantation), St, Louis County, Missouri, on December 17, 1820. He was admitted to West Point in 1839 and graduated in 1843 (33/39). During his last year at "the Point," his roommate was Ulysses S. Grant, with whom he became close friends. Grant accepted an invitation to visit the Dent plantation, met Dent's sister Julia, and married her in 1848. Meanwhile, Dent was commissioned second lieutenant in the 5th Infantry, and was initially stationed in Indian Territory (now Oklahoma). He fought in Mexico and was breveted first lieutenant for his conduct in the Battles of Contreras and  Churubusco and captain for Molino del Rey, where he was wounded during Winfield Scott's drive on Mexico City. He was promoted to captain, substantive rank, in 1855, to major (March 9, 1863), and to lieutenant colonel, Regular Army, on March 20, 1864. Meanwhile, he served sixteen years of duty on the frontier (west Texas and the Pacific Northwest), where he fought in the Yakima War (1855–58). He was stationed in San Francisco when the Civil War began and remained there until March 1863, when he was transferred to New York City. He became an aide to General Grant in the spring of 1864 and was promoted to brigadier general on April 5, 1865, although President Lincoln did not submit his nomination to the Senate as of April 15, the day he died. President Johnson did submit it on January 13, 1866, and he was confirmed on February 23. He was mustered out of the volunteer army on April 30, 1866.

Dent reverted to lieutenant colonel of the 5th Artillery after the war. He was Grant's military secretary from 1866 to 1873, commander of Fort

Trumbull, Connecticut (1873–75), commandant of St. Augustine (1875–81) and colonel of the 1st Artillery (1881–82), and the 3rd Artillery (1882–83). He suffered a stroke and was on sick leave for much of January 1881 to December 1883 period, when he retired with more than forty years' service. Dent initially lived in Washington, D.C., but later moved to Denver, where one of his sons was a lawyer. He died there on December 12, 1892, at age seventy-one. Initially buried at Fort Leavenworth, he is now interred in Arlington National Cemetery. One of Grant's children, Brigadier General Frederick Dent Grant (1850–1912), was named after him.

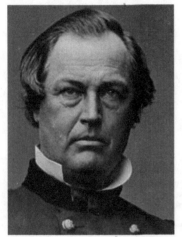

JAMES WILLIAM "JIM" DENVER was born in Winchester, Virginia, on October 23, 1817. His family moved to Ohio in 1830, and he attended public schools in Virginia and in Wilmington, Ohio. He taught school in Missouri in 1841 and then attended law school at Cincinnati College, from which he graduated in 1844. A restless young man, he practiced at Xenia, Ohio, before moving to Platte City, Missouri, in 1845, where he again practiced law. In 1847, he recruited a company of foot soldiers which became part of the 12th U.S. Volunteer Infantry. Jim Denver was its captain. It was part of Scott's drive on Mexico City in 1847.

Denver moved to California in 1850 and became a trader. He fought a duel in 1852 and killed Edward Gilbert, a newspaper editor, a fellow Democrat, and a former U.S. Congressman, who accused him of "negligence and gross mismanagement" in handling wagon trains that were hauling supplies to aid destitute immigrants. This did not affect Denver's popularity. He was elected to the California State Senate later that year. Shortly thereafter, he was appointed secretary of state of California. He was elected to Congress in 1854 and served from 1855 to 1857. He sought election to the U.S. Senate in 1856 but was defeated.

President James Buchanan appointed Denver Commissioner of Indian Affairs in April 1857. Buchanan named him territorial governor of Kansas in December 1857. He was unable to solve the problems of "Bleeding Kansas," and indeed, it is probable that no one could have. Meanwhile,

William Larimer, Jr., a land speculator, founded "Denver City," present-day Denver, Colorado, and named it after the governor. (Ironically, Jim Denver visited the site of the Mile High City only once.) Denver, who did not like Kansas, resigned his post on October 10, 1858, and left office in November. He was Commissioner of Indian Affairs from November 1858 to March 31, 1859, when he resigned.

Lincoln appointed James Denver brigadier general on August 14, 1861, for strictly political reasons. He initially recruited troops in Kansas and later was commander of all troops in the state. He was formally named commander of the District of Kansas in March 1862, but was ordered east of the Mississippi the following month. After briefly commanding the District of West Tennessee, he led a brigade in the Siege of Corinth under William T. Sherman. Both Sherman and Grant praised his performance as a commander. He was given command of a division in Hulbert's XVI Corps. This was mostly a garrison job; his main responsibility was guarding 65 miles of the Memphis & Charleston Railroad. He resigned from the army on March 5, 1863. He left his command on March 18. Why he resigned is unclear. It is known that Denver was frustrated at guarding railroads and not being involved in combat duty. It is also known that the Radical Republicans dislike him, as did Regular Army officers, who looked down on volunteers. It is known that he was personally honest and incorruptible in a very corrupt time and he considered certain of his superiors "scoundrels, whom I have so often thwarted in their rascalitys." Whatever the cause, the North lost a pretty good general.

Denver practiced law in Wilmington, Ohio, and Washington, D.C. for the rest of his life. He died of kidney failure in Washington on August 9, 1892, at the age of seventy-four. He is buried in the Sugar Grove Cemetery in Wilmington. Matthew R. Denver, one of his four children, also lived in Wilmington and was a bank president and a U.S. Congressman from 1907 to 1913.

GUSTAVUS ADOLPHUS DE RUSSY was born on November 3, 1818, in Brooklyn, New York. He was a member of a prominent military family; his father was Brevet Brigadier General Rene Edward De Russy, who refugeed from Haiti during the slave revolt of 1791. Like his father and uncle,

Gustavus was admitted to West Point (in his case in 1835), but he was expelled for drinking in 1838. He did not secure a commission as second lieutenant until 1847, during the Mexican War. He served with the 4th Artillery and was brevetted first lieutenant for gallantry at Contreras and Churubusco and earned a brevet captaincy at the Battle of Chapultepec. Remaining in the army, he was quartermaster at Fort Monroe (the home of the artillery school) from 1848 to 1857. He was promoted to first lieutenant in 1849 and to captain in 1857.

De Russy remained in the 4th Artillery until May 1862, when he was named commander of the Reserve Artillery of the III Corps, which he directed during the Peninsula campaign and in the Seven Days battles. Still a member of the Regular Army only, he received a brevet to major for Seven Pines and a brevet lieutenant colonelcy for his part in the victory at Malvern Hill. He commanded the artillery for the Left Grand Division in the Battle of Fredericksburg. He did not join the volunteer army until March 17, 1863, when he assumed command of the 4th New York Artillery Regiment. After the Army of the Potomac was thoroughly thrashed at Chancellorsville, De Russy was placed in charge of the southern defenses of Washington, D.C. He was promoted to brigadier general on May 23. He remained here until the end of the war.

De Russy's original commission as brigadier general expired on July 4, 1864. He was reappointed on July 6. This time it was confirmed by the Senate. He was discharged from volunteer service on January 15, 1866, and reverted to his Regular Army rank of major.

Gustavus De Russy spent the rest of his career with the 3rd or 4th Artillery Regiments. He was promoted to lieutenant colonel in 1879 and to colonel of the 3rd Artillery in 1882, the year he retired. He settled in Detroit, Michigan, where he died on May 29, 1891, at age seventy-two. He is buried there in Elmwood Cemetery.

PHILIPPE REGIS "PHILIP" DENIS DE KEREDERN DE TROBRIAND (pronounced Duh-troh-Bre-ahn) was born at Chateau des

Rochettes, near Tours, on June 4, 1816. He came from a family with a long military tradition. His father was a baron and one of Napoleon's generals. Philip graduated from the College of Saint-Louis in Paris with a baccalaureate degree; then he studied law. He also wrote poetry and prose, authored two novels, became an expert swordsman, and fought a number of duels. He received the title "Baron" in 1840. De Trobriand emigrated to New York in 1841 and married the daughter of a rich banker. They lived in Venice for a time and had two daughters. After he returned to New York, he became a writer and editor for a pair of French-language publications.

After the Civil War began, de Trobriand became an American citizen and was commissioned colonel of the 55th New York on August 28, 1861. He fought in the Peninsula (including the Siege of Yorktown and the Battle of Williamsburg) and the Battle of Seven Pines. He then fell ill with "swamp fever" and missed the Seven Days battles, where the regiment was commanded by its lieutenant colonel. He returned to duty in July 1862. The 55th (which was called the "Lafayette Guards") was in reserve during the Second Bull Run and in the Washington defenses during the Battle of Antietam. It was lightly engaged at Fredericksburg.

On December 21, 1862, the 55th was absorbed by the 38th New York with de Trobriand as the colonel. It fought at Chancellorsville, where it was again lightly engaged, losing 3 men killed, 15 wounded, and 18 captured or missing. Trobriand was in command of a brigade at Gettysburg, where he distinguished himself in the Wheatfield on July 2, 1863, fighting John Bell Hood's division. Trobriand's brigade lost one-third of its men. When the expected appointment to brigadier general did not materialize, de Trobriand resigned in November. Abraham Lincoln corrected this situation on April 10, 1864, when he appointed him brigadier general. Oddly enough, the Senate had already confirmed his appointment. Meanwhile, Brigadier General J. H. Hobart Ward was dismissed from the army for intoxication. De Trobriand was given his brigade.

General de Trobriand (who was called "Froggy" by his men) fought in the Siege of Petersburg and the Appomattox Campaign, did an excellent job, and occasionally commanded a division. He succeeded Gershom Mott as divisional commander when he was wounded on April 6, 1865. De Trobriand was present at Appomattox. He was brevetted major general on January 13, 1866, and was mustered out of volunteer service three days later.

After the war, de Trobriand returned to France and wrote a book about his Civil War experiences. General Grant appointed him colonel of the 31st Infantry in 1866. He accepted the appointment in July 1867, and he fought in the Indian Wars. In his spare time, he painted portraits of American Indians and landscapes and proved to be a talented artist. He commanded the 13th Infantry Regiment in New Orleans (a largely French-speaking city) from 1872 to 1877 and directed Federal troops in Pittsburgh during the Great Strike of 1877. He retired to New Orleans in 1879, lived in the French Quarter, farmed a large garden, painted, read, and wrote a number of books. He and his wife frequently visited their daughters in Bayport, New York, and France. He died in Bayport on July 15, 1897, at age eighty-one. He was interred in St. Anne's Cemetery, Sayville, New York.

CHARLES DEVENS, JR. was born on April 4, 1820, in Charlestown, Massachusetts, which is now part of Boston. He was educated at Boston Latin School and Harvard College, from which he graduated in 1838. He graduated from Harvard Law School in 1840, was admitted to the bar in 1841, and practiced law in Franklin County from 1841 to 1849. He was elected to the Massachusetts State Senate as a Whig in 1848. Devens was also U.S. Marshal for Massachusetts from 1849 to 1853. He enforced the fugitive slave laws, despite his personal opposition to them. He engaged in private practice in Worcester from 1853 to 1861. Meanwhile, he became a brigadier general in the Massachusetts Militia.

Confederates fired on Fort Sumter on April 12, 1861. Seven days later, Devens was major of the 3rd Massachusetts Rifle Battalion, a 90-day unit. It was stationed at Fort McHenry, Baltimore, Maryland, to help keep that state in the Union. Devens became colonel of the 15th Massachusetts Infantry on July 24 and was wounded in the Battle of Ball's Bluff on October

21. He was still not fully recovered on April 16, 1862, when he was promoted to brigadier general. He led his brigade at Seven Pines, where he was shot in the leg but refused to leave the field until the fighting was over. It took him most of the summer to recover. His brigade was lightly engaged in the Maryland Campaign and Fredericksburg.

Author Bruce Catton referred to Devens as "a fierce disciplinarian." After Oliver Howard assumed command of the XI Corps in April 1863, he named Devens a division commander. On May 2, he was wounded again during the Battle of Chancellorsville, this time in the right foot, while Stonewall Jackson smashed his division. When he returned to duty on July 4, he was on light duty, commanding the Boston Draft Depot.

Devens joined the Army of the James on May 30, 1864, as a divisional commander. He fought in the Bermuda Hundred, Cold Harbor, the Second Battle of Petersburg, the Siege of Petersburg, and the Appomattox Campaign. For two weeks in January 1865, he was acting commander of the XXIV Corps. His troops were the first to occupy Richmond, for which he was brevetted major general in 1866. After the war, he commanded the Military District of Charleston, South Carolina. He was mustered out on June 2, 1866.

General Devens returned to Massachusetts and became a judge in the State Superior court from 1867 to 1873. He was an associate justice on the Massachusetts Supreme Court from 1873 to 1877 and from 1881 to 1891, and attorney general of the United States under President Rutherford B. Hayes from 1877 to 1881. Active in veterans' affairs, he served as commander-in-chief of the Grand Army of the Republic from 1873 to 1875.

Charles Devens died of heart failure in Cambridge, Massachusetts, on January 7, 1891, at age seventy. He was buried in the Mount Auburn Cemetery, Cambridge.

THOMAS CASIMER "TOMMY" DEVIN was born on December 10, 1822, in New York City, the child of Irish immigrants. He was a house painter and partner with his brother in a paint and varnish firm. Meanwhile, he was a member of the New York Militia and rose to the rank of lieutenant colonel in the 1st Cavalry Regiment, New York Militia.

When the Civil War began, he joined the 1st New York Cavalry Regiment as a captain and company commander. On November 18, 1861, he became colonel of the 6th New York Cavalry, which was stationed at York, Pennsylvania. Initially, it was not employed as a single unit but was scattered all over the map. It was not fully mounted by May 1862. It first saw action as a unit in the Maryland Campaign, including the Battle of Antietam. During the Battle of Fredericksburg, George D. Bayard, the cavalry commander of the III Corps, was mortally wounded by Southern artillery fire, and David Gregg replaced him. Devin took Gregg's place as brigade commander. During the Battle of Chancellorsville, Devin's brigade remained with the main body of the Army of the Potomac (i.e., he was not part of Stoneman's raid) and suffered heavy casualties fighting Confederate infantry.

Devin led his brigade at Brandy Station (June 9, 1863) and Gettysburg. He was a favorite of his division commander, John Buford, and his men called him "Uncle Tommy." He was an excellent brigade commander. On the first day of the Battle of Gettysburg, he successfully delayed Heth's infantry division until I Corps could deploy. He led his brigade throughout the Overland Campaign and the Sheridan's Shenandoah Valley Campaign of 1864, and Lincoln appointed Devin to the rank of brigadier general on November 30, 1864. He occasionally served as acting divisional commander, assumed permanent command of the 1st Cavalry Division in March 1865, and led it at Five Forks. He sustained only one severe wound during the war, when he was struck in the foot by a Rebel minié ball on August 16, 1864, but returned to duty two weeks later. He was brevetted major general on January 13, 1866, and was mustered out of the volunteer service two days later.

General Grant reportedly ranked Devin second only to Sheridan as a cavalry officer. After the war, Devin accepted a commission as a lieutenant colonel in the Regular Army. He was assigned to the 8th Cavalry Regiment and served in New Mexico and Arizona. He became colonel of the 3rd Cavalry in June 1877, but soon took sick leave and returned home to New York City. He was suffering from stomach cancer. General Devin died on April 4, 1878, at age fifty-five. He was buried in the Calvary Cemetery on

Long Island, but nineteen years later his remains were reinterred in the West Point Cemetery, even though he never attended the Academy.

JOEL ALLEN DEWEY was born on September 20, 1840, in Georgia, Vermont. He attended Oberlin College, Ohio, but left school in October 1861, to accept a second lieutenant's commission in the 58th Ohio Infantry. He was promoted to captain in the 43rd Ohio in January 1862 and fought at New Madrid and Island No. 10. Later he took part in the battles of Iuka and Second Corinth. His regiment performed occupation and garrison duty in 1863. In early 1864, he became lieutenant colonel of the 1st Alabama (U.S.) Infantry, which consisted of "home grown" Yankees. He made another lateral transfer on June 25, 1864, when he became lieutenant colonel of the 111th United States Colored Troops (USCT) Infantry Regiment, which was mostly employed guarding the Nashville & Northwestern Railroad line.

Colonel Dewey was captured by Nathan Bedford Forrest at Athens, Alabama, in September 1864. He was exchanged in November and returned to his regiment, which he eventually commanded. He was promoted to colonel on April 29, 1865.

On November 25, 1865, at the extremely young age of twenty-five, Andrew Johnson promoted him to brigadier general of volunteers. Why is not known, but he obviously had political influence with the president. The Confederacy no longer existed, there was no need for more generals, literally dozens of colonels were better qualified than he for such a reward and, while his record was credible, it was certainly not extraordinary. The Senate confirmed his promotion on February 23, 1866. Joel Dewey can thus claim the distinction of being the last Civil War general. He was offered a captaincy in the Regular Army but turned it down. He was mustered out of the service on January 31, 1866.

After the war, Dewey studied law in Albany, New York, and was admitted to the bar in 1867. That same year, he was admitted to the Tennessee bar and moved to Dandridge, east Tennessee. He married into a locally prominent Jefferson County family in 1871. Under the corrupt regime of Governor "Parson" Brownlow, he was elected Second Judicial District Attorney in 1869 and re-elected in 1871.

By now, General Dewey suffered from heart disease. He collapsed in a courtroom in Knoxville, Tennessee, and died on June 17, 1873, at age thirty-two. He is buried in the Dandridge Revolutionary War Graveyard in Dandridge, Tennessee.

JOHN ADAMS DIX was born in Boscawen, New Hampshire, on July 24, 1798. His father was Lieutenant Colonel Timothy Dix, Jr., a wealthy merchant who commanded the 14th Infantry Regiment in the War of 1812 until he died of pneumonia in late 1813. John, meanwhile, was educated at the Phillips Exeter Academy and was fluent in Spanish and French. His father obtained an ensign's commission for him, and he entered the army in May 1813 at age fourteen. He fought in the War of 1812 and became a captain before he resigned from the army in 1828. Meanwhile, he studied law and was admitted to the bar.

Dix moved to Cooperstown, New York, where he practiced law and managed his father-in-law's property. He became adjutant general of the New York Militia in 1830 and relocated to Albany. He was New York's secretary of state from 1833 to 1839 and was a member of the New York State Assembly in 1842.

John Dix was a Free Soil Democrat. In 1845, he was elected to fill a vacancy in the U.S. Senate. He ran for governor in 1848 but was defeated by a Whig. He lost his seat in the Senate to William H. Seward, the Whig candidate, in 1849. He returned to the business world and became president of the Mississippi & Missouri Railroad in 1853. He served as postmaster of New York City from 1860 to early 1861. President Buchanan appointed him secretary of the treasury in January 1861 but he only served until March 4. Dix became a major general in the New York Militia on May 6, and Abraham Lincoln appointed him major general on June 14, to rank from May 16. He was thus the senior volunteer officer for most of the war.

Dix was initially commander of the Department of Maryland. To prevent the state from seceding, he suppressed opposition to the Lincoln regime and even arrested several members of the legislature. He thus earned Lincoln's gratitude. Thereafter, he commanded the Department of Pennsylvania, "Dix's Command" (an ad hoc organization), the Department of Virginia, the VII Corps (June 1862–July 1863), and the Department of the East (1863–65). He was considered too old for field command. On July 22, 1862, he and Confederate General D. H. Hill concluded a system of prisoner-of-war exchange (the Dix-Hill Cartel), which worked well for several months, but broke down when the Rebels insisted on returning black POWs to slavery.

General Dix resigned his commission on November 30, 1865. He resumed his political career and was U.S. minister to France, 1866–1869, and was governor of New York, 1873–1874, as a Republican. He was defeated for re-election by Samuel Tilden. He also ran for mayor of New York City but was defeated. Dix was also at various times president of the Union Pacific Railroad and the Erie Railroad.

General Dix died in New York City on April 21, 1879, at age eighty. He is buried in the Trinity Church Cemetery, Manhattan, New York.

CHARLES CLEVELAND DODGE was born in Plainfield, New Jersey, on September 16, 1841, the son of Congressman William E. Dodge, a fervent abolitionist who was known as the "Merchant Prince" and was an owner of the Phelps-Dodge Mining Corporation.

Dodge entered the service on May 12, 1861, as a captain in the 1st New York Mounted Rifle Battalion, which later became the 7th New York Cavalry Regiment. Dodge became its major (January 3, 1862), lieutenant colonel (July 1), and colonel (August 13). Meanwhile, he was involved in the successful attempt to capture the Gosport Naval Yard at Norfolk and the town of Suffolk, Virginia. In the clash between the *Monitor* and the *Merrimac* ironclads, Dodge's men fired on the Rebel vessel from the shore.

Partially because of the political influence of prominent New Yorkers, Dodge was promoted to brigadier general on April 4, 1863, at age twenty-one. He engaged in reconnaissance and skirmishing with Confederate forces, and his performance was credible, but he was passed over for command of the cavalry in the Suffolk sector by General John J. Peck, his immediate commander, and by General Dix, his departmental commander, who had little use for Dodge. Peck preferred an older and more experienced officer and was not pleased at the plundering, desertion, and lack of discipline exhibited by Dodge's men. Unhappy with the attitude of his superiors, Dodge refused to subordinate himself to an officer junior to himself in rank (even if that officer was old enough to be his father) and resigned from the service on June 12, 1863. He returned home and the following month helped suppress the New York Draft Riots, for which he was commended by General John E. Wool. It was his last military service in the Civil War.

Post-war, Charles Dodge participated in many business activities and for years was president of the New York, Boston, and Cape Cod Canal Company. He died in New York City on November 4, 1910, at age sixty-nine. He was buried in Woodlawn Cemetery, the Bronx, New York.

GRENVILLE MELLEN DODGE, an American railroad pioneer, was born on April 12, 1831, in Danvers, Massachusetts. He and his family moved frequently when he was a child. He attended Durham Academy, New Hampshire, and Partridge Academy in Norwich, Vermont, and obtained a degree in civil engineering from Norwich University in 1850. He worked as a surveyor for the Illinois Central and the Chicago and Rock Island Railroads. Dodge eventually settled in Council Bluffs, Iowa, and worked as a surveyor for the Union Pacific and other railroads. He was a member of the city council in 1860, established a bank, and organized a militia company, the Council Bluffs Guards, in 1856.

Dodge was mustered into the Union Army as colonel of the 4th Iowa Infantry on July 6, 1861. He served in Missouri and, near Rolla on December 27, accidentally shot himself in the left leg with his own pistol.

He commanded a brigade at Pea Ridge, where he had three horses shot out from under him and was severely wounded in the side and the hand. He performed well, however, and as a result was promoted to brigadier general on April 11, 1862.

Dodge's responsibilities increased as the war progressed: commander of the Central District, Department of Mississippi (1862); division commander, District of Tennessee; division commander, District of Corinth; and division commander, Army of the Tennessee (1862–63), where he was mainly engaged in building blockhouses and rebuilding railroads and bridges. In the spring of 1863, he organized the 1st Alabama Cavalry (African Descent) at Corinth. He was involved in the operations around Iuka, Corinth, Vicksburg, and northern Alabama. In addition, he rebuilt the Mobile & Ohio and the Richfield & Decatur railroads. As Grant was preparing for the Chattanooga offensive, he wrote to Sherman: "Bring Dodge along. He is an officer on whom we can rely in an emergency." He was promoted to major general on June 8, 1864.

Grenville Dodge commanded the XVI Corps during the drive on Atlanta, where he was wounded in the head by a Rebel sharpshooter on August 19. He did not return to active duty until December, when he was named commander of the Department of Missouri. Later it was expanded to include Kansas, Nebraska, and Utah as well. He left the army on May 30, 1866.

After the war, Dodge was chief civil engineer of the Union Pacific Railroad and the Texas & Pacific Railroad, and worked on other railroads in the United States and Europe. He was one of the main people responsible for building the Transcontinental Railroad. He also served a term in the U.S. House of Representatives as a Republican from 1867 to 1869. He built a railroad in Cuba during the Spanish-American War (1898).

In his last years, Dodge was Commander-in-Chief, Military Order of the Loyal Legion of the United States (MOLLUS) (1907–1909). He also wrote two books about the Civil War (see Bibliography). General Dodge became bedridden with cancer in 1914 and died in Council Bluffs, Iowa, on January 3, 1916. He was eighty-four years old. He is buried in Walnut Hill Cemetery, Council Bluffs.

CHARLES CAMP DOOLITTLE was born on March 16, 1832, at Burlington, Vermont. He attended school in Montreal, Canada, but dropped out because of his father's financial difficulties. He moved to New York City for a time before settling in Hillsdale, Michigan, where he was employed as a store clerk and a glassworker.

On June 30, 1861, Doolittle joined the Union Army as a first lieutenant in the 4th Michigan Infantry. He was promoted to captain and company commander on August 20. Sent to the Eastern Front, he took part in the Peninsula Campaign and the Seven Days battles, where his regiment suffered 249 casualties. He was wounded at Gaines' Mill on June 28, 1862. Doolittle was promoted to colonel of the 18th Michigan Infantry on August 13; the unit was mustered into Federal service at Hillsdale on August 26. It was quickly sent to Kentucky but was not present in the Battle of Perryville. Thereafter, Doolittle was involved in minor operations in Kentucky or part of the provost guard in Nashville, Tennessee, until he was sent to northern Alabama in June 1864. Meanwhile, he was given command of a brigade on June 2, 1864. (He had served a couple of stints as acting brigade commander before this.) On October 30, 1864, he was part of General Granger's command when he successfully defended Decatur from John Bell Hood's Army of Tennessee and imposed a significant delay on his invasion of Tennessee. He fought in the Battles of Franklin and Nashville in late 1864 and was promoted to brigadier general on April 22, 1865.

Following the South's surrender, Doolittle commanded the post of Nashville, Tennessee, and the District of Northeast Louisiana. He was mustered out of the service in November 1865, and brevetted major general in 1866.

After the war, General Doolittle moved to Ohio and became main cashier of the Merchants' National Bank in Toledo. He was also an Elder of the Westminster [Presbyterian] Church.

During the war, General Doolittle developed acute inflammatory rheumatism, which resulted in heart disease. He died in Toledo on February 20, 1903, at age seventy. He was buried in the Woodlawn Cemetery, Toledo. His son Charles was a missionary in Syria for twenty-nine years.

ABNER DOUBLEDAY was born into humble beginnings in Ballston Spa, New York, on June 26, 1819. For a time, his entire family lived in a one-room house, and all slept in the attic. His father made something of himself, however, and became a newspaper and book publisher and served two terms in the U.S. House of Representatives. Abner lived in Auburn and Cooperstown, New York, in his youth and was admitted to West Point in 1838. He graduated in 1842 (24/56) and was commissioned brevet second lieutenant in the 3rd Artillery. He was promoted to second lieutenant in 1845, first lieutenant in 1847, captain in 1855, and major on May 14, 1861. He fought at Monterrey and Buena Vista during the Mexican War and commanded a supply depot in Camargo but did not earn any brevets. In 1856, he was transferred to Florida, where he participated in the Third Seminole War.

Doubleday was on garrison duty in Charleston, South Carolina, when secession came and war burst upon them. As second-in-command of the Fort Sumter garrison, he aimed the first gun to return fire on the Confederates. After the garrison surrendered and was released, Doubleday commanded the artillery for the Department of the Shenandoah and for Banks's forces until May 6, 1862, when he was given command of an infantry brigade in John Pope's Army of Virginia. Meanwhile, he was promoted to brigadier general on February 6, 1862. After Pope's defeat at the Second Bull Run, he was given a division, which he led at South Mountain, Antietam, Fredericksburg, and Chancellorsville. His promotion to major general was dated March 10, 1863.

After General Reynolds was killed at Gettysburg on July 1, 1863, Doubleday became acting commander of the I Corps, but was unable to halt the Rebels; his corps and Howard's XI Corps were driven through the town. General Meade, the army commander, distrusted Doubleday's ability, and he had the reputation for being slow, so Meade relieved him of his command. Doubleday returned to his division and was wounded in the neck on July 3.

General Doubleday received no further field commands after Gettysburg and was mainly on duty in Washington, D.C. He was promoted to lieutenant colonel in the regular army on September 30, 1863, and was mustered out of the volunteer service on August 24, 1865.

After the war, Doubleday briefly served as assistant director of the Freedmen's Bureau. He was named colonel of the 35th Infantry in 1867 but gave up command in 1869 and was unemployed for more than a year. In 1870, he commanded the 24th Infantry at Fort McKavett, Texas. This was an African American regiment. He retired in late 1873 and settled in New Jersey, where he wrote *Reminiscences of Forts Sumter and Moultrie in 1860–1861* (1876), *Gettysburg and Chancellorsville* (1882), and *Gettysburg Made Plain* (1888). He died of heart disease in Mendham, New Jersey, on January 26, 1893, at age seventy-three. He is buried in Arlington National Cemetery. His brother, Brevet Brigadier General Ulysses Doubleday, commanded a brigade in the Army of the James. Another brother, Thomas, was a colonel and commander of the 4th New York Heavy Artillery. He was run over and killed by an omnibus on Broadway in May 1864.

After the war, the legend spread that Abner Doubleday invented baseball. He never claimed this distinction, and baseball historians have thoroughly debunked this myth.

NEAL DOW was born in Portland, Maine, on March 20, 1804. He was a Quaker who hated drunkenness and alcoholic beverages. (In that era, the average man drank about three times as much alcohol as the average person does today.) He was educated in Quaker schools and became locally prominent, serving as chief of the volunteer fire department, mayor of Portland (1851–52 and 1855–56), and two terms in the Maine House of Representatives. He also ran a successful tanning business.

Although highly competent, he sometimes allowed his anti-alcohol views to affect his official duties. For example, when a liquor store caught fire, Fire Chief Dow refused to put it out, and it burned to the ground. He also had a temper. As mayor, he ordered the local militia to fire on anti-temperance rioters; several were wounded and one was killed.

Today, Dow is best known for writing the "Maine Law," America's first alcohol prohibition statute. It became law in 1851. By 1861, Dow was a national leader in the temperance movement. He was later known as "the Father of Prohibition" and "the Napoleon of Temperance." He was also a fervent abolitionist. He joined the Union Army on November 23, 1861, as the colonel of the 13th Maine Infantry. Many of his officers were former associates from the prohibition movement. Some of the enlisted men favored the other side and would occasionally spike his lemonade.

Dow and his regiment were sent to the Department of the Gulf in February 1862. He disliked his commander, General Butler, whom he regarded as soft on slavery and pro-alcohol. He was promoted to brigadier general on April 28, 1862. He led a brigade in Florida and eventually became commander of the District of Pensacola, where he recruited black troops without authorization and banned alcohol in his area of operations.

Dow's only major battle was the Siege of Port Hudson. During the unsuccessful attack of May 27, which Dow was against, he was wounded in the right arm and left thigh. He was taken to the rear, where he was captured by Confederate raiders. He was transported to Libby Prison in Richmond. Here, the Rebel authorities allowed Dow to give anti-alcohol sermons. They made attendance mandatory for Union officers, although they did not attend them themselves. They thought this was funny. (So do I.)

In February 1864, Dow was exchanged for Confederate General W. H. F. "Rooney" Lee, Robert E. Lee's son. His health was undermined by wounds and his months in prison. Because of this, he resigned his commission on November 30, 1864.

Dow resumed his temperance activities after the war and was the Prohibition Party's presidential nominee in 1880. He was writing *The Reminiscences of Neal Dow* when he died in Portland on October 2, 1897, at the age of ninety-three. He was buried in the Evergreen Cemetery in Portland, Maine.

ALFRED NAPOLEON ALEXANDER "NATTI" DUFFIE (pronounced DU-FEE-YAY) was born on May 1, 1833, in Paris, France. Details of his early life are contradictory and misleading because he tended to exaggerate his accomplishments. He did not, for example, graduate from the French military academy at St. Cyr or hold the

ENCYCLOPEDIA OF UNION GENERALS

Legion of Honor, although he wore it on occasion, and his father was not a count. It is known, however, that he was fearless and led a life of adventure. He joined the French Imperial Cavalry in 1851 as a private in the 6th Dragoons. He served in Algiers, Senegal, and in the Crimean War, including the battles of Balaclava, Alma, Sevastopol, and others. He was highly decorated in Russia and was severely wounded in the Battle of Solferino, Italy, in 1859. (Here, Napoleon III and his Piedmont-Sardinian allies defeated the Austrian emperor.) He was promoted to first sergeant in 1858 and enlisted for another seven-year term. He was promoted to second lieutenant in the 3rd Hussars in June 1859.

Meanwhile, Duffie met a thirty-two-year-old American named Mary Ann Pelton, who was serving as a nurse in France. She was the daughter of a rich Staten Island family. He proposed and submitted his resignation from the army. When it was refused, he left for New York anyway; consequently, he was charged with desertion and sentenced to five years imprisonment *in absentia*. He never saw France again but was married in August 1860.

Duffie joined the 2nd New York Cavalry as a captain in August 1861. He was promoted to major in October and to colonel of the 1st Rhode Island Cavalry on July 6, 1862. He had a quarrelsome temper and was arrested several times for altercations with other officers. He even challenged General Fitz John Porter to a duel. The Rhode Islanders initially refused to accept him as their regimental commander, but he told them, "You not like me now, you like me by and by." He managed to win them over because he was firm but fair, trained them well, was fearless, and had a wry sense of humor, liberally laced with profanity. On August 28, during the Battle of Groveton in the Second Bull Run Campaign, he halted on a road, within range of Confederate artillery fire, and calmly rolled a cigarette. An enemy round exploded nearby and covered him with dirt; he simply brushed it off and lit his smoke.

Colonel Duffie also participated in the battles of Cedar Mountain, Second Bull Run, Chantilly, Fredericksburg, and in several small cavalry actions along the Potomac and on the Eastern Front. He was given command of a brigade on February 16, 1863, and so distinguished himself in the Battle of Kelly's Ford (March 17) that General Hooker recommended him for promotion to brigadier general. (His legs were injured in this battle when his horse was shot and fell on him.) When the cavalry was reorganized, he

194

was named commander of a cavalry division on May 16. He disobeyed orders in the Battle of Brandy Station (June 9), however, and was demoted back to regimental command. (General Pleasanton, the commander of the Cavalry Corps, openly distrusted foreigners and did not like Duffie.)

On June 16, Pleasanton sent Duffie men on what amounted to a suicide mission behind Rebel lines. The next day, near Middleburg, Virginia, he rode into an ambush and was smashed by Confederate cavalry. Duffie's brigade commander, Judson Kilpatrick, ignored Duffie's frantic calls for help. Of the 280 men who rode with Duffie on this mission, 225 were killed, missing, or captured. Duffie managed to escape; he then gave up his command and returned to Washington, D.C. Ironically, his promotion to brigadier general came through on June 23.

Duffie was unemployed until August 11, when he was given command of a cavalry brigade in West Virginia. He trained it, led it in a few minor operations, and performed well during Hunter's Shenandoah Valley Campaign of 1864. Elevated to divisional command, he bragged that he would capture John Singleton Mosby, the famous Rebel guerrilla leader, and bring him back to Washington; instead, Mosby captured Duffie on October 20, 1864. This led Phil Sheridan to denounce him as a poor soldier and to demand that he be dismissed from the army.

General Duffie was incarcerated in Danville, Virginia, and exchanged on February 22, 1865, and transferred to the Department of Arkansas. He was ordered to Texas, but the war ended before he arrived. He was mustered out of the service in August without the usual brevet to major general.

Duffie returned to Staten Island and became a naturalized American citizen. In 1869, he was appointed U.S. consul to Cadiz, Spain. He died here from tuberculosis on November 8, 1880, at the age of forty-seven. He is buried in the Fountain Cemetery on Staten Island. His former officers in the 1st Rhode Island thought enough of him to purchase a monument for him.

EBENEZER DUMONT was born on November 23, 1814, in Vevay, Indiana, the son of a prominent attorney, a member of the state legislature, and an unsuccessful gubernatorial candidate. Ebenezer graduated from the University of Indiana in 1834, where he studied law. That same year, he founded the Marion County Seminary, which became a leading boys school in central Indiana. Dumont was admitted to the bar around 1835, and set up a practice in Vevay, near the Ohio River. He was elected to the legislature as a Democrat in 1838, was county treasurer (1839–45), and fought in the Mexican War as captain and then lieutenant colonel of the 4th Indiana Infantry, which part of Winfield Scott's army. He returned home in 1848, was re-elected to the legislature in 1850, and served a term as speaker of the house. He moved to Indianapolis and became president of the State Bank of Indiana (1852–59).

Dumont joined the Republican Party in 1861. On April 27, he rejoined the U.S. Army as colonel of the 7th Indiana Militia, a 90-day regiment which re-mustered as a three-year unit in September. He took part in McClellan's Western Virginia Campaign, including the Battle of Cheat Mountain, and did well, which led to his promotion to brigadier general on September 3, 1861. He assumed command of a brigade in the Army of the Ohio in December and a division in September 1862. Meanwhile, he defeated Confederate General John Hunt Morgan at Lebanon, Kentucky (May 1862) and participated in the Kentucky Campaign of 1862. That winter, his health failed him, and he resigned his commission on February 28, 1863. Later that year, he was elected to Congress. He served from 1863 to 1867 but was not a candidate for re-election in 1866. He returned to Indianapolis and the practice of law.

President Grant appointed Dumont territorial governor of Idaho on March 15, 1871, but he passed away in Indianapolis on April 16, 1871, before he assumed the office. He died of prostration caused by diarrhea, from which he suffered for years. He is buried there in the Crown Hill Cemetery. He was fifty-six years old.

ABRAM DURYEE (pronounced DUR-YAY) was born in New York City on April 29, 1815, the descendent of French Huguenots. His father and two uncles were officers in the War of 1812. Abram attended Columbia College and became a wealthy mahogany importer. He joined the New York Militia as a private in 1833 and rose to the command of the 4th New York Militia Regiment in 1849.

When the Civil War began, Duryee recruited and organized the 5th New York Infantry—a Zouave unit—and became its colonel on May 14, 1861. The regiment's uniforms were modeled after the French Zouaves and featured a dark jacket with red trim, extremely baggy red pantaloons, and a red fez. It first saw action at Big Bethel (June 10, 1861), the first Union defeat of the war. General McClellan was nevertheless impressed with the unit's discipline and recommended Duryee for promotion. He became a brigadier general on August 31, 1861.

Duryee was given command of a brigade in Irvin McDowell's corps in the Washington area and thus missed the Peninsula Campaign and the Seven Days battles. Among other actions, he fought at Cedar Mountain, the Second Bull Run, and Antietam, and was wounded in all three battles and thrown from his horse. He was forced to wear a truss for the rest of his life. Duryee returned home on furlough, but when he returned, he found he had been replaced by John Gibbon, who was junior to him in rank. When his petition to be restored to command was rejected, he resigned his commission on January 5, 1863. He was offered other New York commands later in the war but declined them all. He saw no further service but was nevertheless brevetted major general in 1866.

General Duryee returned to the business world in 1863. Ten years later, he was named police commissioner of New York City where he was accused of brutality for suppressing a labor protest in Tompkins Square Park in 1874. For this action, he was forced to resign. He became Dock Master of New York City in 1884 and served until 1887, when he was incapacitated by a stroke.

Duryee died in New York City on September 27, 1890, after a three-year illness. He was seventy-five years old. He is buried in the Green-Wood Cemetery in Brooklyn. His son, Jacob Eugene Duryee (1839–1918), began the war as a private in his father's regiment but ended it commanding the 2nd Maryland (U.S.) Infantry. He was brevetted brigadier general at the end of the war.

ISAAC HARDIN DUVAL was born at Wellsburg, in that strip of Virginia (now West Virginia) between Ohio and Pennsylvania, on September 1, 1824. He attended local schools and became a trader, the manager of a trading post at Fort Smith, Arkansas, a scout, a hunter, and a 49er. He also travelled in Mexico, Central America, and South America, and was a filibuster in Cuba in 1851. He returned to Wellsburg in 1853 and became a merchant.

Duval was mustered into the Union Army as major of the 1st Virginia (U.S.) Infantry Regiment on June 1, 1861.

He fought in thirty-six engagements during the war, was wounded three times, and had eleven horses shot out from under him. He took part in the Shenandoah Valley Campaign of 1862, where he was wounded in the foot at Port Republic (June 8). He was wounded again, this time in the head, at Cedar Mountain on August 9. He fought at Antietam and was promoted to colonel and commander of the 9th West Virginia Infantry on September 19.

Colonel Duval took part in the Kanawha Valley Campaign of late 1863, in the Second Battle of Winchester (June 1863), and in minor battles in West Virginia, including operations against the Virginia & Tennessee Railroad. He fought at Cloyd's Mountain in May 1864 (where his regiment suffered 30 percent casualties) and in the Third Battle of Winchester, a.k.a. the Battle of Opequon (September 19), where he was wounded in the left thigh. A brigade commander since July, he was promoted to brigadier general on September 24, 1864. After he recovered, he assumed command of a brigade in Crook's Army of West Virginia and briefly led a division in early 1865. He was discharged on January 15, 1866, and brevetted major general on February 24.

After the war, Duval (a Republican) was a West Virginia state senator, state adjutant general, U.S. Congressman (1869–71), state assessor of internal revenue (1871–72), U.S. collector of internal revenue (1872–84), and a member of the West Virginia House of Delegates (1887–89). He refused to run for re-election to Congress in 1870. He died in the town of his birth on July 10, 1902, at age seventy-seven. He is buried in Brooke Cemetery, Wellsburg, West Virginia.

WILLIAM DWIGHT was born in Springfield, Massachusetts, on July 14, 1831. He attended a private military school and entered West Point in 1849 but was discharged (flunked out) on January 31, 1853, due to deficiencies in mathematics. He then engaged in manufacturing in Boston and Philadelphia until the outbreak of the Civil War.

Dwight became a captain in the 70th New York Infantry in May 1861 but was promoted to lieutenant colonel on June 29 and to full colonel on July 1. He led the 70th New York in the Peninsula Campaign until the Battle of Williamsburg (May 5, 1862), where he lost half his command and was wounded in the right leg, thigh, and abdomen. Left for dead, he was captured by the Rebels and nursed back to health. He was exchanged on November 15 and promoted to brigadier general on March 4, 1863. He was transferred to Louisiana and commanded a brigade in the Siege of Port Hudson. At one point he ordered two African American regiments to charge the Confederate fortifications, but their colonels refused because the attack would be suicidal, and Dwight was so inebriated he could barely stand up. The colonels were not punished.

Dwight was outspoken, loud-mouthed, and somewhat rude. He was, however, friends with Nathaniel Banks, the commander of the Army of the Gulf, who promoted him to division commander during the Siege of Port Hudson. He served as Banks's chief of staff during the disastrous Red River Campaign of 1864. He was present during the battles of Mansfield and Pleasant Hill, but his main interest was seizing cotton from civilians and transporting it to New England. It is likely that kickbacks were involved in these dubious transactions.

In July 1864, after Banks was sacked, Dwight was given command of a division in the XIX Corps and transferred to the Shenandoah Valley, where he was relieved of his command and arrested because, during the Third Battle of Winchester, he left his men in combat and retired to a place of safety, so he could eat his lunch in peace. He held no further commands of importance and was mustered out of the service on January 15, 1866, without the usual brevet to major general.

After the war, Dwight went into the railroad business in Cincinnati. He died in Boston on April 21, 1888, at age fifty-six. He is buried in Forest Hills Cemetery, Jamaica Plain, Massachusetts. His brother, Lieutenant Colonel Howard Dwight of the 2nd Massachusetts Infantry, was mortally wounded at Antietam.

ALEXANDER BRYDIE DYER was born in Richmond, Virginia, on January 10, 1815. He entered West Point in 1833 and graduated in 1837 (6/50), just behind Braxton Bragg. Commissioned second lieutenant in the 3rd Artillery, he served in Florida during the Second Seminole War but transferred to the Ordnance Branch in 1838. He was chief of ordnance on the staff of General Stephen W. Kearny's army when it invaded New Mexico. He was wounded in action near Canada, New Mexico, on February 4, 1847. He was promoted to first lieutenant the following month and to captain in 1855. He was brevetted to that rank in 1848 for his gallantry in the Battle of Santa Cruz de Rosales, Mexico.

His career between the Mexican and Civil Wars was unremarkable and consisted almost exclusively of garrison duty at various arsenals, including St. Louis, Fort Monroe, and in North Carolina. In August 1861, he was put in charge of the Springfield Armory, where his performance was astonishing. He quadrupled production and was soon manufacturing a thousand rifles a day. Lincoln was so impressed that he offered him the position of chief of ordnance, but Dyer declined out of respect for the incumbent, General James W. Ripley. After Ripley retired in 1864, Dyer (a major since 1863) was named chief of ordnance on September 12, 1864. He was promoted to brigadier general, Regular Army, the next day, bypassing the ranks of lieutenant colonel and colonel altogether.

General Dyer was scrupulously honest, but many inventors and arms contractors were not. Because he refused to accept their bribes, they sought to get rid of him by other means and tried to "frame up" on him. Facing their rumors and false charges, Dyer demanded a court-martial. That request was rejected, so he demanded a court of inquiry. An exhaustive investigation not only exonerated him but declared his management of the Ordnance Department exemplary and himself worthy of emulation. And indeed, he was! For example, Dyer invented a new artillery projectile but refused to accept any personal profit for it. The proceeds were passed on to the government.

Alexander Dyer was brevetted major general, Regular Army, in 1866. He died in office in Washington, D.C. on May 20, 1874. He is buried in Arlington National Cemetery. One of his six children, Alexander B. Dyer, Jr., graduated from West Point in 1874 and retired as a colonel of artillery in 1909.

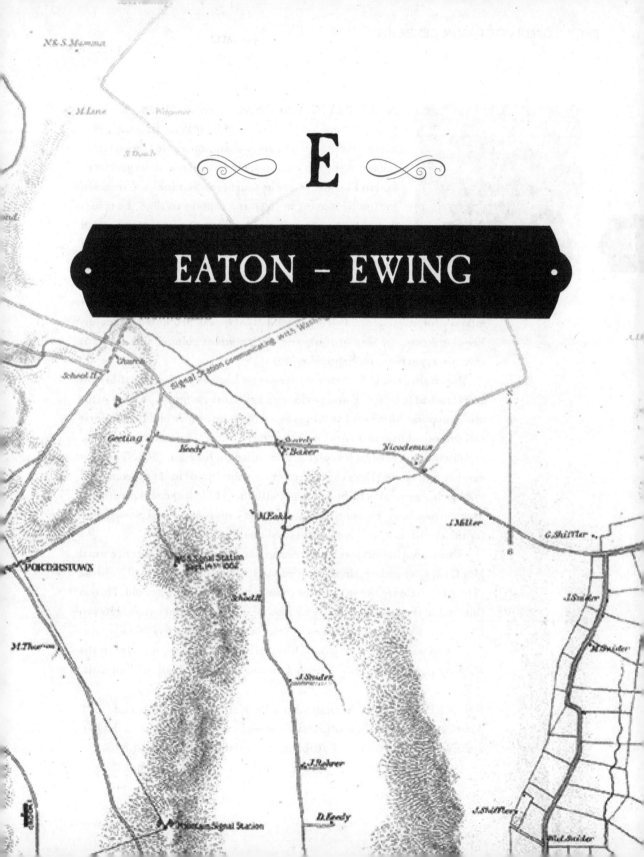

E
EATON – EWING

AMOS BEEBE EATON was born on May 12, 1806, in Catskill, New York. He entered West Point in 1822, graduated in 1826 (36/41), and was commissioned second lieutenant in the 4th Infantry. He served in various garrisons and in Florida, where he fought the Seminoles. Promoted to first lieutenant in 1834 and captain in 1838, he transferred to the commissary department that same year and remained there for thirty-six years. Meanwhile, he served in northern Mexico under Zachary Taylor and earned a brevet to major for gallantry at Buena Vista. From 1855 until the outbreak of the Civil War, he was assistant commissary for subsistence in New York City. He was promoted to major, Regular Army, on May 9, 1861, and to lieutenant colonel and assistant commissary general on September 29.

Naturally, the U.S. Army underwent a huge expansion in 1861 and everyone had to be fed. Eaton performed brilliantly, acquiring and distributing supplies. Abraham Lincoln grasped the significance of Eaton's efforts and promoted him to colonel on February 9, 1863. The commissary general, Brigadier General Joseph P. Taylor, died on June 29, 1864. The next day, Lincoln named Eaton his successor and nominated him for promotion to brigadier general. The Senate acted with incredible speed and confirmed him two days later. He continued to keep the Union Army well provisioned for the rest of the war. He was brevetted major general in 1866.

Eaton continued to serve as commissary general of subsistence until May 1, 1874, when he retired. He died suddenly on February 21, 1877, while sitting in a Yale University lecture room. He was seventy years old. He was interred in the Grove Street Cemetery, New Haven, Connecticut. His son Daniel was a professor of botany at Yale for more than thirty years.

Eaton was the first cousin of Elizabeth Cady Stanton, a leader in the women's rights movement. He was a distant cousin of Winston Churchill.

JOHN EDWARDS was born in Louisville, Kentucky, on October 24, 1815. After receiving a limited education, he read law, was admitted to the bar, and moved to Indiana, to California during the Gold Rush, and back to Indiana. A Whig, he was a state senator from 1852 to 1854, but then he moved to Iowa after his first wife (with whom he had seven children) died. He remarried twice and had five more children. Meanwhile, he was elected to the Iowa House of Representatives as a Republican and was speaker from 1858 to 1860. He also founded a newspaper.

When the Civil War began, Iowa Governor Samuel J. Kirkwood appointed Edwards to his staff as an aide with the rank of lieutenant colonel (May 21, 1861). He was tasked with guarding the Iowa border from invasion by Rebels from Missouri. On August 8, 1862, he was promoted to colonel and commander of the 18th Iowa Infantry. During the war, it lost thirty-five men killed in action or died of wounds and 132 who died of disease. Meanwhile, Edwards was elevated to brigade commander in December 1863 and served in Missouri and northern Arkansas, mostly as post commander at Springfield, Missouri, or Fort Smith, Arkansas. In 1864, he was part of the Camden Expedition and fought at Prairie d'Ane and Jenkins' Ferry. He was promoted to brigadier general on September 26, 1864. In December, he was given command of a division at Fort Smith, where he was when the war ended. He was discharged on January 15, 1866, but remained in Fort Smith as a permanent resident.

President Andrew Johnson appointed Edwards assessor for internal revenue (1866–69). He was elected to Congress as a Liberal Republican and served from March 4, 1871 to February 8, 1872, when he was removed from office after his opponent successfully contested the election. Edwards accepted the verdict and retired from public life. He remained in Washington, D.C. and worked in the legal field until his death, which occurred in Washington on April 18, 1894, at age seventy-eight. He is buried in Arlington National Cemetery.

OLIVER EDWARDS was born on January 30, 1835, in Springfield, Massachusetts. He developed a lifelong interest in mechanics and secured an apprenticeship at the Springfield Armory. He moved to Illinois when he was twenty-one and eventually settled in Warsaw, where he and a partner established a foundry.

Edwards returned to Massachusetts when the Civil War began, recruited a company, and joined the army in May 1861. The following month, he was promoted to first lieutenant and adjutant of the 10th Massachusetts Infantry. Later that month, General Darius Couch tapped him as an aide-de-camp. Edwards served in the Peninsula Campaign and, on August 9, 1862, was named major and commander of the 37th Massachusetts Infantry, which was then forming. He was promoted to colonel on September 9.

The 37th was sent to Virginia in October 1862 and fought at Fredericksburg, Chancellorsville, and Gettysburg, where as part of the VI Corps, it lost forty-seven men out of 593 engaged. The regiment was then redeployed to New York City, where it helped suppress the draft riots. It rejoined the Army of the Potomac in October 1863 and took part in the victory at Rappahannock Station (November 7) and in the Mine Run Campaign (November 26–December 2). On May 6, 1864, during the Battle of the Wilderness, the regiment was surrounded by Confederates. Edwards kept the 37th well in hand and directed a successful retreat, although the 37th did suffer 25 percent casualties. Three days later, Edwards was given command of a brigade.

Colonel Edwards led his new command in the battles of Spotsylvania Court House, North Anna, and Cold Harbor. In July, the brigade was transferred to Sheridan's Army of the Shenandoah and fought in the Valley Campaign of 1864. Edwards particularly distinguished himself in the Battle of Opequon (a.k.a. the Third Battle of Winchester), where he temporarily commanded a division. He also impressed General Sheridan, who offered him the post of provost marshal for the army. Edwards, however, preferred to remain with his brigade. He was brevetted brigadier general on December 12.

In 1865, Edwards's brigade fought in the Siege of Petersburg and was the first to break Lee's line on April 2, 1865. He personally received the surrender of the mayor of Petersburg. During the Appomattox Campaign, he fought in the Battle of Sayler's Creek, where his men captured Confederate Generals Richard S. Ewell and Custis Lee, Robert E. Lee's son, as well as hundreds of other prisoners.

Oliver Edwards was undoubtedly a fine regimental and brigade commander and also did well commanding a division, although he did this for only a limited time. This author is unable to explain why he was not promoted to brigadier general until May 19, 1865. He was offered a Regular Army position after Lee surrendered but turned it down. He was mustered out on January 15, 1866. Later that year, he was brevetted major general.

After the war, Edwards returned to Warsaw, where he served three years as the town's postmaster. In 1870, the Florence Machine Company of Northampton, Massachusetts, hired him, and he eventually became its superintendent. He was also a successful inventor, patenting the Florence ice skates and the Florence oil stove, among others. He retired to Warsaw in 1875 but moved to England in 1882, as general manager of the Gardner Machine and Gun Company. Eventually, however, his health failed, so he returned to Warsaw. He died there on April 28, 1904, at the age of sixty-nine, and is buried in Oakland Cemetery, Warsaw.

THOMAS WILBERFORCE "TOM" EGAN, the child of Irish immigrants, was born in Watervliet, New York, on June 14, 1834. Little is known of his life before April 1861, when he enlisted in the 40th New York (also known as "the Mozart Regiment" or "the Constitution Guard") as a private. The 40th suffered more casualties than any other New York regiment except the 69th New York of the Irish Brigade. Egan was promoted to lieutenant colonel on July 1.

Egan first saw action in the Ball's Bluff disaster of October 21. He fought in the Peninsula Campaign and the Battle of Seven Pines, where he displayed conspicuous gallantry and was wounded in the head. Here, the regiment lost ninety-six men out of 231 engaged, and every member of the color guard was killed or wounded. Egan also arrested his commanding officer for misconduct and assumed command of the regiment himself. His actions must have been valid because he was promoted to colonel on June 5.

Egan continued to lead the Mozart Regiment in all the major battles of the Army of the Potomac, including the Second Bull Run, Chantilly, South

Mountain, Antietam, Fredericksburg, Chancellorsville, Gettysburg, and the Wilderness. Occasionally he was an acting brigade commander in the II Corps, but he was not appointed to this position on a permanent basis until May 12, 1864, at age twenty-nine. He fought at Spotsylvania, North Anna, and Cold Harbor and was wounded by Rebel shrapnel near the spine and right kidney close to Petersburg on June 16. He suffered from partial paralysis of the legs for the rest of his life. He did not return to duty until August 27. He was promoted to brigadier general on September 3, 1864, and was given command of a division in the II Corps the next day. Egan was brevetted major general on October 27.

On November 14, while fighting in the Siege of Petersburg, he was wounded by a minié ball to the right forearm and he could hardly use the arm after that. Egan returned to duty on March 15, 1865, as commander of a provisional division at Charles Town, West Virginia, under his old chief, General Hancock. He remained here until August and was discharged from the service on January 15, 1866. He had proven himself a brave and highly competent commander.

Post-war, Egan was deputy collector in the New York Customs House, a position he held until about 1881. Meanwhile, he turned to alcohol to assuage his physical and emotional pain and financial stress. For a time, he was placed in an insane asylum. He died, alone and in obscurity, at a charity hospital in New York City on February 24, 1887. He was fifty or fifty-one

years old. Members of the Grand Army of the Republic stepped in to cover his burial expenses, or he would have been interred in a potters' field. He is buried in Cypress Hills National Cemetery, Brooklyn, New York. Egan married an actress named Marie Gordon antebellum, but they had long since gone their separate ways. (He caught her in bed with another man in 1866 and quickly divorced her.) She remarried in 1867 and emigrated to London, taking their only child, a son, with her.

ALFRED WASHINGTON ELLET was born in Bucks County, Pennsylvania, on October 11, 1820. He was the thirteenth of fourteen children. His family moved to a farm near Philadelphia when he was four. He worked on the family farm and studied civil engineering at Bristol Academy. Later, he moved to Bunker Hill, Illinois, and worked as a civil engineer until August 20, 1861, when he joined the 59th Illinois as a captain. He fought in the Battle of Pea Ridge in March 1862. The following month, he was promoted to lieutenant colonel and named aide-de-camp to General Fremont, who was then commander of the Western Department.

Meanwhile, Ellet's older brother, Colonel Charles Ellet, Jr., organized the United States Ram Fleet and Alfred became his second-in-command. They fought in the Battle of Memphis on June 6, where they sank eight of the nine Confederate warships involved in the action; unfortunately, Charles was shot in the knee by a Rebel sharpshooter. The wound became infected, and he died on June 21. His brother assumed command of the fleet and led it in the Battle of Liverpool, Mississippi, on the Yazoo River, on June 26. The Confederates were forced to scuttle three gunboats. The Ram Fleet suffered no casualties.

On November 6, 1862, Ellet was promoted to brigadier general and was ordered to form the Mississippi Marine Brigade, an amphibious raiding formation under General Grant's overall command. It was an ill-disciplined lot and bore little resemblance to what the modern American thinks of when they hear the word "Marine." It occasionally skirmished with Confederate forces, but mostly engaged in plundering plantations along the Mississippi River and its tributaries. Ellet himself was accused of war profiteering and illegally selling seized Confederate cotton. His brigade was disbanded in August 1864. Ellet resigned his commission on December 31, 1864, possibly to avoid a court-martial. He did not receive the standard brevet of major general at the end of the war.

Ellet settled in El Dorado, Kansas, and quickly became a prominent business leader and president of a local bank. He persuaded what became the Santa Fe Railroad to lay its main line through El Dorado. He died on January 9, 1895, and was buried in the Buena Vista Cemetery, El Dorado. He was seventy-four years old.

WASHINGTON LAFAYETTE ELLIOTT was born in Carlisle, Pennsylvania, on March 31, 1825. His father was Commodore Jesse Elliott,

who took him on several of his voyages as a boy, including one to the West Indies. He attended Dickinson College but dropped out in 1841 to attend West Point; he resigned for unknown reasons in 1844. He studied medicine but abandoned this course in 1846 to accept a second lieutenancy in the Mounted Rifles Regiment during the Mexican War. He fought in the Siege of Vera Cruz but then fell ill, returned to the states, and spent the rest of the war on recruiting duty. He eventually became a quartermaster and was promoted to first lieutenant in 1847, captain in 1854, and to major, Regular Army, on November 5, 1861. Meanwhile, he served at Fort Laramie; on the Oregon Trail (1849–51); in Texas (1852–56); and in New Mexico (1856–61), where he fought Comanches and Navajos.

Sent to Missouri when the war broke out, Elliott distinguished himself in the Battle of Wilson's Creek (August 10). Afterward, he transferred to the cavalry and became colonel of the 2nd Iowa Cavalry on September 14. As part of John Pope's Army of the Mississippi, he fought at Island No. 10 (February 28 to April 8, 1862) and commanded a brigade in the Siege of Corinth. He led a successful raid on the Mobile & Ohio Railroad, which was one of the few Union cavalry successes early in the war. As a result, he was promoted to brigadier general on June 12, 1862, and was named chief of staff of the Army of the Mississippi.

When General Pope was transferred to the east, he took Elliott with him as cavalry commander for the Army of Virginia. He was less successful against Jeb Stuart and was wounded in the arm in the Second Battle of Bull Run. In disgrace, Pope was sent to command the Department of the Northwest. Elliott was also sent into professional exile as commander of the District of Wisconsin. Unlike Pope, Elliott was recalled to Virginia, where he led a cavalry brigade from February 1863. He and most of his men escaped the debacle that was the Second Battle of Winchester in June. He was given command of an infantry division on July 10.

In the fall of 1863, Elliott was given command of a cavalry division in the West and played a role in the relief of Knoxville in late 1863. He commanded the cavalry corps of the Army of the Cumberland in the Atlanta

Campaign but was sent back to the infantry that fall and directed a division of the IV Corps during the Battle of Nashville. After the Southern surrender, he commanded the District of Kansas. He was mustered out of volunteer service on March 1, 1866, and was brevetted major general later that year.

Washington Elliott remained in the service after the war and reverted to the rank of major in the 1st Cavalry. He was promoted to lieutenant colonel in 1866 and to colonel of the 3rd Cavalry in 1878. Suffering from rheumatism and heart disease, he retired the following year and settled in San Francisco, where he became a banker. He died in San Francisco on June 29, 1888, at age sixty-three. He was buried in The Presidio of San Francisco.

WILLIAM HEMSLEY EMORY was born on September 7, 1811, in Queen Anne's County, Maryland, into a wealthy East Shore, slave-owning family. Ironically, his appointment came from John C. Calhoun. He entered West Point in 1826, graduated in 1831 (14/33), and was commissioned second lieutenant in the 4th Artillery. He resigned his commission in 1836 to become a civil engineer, but employment opportunities were not what he hoped, so he rejoined the army in 1838 as a second lieutenant in the newly formed corps of topographical engineers. He specialized in mapping the borders of the United States and was a great cartographer. His maps were so good that all previous maps were considered obsolete. Among other

things, he mapped the U.S.–Canadian border, the Texas claims west of the Rio Grande, the Texas–Mexico border, and the Gadsden Purchase. He was chief engineer in General Stephen W. Kearny's drive to California during the Mexican War and earned a brevet captaincy for his conduct in the Battle of San Pasqual. He was brevetted major for San Gabriel and Mesa. He was promoted to captain, Regular Army (1851); major (1855); and lieutenant colonel (January 31, 1861). He was brevetted lieutenant colonel for his surveying work on the U.S.–Mexico border in 1857. Meanwhile, he transferred to the cavalry branch in 1855, where the scope of promotion was greater.

Emory was in Indian Territory when the war began. With the aid of friendly Indians, he escaped to Kansas with his entire command and eventually made his way to Washington, D.C. He became lieutenant colonel of the 3rd (later 6th) U.S. Cavalry, which was in the process of forming. He assumed command of the regiment on May 17, when its colonel, David Hunter was promoted to brigadier general. The 6th Cavalry was declared ready for field service on December 31. Its strength was 984 men.

On March 13, 1862, Emory was given command of a cavalry brigade in the Army of the Potomac. He was promoted to brigadier general seven days later. He fought in the Peninsula Campaign and the Seven Days battles, and then was given command of an infantry brigade in the IV Corps. He was in charge of the defenses of Baltimore during the Maryland Campaign and thus missed the Battle of Antietam. He engaged in training an infantry division from September to December 1862 and was sent to Louisiana as part of the XIX Corps.

General Emory fought in Louisiana in 1863 and 1864 and took part in the disastrous Red River Campaign, including the Battle of Mansfield (April 8, 1865). When the XIX Corps was sent to Virginia, he went with it and fought in the Shenandoah Valley. He was an excellent division commander, saving the Army of the Shenandoah in the Battle of Cedar Creek (October 19, 1864), and he may have saved the Army of the Gulf at Mansfield. He assumed command of the XIX Corps on August 6, 1864, and led it until Appomattox. He directed the Department of West Virginia after that and was promoted to major general on September 25, 1865. He was discharged from volunteer service on January 15, 1866.

Emory commanded a number of departments until 1876, when General Sheridan relieved him of his command as part of a political intrigue and forced him into retirement. (This was the same man whose army Emory had saved at Cedar Creek.) He died in Washington, D.C. on December 1, 1887 at age seventy-six, and is buried in the Congressional Cemetery.

General Emory's wife, Matilda Bache, was the great-granddaughter of Benjamin Franklin. She bore ten children. One of them, William H. Emory, became a rear admiral in the U.S. Navy. Another was a lieutenant colonel and an aide to General Meade in the Battle of Gettysburg.

GEORGE PEABODY ESTEY (sometimes spelled Este) was born in Nashua, New Hampshire, on April 24, 1829. He attended Dartmouth, dropped out, and went to California during the Gold Rush. He returned east, read law in Galena, Illinois, and set up a law practice in Toledo, Ohio, where his law partner was Morrison R. Waite, a future chief justice of the U.S. Supreme Court.

Estey was appointed lieutenant colonel of the 14th Ohio on April 24, 1861. It was originally a 90-day unit but was reorganized in August as a three-year regiment. It departed Toledo on August 23 and went to Kentucky, where it first engaged the Confederates at the town of Wild Cat on October 21 and won a minor victory for the Union. The 14th participated in the Western Virginia Campaign and fought in the Battle of Mill Springs in January 1862; it was then transferred to Pittsburg Landing, Tennessee. It arrived in Shiloh late in the day of April 7, however, and basically missed the battle. It took part in the Siege of Corinth and the Kentucky Campaign, although it did not arrive at Perryville until after the battle was over. It was on garrison duty in Nashville during the Stones River Campaign.

George Estey assumed command of the regiment and was promoted to colonel on November 20, 1862. The 14th Ohio took part in the Tullahoma Campaign and was mauled in the Battle of Chickamauga (September 19–20, 1863), where it lost 233 men out of 449 engaged. It remained in the line and fought in the Siege of Chattanooga, including the Battle of Missionary Ridge, where it captured three Rebel cannons. Estey was not in either battle, however, because the regiment was commanded by its lieutenant colonel. In any case, he was given command of a brigade on April 1, 1864.

Colonel Estey fought well in the Atlanta Campaign, the March to the Sea, and the Carolinas Campaign. He was wounded at Jonesboro, Georgia (September 1, 1864), where he distinguished himself, led a bayonet charge, and possibly saved the day for the Union. His brigade lost 346 out of 1,300 men engaged that day. Estey was brevetted brigadier general on December 9, 1864, but was not promoted to full rank until June 26, 1865. He resigned his commission on December 4.

Postwar, General Estey settled in Washington, D.C., where he practiced law until his death, which occurred in New York City on February 6, 1881. He was fifty-one years old. He was buried in the Universalist Church Cemetery in the town of his birth.

HENRY LAWRENCE EUSTIS was born on February 1, 1819, in Fort Independence, Boston, where his father was stationed. At that time a major, Abraham Eustis became a colonel and brevet brigadier general. He died while still on active duty in 1843. Henry's mother died when he was two, and he was raised in boarding schools, including one across from West Point. He enrolled in Harvard in 1838, but resigned that same year to accept an appointment to West Point. He graduated at the top of his class (1/56) in 1842 and was commissioned second lieutenant of engineers—the most coveted of all branches. He worked on building and improving Fort Warren in Boston Harbor and was professor of engineering at West Point from 1847 to 1849. He resigned his commission in late 1849 to accept an appointment as a professor of engineering at Harvard. Despite fragile health, he left the university to accept the job of colonel of the 10th Massachusetts Infantry on August 10, 1862—a year and a half after the war began. As part of the IV Corps, he took part in the Maryland Campaign but was not present at Antietam. Four months later, in December 1862, he was given command of a brigade under General Newton, an old West Point comrade.

Eustis fought at Fredericksburg, Chancellorsville, and (after a forced march of thirty-five miles) at Gettysburg. He was promoted to brigadier general on September 12, 1863, and took part in the Rappahannock Station and Mine Run campaigns; however, his performance in the Overland Campaign of 1864 left much to be desired. He was relieved of his command on June 6, 1864, and Assistant Secretary of War C. A. Dana offered him a choice: resign or be court-martialed for neglect of duty and general inefficiency. (It was said he ate opium.) He resigned June 27, 1864.

General Eustis returned to the classroom at Harvard, where he had a reputation as an excellent and popular professor. He taught until his death, which occurred at his home in Cambridge, Massachusetts, on January 11, 1885, after a long illness. He was sixty-five. He is buried in the Mount Auburn Cemetery, Cambridge.

CHARLES EWING, the brother of Union Generals Hugh B. Ewing and Thomas Ewing, Jr., and brother-in-law of William Tecumseh Sherman, was born in Lancaster, Ohio, on March 6, 1835. His father was Thomas Ewing, who at various times was a U.S. senator, secretary of the treasury, and secretary of the interior. Charles was educated locally, at St. Joseph's College (a Dominican school), and at the University of Virginia. He read law and was practicing in St. Louis when the war began. He was commissioned captain in the 13th U.S. Infantry Regiment on his May 24, 1861. His *de facto* foster brother Sherman was the regimental commander.

As Sherman moved up, so did Ewing. He became inspector-general on Sherman's staff. This is not to imply that Ewing owed his advancement strictly to nepotism, although that certainly was a factor. He was a good officer and a courageous one. The regiment was posted at Alton, Illinois, guarding Confederate prisoners, until October 1862, when it was stationed in Memphis. After Bragg's invasion of Kentucky was defeated, it took part in the Vicksburg campaigns, including the Battle of Chickasaw Bluffs. In the major Union assault on Vicksburg (May 22, 1863), Ewing—despite being a staff officer—personally spearheaded an attack and planted the regimental colors on the Confederate works. He was shot in the hand for his pains. He was brevetted major for this action—the first of three brevets he received during the war. He was promoted to lieutenant colonel (substantive rank) on June 22.

Charles Ewing was Sherman's assistant inspector general when he commanded XV Corps and later the Army of the Tennessee. He took part in the Atlanta Campaign, the March to the Sea, and the Carolinas Campaign. He was promoted to brigadier general on March 13, 1865, bypassing the rank of colonel altogether. He was given command of a brigade on April 3.

Ewing was mustered out of volunteer service on December 1, 1865. He accepted a Regular Army commission as a captain in the 22nd Infantry but resigned from the army in 1867 and opened a law practice in Washington, D.C. In 1874, he became Catholic Commissioner for Indian Missions, which became the Bureau of Catholic Indian Missions. He still occupied this office when he died in Washington, D.C. of pneumonia and typhoid fever on June 20, 1883. He was forty-eight years old. He is buried in Arlington National Cemetery.

HUGH BOYLE EWING was one of three brothers who became Union generals. He was born in Lancaster, Ohio, on October 31, 1826. His well-connected family was wealthy, and he received an excellent education from private tutors and entered West Point in 1844. He resigned in May 1848, less than two months before he should have graduated, because he was failing engineering. He went to California during the gold rush of 1849 but was not successful. He returned to the east in 1852 and became a lawyer in St. Louis and then Leavenworth, Kansas. He returned to Ohio in 1858 to manage his father's salt works.

Ewing was appointed to the staff of the Ohio Militia when the Civil War began. Initially engaged in training recruits at Camp Dennison, he served with McClellan and Rosecrans in the Western Virginia Campaign and became colonel of the 30th Ohio Infantry on August 20, 1861. He participated in the Union victories at Rich Mountain (July 11) and Carnifex Ferry (September 10). In November 1861, his brother-in-law, William T. Sherman, was relieved of his command and sent home in disgrace. Hugh Ewing personally lobbied Abraham Lincoln and, with the help of his younger sister, succeeded in getting Sherman to return to active duty. Meanwhile, Ewing served in western Virginia and Maryland and became a brigade commander after General Reno was killed in action on September 14. He fought in the battles of South Mountain and Antietam, where he distinguished himself. Shortly afterward, he was sent on medical leave due to chronic dysentery.

Hugh Ewing returned to duty in January 1863 as a brigade commander in Sherman's XV Corps. He was promoted to brigadier general on April 4. He performed well and was given command of a division on July 20 after the fall of Vicksburg. He fought in the Siege of Chattanooga and the Battle of Missionary Ridge.

Ewing was hampered throughout his military career by debilitating rheumatism. In April 1864, he was transferred to a rear area assignment as commandant of Louisville, Kentucky, where he opposed the extreme policies of Major General Stephen Burbridge. He was sent to North Carolina in the closing weeks of the war. He was brevetted major general on January 13, 1866, and was discharged two days later.

After the South surrendered, Ewing continued to be plagued by painful attacks of rheumatism and was often bedridden for weeks at a time. He nevertheless served as U.S. minister to the Netherlands from 1866 to 1870. When he returned home, he retired to his farm near Lancaster, Ohio, where he wrote three books about California. He died on June 30, 1905, at the age of seventy-eight. He was buried in the Saint Mary Cemetery, Lancaster.

THOMAS EWING, JR. was born on August 7, 1829, in Lancaster, Ohio. His family was highly prominent politically and two of his brothers became Union generals. Although never formally adopted, William T. Sherman was his *de facto* foster brother and married Ewing's sister. Thomas and Sherman were close their entire lives.

Ewing attended Brown University but, at age nineteen, dropped out to become private secretary to President Zachary Taylor, while Ewing's father was secretary of the interior. After Taylor died, Thomas returned to Ohio, where he studied law, was admitted to the bar, and moved to Leavenworth, Kansas, in 1856. He became a fervent abolitionist, dabbled in politics, and was elected the first chief justice of the state of Kansas in 1861.

Ewing resigned his judgeship in 1862 and, on September 15, was named colonel of the 11th Kansas Infantry, a regiment he was largely responsible for raising. He fought in a few minor battles on the Kansas–Missouri line, as well as in the Battle of Prairie Grove, where he distinguished himself. As a result of this action and his political connections, he was promoted to brigadier general on March 17, 1863, despite his lack of military experience. He was given command of a division in the Army of the Frontier the following month. In June, he assumed command of the District of the Border. Here, on August 25, 1863, he issued the infamous General Order No. 11, requiring all citizens loyal to the South in three Missouri counties and part of a fourth to leave the area by September 9. Those who remained were to be expelled by Union cavalry. The order affected twenty thousand people, mostly old men, women, and children.

Ewing held several minor district commands in Missouri after that and dealt harshly with non-combatants. He also fought against Confederate General Sterling Price's invasion of Missouri, where he defended and successfully evacuated Fort Davidson, despite being badly outnumbered (September 27–29, 1864).

Ewing resigned his commission on February 23, 1865, and returned to civilian life. He was brevetted major general in 1866. He practiced law in Washington, D.C., from 1865 to 1870 and defended three of John Wilkes Booth's associates in the Lincoln assassination trials. He successfully kept them from the gallows, although four others were hanged. Meanwhile, he was offered the posts of secretary of war and attorney general by President Andrew Johnson but refused them. He returned to Ohio in 1870 and made several wise investments, especially in the railroad industry, which he was involved with since his Kansas days. He was elected to Congress as a Democrat in 1876 and served from 1877 to 1881. He narrowly lost the governor's race in 1879. After he left Congress, Ewing moved to New York City, set up a law practice, and never sought public office again. On January 20, 1896, he was struck by an omnibus and died the next day at age sixty-six. He is buried in Oakland Cemetery, Yonkers, New York.

F

FAIRCHILD – FULLER

LUCIUS "LOOSH" FAIRCHILD was born in Franklin Mills, Ohio, on December 27, 1831, while his parents were moving to Wisconsin. His father, a Democrat, later became the mayor of Madison and the treasurer of the state. Lucius attended Carroll College at Waukesha but heeded the call of adventure in 1849 and went to the gold fields of California, where he stayed for six years. He returned home a wealthy man in 1855. (He made more as a businessman selling food and supplies to miners than digging for gold.) He was elected clerk of court for Dane County as a Democrat in 1858. He was admitted to the bar in 1861 and switched to the Republican Party when the war broke out.

Fairchild enlisted as a private in the 1st Wisconsin Infantry on April 17, 1861, but became a captain on May 17, and fought in the First Battle of Bull Run. After the enlistments of his 90-day regiment expired, he accepted a captaincy in the Regular Army (16th U.S. Infantry Regiment) on August 5, but was soon named major in the 1st Wisconsin Infantry Regiment. He became lieutenant colonel of the 2nd Wisconsin Infantry, which was part of the Iron Brigade, on August 20. He fought in all the major battles on the Eastern Front in 1862 and 1863 and was promoted to colonel and commander of the 2nd Wisconsin on September 8, 1862. At Gettysburg, on the morning of July 1, Fairchild and his men launched an attack and captured James J. Archer, the first Confederate general from the Army of Northern Virginia to be taken prisoner. The regiment soon walked into an ambush, however, and lost 77 percent of its men. Fairchild was shot in the upper left arm and captured. The Rebel surgeons had to amputate the limb. He was returned to Virginia and exchanged on August 20.

Abraham Lincoln promoted Fairchild to brigadier general on October 19, 1863, but, no longer capable of field service, he resigned his commission on November 2. He returned home and resumed his political career. He was appointed secretary of state of Wisconsin in 1864 and served until 1866, when he was elected governor at age thirty-four. After three terms (1866–72), he held a series of diplomatic positions in Europe, including U.S.

consul to Liverpool, consult general to Paris, and envoy extraordinary and minister plenipotentiary to Spain. He returned home in 1881.

Fairchild was an outspoken Radical Republican who openly favored civil rights for African Americans and a longer and harsher Reconstruction. He was active in Union veterans affairs, served as commander-in-chief of the Grand Army of the Republic (1886–87), and was commander-in-chief of the Military Order of the Loyal Legion of the United States (1893–95). General Fairchild died in Madison on May 23, 1896, at age sixty-four. He is buried in Forest Hill Cemetery, Madison.

Fairchild's brother Cassius commanded an Ohio regiment and was brevetted brigadier general at the end of the war. He suffered from a wound he received at Shiloh for the rest of his life. In 1868, while serving as a pall bearer for a friend, his wound opened, and he bled to death. He was married ten days earlier.

ELON JOHN FARNSWORTH was born in Green Oak, Michigan, on July 30, 1837. He moved to Illinois with his parents in 1854. Elon attended the University of Michigan (1857–58) but was expelled for his part in a drunken party, during which a classmate was thrown out a window and killed. He promptly joined the army as a civilian foragemaster and took part in Albert Sidney Johnston's expedition against the Mormons. He also became a scout, freighter, and buffalo hunter in the Colorado Territory.

Farnsworth returned to Illinois when the Civil War began and joined the Union Army as a first lieutenant in the 8th Illinois Cavalry on September 18, 1861. His commanding officer was his uncle, John F. Farnsworth, who was later a brevet brigadier general and a member of Congress. Elon was promoted to captain on December 25 and became assistant chief quartermaster of the IV Corps, which fought in the Peninsula Campaign and the Seven Days battles. Farnsworth seems to have done a commendable job, but historians are at a loss to explaining why General Alfred Pleasonton, the Cavalry Corps commander, recommended him for promotion to brigadier general on June 28, 1863, and Lincoln nominated him for this rank the next day.

Farnsworth led his brigade against the Confederate cavalry with considerable dash, fighting in the streets of Hanover on July 1 and near Hunterstown on July 2. On July 3, just after the failure of Pickett's Charge, Farnsworth's division commander, Judson Kilpatrick, thought he saw an opportunity to destroy a large part of Robert E. Lee's army as the survivors of the debacle fell back to Seminary Ridge. (Sherman later called Kilpatrick a "hell of a damned fool.") He ordered Farnsworth to charge Hood's division (now commanded by Evander Law) on Longstreet's right flank, below Little Round Top. Farnsworth objected because he saw no hope of success. He only relented after Kilpatrick said he would lead the charge himself if Farnsworth was afraid to. Farnsworth was right. The attack was repulsed with heavy losses, among them General Farnsworth, who was shot at least three times in the chest. Confederate Colonel William C. Oates, who was only fifty paces away, reported that Farnsworth's horse was killed, he was pinned underneath it, and the general shot himself in the heart rather than surrender. Certain post-war historians have denounced this story as untrue. The reader may take his pick. I am of two minds on this issue. It does seem to me that three bullets in the chest would be enough to get the job done. On the other hand, Colonel Oates's account does have the ring of truth to it. In any case, it is certain that Elon Farnsworth died at Gettysburg on July 3, 1863. He was twenty-five years old and had been a general for four days. He was buried in the Rockton Cemetery, Rockton, Illinois.

General Kilpatrick was criticized for launching the rash, suicidal attack of July 3, but he received no punishment.

JOHN FRANKLIN FARNSWORTH was born on March 27, 1820, in Eaton (now Cookshire-Eaton), Quebec. The family moved to Ann Arbor, Michigan, in 1834. He attended the University of Michigan, studied law, was admitted to the bar in 1841, and set up a practice in St. Charles, Illinois. He was a Republican and was twice elected to Congress antebellum, serving from March 4, 1857 to March 3, 1861. He was not a candidate for re-election in 1860.

At the request of his friend, Abraham Lincoln, Farnsworth organized the 8th Illinois Cavalry and was commissioned its colonel on September 18, 1861. He led his regiment in the Peninsula Campaign, fought in the Battle of Williamsburg, and commanded a cavalry brigade in the Maryland Campaign, including the Battle of South Mountain. Lincoln appointed Farnsworth brigadier general on November 29, 1862. The Senate, however, did not confirm his nomination, returned it to the president on February 12, 1863, and Farnsworth reverted to the rank of colonel. Meanwhile, he was re-elected to Congress. He resigned his commission on March 4, 1863, the day the new Congress convened. He served until 1873. Farnsworth was in the room on April 15, 1865, when Abraham Lincoln died.

Farnsworth was a strong Radical Republican and voted in favor of impeaching President Andrew Johnson. After the national sentiment moderated, he was defeated for renomination in 1872. He attempted to shift with the mood of his constituents and ran as a Democrat in 1874 but was again defeated. He then moved to Chicago, where he resumed his law practice. He settled in Washington, D.C. in 1880 and practiced law there until his death on July 14, 1897, at age seventy-seven. He was buried in North Cemetery, St. Charles. He and his wife were married in 1846 and had six children. He was the uncle of Union General Elon J. Farnsworth.

EDWARD FERRERO was born in Granada, Andalusia, Spain, on January 18, 1831. His parents were both Italian and just arrived in Spain when their son was born. Thirteen months later, they emigrated to the United States. His father became a dance instructor in New York and opened a dance academy which catered to the wealthy and the elite of the city. Edward followed in his footsteps with great success. He took over the operation of the academy and became famous as an expert in dance. He was charming, witty, and had a sense of humor. He even wrote a book, *The Art of Dancing*, which was published in 1859. He was also a part-time dance instructor at West Point. Meanwhile, he became a lieutenant colonel in the 11th New York Militia. With his background in choreography and

ENCYCLOPEDIA OF UNION GENERALS

teaching, he soon had a regiment known for its precision on the parade field.

When the Civil War began, Ferrero fielded a regiment at his own expense. On October 14, 1861, he entered Federal service as colonel of the 51st New York Infantry. He led it in Burnside's successful Roanoke Island expedition in North Carolina. He led a brigade in the Union victory at New Bern in March 1862. Transferred north, he fought in the battles of the Second Bull Run, South Mountain, and Antietam, where he showed particular bravery at Burnside's Bridge. Meanwhile, he was promoted to brigadier general on September 10, 1862, and fought at Fredericksburg. His original appointment as brigadier general expired on March 4, 1863, without Senate action, so he reverted to the rank of colonel. He was reappointed on May 6, and this time he was confirmed.

After Fredericksburg, Ferrero and his men were transferred to the Western Front, where they distinguished themselves during the Siege of Vicksburg. As part of Burnside's IX Corps, he commanded the defense of Fort Sanders during the Knoxville Campaign. In late 1863, he had the opportunity to advance if he would assume command of an African American division. He accepted the command. He and the entire IX Corps were transferred to the Eastern Front in early 1864. Ferrero fought in the Siege of Petersburg and on July 30, 1864, his division (4,300 men) played a major role in the Battle of Crater; however, Ferrero remained in a bombproof to the rear while he and another division commander, Brigadier General James H. Ledlie, passed a bottle of rum back and forth. Meanwhile, his troops became a leaderless mass; the Confederates, who were initially stunned, rallied and inflicted a significant defeat on the North; which lost 3,800 men, and Ferrero's division was crushed. A major chance to capture Richmond and end the war was lost.

Ferrero underwent a court of inquiry and was officially censured but was not otherwise punished. He spent most of the rest of the war commanding a division of the Army of the James in the Bermuda Hundred defenses. He was brevetted major general on December 2. Ferrero took part in the Appomattox Campaign and was mustered out of the military on August 24, 1865. His name will live in Civil War infamy as one of the villains in the Crater debacle.

After the war, Ferrero resumed his dancing career and continued to experience his previous success. He even wrote another book, *The History of Dancing*, which is still in print. He died in New York City on December 11, 1899, at age sixty-eight. He was buried in Green-Wood Cemetery, Brooklyn.

ORRIS SANFORD FERRY was born in Bethel, Connecticut, on August 16, 1823. His father was a prosperous manufacturer. Orris attended Yale, where he distinguished himself as a public speaker. He graduated in 1844, was admitted to the bar in 1846, established a practice in Norwalk, and married the daughter of the governor. He spent seven years as a probate judge and three as a state's attorney (1856–1859) as well as two terms in the state senate. He joined the militia in 1847 as lieutenant colonel of the 12th Connecticut. Ferry also ran for Congress as a Republican in 1856 but lost. He won in 1858 but was defeated for re-election by a Democrat in 1860.

Ferry helped form a Connecticut militia formation when the Civil War began. On July 23, 1861, he was named colonel of the 5th Connecticut Infantry. He was sent to Virginia and launched a bold attack on the Rebels at Winchester in early March 1862. This led to Ferry being promoted to brigadier general on March 20. He became a brigade commander on May 1 and fought in the Shenandoah Valley Campaign of 1862 under General James Shields. He later fought under Nathaniel Banks in the Confederate victory at Cedar Mountain (August 9).

After Cedar Mountain, Ferry received only backwater assignments. He was transferred to the Department of the South and commanded a brigade and then a division in North Carolina. After a series of district commands, he led a division in the Army of the James in 1864. His last command was the District of Philadelphia (December 1864–June 1865). He was mustered out on July 15, 1865, and brevetted major general in 1867.

After the war, Ferry returned to the political world. In 1866, the Connecticut legislature deadlocked on who to send to the U.S. Senate. Ferry was chosen as a compromise candidate. A former Radical Republican, he reversed himself as a senator and came out for moderation, including granting amnesty to former Confederates. He was, however, pressured into voting to impeach Andrew Johnson. He voted against the Civil Rights Act of 1875.

In an era noted for its corruption, Ferry was incorruptible. He was re-elected to the Senate in 1872 but was attacked by a rare disease which caused a slow degeneration of the spine. After months of suffering, he died in Norwalk, Connecticut, on November 21, 1875, at age fifty-two. He is buried in the Union Cemetery at Norwalk.

FRANCIS FESSENDEN was born in Portland, Maine, on March 18, 1839, into a politically prominent family. His father was a U.S. senator and secretary of the treasury in Lincoln's cabinet, his older brother James also became a Union general, and two of his uncles were U.S. Congressmen. Another brother, Lieutenant Samuel Fessenden, was mortally wounded in the Second Battle of Bull Run.

Fessenden was well educated in local schools and at Bowdoin College, from which he graduated in 1858. When the war began, he was commissioned captain in the Regular Army, despite having no military background. He was assigned to the 19th U.S. Infantry Regiment and spent much of 1861 as a recruiter. He rejoined his unit in time for the Battle of Shiloh, where he was severely wounded in the arm. After he recovered, he was promoted to colonel (September 29) and given command of the 25th Maine Infantry. The following month, he was placed in command of a brigade in the Washington defenses. He was mustered out of volunteer service in July 1863 and reverted to his Regular Army rank of captain. On January 11, 1864, however, he was re-promoted to the rank of colonel and named commander of the 30th Maine.

Fessenden and his regiment were sent to Louisiana, where they took part in the Red River Campaign, including the disastrous Battle of Mansfield. When Colonel Lewis Benedict was killed in action at Pleasant Hill (April 9, 1864), Fessenden succeeded him as brigade commander.

During the Battle of Monett's Ferry (April 23), Banks's Army of the Gulf was surrounded by the Confederate Army of Western Louisiana. Fessenden led the breakout that saved the army. The cost was high for him personally, however: a Rebel bullet shattered his right leg, which was amputated. He was still recovering on May 13, 1864, when he was promoted to brigadier general.

Francis Fessenden spent the rest of the war on garrison duty in the Washington area or commanding wagon trains. He was promoted to major general on November 9, 1865, an advancement which can only be explained by his father's political prominence. He was a member of the military court that tried Andersonville Prison commandant Henry Wirz and sentenced him to death.

Fessenden was mustered out of volunteer service on September 1, 1866, but briefly remained in the Regular Army as a captain. He retired on November 1 as a brigadier general. He returned to Portland, resumed his legal career, and was elected mayor of the city in 1876. He also wrote a biography of his father, which was published in 1907.

General Francis Fessenden died in Portland on January 2, 1906, at age sixty-six. He is buried in Evergreen Cemetery, Portland, Maine.

JAMES DEERING FESSENDEN was born on September 28, 1833, in Westbrook, Maine, into a nationally prominent political family (see essay on Francis Fessenden). He was educated locally and at Bowdoin College, where he studied law. He was admitted to the bar and joined his father's law firm.

Shortly after the outbreak of the war, he organized a company that became part of the 2nd U.S. Sharpshooters Regiment. He was commissioned captain on November 2, 1861, and was initially posted to the Washington defenses. In March 1862, his father used his influence to have James promoted to lieutenant colonel and assigned to the staff of General David Hunter, who was commanding Union operations against Charleston, South Carolina. Here, Fessenden engaged in organizing the first African American regiment in Federal service—the

1st South Carolina Infantry. His action was subsequently repudiated by the government. He was nevertheless promoted to colonel on July 16, 1862.

Fessenden had a riding accident in January 1863 and did not return to duty until November, when he was appointed an aide-de-camp to General Hooker in Tennessee. Fessenden distinguished himself in the Battle of Missionary Ridge (November 25), and Hooker was so impressed with him, he recommended him for promotion, but no action was taken. Hooker recommended him three additional times during the Atlanta Campaign. The promotion was finally approved on August 8, 1864, but Hooker was transferred elsewhere, and Fessenden did not receive a brigade command until October, with the Army of the Shenandoah. James fought in the Battle of Cedar Creek and then was placed in command of the garrison at Winchester, Virginia. In this post, he also commanded a brigade in the XIX Corps. After the Confederate surrender, he directed occupation forces in South Carolina before being discharged on January 15, 1866. He was brevetted major general in February 1866.

James Fessenden returned to Portland in 1866 and resumed his law practice. He served three terms in the Maine legislature and was U.S. Register of Bankruptcy for his area (1868–78). He died in Portland on November 18, 1882, at age forty-nine. He is buried in the Evergreen Cemetery.

CLINTON BOWEN FISK was born on December 8, 1828, in York County, western New York, the fifth son of a blacksmith. His family relocated to Coldwater, Michigan, shortly after. His father died of typhoid fever in 1832, throwing the family into poverty. Clinton had to start work for a farmer at a young age. His mother remarried when he was thirteen and he was sent to the Wesleyan Seminary in Albion, Michigan. He attended the newly formed Michigan Central College but apparently dropped out because of eye problems. He became an entrepreneur and merchant in Coldwater and eventually established his own small bank. He was financially wiped out in the Panic of 1857. He then moved to St. Louis and went into the insurance business.

In May 1861, Fisk enlisted as a private in the Missouri Militia. When the St. Louis Merchant Exchange appeared likely to influence Missouri in favor of the South, he established the Union Merchants Exchange, which soon absorbed the old exchange.

In July 1862, he began recruiting a regiment for the Union. On September 5, he became colonel of the 33rd Missouri Infantry. He was promoted to brigadier general on November 24, 1862. Fisk spent most of the war in Missouri and Arkansas, fighting Confederate guerrillas and cavalry raids, although he did command a brigade in the Army of the Tennessee from early 1863 until that June. He was successful in his Trans-Mississippi operations and proved to be a good general, despite his lack of military background and training.

Clinton B. Fisk was a fervent abolitionist and prohibitionist who never drank nor swore. He worked hard to improve the lot of recently freed slaves and after the war accepted an appointment as assistant commissioner of the Bureau of Refugees, Freedmen, and Abandoned Lands (called the Freedmen's Bureau) for Kentucky and Tennessee. Working with the American Missionary Association, he made the abandoned barracks in Nashville, Tennessee, available for the creation of Fisk College, which grew into Fisk University, a major seat of African American education. He endowed it with $30,000 of his own money.

After the legislation authorizing the Freedmen's Bureau expired, Fisk was involved in a variety of businesses, including banking, mining, and land speculation. He was vice president and treasurer for the Missouri Pacific Railroad and the Atlantic & Pacific Railroad from 1866 to 1876. He then returned to New York as president of the New York Accident Insurance Company and served on the board of directors of a number of colleges and charitable organizations. In 1889, he was one of the founders of Harriman, a utopian temperance settlement in east Tennessee. He was a humble man from humble beginnings and did not mind spending his own money on causes he considered righteous. He improved a great many lives.

Fisk became the Prohibition Party's nominee for New Jersey governor in 1886 and received the largest number of votes that group ever received in the Garden State (19,808 votes or 8.55 percent). He was the party's presidential nominee in 1888 and garnered a quarter of a million votes.

In the fall of 1889, General Fisk contracted heart disease and later influenza. Confined to his home in New York City, he died on July 9, 1890. He was sixty-one years old. He was buried in Oak Grove Cemetery, Coldwater, Michigan.

MANNING FERGUSON FORCE was born on December 17, 1824, in Washington, D.C., where his father was the mayor. Well-educated in the Benjamin Hallowell School at Alexandria, Virginia, he turned down an appointment from West Point and attended Harvard, from which he graduated in 1845. He then attended Harvard Law School and matriculated in 1848. He was admitted to the Ohio bar in 1850 and started a practice in Cincinnati.

Force joined the Union Army as major of the 20th Ohio Infantry on August 26, 1861. He was promoted to lieutenant colonel (September 11, 1861), colonel (May 1, 1862), and brigadier general (August 11, 1863). In the process, he proved to be an excellent commander. He fought at Fort Donelson, Shiloh, the Siege of Corinth, the various campaigns for Vicksburg, and the Siege of Vicksburg. Promoted to the command of a brigade in the Army of the Tennessee on June 3, 1863, he took part in the Battle of Chickamauga, the Siege of Chattanooga, the Battle of Missionary Ridge, and the Atlanta Campaign. He performed so well that he was awarded the Congressional Medal of Honor for his courage during the Battle of Atlanta (July 22, 1864), a medal which he received in 1892. He was also severely wounded, and his face disfigured for life. After he recovered, General Force took part in the March to the Sea and the Carolinas Campaign. He was given command of a division on April 5, 1865. He was brevetted major general on January 13, 1866, and mustered out on January 15.

After the war, General Force returned to Cincinnati and became was elected judge of the Hamilton County Common Pleas Court. Later, he was elected justice on the Superior Court of Cincinnati. He also was a faculty member of the Cincinnati Law School, authored a several books on the law, early Indian tribes, and Civil War history, was president of the Cincinnati Historical Society, and became a bit of an authority on archeology.

Force suffered a nervous breakdown from stress and overwork in 1887 and resigned his judgeship. He was governor of the Soldiers' Home and Sailors' Home in Sandusky, Ohio, a post he held from 1888 until his death in Cincinnati or Sandusky (depending upon the source) on May 8, 1899, at age seventy-four. He was interred in Spring Grove Cemetery, Cincinnati.

He and General John Pope were brothers-in-law (they married sisters), and he was close friends with Rutherford B. Hayes, who named one of his children after Force.

JAMES WILLIAM FORSYTH was born in Maumee, Ohio, on August 8, 1834. He was educated in local schools and entered West Point in 1851. It took him five years to graduate (28/49), but he was commissioned second lieutenant in the 9th U.S. Infantry. He was sent to San Juan Island in Washington Territory, where his commander was future Confederate General George Pickett. He was promoted to first lieutenant on July 1, 1861, and to captain on October 24. Meanwhile, the Civil War began, and he was recalled to the east, where he was named commander of the 64th Ohio Infantry with the rank of colonel of volunteers on November 1. He assumed temporary command of a brigade in Buell's Army of the Ohio in January 1862. The regular commander, James A. Garfield, returned to duty on April 5, and Forsyth then reverted to the rank of captain and was transferred to the Army of the Potomac, so he missed the Battle of Shiloh.

Forsyth served on McClellan's staff as assistant inspector general during the Peninsula Campaign and Seven Days battles. He was an aide to General Mansfield at Antietam until that officer was killed. He then became provost marshal of the Army of the Potomac until May 1863, when he transferred back to the Western Front. He was Philip Sheridan's adjutant at Chickamauga, where he performed well in a disastrous situation. When Sheridan was promoted to commander of the Cavalry Corps of the Army of the Potomac and later as commander of the Army of the Shenandoah, he carried Forsyth with him as chief of staff. He served in the Overland Campaign, the Valley Campaign of 1864, and the Appomattox Campaign.

Meanwhile, he was promoted to major on April 7, 1864, and to lieutenant colonel twelve days later. He was advanced to the rank of brigadier general on May 19, 1865. He skipped the rank of colonel altogether.

Forsyth once again reverted to the rank of captain in January 1866 but was promoted to major, Regular Army, in July. He became a lieutenant colonel in 1869 and colonel in 1886. He spent almost all his post-war career fighting Indians on the Western Frontier. His opponents included Comanche, Cheyenne, Arapaho, Kiowa, and Lakota Sioux. He also monitored the Crow, Creek, and Atsina Indians. Forsythe did spend a year in Europe, observing the Franco-Prussian War. He assumed command of the 7th U.S. Cavalry in July 1886. On December 29, 1890, he led it during the Wounded Knee Massacre, in which more than 250 men, women, and children were slaughtered, and over fifty were wounded but survived. Thirty-one soldiers were killed and thirty-three were wounded.

James Forsyth became a brigadier general in 1894 and commanded the Department of California. He was promoted to major general on May 11, 1897, and retired three days later. He died in Columbus, Ohio, on October 24, 1906, at age seventy-two. He is buried there in Green Lawn Cemetery.

JOHN GRAY FOSTER was born in Whitefield, New Hampshire, on May 27, 1823. His family moved to Nashua in 1833 and he was educated at Hancock Academy. He entered West Point in 1842 and graduated in 1846 (4/59). Commissioned brevet second lieutenant of engineers, he was attached to the Company of Sappers, Miners, and Pontoniers, and he fought at Vera Cruz, Cerro Gordo, Contreras, and Churubusco in Mexico, where he was brevetted first lieutenant and captain and was severely wounded in the leg at Molino del Rey. He was disabled by his wound and a case of dysentery for several months. His interwar service included constructing fortifications and a tour of duty as an instructor at West Point. He was stationed in Charleston, South Carolina, in 1858, and was second-in-command to Major Robert Anderson during the reduction of Fort Sumter (April 12-13, 1861). Meanwhile, Foster was promoted to second lieutenant in 1848, first lieutenant in 1854, and captain in 1860. He was brevetted major for his gallantry at Fort Sumter.

On October 23, 1861, he was promoted to brigadier general of volunteers and given command of a brigade in Burnside's North Carolina Expedition, in which he played a major role. In April 1862, he was made a division commander and in July assumed command of the Department of North Carolina. He was promoted to major general on August 20, 1862. In this post, he successfully defended Washington, NC, from attacks by D. H. Hill and won a couple of minor victories at Kinston and Goldsboro.

Foster has been criticized for his attitude toward African Americans. He never believed in using black troops and made no attempt to recruit them. He was, however, a man of energy and commanding presence. He was transferred to east Tennessee, where he assumed command of the XVIII Corps in November 1863. He fought in the Knoxville Campaign and was named commander of the Army (and Department) of the Ohio on December 9, 1863. His tenure was short. On February 9, 1864, his horse fell on him and broke his leg. He returned to active duty on May 26 as commander of the Department of the South, which controlled Union forces on the coasts of Florida, Georgia, and the Carolinas. His attempts to take Charleston, however, were noteworthy failures. From July to September 1864, for example, he bombarded Fort Sumter and Charleston for sixty days, and 14,666 rounds of artillery were fired at the fort. Still it held out until February 17, 1865, when the Rebels abandoned it as part of the evacuation of Charleston. Meanwhile, on February 6, 1865, Foster took a leave of absence for health reasons.

Postwar, Foster briefly commanded the Department of Florida and the Military Division of the Gulf until he was mustered out of volunteer service in September 1866 and reverted to his regular army rank of major of engineers. He was promoted to lieutenant colonel in 1867 and colonel in 1871.

Among other duties, Foster was engaged in underwater surveying and became an authority on underwater demolition. He was assistant to the chief of engineers in Washington from 1871 to 1874, and was superintendent of the Harbor of Refuge on Lake Erie in 1874. He died during a visit to his hometown (Nashua, New Hampshire) on September 2, 1874. He was fifty-one years old. He was buried in the Nashua Cemetery.

ROBERT SANFORD "SANDY" FOSTER was born in Vernon, Indiana, on January 27, 1834. He moved to Indianapolis when he was sixteen, worked in his uncle's grocery store, and eventually became a tinsmith. He enlisted as a private in the Indiana volunteers two days after Fort Sumter surrendered, and six days later was promoted to captain and company commander in 11th Indiana Infantry. He married on May 1, 1861, and left for war on May 8. Foster fought at Rich Mountain in the Western Virginia Campaign, where he captured two guns. He moved up rapidly in rank, to major of the 13th Indiana (June 19), lieutenant colonel (October 28), and colonel and regimental commander (April 30, 1862).

Foster fought against Stonewall Jackson in the Valley Campaign of 1862. He was transferred to southeast Virginia after that and was given command of a brigade at Suffolk. He subsequently took part in the Siege of Suffolk when Longstreet unsuccessfully tried to capture the place. He did well in these operations and, in recognition of this fact, was promoted to brigadier general on June 12, 1863. He was soon transferred to the X Corps, which was trying to capture Charleston, South Carolina. Here, the Federal forces were less successful. Foster was nevertheless given command of a division in late 1863.

Sandy Foster served as chief of staff to General Gilmore during the Bermuda Hundred Campaign. He briefly reverted to brigade command before taking charge of a division in the Army of the James. He fought in the Siege of Petersburg and in the Appomattox Campaign. After the surrender, Foster sat on the military commission that tried the conspirators who were involved in the assassination of Abraham Lincoln. He resigned his commission on September 25, 1865, and was brevetted major general in 1866.

Foster declined a Regular Army commission, returned to Indianapolis in 1865, and held a variety of local offices, including alderman, city treasurer (1867–1872), and president of the Board of Trade. President Garfield appointed him U.S. marshal in 1881, a post he held until 1885. He later served as director of Northern Prison and Quartermaster-General of the Indiana National Guard.

At age sixty-nine, General Foster died in Indianapolis on March 3, 1903. He is buried there in Crown Hill Cemetery.

WILLIAM BUEL FRANKLIN was born on February 27, 1823, in York, Pennsylvania. His father was Clerk of the U.S. House of Representatives. William received an appointment to West Point and graduated at the top of the Class of 1843 (1/39). He was commissioned brevet second lieutenant in the Corps of Topographical Engineers and took part in the survey of the Great Lakes and then the Rocky Mountains. He fought in the Mexican War and was brevetted for his conduct at Buena Vista. Meanwhile, he was promoted to second lieutenant in 1846. He became a first lieutenant in 1853 and captain in 1857.

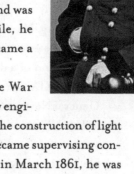

After Mexico, Franklin was assigned to the War Department in Washington. In 1857, he became army engineer secretary of the Light House Board and oversaw the construction of light houses in Maine and New Hampshire. In 1859, he became supervising construction engineer for the U.S. Capitol Dome, and in March 1861, he was appointed supervising architect for the Treasury Building in Washington. He was named colonel of the 12th U.S. Infantry Regiment on May 14, 1861.

Franklin commanded a brigade at the First Bull Run (July 21) and was given command of a division immediately after this defeat. He was promoted to brigadier general on August 6, 1861. As the army expanded, Franklin was named commander of the VI Corps on May 18, 1862, and led it in the Peninsula Campaign and the Seven Days battles. He was promoted to major general on July 16, 1862.

William Franklin arrived too late to see action in the Second Battle of Bull Run and was charged with failure to obey orders by General Pope. It appears the charges were justified. He led VI Corps in the Maryland Campaign, including the Battles of Crampton's Gap (a.k.a South Mountain) and Antietam, where his corps was held in reserve. Franklin begged General Sumner to allow him to attack a weak point in the Confederate center but Sumner, the senior officer, refused. If Franklin had been given his way, they would likely have destroyed the Army of Northern Virginia.

ENCYCLOPEDIA OF UNION GENERALS

Franklin was a good friend of General George McClellan, so he was not considered for command of the Army of the Potomac when Lincoln sacked that officer. He commanded the "Left Grand Division" (the I and VI Corps) in the Battle of Fredericksburg, where his performance was controversial. When George Meade's division breached Stonewall Jackson's lines, Franklin failed to promptly reinforce it, and the Union's best chance to win a victory on that field was lost. He was caught up in the political maneuvering of 1862–63 and joined the cabal which sought to remove General Burnside from command of the Army of the Potomac. In retaliation, Burnside did what he could to damage Franklin's career—with some success. In any case, Franklin's career entered a downward spiral after Fredericksburg. He refused to serve under Joe Hooker (Burnside's replacement) and was unemployed from January 25 to July 28, 1863, when he was given command of a division in the Army of the Gulf. He assumed command of the XIX Corps the following month.

General Newton Curtis recalled: "General Franklin was an officer of general ability, standing among the first rank in the army." When Grant became general-in-chief, he wanted to give him a more important post but was blocked by Secretary of War Stanton. Franklin was definitely on probation when he arrived in Louisiana, where his performance was less than awe-inspiring. At Mansfield (April 8, 1864), the decisive battle of the Red River Campaign, his horse was shot from under him, and he was wounded in the leg. He remained with the troops, but his physical condition deteriorated to the point that he had to give up command on May 2.

General Franklin's career effectively ended in Louisiana. He was never given another command, despite the efforts of his old friend and West Point classmate, Ulysses S. Grant. He did achieve a rather dubious distinction on July 11, 1864. Many historians have written that George Stoneman was the senior Union general captured in the war, but he was not. Franklin was. He was on board a train near Baltimore when he was taken prisoner by partisans commanded by Confederate Major Harry Gilmor. Fortunately for Franklin, the Rebels had been riding for two days, and his guards were exhausted. They fell asleep, and the alert general managed to escape in the pre-dawn darkness of July 12. He was a prisoner for only a few hours.

236

William Franklin resigned his commission on March 15, 1866, settled in Hartford, Connecticut, and became vice president of the Colt Firearms Manufacturing Company, a position he held from 1865 to 1887. Simultaneously, he supervised the construction of the Connecticut State Capitol and other public projects. He also spent two years as adjutant general of Connecticut. He was U.S. commissioner general at the Paris Exposition of 1889.

Franklin was undoubtedly a better engineer than he was a field commander, where his performance was mixed. He died in Hartford from complications of senility on March 8, 1903, at age eighty. He is buried in Prospect Hill Cemetery, York, Pennsylvania. He and Mrs. Franklin had no children. His oldest brother Samuel became a rear admiral in 1885. His youngest brother Walter was a brevet lieutenant colonel.

JOHN CHARLES FREMONT was born on January 21, 1813, in Savannah, Georgia, the son of a French-Canadian school teacher and a woman to whom he was not married, which was considered scandalous in 1813. His life was plagued by drama, controversy, and scandal, exacerbated by his own impetuous behavior. He was, however, handsome, bold, and extremely charismatic.

Fremont enrolled in Charleston College, South Carolina, in 1829 but was expelled for irregular attendance in 1831. He became a navigational mathematics teacher aboard a U.S. Navy sloop in 1833 and sailed to South America. Later, he secured an appointment as a second lieutenant in the U.S. Topographical Corps, where he worked in the mountains of North and South Carolina. He decided to become an explorer, at which he was first rate. He joined Joseph Nicollet and was involved in exploring lands between the Mississippi and Missouri Rivers. Here he came in contact with U.S. Senator Thomas Hart Benton of Missouri, who invited Fremont to his home. Fremont (who was 28) swept Jessie Benton, the senator's sixteen-year-old daughter, off her feet and eloped with her in 1841. Benton (who opposed the marriage) was initially furious but, because of his love for his daughter, eventually became Fremont's patron.

With Benton's backing, Fremont became one of the greatest explorers in American history. Known as "the Pathfinder of the West," he made five expeditions, and his maps guided thousands of American emigrants. The accurate maps covered many places, including the entire Oregon Trail. He fought Indians, played a major role in opening up California, and fought in the Mexican War. He briefly served as military governor of California but was court-martialed for disobedience of orders and misconduct. He was convicted and dismissed from the service in January 1848. President Polk confirmed the conviction but set aside the dismissal. Fremont resigned his commission in early 1848.

Gold was discovered on his California ranch, and Fremont became very wealthy. His worth was estimated at $10,000,000 ($250,000,000 in today's money.) With money, fame, and political influence, he became California's first U.S. senator in 1850. A Free Soiler, Fremont was defeated for reelection by a pro-slavery candidate in 1851. He was the Republican Party's first presidential nominee in 1856. The campaign was brutal and the Democrats (who were better organized and better funded) attacked Fremont's illegitimate birth. Their candidate, James Buchanan, carried nineteen states. Fremont carried eleven, which is still impressive, given the circumstances.

Abraham Lincoln appointed Fremont major general on June 1, 1861, and named him commander of the Department of the West. He arrived in St. Louis on July 25 and immediately engaged in a political feud with the powerful Blair family. He also spent public funds lavishly, lived like a European monarch, doled out contracts to his friends, and was unable to prevent the Confederates from occupying half the state. He also issued the first Emancipation Proclamation, which Lincoln immediately repudiated. The president sacked Fremont on November 2.

On March 29, 1862, Lincoln yielded to political pressure from the abolitionists and Radical Republicans and recalled Fremont to active duty. He was given command of the Mountain Department (i.e., West Virginia) and, along with two other armies, was ordered to trap and destroy Stonewall Jackson. The Rebel, however, defeated all three forces. Fremont (who had 11,500 men) was beaten at Cross Keys on June 8 by 5,800 Rebels and retreated back into West Virginia. He was later named commander of the I

Corps of John Pope's Army of Virginia, but he refused to serve under that officer. He withdrew to New York City expecting another command, but none was forthcoming. He resigned his commission on June 4, 1864.

The Radical Democracy Party nominated Fremont for president in May 1864, but he reluctantly withdrew from the race on September 22. The Pathfinder lost his fortune in railroad adventures, land speculation, and bad investments. President Hayes appointed him governor of Arizona Territory in 1878, but he spent so little time there he was asked to attend to his duties or resign. He resigned in 1881. He was almost destitute in April 1890, when the War Department appointed him major general on the retired list.

General Fremont died of peritonitis (an abdominal infection) in New York City on July 13, 1890, at age seventy-seven. Initially interred in the Trinity Church Cemetery, he was reburied in Rockland Cemetery, Sparkill, New York, in 1891. He had five children, one of whom became a rear admiral.

WILLIAM HENRY "BLINKY" FRENCH was born on January 13, 1815, in Baltimore, Maryland. He attended West Point and graduated with the Class of 1837 (22/50). Appointed second lieutenant in the 1st Artillery, he was promoted to first lieutenant in 1838. He fought in the Seminole War, helped transport the Cherokee Nation from North Carolina to Indian Territory, served on the Northern frontier during the boundary dispute with England, and fought in Mexican War, where he was aide-de-camp to Franklin Pierce and served on the staff of General Patterson. He was brevetted captain for Cerro Gordo and major for Contreras and Churubusco. He was promoted to captain (substantive rank) in 1848.

From 1850 to 1852, he again fought the Seminoles in Florida. Here, one of his lieutenants, the future Stonewall Jackson, filed several charges against him, but he escaped conviction. After Florida, he served on the frontier until the Civil War began. He was in west Texas when Texas seceded but managed to escape with his command. He was promoted to brigadier general on September 28, 1861.

Blinky French served on the Eastern Front from 1861 to 1864, seeing action at Yorktown, Seven Pines, the Seven Days battles, Antietam, Fredericksburg, Chancellorsville, Gettysburg, and the Mine Run Campaign. He assumed command of a division on September 10, 1862, and was promoted to major general on March 11, 1863. After General Sickles was wounded on July 2, he served as acting commander of the III Corps at Gettysburg.

General French's military career was ruined during the Mine Run Campaign, when General Meade accused him of indecisiveness and moving too slowly. When the III Corps was dissolved in the spring of 1864, French was mustered out of volunteer service on May 6. He reverted to his regular army rank of colonel and spent the rest of the war in Washington, serving on various boards.

Cullum called French "a good disciplinarian . . . firm in his convictions . . . and withal was a jovial compassion, full of wit and sparking humor." Postwar, French commanded the 2nd U.S. Artillery Regiment on the Pacific Coast (1865–72). He commanded Fort McHenry near Baltimore from 1875 to 1880, after which he retired. He died in Washington, D.C., on May 20, 1881. He was sixty-six. General French was buried in Rock Creek Cemetery, Washington, D.C.

His grandson, John French Conklin, became a brigadier general in the United States Army.

JAMES BARNET FRY was born on February 22, 1827, in Carrollton, Illinois, the first child of General Jacob G. Fry. He entered the U.S. Military Academy in 1843 and graduated in 1847 (14/38). Commissioned brevet second lieutenant in the artillery, he was retained at West Point as an instructor of artillery. He was sent to Mexico, where he took part in Scott's drive on Mexico City. He remained in the Mexican capital on occupation duty for some months. Later, he performed garrison duty at Fort Columbus in New York harbor; Fort Vancouver, Washington Territory; Astoria, Oregon Territory; Fort Monroe, Virginia; Baton Rouge, Louisiana; and Fort Leavenworth, Kansas. He also did another tour at West Point and helped suppress John Brown's raid on Harpers Ferry in 1859. He commanded a battery of light artillery in Washington, D.C., when the Civil War began. Meanwhile, he was promoted to second lieutenant (1847), first lieutenant (1851), and captain (March 16, 1861).

Fry was chief of staff to Irvin McDowell during the First Bull Run Campaign. In November 1861, he became chief of staff of the Army of the Ohio under Don Carlos Buell and fought at Shiloh, in the Siege of Corinth, and the Battle of Perryville. He was promoted to major (April 22, 1862) and lieutenant colonel (December 31, 1862). He was brevetted brigadier general for his services at Shiloh and Perryville.

General Fry was transferred to the adjutant general's office in Washington, D.C., at the end of 1862. He was promoted to colonel and became provost marshal general of the U.S. Army on March 17, 1863, and was responsible for enforcing military law, finding and arresting deserters, and directing the Invalid Corps. He and his men arrested 76,562 deserters during the war and conscripted 1,120,621 men into the service as part of the draft. He was promoted to brigadier general (substantive rank) on March 22, 1864, and directed the provost office until it was abolished in the autumn of 1866. He was brevetted major general in 1866.

Fry reverted to his regular army rank of lieutenant colonel in 1866 and was on duty in the Division of the Pacific (1866–1869), the Division of the South (1869–1871), the Division of the Missouri (1871–1873), and the Division of the Atlantic (1873–1881). He was promoted to colonel, regular army, in 1875 and retired in 1881. After that, he wrote a number of military history books, including one defending his old chief, Buell, and another generally favorable to Irvin McDowell.

James B. Fry was a fine staff officer and astute and prolific military historian. He died in Newport, Rhode Island, on July 11, 1894, at age sixty-seven. He was interred in Saint James the Less Episcopal Churchyard, Philadelphia.

SPEED SMITH FRY was born in Mercer County (now Boyle County), near Danville, Kentucky, on September 9, 1817. He graduated from Wabash College, Indiana, in 1840 and set up a law practice in Danville. He joined

the 2nd Kentucky Infantry when the Mexican War began, was promoted to captain, and fought at Buena Vista. He practiced law in Mercer County and served as judge from 1857 to 1861.

Fry was appointed colonel in the Kentucky Militia in July 1861. He helped recruit the 4th (U.S.) Kentucky Infantry and on October 9 was named its colonel. He distinguished himself in the Battle of Mill Springs (January 19, 1862), where he personally shot and killed Confederate General Felix Zollicoffer. Fry was promoted to brigadier general on March 22.

General Fry was given a brigade in Buell's Army of the Ohio. He arrived on the field at Shiloh late on April 7—too late to take part in the battle. General Buell made it plain that he was not satisfied with Fry's performance. He served in the Siege of Corinth and in the Battle of Perryville, which was fought within a few miles of his birthplace. After Buell was sacked, Fry was given command of a division in Rosecrans's Army of the Cumberland. Again, he proved too slow and most of his division did not fight in the Battle of Stones River. Rosecrans was also unhappy with his work and sacked him in January 1863.

Speed Fry was unemployed until the summer of 1863, when he took command of Camp Nelson, the Army of the Ohio's massive supply, recruiting, and training base south of Nicholasville, Kentucky. Here he impressed thousands of African Americans into the Union war effort. Initially they were used as laborers to expand the road network, but in 1864 enough volunteered to be soldiers to form eight combat regiments.

Fry's treatment of African Americans was harsh. On August 9, he ordered "that all negro women and children, old and infirm, negro men unfit for any military duty . . . be at once sent beyond the lines with instructions not to return." Even so, on November 6, he was named commander of the Sub-district of North Central Kentucky, but he retained command of Camp Nelson.

When more African American civilians (mostly relatives of soldiers) sought shelter at Camp Nelson that winter, he issued his famous "Impulsion Order" of November 23, which expelled four hundred of them from camp in the middle of a winter storm. Fry's superior officer, General Burbridge, quickly rescinded the order and 250 refugees returned to the camp, but at least 102 of them (mostly women and children) died as a result of Fry's cruel treatment. Fry was suspended from command but only for a week. He was never formally reprimanded and continued commanding the camp until March 29, 1865.

Fry was not given the normal brevet promotion to major general at the end of the war. Mustered out in August 1865, he ran for Congress as a Republican in 1866 but was defeated. He then became supervisor of Internal Revenue Service collections in his local area. He also served as an elder of the local Presbyterian Church.

General Fry died near Louisville on August 1, 1892, at the age of seventy-four. He is buried in the Bellevue Cemetery, Danville, Kentucky.

JOHN WALLACE FULLER was born in Harston, England, on July 28, 1827, the son of a Baptist minister. His family emigrated to Oneida County, New York, when Fuller was six. He was homeschooled, largely by his highly educated father. He began working at a bookstore and later owned a publishing business in Utica. He became the city's treasurer and was active in the militia. His business was destroyed by a fire in 1858, and he moved to Toledo, Ohio, which became his home for the rest of his life. He soon started a book publishing business there.

When the Civil War began, Fuller was sent to Grafton, Virginia (now West Virginia), to drill troops. He was appointed commander of the 27th Ohio Infantry on August 18, 1861. He served in Missouri under John Pope and took part in the capture of New Madrid and Island No. 10 (February 28–April 8, 1862). He assumed command of a brigade in the Army of the Mississippi on September 10 and fought at Iuka and in the Second Battle of Corinth. He distinguished himself in the Battle of Parker's Crossroads on December 31, when (for the only time in the war) he took Nathan Bedford Forrest by surprise, attacked him in the rear, and saved a Union brigade, which was at the point of surrendering. Forrest only just managed

ENCYCLOPEDIA OF UNION GENERALS

to escape, and Parker's Crossroads ended his (Forrest's) Second West Tennessee raid.

Fuller spent most of 1863 on garrison duty, much of it in Memphis. He captured Decatur, Alabama, in March 1864 and was promoted to brigadier general on April 10. He joined the Army of the Tennessee in the spring of 1864 and fought in the Atlanta Campaign, where he earned a commendation from General McPherson. He temporarily commanded a division during the battles around Atlanta in July 1864. He led his brigade in the March to the Sea and the Carolinas Campaign. He resigned from the service on August 15, 1865, and was brevetted major general in 1866.

Postbellum, Fuller returned to the business world and became a wholesaler of boots and shoes. President Grant appointed him collector for the port of Toledo in 1874. He was reappointed by President Hayes and held this post until 1881. General Fuller retired in 1888 and died in Toledo on March 12, 1891, at age sixty-three. He was interred in the Woodlawn Cemetery, Toledo, Ohio.

G

GAMBLE – GROVER

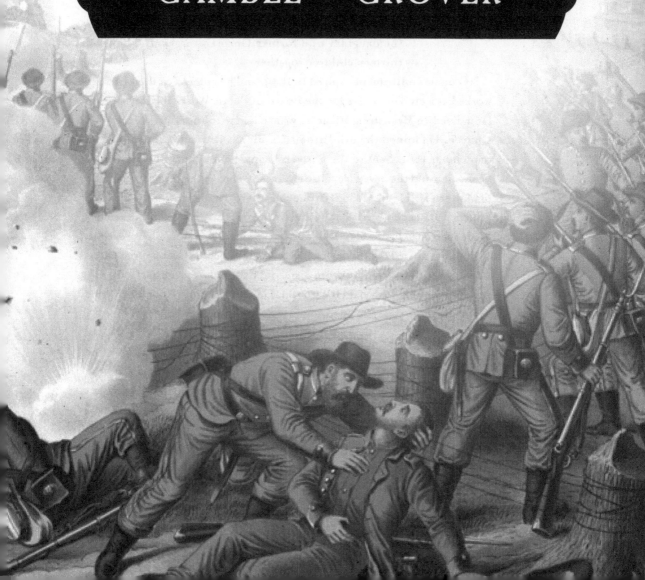

WILLIAM GAMBLE was a native Irishman, born on New Year's Day, 1818. His birthplace is variously cited as County Tyrone, Northern Ireland; Duross; Lisnarick; and County Fermanagh. In any case, he studied surveying and civil engineering, and took part in the Northern Ireland survey. He also served briefly in the British dragoons. (He loved both horses and scholarly pursuits.) Gamble emigrated to the United States in 1838 and enlisted as a private in the 1st Dragoons Regiment. He was promoted rapidly to corporal, sergeant, first sergeant, and sergeant major by early 1839. He fought in the Seminole War and married the daughter of a former German sergeant. They had thirteen children together.

Gamble's enlistment expired in 1843, and he entered civilian life. He worked as a civil engineer for the Board of Public Works in Chicago. He later lived in Evanston, Illinois, where he co-founded the Methodist Church. He joined the 8th Illinois Cavalry as its lieutenant colonel in September 1861. Sent to the Eastern Front, he fought in the Peninsula Campaign and the Seven Days battles. He was shot in the chest in the Battle of Malvern Hill (July 1, 1862). Although still suffering from his wound, he returned to field duty in late 1862 and was promoted to colonel on December 5. He succeeded his good friend John Farnsworth as commander of the 8th Illinois but missed the Battle of Chancellorsville because he was on medical furlough, suffering from rheumatism and neuralgia, as well as the lingering effects of his Malvern Hill wound. Gamble did not return until June 13; he was nevertheless named commander of a cavalry brigade on May 27, 1863.

His brightest moment as a commander came at Gettysburg on the morning of July 1. Despite being greatly outnumbered, he held up the advancing Confederates long enough to allow Wadsworth's infantry division of the I Corps time to arrive and deploy. His men fired the first shots of that legendary battle.

Because of his wound, Gamble was assigned command of a cavalry division in the Washington defenses. Except for some skirmishes with the Confederate guerilla John Singleton Mosby—in which he came out second best—Gamble saw no further combat. He was nevertheless brevetted brigadier general on December 12, 1864, and was promoted to the full volunteer rank of brigadier general on September 25, 1865—one of the last Civil War generals. He was mustered out of volunteer service on March 13, 1866, and reverted to his regular army rank of major. He was assigned to the 8th U.S. Cavalry.

Gamble's regiment was ordered to California in 1866, and Gamble was earmarked to command the Presidio in San Francisco. While stopping in Latin America on his way to the Pacific Ocean, Gamble was stricken by cholera. He died in Virgin Bay, Nicaragua, on December 20, 1866, at age forty-eight. He was buried in the Virgin Grove Cemetery. The waters of the bay eventually swamped the cemetery and destroyed the grave, which is now permanently under water and must be regarded as lost.

JAMES ABRAM GARFIELD was born on November 19, 1831, in Moreland Hills, Ohio. His father died when he was a toddler, and his stepfather abandoned the family, so James grew up in poverty. Many years later, when his stepfather died, Garfield noted his passing with satisfaction. Meanwhile, Garfield was raised by a strong-willed mother who guided him into the Disciples of Christ Church (now called the Church of Christ), which would profoundly impact his life.

Young Garfield was determined to overcome his circumstances and get a good education. He was a voracious reader and, by hard work, gained admission to the nearby Geauga Seminary. He attended school while working as a carpenter's assistant and a teacher. Simultaneously, he became a powerful public speaker and a Disciples of Christ elder and lay preacher. He later transferred to the Western Reserve Eclectic Institute and Williams College in Williamstown, Massachusetts, from which he graduated with honors in 1856. He became the president of Western Reserve College in Hiram, Ohio; simultaneously, he read law. Garfield was highly intelligent. He was also ambidextrous. He could take a quill pen in each hand and write in Greek with one and in Hebrew with the other—simultaneously.

ENCYCLOPEDIA OF UNION GENERALS

Garfield joined the Republican Party and was elected to the Ohio State Senate in 1860. A "true believer" abolitionist, he thought the Civil War should be a holy crusade against slavery. He was disappointed that Abraham Lincoln did not think so at first but thought he would eventually come around. He joined the Union Army as lieutenant colonel of the 42nd Ohio Infantry on August 21, 1861, and became the regiment's colonel on November 27. He was elevated to brigade commander on December 17. Although he had no military background, he read every military manual or book he could get his hands on and was a fast learner. He was also an effective recruiter. His brigade joined Buell's Army of the Ohio in Kentucky in December 1861.

Colonel Garfield defeated a Rebel brigade of about equal strength in the Battle of Middle Creek on January 10, 1862. This victory, along with Mill Springs a week later, secured eastern Kentucky for the Union. As a result, he was promoted to brigadier general on February 20. Garfield and his brigade were then sent to southwestern Tennessee, where they fought in the Battle of Shiloh on April 7. He also took part in the Siege of Corinth before returning to Ohio on sick furlough.

General Garfield served on the court-martial board of Fitz John Porter in late 1862 and early 1863 and voted to convict him. On January 14, 1863, he was named chief of staff of William Rosecrans's Army of the Cumberland. He was an effective chief and, unlike Rosecrans, distinguished himself in the Battle of Chickamauga (September 19–20). He then served in the early stages of the Siege of Chattanooga.

Garfield was not named commander of the Army of the Cumberland, as he hoped; instead, General Grant replaced Rosecrans with George Thomas. After briefly serving as Thomas's chief of staff, Garfield returned to Ohio, where he was elected to the U.S. House of Representatives, although he refused to campaign. Garfield felt his place was in the field and seriously considered resigning his seat. Abraham Lincoln persuaded him to go to Congress, stating that the administration needed supporters in Congress more than it needed generals. He resigned his commission on December 6 and took his seat the next day. In the process, he declined a promotion to major general.

The rest of Garfield's career was political. He remained in Congress until 1880, where he supported Reconstruction, civil rights for African

Americans, and the impeachment of Andrew Johnson. He opposed land grants for railroads, supported high tariffs, and called for the establishment of a U.S. civil service.

James Garfield won the Republican nomination for president in 1880 and defeated General Winfield Scott Hancock in the general election. Although he had only 39,000 more votes than Hancock, he won handily in the Electoral College. He was inaugurated on March 4, 1881.

Garfield's presidency was very brief. On July 2, while waiting for a train at a station in Washington, he was shot twice by a mentally unbalanced office-seeker. Garfield's medical treatment was poor and, after some initial improvement, his condition deteriorated. He was taken to Elberon, New Jersey, to escape the Washington heat, and he died there on September 19, 1881, at age forty-nine. His remains were interred in a crypt beneath the James A. Garfield Memorial at Lake View Cemetery, Cleveland, Ohio.

KENNER GARRARD was born in 1827 in Bourbon County, Kentucky, where his mother was visiting in-laws. (Kenner's grandfather was James Garrard, a former governor of Kentucky.) His exact birth date is unclear but sources list September 21 or 30. His parents lived in Cincinnati, where he was raised. He attended Harvard but dropped out in his sophomore year to attend West Point, from which he graduated in 1851 (8/42). He was commissioned brevet second lieutenant in the 4th Artillery but transferred to the 1st Dragoons in 1852. He was promoted to second lieutenant in 1853, to first lieutenant in 1855, and to captain on February 27, 1861.

Garrard spent most of the antebellum years on frontier duty in New Mexico and Texas. He was stationed in west Texas when the war began, so he was captured by Rebels on April 23, 1861, but was allowed to return to the United States on parole. He was named commandant of cadets at West Point in December and held that post until September 1862; meanwhile, he was exchanged on August 27, and was named commander of the 146th New York Infantry. He fought at Fredericksburg, Chancellorsville, and Gettysburg, where he became a brigade commander after Brigadier General

Stephen H. Weed was killed at Little Round Top. He was promoted to brigadier general on July 23.

Garrard was an officer noted for his personal bravery. He transferred to the Western Front in January 1864 and led a cavalry division in the Atlanta Campaign, where his performance was unimpressive. He is most famous for his raid on Roswell, Georgia, where (in accordance with Sherman's orders) he rounded up factory workers and their families and deported them to the North. These included one hundred men and five hundred women and children. They were treated badly and most of them never saw the lights of home again. Garrard took part in Sherman's March to the Sea and was given command of an infantry division on December 7. He distinguished himself in the Battle of Nashville, where Hood's Confederate army was virtually destroyed. He was brevetted major general on February 1, 1865. He also took part in the capture of Mobile, Alabama, that April.

Postwar, Garrard briefly commanded the District of Mobile but resigned from the Regular Army on November 9, 1866, and returned to Cincinnati, where he worked as a real estate broker and was highly successful. A life-long bachelor, he died in Cincinnati on May 15, 1879, at age fifty-one, and is buried in the Spring Grove Cemetery. Two of Garrard's brothers, Jeptha and Israel, were brevet brigadier generals, and a first cousin, Theophilus, was a brigadier general of volunteers.

THEOPHILUS TOULMIN GARRARD was born at Goose Creek Salt Works, Kentucky, near the town of Manchester, on June 7, 1812. His father, Daniel Garrard, was a wealthy land owner and salt mine owner who served as a colonel during the War of 1812. His father (Theophilus's grandfather) was the second governor of Kentucky. Theophilus, on the other hand, initially became a farmer.

Garrard dabbled in politics during the 1840s. He ran for the Kentucky legislature in 1841 and 1842, but was defeated both times. He was elected in 1843 and re-elected without opposition in 1844. He was a captain in the 16th U.S. Infantry during the Mexican War and was on duty in northern Mexico but did not see combat. He later recalled that his eight months in Mexico were the most pleasant of his life and expressed great fondness for the Mexican people.

Garrard became a 49er after the war but did not find the bonanza gold. He returned to Kentucky in 1850 and was elected to the state senate in 1857. He ran for Congress in 1859 but was defeated. Garrard was re-elected to the state senate in 1861 but decided not to take his seat. The Civil War had begun, and he raised a regiment, the 7th Kentucky Infantry, which was mustered into Union service on September 22, 1861, with Garrard as colonel.

Garrard served in the Cumberland Gap Campaign of 1861 and in the Kentucky (Heartland) Campaign of 1862, during which he fought in the Battle of Perryville. He was given a brigade in Grant's Army of the Tennessee in February 1863. In March, while he was stationed at Milliken's Bend, Louisiana, he suddenly lost central vision in his left eye. He was sent to the Union medical director in Cincinnati, who determined that he had a rare disease which caused a rupture behind the eye, and it was incurable. Promoted to brigadier general on July 23, he returned to active duty in August but because of his medical condition, he could only serve in rear area posts. He commanded the District of Somerset, Kentucky, (December 1863–January 1864) and then the District of the Clinch, which included the Cumberland Gap. He resigned his commission on April 4, 1864, because of his vision issues. He was a salt producer and farmer in Clay County for the rest of his life. He had to rebuild the salt works. Ironically, it was burned by Union soldiers to prevent it falling into Confederate hands. After the war, he lost all vision in his left eye and nearly all in his right.

General Theophilus Garrard died in the same house in which he was born on March 15, 1902, at age eighty-nine. He is buried in the Garrard Family Cemetery in Clay County. He had at least fifteen children by his three wives, two of whom pre-deceased him. At least ten of his children lived into adulthood. One of them was Joseph Garrard (1851–1924), who graduated from West Point in 1873, fought Indians on the frontier and insurgents in the Philippines, and retired as a colonel.

JOHN WHITE GEARY was born on December 30, 1819, in Westmoreland County, Pennsylvania, not far from present-day Pittsburgh, the son of a

Scotch-Irish schoolmaster and iron worker. He attended Jefferson College in Canonsburg, Pennsylvania, but had to drop out for financial reasons after his father died. Antebellum, he labored as a clerk, schoolteacher, surveyor, construction engineer for a railroad, and a land speculator. He also studied law and was admitted to the bar in Kentucky. Geary was active in the Pennsylvania Militia from his teenage years and was commissioned lieutenant at age sixteen. During the Mexican War, he was lieutenant colonel and then colonel of the 2nd Pennsylvania Infantry. He took part in the drive from Vera Cruz to Mexico City, which included the Battle of Chapultepec, where he was wounded five times. (A big man, he stood 6'6", and weighed 260 pounds; he was thus an easy target. He was wounded at least ten times in his military career.) He briefly served as military governor of Mexico City.

Geary launched his political career in early 1849 when President Polk appointed him postmaster of San Francisco. He was elected *alcalde* a year later. In 1850, he became the first mayor of San Francisco and reportedly the youngest. He returned to Pennsylvania in 1852 because of his wife's failing health. After she died, President Pierce offered him the post of territorial governor of Utah, but he declined it. Later, he accepted Pierce's offer to be territorial governor of Kansas.

Although Geary (a Democrat) attempted to steer a neutral course in "Bleeding Kansas," he clashed with the pro-slavery legislature and eventually sided with the abolitionists—but not the factions advocating violence. He served from September 9, 1856 to March 20, 1857. He was fired by President Buchanan on March 12 and then returned to his farm in Pennsylvania.

When the Civil War came, Geary recruited the 28th Pennsylvania Infantry Regiment and became its colonel. It was mustered into Federal service on June 28, 1861. It initially guarded the upper Potomac River crossings. At Bolivar Heights on October 16, Geary was struck in the leg by a piece of enemy shrapnel. On March 8, 1862, he was wounded and captured by Confederate cavalry. He was exchanged almost immediately and promoted to brigadier general on April 26. He led a brigade in Banks's command during the Shenandoah Valley Campaign and at Cedar Mountain (August 9), where he was wounded twice, one of which was serious. When he returned to duty in October, he was promoted to divisional commander.

Geary's division was part of the XII Corps. It fought at Chancellorsville, where on May 3 a Rebel cannonball flew so close to Geary's head that it knocked him out. He fought Culp's Hill during the Battle of Gettysburg and was sent west with the XII Corps. He took part in the Siege of Chattanooga, including the Battle of Wauhatchie, where on October 29, one of his sons, Lieutenant Edward R. Geary, died in his arms. Ironically, the eighteen-year-old officer was advanced to captain that same day, and his father had his orders in his pocket but had not yet given them to Edward when he was hit, so he never knew he was a captain.

General Geary continued to perform well in the Battle of Missionary Ridge, the Atlanta Campaign, and in the March to the Sea, where he distinguished himself in the capture of Savannah. He was brevetted major general on January 12, 1865, for his part in the capture of that city, where he briefly served as military governor.

John Geary was mustered out of volunteer service on January 15, 1866. He returned to Pennsylvania, where he was twice elected governor, serving from January 15, 1867 to January 21, 1873. A Democrat antebellum, he was an independent Republican governor who vetoed numerous special interest bills and sought to minimize the influence of the railroads.

Eighteen days after his second term ended, General Geary suffered a fatal heart attack. He died on February 8, 1873, in Harrisburg, Pennsylvania. He was fifty-three years old. He is buried in Harrisburg Cemetery.

GEORGE WASHINGTON GETTY was born in Georgetown, District of Columbia, on October 2, 1819. He entered West Point in 1836 at age sixteen and graduated in the Class of 1840 (15/42). He was commissioned second lieutenant in the 4th Artillery and served in various garrisons as well as in the Mexican War, where he was brevetted captain for his gallantry at Contreras and Churubusco. He also fought in the Second and Third Seminole Wars

(1849–50 and 1856–57). He was promoted to first lieutenant in 1845 and captain (substantive rank) in 1853.

Getty was transferred to the 5th U.S. Artillery Regiment when the Civil War began. He was promoted to lieutenant colonel and aide-de-camp to General McClellan in September 1861. The following month, he took charge of the artillery of Joseph Hooker's division (four batteries) and led it in the Peninsula Campaign and the Seven Days battles. After briefly commanding the Reserve Artillery Brigade of the Army of the Potomac, he took charge of the artillery of Burnside's IX Corps, which he led in the Maryland Campaign, including the Battles of South Mountain and Antietam. He was promoted to brigadier general on September 25, 1862, and assumed command of an infantry division in the IX Corps on October 4.

Getty directed his new command in the Battle of Fredericksburg, where he was wounded in the right hand. He and his men were sent to Suffolk in March 1863 and successfully resisted Longstreet's attempts to take the place the following month. He continued to operate south of Norfolk until January 1864, when he began a two-month tour as inspector general of the Army of the Potomac. He led a division in the VI Corps at the Wilderness until May 6, when he was again wounded, this time in the shoulder. Getty returned to duty at the end of June. He took part in the Siege of Petersburg and the Shenandoah Valley Campaign, where he distinguished himself and temporarily assumed command of the VI Corps at Cedar Creek after General Ricketts was wounded. For his gallantry here, he was brevetted major general on December 12.

Meanwhile, George Getty returned to the trenches outside Petersburg. He spearheaded the initial Union breakthrough of Lee's lines on April 2, 1865, and was present at Appomattox on April 9. He was mustered out of volunteer service on October 9, 1866, and reverted to his Regular Army rank of colonel. His first assignment was as commander of the 37th U.S. Infantry Regiment, which was stationed at the Little Rock Arsenal. Later, he commanded the District of New Mexico, the 3rd U.S. Infantry, the 3rd U.S. Artillery, the Artillery School at Fort Monroe, Virginia, and the 4th U.S. Artillery. He was also on the board which exonerated Fitz John Porter for his conduct as V Corps commander at the Second Bull Run.

After forty-eight years' service, Getty retired as a colonel in 1883. He was interested in veterans affairs and served a tour as commander-in-chief of the Military Order of the Loyal Legion of the United States (1895–96). He settled on a farm near Forest Glen, Maryland, where he died on October 1, 1901. He was eighty-one. He is buried in Arlington National Cemetery. His son, Robert Nelson Getty (1855–1941), fought in the Indian wars against the Sioux, in Cuba during the Spanish American War, and in the Philippines. He commanded the 88th Infantry Division during World War I and retired as a brigadier general.

JOHN GIBBON was born in Philadelphia, Pennsylvania, on April 20, 1827, the son of a doctor. His family moved to North Carolina in 1838. He entered the U.S. Military Academy in 1842, but his plebe year was characterized by such indiscipline that he was forced to repeat it. He graduated in 1847 (20/38) and was commissioned brevet second lieutenant in the 3rd Artillery. He was promoted to second lieutenant later that year, to first lieutenant in 1850, and to captain in 1859. Meanwhile, he served in Mexico (without seeing combat), in southern Florida against the Seminoles, and at West Point, where he taught artillery tactics for five years, among other posts. He wrote *The Artillerist's Manual* (1859), which was used by both sides during the war. (Gibbons loved books and writing, as well as hunting and fishing.) He was at Camp Floyd in Utah when the war began.

Most of Gibbon's family adhered to the Confederacy, including three of his brothers, two brothers-in-law, and several cousins, including Confederate General J. Johnston Pettigrew, who was killed in the Gettysburg Campaign. His father owned slaves. Although he was a Southern Democrat, Gibbon split with most of his family when he remained in the U.S. Army.

In Union service, Gibbon initially commanded a battery in the 4th U.S. Artillery in the Washington, D.C. area. He was placed in charge of the artillery of Irvin McDowell's division in October and was promoted to brigadier general on May 3, 1862. Four days later, he assumed command of a Wisconsin infantry brigade. He improved its training until it became known as "the Iron Brigade" and became one of the most famous units to fight in the war. He led it in the Second Bull Run Campaign and in the Battle of Antietam, where it suffered heavy casualties in the Cornfield.

John Gibbon was one of the best officers in the Federal army. He led a division in the I Corps at Fredericksburg, where he was wounded in the right hand and wrist. The injury itself was minor, but it became infected, and it took him months to recover. He returned to duty in April 1863 and was lightly engaged in the Battle of Chancellorsville. At Gettysburg, he briefly served as acting commander of the II Corps on July 2 and played the key role in repulsing Pickett's Charge on July 3. Gibbon was seriously wounded in the process when a Rebel bullet ripped through his left arm near the shoulder. He did not return to duty until November, and then it was light duty, commanding the draft depots in Cleveland and Philadelphia.

General Gibbon was back in command of a division in the Overland Campaign of 1864. He distinguished himself at Spotsylvania and was promoted to major general on June 8; meanwhile, his division suffered 47 percent casualties in heavy fighting. He assumed command of the XVIII Corps of the Army of the James on September 4. He became demoralized at Reams' Station when his troops—who suffered severe casualties—refused to attack. He went on extended sick leave and apparently did not return to field duty until January 15, 1865, as commander of the newly formed XXIV Corps. He again excelled on April 2, 1865, when Lee's lines finally broke, and Gibbon captured Fort Gregg. He was present at the surrender at Appomattox. He was mustered out of volunteer service on January 15, 1866. Gibbon reverted to his regular army rank of captain, but he was advanced to colonel when the Regular Army was reorganized later that year, and he assumed command of the 7th U.S. Infantry, which he led against the Sioux in the Montana Territory. His prompt arrival on the Little Bighorn River on June 26, 1876, saved several hundred members of the 7th Cavalry Regiment under Major Marcus Reno. The following year, he defeated the Nez Perce in the Battle of the Big Hole, but Gibbon was severely wounded by a bullet in the thigh and was unable to direct the pursuit.

Gibbon was placed in charge of the Department of the Platte in 1884 and was promoted to brigadier general, Regular Army, in 1885. He subsequently commanded the Department of the Columbia (where he enforced the Chinese Expulsion Act without any qualms) and the Military Division of the Atlantic. He retired in 1891 when he reached the mandatory age of sixty-four. His memoirs, *Personal Recollections of the Civil War*, were published posthumously in 1928.

General Gibbon died of pneumonia in Baltimore on February 6, 1896, at age sixty-eight. He was commander-in-chief of the Military Order of the Loyal Legion at the time of his death. He is buried in Arlington National Cemetery.

ALFRED GIBBS was born on April 22, 1823, on his father's estate near Astoria, Long Island, New York. His family was distinguished, and his grandfather was secretary of the treasury under George Washington and John Adams. Alfred attended Dartmouth before entering West Point in 1842. He graduated in 1846 (42/59) and was commissioned brevet second lieutenant in the Mounted Rifles Regiment. He was promoted to second lieutenant in late 1846.

Gibbs distinguished himself as part of Winfield Scott's drive from Vera Cruz to the Mexican capital. He was wounded at Cerro Gordo and was brevetted first lieutenant for his courage there. He was brevetted captain for his part in storming the Belen Gate at Mexico City. He later served as an aide to General Persifor Smith in Texas and Kansas (1850–56) and on the Western frontier (1857–61) and was wounded fighting Apache in New Mexico Territory in 1857. Still in the West when the war began, he tried to escape with his company but was surrounded by Texas Confederates and captured at San Augustine, New Mexico, on July 8, 1861. He was paroled but not exchanged until August 1862. In the meantime, he was promoted to captain on May 11, 1861, and was stationed at Detroit.

On September 6, 1862, Gibbs was named commander of the 130th New York Infantry and was promoted to colonel. The newly formed regiment was sent to Suffolk. He was placed in charge of a brigade, which he led in the Battle of Deserted House (a.k.a. Kelly's Store). Here, General Corcoran arrested him for disobedience. Although under arrest and without a horse or a gun, Gibbs grabbed a flag and led a desperate charge which won the battle for the Union. He took part in the Siege of Suffolk in April and early May 1863.

Gibbs reverted to regimental command in the summer of 1863 and oversaw the conversion of the 130th New York into the 1st New York Dragoons, which was also known as the 19th New York Cavalry. He occasionally served as a brigade commander.

In November, Gibbs assumed command of the Reserve Cavalry Brigade of the Army of the Shenandoah. He spent the rest of the war with this army and fought in the Overland Campaign, at Yellow Tavern, and Trevilian Station, where he suffered sunstroke. He was promoted to brigadier general on November 30, 1864, and led his brigade in the Battle of Five Forks and the Appomattox Campaign.

After the surrender, Gibbs briefly commanded a division in the Military Division of the Gulf. He was mustered out of volunteer service on February 1, 1866, and brevetted major general on March 12, 1866. Meanwhile, he reverted to his regular army rank of major in the 7th U.S. Cavalry and was sent to Kansas.

General Gibbs was a rigid disciplinarian but was loved by his men. Off-duty, Cullum described him as "very compassionate, cheery, jocose, fond of music, [and] attractive to all of his fellows . . ." He died at Fort Leavenworth on December 26, 1868, of "congestion of the brain" at age forty-five. He is buried in Saint Mary's Episcopal Churchyard in Portsmouth, Rhode Island. One of his sons became a surgeon and was killed in action at Guantanamo Bay, Cuba, in 1898.

CHARLES CHAMPION GILBERT, the brother of General James I. Gilbert, was born on March 1, 1822, in Zanesville, Ohio. He attended Yale in 1839 but was expelled, apparently for hazing a professor. He enrolled in Ohio University in Athens in 1840 but left in 1842 to attend West Point, graduated with the Class of 1846 (21/59), and was commissioned brevet second lieutenant in the 3rd U.S. Infantry Regiment. He was promoted to second lieutenant in September.

Gilbert took part in the Siege of Vera Cruz and was later on garrison duty there. He then spent two years on the Texas frontier and became a professor of geography, history, and ethics at West Point in 1850. He was promoted to first lieutenant that same year and to captain in 1855. He was sent back to Texas in 1855 and fought Comanches with the 1st Infantry Regiment.

When the Civil War began, Gilbert was commander of Fort Cobb, Indian Territory. He led a company of 1st Regular Infantry in the Battle of Wilson's Creek (August 10, 1861), where he was badly wounded in the shoulder. After he recovered, he was named inspector general of the Army of the Ohio and participated in the Battle of Shiloh and the Siege of Corinth.

During the Kentucky (Heartland) Campaign of 1862, General "Bull" Nelson's Army of Kentucky was crushed in the Battle of Richmond. Nelson was wounded, and it became the duty of General Horatio Wright, commander of the Department of the Ohio, to appoint his replacement. After the two senior officers available declined the promotion, Wright assigned Gilbert to duty as an "acting" major general. President Lincoln promoted Gilbert to brigadier general of volunteers on September 4. General Buell, the commander of the Army of the Ohio, appointed him commander of the III Provisional Corps (the former Army of Kentucky).

Until this point, Gilbert's performance in the Civil War was exemplary. Commanding a corps, however, was too much for him, and his troops hated him because he was a martinet. He fought in the Battle of Perryville (October 8), where he moved slowly and failed to support McCook's corps on his left, which was forced back, exposing Gilbert's own left flank. He was condemned in a subsequent investigation.

The Senate did not act on Gilbert's appointment, which expired on March 4, 1863. He reverted to his Regular Army rank of major and held only minor administrative rear-area posts (mostly in Philadelphia) for the rest of the war.

After the surrender, Gilbert served in infantry units in Arkansas (1865–68) and Florida (1868–69), and in Wyoming Territory; Montana Territory; Minnesota; and Dakota Territory. He was promoted to lieutenant colonel in 1868 and to colonel and commander of the 17th U.S. Infantry Regiment in 1881. He retired in 1886 after forty years' service.

General Gilbert died in Baltimore, Maryland, on January 17, 1903, at age eighty. He is buried in Cave Hill Cemetery, Louisville, Kentucky.

JAMES ISHAM GILBERT, the brother of Charles C. Gilbert, was born on July 16, 1823, in Louisville, Kentucky. As an infant and a child, he moved with his family to Illinois and Prairie du Chien, Wisconsin, where he was educated. He lived a frontier life before the war, rafting lumber down the Mississippi and its tributaries, engaging in trading with the Indians, land speculation, and operating livery stables. He helped found the town of Lansing, Iowa, where he lived from 1851 to 1862. A late volunteer, he became colonel of the 27th Iowa Infantry and was mustered into Union service on October 3, 1862.

Gilbert took part in Steele's Little Rock Expedition and, after a period of garrison duty in Arkansas, was transferred to A. J. Smith's XVI Corps, with which he served in the Meridian Expedition of February 1864. Sent to the Army of the Gulf, he first saw serious action in the Red River Campaign, where he earned commendations for his performances at Fort DeRussy and Pleasant Hill. He was wounded in the left hand but remained on the field until the fighting was over.

In June 1864, Gilbert was given command of a brigade. He and the XVI Corps were sent to Mississippi, where they fought at Tupelo. Later, they were sent to Missouri, where he was part of Smith's pursuit of General Sterling Price.

Gilbert led a brigade in the Battle of Nashville in December 1864 and played a significant role in that victory. He was then sent to Alabama and took part in the Battle of Fort Blakeley (April 2–9, 1865). Mobile fell on April 12 and Gilbert was promoted to brigadier general on April 21. In 1866, he was brevetted major general for his part in this campaign. Meanwhile, he was mustered out on August 25, 1865.

General Gilbert was a modest and unassuming man, though a brave and highly competent one. Post-war, Gilbert returned to Iowa and the lumber business. He later went to Colorado, where he engaged in mining.

He settled in Kansas and was president of the Topeka Coal Economizing Company. He died in his sleep in Topeka on February 9, 1884, at age sixty. He is buried in the Aspen Grove Cemetery, Burlington, Iowa, where his brother was a wealthy and prominent citizen.

ALVAN CULLEM GILLEM was a Southerner, born in Gainesboro, Tennessee, on July 20, 1830. He entered West Point in 1847, graduated in 1851 (11/42), and was commissioned brevet second lieutenant in the 1st U.S. Artillery. He was promoted to second lieutenant at the end of the year, to first lieutenant in 1855, and to captain on May 14, 1861. Meanwhile, he fought in the Third Seminole War in Florida and served on the Texas frontier. He also became interested in logistics.

Gillem served as assistant quartermaster of the Army of the Ohio under Don Carlos Buell. Despite the rear area nature of his position, he earned a Regular Army brevet to major for his courage at the Battle of Mill Springs (January 19, 1862). He took part in the Battle of Shiloh and on May 13 was named colonel of the 10th (U.S.) Tennessee Infantry. From August to December, he was provost of Nashville. On December 24, he was given command of a brigade in the Army of the Cumberland.

The Union high command realized that Gillem could perform his best service in his native Tennessee, so at the request of Andrew Johnson, the military governor of Tennessee, they named him adjutant general of the state on June 1, 1863—a post he held until the end of the war. He was promoted to brigadier general on August 17, 1863. He defeated and killed Confederate raider John Hunt Morgan (September 4, 1864) and routed his command. He was less successful against John C. Breckinridge, who routed his forces in the Battle of Bull's Gap (November 13, 1864). His overall performance, however, was judged positively by his superiors. He was given command of a cavalry division in East Tennessee near the end of the war and was brevetted major general in 1866. Meanwhile, he took part in the capture of Saltville, Virginia (December 22, 1864) and became a member of the Tennessee House of Representatives in March 1865. He participated in the capture of Salisbury, North Carolina, on April 12, 1865.

Postwar, Gillem commanded the District of East Tennessee (July 1865–July 1866). He was mustered out of volunteer service on July 28, 1866, and became a colonel in the Regular Army and commander of the 28th U.S. Infantry Regiment. He assumed command of the Fourth Military District (Arkansas and Mississippi) in January 1868. His policies of forgiveness, conciliation, and moderation were not looked upon favorably by the Radical Republicans, and he was transferred to Texas in 1869 and to California two years later; here he fought the Modoc Indians. He was not successful, and General Jefferson C. Davis relieved him of his command in 1873.

Gillem became seriously ill in 1873 and returned to Tennessee to die. He passed away near Nashville on December 2, 1875, at age forty-five. He is buried in Mount Olivet Cemetery, Nashville. His son Alvin joined the army during the Spanish-American War and retired as a colonel of cavalry. His grandson, Alvan C. Gillem, Jr., commanded the U.S. XIII Corps during World War II and took 247,000 prisoners in France and Germany. He retired as a lieutenant general. His great-grandson, Alvan C. Gillem, II, became a lieutenant general in the U.S. Air Force.

QUINCY ADAMS GILLMORE was born on February 28, 1825, in Black River (now Lorain), Ohio. He entered West Point in 1845 and graduated at the top of his class in 1849 (1/43). He was commissioned brevet second lieutenant of engineers and was promoted to second lieutenant in 1853, first lieutenant in 1856, and to captain on August 6, 1861. Antebellum, he served mainly as an instructor of Practical Military Engineering at West Point and as a construction engineer at Hampton Roads, Virginia. He was purchasing agent in New York City when the Civil War began.

Gillmore was chief engineer on the staff of General Thomas W. Sherman on the Port Royal Expedition. He directed Union forces in the Battle of Fort Pulaski, Georgia, where he employed rifled artillery against the fort's exterior stone walls, fired more than five thousand artillery shells from a range of 1,700 yards, and forced the garrison to surrender. This action essentially made stone wall fortifications obsolete throughout the globe, and Gillmore became internationally famous. As a result, he was promoted to brigadier general on April 30, 1862.

From October to May 1863, he commanded a cavalry division in the Army of the Ohio and defeated Confederate General John Pegram in the Battle of Somerset (March 31, 1863). Earmarked for greater things, he was given command of the X Corps in the Department of the South in July after its commander, General Ormsby Mitchel, died of yellow fever. Gillmore was promoted to major general on September 12, 1863. His main mission was to capture Charleston, South Carolina. He was not successful, and his orders to launch a frontal assault on the Battery Wagner on Morris Island led to the slaughter of the 54th Massachusetts Infantry. (This was predictable. A similar attack by a white regiment the week before had also been slaughtered.) He now lay siege to the place, which the Rebels abandoned on September 7, 1863. Now within artillery range, he blasted the city to pieces but was not able to capture it.

Major Adam J. Lewis of the U.S. Army's Command and General Staff College concluded that Gillmore was unable to handle the transition from the tactical to the operational level of command (i.e., the operations of an army or an independent corps) or successfully deal with the expanded logistical factors at that level. Consequently, he failed before Charleston. His efforts to capture Tallahassee and cut off the Southern supply of beef from south Florida were defeated at the Battle of Olustee, a.k.a. Ocean Pond (February 20, 1864).

Gillmore and his corps were transferred to the Army of the James in Virginia. Here, he was not highly respected by his men and feuded with the army commander, General Butler, whom he correctly considered incompetent. He participated in the disastrous Battle of Drewry's Bluff (May 12–16), in which Butler was crushed by numerically inferior Rebel forces under General Beauregard. Gillmore asked to be transferred and happened to be in Washington, D.C. when Confederate General Early advanced on the capital. Gillmore personally assumed command of much of the garrison. Early was checked at Fort Stevens on July 11 and 12.

Quincy Gillmore was severely injured on July 14, when his horse fell and smashed his foot. He did not return to duty until December as inspector of military fortifications in the Military Division of Western Mississippi. He was again named commander of the Department of the South at the end of the war. He resigned his volunteers' commission on December 5, 1865, and reverted to his regular army rank of major of engineers. He was initially stationed in New York City.

Gillmore resumed normal engineer duties and was promoted to lieutenant colonel (1874) and colonel (1883). In his sunset years, he suffered from kidney and liver problems. He died on April 7, 1888, in Brooklyn, New York. He was sixty-three years old. He was interred in the West Point Cemetery. He is buried beside his son and grandson, both of whom graduated from West Point and became generals in the New Jersey National Guard.

GEORGE HENRY GORDON was born in Charlestown, Massachusetts, on July 19, 1823. His widowed mother moved to Framingham when he was five. He attended the Framingham Academy, was admitted to West Point in 1842, and graduated with the Class of 1846 (43/59). Commissioned brevet second lieutenant in the Mounted Rifle Regiment and sent to Mexico, he was wounded at Cerro Gordo and at San Juan Bridge, where the fighting was hand-to-hand. Gordon was brevetted for Cerro Gordo, was promoted to second lieutenant in 1848, and to first lieutenant in 1853. In the six years after Mexico, he spent mainly on frontier duty in Washington Territory, Kansas, and Dakota Territory. He resigned his commission in 1854 to attend Harvard Law School. He was admitted to the bar in 1857 and practiced law in Boston until the Civil War began.

Gordon organized the 2nd Massachusetts Infantry Regiment and became its colonel on May 25. He guarded fords on the upper Potomac until March 1862, when he was given a brigade command in Nathaniel Banks's Army of the Shenandoah. He fought Stonewall Jackson in the Valley but without success. Later he took part in the Battle of Cedar Mountain, the

Second Bull Run Campaign, and the Battle of Antietam, where he was an acting division commander. Meanwhile, he was promoted to brigadier general on June 12, 1862.

George Gordon reverted to brigade command after the Maryland Campaign. He fought in the Battle of Fredericksburg and the Siege of Suffolk and was later transferred to the Department of the South, where he again directed a division on Folly Island, South Carolina. For reasons not made clear by the records, he was never promoted to major general, despite lengthy service as a division commander. He was chief of staff of the District of New York (November 1864–February 1865) and commander of the District of Eastern Virginia (February–August 1865). He resigned from the army on August 25. He was brevetted major general in 1866.

After the war, Gordon returned to his law practice in Boston. He was one of the founders of the prestigious Military Historical Society of Massachusetts. He also wrote four books on the Civil War (see bibliography) and was an unswerving supporter of Fitz John Porter. General Gordon died in Framingham on August 30, 1886, at age sixty-three. Eulogized as a "gallant soldier, a loving husband and an upright citizen," he was buried in Edgell Grove Cemetery and Mausoleum, Framingham, Massachusetts.

WILLIS ARNOLD GORMAN, the son of Irish immigrants, was born on January 12, 1816, in Flemingsburg, Kentucky. The family moved to Bloomington, Indiana, in 1835. Gorman attended Indiana University, read law, and was admitted to the bar. He began his political career by becoming a clerk in the Indiana State Senate in 1837. He was subsequently elected to the Indiana House of Representatives, where he served three terms from 1841 to 1844.

Gorman began his military career as 1st Sergeant of the 3rd Indiana Infantry on June 22, 1846. Promoted to major four days later, he fought at Buena Vista, where he was injured when he fell from his horse. When his regiment's term of enlistment expired, Gorman was selected to be colonel of the 4th Indiana, which fought in the Battle of Huamantla (October 9, 1847) late in the war. It also played a role in the relief of the Siege of Puebla.

After the war, Willis Gorman returned to Indiana and re-entered the political arena. A Democrat, he was twice elected congressman (1849–1853). Franklin Pierce appointed him the second territorial governor of Minnesota, where he unsuccessfully attempted to have the capitol moved from St. Paul to St. Peter and onto land he owned. He served as governor from 1853–1857 and remained in Minnesota after his term expired, practicing law. He was a delegate to the state constitutional convention in 1859, served in the state legislature (1858–1861), and was a presidential elector for Stephen A. Douglas in 1860.

Gorman joined the Federal army as colonel of the 1st Minnesota Infantry on April 29, 1861, and fought well in the 1st Battle of Bull Run. Afterward, he was given command of a brigade and was promoted to brigadier general on September 7, 1861. He participated in the Ball's Bluff's disaster (October 9), the Peninsula Campaign, the Battle of Seven Pines, the Seven Days battles, and the Battle of Antietam. Here his men suffered heavy casualties because he launched an ill-advised attack on Rebel positions in the West Woods.

General Gordon was named commander of the District of Eastern Arkansas on December 3, 1862, but stepped down in mid-February 1863. Apparently unemployed for more than a year, he resigned his commission and was mustered out on May 4, 1864. He returned to St. Paul, where he resumed the practice of law. He was elected city attorney in 1869 and held that position until his death, which occurred in St. Paul on May 20, 1876. He was sixty years old. He was buried in the Oakland Cemetery in Saint Paul.

CHARLES KINNAIRD GRAHAM was born in New York City on June 3, 1824. He joined the navy as a midshipman in October 1841 and was involved in the Siege of Vera Cruz during the Mexican War, but resigned in 1848. He then studied both law and engineering and was fully qualified in both professions. He helped design Central Park and constructed the dry docks at the Brooklyn Naval Yard. Meanwhile, he joined the New York Militia as a major and was successively promoted to lieutenant colonel and colonel antebellum.

Graham joined the Union Army as colonel of the 74th New York (part of the Excelsior Brigade) on May 26, 1861. He fought in the Peninsula Campaign, in the Battle of Seven Pines, and in the Seven Days battles. He was promoted to brigadier general on November 9, 1862, and was given command of a brigade. He fought in the Battle of Chancellorsville and was part of Sickles's III Corps at Gettysburg. He was defending Union positions on the Emmitsburg Road and the Peach Orchard on July 2 when the Confederates smashed his brigade. Graham was wounded in the right hip and both shoulders before he was captured. He was taken to a prisoner-of-war camp in Richmond and remained there until September 19, when he was exchanged for James L. Kemper.

It was April 28, 1864, before Graham recovered enough to undertake a new field assignment. He was named commander of the Naval Brigade of the gunboat flotilla attached to the Army of the James. He served in Benjamin Butler's spectacularly unsuccessful operations around Petersburg, the Bermuda Hundred, and the First Battle of Fort Fisher, North Carolina. He was commander of the Norfolk, Virginia, garrison from March 19, 1865, until the end of the war. He was mustered out of the service on August 24, 1865. Charles Graham was brevetted major general on January 13, 1866.

After the war, Graham returned to New York City as a civil engineer. He spent most of the rest of his career working on the port of New York in various capacities. He died of pneumonia in Lakewood, New Jersey, on April 15, 1889, at age sixty-four. General Graham is buried in Woodlawn Cemetery, The Bronx, New York.

LAWRENCE PIKE GRAHAM was born on January 8, 1815, in his father's country home, "the Wigwam," in Amelia County, Virginia. His family was well connected and three of his brothers graduated from West Point. Despite their Southern roots, all four brothers supported the Union during the Civil War. Lawrence, who was well educated by private tutors, chose not to attend the Academy; instead, he was commissioned directly into the army as a second lieutenant in the 2nd Dragoons in 1837. He was promoted to first lieutenant in 1839 and to captain in 1843. He fought in the Seminole War in Florida and in northern Mexico in 1846 and was breveted major for his conduct at Palo Alto and Resaca de la Palma. He was promoted to major (substantive rank) in 1858.

Graham was stationed at Carlisle Barracks, Pennsylvania (then the home of the Cavalry School), when the Civil War erupted. He transferred to the 2nd Cavalry that autumn but was almost immediately placed in charge of a cavalry brigade in the Army of the Potomac. He was promoted to brigadier general of volunteers on August 31, 1861.

General Graham's brigade was part of Couch's division (IV Corps) during the Siege of Yorktown (April 1862), but he fell ill and took no further part in the Peninsula Campaign and indeed held no further field commands for more than two years. By June, he recovered and was named chief instructor at the Cavalry Instruction Camp near Annapolis, Maryland. He was considered an excellent training officer. He was later transferred to St. Louis, where he was president of a number of court-martials and on the Board of Examination of Invalid Officers at Annapolis. He never commanded a brigade again.

Graham was promoted to lieutenant colonel, Regular Army, in the 4th U.S. Cavalry in May 1864. The regiment, scattered over hundreds of miles in the 1861–63 period, was reunited in 1864 and fought on the Western Front. Graham was promoted to colonel and commander of the 4th Cavalry on May 9, 1864. Although he did not resign his volunteer commission, he led this Regular Army regiment for the rest of the war. It took part in the Battle of Nashville and was with General Wilson in the Battle of Selma (April 2, 1865), where Forrest's Cavalry was finally defeated. Graham was mustered out of volunteer service on August 24, 1865, but retained command of his regiment. After the war, Graham served on the Western frontier in western Texas, where his regiment fought Indians and was again scattered all over the map.

General Graham retired from the army in 1870 and settled in Washington, D.C. Over the thirty-five years of life remaining to him, he became a famous Shakespearian scholar and authority. He fractured his hip in 1905, which led to his death in Washington, D.C. on September 12, 1905, at age ninety. He was buried in Arlington National Cemetery beside his wife, to whom he was married for sixty-two years.

GORDON GRANGER was an important and highly effective Union commander who is virtually unknown today. He was born in Joy, New York, on November 6, 1821. His mother died when he was three, and he was raised by grandparents in Phelps, New York. He was admitted to West Point in 1841, graduated in 1845 (35/41), and was commissioned brevet second lieutenant in the 2nd U.S. Infantry Regiment. At the U.S. Military Academy, he and Ulysses S. Grant developed a lifelong dislike for each other, due in large part to Granger's abrasive personality, which occasionally bordered on insubordination. He also established a strong friendship with John Pope.

Granger was initially stationed in Detroit, Michigan but transferred to the Mounted Rifles Regiment in 1846. He was part of Scott's Army of Mexico and fought from Vera Cruz to Mexico City in 1847. He was brevetted first lieutenant for his gallantry at Contreras and Churubusco and to captain for his actions at Chapultepec. He was promoted to first lieutenant (substantive rank) in 1852 and to captain on May 5, 1861.

Gordon Granger was assistant adjutant general on the staff of George McClellan when the North mobilized. He later briefly returned to his regiment (then in Missouri) and was on the staff of Nathaniel Lyon until that officer was killed at Wilson's Creek on August 10, 1861. He was named colonel of the 2nd Michigan Cavalry on September 2, where he proved to be a master at winning the respect of his men and vastly improving their performance, despite his gruff manner and attention to the smallest detail.

He joined Pope in the advance on New Madrid, Missouri, and was given command of a small cavalry brigade and then a cavalry division. He was promoted to brigadier general on March 26, 1862, and led his command in the victory at New Madrid and in the Siege of Corinth. He was promoted to major general on September 17. He commanded the cavalry division of the Army of the Mississippi under Pope and later John McClernand, and led the Army of Kentucky (October 7, 1862 to January 20, 1863). This formation was reorganized as the Reserve Corps, with Granger retaining command.

ENCYCLOPEDIA OF UNION GENERALS

The high point of his war occurred on September 20, 1863, when the Union Army was badly defeated in the Battle of Chickamauga. Here, General Thomas saved the army, and General Granger saved Thomas, whom he reinforced at a critical moment on his own initiative and without orders. He later distinguished himself commanding the IV Corps in the Battle of Missionary Ridge and in lifting the Siege of Knoxville. Despite his performance, which was nothing short of brilliant, Grant continued to hate him and saw to it that he was not given any assignments more prominent than what he already had. He was placed under General Canby's Department of the Gulf, where he was given command of the Reserve Corps. He again distinguished himself in the capture of Forts Morgan and Gaines, Alabama, and isolating Mobile in August 1864. Placed in charge of the XIII Corps in February 1865, he played the major in the capture of Fort Blakeley in April, which led to the fall of Mobile.

Granger commanded the Department of Texas after the war and issued General Order No. 3, dated June 19, 1865. It declared all slaves in Texas to be free, equal citizens, and led to celebrations, which originated what became the Juneteenth holiday.

Gordon Granger supported President Andrew Johnson's moderate Reconstruction plans, which alienated the Radical Republicans, including Grant. Granger was mustered out of volunteer service on January 15, 1866, and reverted to his Regular Army rank of colonel. He briefly commanded the District of Memphis and then the 25th U.S. Infantry Regiment (1866–1869) but, thanks to Grant, was unemployed for more than a year and a half (1869–1870).

He finally managed to secure command of the 15th U.S. Infantry Regiment and the District of New Mexico on December 20, 1870. Here, he fought the Chiricahua Apache under Cochise. Meanwhile, Granger, who had health issues since he was a teenager, lost the vision in his left eye. Medical furloughs did not help. He returned to active duty and died in Santa Fe, New Mexico, on January 10, 1876, at age fifty-four. He was interred in the Lexington Cemetery, Lexington, Kentucky.

ROBERT SEAMAN GRANGER was born in Zanesville, Ohio, on May 24, 1816. His uncle was U.S. Attorney General Henry Stanbery. He entered the U.S. Military Academy in 1833 but was set back a year and did not graduate until 1838 (28/45). He was commissioned second lieutenant in the 1st Infantry Regiment. He served on the frontier in Minnesota and Wisconsin and fought in the Seminole War and served as a tactical instructor at West Point (1843–44). He played an undistinguished role in the Mexican War (mostly on garrison duty in Vera Cruz), after which he spent several years on the west Texas frontier. Granger was promoted to first lieutenant in 1839, to captain in 1847, and to major on September 9, 1861. He was in west Texas when that state seceded and was captured by Confederates near Lavaca, Texas, on April 25, 1861. He was paroled but, under the terms of his parole, he was not allowed to serve in the field until he was exchanged. This did not occur until August 15, 1862. He was on recruiting duty in Ohio until that time.

Robert Granger was appointed brigadier general in the Kentucky Militia on September 1, 1862, and to brigadier general of volunteers on October 22, 1862. Although he briefly commanded brigades and divisions in the armies of the Ohio and Cumberland in 1862 and 1863, he mainly labored in rear area assignments, principally in Nashville and the District of Middle Tennessee. In 1864, he directed the District of Northern Alabama, where he overran General Rodney's camp and repulsed raids by Joseph Wheeler. Against Nathan Bedford Forrest, he was less successful. His brightest moment occurred in October 1864, when he successfully defeated Army of Tennessee sorties against Decatur, Alabama. He remained in northern Alabama until after the surrender. He was discharged from the volunteer service on August 24, 1865, and was brevetted major general in the omnibus promotions in 1866.

Granger was promoted to lieutenant colonel in the Regular Army in June 1865 and served in the 11th and 16th (U.S.) Infantry Regiments. Simultaneously, he exercised territorial command in Richmond, Virginia, and Jackson, Mississippi. He also did a short tour as a recruiter in San Francisco in 1871. Granger was promoted to colonel and commander of the 16th Infantry Regiment in August 1871 and retired in 1873 after more than thirty years' service.

General Granger died of nephritis (kidney inflammation) in Washington, D.C. on April 25, 1894. He was seventy-seven years old. He was buried in Woodlawn Cemetery, Zanesville, Ohio.

LEWIS ADDISON GRANT was born on January 17, 1828, in Winhall, Vermont, the son of a farmer and schoolteacher. He attended public schools in Townshend, Vermont, and an academy in Chester. He then became a schoolteacher for five years while he read law. He was admitted to the bar in 1855 and set up a practice in Bellows Falls, Vermont. His first wife died in childbirth after they had been married only two years. His second wife was a niece of Franklin Pierce.

Grant was mustered into Federal service as major of the 5th Vermont Infantry on August 15, 1861. He became its lieutenant colonel in September 1861. The 5th was a distinguished regiment which mustered in 1,618 soldiers during the war. Part of the famous Vermont Brigade, it lost 339 dead during the conflict, of which 201 were killed in action or died of wounds. The 5th (and the Vermont Brigade) fought in the Peninsula Campaign (including the Siege of Yorktown and the Battle of Williamsburg), the Seven Days battles, Antietam, Fredericksburg, Salem Church during the Chancellorsville Campaign, Gettysburg, and the Overland Campaign, including the Wilderness, Spotsylvania, Cold Harbor, and the Siege of Petersburg. Meanwhile, Grant became its commander and was promoted to colonel on September 16, 1862.

Lewis Grant was wounded in the leg in the Battle of Fredericksburg and, upon recovery, was named commander of the Vermont Brigade on February 2, 1863. He distinguished himself at Salem Church on May 3, where his brigade played a significant role in the escape of the VI Corps. In 1893, Grant was awarded the Congressional Medal of Honor for his part in this battle. He was also severely wounded but managed to return and fight in the Battle of Gettysburg. He was finally promoted to brigadier general on April 30, 1864.

Grant served with a division in the Army of the Shenandoah (August 1864–February 1865) and earned a brevet to major general for rallying Union troops in the Battle of Cedar Creek, and briefly commanded a division. He was back in brigade command on April 2, 1865, when he was wounded in the head during the Battle of Fort Welch (Petersburg) but returned for the Battle of Sayler's Creek (April 6) and was present at Appomattox. An extremely solid officer, he was offered a regular army commission after the war but declined it and was discharged from the service on August 24, 1865. He was already brevetted major general for his courage in the Shenandoah, October 1864.

General Grant returned to Vermont in 1865 but later moved to Chicago, Des Moines, and Minnesota. He engaged in the banking business and was assistant secretary of war during the administration of Benjamin Harrison (1890–93). After an illness of several years, he died in Minneapolis on March 20, 1918, at age ninety, outliving all but seven Union generals (excluding brevets). He is buried in Lakewood Cemetery, Minneapolis, Minnesota.

ULYSSES SIMPSON GRANT, the general-in-chief of the Union Army (1864–1865) and the eighteenth president of the United States, was born Hiram Ulysses Grant on April 27, 1822, in Point Pleasant, Ohio. When he was appointed to West Point, however, the congressman who sponsored him erroneously listed him as Ulysses Simpson Grant, and the name stuck. (In any case, he did not like his original initials, "H.U.G."). His colleagues at the Military Academy nicknamed him "Sam" after "Uncle Sam," whose initials were also "U.S." He graduated with the Class of 1843 (21/43).

Cadet Grant was considered the best equestrian at West Point, but there were no vacancies in the cavalry at that time, so he was commissioned brevet second lieutenant in the 7th Infantry. (He later remarked that the happiest day of his life was the day he left the presidency; after that was the day he left the Academy.) He was promoted to second lieutenant (1845), first lieutenant (1847), and captain (1853). Meanwhile, he was stationed at

Jefferson Barracks, Missouri, and fought in the Mexican War, serving under both Taylor and Scott. Although he was the regimental quartermaster, he sought combat and earned brevets for his courage and initiative at Molino del Rey and Chapultepec.

Stationed in the Pacific Northwest after the war, Sam Grant developed a drinking problem and was forced to resign his commission in 1854. The next seven years were the most difficult of his life. He labored as a farmer, firewood salesman, real estate agent, bill collector, and clerk in his father's leather goods business in Galena, Illinois. He was, initially, a slave holder (through his wife) and a Democrat, and he voted for Stephen A. Douglas against Abraham Lincoln in 1860.

When the war began, Grant had difficulty obtaining a position but became colonel of the 21st Illinois on June 15, 1861, thanks to the aid of his political mentor, Congressman Elihu B. Washburne. Grant imposed discipline on the unruly 21st and after that he rose rapidly to brigadier general (August 9, 1861), major general of volunteers (September 20, 1862), major general, Regular Army (July 4, 1863), lieutenant general (March 4, 1864), general-in-chief of the U.S. Army (March 12, 1864–1869), and full ("four star") general (January 25, 1866). He quickly developed a well-deserved reputation as a fighter, and his strategy (defeat the Confederate Army by attrition) won the war for the Union. Whether this task could have been accomplished with fewer casualties is a controversy which rages to this day.

Although he was undoubtedly an excellent strategic thinker and is nearly worshipped by certain historians, Grant's record as a tactician is mixed and varies from brilliant to below mediocre. His last Vicksburg Campaign was unquestionably a stroke of genius, as was his crossing of the James in 1864, although he failed to take Petersburg because of the timidity of his subordinates and through no fault of his own. On the other hand, he was taken by surprise by Rebel counterattacks at Fort Donelson, Shiloh, Champion Hill, and the Wilderness. He also lost seven thousand in thirty minutes at Cold Harbor—a record which still stands as the highest number of casualties suffered by an American army in such a short period of time. Grant's campaigns are well known and space does not allow me to go into detail, but they culminated with Robert E. Lee's surrender on April 9, 1865. He gave General Lee generous terms.

Grant's subsequent political career is also controversial. Although he was among the last people in the United States to free his slaves, he eventually advocated African American citizenship. He was easily elected president of the USA in 1868 and served from March 9, 1869 to March 4, 1877. He was somewhat gullible politically and was unable to control the corruption, which was rampant in his administration, although he was not personally corrupt. His Reconstruction, Indian, and economic policies were failures, and scandals discredited him as a chief executive by 1876. The Democrats took control of the U.S. House of Representatives in 1875. Grant chose not to run for re-election and was succeeded by Rutherford B. Hayes in 1877.

General and Mrs. Grant did a world tour, and after returning home, he attempted a political comeback. His efforts for a third term were defeated when the GOP picked compromise candidate James A. Garfield as their nominee. Grant campaigned for Garfield but refused to criticize Democratic nominee Winfield Scott Hancock, who was one of his former generals. Grant subsequently failed in several business ventures and was financially broke by 1884, when he was diagnosed as having throat cancer caused by his constant cigar smoking. He was greatly worried that he might die and leave his wife in poverty. With the help of his friend, Mark Twain, he wrote his memoirs, which are very successful, highly readable, and remain in print to this day. He finished them five days before his death, which occurred on July 23, 1885, in Wilton, New York. He was sixty-three years old. He is buried in Grant's Tomb in New York City. It is said to be the largest mausoleum in North America.

GEORGE SEARS GREENE, who was called "Pop," "Pap" or "Pappy" by his men, was born on May 6, 1801, in Apponaug, Rhode Island. His second cousin was Revolutionary War hero General Nathanael Greene. George's father was a shipbuilder who was ruined by Thomas Jefferson's Embargo of 1807 and the War of 1812. Financially unable to attend Brown University (his school of choice), George Greene secured an appointment to West

ENCYCLOPEDIA OF UNION GENERALS

Point in 1819. He graduated in 1823 (2/35) and was commissioned second lieutenant but selected the artillery as his branch, instead of the engineers. He spent his first four years on active duty as an assistant professor of mathematics at West Point.

Greene married in 1828. His wife bore three children in four years; they all died (the wife included) within seven months. Greene threw himself into his studies and became a qualified lawyer and a civil engineer. He resigned his commission in 1836.

George S. Greene was a brilliant engineer. He designed the sewage and water systems for Washington, D.C. and Detroit, Michigan, among others, designed the Croton Aqueduct reservoir in New York City and helped to build Central Park. He also constructed railroads in six states. He was sixty years old when the Civil War began.

Like many Union officers, Greene was not an abolitionist but firmly believed in restoring the Union. Initially, his efforts to rejoin the army were rejected because of his age. Governor Morgan named him commander of the 60th New York Infantry on January 1862. Although he was a strict disciplinarian and made an intimidating first impression, and presented a rough interior, his men grew to love him. He served in the Washington defenses until April 30, 1862, when he was promoted to brigadier general. He led a brigade in General Banks's Shenandoah Valley Campaign of 1862 and proved to be an effective commander, despite his advanced age. He took command of a division after Brigadier General John W. Geary was wounded at Cedar Mountain. He distinguished himself in the Battle of Antietam, where his men penetrated further than any others against Stonewall Jackson's corps.

Greene reverted to brigade command at the end of October. He was not engaged in the Battle of Fredericksburg but fought at Chancellorsville, where his brigade collapsed to Jackson's famous flanking attack of May 2, 1863. His finest hour occurred at Gettysburg on July 1 and 2, when his foresight in strengthening his positions allowed the Union to hold Culp's Hill. His son and aide, Lieutenant Charles Greene, lost a leg due to a Confederate Army shell in this battle. Sent to the Western Front that autumn, General Greene participated in the Siege of Chattanooga. At the Battle of Wauhatchie, he was severely wounded in the face when the

Confederates launched a surprise night attack (October 28–29), and he lost several teeth. He never fully recovered from this wound and was on court-martial or light duty until January 1865, when he assumed command of a brigade in Sherman's army. He took part in overrunning North Carolina and capturing Raleigh.

Greene was brevetted major general in January 1866 and was discharged from the service on April 30, 1866. He continued to be active and served a term as president of the American Society of Civil Engineers. Wanting to secure a lifetime pension for his second wife, Greene petitioned Congress for a captain's pension in 1892. Congress granted him only the rank of first lieutenant based on his highest regular army rank. He was sworn in in 1894 and, at age ninety-three, was perhaps the oldest lieutenant in U.S. history.

General Greene died in Morristown, New Jersey, on January 28, 1899. He was ninety-seven years old. He was interred in the George Sears Greene Family Cemetery (a.k.a. Rhode Island Historical Cemetery, Warwick #23), which is currently undergoing restoration. His gravestone is a boulder from Culp's Hill.

Greene's youngest son, Francis, was too young to fight in the Civil War, but he did fight in the Philippines during the Spanish-American War. He retired as a major general.

DAVID MCMURTRIE GREGG was born in Huntington, Pennsylvania, on April 10, 1833. His grandfather was a congressman and U.S. senator, and his first cousin was Andrew Curtin, the wartime governor of Pennsylvania (1861–1867). Gregg was educated by private tutors and attended the University of Lewisburg (now Bucknell University) in Pennsylvania and was admitted to West Point in 1851. He graduated in the Class of 1855 (8/34) and was commissioned brevet second lieutenant in the dragoons. He was promoted to second lieutenant later that year. Stationed on the Northwestern frontier, he became a company commander in the 1st Dragoons. He was later sent to California and traveled there with his

close friend, Dorsey Pender, who later became a Confederate general. The two young officers bought a racehorse together.

Gregg and his company were stationed at Fort Vancouver, Washington Territory, in 1857. At one time, his 160 men were surrounded by 1,000 hostile Indians. After a three-day battle, Gregg managed to extricate his command with only minor casualties. He was promoted to first lieutenant in March 1861 and was stationed at Fort Tejon, California, when the Civil War began. He became a captain in the 3rd U.S. Cavalry on May 14, 1861.

In August, Gregg was transferred to the 6th U.S. Cavalry of the Army of the Potomac. He was stricken with typhoid fever and was almost roasted alive when his Washington, D.C. hospital caught fire. In January 1862, he was named colonel of the 8th Pennsylvania Cavalry and distinguished himself in Seven Days battles, screening retreating Union infantry. He fought in the Maryland Campaign and at Fredericksburg, where he commanded a brigade. He was promoted to brigadier general on November 29. He assumed command of a division when General Hooker reorganized the Union cavalry in February 1863.

General Gregg was part of Stoneman's Raid during the Chancellorsville Campaign, fought in the Battle of Brandy Station and at Gettysburg, where he clashed indecisively with Confederate horsemen in the East Cavalry Field. He briefly commanded the Cavalry Corps of the Army of the Potomac on three occasions (1864–65) and was brevetted major general on August 1, 1864. He led the Union cavalry in the Petersburg sector until, after three years of constant field service and dozens of battles, his nerves apparently failed him. To the regret of General Sheridan, whom Gregg cordially despised, he resigned his commission on February 3, 1865.

Gregg was a taciturn man noted for his cool, unemotional demeanor. Post-war, General Gregg became a farmer in Reading, Pennsylvania (his wife's hometown), and Milford, Delaware, but he considered this life dull and regretted leaving the army. His application to rejoin the cavalry, however, was unsuccessful. President Grant appointed him U.S. consul to Prague in 1874, but he returned home after a short time because his wife was homesick. He was elected auditor general of Pennsylvania in 1891. He declined nomination as state treasurer in 1899 because of declining health.

General Gregg was commander-in-chief of the Military Order of the Loyal Legion United States from 1903 to 1905. He was the author of *The Second Cavalry Division of the Army of the Potomac in the Gettysburg Campaign*, which was published in 1907. He died in Reading, Pennsylvania, on August 7, 1916, at age eighty-three. He was buried in the Charles Evans Cemetery, Reading.

WALTER QUINTIN GRESHAM was born on March 17, 1832, near Lanesville, Indiana. He was educated in a log cabin schoolhouse, after which he became a schoolteacher and a minor county official. Meanwhile, he studied law, was admitted to the bar in 1854, and practiced in Corydon, Indiana, from then until 1860.

Gresham was a Republican in a strongly Democrat area and lost several local elections. He was finally elected to the legislature in 1860 and, as chairman on the Military Affairs Committee, did a great deal toward preparing Indiana for war. When the war broke out, he enlisted in the 38th Indiana as a private. He was promoted to lieutenant colonel in September 1861 and was named colonel of the 53rd Indiana in December. His regiment fought in the Siege of Corinth and in Grant's various Vicksburg campaigns. He led a brigade in the Siege of Vicksburg and was promoted to brigadier general on August 11, 1863. After directing Federal forces in the Natchez area, he and his men fought in Sherman's Atlanta Campaign. Here, on July 20, 1864, a Rebel bullet struck his left knee, maimed him for life, and ended his military career. He was brevetted major general in February 1866 and was discharged on April 30, 1866.

Gresham returned home on crutches and, despite his excellent military record, was defeated in contests for the U.S. House of Representatives and Senate. He nevertheless had a distinguished post-war career, serving as a U.S. district judge (1869–1883), postmaster general (1883–1884), U.S. secretary of the treasury (1884), U.S. circuit court judge (1884–1891), and U.S. secretary of state (1893–1895). He was a serious candidate for the presidency of the United States in 1884 and 1888, because of his sympathy for the American small farmer, and his dislike for the Republican Party's high tariff policies, he switched to the Democratic Party and was appointed secretary of state in President Grover Cleveland's second term. He died in office in Washington, D.C. on May 25, 1895. He was buried in Arlington National Cemetery.

BENJAMIN HENRY GRIERSON was born in Allegheny, Pennsylvania (now part of Pittsburgh), on July 8, 1826. When he was eight years old, he was kicked by a horse and almost died. He hated horses for the rest of his life; he nevertheless became a fine cavalry commander. General Sherman once called him the best cavalry commander he ever met. Meanwhile, he moved to Ohio and became a music teacher. Later, he settled in Illinois and became a band leader and a music instructor.

Grierson joined the Union Army on May 8, 1861, as a volunteer aide for General Prentiss. He became major of the 6th Illinois Cavalry in October and was promoted to colonel and commander of the regiment on April 12, 1862. He fought in numerous skirmishes and small actions in western Tennessee and northern Mississippi. He was wounded in the left hand at Olive Branch, Mississippi, on September 6, 1862. He assumed command of a cavalry brigade in November.

Grierson's most famous accomplishment was a raid he launched deep into Mississippi. Departing Union lines with 1,700 men on April 17, 1863, he rode 800 miles in 17 days, crippled two railroads, captured dozens of prisoners and horses, and destroyed tons of supplies. He reached Baton Rouge on May 2. Sherman called his raid "the most brilliant expedition of the war." It was the first major raid launched by the Union cavalry in the conflict.

Grierson was promoted to brigadier general on June 3, 1863. He took part in the Siege of Port Hudson as cavalry commander of the XIX Corps. He accompanied Sherman in his Meridian Expedition in February 1864. He was less successful fighting Nathan Bedford Forrest at Brice's Cross Roads in June 1864, where his command was routed; in fact, he was successful every time he fought the Confederate cavalry unless it was commanded by Forrest, whom he never managed to defeat.

Benjamin Grierson also fought as a gentleman. He kept his men under a tight control and never allowed them to loot or terrorize Southern civilians, who held him in high esteem, even if begrudgingly so.

Grierson assumed command of the cavalry division of the District of West Tennessee in late December 1864. He launched a successful raid against Verona, Mississippi, and destroyed Forrest's dismounted instructional camp. He also smashed the Mobile and Ohio Railroad and took five hundred prisoners. In 1865, he took part in the drive on Mobile, which fell on April 12. He was promoted to major general of volunteers on March 19, 1866, and was mustered out of volunteer service on April 30.

Grierson joined the Regular Army after the war and was commissioned colonel in 1866. This was unusual because he lacked West Point credentials, so he was looked upon with suspicion by many of his peers. He recognized the military potential of the African American and was an enthusiastic supporter of the Buffalo soldier. He was also sympathetic to the Indians, which led many of his colleagues to ostracize him, at least to a degree. Given command of the 10th Cavalry Regiment ("Buffalo soldiers"), he and his men excelled on the Western frontier, and in the summer of 1880 defeated the legendary Apache War Chief Victorio, ending the Indian threat to west Texas. This led to offers for him to command a "real" cavalry regiment, but he preferred to remain with his men. This led to further suspicion. Despite a solid record of accomplishment in New Mexico, Arizona, and the Indian Territory (he even founded Fort Sill, Oklahoma), Grierson was not promoted to brigadier general until April 1890. He reached the mandatory retirement age of sixty-four three months later. Meanwhile, he organized a railroad promotion company and successfully engaged in land speculation.

General Grierson lived in Jacksonville, Illinois, after he left the service, and had a ranch near Fort Concho, Texas. (Grierson and his wife loved west Texas.) He also had a summer home in Omena, Michigan. Here, he suffered a debilitating stroke in 1907 and spent most of the rest of his life in a sick bed. He died in Omena on September 1, 1911, at age eighty-five. He is buried in the Jacksonville East Cemetery, Illinois. He fathered seven children, one of whom served in the 10th Cavalry and retired as a colonel in 1915. The character Colonel Marlowe, played by John Wayne in the movie *The Horse Soldiers*, is very loosely based on him.

CHARLES GRIFFIN was born on December 18, 1825, in Granville, Ohio. He attended Kenyon College in Gambier, Ohio, before transferring to West Point in 1843. He graduated in the Class of 1847 (23/38) and was commissioned brevet second lieutenant in the 2nd U.S. Artillery. Griffin joined General Scott's army just before the fall of Mexico City. Afterward, he served in the American Southwest and fought Navajos in the New Mexico Territory. In 1854, he became an instructor of artillery tactics at West Point, where he was when the Civil War began. He was promoted to second lieutenant (1847), first lieutenant (1849), and captain (April 25, 1861).

Griffin turned the Academy's guns and enlisted men into a battery (Battery D, 5th Artillery), which he led in the First Battle of Bull Run and in the Peninsula Campaign. Because of the shortage of competent officers, he was promoted to brigadier general on June 12, 1862, and was given command of an infantry brigade. He distinguished himself at Gaines' Mill and Malvern Hill during the Seven Days battles. He was held in reserve at the Second Bull Run and lightly engaged at Antietam.

Charles Griffin had an irascible temperament and frequently quarreled with his superiors but was popular with his men. He led a division at Fredericksburg and Chancellorsville; he then fell ill and only rejoined the army at the very end of the Battle of Gettysburg. He later served in the Mine Run and Overland Campaigns and the Siege of Petersburg and was brevetted major general in December 1864. He commanded the V Corps during the Appomattox Campaign. He was appointed major general of volunteers on July 12, 1865.

Postwar, Griffin was commander of the District of Maine; then he was named colonel, Regular Army, and commander of the 35th Infantry Regiment. He was transferred to Galveston, Texas, in 1867, as assistant commander of the Freedmen's Bureau for Texas. His immediate superior was Philip Sheridan. Griffin and Sheridan used their power to remove several Democrats from office and even replaced the governor. Meanwhile, a yellow fever epidemic swept through the Lone Star State. Griffin caught it and died in Galveston on September 15, 1867. He was forty-one years old. He was interred in Oak Hill Cemetery, Washington, D.C.

Griffin and his wife had two children, both of whom died before age six. She later married Count Maximilian Esterhazy and became an Austrian countess.

SIMON GOODELL GRIFFIN was born in Nelson, New Hampshire, on August 9, 1824. He attended local schools when he was not working on his uncle's farm. He eventually became a teacher, was elected to the state legislature, read law, and was admitted to the bar in 1860.

Griffin joined the U.S. Army as a captain in the 2nd New Hampshire Infantry on June 1, 1861, and with it at the First Battle of Bull Run. In October, he was promoted to lieutenant colonel of the 6th New Hampshire Infantry and led it brilliantly in the capture of Elizabeth City, North Carolina, on April 7, 1862, and in the Union victory at Camden on April 19. As a result, he was promoted to colonel on April 22, 1862. Sent back to Virginia, he fought in the Second Battle of Bull Run, Chantilly, and Antietam, where his regiment and the 2nd Maryland stormed Burnside's Bridge. Both units suffered heavy casualties. Griffin was less successful at Fredericksburg on December 13, where a third of the men were killed or wounded. Griffin was promoted to brigade commander in February 1863.

Sent west, Griffin took part in the final Vicksburg Campaign, where it was posted in the rear, to prevent any Confederate attempt to relieve the fortress. He was with Sherman in his Meridian Expedition of February 1864. He occasionally served as an acting division commander and was promoted to brigadier general on May 30, 1864.

After helping to get men from New Hampshire to re-enlist, he returned to the Army of the Potomac and fought in the Overland Campaign and the Siege of Petersburg with the IX Corps. He participated in the Appomattox Campaign and was promoted to major general on July 12, 1865. He was mustered out on August 24, 1865, having never missed a single day's duty in the entire war. He was a fine commander at every level in which he exercised command.

Simon Griffin returned to New Hampshire, where he became a manufacturer, served three more terms in the legislature (the last two as speaker), and was twice defeated in races for Congress. He went to Texas in 1873 and spent several years in land speculation and railroad development. He returned to New Hampshire and settled in Keene, where he became a local historian. He died on June 14, 1902, at age seventy-seven. He is buried in Woodland Cemetery, Keene, New Hampshire.

WILLIAM GROSE was born on December 16, 1812, in Dayton, Ohio. His family moved to Fayette County, Indiana, and then to Henry County. As a youth, Grose worked in a local brickyard and as a farm laborer. Wanting more, he studied law, passed the bar in 1842, and settled in New Castle, Indiana, where he lived for the rest of his life. He ran for Congress as a Democrat in 1852 but was defeated. By 1856, however, he joined the Republican Party, and was elected to the legislature that same year. He was elected judge of the Henry County Common Pleas Court in 1860 but resigned when the war began.

Grose recruited the 36th Indiana Infantry and was appointed its colonel in October 1861. Throughout his military career, Grose was noted for his courage and a tendency to gravitate to wherever the fighting was heaviest. He first saw action at Shiloh, where his horse was shot out from under him, and he was wounded in the left shoulder. He was slightly wounded in the head on May 30, during the Siege of Corinth. When Jacob Ammen was wounded in June, Colonel Grose assumed command of his brigade. He fought in all the major battles of the Army of the Cumberland, including the Kentucky (Heartland) Campaign, the Battle of Stones River (where another horse was shot from under him), Vicksburg, Chickamauga, the Tullahoma Campaign, the Siege of Chattanooga, and the attack on Lookout Mountain, where he was wounded in the neck. On July 30, 1864, during the Atlanta Campaign, he was promoted to brigadier general on the recommendations of Sherman and Thomas. He opposed Hood's invasion of Tennessee, including the Battles of Franklin and Nashville. He left the army on December 31, 1865, and was brevetted major general the following month.

Grose was a collector of internal revenue from 1866 to 1874. After he left Federal employment, Grose began rebuilding his law practice. He was also involved in building a number of mental hospitals in Indiana. In 1878, he ran for Congress again but lost. He wrote a history of the 36th Indiana, which was published in 1891. Meanwhile, he served a term as state senator in the late 1880s.

General Grose had to give up the practice of law around 1890 because of deafness. Senile and suffering from severe rheumatism in his last years, he died in New Castle on July 30, 1900, at age eighty-seven. His former home is now the headquarters of the Henry County Historical Society. Grose is buried in South Mound Cemetery, New Castle, Indiana.

CUVIER GROVER was born in Bethel, Maine, on July 24, 1828. He entered West Point in 1846 at the age of seventeen and graduated in 1850 (4/44). He was commissioned brevet second lieutenant in the 4th Artillery and was promoted to second lieutenant (1850), first lieutenant (1855), and captain (1858). He spent his antebellum career on the Western frontier, where he explored routes for the Northern Pacific Railroad and took part in operations against the Mormons in Utah. Grover was stationed at Fort Union, New Mexico Territory, when the war began.

Grover returned to the East in November 1861 and took a leave of absence for six months. He returned to duty in April 1862, was immediately given a brigade in the Army of the Potomac, and was promoted to brigadier general of volunteers on April 15. He was a good brigade commander and distinguished himself at the battles of Williamsburg and Seven Pines. Transferred to the Army of Virginia, he led a bayonet attack against Stonewall Jackson in the Battle of Groveton during the Second Bull Run Campaign and won accolades from John Pope. He lost five hundred men in this action. Perhaps someone thought this was too many; in any case, Grover was transferred to Louisiana, where he commanded a division in the XIX Corps.

Cuvier Grover fought in the Louisiana Campaigns of 1863 and commanded the Union right wing during Banks's Siege of Port Hudson. In 1864, he served in the Red River Campaign before he was transferred to Virginia. He fought in the Shenandoah Valley Campaign and performed well at Winchester and Fisher's Hill. He distinguished himself in the Battle of Cedar Creek (October 19), where he was wounded in the left arm and foot, and for which he was brevetted major general. He was in command of the District of Savannah when the war ended. He was mustered out of volunteer service on August 24, 1865.

Grover reverted to his regular army rank (major) and was promoted to lieutenant colonel in 1866. He served on the frontier in Kansas and New Mexico and on garrison duty at Jefferson Barracks, Missouri and briefly commanded the 38th U.S. Infantry, an African American regiment, after the army reorganized in 1866. He was unemployed for a year (1869–70), after which he served in the 3rd Cavalry. He was named commander of the 1st Cavalry in 1875 and was promoted to colonel. He served in Washington and Montana territories.

Ill for some time, General Grover went to Atlantic City, New Jersey, to improve his health. He died there on June 5, 1885, at age fifty-six. He was interred in the West Point Cemetery. His younger brother was La Fayette Grover, who was governor of Oregon from 1870 to 1877 and U.S. senator (1877–1883).

H

HACKLEMAN – HURLBUT

PLEASANT ADAMS HACKLEMAN was born on November 15, 1814, in Franklin County, Indiana. He married in 1833 and became a farmer. He and his wife had at least eight children, seven of whom lived into adulthood. Meanwhile, he studied law and passed his bar exam. He was probate judge of Rush County from 1837 to 1840, when he became editor of the *Rushville Republican* (a position he held until 1861) and was elected to the Indiana House of Representatives in 1841. He also served as county clerk and ran for Congress in 1848 and 1858 but was not successful either time. An abolitionist, he was a delegate to the Republican National Convention which nominated Lincoln for president in 1860, and Hackleman was a delegate to the "Washington Peace Conference" of 1861, but it was unsuccessful in preventing the war.

Indiana Governor Oliver P. Morton appointed Hackleman colonel of the 16th Indiana Infantry on May 20, 1861. It was sent to the Eastern Front and fought in the Battle of Ball's Bluff (October 21). The regiment remained in Maryland and Virginia, but on April 30, 1862, Hackleman was promoted to brigadier general and sent to the Western Front, where he was given command of a brigade in the Army of the Tennessee. Transferred to Rosecrans's Army of the Mississippi, he was at Corinth when the Confederates attacked on October 3, 1862. They pushed through Union lines, which fell back in confusion. Showing considerable courage, Hackleman attempted to rally his brigade but was shot through the neck. Taken to the Tishomingo Hotel in the rear, he died later that day. His last words were: "I am dying, but I die for my country." He was forty-seven years of age. General Hackleman is buried in the East Hill Cemetery, Rushville, Indiana.

HENRY WAGER HALLECK was born in Westernville, New York, on January 15, 1815. He detested life on the farm and ran away at an early age to be raised by an uncle in Utica. He attended Hudson Academy and Union College before gaining admission to West Point in 1835. He graduated in 1839 (3/31) and was commissioned second lieutenant of engineers, the most coveted and prestigious of all the branches. He spent two years improving the defenses of New York Harbor before being sent to Europe, where he studied European fortifications and techniques. After he returned home, he gave a dozen lectures which he published as a book, *Elements of Military Arts and Science*, in 1846. This earned him the nickname "Old Brains." It eventually became a derogatory sobriquet.

In many ways, Halleck was more of a scholar than a soldier. Sent to California during the Mexican War, he used the seven-month sea voyage to translate Antoine-Henri Jomini's work on Napoleon into English. He fought in the Battle of Mazatlán and earned a brevet to captain for his service on the west coast. Meanwhile, Halleck was promoted to first lieutenant in 1845 and to captain, regular army, in 1853. He studied law in his spare time and founded a law firm. It was so successful that he resigned from the service in 1854. He was also successful at land speculation and ranching. His Rancho Nicasio covered thirty thousand acres. He became president of the Atlantic and Pacific Railroad and turned down a seat on the California Supreme Court and in the U.S. Senate. He was a major general in the California Militia when the Civil War began.

A Democrat who was sympathetic to the South, he nevertheless opposed breaking up the Union. After the Bull Run disaster, Winfield Scott arranged for him to join the Federal (regular) army as a major general on August 19, 1861. He succeeded Fremont as commander of the Department of the Missouri on November 9. Halleck had a talent for logistics and established order out of the chaos and corruption left by Fremont. He was a brilliant organizer but not an easy man to work for; he was also an easy man to hate. Early in the war, his subordinates won major victories—Grant at Forts Henry and Donelson, Curtis at Pea Ridge, Pope at Island No. 10, and Grant at Shiloh. This led to the expansion of Halleck's department, and eventually he was placed in charge of the Department of the Mississippi.

Henry Halleck was not a good field commander. The only field operation he personally directed was the Siege of Corinth (April–May 1862). The Rebel leader, General Beauregard, was outnumbered almost three to one, but he clearly outclassed Halleck as a commander, who advanced at glacial speed. He finally captured the place, but the Confederates escaped with almost no loss. Even so, Lincoln promoted him to general-in-chief of the U. S. Army on July 23, 1862.

The admiration he gained from his unquestionably brilliant antebellum accomplishments eventually deteriorated to the point that few people in Washington, D.C. respected him. Lincoln called him "little more than a first-rate clerk" and Secretary of the Navy Gideon Welles said he "takes no responsibility, plans nothing, suggests nothing, is good for nothing." He continually tried to shift responsibility from his own shoulders and to find scapegoats. He was replaced as general-in-chief by Ulysses S. Grant on March 9, 1864.

General Halleck devised the Union's strategy for 1864, and it was flawed. He arranged for the major Union targets to be Richmond, Atlanta, and Shreveport, Louisiana, instead of the Richmond-Atlanta-Mobile strategy advocated by Grant. By the time Grant took charge, it was too late to change the strategy. This meant Sherman had to advance on Atlanta with ten thousand fewer men than he planned (they were tied down in Louisiana), while the Rebels were able to reinforce Atlanta with fourteen thousand men, initially earmarked to defend Mobile. This was a swing of twenty-four thousand men in favor of the South, which might have cost the Union the war. (Lincoln believed he would lose the election of 1864 until Atlanta fell; that changed everything.) It also brought the Confederate Army of Western Louisiana, which could not cross the Mississippi River to aid its comrades west of the river, into combat, with unhappy results for the Union.

Fortunately for the North, General Grant recognized Halleck would be a very effective chief of staff, U.S. Army. He served in this position from March 12, 1864, until the end of the war. He was a fine administrator and kept the Union armies well supplied and equipped. He meshed well with Grant, whose forte was aggressive field command.

After the war, Halleck briefly commanded the Military Division of the James before he was transferred to the Department of the Pacific, which was headquartered in San Francisco. In 1869, he was given command of the Department of the South. He died of liver disease at his headquarters in Louisville, Kentucky, on January 9, 1872, at age fifty-six. He is buried in the Green-Wood Cemetery, Brooklyn, New York.

JOSEPH ELDRIDGE HAMBLIN was born in Yarmouth, Massachusetts, on January 13, 1828. His Puritan ancestors came to America in 1639. He was educated in public schools in Boston, took a voyage to China, and worked for a firm which built engines. He became an insurance broker in New York City and joined the 7th New York Militia Regiment. He moved to St. Louis, Missouri, in 1857 but returned to New York when the war began and entered Union service on April 27, 1861. He was commissioned first lieutenant in the 5th New York Infantry (a Zouave regiment) on May 10, 1861, and served as regimental adjutant. He was promoted to captain on August 10.

Hamblin was a fearless warrior who was repeatedly commended by his superiors. He fought at Big Bethel, the Peninsula Campaign, the Maryland Campaign, Fredericksburg, Chancellorsville, Gettysburg, the Wilderness, the opening battles for Petersburg, and the Shenandoah Valley Campaign of 1864, including the battles of Fisher's Hill and Cedar Creek, where he led a charge that helped win the battle. Here, he was severely wounded in the right leg and was brevetted brigadier general for his gallantry. He returned to the Petersburg trenches in February 1865 and earned a brevet to major general for his part in the victory at Sayler's Creek. Meanwhile, he was promoted rapidly, to captain (September 8, 1861); major of the 65th New York (November 4, 1861); lieutenant colonel (July 20, 1862); colonel and regimental commander (May 26, 1863); and brigade commander (December 30, 1863). He was promoted to brigadier general of volunteers on May 19, 1865, and was discharged from the service on January 15, 1866.

General Hamblin returned to New York City and the insurance business but remained active in the New York Militia, initially serving as a colonel. He became adjutant general and chief of staff of the New York National Guard in 1867. Meanwhile, he became superintendent of agencies for the Commonwealth Fire Insurance Company. He died in New York City on July 3, 1870, at the age of forty-two and was buried in Woodside Cemetery in the town of his birth.

ANDREW JACKSON HAMILTON was born in Huntsville, Alabama, on January 18, 1815. He studied law, was admitted to the bar in 1841, and moved to Fayette County, Texas, in 1847. Here, he launched a successful political career, serving as attorney general of Texas (1849–50), a member of the Texas House of Representatives (1851–53), and a member of the U.S. House of Representatives (1859–61). He did not run for re-election in 1860.

Hamilton was an uncompromising Unionist, although he was a Democrat and advocated conciliation with the South. Even though Texas seceded on February 1, 1861, Hamilton retained his seat in Congress until his term expired on March 3. He then returned to the Lone Star State and was elected to the state senate as an opponent of secession. His views were not particularly appreciated at home, and he fled to Mexico in July 1862, after his life was threatened. He then returned to the United States and gave speeches in the Northeast, where he denounced slave power.

On November 4, 1862, Abraham Lincoln appointed him brigadier general and named him military governor of Texas. He was not well liked in Washington. Secretary of the Navy Gideon Welles described him as "deceptive, vain, [and] self-conceited." His initial appointment was never ratified by the Senate and expired on March 4, 1863. Lincoln, however, reappointed him on September 18. Meanwhile, the Union attempts to invade Texas failed in 1863 and again in 1864. Hamilton had no real power and spent most of his time in New Orleans. His attempts to pay off his personal creditors by giving them the opportunity to speculate on Texas cotton failed, which is why General Banks commented that Hamilton was "without force of character."

President Andrew Johnson appointed Hamilton provisional (civilian) governor of Texas on June 17, 1865. As the first Reconstruction governor of the state, he faced huge problems, including Indian excursions, financial chaos, general lawlessness, and the issue of what to do with the newly freed African Americans. He soon broke with President Johnson, aligned himself with the Radical Republicans, and advocated suffrage for the blacks, but not to former Confederates. He resigned his governorship on August 9, 1866, and became a bankruptcy judge in New Orleans in 1867. Later that year, he returned to Texas as a member of the state Supreme Court. He ran for governor in 1869 but was defeated. Meanwhile, he reversed his position on suffrage and opposed giving the vote to African Americans. He also broke with the Radicals, changed his views on Reconstruction, and advocated ending it quickly.

General Hamilton never stood for office again after his 1869 defeat. He returned to his farm, practiced law, and died of tuberculosis in Austin on April 11, 1875, at age sixty. He was buried in Oakwood Cemetery, Austin.

CHARLES SMITH HAMILTON was born on November 16, 1822, in Westernville, New York. He attended West Point from 1839 to 1843 (26/39), where he was Ulysses S. Grant's classmate. He was commissioned brevet second lieutenant in the 2nd U.S. Infantry and served in the Mexican War, where he fought at Monterrey, Vera Cruz, Cerro Gordo, Contreras, and Churubusco. He was promoted to second lieutenant in 1845, to first lieutenant in 1847, and was brevetted captain for his actions at Churubusco. During the Battle of Molino del Rey (September 8, 1847), he was shot through the shoulder and spent six months recuperating.

Hamilton's next duty assignment was as a recruiter in Rochester, New York. In 1850, he returned to the field, fighting Comanches in Texas. He resigned his commission in 1853 and moved to Fond du Lac, Wisconsin, where he farmed and operated a linseed mill.

Charles Hamilton was eager to return to the colors in 1861 and accepted the colonelcy of the 3rd Wisconsin Infantry on May 11. He was sent to Harpers Ferry, Virginia, and was promoted to brigadier general on August 7. He was given a brigade and guarded the Potomac crossings until March 1862, when he took command of a division in General McClellan's army.

Hamilton fought in the Siege of Yorktown but clashed with McClellan, who declared he was not fit to lead a division and relieved him of his command for insubordination on April 30. Abraham Lincoln felt McClellan acted improperly, but the general responded: "You cannot do anything better calculated to injure my army . . . than to restore Gen. Hamilton to his division." Because of McClellan's uncompromising attitude, Lincoln transferred Hamilton to the Western Front.

Given command of a division in the Army of the Mississippi, Hamilton performed very well in the battles of Iuka and Corinth and was promoted to major general on November 29, 1862. Over the next five months, he commanded the District of Corinth, the Left Wing of the XIII Corps, the XVI Corps, the District of West Tennessee, and the Left Wing of the XVI Corps. He could not stay out of army politics, however. Although he assured Grant of his support, for example, he simultaneously denounced him as a "drunkard" to U.S. Senator James R. Doolittle. He also intrigued against generals Hurlbut and McPherson. When Grant ordered him to the Vicksburg sector to serve under John McClernand, Hamilton submitted his resignation, which Grant happily accepted. He was discharged on April 13, 1863.

Hamilton was not the first general ruined by politics. He returned to Wisconsin, where he became a successful businessman. Ironically, in 1869, President Grant appointed him U.S. marshal in Milwaukee. He later became president of the Board of Regents of the University of Wisconsin.

Charles Hamilton died in Milwaukee on April 17, 1891. He was sixty-eight. He was buried in the Forest Home Cemetery, Milwaukee.

SCHUYLER HAMILTON was born in New York City on July 22, 1822. His grandfather was founding father Alexander Hamilton, the first U.S. secretary of the treasury. His maternal grandfather was Baron Cornelis van den Heuvel, the governor of Dutch Guiana. His sister was married to General Halleck and, after he died, married General George W. Cullum.

The extremely well-connected Hamilton entered West Point in 1837 at age fifteen. He graduated in 1841 (24/52) and was commissioned second lieutenant in the 1st U.S. Infantry Regiment. He served on the Western frontier, as an assistant professor of tactics at West Point, and in the

Mexican War, where he was brevetted first lieutenant and captain. He was also shot in the stomach and had a lance go completely through his chest, piercing a lung, in the fighting around Monterrey, northern Mexico. After he recovered, he was an aide to General Scott for seven years. Meanwhile, he was promoted to first lieutenant, Regular Army, in 1848. He resigned his commission in 1855 and moved to California, where he briefly interned in William Tecumseh Sherman's bank. He also engaged in mercury mining. In 1858, he returned to the East and became a farmer in Branford, Connecticut.

Six days after the fall of Fort Sumter, Hamilton enlisted in the 7th New York Militia Regiment as a private. On May 9, 1861, he was promoted to lieutenant colonel and military secretary to Winfield Scott. He was promoted to brigadier general on November 12, 1861, and was named assistant chief of staff of the Department of the Missouri. He commanded a division in the Battle of Island No. 10 and the Siege of Corinth, after which he was given command of the Right Wing of the Army of the Mississippi, which consisted of two divisions.

Hamilton was appointed major general on November 29, 1862, but his appointment was never confirmed due to illness. Schuyler Hamilton was a fine general, but his health would not allow him to do prolonged field service. He suffered from liver problems, violent diarrhea, severe cramps, malaria, and dysentery. He resigned from the army on February 27, 1863. Abraham Lincoln, with whom he corresponded, wrote him a letter lamenting his decision.

General Hamilton returned to his farm in Connecticut but in 1866 moved back to New York City. He worked as a hydrographic engineer and in the city's Department of Docks. He also attempted to be placed on the U.S. Army's retirement list but without success. He retired for health reasons in 1875. An invalid for years, General Hamilton died at his home in New York City on March 18, 1903. He was eighty years old. He was interred in the Green-Wood Cemetery, Brooklyn, New York.

CYRUS HAMLIN was born in Hampden, Maine, (a suburb of Bangor), on April 26, 1839, the son of prominent Maine politician Hannibal Hamlin, who became Lincoln's first vice president (1861–65). Cyrus was

educated at Hampden Academy and Waterville College (now Colby College), Maine, but dropped out to study law. He was admitted to the bar in 1860 and set up a practice in Kittery, Maine.

Hamlin joined the Union Army in April 1862 as a captain and aide-de-camp to John C. Fremont in western Virginia. He was one of the first officers to advocate enlisting African Americans into the U.S. Army. He was sent to Louisiana where, on February 12, 1863, he was named colonel of the 8th *Corps d'Afrique*, which became the 80th United States Colored Troops (USCT) Infantry Regiment in April. He took part in the Siege of Port Hudson and was given command of a USCT brigade in September. He remained in the Department of the Gulf for the rest of the war and became commander of a black division in April 1864. Mostly his men were used to secure the Union rear. Hamlin was promoted to brigadier general on December 3, 1864, and was named commander of the District of Port Hudson in February 1865. He was mustered out of volunteer service on January 15, 1866, and brevetted major general on February 21, 1866.

A Carpetbagger, Hamlin remained in Louisiana after the war. He died of yellow fever in New Orleans on August 28, 1867. He was twenty-eight years old. He was buried in Mount Hope Cemetery, Bangor, Maine. His brother, Major Charles Hamlin, was brevetted brigadier general in March 1866.

WILLIAM ALEXANDER HAMMOND was born on August 28, 1828, in Annapolis, Maryland, but grew up in Harrisburg, Pennsylvania. He received his MD degree from New York University Medical College in 1848 at age twenty. He specialized in neurology, the branch of medicine dealing with the diagnosis and treatment of diseases involving the brain, the spinal cord, and the nervous system. He had a dynamic personality and attracted followers and foes wherever he went. After an internship and a brief period in private practice, he became an assistant surgeon in the U.S. Army from 1849 to 1860. He served in New Mexico, participated in the First Sioux War in Wyoming and Nebraska, and was medical director at Fort Riley, Kansas, when he resigned his commission in 1860. Dr. Hammond wrote a paper which won a prize from the American Medical Association and was offered the chair of anatomy and physiology at the University of Maryland School of Medicine in Baltimore, which he accepted.

Hammond rejoined the army on May 28, 1861, and, as a surgeon, was sent to western Virginia, where he and Jonathan Letterman designed a new ambulance wagon. The medical services at that time were noted for its personality conflicts and internal politics. In 1862, Secretary of War Edwin M. Stanton fired Surgeon General Clement Finley after an argument, so Abraham Lincoln appointed Hammond surgeon general—against Stanton's advice. He was promoted to brigadier general on April 25, 1862.

Hammond was young (thirty-four years old), tall, brilliant, and energetic. He was also somewhat inflexible and didn't mind stepping on toes. He raised requirements for entry into the Army Medical Corps, reorganized the corps, successfully lobbied for more funding (which increased ten-fold), set up an efficient ambulance system throughout the Union Army, and saw to it that personal decisions were based on merit rather than political favoritism. His reforms saved a significant number of Yankee lives, but they also alienated Stanton, who sent him on an inspection tour of the South on September 8, 1863. He then effectively replaced Hammond with Joseph Barnes, Stanton's personal physician, who became "acting Surgeon General."

General Hammond bristled at Stanton's high-handed action and demanded to be reinstated or court-martialed. He was court-martialed. Stanton stacked the court against him and used fabricated data (false evidence) to convict Hammond for "irregularities" in the purchase of medical furniture. He was dismissed from the service on August 18, 1864.

In civilian life, Dr. Hammond recovered his reputation quickly. He established himself at Bellevue Hospital in New York City, became a pioneer in the treatment of nervous and mental diseases, and he wrote numerous articles on a staggering number of medical topics. He was a founder of the American Neurological Association, became a professor of nervous and mental disorders at New York University, was co-editor of *The Medical and*

Surgical History of the War of the Rebellion (1870–1888), and even wrote novels. Space does not allow me to list all his accomplishments. In 1878, his court-martial was reversed, he was declared acquitted, and was restored to the rank of brigadier general, U.S. Army, retired, but without back pay or benefits.

Dr. Hammond was undoubtedly a genius of the first order who made a significant contribution to the Union war effort. He died in Washington, D.C., on January 5, 1900, at seventy-one years old. He was interred in Arlington National Cemetery.

WINFIELD SCOTT HANCOCK was born on February 14, 1824, in Montgomeryville, Pennsylvania (a hamlet just northwest of Philadelphia), along with Hilary Baker Hancock, his identical twin brother. He was educated in public schools and at Norristown Academy. He entered the United States Military Academy at West Point in 1840 and graduated in 1844 (18/25). Commissioned brevet second lieutenant in the 6th U.S. Infantry, he was stationed in the Indian Territory and was promoted to second lieutenant in 1846. He fought in Mexico, where he was wounded in the knee at Churubusco and was brevetted first lieutenant for Contreras and Churubusco. He later served as regimental quartermaster and then regimental adjutant, being stationed mainly in Fort Snelling, Minnesota; Jefferson Barracks, St. Louis, Missouri; Florida; and Utah. He was an assistant quartermaster on the staff of the District of California from 1855 to 1861 and was promoted to first lieutenant (1853) and captain (1855). He was in the Golden State when the Civil War began.

After the First Bull Run, Hancock was recalled to the East and was promoted to brigadier general on September 23, 1861. He commanded a brigade in the Army of the Potomac, fought in the Peninsula Campaign, and led a vital counterattack in the Battle of Williamsburg (May 5, 1862). General McClellan praised his performance as "Superb," which became his nickname.

When Major General Israel Richardson was mortally wounded at Antietam on September 17, Hancock took command of his division. The appointment was made permanent, and he was promoted to major general on November 29, 1862. By now, he was generally recognized as one of the best generals in the Union Army. He was part of Burnside's disastrous attack on Marye's Heights during the Battle of Fredericksburg, where he was grazed in the abdomen by a Confederate bullet. He was wounded again on May 3, 1863, during the Battle of Chancellorsville. He assumed command of the II Corps on May 22.

Hancock's most famous service came at Gettysburg. After his friend, General Reynolds, was killed, Meade gave Hancock temporary command of the northern wing of the army, which included the I, II, III, and IX Corps. He had the authority to withdraw, but he made the decision to fight at Gettysburg on July 1. Meade arrived on the field and assumed command that night.

Hancock's II Corps held the center of the Union line at Cemetery Ridge on July 2 and 3. He rushed units to critical spots in the battle and exhibited a sure tactical feel throughout the battle. On July 3, he bore the brunt of Pickett's Charge. Here, a bullet struck the pommel of his saddle and ricocheted into his thigh, along with pieces of wood and a small nail. Although in great pain, Hancock would not leave the field until the fighting was over.

After he partially recovered from his wound, Hancock was sent on recruiting duty (i.e., light duty) that winter. He suffered from his Gettysburg wound for the rest of the war. He nevertheless performed well in the Overland Campaign, although he did not have his former energy. His corps suffered enormous casualties during Grant's futile assault at Cold Harbor. He suffered his only significant defeat of the war at Reams' Station on August 25, 1864, when Confederate forces under General Heth launched a surprise attack, caught the II Corps flat-footed, and took many prisoners. This action, along with the lingering effects of his Gettysburg wound, led to Hancock's decision to give up field command in November, despite having won a significant victory in the Battle of the Boydton Plank Road on October 27 and 28. He commanded the largely ceremonial I Veteran Corps and replaced Sheridan as commander of the Shenandoah Valley after it was basically cleared of Rebel forces. After the end of the war, he supervised the execution of the Lincoln assassination conspirators. He did not want to hang Mary Surratt, but President Johnson ordered it, so Hancock carried it out.

Winfield Hancock was promoted to brigadier general, Regular Army, on August 12, 1864, and was scheduled to revert to that rank when he was discharged from volunteer service on July 26, 1866. General Grant, who had nothing but praise for his integrity, his competence, genial personality, and courage, arranged for him to be promoted to major general that same day. Post-war, he briefly commanded the Department of Kansas. He was given command of the Fifth Military District, which included Louisiana and Texas, and treated the civilians well, in accordance with President Johnson's policies. He refused to use his power to overturn elections and jury verdicts, and restored habeas corpus and the freedom of the press.

After commanding the Department of Dakota and the Division of the Atlantic, Hancock was the Democratic nominee for president in 1880 but was narrowly defeated by James A. Garfield. Hancock lost the popular vote 4,446,158 to 4,444,260. He exhibited his typical class and good grace in defeat.

In later life, Hancock was the president of the National Rifle Association and served as commander-in-chief of the Military Order of the Loyal Legion (MOLLUS) from 1879 until his death, which occurred in New York City on February 9, 1886. He was sixty-one years old. General Hancock was laid to rest in the Montgomery Cemetery, West Norristown Township, Montgomery County, Pennsylvania.

JAMES ALLEN HARDIE was born in New York City on May 5, 1823. He attended the Western Collegiate Institute at Pittsburgh and the Poughkeepsie Collegiate Institute in New York, before attending the United States Military Academy for four years. Just after his twentieth birthday, he graduated with the Class of 1843 (11/39), was commissioned brevet second lieutenant of artillery, and was assigned to the 3rd U.S. Artillery Regiment. He spent the Mexican War years in California as a major in the 1st New York Infantry and became commandant of San Francisco between routine garrison assignment. Later, he fought Indians in Oregon and Washington territories and was an aide to General John E. Wool. He was promoted to second lieutenant (1846), first lieutenant (1847), and captain (1857). He was stationed in Oregon when the Civil War began.

Hardie was promoted to lieutenant colonel on September 28, 1861, and was named aide to General George C. McClellan. He served with that general until Lincoln sacked him in November 1862; then he remained on the staff of McClellan's successor, General Burnside. He was appointed brigadier general on November 29, 1862, but the appointment was revoked on January 22, 1863—probably because Burnside was in disgrace after the Battle of Fredericksburg and Hooker did not want Hardie. In any case, he was named major and assistant adjutant general in the regular army in February. It was he who delivered the order to General Meade, naming him commander of the Army of the Potomac on June 28, 1863.

Hardie was promoted to colonel, Regular Army, in March 1864. A staff officer throughout the war, he was brevetted brigadier general on March 3, 1865 and major general in 1866. Postbellum, Hardie was one of four inspectors general holding the rank of colonel. He continued on active duty until his death, which occurred in Washington, D.C. on December 14, 1876. He was fifty-three years old. He was buried in the Green-Wood Cemetery, Brooklyn.

MARTIN DAVIS HARDIN was born in Jacksonville, Illinois, on June 26, 1837. One of his ancestors served at Valley Forge, his grandfather was a U.S. senator from Kentucky, and his father was Major General of Illinois Militia John J. Hardin, who was killed in action at Buena Vista in the Mexican War. Prior to that, John Hardin was close, personal friends with a fellow Illinois lawyer, Abraham Lincoln, who reportedly met his future wife in Hardin's home. Martin entered West Point in 1854 (the first five-year class at the Academy), graduated in 1859 (11/22), and was commissioned brevet second lieutenant in the 3rd Artillery. He was promoted to second lieutenant in 1860.

One of Hardin's first assignments was as an aide to Colonel Robert E. Lee in the hanging of John Brown in

December 1859. He was sent to Oregon soon after and was stationed at Fort Umpqua when the war broke out. Sent to the Eastern Front, he was promoted to first lieutenant on May 1, 1861, and was aide-de-camp to Henry Hunt from May 1861 to June 1862. After serving in the Peninsula Campaign, he was elected lieutenant colonel of the 12th Pennsylvania Reserve Infantry Regiment on April 1, 1862, and led it in the Peninsula Campaign, the Seven Days battles, and the Battle of Groveton (August 28), where he was slightly wounded in the head. The next day, during the Second Battle of Bull Run, he became acting brigade commander. Here, he was severely wounded twice, in the side and in the chest. Promoted to colonel on July 8, he was unable to participate in the battle of Antietam or Fredericksburg, where the 12th was commanded by its senior captain. He returned to duty in February 1863, but his regiment was on provost duty in Washington, D.C., during the Battle of Chancellorsville.

Colonel Hardin distinguished himself at Gettysburg, where his regiment held part of Big Round Top on July 2 and 3. Hardin was given command of a brigade in the V Corps in September. In December, during the Mine Run Campaign, he was assigned the task of guarding the Orange & Alexander Railroad. Here, near Catlett's Station, Virginia, he was seriously wounded when a group of Rebels, guerrillas dressed in blue uniforms, ambushed him, and his left arm had to be amputated.

Hardin returned to duty in March 1864 as commander of the Pittsburgh Draft Depot. He soon returned to the main army and took part in the Overland Campaign, where he was wounded on the North Anna River on May 23. He was promoted to brigadier general on July 6, 1864, and took command of a division in the XXII Corps, District of Washington, six days later. He fought against General Early's raid on Washington at Fort Stevens. He remained in the capital city area for the rest of the war on provost and court-martial duty.

Hardin was discharged from volunteer service on January 15, 1866, and reverted to the Regular Army rank of major in the 43rd U.S. Infantry. He spent the rest of his military career on recruiting and garrison duty. He retired in December 1870 as a brigadier general and became a lawyer in Chicago. Hardin was a strong Roman Catholic and an ardent fisherman. He also wrote a history of the 12th Pennsylvania Reserves. From 1886, he spent his winters in his summer house in St. Augustine, Florida, where he died on December 12, 1923, at age eighty-six. He was the last member of his West Point class and one of the last Civil War generals to pass away. General Hardin is buried in the St. Augustine National Cemetery.

ABNER CLARK HARDING was born on February 10, 1807, in East Hampton, Connecticut. His family moved to Plainfield, New York, where he was raised. He engaged in various occupations as a young man, including teaching. He studied law at Hamilton College in Clinton, New York, graduated with honors, passed the bar, and set up a practice in Oneida County, New York, circa 1827. He moved to Monmouth, Illinois, in 1838 and resumed his legal practice there. He was a member of the Illinois Constitutional Convention in 1848 and was elected to the state legislature that same year. He served until 1850. Harding also became a banker and a railroad executive; indeed, railroads became his passion.

In 1862, he enlisted as a private in the 83rd Illinois, despite being fifty-five years old already. He was commissioned its colonel on August 21, 1862, and helped organize the regiment at Monmouth and Cairo, Illinois. It was then sent to western Tennessee, where it was used essentially as a security formation, guarding the Union line of communication and skirmishing with guerrillas.

Harding only fought one battle in the Civil War, but it was a brilliant one. On February 3, 1863, at Fort Donelson, he repulsed an attack by Confederate General "Fighting Joe" Wheeler, who had about three thousand cavalrymen. Harding had about nine hundred total. Harding showed such skill in this action, which was also called the Battle of Dover, that he was promoted to brigadier general on April 9.

Unfortunately for the Union, failing eyesight forced Abner Harding to resign on June 3. He nevertheless ran for Congress in 1864 and was elected twice, serving from 1865 to 1869. He did not seek re-election in 1868.

General Harding spent the rest of his life banking and building railroads and amassed a fortune estimated at $2,000,000 ($54,000,000 in

2022 money). He died of Bright's Disease in Monmouth, Illinois, after a long and painful illness, on July 19, 1874, at age sixty-seven. He is buried in the Monmouth Cemetery.

CHARLES GARRISON HARKER was born on December 2, 1837, in Swedesboro, New Jersey. Orphaned at an early age, he went to work as a clerk in a business owned by Nathan T. Stratton, who served in Congress from 1851 to 1855. In 1854, he gave Harker an appointment to West Point. Harker graduated in 1858 (16/27) and was named brevet second lieutenant in the 9th U.S. Infantry. He was promoted to second lieutenant in August. He did garrison duty in New York City and escorted wagon trains to Oregon and Washington. He was promoted to first lieutenant on May 14, 1861, and was assigned the task of drilling Ohio troops. He was promoted to captain on October 24 and to colonel of the 65th Ohio Infantry on November 11.

Harker's regiment fought at Shiloh on the second day (April 7, 1862), in the Siege of Corinth, and at Perryville. He became a brigade commander in July and performed so well at Stone River that he was recommended for brigadier general, although this recommendation was not acted on until after the Battle of Chickamauga, where he again distinguished himself and helped save the Union army. After taking part in the relief of Knoxville, he was promoted on April 10, 1864, but his date of rank was September 20, 1863, i.e., from the second day of Chickamauga. He commanded nine regiments in the Atlanta Campaign.

Harker was a promising young officer of the first order, but for some reason, he went into the Battle of Kennesaw Mountain mounted. He had already had four horses shot out from under him in earlier battles, but he was never seriously wounded. On June 26, 1864, however, he was an easy target for Rebel sharpshooters, who cut him down as he led an attack. One minié ball fractured his right arm and buried itself in his chest. He died in a Union field hospital a few hours later. General Harker was twenty-six years old. He is buried in the New Episcopal Cemetery in the town of his birth. After the war, the veterans of his old regiment erected a monument on his gravesite.

EDWARD "NED" HARLAND was born on June 24, 1832, in Norwich, Connecticut. He attended Yale University, graduated in 1853, and became a lawyer. He was the secretary of the Connecticut State Democratic Convention in 1855, but a Republican supporting Abraham Lincoln by 1860.

Harland joined the Union Army as a captain in the 3rd Connecticut Infantry in April 1861 and fought at Bull Run. After briefly serving as lieutenant colonel of the 6th Connecticut Infantry (September 1861), Governor Buckingham appointed him colonel of the 8th Connecticut Infantry on October 5. After taking part in Burnside's North Carolina Expedition, Harland returned to Virginia with Burnside's newly formed IX Corps. He was promoted to brigade commander in July 1862 and fought at Antietam. As a brigade commander, Harland was noted for his competence and inexhaustible energy. After the Confederate defenders of Burnside's Bridge were outflanked, he and General Isaac P. Rodman advanced on Sharpsburg, but Harland allowed his regiments to become badly separated. Rodman tried to hurry Harland's two trailing regiments along but was mortally wounded, and Harland's horse was shot from under him. He assumed command of the division and continued to try to move forward, but Confederate reinforcements arrived in time to check the advance. Harland was replaced as division commander by Brigadier General George W. Getty on October 4 and reverted to brigade commander.

Harland's brigade was lightly engaged at Fredericksburg. Sent to the Tidewater sector, Harland was promoted to brigadier general on April 4, 1863. He and his men helped check Longstreet in the Siege of Suffolk (April 11–May 4, 1863). After Longstreet retreated, Harland and his troops returned to North Carolina, where he commanded the Sub-District of Pamlico. In July 1864, he was placed in charge of the defenses of New Bern, where he remained until Sherman's men arrived. He briefly commanded the District of Beaufort but resigned his commission on June 22, 1865.

After the war, Harland returned to his law practice in Norwich. He served in both houses of the Connecticut legislature and was adjutant general of the state. He also worked as a probate judge and was president of the Chelsea Savings Bank. General Harland died in Norwich on March 9, 1915, at age eighty-two. He is buried in the Yantic Cemetery, Norwich.

WILLIAM SELBY HARNEY was born in Haysboro, Tennessee, on August 22, 1800, the son of a former army officer. Harney was educated at a local private academy and was commissioned directly into the army as a second lieutenant in 1818. President Monroe offered him a naval commission, but he opted for the army. He had a distinguished antebellum career and was promoted to first lieutenant (1819), captain (1825), major (1833), lieutenant colonel (1836), colonel (1846), and brigadier general (June 14, 1858).

A tall, 6'3," blue-eyed, red-haired officer who established and used political contacts, Harney's mentor was Andrew Jackson, whom he served in Louisiana and helped force pirate Jean Lafitte to leave U.S. territory. He was also friends with Jefferson Davis, who called him "physically, the finest specimen of a man I ever saw." He fought in the Black Hawk War against the Sauk, Kickapoo, and Fox tribes, was brevetted colonel for his courage in combat during the Second Seminole War in Florida, served on the Western frontier, and fought in the Battle of Buena Vista with Zachary Taylor. Here, he commanded the 2nd Dragoons. He was brevetted brigadier general for his gallantry in the Battle of Cerro Gordo. He was, however, opinionated and headstrong, intimidated and occasionally assaulted subordinates, and was court-martialed for insubordination at Monterrey. President Polk set aside Harney's conviction, and he led Winfield Scott's cavalry on the drive on Mexico City.

Harney possessed a violent temper and, in 1834, beat a slave girl to death after torturing her for three days. His action caused outrage even in slave-holding St. Louis, and he fled the Gateway City to escape mob justice. He was indicted and tried for murder, but was acquitted in a secretive trial. The judge in the case was known to be favorable toward Harney. Later, in Mexico, he was accused of brutal treatment toward prisoners-of-war, deserters, and escaped slaves. On the other hand, he was always fair to the

Indians. On the plains, the Sioux called him by an Indian name which meant "Man-who-always-kept-his-word." He was also known as "Big Chief Who Swears." Over the course of his career, he negotiated peace treaties with the Comanche, Kiowa, and Brule Sioux, and fought Yakama, Palouse, Spokane, Coeur d'Alene, and other Native American tribes.

Dedicated to his career, Harney fathered a daughter by a mixed-race Winnebago woman but abandoned them when he was reassigned. He married into a rich family and fathered three children, but only saw them twice after 1850. His wife left him in 1853 and relocated to France, where she died in 1860.

William Harney was one of five generals in the U.S. Army in 1860. When the Civil War began, he was commander of the Department of the West with headquarters in St. Louis, but he was distrusted by the Lincoln administration because of his Southern roots and sympathies. On or about April 25, 1861, he was on board a train passing through Harpers Ferry, Virginia, when he was captured by Confederates. Robert E. Lee offered him a commission, but he declined it; even so, the Rebels released him on April 29. This did nothing to allay the suspicions of Lincoln's supporters, who thought him too moderate toward pro-secession Missourians. He was sacked on May 31, 1861, and never re-employed. He retired on August 1, 1863. He was nevertheless brevetted major general in 1866. After the surrender, President Johnson occasionally employed him as a peace commissioner to the Indians.

Harney retired to Pass Christian, Mississippi, and remarried in 1884. While here, he often met with his close friend, Jefferson Davis. Harney later moved to Orlando, Florida, where he died on May 9, 1889. He was eighty-eight years old. He is buried in Arlington National Cemetery.

THOMAS MALEY HARRIS was born on June 17, 1817, in Wood County, Virginia (now Ritchie County, West Virginia). Some sources say he was born in 1813. He was raised in Solus, (West) Virginia, where he received a limited education, attended Marietta College, studied medicine at Louisville Medical College, and practiced in Solus (now Harrisville). He moved to Glenville in 1856 and practiced medicine there until the second half of 1861, when he helped recruit the 10th West Virginia Infantry. He became its lieutenant colonel in March 1862 and its colonel on May 20.

Harris's regiment first saw action in the Shenandoah Valley in 1862, where it was lightly engaged. Used largely to guard railroads, it was involved in a few minor operations in 1863 and fought in the Battle of Cloyd's Mountain in May 1864, where Confederate General Jenkins was mortally wounded, and his command scattered. Given command of a brigade in July, Harris opposed Jubal Early's raid on Washington, D.C., and later took part in the Shenandoah Valley Campaign of 1864, where he distinguished himself at Winchester and Cedar Creek. He was subsequently assigned to the Army of the James and was promoted to brigadier general on March 29, 1865. He was brevetted major general in 1867 for his part in breaking Lee's lines on April 2, 1865.

After the war, Harris served on the military commission which sentenced the Lincoln conspirators, including Mary Surratt, to death. He later wrote two prejudiced books on the subject. After commanding a brigade in the Fredericksburg area, he was mustered out of the service on April 30, 1866. Secretary of War Stanton offered him a lieutenant colonel commission in the 37th Infantry Regiment, but he declined it and returned to West Virginia. As a Republican, Harris was elected to the West Virginia legislature in 1867. He also served a term as mayor of Solus, a town which was later named after him. He was adjutant general of West Virginia (1869–70) and a pension agent at Wheeling (1871–77). He returned to the practice of medicine and wrote numerous articles, including a religious tract, "Calvinism Vindicated."

General Harris died at Harrisville on September 30, 1906, at age eighty-nine or ninety-three, depending on the source. He is buried in the Harrisville Cemetery.

WILLIAM HARROW was born on November 14, 1822, in Winchester, Kentucky, but his family moved to Lawrenceville, Illinois, when he was a child. Educated in local schools, he read law and was admitted to the bar. He was a friend of Abraham Lincoln and often traveled the judicial circuit with him. Harrow moved to Vincennes, Indiana, in the late 1850s and married the daughter of a wealthy man. He also prospered and became captain of the local militia company.

A man with political connections, Harrow joined the Union Army as a captain in April 1861 and became major of the 14th Indiana Infantry in June. He served in the Western Virginia Campaign of 1861 and fought at Cheat Mountain and on the Greenbrier River. He was promoted to lieutenant colonel in February 1862 and to colonel and regimental commander in April. Harrow served in the Valley Campaign against Stonewall Jackson and fought at Kernstown but was relieved of his command for drunkenness in July. He resigned his commission but was restored to command in August; apparently, 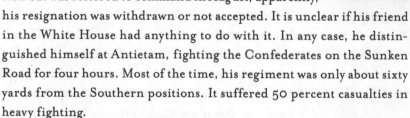 his resignation was withdrawn or not accepted. It is unclear if his friend in the White House had anything to do with it. In any case, he distinguished himself at Antietam, fighting the Confederates on the Sunken Road for four hours. Most of the time, his regiment was only about sixty yards from the Southern positions. It suffered 50 percent casualties in heavy fighting.

William Harrow was rewarded for his courage and tenacity by being given a brigade command, and President Lincoln wrote a letter to the War Department on October 16, recommending that he be promoted to brigadier general. Stanton took his time initiating the process, but Harrow was promoted on April 4, 1863.

Harrow was apparently not present at Chancellorsville, but commanded the 1st Brigade, 2nd Division, II Corps at Gettysburg. Here, his brigade—which consisted of four regiments—lost five regimental commanders, two of whom died. Harrow succeeded John Gibbon as division commander after that officer was wounded on July 1 and led it against Pickett's Charge on July 3. In heavy fighting, the division suffered more than 1,600 casualties out of less than 3,800 men engaged. Significantly, however, in his official report, Gibbon did not praise Harrow for his performance at Gettysburg, although he did praise his other brigade commanders. (Harrow was ill-tempered and officious.) Shortly after, Harrow was relieved of his command, but Abraham Lincoln personally revoked this order. The situation was solved by transferring Harrow to a divisional command on the Western Front.

Harrow's problems were the bottle and a bad temper. He was also a harsh disciplinarian. Certainly, he did not inspire the confidence of his men or his superiors. His division nevertheless fought well during the Atlanta Campaign. In September 1864, after the city fell, the army was reorganized, and Harrow was left without a command. Because of his reputation, neither Oliver O. Howard, William T. Sherman, or Winfield Scott Hancock would accept him as a commander. Without an assignment for months, Harrow resigned his commission on April 7, 1865, and returned to Indiana.

The former general took an interest in politics after the war. On September 27, 1872, he was en route to deliver a speech on behalf of presidential candidate Horace Greeley, when his train derailed near New Albany, Indiana, and he was killed. He was forty-nine. General Harrow was buried in the Bellefontaine Cemetery, Vernon, Illinois.

JOHN FREDERICK "OLD JOHNNY" HARTRANFT was born on December 16, 1830, in New Hanover Township, Pennsylvania, the child of German American parents. His father worked hard, established an inn and stagecoach line in Norristown, and eventually worked in real estate. John attended local schools and Marshall College before graduating from Union College in 1853. Initially, he was a civil engineer for the Mauch Chunk & Wilkes-Barre Railroad. He later became deputy sheriff and was admitted to the bar in 1860. Meanwhile, he joined the militia and rose to lieutenant colonel.

Hartranft became commander of the 4th Pennsylvania Militia Regiment, a 90-day unit, on April 21, 1861. He led it to the Plains of Manassas, but on July 21, its enlistments expired and the men turned around and went home, despite a personal appeal from General McDowell and the fact that they were within hearing distance of Confederate musket fire. Humiliated by this behavior, Colonel Hartranft went into the First Battle of Bull Run as a volunteer aide and bravely rallied several disorganized regiments. Twenty-five years later, he was awarded the Congressional Medal of Honor for the courage he exhibited that day.

After Bull Run, Hartranft returned to the Keystone State and organized the 51st Pennsylvania Infantry—a three-year regiment. He led it in Burnside's North Carolina Expedition, including the battles of Roanoke Island and New Bern. Transferred back to Virginia, he fought at the Second Bull Run, South Mountain, and Antietam, where he led a charge over Burnside's Brigade. He served in the Battle of Fredericksburg before he and his men were sent to the Western Front. He led a brigade in the Vicksburg Campaign and occasionally commanded a division, despite only being a colonel. Sent to east Tennessee that fall, he took part in the Knoxville Campaign.

John Hartranft was promoted to brigadier general on May 14, 1864. He served in the Overland Campaign and the Siege of Petersburg and was given command of a division of new Pennsylvania recruits in early 1865. He checked General Lee's Fort Stedman attack (the last offensive of the Army of Northern Virginia) and took part in the Appomattox Campaign. Overall, he fought in twenty-three major battles.

Hartranft was named commandant of the Old Capitol Prison and was provost marshal at the trial and execution of the Lincoln assassins. Two of them praised him for his kindness on the day of their executions. He was brevetted major general on January 13, 1866, and was mustered out two days later.

A pre-war Democrat, General Hartranft was now a Radical Republican. He served as Pennsylvania state auditor from 1867 to 1873. An opponent of the corrupt Simon Cameron political machine, he ran for governor in 1872 and—with the support of the railroads—was elected twice, serving from 1873 to 1879. He advocated suffrage for the African American and strongly supported education and the rights of workers to organize. He was in contention for the presidential nomination in 1876, but the Republicans selected Rutherford B. Hayes instead.

Hartranft was commander-in-chief of the Grand Army of the Republic from 1875 to 1877. After he left the governor's office, he was postmaster of Norristown, near his home in Montgomery County. He later worked as collector for the port of Philadelphia and commander of the Pennsylvania

National Guard. At the age of fifty-eight, he died of Bright's Disease in Norristown on October 17, 1889. He is buried in the nearby Montgomery Cemetery, West Norristown Township.

GEORGE LUCAS HARTSUFF was born in Tyre, New York, on May 28, 1830. When he was twelve, his family moved to a farm in Livingston County, Michigan, where Hartsuff worked until he secured a cadetship at West Point in 1848. He graduated in 1852 (19/43) and was commissioned brevet second lieutenant and assigned to the 4th U.S. Artillery Regiment.

Hartsuff was a deeply religious, kind, temperate man with a highly positive mental attitude, and of impressive physique. He would need it to survive many diseases and wounds. Assigned to Fort Brown, Texas, as his first assignment, in late 1852 he was attacked by yellow fever, which reached the worst and generally fatal stage—black vomit. He nevertheless survived. He later fought against the Seminoles in Florida, where he was severely wounded twice on December 20, 1855. After personally shooting two of the Indians with a pistol, he was forced to take cover in a pond. After three hours, he was driven out by alligators, which were attracted by his blood. He then walked fifteen miles before coming across soldiers who were looking for him. The bullet in his lung, however, could not be removed.

After three years teaching artillery tactics at West Point (1856–59), Lieutenant Hartsuff was sent to the Great Lakes, where he survived a shipwreck in Lake Michigan in September 1860. He heroically provided life preservers for women and children but not for himself. He clung to a piece of wreckage for eleven hours before he was rescued. Three hundred seventy-three other passengers perished.

Promoted to brevet captain and sent to Florida in early 1861, he secretly helped reinforce Fort Pinkens, in violation of an agreement with Florida and Confederate authorities. He was transferred to western Virginia after the war began and was chief of staff of the Departments of the Ohio and West Virginia (i.e., General Rosecrans). Here, he was given command of a brigade and promoted to brigadier general on April 16, 1862. After fighting in the Shenandoah and in Battle of Cedar Mountain, General McDowell relieved him of his command because he was too sick to keep any food down. He was back in action at Antietam, where he was so severely wounded in the hip that the doctors at first thought he would die. He did not, and after he partially recovered, Hartsuff was given light duty, writing army regulations and sitting on court-martials. He could not return to field duty until May 1863, when he assumed command of the XXIII Corps of the Army of the Ohio. Meanwhile, he was promoted to major general on November 29, 1862.

Hartsuff returned to field duty too soon and had to give up his corps command in September 1863 for health reasons. He was either on light duty or awaiting orders from then until January 1865, when he became an assistant inspector general in the Army of the Ohio. On March 19, he assumed command of the XVIII Corps of the Army of the James, which was in the trenches of the Bermuda Hundred peninsula. After Lee surrendered, Hartsuff briefly commanded the District of Nottoway, which headquartered in Petersburg. He was mustered out on August 24, 1865, and reverted to his regular army rank of lieutenant colonel.

A man of courage and character, General Hartsuff was a solid soldier whose only major weakness was a tendency to attract enemy bullets. Postwar, he served in Louisiana and Texas (1866–68), in New York City (1868–69), and in Missouri (1869–71) as an adjutant general. He retired for disabilities caused by wounds received in battle on June 29, 1871. Because his health was shattered due to wounds, he was allowed to retire as a major general.

General Hartsuff died at his home in New York City on May 16, 1874. He was forty-one years old. An autopsy revealed that the infection that caused his death was from the scar on his lung, which he received fighting the Seminoles in Florida in 1855. He was buried in the West Point Cemetery. His brother, William Hartsuff, was brevetted brigadier general for his performance at Franklin and Nashville.

MILO SMITH HASCALL was born in LeRoy, Genesee County, New York, on August 5, 1829. He moved to Goshen, Indiana, in 1846, where he clerked in a store owned by his three brothers. He also taught school. In 1848, he

received an appointment to West Point, from which he graduated in 1852 (14/43). Commissioned brevet second lieutenant, he was assigned to the 2nd U.S. Artillery and stationed at Fort Adams, Newport Harbor, Rhode Island, until he resigned his commission in September 1853.

Hascall returned to Goshen, became a railroad contractor, a lawyer, district attorney, and clerk of the county court and common pleas court. When the war began, he volunteered immediately and was appointed captain and aide-de-camp to Brigadier General Thomas A. Morris of the Indiana Militia. In June, he became colonel of the 17th Indiana Infantry and led it in western Virginia, where it was involved in some minor actions. In late November, he was summoned to Louisville, Kentucky, and given command of a brigade in the Army of the Ohio. It arrived at Shiloh the day after the battle. Hascall was nevertheless promoted to brigadier general on April 26, 1862. He took part in the Siege of Corinth, the Kentucky Campaign (including the Battle of Perryville), and Stones River, where he temporarily commanded a division after Thomas J. Wood was wounded. He performed well.

After Stones River, Hascall assumed command of the District of Indiana, where his job was to round up deserters. He also suppressed anti-Lincoln newspapers, including the *Plymouth Democrat*. In June 1863, he was given command of a division in the Army of the Ohio. He took part in the Tullahoma Campaign, the Battle of Chickamauga, and the Siege of Chattanooga. For reasons not made clear by the records, he was demoted back to brigade command in March 1864, but was again given a division in May. He led it in the Atlanta Campaign, after which John Schofield, the commander of the Army of the Ohio, enthusiastically recommended Hascall for promotion to major general on September 12, 1864, but when no action was taken, he resigned his commission. His resignation was accepted on October 27, and Hascall's military career was over.

He returned to Goshen and became a banker but moved to Chicago in 1890 and engaged in the real estate business. He died in Oak Park, Illinois, on August 30, 1904, at age seventy-five. He was buried in Forest Home Cemetery, Chicago, Illinois.

JOSEPH ABEL HASKIN was born on June 21, 1818, in Troy, New York, where his father became sheriff. Admitted to West Point, he graduated in 1839 (10/31) and was assigned to the 1st U.S. Artillery. Initially posted to northern Maine during the border dispute with Britain, he was a first lieutenant when the Mexican War erupted. During Scott's drive on Mexico City, he was brevetted captain for Cerro Gordo and major for Chapultepec, where he lost his left arm. He became a captain in the quartermaster department in 1848.

Captain Haskin was commander of the Baton Rouge Barracks on January 10, 1861, when he was forced to surrender to Louisiana state forces. He was not exchanged until early 1862, so he was prohibited from engaging in combat with Rebel forces until then. Promoted to lieutenant colonel in 1861, he was assigned to the Department of Washington and placed in charge of the defenses of the city north of the Potomac. His only Civil War action was against Jubal Early, who threatened the capital in June 8. He led a division in XXII Corps (four thousand men) until he was superseded by Martin D. Hardin. Haskin directed a brigade during the Battle of Fort Stevens, where Early's probe was repulsed. For his services here, he was promoted to brigadier general on August 5, 1864.

Haskin remained in Washington until he was mustered out of volunteer service in April 1866. He reverted to his Regular Army rank of lieutenant colonel and commanded Fort Independence in Boston Harbor. He retired on December 15, 1870. The general died at Oswego, New York, on August 3, 1874. He was fifty-six. He was interred in Arlington National Cemetery. His son, William Lawrence Haskin, also retired as a brigadier general.

EDWARD HATCH was born on December 22, 1832, in Bangor, Maine. He attended local schools and spent two years at the Norwich Military Academy in Vermont. After spending time as a merchant seaman, he settled in Muscatine, Iowa, and worked in the lumber business. In August 1861, he joined the Union Army as a captain in the 2nd Iowa Cavalry, which he helped raise. He was promoted to major the following month.

Hatch fought at New Madrid, Island No. 10, the Siege of Corinth, and the (Second) Battle of Corinth. Meanwhile, on June 13, 1862, he became colonel and commander of his regiment after Washington L. Elliott was promoted to brigadier general. Advanced to brigade commander in August, he served in Grant's Vicksburg campaigns and was part of Grierson's cavalry during his famous raid of May 1863. Transferred to the Army of the Tennessee, he operated in northern Mississippi and northern Alabama during the winter of 1863/64 and was wounded in the right lung during a skirmish at Moscow, Tennessee, on December 3. While he recovered, he commanded the cavalry depot at St. Louis. He was promoted to brigadier general on April 30, 1864.

Hatch fought against Nathan Bedford Forrest in northern Mississippi but experienced no success against "the Wizard of the Saddle." Warner stated that he was "clearly outclassed" by Forrest. Hatch did, however, plunder the home of Confederate Colonel Jacob Thompson, taking the modern equivalent of more than $1,000,000 worth of furnishing and hauling it off in U.S. Army ambulances. Then he burned the house.

General Hatch was much more successful in the Franklin-Nashville Campaign of 1864/65 and in February 1865 was brevetted major general for his actions at Nashville in December 1864. His division spent the last campaign of the war in Eastport, northern Mississippi. Mustered out of the volunteer service in January 1866, he was appointed colonel, Regular Army, and commander of the 9th U.S. Cavalry—a Buffalo soldiers unit—that same year. In this post, he defeated Geronimo and his Apache in the southwest. He succeeded Gordon Granger as commander of the District of New Mexico in 1876 and developed a reputation as a brilliant Indian fighter.

On March 27, 1889, he had an accident and fractured his right leg. He died from a cerebral blood clot at Fort Robinson, Nebraska, on April 11, 1889. He is buried in the Fort Leavenworth National Cemetery, Fort Leavenworth, Kansas.

JOHN PORTER HATCH was born on January 9, 1822, in Oswego, New York. He entered the U.S. Military Academy at West Point as a cadet in 1840 and graduated in the class of 1845 (17/41) as a brevet second lieutenant of infantry. Sent to Texas, he was with the 3rd U.S. Infantry Regiment during Zachary Taylor's victories at Palo Alto and Resaca de la Palma but transferred to the Mounted Rifles Regiment shortly after. As part of Winfield Scott's Army of Mexico, he earned a brevet to first lieutenant for gallantry at Contreras and Churubusco and to captain for his courage at Chapultepec. He subsequently served on the Western frontier and in Oregon and was promoted to captain (substantive rank) in 1860. He was chief commissary officer for the Department of New Mexico when the Civil War began.

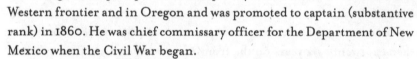

Hatch was transferred to the Eastern theater in 1861, where he worked under George B. McClellan. He jumped three grades of rank and was promoted to brigadier general on September 28, 1861, and assumed command of a cavalry brigade in December. That winter, he engaged in a number of raids along the Rapidan and Rappahannock rivers and skirmished against Jeb Stuart. In March 1862, he was given command of Nathaniel Banks's cavalry and fought against Stonewall Jackson in the Valley Campaign of 1862. Following that disaster, he was transferred to John Pope's Army of Virginia.

General Hatch launched two unsuccessful raids against Lee's army in the summer of 1862, incurring General Pope's wrath. He was stripped of his cavalry command and transferred to the infantry. He led a brigade in the III Corps during the Second Manassas Campaign and briefly commanded a division after General Rufus King fell ill with epilepsy on August 28. Two days later, during the Second Battle of Bull Run, Hatch was wounded but was back in command of an infantry division on September 14, during the Battle of South Mountain, where he was shot in the leg. Thirty-one years later, he was awarded the Congressional Medal of Honor for his courage in this battle.

John Hatch was unable to return to duty until February 1863, when he sat on a court-martial board. He was still on light duty in July, when he took command of the Draft Depot at Philadelphia. In December, he was transferred to St. Louis, where he directed the Cavalry Depot. He was sent to the Department of the South in March 1864, where he commanded the Coastal Division. He tried to aid Sherman's forces during their March to the Sea by cutting the Charleston & Savannah Railroad, but was defeated in the Battle of Honey Hill on November 30, 1864, by the Georgia Militia and the 3rd South Carolina Infantry, despite outnumbering them 5,000 to 1,400. He suffered 755 casualties as opposed to 47 for the Rebels.

After Charleston fell in February 1865, Hatch commanded the District of Charleston from then until January 1866, when he was mustered out of volunteer service. He was brevetted major general in the omnibus promotions of 1866.

Hatch reverted to his Regular Army rank of major in 1866 and spent the next twenty-six years on the frontier, serving in west Texas, Indian Territory, Montana Territory, and Washington Territory. Hatch was promoted to lieutenant colonel in 1873 and colonel of the 2nd U.S. Cavalry in 1881. He reached the mandatory retirement age in January 1886 and settled in New York City, where he died on April 12, 1901, at age seventy-nine. He was buried in Arlington National Cemetery.

HERMAN HAUPT, whose Christian name is sometimes spelled Hermann, was born in Philadelphia on March 26, 1817. President Andrew Jackson gave him an appointment to the U.S. Military Academy in 1831, when he was fourteen years old. He graduated in 1835 (31/56), but resigned his commission three months later and became a civil engineer.

He spent his antebellum career in the railroad business, mainly in Pennsylvania, where he pioneered the construction of railroad bridges and made a fortune. Some of the trusses he constructed are still in use. He did not join the Union war effort until April 27, 1862, when he became a colonel and aide-de-camp to Major General Irvin McDowell. The following month, he was named chief of construction and transportation on U.S. Military Railroads (i.e., lines taken over by the government). Abraham Lincoln, for one, was highly impressed by Haupt. "That man Haupt has built a bridge 400 feet long and 100 feet high, across Potomac creek, on which loaded trains are passing every hour, and upon my word, gentlemen, there is nothing in it but cornstalks and beanpoles," he declared. He promoted Haupt to brigadier general of volunteers on September 5, 1862, but Haupt initially declined the appointment. He preferred to work without pay or rank. He hated the military bureaucracy and felt many Union generals were causing his bureau more trouble than they were causing the enemy. He finally accepted the appointment on March 4, 1863, but he could not work with the War Department and vacated (retroactively declined) his appointment on September 14, 1863.

Haupt's postbellum career was also brilliant. He was general manager of the Piedmont Air Line Railroad (1872–76), chief engineer of the Pennsylvania Transportation Company (1876–78), consulting engineer for the Northern Pacific Railroad (1878–81), general manager of the Northern Pacific Railroad (1881–85), and president of the Dakota and Great Southern Railway (1885–86). He spent the years 1886 to 1905 as a consulting engineer in Washington, D.C., and he was the first person to prove the practicality of transporting oil via pipelines. Unfortunately, he lost most of his fortune in a lawsuit involving political complications and a tunnel. In his latter years, he and his wife purchased and operated a small resort hotel in Mountain Lake, Virginia. While on a trip from New York to Philadelphia, General Haupt died of a heart attack in Jersey City, New Jersey, December 14, 1905, at age eighty-eight. He is buried in the West Laurel Hill Cemetery, Bala Cynwyd, Pennsylvania.

JOHN PARKER HAWKINS was born in Indianapolis, Indiana, on September 29, 1830. He could trace his military lineage back to 1588, when Royal Navy Captain William Hawkins fought the Spanish Armada. John entered West Point in 1848 and graduated in 1852 (40/43). An infantry officer, his antebellum service was almost entirely in frontier garrisons, with stops in Fort Kearny, Nebraska Territory; Fort Randall, Dakota Territory; Fort

Ridgely, Minnesota Territory; and Fort Abercrombie, Dakota Territory. He was a first lieutenant and chief quartermaster of the 6th U.S. Infantry when the war broke out. He was promoted to captain, staff, on August 3, 1861.

Initially posted to Washington, D.C. as assistant commissary for subsistence, for a brigade in the capital defenses, he moved up steadily in that branch and was commissary for subsistence for the Sub-District of Southwest Missouri by late August. He was named commissary for the XIII Corps and promoted to lieutenant colonel on November 1, 1862. The following month, Hawkins was promoted to commissary for subsistence for Grant's Army of the Tennessee. President Lincoln named him brigadier general on April 25, 1863. The Senate, however, returned the nomination to Lincoln on April 1, 1864, without acting on it. The next day, Lincoln resubmitted the nomination, which was subsequently confirmed.

Meanwhile, Hawkins assumed command of the USCT (United States Colored Troops) in the District of Central Kentucky in May 1863. He took charge of a USCT brigade in northeast Louisiana in August and a USCT division in the District of Vicksburg in February 1864. His command essentially acted as a security unit, protecting the Union supply lines. He held this position until February 1865, when he assumed command of another USCT division, this time in Florida. He led his regiments in the Battle of Fort Blakely on April 9, which led to the capture of Mobile on April 12.

General Hawkins commanded the Western District of Louisiana after the war. He was brevetted major general on January 13, 1866, and mustered out on February 1. He reverted to his regular army rank of captain and returned to the Subsistence Department. Once again, he was steadily promoted: major (1874), lieutenant colonel (1889), and colonel (1892). In late 1892, he was promoted to commissary general of subsistence for the U.S. Army with the rank of brigadier general. He retired when he reached the mandatory retirement age of sixty-four in 1894 after forty-two years' service.

Hawkins returned to his hometown of Indianapolis, where he wrote a book on physical fitness. He died in Indianapolis on February 7, 1914, at age eighty-three. He is buried in the Crown Hill Cemetery, Indianapolis. His brothers-in-law included Generals Edward R. S. Canby and Henry J. Hunt.

JOSEPH ROSWELL HAWLEY was born on October 31, 1826, in the village of Stewartsville, North Carolina, where his father (a native of Farmington, Connecticut) was the pastor of a Baptist church. Joseph could trace his New England roots back to 1629. The elder Hawley was a fervent abolitionist who strongly influenced his son's subsequent career. Joseph was attending school in Cheraw, South Carolina, during the Nullification Crisis of 1832–33. He recalled that only he and one other boy were Unionists, and the other child also had a Northern father. Physically threatened by pro-slavery elements, Rev. Hawley left North Carolina with his family in 1837 and never returned.

Joseph Hawley worked on the family farm and resumed his education at Hartford Grammar School in Connecticut and at Hamilton College, New York, from which he graduated with honors in 1847. He read law, was admitted to the bar in 1850, and practiced in Hartford, Connecticut, for six years.

Like his father, Hawley was a Free Soiler and fervent opponent of slavery. He was also a superb orator. He played a major role in organizing the Republican Party in Connecticut and, in 1856, became the editor of the party's newspaper, the *Charter Oak*. In 1857, he became editor of the *Hartford Evening Press*, a Republican newspaper, and was an early supporter of Abraham Lincoln. In April 1861, he joined the 1st Connecticut Infantry (a 30-day regiment) as a first lieutenant and was promoted to captain within days. He fought in the First Battle of Bull Run, where he won the praise of General Keyes. When his regiment's enlistments expired, he helped form the 7th Connecticut and became its lieutenant colonel in September.

Hawley took part in the Port Royal (South Carolina) Expedition and helped establish a Union base between Charleston and Savannah. He participated in the Siege of Fort Pulaski, which fell in April 1862. In June, he was named commander of the 10th Connecticut Infantry, which he led in the coastal battles in South Carolina and Florida. He took part in the Siege of Charleston, including operations against Fort Wagner in September 1863, where he commanded a brigade. He continued in that role and fought in the unsuccessful Battle of Olustee, Florida, in February 1864.

Sent to Virginia, he took part in the Siege of Petersburg and was promoted to brigadier general on September 13, 1864. He led a division in the Second Battle of Fort Fisher (January 1865) and ended the war as commander of District of Wilmington. He was brevetted major general and discharged in January 1866.

Hawley owed his rapid advancement in the Union Army to his tactical abilities, courage, energy, and dynamic personality. The fact he had political influence also contributed.

Postwar, Hawley had a political career. A Radical Republican, he was elected governor of Connecticut (1866–67) but was defeated for re-election. He won and lost several elections and served as a congressman (1872–75 and 1879–81) and a U.S. senator (1881–1905). He was a "favorite son" candidate for president in 1872, 1886, and 1880, but Connecticut was an inadequate base for his presidential ambitions. He did, however, have a reputation for integrity. Mark Twain once introduced him as an honest U.S. senator and quipped that he must be "mighty lonely there." He did not run for re-election in 1904. Hawley died in Washington, D.C. on March 18, 1905, two weeks after his fourth term in the senate expired. He was seventy-eight. He was buried in the Cedar Hill Cemetery, Hartford.

JOSEPH HAYES was born on September 14, 1835, in South Berwick, Maine, the son of a highly respected judge. He attended the Phillips Exeter Academy (a highly selective preparatory school in New Hampshire) and Harvard, from which he graduated in 1855. He moved to Wisconsin and worked in the banking business and took a course in civil engineering. He then went west and worked as a surveyor for the Chicago & Rock Island Railroad. He returned to Boston in 1859 and later became a real estate broker.

Hayes was appointed captain and company commander in the 20th Massachusetts Infantry on August 23, 1861, but was advanced to the rank of major of the 18th Massachusetts the next day. The regiment left Boston for Washington, D.C. on August 28. It joined the Army of the Potomac and fought in the Siege of Yorktown, the Battle of Hanover Court House (May 27, 1862), the Seven

Days battles (June 25–July 1), the Second Bull Run, and Antietam. Hayes, meanwhile, was promoted to lieutenant colonel on August 25. He particularly distinguished himself at Fredericksburg, where he commanded the regiment and led three successive charges on Marye's Heights. More than half the men of the 20th Massachusetts were killed or wounded in this battle.

The commander of the 20th, James Barnes, was promoted to brigadier general, and Hayes succeeded him as regimental commander. He was promoted to colonel on March 1, 1863. He fought at Chancellorsville and Gettysburg, where he suffered a concussion and a dislocated shoulder when he was thrown from his horse on July 2. He also took part in the Overland Campaign. On May 5, 1864, during the Battle of the Wilderness, a Rebel bullet cut a deep furrow in his skull. He was in a hospital in Washington when he was promoted to brigadier general on May 12.

Hayes returned to the field on June 20 and fought in the Siege of Petersburg. He cut the Weldon Railroad on August 21 and checked a major Southern counterattack, during which both of Hayes's aides were killed by his side. The next day, he went too far forward on a reconnaissance and was captured by the Confederates. He was held in Libby Prison for almost six months. Here he was selected to distribute supplies to Union POWs in the South. Finally exchanged in February 1865, he took part in the Appomattox Campaign and was mustered out in August 1865. He was brevetted major general in 1866.

Hayes declined a Regular Army commission after the war and worked as a mining engineer, mainly in Colombia, South America. He died in New York City on August 20, 1912, at age seventy-six. He was buried in the Old Fields Cemetery, South Berwick, Maine. He was a life-long bachelor.

RUTHERFORD BIRCHARD HAYES, the 19th President of the United States, was born on October 4, 1822, in Delaware, Ohio. His father, a native of Vermont, was a storekeeper who died ten weeks after Rutherford's birth, and he was raised by his mother and her younger brother. He attended local schools, the Methodist

Norwalk Seminary, the Webb School (a college preparatory school in Connecticut), and Kenyon College, from which he graduated as valedictorian in 1842. He then attended Harvard Law School and was admitted to the bar in 1845.

Hayes set up a practice in Lower Sandusky (now Fremont), Ohio, and later in Cincinnati, where he gained prominence as a criminal defense attorney. He also became a Republican and an abolitionist who defended fugitive slaves. As such, he rose to prominence within the party and, after declining a judgeship, became city solicitor in 1858. Even though Hayes thought it might be best if the United States let the Southern states go, he joined the Union Army as a major in the 23rd Ohio Infantry in June 1861.

Hayes first saw action in western Virginia in September. He proved to be a brave, useful officer, and was promoted to lieutenant colonel in October. He often led charges personally and was wounded five times. He was wounded in the right knee at Giles Court House on May 10, 1862, and was shot through the left arm at South Mountain on September 14. He tied a handkerchief above the wound to slow the bleeding and continued to fight. He was eventually carried to the hospital and thus missed the Battle of Antietam but was nevertheless promoted to colonel on October 24. He was placed in charge of a brigade in March 1863.

Hayes's command was sent to Charleston, (West) Virginia, during the winter of 1862–63 and was not directly involved in the Fredericksburg or Chancellorsville campaigns. It was deeply involved in the destruction of John Hunt Morgan's Confederate raiders and fought in the Battle of Buffington Island, where Morgan's command was shattered on July 19, 1863. Assigned to the Army of West Virginia, Hayes played a prominent role in the Union victory at Cloyd's Mountain (May 9, 1864) and in the Shenandoah Valley Campaign of 1864, where he impressed Generals Sheridan and Grant, among others. He was promoted to brigadier general on November 30, 1864. He was given command of a division in West Virginia in February 1865. After Appomattox, General Hayes resigned from the army on June 8. He was brevetted major general in February 1866.

In November 1864, Hayes was elected to the U.S. House of Representatives. He defeated the incumbent despite the fact that he refused to leave the army and therefore did not campaign. He served in the House until July 1867, when he resigned to run for governor. He voted with the Radical Republicans and favored the impeachment of President Johnson.

Hayes favored allowing black males to vote. He was narrowly elected governor in 1867 was re-elected in 1869. Hayes did not seek reelection in 1871 and retired from politics, but the Panic of 1873 depleted Hayes's finances and compelled him to seek the governorship again in 1875. He was elected and served from 1868 to 1872 and from 1876 to 1877. He was the first three-term governor in Ohio history.

Rutherford B. Hayes was elected president of the United States in 1876. The election was disputed, and he received 185 votes in the Electoral College, as opposed to 184 for his opponent. In order to be elected, he compromised with former Confederates and agreed to end Reconstruction in the South, which he did. Hayes hated the job of president. He was the nation's CEO from 1877 to 1881, when he retired to Spiegel Grove, his summer home in Fremont. While he was overjoyed at leaving the White House, he remained active in veterans' affairs and was commander-in-chief of the MOLLUS, (the Military Order of the Loyal Legion of the United States) (1886 and 1888–1893). President Hayes died in Fremont, Ohio, on January 17, 1893, at age seventy. He is buried in what is now the Spiegel Grove State Park in Fremont.

ISHAM NICHOLAS HAYNIE was born in Dover, Tennessee, on November 18, 1824. His family moved to Illinois during his early childhood, and he worked on the family farm to accumulate enough money to study law. His studies were interrupted in 1846, when he volunteered for service in the Mexican War. Part of the 6th Illinois Infantry, he was discharged as a first lieutenant in 1848. After the war, he attended the Kentucky Law School, graduated with the highest honors, and was admitted to the bar in 1853. He was elected to the Illinois legislature in 1850, was appointed judge of the Court of Common Pleas in Cairo, Illinois, in 1857, and was a presidential elector for Stephen A. Douglas in 1860.

Haynie recruited the 48th Illinois Infantry and was mustered in as its colonel in November 1861. He took part in the capture of Fort Henry (February 6, 1862) and in the Battle of Fort Donelson (February 12–16), where he temporarily commanded a brigade in McClernand's division and led an unsuccessful attack on Rebel lines. Ironically, Haynie's birthplace was part of the Fort Donelson complex.

Still part of Grant's army, Haynie led his regiment with gallantry at Shiloh until he was shot through the left thigh and was forced to turn over his command on April 6. He returned to southern Illinois, where he ran for Congress as a "War Democrat." He lost to a "Peace Democrat" by seven hundred votes out of twelve thousand ballots cast. After he returned to active duty, he was given command of a brigade. Returning to Tennessee, he was the commander of the post of Bethel (one of Grant's two major supply depots) from the fall of 1862 to early 1863. He was appointed brigadier general on or about November 29, 1862.

Haynie took part in the Yazoo Pass Expedition (February–March 1863); meanwhile, the U.S. Senate failed to confirm this appointment, which cost the Union a pretty good commander. His general's commission expired on March 4, 1863. Rather than revert to colonel, Haynie resigned two days later. He returned to Illinois and was named adjutant general of the state militia. Haynie was in Washington on April 14, 1865, and spent more than an hour with Abraham Lincoln on the last day of his life. He was in the room when Lincoln died and accompanied the President's body back to Springfield. General Haynie died in Springfield on May 22, 1868, at age forty-three, and is buried there in the Sangamon Cemetery.

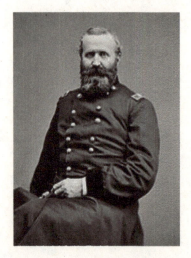

ALEXANDER "SANDY" HAYS was born in Franklin, Pennsylvania, on July 8, 1819, the son of a congressman and general in the Pennsylvania militia. He attended Allegheny College until his senior year (1840), when he transferred to West Point. He graduated in 1844 (20/25) and was commissioned brevet second lieutenant of infantry. He fought in the Mexican War, where he was wounded in the leg at Resaca de la Palma and was brevetted first lieutenant. After taking part in Scott's drive on Mexico City, he resigned from the army in 1848 and returned to Pennsylvania, where he worked in the iron business. Unsuccessful, he went to California in 1850, where he was part of the gold rush. Again unsuccessful, he returned to western Pennsylvania and settled in Pittsburgh, where he became a civil engineer, specializing in the construction of railroad bridges.

Hays was a captain in the militia when the war began. He was promoted to major of the 12th Pennsylvania on April 25, 1861, and became colonel of the 63rd Pennsylvania Infantry in October. Known for his fearlessness and heavy drinking, he was widely admired by the volunteers. He fought at Yorktown, Williamsburg, Seven Pines, Savage Station, and Malvern Hill, among other battles in 1862. Wounded and suffering from partial blindness in his right eye and paralysis of his left arm, he took a month's medical furlough. He was back in action at the Second Bull Run, where on August 29 his left leg was shattered by Rebel fire. He was still recovering on September 29, when he was promoted to brigadier general. He missed the Maryland and Fredericksburg campaigns.

General Hays was initially given command of a brigade in the Washington defenses. He commanded a division in the Battle of Gettysburg, where he defended part of Cemetery Ridge and had two horses shot out from under him. After Pickett's Charge was repulsed, he mounted a third horse and dragged a captured Confederate battle flag through the dirt, much to the delight of some of his men. He later participated in the Bristoe and Mine Run campaigns.

Because he lacked seniority, Hays was demoted to brigade command when the army reorganized in early 1864, despite his close friendship with Ulysses S. Grant, a former classmate at West Point. He almost certainly would have been given a division later in the war but, on May 5, 1864, at the beginning of the Battle of the Wilderness, a Confederate marksman shot him through the head. He died three hours later. He was forty-four years old.

General Hays was brevetted major general on June 27, 1864. He was buried in the Allegheny Cemetery, Pittsburgh. After the war, when he was running for president, General Grant made a campaign stop in Pittsburgh. He took the time to visit Hays's grave and openly wept.

WILLIAM HAYS was born on May 9, 1819, in Richmond, Virginia. His family later moved to Nashville, Tennessee, where he lived when President Andrew Jackson granted him an appointment to West Point in 1836. He graduated in 1840 (18/42) and was commissioned second lieutenant of artillery. He was stationed on the New York–Canada border during the border disturbances of the 1840s. He was sent to Louisiana in 1845 and took part in the military occupation of Texas in 1846. Serving in the light artillery, Hays fought at Palo Alto, Resaca de la Palma, and Monterrey. Transferred to Scott's army, he participated in the Siege of Vera Cruz and the subsequent drive inland. He earned a brevet to captain for Contreras and Churubusco and to major for Chapultepec. He was wounded at Molino del Rey on September 8, 1847, but still took part in the capture of Mexico City (September 13–14).

Hays remained in the army after Mexico and saw action in the Seminole War in Florida (1853–54), between routine garrison tours. He was promoted to captain in 1853 and was on frontier duty when the Civil War broke out. Transferred to the East, he was promoted to lieutenant colonel of volunteers and served in the Washington defenses and as an aide to General George B. McClellan. On May 18, 1862, he was given command of a brigade of horse artillery, which he led in the latter part of the Peninsula Campaign, in the Battle of Seven Pines (where he distinguished himself), and in the Seven Days battles. He directed the V Corps Artillery at Antietam and the reserve artillery of the Army of the Potomac from September 1862 to February 1863. He was promoted to brigadier general on December 27, 1862.

William Hays assumed command of an infantry brigade in February 1863. On May 3, during the Battle of Chancellorsville, he was injured when his horse fell on him. He was taken prisoner, along with all but one member of his staff. He was quickly exchanged and fought at Gettysburg. On the evening of July 3, after Pickett's Charge was repulsed, Hays was named acting commander of the II Corps, despite his junior rank. He held the command until mid-August, when he was replaced by Gouverneur K. Warren.

After Gettysburg, Hays was provost marshal for the Southern District of New York, a post he held until February 1865, when he returned to the Army of the Potomac as a division commander in the II Corps. He took part in the Siege of Petersburg and the subsequent pursuit of Lee's army toward Appomattox. At 6:30 a.m. on April 6, his corps commander, General Humphreys, caught him sleeping on duty, along with his entire headquarters. He relieved Hays of his command, and his previous brevets were revoked as punishment. Hays was nevertheless named commander of the Artillery Reserve of the Army of the Potomac on April 6. He was discharged from volunteer service in January 1866.

Hays reverted to his regular army rank of major and, because of the April 6 incident, was not brevetted major general or promoted beyond major in the postwar army. He commanded a variety of posts until April 1873, when he assumed command of Fort Independence in Boston Harbor. He died in Boston on February 7, 1875, at age fifty-five. He was buried in Yonkers, New York, but was reinterred in the West Point Cemetery in 1894.

WILLIAM BABCOCK HAZEN was born in West Hartford, Vermont, on September 27, 1830. His family moved to Hiram, Ohio, when he was three. Future President James A. Garfield was a boyhood friend. Hazen spent four years at West Point and was commissioned brevet second lieutenant in the 4th U.S. Infantry in 1855 (28/34). He would have finished considerably higher but for the fact he accumulated 150 demerits his senior year. His antebellum service was primarily in the Pacific Northwest and on the Texas frontier, where he fought Indians. On November 3, 1859, during a battle with the Comanches on the Llano River, he was severely wounded. A bullet passed through his right hand, through the right side of his chest, and lodged in his rib cage. He carried the bullet for the rest of his life. He did not return to active duty until January 1861, when he became an assistant professor of infantry tactics at West Point. He was at the Academy when the Civil War began in April 1861.

A talented soldier, Hazen was promoted rapidly: first lieutenant in April; captain in May; and (with the help of Garfield) colonel of the 41st

Ohio Infantry in October. He became a brigade commander in Buell's Army of the Ohio in January 1862 and fought at Shiloh on April 7. He also saw action at Perryville, but his most famous battle was Stones River, near Murfreesboro, Tennessee, where he defended the "Round Forest" and repulsed several Confederate attacks. He probably saved the Army of the Cumberland from a thorough defeat. Hazen was also wounded in the shoulder. He was promoted to brigadier general on April 4, 1863.

General Hazen took part in the Tullahoma Campaign and the Battle of Chickamauga, where he helped hold the vital position of Snodgrass Hill. Next, he fought in the Siege of Chattanooga, where he played a major role in opening the "Cracker Line" and resupplying the Army of the Cumberland, which was in desperate trouble before that. He later took part in the Atlanta Campaign, the March to the Sea, and the Carolinas Campaign. He assumed command of a division on August 17, 1864, and was promoted to major general on April 20, 1865. He took command of the XV Corps on May 23, 1865, after the Southern armies east of the Mississippi had surrendered. He was mustered out of volunteer service in January 1866.

After the war, Hazen was named colonel of the 38th (later 6th) U.S. Infantry, which consisted of Buffalo soldiers. He served primarily on the Western frontier and was stationed at Fort Buford in the Dakota Territory from 1872 to 1880. He was on detached duty to Prussia (1870–71), where he was an observer during the Franco-Prussian War. He wrote a book about the French and German military systems. Later, Hazen gave testimony against the corruption in the War Department and played a major role in forcing Grant's secretary of war, William W. Belknap, to resign. He also squabbled with George Armstrong Custer, William T. Sherman, and David S. Stanley, among others.

William Hazen was a perfectionist, a talented officer, and a fractious man. His combative nature served him well on the battlefield against Indians and Confederates, but not so much in the halls of Washington, D.C. He was nevertheless promoted to brigadier general by President Hayes in 1880 and named chief signal officer of the U.S. Army. He was also involved in a controversy with Secretary of War Robert Todd Lincoln, who had him censured and court-martialed. Hazen accused Lincoln of failing to provide timely rescue for an Arctic expedition trapped in the snow. Public opinion was on Hazen's side, however, and rightly so. He escaped with a mild reprimand from President Arthur.

General Hazen died in office of kidney poisoning on January 16, 1887, at age fifty-six. He is buried in Arlington National Cemetery. His widow, Mildred McLean, later married Admiral George Dewey.

CHARLES ADAM HECKMAN was born on December 3, 1822, in Easton, Pennsylvania, and graduated from Minerva Seminary in Eaton in 1837 at age fifteen. He was a clerk in a hardware store in 1846 when the Mexican War began. He enlisted in the Voltigeurs Regiment and took part in several battles and the drive on Mexico City. He was discharged as a sergeant in 1848 and became a conductor on the New Jersey Central Railroad.

Heckman joined the Union Army as a captain in the 1st Pennsylvania Infantry immediately after the Rebels fired on Fort Sumter in April 1861. He became major of the 9th New Jersey the following month and was promoted to lieutenant colonel in October. He was part of Burnside's North Carolina Expedition and fought in the Battle of Roanoke Island (February 7–8, 1862). He performed so well in this Union victory that he was promoted to colonel on February 10. He also fought in the Battle of New Bern (March 14), where he was wounded. He continued to serve in North Carolina after he recovered and was given a brigade command in July. He was promoted to brigadier general on November 29. Meanwhile, he fought at Kinston, White Hall, and Goldsboro. He spent most of 1863 commanding the District of Beaufort, although he did take part in the defense of New Bern.

Heckman briefly commanded the garrison at Newport News, Virginia in late 1863 and early 1864. Assigned command of a brigade in the Army of the James, he was wounded at Port Walthall (May 7) and was captured in the Battle of Chaffin's Farm on May 16. After a few months in Libby Prison, he was exchanged in September and was given command of a division. During the fighting at Fort Harrison on September 29, the commander of the XVIII Corps, Edward O. C. Ord, was severely wounded, and Heckman took command of the corps. His performance at this level was substandard, and the army commander, Benjamin Butler, relieved him and replaced him with his own chief of staff, General Weitzel, on October 1. Heckman then resumed command of his old division.

Charles Heckman commanded the newly created XXV Corps in January and early February 1865, but was again relieved. He held no further assignments and resigned his commission on May 25, 1865. He did not receive a brevet to major general in the omnibus promotions after the war.

Heckman returned to work as a conductor and railroad dispatcher for the New Jersey Central in 1865. He died in Germantown, Pennsylvania, on January 14, 1896, at age seventy-three. He is buried in the Easton Cemetery in the town of his birth.

SAMUEL PETER HEINTZELMAN was born in Manheim, Pennsylvania, on September 30, 1805. He attended West Point and graduated in the Class of 1826 (17/41). Commissioned brevet second lieutenant in the infantry, he was stationed in Michigan on the northern frontier for several years before being transferred to Florida, where he performed quartermaster duty in the Second Seminole War (1835–37). He served in the Quartermaster Department from 1838 to 1846 and fought in the Mexican War, where he was brevetted major during Scott's drive on Mexico City. He accompanied his regiment (the 2nd U.S. Infantry) to California and fought against the Yuma Indians in Arizona Territory, where he earned a brevet to lieutenant colonel. Heintzelman was promoted to major in 1855 and distinguished himself in the First Cortina War in west Texas, where he played a major role in defeating Juan Cortina, a Mexican paramilitary and outlaw leader. He spent two years on recruiting duty (1855–57) before being assigned to frontier duty in west Texas.

An experienced military commander at a time when they were in short supply, Heintzelman was recalled to Washington and named colonel of the 17th U.S. Infantry. He was promoted to brigadier general three days later, on May 17, 1861. He led a division in the First Battle of Bull Run, where he was wounded in the right elbow. When the army was reorganized in March 1862, Heintzelman was given command of the III Corps of the Army of the Potomac.

During the Peninsula Campaign, Heintzelman played a major role in the Siege of Yorktown, the Battles of Williamsburg and Seven Pines, and the Seven Days Battles. During Lee's counteroffensive of June 1862, he was wounded in the Battle of Frayser's Farm (Glendale) and could not use his left arm for some weeks. Promoted to major general on July 16, he also fought at the Second Bull Run, where the Union forces were routed. His corps was stationed in the Washington defenses during the Maryland Campaign.

Samuel Heintzelman's star fell rapidly. Too old and insufficiently aggressive to be an effective corps commander, he had been promoted above his level of competence. He was relieved of his command on October 12. He spent the next year and a half commanding a portion of the Washington, D.C. defenses. He commanded the XXII Corps from February to October 1863. From January 1864, he directed the Northern Department, headquartered in Columbus, Ohio, and sat on court-martial boards. He was discharged from volunteer service in August 1865 and reverted to the rank of colonel. Postwar, he served on boards of inquiry and in Texas, until he reached the mandatory retirement age of sixty-four in 1869. By a special act of Congress, he retired as a major general because of wounds suffered in the line of duty.

General Heintzelman served as president of a mining company and on the board of directors of various corporations in New York and Washington before retiring altogether in 1874. He died in Washington, D.C. on May 1, 1880, at age seventy-four. He was buried in the Forest Lawn Cemetery, Buffalo, New York.

His grandson, Stuart Heintzelman, distinguished himself as a General Staff officer during World War I and died as a major general in 1935.

FRANCIS JAY HERRON was born in Pittsburgh on February 17, 1837. He attended the Western University of Pennsylvania (now the University of Pittsburgh) but did not complete his degree; instead, he became a bank clerk.

In 1855, he and his three brothers established a bank in Dubuque, Iowa. As the Civil War approached, Herron organized a militia company, the "Governor's Greys," which he offered to President-elect Lincoln in January 1861. He became a captain and company commander in the 1st Iowa Infantry and took part in the Union victory in the Battle of Boonville on June 17 and in the disaster at Wilson's Creek on August 10. Promoted to lieutenant colonel in the 9th Iowa in September, he distinguished himself in the Battle of Pea Ridge, where he was wounded and captured. He was exchanged within two weeks and was promoted to brigadier general on July 18. He would be awarded the Congressional Medal of Honor in 1893 for his actions at Pea Ridge. Given command of a division, he played a major role in the Federal victory at Prairie Grove, Arkansas, on December 7. By marching more than 100 miles in three days, he arrived just in time to check the Confederates. This earned him a promotion to major general on March 10, 1863. He was the youngest major general on either side at that time. He was acting commander of the Army of the Frontier from March 30 to June 5, 1863.

General Herron's division joined Grant's army in June 1863 and took part in the Siege of Vicksburg. He was one of the three generals Grant appointed to accept the formal surrender of the city. After Vicksburg, he led an expedition against Yazoo City, which he also captured. He was then sent to Brownsville, Texas, where he commanded part of the XIII Corps. Here he aided Benito Juarez and helped prevent French troops from establishing a foothold on the Rio Grande. He briefly commanded the Baton Rouge-Port Hudson district and ended the war as commander of the District of Northern Louisiana. He resigned from the army on June 27, 1865.

Herron was not as successful as a civilian as he was a soldier. He was a carpetbagger lawyer, tax collector, and U.S. marshal in Louisiana (1867–69) and Louisiana secretary of state (1871–72). When Reconstruction ended in 1877, he moved to New York City, where his fortunes declined, and he descended into poverty. He died at age sixty-four in a tenement in the Big Apple on January 8, 1902. He was buried in the Calvary Cemetery, Queens, New York.

EDWARD WINSLOW "WARD" HINCKS was born in Bucksport, Maine, on May 30, 1830. He later changed the spelling of his name to "Hinks" but, after he retired from the army, went back to "Hincks." He was educated in local schools and moved to Bangor in 1845, where he became a printer for a Whig newspaper. He moved to Boston in 1849 and was elected to the Massachusetts legislature in the 1850s. He also served on the Boston City Council.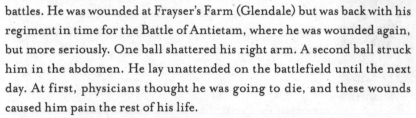

On April 26, 1861, a political ally secured for him a Regular Army commission as a second lieutenant in the 2nd U.S. Cavalry, but he was promoted to lieutenant colonel four days later. In August, he assumed command of the 19th Massachusetts Infantry. He led the 19th at Ball's Bluff, in the Peninsula Campaign, and in the Seven Days battles. He was wounded at Frayser's Farm (Glendale) but was back with his regiment in time for the Battle of Antietam, where he was wounded again, but more seriously. One ball shattered his right arm. A second ball struck him in the abdomen. He lay unattended on the battlefield until the next day. At first, physicians thought he was going to die, and these wounds caused him pain the rest of his life.

Hincks was promoted to brigadier general on April 4, 1863. Apparently still troubled by his wounds, he spent the next several months in rear area duties, including a short tour as commandant of the infamous Point Lookout prison camp. On April 20, 1864, he was given command of a division of USCT troops. He took part in the unsuccessful First Battle of Petersburg (June 9) and the early stages of the Siege of Petersburg. He was severely injured in late June when his horse fell on him.

General Hincks spent the rest of the war in rear area duties, mainly involving recruiting and enforcing the draft in New York City and provost marshal general of New Hampshire. He resigned from the volunteer service on June 30, 1865, although he was brevetted major general in 1866. He reverted to his Regular Army rank of lieutenant colonel in the 40th U.S. Infantry and retired because of his disabilities in 1870. Later, he was promoted to colonel on the retired list.

Hincks served as governor of the National Military Home for Disabled Veterans in Hampton, Virginia, from 1870 to 1873, and the home in Milwaukee from 1873 to 1880. He retired to Cambridge, Massachusetts, where he served on the Board of Aldermen. General Hinck died of cirrhosis of the liver in Cambridge, Massachusetts, on February 14, 1894, after a long and painful illness. He was sixty-three. He was interred in the Mount Auburn Cemetery, Cambridge.

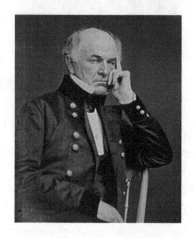

ETHAN ALLEN HITCHCOCK was born on May 18, 1798, in Vergennes, Vermont, the son of a U.S. district judge. His mother was the daughter of Revolutionary War General Ethan Allen, whom Hitchcock strongly resembled. He attended West Point from 1814 to 1817 (17/19) and was commissioned third lieutenant in the artillery. He spent several years in routine garrison duty, mostly in Louisiana and Mississippi. Promoted to second lieutenant (1818), first lieutenant (1818), and captain (1824), he became commandant of cadets at West Point (1829–33), and fought the Seminoles in Florida and various Indian tribes in the Pacific Northwest. He was promoted to major in 1838 and was a lieutenant colonel in the 3rd U.S. Infantry Regiment and commander of Fort Stansbury (south of Tallahassee, Florida) by 1842. He was twice offered the post of governor of Liberia by the American Colonization Society but declined it both times.

Hitchcock served as Winfield Scott's inspector general during the Mexican War, earned a brevet to colonel for Contreras and Churubusco, and was brevetted brigadier general for his gallantry at Molino del Rey. He became the colonel (full rank) of the 2nd U.S. Infantry Regiment in California in 1851, after which he commanded the Pacific Division and then the Department of the Pacific. He took a four-month leave of absence for reasons of health in the summer of 1855. When Secretary of War Jefferson Davis (who disliked him) refused to extend his leave, Hitchcock resigned his commission in October. He retired to St. Louis, where he studied literature and philosophy and published several books on those subjects.

When the Civil War began, Hitchcock went to Washington and applied to return to active duty but was rejected. He returned to St. Louis and worked as a civilian adviser to Generals Harney and Halleck. Winfield Scott used his influence with Secretary of War Stanton on Hitchcock's behalf, and he was commissioned major general, Regular Army, on February 12, 1862. He was named special advisor to Secretary of War Edwin Stanton. He also advised Abraham Lincoln, became commissioner for the exchange of prisoners, in November 1862, and Commissioner for Prisoners in 1865. He was mustered out in October 1867.

General Hitchcock was famous for his collection of books on the flute and the subject of alchemy. He moved to Charleston, South Carolina, after the war and then to Glen Mary Plantation in Sparta, Georgia, where he died on August 5, 1870, at age seventy-three. He was buried in the West Point Cemetery.

EDWARD HENRY HOBSON was born in Greensburg, a village on the Green River in central Kentucky, on July 11, 1825, the son of a steamboat captain and merchant. He was educated in local public schools in Greensburg and Danville. In 1846, at age eighteen, he enlisted in the 2nd Kentucky Infantry, was promoted to first lieutenant, and fought in the Battle of Buena Vista in northern Mexico in February 1847. Mustered out in June, he returned to Kentucky, where he became a merchant and bank president. Meanwhile, he married Governor John Adair's niece. They had seven children.

When the war began, Hobson organized the 13th Kentucky Infantry and became its colonel. Part of Buell's army, he fought at Shiloh on April 7, 1862. He was then sent back to the Bluegrass State and became commander of the District of Western Kentucky. He was promoted to brigadier general on April 15, 1863.

Most of Hobson's services during the rest of the war were in his home state as a brigade or district commander. He defeated and captured John Hunt Morgan on July 26, 1863. He was named commander of Burnside's cavalry corps, but his health prevented him from taking the post.

In a turn of fate, Hobson and 750 of his men were captured by Morgan near Cynthiana, Kentucky, on June 11, 1864. Hobson was wounded in the left arm during this battle. Quickly released and declared exchanged, he fought in the First Battle of Saltville, Virginia, on October 2, where the Union forces were badly defeated. Edward Hobson directed a brigade of cavalry and mounted infantry in Kentucky from then until the end of the war. He was mustered out in August 1865.

After the war, Hobson became a Radical Republican and ran for clerk of the state Court of Appeals but lost. In 1868, he was a delegate to the Republican National Convention, where he strongly supported Ulysses S. Grant. In 1869, President Grant rewarded him by appointing the district collector for the Internal Revenue Service. He ran for Congress in 1872 but lost.

Hobson later became president of the Southern Division of the Chesapeake and Ohio Railroad. He was very active in the Grand Army of the Republic and died at one of their encampments in Cleveland, Ohio, on September 14, 1901. He was seventy-six. He was buried in the Hobson family cemetery, Greensburg, Kentucky.

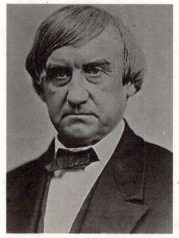

JOSEPH HOLT was born on January 6, 1807, in Breckinridge County, Kentucky. He was educated at St. Joseph's College in Bardstown and Centre College in Danville, Kentucky. He read law, passed the bar, and set up an office in Elizabethtown. He moved to Louisville in 1832 and became an assistant newspaper editor and Commonwealth Attorney (1833 to 1835). He moved to Port Gibson, Mississippi, and practiced law there and in Vicksburg and Natchez, Mississippi, which was the home of one-third of all U.S. millionaires in 1860. Meanwhile, Holt (who was now wealthy) contracted tuberculosis and partially retired in 1842.

Holt was an excellent public speaker and was highly sought after by Democratic politicians. He was, however, strongly anti-slavery and pro-Union. He recovered from his disease, moved to Washington, D.C., and joined the Buchanan administration as Commissioner of Patents in 1857. He became postmaster general in March 1859.

When the South seceded in early 1861, many prominent politicians resigned and "went South," including Secretary of War John B. Floyd. President Buchanan appointed Holt secretary of war, but he had the job only from January 18 to March 5. He then returned to Kentucky and worked to keep that state in the Union.

Lincoln also strained every muscle to keep the Bluegrass State in the union, as did Holt's friend, Erwin Stanton, who became secretary of war in January 1862. He appointed Holt judge advocate general of the U.S. Army, a post he held from September 1862 to December 1875. Initially a colonel, he was promoted to brigadier general on June 24, 1864.

Holt was a man of dubious integrity. Among other constitutionally questionable actions, he suppressed more than three hundred newspapers, harassed Copperheads, and was behind legislation stripping Union Army deserters of their citizenship. He even had U.S. Congressman Benjamin G. Harris of Maryland arrested because he "uttered treasonous statements" on the floor of the U.S. House of Representatives.

Abraham Lincoln was impressed by Holt's work and strongly pro-emancipation, pro-Union efforts. The President, Holt, and John G. Nicolay met almost daily from 1862 on to consider court-martial cases. Of the three, Holt almost always took the harder line. In 1864, Lincoln offered Holt the positions of secretary of the interior and attorney general, but he declined both portfolios. He was also considered for the vice presidential slot in the 1864 elections, but Lincoln settled on Andrew Johnson instead. Holt was later chief prosecutor of the conspirators involved in the Lincoln assassination. Among others, he prosecuted Mary Surratt, the first woman ever executed by the Federal government. (Although she was undoubtedly involved in the plot to kidnap Lincoln, the evidence that she was involved in the assassination plot was dubious.) Holt was also behind the execution of Henry Wirz, the commandant of Andersonville, where some of Holt's witnesses perjured themselves.

Joseph Holt's reputation was further degraded by his prosecution of the Lincoln conspirators and his sensitivity to criticism. He retired in 1875 and lived quietly in Washington, D.C. until his death on August 1, 1894. He was eighty-seven. He was interred in the Holt Family Cemetery in Addison, Kentucky.

JOSEPH "FIGHTING JOE" HOOKER was born in Hadley, Massachusetts, on November 13, 1814. He was educated at the Hopkins Academy in Hadley and at West Point, from which he graduated in 1837 (29/50). Commissioned in the artillery, he fought in the Second Seminole War in Florida and as a captain in Mexico. He served in both Taylor's and Scott's armies and was one of the very few men to receive three brevets, the last one to lieutenant colonel for Chapultepec. (Some authors have opined that three brevets in 1846/48 were equal to the Congressional Medal of Honor of later decades. I tend to agree.) Hooker also had considerable success seducing local women.

After the war, Joe Hooker was assistant adjutant general of the Pacific Division but resigned his commission in 1853. He took up farming at Sonoma but was a failure in agriculture. He applied to return to the army as a lieutenant colonel but was rejected by Secretary of War John Floyd. Although he did obtain a colonelcy in the California Militia, he was in poverty when the Civil War began. He borrowed money to travel to Washington, where he witnessed the First Battle of Bull Run. He then wrote Lincoln a letter, denouncing the mismanagement of Scott's army and promoting his own qualifications. It worked. He was appointed brigadier general on August 6, 1861. He commanded a brigade from August to October, when he was given a division.

Hooker was a good, aggressive division commander. He fought in the Peninsula Campaign and distinguished himself at Williamsburg and Seven Pines. He openly criticized his army commander, General McClellan, for not counterattacking Lee during the Seven Days battles. Promoted to major general on July 16, 1862, Hooker was given command of the III Corps of the Army of Virginia after the Second Bull Run disaster, replacing Irvin McDowell. His command was redesignated I Corps six days later.

Joe Hooker was a man of the world. His HQ was noted for drinking, gambling, wild parties, and loose women, so that the word "hooker" became synonymous with prostitute in popular slang. It was said of his headquarters that it was a place no gentleman would care to go and no lady could go. Hooker himself was a hard drinker, even on the battlefield.

Joe Hooker fought aggressively in the Union victories at South Mountain and Antietam, where he was shot in the right foot. He later claimed that, if he was not forced to leave the field, Lee's army would have been destroyed. After he recovered, he was named commander of the V Corps and led the Center Grand Division (III and V Corps) at Fredericksburg. He protested the plan and correctly predicted a disaster. His grand division launched fourteen attacks on the Confederate line—all unsuccessful. Burnside looked for scapegoats, and Hooker was one of them. He denounced Fighting Joe as "unfit to hold an important commission." But Lincoln sacked Burnside instead, and Hooker assumed command of the Army of the Potomac on January 26.

From his appointment until the end of April, Hooker was a fine army commander. He was a good administrator, restored the sagging morale of the army, consolidated the Union cavalry, created a cavalry corps, and improved the Union horse to the point it was almost equal to that of Jeb Stuart's—something he is rarely given credit for. He entered the Chancellorsville Campaign with his usual bravado, saying: "May God have mercy on General Lee, for I will have none." He vowed not to drink until the Rebels were defeated. This was probably a mistake and may have affected his subsequent poor performance. He was also injured on May 3, when a Confederate cannonball hit the Chancellor Tavern. It knocked off a portion of a wooden column, which struck Hooker in the head and left him sense- less for several hours. His tactical mistakes and errors in judgment are too numerous to discuss here, but they were serious. His subordinates also made mistakes and let him down. His 134,000-man army was smashed by Robert E. Lee, who had only 58,000 men.

Hooker was unable to prevent Lee from invading the North. In a dis- pute with General Halleck over reinforcements, Hooker impulsively sub- mitted his resignation on June 28. It was promptly accepted, and he was replaced by George G. Meade, who led the Army of the Potomac to victory at Gettysburg the following week.

Although he was no match for Robert E. Lee and Stonewall Jackson, Hooker was a solid corps commander and was given command of the XI and XII Corps, which were consolidated to form the XX Corps. He led it with considerable success in the Battle of Lookout Mountain and breaking the Siege of Chattanooga. He also performed well in the Atlanta Campaign. His old friend Sherman, however, promoted O. O. Howard to command of the Army of the Tennessee after General McPherson was killed in action. Howard was junior to Hooker and had commanded the XI Corps under Hooker at Chancellorsville; in fact, Hooker blamed him in large part for the ensuing disaster—and with considerable justification. Angry, Hooker submitted his resignation, which Sherman promptly accepted.

On October 1, Hooker assumed command of the Northern Department (Ohio, Indiana, Illinois, and Michigan) and directed it for the rest of the war. He was mustered out of volunteer service in September 1866, reverted to his regular army rank of brigadier general, and commanded the Department of the East (1865–66) and the Department of the [Great] Lakes (1866–68). He suffered a stroke in November 1865, was partially paralyzed, and was in poor health for the rest of his life. He retired in 1868 and died in Garden City, New York, on October 31, 1879, at the age of sixty-four. He was interred in Spring Grove Cemetery in Cincinnati, Ohio, his wife's hometown.

ALVIN PETERSON HOVEY was born in Mount Vernon, Indiana, probably on September 26, 1821. (Sources differ slightly concerning the exact date.) His father died when he was young, and he grew up in poverty. Sent to an orphanage at age fifteen, he was turned out when he reached age eighteen. He worked as a bricklayer in the daytime and studied law at night, using law books loaned to him by a local attorney. He passed the bar in 1843 and opened his own law office.

Hovey launched his political career as a Democrat in 1850, when he was elected as a delegate to the Constitutional Convention. Here, he opposed black and women's suffrage and introduced a resolution that banned free African Americans from entering the state. It passed, although it was later declared unconstitutional by the U.S. Supreme Court. In 1854, he was appointed to the Indiana

Supreme Court to fill a vacancy until a special election could be held. He ran for a full term but was defeated and held the office for only six months.

President Pierce named Hovey U.S. Attorney for Indiana in 1855, but he was strongly anti-slavery. The pro-slavery faction expelled him from the Democrat Party in 1858, and President Buchanan fired him in 1859. Hovey responded by running for Congress as an independent but lost handily. He then joined the Republican Party.

Hovey received a commission as a first lieutenant in the 2nd Indiana Infantry in 1846, but did not see combat in Mexico. He remained active in the militia and was a colonel by 1861. He joined the Union Army on July 31 as the colonel of the 24th Indiana Infantry. After some initial service in Missouri, he fought in the Battle of Shiloh (April 6–7, 1862), where he performed well. He was promoted to brigadier general on April 30 and assumed command of a brigade in the Army of the Tennessee the following month.

Alvin Hovey was a good commander, and some of his friends said that Hovey believed himself to be the reincarnation of Napoleon. He fought in the Siege of Corinth and in Grant's subsequent Vicksburg campaigns, including the final, successful one. After briefly commanding the District of Eastern Arkansas (November 2–December 3), he was elevated to divisional command in February 1863 and particularly distinguished himself in the Battle of Champion Hill on May 16. He also did well in the Siege of Vicksburg and was praised by General Grant.

Hovey's wife died on November 16, and General Hovey was emotionally devastated. He returned to Indiana and set up guardianships for his children. (He had five but only two reached adulthood.) He briefly commanded a division in the Atlanta Campaign (April–June 1864) but returned home on furlough. General Sherman thought the middle of a decisive campaign was no time to go on leave, so he disbanded Hovey's division. Hovey then became commander of the District of Indiana. Here, he raised a division of ten thousand men and suppressed a potential Sons of Liberty (Copperhead) revolution. The young men of his division were called "Hovey's babies." He was brevetted major general on July 4, 1864, and resigned his commission in October 1865.

After the war, Hovey remarried and served as ambassador to Peru (1866–1870), before returning to Mount Vernon and resuming his law practice. He declined the Republican nomination for governor in 1872. He was elected to Congress in 1886 but only served a single term (1887–1889). He finally accepted the gubernatorial nomination in 1888 and rode Benjamin Harrison's coattails to victory, although the election was very close. He won with 49 percent of the vote, having less than two thousand more than the Democratic nominee, who got 48.8 percent. A Prohibition Party candidate accounted for the other 2.2 percent.

Hovey served as governor from January 14, 1889. Both houses of the legislature were controlled by Democrats, who defeated Hovey's legislative agenda, except for his election reform measures. He created the secret ballot, standardized ballots, and instituted tighter supervision of polling stations. He also suppressed vigilante groups who were hanging outlaws, known local criminals, alcoholics, and deadbeat fathers, as well as dishing out corporal punishment.

General Hovey died in office in Indianapolis on November 23, 1891. He was seventy years old. He is buried in Bellefontaine Cemetery in the town of his birth.

CHARLES EDWARD HOVEY, a distant cousin of General Alvin Hovey, was born in Thetford, Vermont, on April 26, 1827. A man of limited financial means, he worked as a lumberjack or schoolteacher during the summers and attended Dartmouth University when he could afford it. He graduated in 1852. After teaching high school at Framingham, Massachusetts, where he became principal, he moved to Illinois in 1854 and became superintendent of the Peoria schools in 1856. He became the founding president of Illinois State Normal University, now Illinois State University, in 1857.

Hovey resigned his presidency and joined the Union Army as a colonel and commander of the 33rd Illinois Infantry on August 15, 1861. He was largely responsible for forming the regiment, which included many of his former teachers and students and was known as "the Teachers' Regiment." Sent to Missouri, the 33rd fought in several minor engagements. Hovey distinguished himself in the Battle of Cotton Plant,

Arkansas, on July 7, 1862, where he checked a series of poorly coordinated Texas cavalry attacks and was largely responsible for the Union victory. He was promoted to brigadier general to rank from September 5 and was given command of a brigade in November.

General Hovey was severely wounded when Rebel bullets went through both of his arms and shrapnel struck his left knee during the Battle of Arkansas Post on January 11, 1863. He nevertheless remained in command of his brigade until the post fell. While he was still recovering, the U.S. Senate adjourned without acting on his nomination within the statutory period, and he reverted to colonel on March 4. Due to his wounds, he never returned to active duty and resigned his commission in June 1864. He was brevetted major general in 1868.

Charles Hovey moved to Washington, D.C. after the war and worked as a lobbyist and a pension agent. He also passed the bar and worked as an attorney. He died in Washington on November 17, 1897, at age seventy, and was buried in Arlington National Cemetery.

OLIVER OTIS HOWARD was born on November 8, 1830, in Leeds, Maine. He attended Monmouth Academy and North Yarmouth Academy, both in Maine, and graduated from Bowdoin College in 1850 at age nineteen. He then entered West Point, graduating in 1854 (4/46) and was commissioned brevet second lieutenant of ordnance. He was promoted to second lieutenant the following year. After serving in the Watervliet and Kennebec arsenals, he was sent to Florida in 1857 and took part in the Third Seminole War. While there, he converted to Christianity and was a strong evangelical Christian for the rest of his life. He was promoted to first lieutenant in 1857 and became an assistant professor of mathematics at West Point in 1858.

On June 4, 1861, Howard was promoted to colonel of volunteers and named commander of the 3rd Maine Infantry Regiment. He was given a brigade on July 8 and fought in the First Battle of Bull Run, where his command was routed. Even so, he was promoted to brigadier general on

September 3 and fought in the Peninsula Campaign. On June 1, 1862, during the Battle of Seven Pines (Fair Oaks), he was wounded twice in the right arm, which had to be amputated. He received the Congressional Medal of Honor in 1893 for his courage in this battle. He rejoined the army in time to command the rearguard of Pope's army after it was smashed in the Second Bull Run. He fought at Antietam (September 17), where he commanded John Sedgwick's Division after that officer was wounded. He was promoted to major general on November 29, 1862, and replaced Franz Sigel as commander of the XI Corps on March 31, 1863.

O. O. Howard was on the right flank of the Union Army on May 2. He ignored General Hooker's orders to guard against a Confederate offensive and was taken by surprise when Stonewall Jackson launched his famous flank attack, and was thus largely responsible for the disaster at Chancellorsville. His performance at Gettysburg was mixed. He was indecisive, and his corps was largely routed on July 1; the Rebels chased it through the streets of the town, but Howard's decision to place his reserves on Cemetery Hill and hold it as the key position in the defense was a major factor in the Union victory, and he showed great personal courage in rallying Union troops there. Cowardice was not in his nature.

Howard was sent to the Western Front in 1864 and was given command of the IV Corps of the Army of the Cumberland in April. Part of Sherman's drive on Atlanta, he was wounded in the left foot at Pickett's Mill on May 27. After he recovered, Sherman appointed him commander of the Army of the Tennessee on July 27. He led it for the rest of the war, including the capture of Atlanta, the March to the Sea, the capture of Savannah, and the Carolinas Campaign. The last U.S.V. general, he was mustered out on January 1, 1869.

O. O. Howard was an abolitionist from his cadet days and was gravely concerned about the fate of the African American. Postwar, he headed the Freedman's Bureau. Although personally incorruptible, he was a poor administrator and proved incapable of controlling the fraud, thief, incompetence, and corruption which permeated that agency. He stepped down in January 1871 but continued to be interested in the welfare of the African American. He was instrumental in establishing Howard University, an all-black school in Washington, D.C., and was its founding president. Later, as a brigadier general, Regular Army, he took part in several Indian campaigns on the Western frontier and fought Apache, Nez Perce, Bannocks and Paiutes, and did a tour as superintendent of West Point (1881–82). He was promoted to major general in 1886 and retired in 1894.

General Howard died in Burlington, Vermont, on October 26, 1909, at age seventy-eight. He is buried in Lakeview Cemetery, Burlington. His brother was Brevet Brigadier General Charles H. Howard (1838–1880), who was commander of the 128th USCT Infantry Regiment at the end of the war.

ALBION PARRIS HOWE was born on March 13, 1818, in Standish, Maine. He entered the U.S. Military Academy in 1837, graduated in 1841 (8/52), and was commissioned second lieutenant in the artillery. He served along the Michigan–Canada border, at Sackett's Harbor, New York, at Fort Severn, Maryland, as an instructor of mathematics at West Point, and at Fort Monroe, Virginia, until 1846, when the Mexican War broke out. Promoted to first lieutenant in 1846, he earned a brevet to captain for his gallantry at Contreras and Churubusco. From 1848 to 1861 he alternated between posts on the Western frontier and assignments back east. He was promoted to captain (substantive rank) in 1855. He was on frontier duty at Fort Randall, Dakota Territory, when the war began.

Howe served under George B. McClellan in the Western Virginia Campaign of 1861. Still under McClellan, he directed an artillery brigade in the Peninsula Campaign. He transferred to the infantry that summer and was promoted to brigadier general on June 13, 1862. He took command of a mixed New York–Pennsylvania brigade just before the Seven Days battles and distinguished himself at Malvern Hill.

Howe fought at South Mountain and Antietam, after which he was given command of a division, which he led at Fredericksburg, in the Battle of Salem Church during the Chancellorsville Campaign, Gettysburg (where his division was minimally engaged), and in the Bristoe and Mine Run campaigns. His relationship with his corps commander, John Sedgwick, was bad, and his relationship with George G. Meade, the commander of the Army of the Potomac, was poor. (He was a supporter of "Fighting Joe" Hooker.) Who initiated his removal is not clear, but he was replaced by George W. Getty in early March 1864. He was demoted to the command of the Artillery Depot at Washington, D.C. for the rest of the war except for the period July–August 1864, when he was commandant of Harpers Ferry. He was brevetted major general in January 1866 and discharged from volunteer service in July. He reverted to his Regular Army rank of major.

Postwar, Howe was member of the military commission that tried the Lincoln conspirators, and briefly worked for the Freedman's Bureau. He remained in the artillery, was promoted to lieutenant colonel in 1879, and became colonel of the 4th Artillery Regiment in the spring of 1882. He retired ten weeks later.

General Howe settled in Cambridge, Massachusetts, where he died on January 25, 1897. He was seventy-eight. He is buried in Mount Auburn Cemetery, Cambridge.

JOSHUA BLACKWOOD HOWELL was born on September 11, 1806, at "Fancy Hill," his family's estate near Woodbury, New Jersey. His family owned this property on the Delaware River since 1688. He was the tenth child of Joshua Ladd Howell, who served as a colonel in the War of 1812, and his grandfather held the same rank in the quartermaster branch during the American Revolution. The future Union general was educated locally, studied law in Philadelphia, was admitted to the bar, and set up a practice in Uniontown, Pennsylvania. Politically, he was a Douglas Democrat. He was a brigadier general in the Pennsylvania Militia for several years when the Civil War began.

Howell was commissioned colonel of the 85th Pennsylvania on November 12, 1861, the day the regiment left for Washington, D.C. It remained in the capital's defenses until late March 1862, when it was transported to the Virginia Peninsula. It fought in the Siege of Yorktown and the Battle of Williamsburg. Part of the IV Corps, Howell assumed command of a brigade on May 18 but returned to his regiment on May 24. He fought at Seven Pines (Fair Oaks), and the Seven Days battles, including Malvern Hill. The 85th Pennsylvania was posted at Suffolk, Virginia, from September until December, when it was transferred to New Bern, North Carolina. Howell was given command of a brigade in January 1863 and served in the Department of the South, where he took part in the operations against Charleston, South Carolina. He was involved in the reduction of Fort Wagner on Morris Island, where he was slightly wounded in the head by Rebel shrapnel on August 16, 1863. His brigade spent December 1863 to April 1864 on Hilton Head, when it was transferred to the Army of the James. It fought south of Petersburg, Virginia, including the Battle of Drewry's Bluff (May 14–16, 1864) and the Bermuda Hundred (from May 17). Howell distinguished himself on May 20, when he launched a quick counterattack and recaptured some rifle pits previously lost to the Confederates.

Howell took part in the Siege of Petersburg and was acting commander of a division on September 12. He mounted his horse that day, but it reared up, fell over backward, and landed on top of the colonel. They took him to X Corps Headquarters and then to the 85th Pennsylvania's field hospital, where he died on September 14, 1864. He was fifty-eight. Six months later, he was posthumously promoted to brigadier general. His remains lie in the Eglington Cemetery, Clarksboro, New Jersey.

ANDREW ATKINSON HUMPHREYS was born into a Quaker family in Philadelphia on November 2, 1810. His grandfather, Joshua, was known as "the Father of the American Navy." Andrew matriculated from Nazareth Hall (now Moravian University) and the U.S. Military Academy, from which he graduated in 1831 (13/33). Commissioned in the artillery, he was stationed in Charleston, South Carolina, and fought in the Second Seminole War in 1836. He resigned his commission later that year (apparently he caught yellow fever) but was reinstated in 1838 as a first lieutenant in the newly formed topographical engineers. He stayed in this branch for the next twenty-three years. Antebellum, his duty stations

included Chicago; Oswego Harbor, New York; Washington, D.C.; another tour of duty against the Seminoles in Florida; Europe; Washington, D.C. again; the lower Mississippi Delta in Louisiana; and West Point. He was considered one of America's top scientists when the Civil War began.

Humphreys was promoted to major on August 6, 1861, and was an aide to George B. McClellan. His advancement was hampered because of his previous close relationship with Jefferson Davis. He helped plan the defenses of Washington, D.C. and was transferred to McClellan's Army of the Potomac in March 1862. This led to his promotion to brigadier general on April 29. He never commanded a brigade but was promoted directly to division commander in the V Corps on September 12. His unit was in reserve at Antietam, but at Fredericksburg, it advanced further than any Union formation in the attack on Marye's Heights. Five of the seven members of his staff were killed or wounded, and Humphreys had two horses shot out from under him. His uniform was punctured several times by Southern bullets, but the general remained unharmed.

Humphreys was respected by his men but not liked by them. He was a strict disciplinarian and hard taskmaster noted for his profanity. They called him "Old Goggle Eyes" because of his eyeglasses. In social situations, however, he was genial and courteous, and a dignified gentleman. He was also good at handling large bodies of troops.

After fighting at Chancellorsville, Humphreys was transferred to the command of a division in the Sickles's III Corps. Because Sickles disobeyed orders, it was slaughtered at Gettysburg on July 2, 1863. Humphreys did the best he could in a bad situation and was eventually able to re-form the survivors. He was promoted to major general on July 8 and (at General Meade's request) became chief of staff of the Army of the Potomac the next day. He held this post until November 1864, when he assumed command of the II Corps. He fought in the Siege of Petersburg and in the Appomattox Campaign, including Sayler's Creek, where he distinguished himself.

Humphreys fought in seventy engagements during the Civil War. He was mustered out of volunteer service in September 1866 and reverted to the rank of brigadier general and chief of engineers. He retired in 1879.

General Humphreys spent his retirement writing scientific and philosophical articles and two books on the war. He was also an incorporator of the National Academy of Sciences. He died in Washington, D.C., on December 27, 1883, at age seventy-three. He is buried there in the Congressional Cemetery.

HENRY JACKSON HUNT was born on September 14, 1819, in Detroit Barracks, Michigan. His younger brother Lewis also became a Union general but by brevet only. His father was an infantry officer who died when he was ten. Supported financially by family and friends, he received a good education, was admitted to West Point in 1835 and graduated four years later (19/31). While there, he became interested in light artillery tactics, became a second lieutenant in the 2nd U.S. Artillery in 1839, and went on to become arguably the foremost artilleryman and artillery tactician of the entire Civil War era.

Promoted to first lieutenant in 1846, Hunt fought in Mexico and won brevets to captain for Contreras and Churubusco and to major for Chapultepec. He was wounded twice at Molino del Rey (September 8, 1847), but not seriously. After Mexico, he did garrison duty at various locations, including the frontier, took part in the Utah War of 1857 against the Mormons, and helped quell disturbances in "Bleeding Kansas" (1857–58). A Regular Army captain as of 1852, in 1856 he was named to a three-member board to revise artillery tactics for the entire army. His *Instructions for Field Artillery* was published in 1861 and became the guiding star of U.S. artillery during the Civil War. It called for infantry brigades to keep their artillery batteries for close support, but divisional and corps batteries were assigned to a central Artillery Reserve under army headquarters control.

Hunt was promoted to major on May 14, 1861, commanded a four-gun battery at the First Bull Run (July 21), and distinguished himself covering the Union retreat. To fire more rapidly, he ordered his men to reload without pausing to sponge the cannons—a dangerous procedure, but it worked for him. He was named commander of artillery for the Washington, D.C., defenses two days later. He was promoted to colonel on September 28 and joined the staff of General George McClellan, where he commanded the Artillery Reserve of the Army of the Potomac during the Peninsula and

Seven Days campaigns. His 250 guns slaughtered the Confederates at Malvern Hill on July 1, 1862, and led to his promotion to chief of artillery of the Army of the Potomac and brigadier general on September 15. He fought at Antietam and Fredericksburg, where he commanded 147 guns.

When General Hooker commanded the Army of the Potomac, he reduced Hunt to an administrative role. As a result, Union artillery coordination was poor during the Battle of Chancellorsville, and its overall performance was substandard. Hooker realized his mistake and restored Hunt to overall artillery command after the battle.

Henry Hunt was a hero at the Battle of Gettysburg. On July 3, he concentrated seventy-seven guns along a narrow front on Cemetery Hill and resisted pressure to engage in counterbattery fire. As a result, he had enough ammunition left to smash Pickett's Charge. When the Rebels broke through the Union line at The Angle, Hunt rushed forward with the reinforcements, firing his pistol at the enemy, until his horse was killed, and he was pinned beneath it. Fortunately for him, some of his men saw the incident, ran forward and rescued him. His actions that day earned him a brevet promotion to major general and a Regular Army promotion to lieutenant colonel. He continued to serve as chief of artillery during the Overland Campaign, the Siege of Petersburg, and the Appomattox Campaign. He was mustered out of volunteer service in 1866 and reverted to the rank of lieutenant colonel. He was promoted to colonel in 1869 as commander of Fort Adams, Rhode Island, and the 5th U.S. Artillery. He became president of the permanent Artillery Board in 1875. He retired in 1883.

General Hunt was governor of the Soldiers' Home in Washington from 1883 until his death, which occurred there on February 11, 1889. He was sixty-nine. He is buried in the Soldiers' and Airmen's Home National Cemetery, Washington, D.C. He was one of the great unsung Union heroes of the war.

LEWIS CASS HUNT was born on February 23, 1824, at Fort Howard, on Green Bay, Michigan Territory, the son of an army officer. His older brother was future Union General Henry J. Hunt. He became a cadet at West Point in 1843, graduated in 1847 (33/38), and was commissioned brevet second lieutenant in the 3rd Infantry Regiment. He transferred to the 4th Infantry later that year. He served in Mexico and then did garrison duty in East

Pascagoula, Mississippi, and Sackett's Harbor, New York. Frontier duty at Fort Humboldt, California, and action against the Trinity River Indians followed. He took a leave of absence from 1854 to 1858 before conducting recruits to Utah in 1858. He served in Washington Territory and California from 1859 to 1861. Meanwhile, he was promoted to second lieutenant (1847), first lieutenant (1852), and captain (1855). His wife was the daughter of future Union General Silas Casey.

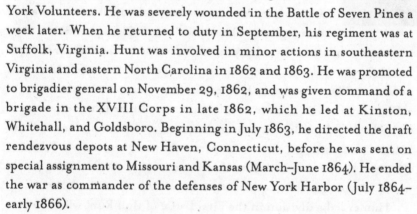

In early 1862, Hunt was transferred to the Washington defenses and then the Eastern Front, where he fought in the Peninsula Campaign, including the Siege of Yorktown and the Battle of Williamsburg. On May 25, he was promoted to colonel and assumed command of the 92nd New York Volunteers. He was severely wounded in the Battle of Seven Pines a week later. When he returned to duty in September, his regiment was at Suffolk, Virginia. Hunt was involved in minor actions in southeastern Virginia and eastern North Carolina in 1862 and 1863. He was promoted to brigadier general on November 29, 1862, and was given command of a brigade in the XVIII Corps in late 1862, which he led at Kinston, Whitehall, and Goldsboro. Beginning in July 1863, he directed the draft rendezvous depots at New Haven, Connecticut, before he was sent on special assignment to Missouri and Kansas (March–June 1864). He ended the war as commander of the defenses of New York Harbor (July 1864–early 1866).

Hunt returned to the Regular Army as a major in 1866. He served on the Michigan and Minnesota frontiers, Louisiana, in the Dakota Territory, and in Texas. He was promoted to lieutenant colonel in 1868 and colonel and commander of the 14th Infantry in 1881. His service with the 14th was spotty, however, because of his fragile health. Finally placed on light duty, he was transferred to Fort Union, New Mexico, hoping he might regain his health. Instead, he died there on September 6, 1886, at age sixty-three. Initially interred in the post cemetery, he was reburied in the Fort Leavenworth National Cemetery. He is sometimes confused with his cousin,

also named Lewis Cass Hunt (1831–1868), a brevet brigadier general in the Civil War.

DAVID "BLACK DAVE" HUNTER was born on July 21, 1802. Sources differ as to his birthplace, with Troy, New York; Princeton, New Jersey; and Washington, D.C., being cited by various sources. In 1872, Hunter himself said he was born in New Jersey. He was a grandson of Richard Stockton, a signer of the Declaration of Independence.

Hunter graduated from West Point in 1822 (25/40) and was assigned to the 5th Artillery Regiment, which served in the old Northwest, including Fort Snelling, Minnesota, and Fort Dearborn, Chicago, Illinois, where Hunter met his wife. He was promoted to captain in the 1st Dragoons in 1833 and resigned his commission in 1836. He worked as a real estate agent and land speculator in Chicago until late 1841, when he rejoined the army as a paymaster. He was promoted to major in 1842.

Hunter served with Taylor's army in northern Mexico where he earned no brevets. There are gaps in Hunter's service record, but he next emerges at Fort Leavenworth, Kansas, in 1860, when he initiated a correspondence with Abraham Lincoln. Lincoln was impressed with Hunter, invited him to travel to Washington with him as part of the inaugural train in February 1861, and he guarded the White House and lived in the East Wing for six weeks. Lincoln gave him command of the 6th U.S. Cavalry on May 14.

Hunter led a division in the First Battle of Bull Run, where he was wounded in the neck and cheek. When he recovered, he was promoted to brigadier general on August 7 and to major general on August 13. It was one of Lincoln's more unfortunate appointments. Transferred to the West, Hunter briefly commanded a division in Missouri and succeeded John C. Fremont as commander of the Department of the West. He was relieved of this job by General-in-Chief McClellan on November 8 and was named commander of the Department of Kansas. Unhappy in this backwater post, he ignored the chain of command again and wrote several letters of protest to his friend in the White House, who finally yielded to his complaints and named him commander of the Department of the South and X Corps in March 1862.

David Hunter was a strong advocate of arming African Americans to fight for the Union. He formed the 1st [U.S.] South Carolina Infantry Regiment (African Descent) without the permission of the War Department, and on May 9, he ordered the emancipation of the slaves in his district, which included the states of South Carolina, Georgia, and Florida. Lincoln immediately repudiated and revoked this order. The 1st South Carolina, meanwhile, was disbanded and its soldiers discharged without pay. Jefferson Davis, meanwhile, branded Hunter a felon for instigating servile insurrection and ordered that he be executed if captured. This never happened, but he was defeated in the Battle of Secessionville, and all his efforts to take Charleston failed.

In the winter of 1862–63, Hunter was on temporary duty in Washington, D.C., where he presided over the court-martial of Fitz John Porter, who was railroaded and discharged from the service for political reasons. Hunter then returned to his headquarters at Port Royal, South Carolina.

David Hunter was relieved of the command of the Department of the South in June 1863 and was an inspector in Tennessee and Louisiana until General Sigel, the commander of the Army of the Shenandoah, was defeated at New Market in May 1864. Hunter was selected to replace him. On General Grant's orders, he instituted a scorched earth campaign in the Valley. It ended at Lynchburg (June 17–19), where he suffered a minor defeat at the hands of Confederate General Early. He then fled into the mountains of West Virginia, took his army with him, and exposed Washington, D.C., to potential capture by General Early. After the war, Hunter wrote to Robert E. Lee and asked him to declare that his (Hunter's) retreat was justified. Lee (who despised Hunter for burning private homes, colleges, and libraries, and leaving women and children without shelter) wrote back that he did not understand the strategy behind removing an entire Union army to West Virginia, but that it was an immense help to the Confederate Army.

General Grant ordered that Hunter be relegated to a figurehead position after Lynchburg and that field operations be conducted by General Sheridan. Hunter refused to accept this, so Grant sacked him on August 8. He held no further commands in the Civil War. He retired from the army as a colonel of cavalry in 1866. He wrote a self-serving memoir, which was published in 1873. He, however, could not disguise the fact that he was one of the least successful and least capable Union generals.

David Hunter lapsed into obscurity after the war. He died in Washington, D.C., on February 2, 1886, at age eighty-three. He is buried in the Princeton Cemetery, Princeton, New Jersey.

STEPHEN AUGUSTUS HURLBUT was born in Charleston, South Carolina, on November 29, 1815, the son of a Unitarian minister. He became a lawyer and a first lieutenant in the South Carolina Militia and served as a regimental adjutant during the Second Seminole War.

Hurlbut fled South Carolina in 1845 to escape his creditors. He settled in Belvidere, Illinois, established a law practice, and became close friends with another Illinois lawyer, Abraham Lincoln. He was a member of the Illinois Constitutional Convention in 1847 as a Whig. After that party collapsed in 1854, he joined the Republicans and was elected to the legislature in 1859 and 1861. He campaigned for his friend Lincoln in 1860. He returned to Charleston on a fact-finding mission for Lincoln for three days in March 1861. Despite his minimal qualifications, Lincoln appointed him brigadier general of volunteers on June 14, 1861. He was given command of a division in the Army of the Tennessee in February 1862. In this position, his courageous decision to abandon Prentiss's Division to defend Pittsburg Landing probably saved Grant's army. After participating in the Siege of Corinth and the Corinth-Iuka Campaign (September–October 1862), he was given command of the XVI Corps in Memphis. He was promoted to major general on September 17.

War brings out the best in some people and the worst in others. It brought out both in General Hurlbut. Like General Grant, Hurlbut hated Jews. Unlike Grant, who expelled them from Memphis, Hurlbut wanted wealthy Jews to stay in the River City. He could then arrest them, throw them in a dungeon called Fort Putnam, and hold them until their families could pay a ransom. He also confiscated their property. Meanwhile, his efforts to deal with Confederate General Nathan Bedford Forrest were totally ineffective.

Cotton was called "White Gold" in those days. The price of cotton increased from $.06 a pound pre-war to $1.09 a pound in 1864, with spikes even higher. Hurlbut confiscated corps and sold permits to corrupt cotton brokers. He used Fort Pillow, about fifty miles north of Memphis, to ship the illicit cotton to the North, where the textile industry desperately needed the raw material. General Sherman, meanwhile, needed men, so he ordered Fort Pillow (which no longer served a military purpose) closed. Hurlbut did close it but then secretly reopened it. The Union high command was shocked when General Forrest captured it on April 12, 1864, and slaughtered the garrison. Sherman sacked Hurlbut on April 17.

Hurlbut's friend Lincoln rescued the hard-drinking general from professional obscurity in September 1864, when he appointed him commander of the Department of the Gulf. Here, he continued his corrupt practices until Edward R. S. Canby, the straight-laced commander of the Army of the Gulf, had him arrested for embezzlement on April 22, 1865. Hurlbut, however, was allowed to resign his commission on June 20.

The now wealthy former general was a founder of the Grand Army of the Republic and served as its commander-in-chief from 1866 to 1868. He served as minister resident to Colombia from 1869 to 1872, when he was elected to Congress. Re-elected in 1874, he was defeated in 1876. He was named ambassador to Peru in 1881. One of the more corrupt Union generals, Hurlbut died in Lima, Peru, on March 27, 1882. He was sixty-six years old. He was buried in the Belvidere Cemetery, Boone County, Illinois.

I

INGALLS

RUFUS INGALLS was born in Denmark, Maine, on August 23, 1818. He graduated from West Point in 1843 (32/39) and was commissioned brevet second lieutenant in the Mounted Rifles Regiment. Assigned to the 1st Dragoons, he fought in northern Mexico and New Mexico Territory and was brevetted first lieutenant for his gallantry at Embudo and Taos. He transferred to the quartermaster branch in 1848 and made his career there. Ingalls was stationed in a variety of duty stationed antebellum, including Los Angeles (1848), Oregon Territory (1849-52), Fort Vancouver, Washington Territory (1852-53), Washington, D.C. (1853-54), and Fort Leavenworth, Kansas (1854). He accompanied the Steptoe Expedition across the continent from Kansas through Utah Territory to California. He was assistant quartermaster of the Department of Florida and was stationed at Fort Pickens when the Civil War began.

Ingalls (a captain since 1854) was known to be a highly competent quartermaster and logistician. He was almost immediately promoted to major and then lieutenant colonel of volunteers. He was on George B. McClellan's staff in the Western Virginia Campaign and followed him east. In April 1862, Ingalls became quartermaster of the Army of the Potomac, where he did what seemed to be impossible: in succession, he satisfied Generals McClellan, Burnside, Hooker, Meade, and Grant. He and Grant were old friends from their Fort Vancouver days, and Grant named him chief quartermaster for all the armies in Virginia in June 1864. Meanwhile, he was promoted to brigadier general on May 23, 1863. During the Siege of Petersburg, his base at City Point, Virginia, became the largest port operation in the Western Hemisphere. Grant later wrote: "There never was a corps better organized than was the Quartermaster Corps with the Army of the Potomac in 1864."

Rufus Ingalls was indeed an unsung hero of the Union war effort. He was present at Appomattox when General Lee surrendered. He was brevetted major general in January 1866 and reverted to his Regular Army rank of lieutenant colonel on July 28. He was promoted to colonel the next day. Over the next sixteen years, he was stationed in a number of places, including New York City, San Francisco, and Chicago. In 1882, he became Quartermaster General of the Army and was promoted to brigadier general, Regular Army. He retired fifteen months later after forty years' service. He moved to Oregon and then in 1891 to New York City, where he died on January 15, 1893, at age seventy-four. He was buried in Arlington National Cemetery.

J

JACKSON – JUDAH

CONRAD FEGER JACKSON was born on September 11, 1813, in Alsace Township, Berks County, Pennsylvania. His father served in the War of 1812, where he contracted a disease which killed him in 1818, and Conrad was raised in the home of an uncle. His family were Quakers, and he was educated in local Quaker schools. He was called by his middle name. As a young adult, he worked in a warehouse in Philadelphia and then became a conductor on the Philadelphia & Reading Railroad. A militia lieutenant, he served as a dispatch rider in General Scott's Army of Mexico in 1847. He returned to Pennsylvania and worked for the United States Revenue Service after the war. He was the manager of a petroleum oil company in western Virginia when the North and South came to blows in 1861.

Jackson at once quit his civilian job, went to Pittsburgh, and organized the 9th Pennsylvania Reserve, of which he was appointed colonel by the governor. His regiment, which was also known as the 38th Pennsylvania Infantry, arrived in Washington, D.C., a few days after the First Battle of Bull Run, and remained in the capital defenses that winter. Jackson distinguished himself in the Peninsula Campaign. He was given command of the 3rd Brigade of the Pennsylvania Reserves near the end of the Seven Days battles and was promoted to brigadier general on July 19, 1862. He fought in the Second Battle of Bull Run but missed most of the Maryland Campaign, including the Battles of South Mountain and Antietam, due to illness.

General Jackson was killed in action during the Battle of Fredericksburg on December 13, 1862. There are two accounts of his death. According to one, he rode forward to give his brigade an order, when he and his aide were cut down by a Confederate volley. According to the other, his men were pinned down in a three-foot ditch on the eastern side of the Richmond, Fredericksburg & Piedmont Railroad. Jackson rode forward to get them moving forward again when his horse was killed. He got up, leapt on to the railroad bed, and waved his sword, to encourage his men to advance. This attracted the fire of a Tennessee regiment. One of the bullets struck him in the head and killed him instantly. He was forty-nine years old. In writing about his death, General Meade spoke highly of him as an officer of merit and gallantry. General Jackson is buried in Allegheny Cemetery, Pittsburgh.

JAMES STRESHLY JACKSON was born in Fayette County, Kentucky, on September 27, 1823. He received a classical education at Centre College in Danville, Tennessee, and at Jefferson College, Canonsburg, Pennsylvania, from which he graduated in 1844. Jackson then pursued a legal education at Transylvania University in Lexington and was admitted to the bar in 1845. He began practicing in Greenupsburg, Kentucky, but his business was interrupted by the Mexican War. He enlisted as a private on June 9, 1846, and was elected third lieutenant in July. Then a quarrel with Thomas Francis Marshall led to a duel. Although neither man was hurt, Jackson feared he would be court-martialed because Marshall was a captain, and he had thus tried to kill a superior officer. To avoid this contingency, he resigned his commission on October 10. This was not his only duel. He was a gruff, overbearing, and quarrelsome man who reportedly later killed a man in an altercation on the streets of Hopkinsville.

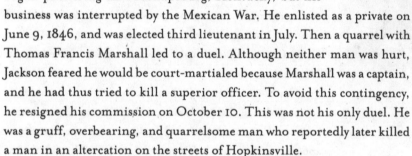

Jackson returned to Greenupsburg in 1846 and practiced there until 1859, when he moved to Hopkinsville. He owned thirteen slaves in 1860. He ran for Congress that year on the Unionist Party ticket and was elected, serving from March 4 to December 31, 1861. Meanwhile, on December 13, he was elected colonel of the 3rd (U.S.) Kentucky Cavalry. He and his men arrived at Shiloh with Buell's army on April 7, 1862, too late to fight in the battle. He was nevertheless appointed brigadier general on July 19, 1862, largely because of Lincoln's policy of advancing local border-state politicians to higher rank, regardless of their qualifications or lack thereof. In any case, Jackson was placed in charge of "Bull" Nelson's cavalry but did not join him until the day after Nelson's forces were slaughtered in the Battle of Richmond. Buell transferred him to the command of a two-brigade infantry division on September 29.

Jackson's division was in the thick of the Battle of Perryville on October 8. Both of Jackson's brigade commanders were killed and his command suffered 1,172 casualties. Jackson was shot in the chest and died instantly or almost so. He was thirty-nine years old. He was buried in the Cave Hill Cemetery in Louisville but was later reinterred in the Riverside Cemetery, Hopkinsville.

NATHANIEL JAMES JACKSON was born on July 28, 1818, in Newburyport, Massachusetts. He became a machinist and, when the Civil War broke out, he was superintendent of the Hill Mill at Lewiston, Maine. Active in the militia, he became a colonel and commander of the 1st Maine Infantry (a 90-day unit) on May 3, 1861. (Eight of the regiment's ten companies were former militia units.) The 1st Maine did not see combat in the Bull Run Campaign, and Jackson and his men were mustered out on August 3.

On September 3, Jackson returned to the colors as commander of the 5th Maine, a three-year unit recruited from militiamen. Colonel Jackson was not a popular appointment; several officers resigned, and the 5th almost mutinied. Jackson and his men fought in the Peninsula Campaign. At Gaines' Mill, the 5th Maine suffered ten killed, sixteen missing, and sixty-nine wounded. One of the casualties was Jackson, who was wounded in the right elbow. He returned to duty in time to take part in the Battle of South Mountain (September 14), where he was wounded in the knee at Crampton's Gap. He nevertheless fought at Antietam on September 17.

Nathaniel Jackson was given command of a brigade in the XII Corps and was promoted to brigadier general on September 24, 1862. His brigade was stationed at Harper's Ferry that winter and thus missed the Battle of Fredericksburg. He suffered a severe accident that spring and missed the Battle of Chancellorsville. He was capable of performing only light duty that summer and was given command of the draft rendezvous depot on Rikers Island in New York Harbor. On September 20, he was ordered to the Western Front, where Sherman assigned him to command the 1st

Division of the XX Corps, a vacancy caused by the temporary incapacitation of General Mower. Later, he was temporary commander of General A. S. Williams's Division when that officer commanded a corps. He led this command in the March to the Sea and the Carolinas Campaign, including the Battle of Bentonville, even though he was shot in the ankle in December 1864. When Williams returned to duty on April 2, 1865, Jackson was left without a command. He was brevetted major general on March 15, 1865, and mustered out in August.

Postwar, Jackson operated a coal mine and spent his summers in Newburyport, where he had many friends. He suffered a stroke in 1891 and died of a cerebral hemorrhage at the home of a son in Jamestown, New York, on April 21, 1892. He was seventy-three years old. He was buried in Oak Hill Cemetery, Newburyport.

RICHARD HENRY JACKSON was born in Kinnegad, County Westmeath, Ireland on July 14, 1830. He emigrated to the United States and enlisted in the 4th U.S. Artillery as a private on December 12, 1851, and fought Indians on the Plains. He was successively promoted to corporal, sergeant, and first sergeant. In 1859, he took the very difficult Competitive Officers' Exam, passed it, and was promoted to brevet second lieutenant on September 13. He was promoted to second lieutenant in 1860 and to first lieutenant on May 14, 1861.

Jackson was stationed at Fort Pickens, Florida, when the war began. He defended the fort and fought in the Battle of Santa Rosa Island, when the Confederates unsuccessfully tried to capture the place. In early 1862 he was promoted to captain and transferred to the staff of the X Corps, Department of the South, as an inspector general. He was part of the unsuccessful attempts to take Fort Sumter and Battery Wagner and was with X Corps when it was transferred to the Army of the James in Virginia in 1864. Meanwhile, he was promoted to lieutenant colonel in April 1863.

Jackson distinguished himself in the Battle of Drewry's Bluff, just southeast of Richmond, on May 15, 1864. In September, he was named chief of artillery of the X Corps. He did a fine job in this post and was named chief of staff of the Army of the James in January 1865. On April 10, 1865, the day after General Lee surrendered, he was given command of a U.S. Colored Troops division in the XXV Corps. He and his men were sent to Texas almost immediately. Jackson was promoted to brigadier general on May 19.

It was thought that the Union Army might have to be employed against the French in Mexico, but this proved unnecessary. Jackson was brevetted major general in November 1865 and mustered out of volunteer service in February 1866. He reverted to his Regular Army rank of captain and was not promoted to major until 1880. Perhaps his closest brush with death occurred when he was hit by lightning while standing in the honor guard for Ulysses S. Grant's body at Mount McGregor, New York, on July 30, 1885. He recovered from his burns and was promoted to lieutenant colonel of the 4th Artillery in late 1888. He died of acute inflammatory rheumatism at Fort McPherson in Atlanta, Georgia, on November 28, 1892. He was sixty-two years old.

Jackson's only son, Franklin, was a West Point cadet who, at age twenty, died on New Year's Eve, 1888. He was buried in the West Point Cemetery, and his father, General Jackson, was buried beside him.

CHARLES DAVIS JAMESON was born in Orono, Maine, or Gorham, Maine (depending on your source) on February 24, 1827. His family moved to Old Town, Maine, when he was young. He obtained a limited education locally. He became a lumberman and was quite successful. He was also active in the militia, rising to the rank of colonel. He was a delegate to the Democratic National Convention in 1860 and backed Stephen A. Douglas. A "War Democrat," he was the party's nominee for governor of Maine in 1861 and 1862. Meanwhile, on May 28, 1861, he was elected colonel of the 2nd Maine Infantry, a 90-day regiment whose enlistments were later extended to two years. It was the first unit to leave the state and Jameson led it in the First Battle of Bull Run. He helped cover the routed army's retreat to Centreville, which led to his promotion to brigadier general on September 3. He was given command of a brigade in the III Corps.

Jameson took part in the Peninsula Campaign and was the first to discover that the Confederates had evacuated Yorktown. He fought in the Battle of Seven Pines, where he distinguished himself. He also had a horse shot out from under him. Shortly thereafter, he came down with "camp fever" (probably typhoid fever) and was granted leave. He died on a steamboat between Boston and Bangor on November 6, 1862. He was thirty-five years old. He is buried in Stillwater Riverside Cemetery, Old Town, Maine.

ANDREW "ANDY" JOHNSON, the 17th President of the United States, was born on December 29, 1808, in a two-room shack in Raleigh, North Carolina. He grew up in poverty and never attended school. His father died when he was three and his mother, a tavern servant and laundress, raised him. At age ten, his mother apprenticed him to a tailor, and he was taught rudimentary literary proficiency from a fellow apprentice. He quickly developed a lifelong love of reading and education. He soon developed into a skilled orator and an effective debater. On the other hand, he could be stubborn and arrogant.

Not happy at the shop, but legally bound until age twenty-one, Johnson ran away when he was fifteen and eventually settled in Greeneville, Tennessee, where he established a successful tailoring business. He made several successful real estate investments, became prosperous, and ultimately owned ten slaves, which he freed in August 1863.

Meanwhile, Johnson entered politics as a Democrat. (He fervently admired fellow Tennessean Andrew Jackson.) He was successively an alderman, mayor of Greeneville, member of the Tennessee House of Representatives (1835–42), state senator (1842–43), Congressman (1843–53), two-term governor (1853–57), and United States Senator (1857–62). He also joined the militia and rose to the rank of colonel.

Johnson was a conservative who believed in limited government. He also believed that the Constitution prohibited the Federal Government

ENCYCLOPEDIA OF UNION GENERALS

from abolishing slavery or restricting it in the territories, and he opposed protective tariffs and subsidizing the railroads. He did not, however, believe in secession. When the South left the Union, he was the only member of a seceded state to remain in the Senate.

In early 1862, Lincoln appointed Johnson military governor of Tennessee, and he became a brigadier general on March 5. The Confederacy responded by seizing his property and his slaves. In Nashville, Johnson demanded loyalty oaths from state officials. Like most military governors, he exercised arbitrary power, but he succeeded in restoring civil government in areas behind Union lines. When Lincoln issued the Emancipation Proclamation, the areas of Tennessee still in Confederate hands were exempted at Johnson's request.

Lincoln ran for re-election in 1864 on a National Union Party ticket, and he needed a War Democrat as his running mate to balance the ticket. He chose Johnson, who actively campaigned for Lincoln. It was considered unusual for president or vice-presidential candidates to actively campaign at that time. After Atlanta fell, the Lincoln-Johnson ticket was easily elected, and the Tennessean was inaugurated on March 4, 1865. He was clearly intoxicated at the time and was almost incoherent.

Abraham Lincoln was shot on April 14 and died the following morning. President Johnson was initially in favor of treating former Confederates harshly but quickly changed his mind. His policy became conciliatory as he attempted to reinstate the Southern states into the Union and restore the civil rights of most of the former Confederates. This led to a break with the Radical Republicans, who attempted to impeach him. Johnson's arrogance and stubbornness did not help his cause. The Radicals' efforts failed by one vote in the Senate. They did, however, succeed in imposing Radical Reconstruction on the South.

Modern historians generally focus solely on Johnson's failure to support African American suffrage and rank him as one of the worst presidents ever, but he did have some successes. He forced the French to leave Mexico and purchased Alaska from Russia. He also established an eight-hour workday for Federal employees, issued a general amnesty for all former Confederates, and tried to heal the scars left by the Civil War. He was nevertheless denied renomination for the presidency at the Democratic National Convention in 1868.

After he left the White House, Johnson was defeated in bids for the U.S. Senate and House of Representatives. In January 1875, however, he completed his political comeback when he was elected to the U.S. Senate—the only former president to have ever done so. He felt vindicated. He only held the seat for five months, however, dying of a stroke at Carter's Station, Tennessee, on July 31, 1875. He was sixty-six. His remains were interred in the Andrew Johnson National Cemetery, Greeneville, Tennessee.

RICHARD W JOHNSON (just an initial—no middle name) was born on February 27, 1827, near Smithland, Kentucky, at the confluence of the Ohio and Cumberland Rivers. (One source said his middle name was "Woodhouse," and another declared that it was "Washington.") His brother, Dr. John M. Johnson, secured him an appointment to West Point. John was later Confederate post surgeon of Atlanta and chief surgeon of Cleburne's division. Richard entered the U.S. Military Academy in 1844 and graduated in 1849 (30/43) as a brevet second lieutenant of infantry. He was initially assigned to Fort Snelling, Minnesota, but was sent to Texas in 1851. He transferred to the cavalry in 1853, became quartermaster of the 2nd U.S. Cavalry in 1855, and served in various  garrisons and on the Texas frontier, where he fought Comanches. He was promoted to second lieutenant in 1850, first lieutenant in 1855, and captain on August 3, 1861. Meanwhile, as a member of the 5th Cavalry, he took part in the engagement at Falling Waters on July 2.

When Kentucky entered the war in September, Johnson became lieutenant colonel of the 3rd Kentucky Cavalry. On October 3, he assumed command of a brigade of infantry in the Army of the Cumberland and was promoted to brigadier general eight days later. He served on the Western Front but missed the Battle of Shiloh due to illness. In the summer of 1862, he promised to bring Confederate raider John Hunt Morgan back in a bandbox. Morgan, however, defeated Johnson and forced him to surrender near Gallatin, Tennessee, on August 20. Johnson was quickly exchanged and was given command of an infantry division in November.

Richard Johnson fought in the battles of Stones River and Chickamauga, and in the Siege of Chattanooga, where he distinguished himself on November 25, 1863, when the Union Army stormed Missionary Ridge. He took part in the Atlanta Campaign until May 27, 1864, when he was severely wounded in the right side during the Battle of New Hope Church.

After he recovered, Johnson returned to divisional command and briefly directed the XIV Corps in August 1864. From August 24 to October 29, he commanded the Cavalry Corps of the Army of the Cumberland. He later led a cavalry division under General Wilson in the Battle of Nashville. He remained in Tennessee during the last campaigns of the war.

Johnson was brevetted major general for his conduct at Nashville. He was discharged from the volunteer service in January 1866 and retired in 1867 as a major general because of wounds suffered in the line of duty. His retired rank was downgraded to brigadier general in 1875. He nevertheless served as the professor of military science at Missouri State University (1868–69). Meanwhile, he wrote his memoirs and a book about General George Thomas. He was the Democrat Party nominee for governor of Minnesota in 1881 but lost the general election.

General Johnson died in St. Paul, Minnesota, on April 21, 1897, at age seventy. He was buried in the Oakland Cemetery, St. Paul.

PATRICK HENRY JONES was born on November 20, 1830, in Clonmellon, County Westmeath, Ireland. He attended grammar school for three years before emigrating to the United States with his parents in 1840. He spent most of his childhood on the family farm in Cattaraugus County, New York. Despite his poor education, he learned to write well, became a newspaper correspondent, managed to read law, and was admitted to the bar in 1856. He was practicing law in Ellicottville when the Civil War began.

Jones was a War Democrat. He joined the 37th New York Infantry (the "Irish Rifles") as a second lieutenant on June 7, 1861. His regiment was in reserve during the First Battle of Bull Run. He rose rapidly in rank, successively becoming regimental adjutant, first lieutenant (November 4), and major (January 21, 1862). He fought in the Peninsula Campaign, the Battle of Seven Pines, and the Seven Days battles. After that, he came down with malaria and was hospitalized in Washington, D.C., when he was promoted to colonel of the 154th New York on October 8.

Jones's regiment was ambushed by Stonewall Jackson's men during the Battle of Chancellorsville, and he was wounded in the right hip and captured (May 2, 1863). He was paroled two weeks later but was not exchanged until October. He was on light duty for a time while he recovered from his wounds and imprisonment. He accompanied the XI Corps when it was transferred to the Western Front in the autumn of 1863. When the XI and XII Corps were consolidated to form the XX Corps, Jones was given command of one of its brigades. He fought in the Atlanta Campaign and was severely injured in a skirmish at Buzzard's Roost (Mill Creek Gap) during the Battle of Rocky Face Ridge on May 8, 1864, and was forced to take at least two medical furloughs. He returned to duty on June 7 and took part in the capture of Atlanta and the March to the Sea. Meanwhile, he developed chronic diarrhea and, after the fall of Savannah, was sent north to recuperate. He missed much of the Carolinas Campaign but rejoined his command on March 30, 1865. On the recommendations of Generals Hooker and Howard, and with the endorsement of General Sherman, he was belatedly promoted to brigadier general on April 18, 1865. He resigned his commission on June 17.

Jones was a good tactical commander and had a talent for getting divided factions to work together. He was also a good organizer.

Postwar, Jones practiced law and held a number of public offices in New York City, including that of postmaster. He never fully regained his health after the war, suffering from deafness (caused by artillery fire), chronic diarrhea, and continuing pain from his Chancellorsville wound. His last years were marred by scandal, alcoholism, and poverty. His subordinates embezzled a substantial sum from the post office, and Jones was held responsible for much of it. His political enemies also accused him of being involved in the "kidnapping" of the body of A. T. Stewart, a wealthy businessman. Eventually, Jones had to live on his military pension ($20 a month). He died from cardiac failure at his home in Port Richmond, Staten

Island, New York, on July 23, 1900, at age sixty-nine. He is buried in St. Peter's Cemetery, West New Brighton, Staten Island.

HENRY MOSES JUDAH was born in Snow Hill, Maryland, on June 12, 1821, the son of an Episcopal preacher from Connecticut. He graduated from West Point in 1843 (35/39), was commissioned brevet second lieutenant in the 8th Infantry and served in Florida (1843–45), before being sent to Louisiana. He took part in the occupation of Texas and the subsequent battles at Palo Alto, Resaca de la Palma, and Monterey. Transferred to Scott's Army of Mexico, he fought in the Siege of Vera Cruz and the drive to Mexico City; meanwhile, he earned brevets for gallant and meritorious service Molino del Rey and Chapultepec. His subsequent antebellum service was mainly in California and Washington Territory, where he fought Indians. He narrowly avoided a court-martial for being drunk on duty and only escaped by agreeing to ask for a transfer. Alcohol would plague Judah throughout his career. He was nevertheless promoted to captain (permanent rank) in 1853.

Captain Judah was in California when the Civil War began. He commanded the 4th California Infantry Battalion at Fort Yuma as a colonel of volunteers until November, when he resigned from state service and returned to the East. He was stationed in the Washington, D.C. defenses and, on March 22, 1862, was promoted to brigadier general. He then joined the staff of his friend and fellow classmate, Ulysses S. Grant, as an inspector general and took part in the Battle of Shiloh.

In May 1862, Judah was given command of an infantry division under General Halleck and participated in the Siege of Corinth. He was then sent to Cincinnati, where he performed administrative duties and became acting inspector general of the Army of the Ohio. He was given command of a division in the XXIII Corps (also stationed in Cincinnati) in June 1863.

Judah was given the task of capturing John Hunt Morgan when he launched his famous raid into Ohio that summer. The Rebel general successfully evaded Judah, whose performance left much to be desired. Morgan was captured by other Federal troops. Judah was nevertheless sent to Tennessee, where he commanded a division in the Atlanta Campaign. His immediate superior was John M. Schofield, commander of the Army of the Ohio, who previously disciplined him for alcoholism. Realizing this was his last chance, Judah recklessly launched a hasty attack on Resaca on May 14. He failed to conduct a reconnaissance or use his artillery to soften up the Confederate positions, and his attack was repulsed with heavy losses. Schofield relieved him of his command shortly after. He was then given an administrative post at Marietta, Georgia. After the surrender, Judah issued corn and bacon to needy civilians until they could harvest their first postwar crop. He thus saved thousands of lives.

Mustered out of volunteer service on August 24, 1865, Judah reverted to the rank of major, Regular Army. He was stationed at Plattsburgh, New York, where he died on February 14, 1866. He was forty-four. He is buried in the Kings Highway Cemetery, Westport, Connecticut.

K

· KANE – KRZYZANOWSKI ·

THOMAS LEIPER KANE was born in Philadelphia on January 27, 1822, the son of a federal district judge. After receiving a local education, he was sent to Europe and studied in England and France for several years. His Paris apartment was raided by police, who suspected him of being a revolutionary. He then returned home, read law under his father, and was admitted to the bar in 1846.

Kane was a fervent abolitionist. He fell out with his father because the latter enforced the Fugitive Slave Law, which he was legally obligated to do. The feud ended when the judge had his own son thrown into jail for contempt of court. (They later reconciled.) After his release, the younger Kane became even more involved in the abolitionist movement, was an agent for the Underground Railroad, and represented the Church of Jesus Christ of Latter-day Saints (the Mormons) in their conflicts with the U.S. government. Kane later worked to secure Utah's admission to the Union. He was instrumental in creating the Mormon Battalion for service during the Mexican War. In 1850, President Fillmore offered Kane the governorship of Utah Territory, but he declined and recommended Brigham Young instead. In 1858, Kane convinced Young that further resistance to the U.S. Army would end in disaster. When his father died in 1858, Kane returned to Pennsylvania, where he founded the village of Kane in northwest Pennsylvania.

Kane was a small man who suffered from ill health much of his life. When the Civil War began, he nevertheless recruited the 13th Pennsylvania Reserves, which became famous as the "Bucktails." (It was also known as the 42nd Pennsylvania Infantry.) Kane was initially elected colonel but demoted himself to lieutenant colonel so an officer with more military experience could command the regiment. He first saw action at Dranesville, Virginia (December 20, 1861), where he was shot in the face. He lost several teeth, and his wound permanently affected his vision.

When his colonel resigned to take a seat in Congress, Kane replaced him. He fought against Stonewall Jackson in the Valley Campaign of 1862. Near Harrisonburg on June 6, while attempting to rescue a regiment Jackson ambushed, a Confederate bullet struck him just below the right knee, splitting the bone. He was also wounded in the chest. As his men fled the field, Kane continued to resist until a Rebel soldier butt-stroked him in the chest with his rifle and broke his breastbone. Unconscious, he was taken prisoner and not exchanged until August.

Kane was promoted to brigadier general on September 7, 1862, and was given command of a brigade, but it was mustered out in March 1863, before Kane could lead it in action. He was given command of another brigade, but on April 28, 1863, his horse dumped him in the Rapidan River and he developed pneumonia. He was in a hospital while his men fought at Chancellorsville. He rejoined his command at Gettysburg on the morning of July 2. He fought at Culp's Hill until he fell ill and had to leave the field the next day. Unable to perform field duty, he commanded the draft depot at Pittsburgh until November 7, 1863, when he resigned his commission. He was brevetted major general in the omnibus promotions of 1866.

After the war, Kane lived in western Pennsylvania, where he owned more than one hundred thousand acres of timberland. He also worked in various charities, although he never really regained his health. He died of pneumonia in the city of his birth on December 26, 1883, at age sixty-one. Initially buried in Philadelphia, his remains now lie in the Kane Memorial Chapel Cemetery, Kane, Pennsylvania.

AUGUST VALENTINE "DUTCH" KAUTZ was born on January 5, 1828 at Ispringen (Pforzheim) in the Grand Duchy of Baden, Germany. His family immigrated to the United States in 1832 and settled in Brown County, Ohio. After getting an education in local schools, he enlisted in the 1st Ohio Infantry as a private and served in the Mexican War. After he was discharged, he attended West Point, where he graduated with the Class of 1852 (35/43). In the antebellum years, he was stationed in the Pacific Northwest, where he was wounded in the chest in a skirmish with the Rogue River Indians (now in southern Oregon). Fortunately for him, he was carrying two books. The bullet passed through one and lodged in the second. Instead of killing him, it just knocked him down. He also fought in the Puget Sound War of 1855–56, in

which several small tribes were defeated. In the process, in March 1856, he was wounded in the leg during a firefight on the Muckleshoot Prairie.

Kautz "married" a Nisqually woman, Tenas Puss (Little Kitten), who bore two sons. Later, Kautz married three white wives and outlived two of them. He had at least five children, one of whom became a U.S. Navy captain during World War I. The future Union general was also a noted mountain climber and is said by some to be the first man to climb Mount Rainier.

Shortly after the Rebels fired on Fort Sumter, the U.S. Regular Army was reorganized and Kautz became a captain in the 6th U.S. Cavalry. He returned to the East, served in the Washington defenses, and took part in the Peninsula Campaign and Seven Days battles. In September 1862, he became colonel of the 2nd Ohio Cavalry and was sent to Fort Scott, Kansas. In 1863, Kautz was commandant of Camp Chase, Ohio, and played a role in the apprehension of Confederate raider John Hunt Morgan in July. He was rewarded by being given command of a cavalry brigade in the Army of the Ohio later that month. He served under Ambrose Burnside during the East Tennessee Campaign and fought in the Battle of Knoxville.

In April 1864, he was given command of a cavalry division in the Army of the James and was promoted to brigadier general on April 16. He took part in the attacks on Petersburg and in the Bermuda Hundred Campaign, where his performance was undistinguished. On June 9, for example, he led more than 2,300 men against Archer's Battalion—125 men and two guns—which was all that stood between him and Petersburg. His first assault was checked by this home guard battalion (old men and boys), and they delayed him long enough for the Confederates to reinforce the sector. Petersburg would not fall for another ten months. Abraham Lincoln nevertheless promoted him to brevet major general in December 1864. In March 1865, Kautz was given command of an African American division in the XXV Corps, which was considered a demotion in those days. He led it into Richmond on April 3. After the surrender, he was a member of the commission that tried the Lincoln conspirators. He was mustered out of volunteer service in January 1866. Kautz reverted to the rank of lieutenant colonel in the 34th U.S. Infantry Regiment.

Most of Kautz's post-war service was in the southwest. He became colonel of the 8th U.S. Infantry in 1874 and to brigadier general in 1891. He was quite effective in operations against the Indians. General Kautz retired to Seattle, Washington, in 1892 and died there on September 4, 1895, at age sixty-seven. He is buried in Arlington National Cemetery.

PHILIP KEARNY, JR., (pronounced CAR' NEY) was born in New York City on June 1, 1815, into a wealthy Irish American family, which owned ships, mills, banks, factories, and various other businesses. His father was a founder of the New York Stock Exchange.

Early in life, Kearny, Junior, decided upon a military career. After his parents died, however, his grandfather (who raised him) insisted he become a lawyer. He graduated from Columbia College with a law degree in 1833. When his grandfather died in 1836, Kearny inherited a fortune worth more than $25,000,000 today. Even so, he obtained a commission in the 1st Dragoons, which was commanded by his uncle, Colonel Stephen W. Kearny. Its adjutant was Jefferson Davis.

Philip Kearny initially served on the Western frontier. In 1839, he was sent to Europe and studied at the famous French cavalry school at Saumur. He also went to Algeria and fought in several engagements with the *Chasseurs d'Afrique* (French light cavalry). After he returned to the United States, he wrote a cavalry manual based on his experiences.

In 1846, he was ordered to form an Indiana company for the 1st Dragoons. He recruited 120 men and outfitted them at his own expense, including dapple gray horses. It was soon made the personal bodyguard for General Scott. Kearny fought at Contreras and Churubusco, where he led a daring charge, and his left arm was shattered by Mexican grapeshot. Brigadier General and future President Franklin Pierce held him down as a surgeon amputated the limb. The loss of his arm did not slow him down, however. General Scott later called him "the perfect soldier" and "the bravest man I ever knew." Meanwhile, he was brevetted major.

After Mexico, Kearny served in the Oregon Territory and fought in the Rogue River War against hostile Indians in 1851. He married Diana

Bullett of Kentucky in 1841, and she bore him five children. He returned to the East in the early 1850s, when his marriage failed. She refused to grant him a divorce, so he moved in with his lover, which caused a major scandal. He resigned his commission in disgrace. When his wife finally relented and granted him a divorce, he moved to Paris and married his mistress (who had already bore him a child) in 1859. Meanwhile, he served in Napoleon III's Imperial Guard against the Austrians. He led such a bold charge in the Battle of Solferino, Italy, that the emperor awarded him the Legion of Honor. He was the first American to receive this honor.

Phil Kearny was a patriot. He was living a millionaire's lifestyle in Paris. He nevertheless returned to the United States when the Civil War began and was appointed brigadier general on August 7, 1861. He was given command of the 1st New Jersey Infantry Brigade, which he trained. He led a division in the Peninsula Campaign, where he distinguished himself in the Battle of Frayser's Farm (Glendale). Here, he was wounded in the chest by shell fragments, but not seriously. Meanwhile, he introduced what became the first U.S. Army shoulder patch, now worn by every American soldier.

Despite his fierce, short temper, General Kearny was very popular with his men, who called him "Kearny the Magnificent." He was promoted to major general on July 25. In the fall of 1862, there were rumors that Abraham Lincoln was considering replacing George McClellan, the commander of the Army of the Potomac, with Kearny.

Philip Kearny fought in the disastrous Second Battle of Bull Run (August 28–30, 1862). The Confederates under Stonewall Jackson pursued and, on September 1, again met Kearny's division in battle, this time at Chantilly (Ox Hill). During a violent thunderstorm, he accidentally rode into Confederate lines. Ignoring demands to surrender, he turned and fled. His last words were: "They can't hit a barn!" Soldiers from the 49th Georgia fired on him, killing him instantly. Confederate General A. P. Hill arrived on the scene a few moments later, identified the body, and commented that Phil Kearny deserved a better fate than to die in the mud. He was forty-seven years old. General Lee—another personal friend—had his body returned to Union lines, along with a note of condolence.

General Kearny was buried in the Trinity Churchyard in New York. His remains were reinterred in Arlington National Cemetery in 1912.

WILLIAM HIGH KEIM was born in Berks County, near Reading, Pennsylvania, on June 13, 1813. His uncle was a U.S. Congressman. Keim attended Mount Airy Military School in his home state and took a great interest in militia affairs. He advanced steadily in rank until April 20, 1861, when he was promoted to major general in the Pennsylvania Militia. Meanwhile, as a Whig, he served as mayor of Reading (1848–49) and, as a Republican, he was surveyor general of Pennsylvania (1860–61).

In 1858, U.S. Congressman John Roe was defeated for re-election. Rather than remain in Washington, he resigned, and Keim (now a Republican) was chosen to finish his term. He served from November 30, 1858 to March 3, 1859, but did not run for election to a full term.

On April 21, 1861, Keim was called to active duty for ninety days. He commanded the 2nd Division, Pennsylvania Militia, until July 21, and was involved in General Patterson's failed attempt to prevent Confederate General Joseph E. Johnston from reinforcing General Beauregard at Manassas. On the day of that battle, July 21, Keim was mustered out of the service. Six months later, when it was obvious that there was not going to be a quick victory, Keim returned to the colors. He was commissioned brigadier general of volunteers on December 21, 1861, was given command of a brigade in the IV Corps of Army of the Potomac and took part in the Peninsula Campaign. His tenure was short. He fought in the Battle of Williamsburg on May 5, 1861, but was so ill he could barely remain on his horse. It is unclear if he had camp fever or typhus. In any case, General Keim returned home on medical leave but died on May 18, 1862, in Harrisburg, Pennsylvania. He was forty-eight years old. He is buried in Charles Evans Cemetery, Reading, Pennsylvania.

BENJAMIN FRANKLIN KELLEY was born on April 10, 1807, in New Hampton, New Hampshire. He attended Partridge Military Academy, and in 1826, when he was nineteen, he moved to Wheeling, Virginia (now West Virginia), where he worked in the merchandising business. He was known for his integrity, courtesy, and commanding presence. In 1851, he moved

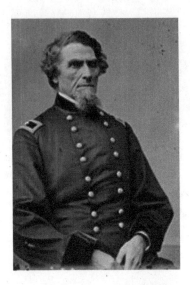

to Philadelphia, to be near his wife, who was confined to the Pennsylvania Insane Asylum. He took a job as a freight agent for the Baltimore & Ohio Railroad. Mrs. Kelley died in 1860. Benjamin was still working for the B & O in Philadelphia when the war began. Kelley returned to Wheeling and assumed command of the 1st (West) Virginia Infantry Regiment (formerly the 4th Virginia Militia), which he led in McClellan's Western Virginia Campaign. He fought in the Battle of Philippi (June 3), where he overran the Confederate camp but was badly wounded in the chest in the process.

Kelley was promoted to brigadier general on August 6. After he recovered, he took part in a series of minor Union victories in the mountains and commanded the districts of Grafton and Harpers Ferry. In 1862, he commanded the Railroad Division of the Department of West Virginia (ten thousand men) and was tasked with defending the B & O from Confederate raiders. He was not particularly successful in this mission but probably did as well as anyone could have.

After Gettysburg, Kelley took part in the pursuit of the Army of Northern Virginia. He overran Confederate General Imboden's camp in November 1863 and participated in the Battle of Moorefield, West Virginia, on August 7, 1864, in which Confederate General John McCausland's cavalry was defeated. He was brevetted major general effective August 5. In November, a Confederate raiding party captured the Union depot at New Creek, West Virginia, which was within Kelley's area of operations. He also botched the ensuing pursuit and was severely criticized by General Sheridan.

In August 1863, Kelley ordered the arrest of Confederate guerrilla Captain John H. McNeill's wife and four-year-old son. Seeking revenge, McNeill raided Cumberland, Maryland, on February 21, 1865, where he captured Kelley and his immediate superior, General George Crook. (They were both courting local belles whom they subsequently married.) Both Union generals were exchanged in March. Kelley resigned his commission on June 1.

After the war, Benjamin Kelley held a number of minor government posts, including collector of internal reserve for West Virginia, superintendent of the Hot Springs Military Reserve in Arkansas, and examiner of pensions in Washington, D.C. He died on July 16, 1891, in Oakland, Maryland. He was eighty-four. He is buried in Arlington National Cemetery.

JOHN REESE KENLY was born in Baltimore on January 11, 1818. He was educated in local public schools, read law, and was admitted to the bar in 1845. Active in the Maryland Militia, he was a lieutenant in the Eagle Artillery of Baltimore when the Mexican War began. Sent to northern Mexico, he was part of the Maryland and District of Columbia Battalion and so distinguished himself in the Battle of Monterrey that the Maryland legislature gave him a vote of thanks. The battalion later served in General Scott's army. Kenly was a major when the war ended. He returned to his law practice in Baltimore in 1848.

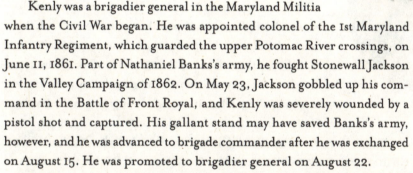

Kenly was a brigadier general in the Maryland Militia when the Civil War began. He was appointed colonel of the 1st Maryland Infantry Regiment, which guarded the upper Potomac River crossings, on June 11, 1861. Part of Nathaniel Banks's army, he fought Stonewall Jackson in the Valley Campaign of 1862. On May 23, Jackson gobbled up his command in the Battle of Front Royal, and Kenly was severely wounded by a pistol shot and captured. His gallant stand may have saved Banks's army, however, and he was advanced to brigade commander after he was exchanged on August 15. He was promoted to brigadier general on August 22.

Kenly was given command of the "Maryland Brigade," which joined the Army of the Potomac after Antietam. It was posted to western Maryland, where it fought against Confederate raiders attempting to cut the B & O Railroad, with mixed success. He briefly commanded a division in the I Corps in late 1863 and took part in the Bristoe and Mine River campaigns. He was transferred to Wilmington, where he was the commander of the District of Delaware in May 1864.

General Kenly was part of the Union force pursuing Jubal Early after he threatened Washington in July 1864. He allowed the Rebels to capture an important train, which led to an official court of inquiry. This led to his being assigned to command the District of the East Shore, Maryland, a post which was enlarged to include Delaware in March 1865. At the end of the war, the Maryland legislature gave him a vote of thanks and the city of Baltimore presented him with a sword. He was discharged from the army on August 24, 1865, and brevetted major general in 1866.

John Kenly returned to Baltimore, where he resumed his law practice and devoted much of his time to studying literature. He also wrote *Memories of a Maryland Volunteer* (Philadelphia: 1873) about his service in Mexico. He died in Baltimore on December 20, 1891. He was seventy-four years old. He was interred in the Green Mount Cemetery in Baltimore.

JOHN HENRY KETCHAM, of descent from the Pilgrims, was born in Dover Plains, New York, on December 21, 1832. He graduated from Suffield Academy in Connecticut and then became a farmer. He was also interested in politics, serving as a supervisor for the town of Dover, a member of the New York Assembly (state legislature) (1856–57), and member of the New York State Senate (1860–61). He joined the Union Army on October 11, 1862, as the colonel of the 150th New York Infantry, a Dutchess County unit which did guard duty at Baltimore until July 1863, when it was lightly engaged in the Battle of Gettysburg as part of the XII Corps.

Transferred to the West, the 150th guarded the Nashville and Chattanooga Railroad between Murfreesboro and Bridgeport until the Atlanta Campaign began. It fought at Resaca, Cassville, Dallas, Kennesaw Mountain, and other battles around the city. Ketcham performed well, was brevetted brigadier general, and was wounded at least once. He rejoined his regiment on December 19, 1864, near the conclusion of the March to the Sea, but was wounded again near Savannah two days later. This time the wound was more serious, and doctors wanted to amputate his leg, but he refused to allow it. He never fully recovered from his wounds and never returned to his command. He was elected to Congress as a Republican in November 1864 and resigned his colonel's commission on March 2, 1865.

Remarkably, even though he never held command above the regimental level, Ketcham was promoted to brigadier general of volunteers on October 23, 1865, months after he resigned and months after the Confederacy ceased to exist. He was also brevetted major general in 1866. This can only be explained by his political prominence. Always a courteous gentleman, he made many friends. He served in Congress from 1865 to 1873, was defeated for re-election in 1872, was re-elected in 1876, and served from 1877 to 1893. After his defeat in 1872, President Grant appointed him a Commissioner of the District of Columbia (1873–77). He did not seek re-election in 1892, but ran again in 1896, serving from March 4, 1897, until his death, which occurred in New York City on November 4, 1906. He was seventy-three. General Ketcham was buried in Valley View Cemetery, Dover Plains, New York.

WILLIAM SCOTT KETCHUM was born in Norwalk, Connecticut, on July 7, 1813. His father, Major Daniel Ketcham, was a Regular Army officer who died in Jefferson Barracks, Missouri, in 1828. William entered West Point in 1830 and graduated four years later (32/36) as a brevet second lieutenant of infantry. He spent most of his antebellum time after that on duty on the Western frontier, where he escorted wagon trains and fought Seminoles (1838–42), Sioux, Cheyenne, Mojave, and Mormons. He also suppressed disturbances in Bleeding Kansas. Meanwhile, he was promoted to second lieutenant (1836), first lieutenant (1837), captain, staff (1839), captain (1842), and major (1860).

Ketcham was commanding Fort Dalles, Oregon Territory, when the war began, protecting settlers from Indian raids. Ordered to San Francisco and then southern California, he was promoted to lieutenant colonel of the 10th U.S. Infantry on November 1, 1861. He was then transferred to Missouri as an assistant inspector general and was promoted to brigadier general of volunteers on February 6, 1862. He spent the entire war in the inspector general branch, mostly in Washington, D.C. He was brevetted major general on February 21, 1866, and mustered out of volunteer service on April 30. 1866.

Reverting to the rank of colonel, William Ketchum spent the next four years in the quartermaster branch, as a special auditor under the Treasury Department, and as a staff officer in the Adjutant General's office. He retired in 1870. He was murdered by poison in Baltimore, Maryland, on June 26, 1871, probably by the landlady of a boarding house he owned (she owed him money). She was tried for the crime but found not guilty. Ketchum was fifty-seven years old when he passed. He was buried in the Rock Creek Cemetery in Washington, D.C.

ERASMUS DARWIN KEYES was born on May 29, 1810, in Brimfield, Massachusetts, but grew up in Maine. He graduated from West Point in 1832 (10/45) and was commissioned brevet second lieutenant in the artillery. He was stationed in Charleston, South Carolina, during the Nullification Crisis, served in various garrisons, fought Indians in the Pacific Northwest in the Puget Sound War (1855–56) and the Coeur d'Alene War in Idaho (1858), and did a tour as Winfield Scott's aide. He was an artillery and cavalry instructor at West Point (1844–48) and thus missed fighting in the Mexican War. Meanwhile, he was promoted to second lieutenant (1833), captain (1838), major (1858), and lieutenant colonel (1860). He was military secretary to General Scott when the Civil War began.

Keyes assumed command of the 11th U.S. Infantry Regiment and was promoted to colonel on May 14, 1861. After briefly serving as chief of staff for New York Governor Edwin D. Morgan, he was given command of an infantry brigade, which he led in the First Battle of Bull Run. He was promoted to brigadier general on August 7, 1861, to rank from May 17, making him the third highest ranking officer in the army. He assumed command of a division in the Army of the Potomac on November 9, replacing Don Carlos Buell.

In March 1862, Abraham Lincoln personally chose the corps commanders for the Army of the Potomac. He picked Keyes to lead the IV Corps. He fought in the Siege of Yorktown, the ensuing Peninsular Campaign and Seven Days battles, where his performance was mediocre.

When McClellan withdrew the Army of the Potomac to Washington, D.C. in August 1862, he left Keyes behind with only one division. Keyes became part of John A. Dix's Department of the James. Meanwhile, Lincoln promoted Keyes was promoted to major general on August 2.

General Keyes fought in a few minor engagements in southeastern Virginia, in 1862 and 1863. He transferred to the command of the VII Corps in the Yorktown sector in December 1862. During the Gettysburg Campaign, Dix demonstrated against Richmond, in hopes of preventing President Davis from reinforcing Robert E. Lee. Keyes moved slowly and allowed the Confederates to reinforce the threatened sector; then he retreated in the face of an inferior number of Rebels, so Dix relieved him of his command on July 18, 1863. General Keyes was relegated to a seat on a retirement board in New York. He resigned his commission on May 6, 1864.

Keyes moved to San Francisco in 1866, where he became very successful financially. He was president of a gold mining company, was involved in the grape industry, and worked in the savings and loan business. While he was on a trip to Europe, he died in Nice, France, on October 14, 1895. He was eighty-five years old. He was buried in the West Point Cemetery.

JAMES LAWLOR KIERNAN was born in Mountbellew, County Galway, Ireland, on October 26, 1837, the son of a retired British naval surgeon. He studied at Trinity College, Dublin, before emigrating to the United States. He attended what became the New York University Academy of Medicine, from which he graduated in 1857, before his twentieth birthday. He opened an office on the Lower East Side of New York City. He also joined the militia and served as co-editor of the *Medical Press* (1859–61).

When the Civil War began, Kiernan was named assistant surgeon of the 69th New York Militia Regiment, which was nicknamed "the Fighting Irish." After participating in the First Battle of Bull Run, he resigned and went west, where he served as surgeon of the 6th Missouri

Cavalry in the Pea Ridge Campaign. He was wounded in the right leg at Elkhorn Tavern.

Dissatisfied in the military medical field, he secured an appointment as major of the 6th Missouri Infantry. He served in Grant's various Vicksburg campaigns and was badly wounded in the left shoulder, lung, and chest at Port Gibson, Mississippi, on May 1. Left for dead, he was captured by Rebels but managed to escape. He resigned his commission on May 24 and returned to New York City to recover from his wounds. Meanwhile, 26 officers recommended him for promotion. They included Generals Grant, Frank Blair, McClelland, Hovey, Hurlbut, Schofield, Sullivan, Osterhaus, Logan, McPherson, Burbridge, and A. J. Smith.

Lincoln promoted him to brigadier general on August 1, 1863. He was appointed commander of the post of Milliken's Bend, Louisiana, but his health remained problematic. He resigned again on February 3, 1864, possibly because his appointment as brigadier general had not been confirmed.

Kiernan was given a consular position at Chinkiang, China, at the end of the war. His health, however, forced him to return to New York, where he worked as an examining physician for the Pension Bureau. Apparently, he was not an effective diplomat. He applied for the position of U.S. minister to Portugal or Turkey, but President Grant would not appoint him to another post. There were rumors that he suffered from alcoholism. He died of "congestion of the lungs" in New York City on November 29, 1869, at age thirty-two. He was interred in Green-Wood Cemetery, Brooklyn.

HUGH JUDSON "KILL CAVALRY" KILPATRICK was born on January 14, 1836, near Deckertown, New Jersey, the son of a colonel. He dropped the "Hugh" from his name and simply became Judson Kilpatrick in 1856. He was educated in local schools and entered West Point in 1856. He graduated on May 6, 1861 (17/45) and was commissioned second lieutenant in the artillery. He became a captain in the 5th New York three days later. Sent to the Virginia Peninsula, he fought at Big Bethel (June

10), the first battle of the war, where he was wounded in the thigh by Southern grapeshot. He was said to be the first Regular Army officer wounded in the conflict. After he recovered, he returned to New York and helped raise the 2nd New York Cavalry. He was named its lieutenant colonel in September.

Kilpatrick saw the mounted arm as the quickest path to fame and prominence. Although unquestionably brave and personally charming, Kilpatrick rapidly developed a reputation for self-promotion and loose morals. His official reports were often fictional. He did not drink, smoke, or play cards, but was very much sexually promiscuous in an era when that was not generally tolerated. He was, however, a bold cavalry commander—although not a good one. His men did not like him because of his willingness to send exhausted troopers headlong into hopeless attacks. Sherman called him "a hell of a damned fool." He was also personally corrupt. His camps were neglected, and his headquarters frequented by prostitutes. He was accused of selling captured Confederate goods for personal gain, for which he was arrested in 1862. He was arrested a second time for accepting bribes in the purchasing of horses for his command.

After the First Bull Run, Kilpatrick spent more than a year in northern Virginia, occupied in reconnaissance missions and minor cavalry skirmishes. He was wounded in the knee near Fredericksburg in April 1862. He was involved in the Second Battle of Bull Run, during which he ordered a suicide charge and lost a full squadron of horsemen. Even so, he was promoted to colonel in December 1862.

When General Hooker reorganized the cavalry of the Army of the Potomac in February 1863, he promoted Kilpatrick to brigade commander. He took part in Stoneman's Raid during the Chancellorsville Campaign and pushed almost to the gates of Richmond. He was promoted to brigadier general on June 14 and was captured on June 21, near Upperville, Virginia, but was quickly rescued. He was given command of a division on June 28 and fought at Gettysburg, where he ordered the foolish charge against Confederate infantry that resulted in the death of General Farnsworth (among others) on July 3. He also directed an unsuccessful raid against Richmond in February and March 1864, which resulted in the death of Lieutenant Colonel Ulrich Dahlgren and the destruction of his spearhead.

Transferred to the Western Front, he was severely wounded in the thigh during the Battle of Resaca, which kept him out of action until July. After that, he experienced considerable success raiding in the Southern rear, burning bridges, tearing up railroads, and wrecking Confederate installations. Kilpatrick delighted in destroying private property. He was less successful against armed men. Confederate General Wade Hampton, for example, took him by surprise one evening in North Carolina while he was entertaining a woman of doubtful morality. The Union general fled in his underclothes while his troops checked the Rebels.

On June 19, 1865, he was promoted to major general of volunteers, but resigned his commission on December 1. Kilpatrick had unrealistic political ambitions, but they never materialized. Despite being arrested for bribery in November 1865, he was appointed minister to Chile by President Johnson that same month. He married a wealthy Chilean woman in the following year. Grant retained him in this post until 1870, when he was recalled. Meanwhile, Kilpatrick lost the New Jersey gubernatorial race of 1865.

Because Grant recalled him, Kilpatrick backed Horace Greeley for the presidency in 1872. He returned to the Republican fold in 1876. He ran for Congress in New Jersey in 1880 but lost. President Garfield appointed him minister to Chile in 1881 but he died on December 4, shortly after his arrival in Santiago. He was forty-five years old. His remains were returned to United States in 1887, and he was reinterred in the West Point Cemetery.

NATHAN KIMBALL was born on November 22, 1822, in the small village of Fredericksburg, Indiana, where he attended the local public school. He went on to attend the Washington County Seminary; Asbury College (now DePauw University); and, after teaching school in Independence, Missouri, the University of Louisville Medical School, from which he graduated in 1844. He set up a practice in Salem and Livonia but closed it when the Mexican War began. He raised a company at Livonia and joined the 2nd Indiana Infantry, which was routed at

Buena Vista. Captain Kimball, however, rallied his company and kept it together when the rest of the regiment fled, even though he was wounded.

Mustered out in June 1847, Kimbell returned to Indiana and ran for the state senate as a Whig but was defeated. He re-established his medical practice at Loogootee. He ran for the Indiana State Senate in 1847 but was again defeated.

Kimball raised another infantry company when the Civil War began, but the governor appointed him colonel of the 14th Indiana Infantry (1,145 men) on June 7. He led it in the Western Virginia Campaign (including the Battle of Cheat Mountain) in 1861. During the Battle of Kernstown (March 23, 1862) he replaced General Shields, who was wounded the day before, and handed Stonewall Jackson one of his few defeats. As a result, he was promoted to brigadier general on April 16. Sent to join the Army of the Potomac, he fought in the Second Bull Run and Maryland campaigns. At Antietam, his brigade was part of several attacks on the Sunken Road, where it lost more than six hundred men. During the Battle of Fredericksburg, it tried to storm Marye's Heights and again suffered heavy casualties. General Kimball was one of them. He was wounded in the thigh and groin. He could not return to duty until March 1863, when he was named commander of a subdistrict at Jackson, Tennessee. Meanwhile, he was nominated for lieutenant governor of Indiana in early 1863 but declined the nomination, preferring to remain in the army.

In June, when he was able to return to field duty, Kimball was given command of a division at Corinth, Mississippi, and was sent to Vicksburg near the end of the siege. Transferred to the VII Corps, Kimball commanded the corps' rear area during the unsuccessful Camden Expedition. Sent back east of the Mississippi, he commanded a brigade in the Atlanta Campaign, where he became a close friend of William T. Sherman. He was placed in charge of a division after the Battle of Peachtree Creek. Following a brief tour of duty in Indiana, where he helped suppress Copperheads, Kimball fought at Franklin and Nashville in the Tennessee Campaign. He was brevetted major general in February 1865.

Kimball was mustered out of the service on August 25, 1865, and was elected state treasurer in 1867. After two terms, he was elected to the Indiana House of Representatives in 1873. He was surveyor general of the

Utah Territory (1873–78) and adopted Ogden as his home. He served as postmaster there from 1879 until his death, which occurred on January 21, 1898. He was seventy-five years old. He is buried in the Aultorest Memorial Park, Ogden.

JOHN HASKELL "IRON BULL" KING was born in Sackets Harbor, New York, on February 19, 1820, the son of a militia colonel. He was unofficially adopted by a relative, Colonel Hugh Brady, the commandant of Fort Wayne, Michigan, and grew up on army bases. In 1837, at age seventeen, he was commissioned directly into the army as a second lieutenant in the 1st U.S. Infantry Regiment. He fought in the Seminole Wars, with Scott's army in Mexico, and against Indians on the frontier. A captain since 1846, he was in Texas when the Civil War began. He ignored the demands of local authorities that he surrender and led nine companies of Regulars out of the Lone Star State to New York. He was rewarded with a promotion to major on May 14, 1861, and was simultaneously ordered to help raise a new regiment, the 15th U.S. Infantry, in Ohio and Kentucky.

Reinforced by several detachments and companies of Regular Army troops, King led 844 Regulars in the Battle of Shiloh. He also fought in the Siege of Corinth and the Kentucky Campaign. King was named commander of a brigade of regulars in the Army of the Cumberland and led it at Stones River, where he was shot twice in the left arm and once in the left hand. He then fell from his horse and dislocated his left shoulder. He was still on medical furlough when he was promoted to brigadier general on April 4, 1863.

King returned to duty in May 1863 and took part in the Tullahoma Campaign and the Battle of Chickamauga, where his brigade suffered an astonishing 56 percent casualties—the highest casualties of any brigade in that battle. King nevertheless took part in the Siege of Chattanooga. He led a division in the IV Corps for part of the Atlanta Campaign but then reverted back to brigade commander. He and his men were later transferred to the District of Etowah, Alabama, where he remained for the rest of the war. He was brevetted major general on January 13, 1866, and mustered out of volunteer service on January 15.

"Iron Bull" was named colonel of the 9th U.S. Infantry in July 1865 and spent more than a decade on the Western Frontier. He retired in 1882 after more than forty-five years' service and settled in Washington, D.C., where he died of pneumonia on April 7, 1888. He was interred in Arlington National Cemetery. One of his sons, Charles B. King, invented the jackhammer.

RUFUS KING was born in New York City on January 26, 1814, into a prominent family. His father was president of Columbia College (now University) and his grandfather was a U.S. senator. After graduating from Columbia's prep school, King entered West Point and graduated with the class of 1833 (4/43). Commissioned brevet second lieutenant in the engineers, he was assistant engineer in the construction of Fort Monroe; on the survey of the Ohio–Michigan border; and on navigational improvements on the Hudson River. He resigned his commission in 1836 to become a civil engineer for the New York & Erie Railroad. Four years later, he made a radical career change and became a newspaper editor. In 1839, Governor William H. Seward, Lincoln's future secretary of state, appointed him state adjutant general, a post he held until 1844.

King moved to Wisconsin Territory in 1845, where he worked as editor of the *Milwaukee Sentinel and Gazette*. He also did a tour as superintendent of the city's schools and became a colonel in the Wisconsin Militia. He was promoted to brigadier general of militia on May 7, 1861.

Lincoln appointed him ambassador to the Papal States in the spring of 1861. He was reportedly on his way to the Vatican when the Civil War erupted, so he took a leave of absence from the State Department and joined the Union Army as a brigadier general on August 7. Meanwhile, he helped organize the famous Iron Brigade, but he never saw battle with this unit. He was promoted to division commander in March 1862.

Rufus King's first and only major campaign was the Second Battle of Bull Run, where on August 28 he fell back against orders, exposing General Ricketts's division at Thoroughfare Gap. This compelled Rickett's to retreat, opened the way for Robert E. Lee to reinforce Stonewall Jackson, which led to the debacle of August 30. King spent most of the battle in an ambulance, suffering from epileptic seizures. John P. Hatch led the division for most of the battle and in the Maryland Campaign, until he was wounded at South Mountain on September 14, when he was succeeded by Abner Doubleday. King was on sick leave (September 19–October 19) and served on the court-martial board of General Fitz John Porter. Unemployed for three months, he returned to field duty as a brigade commander in the VII Corps in southeastern Virginia in April 1863. In June, he assumed command of the forces in the Yorktown area—a backwater sector. From July to October 1863, he directed a division at Fairfax, Virginia, covering the southern approaches to Washington, D.C.

King's condition worsened in 1863, and his seizures became more frequent, so he resigned his commission on October 20. Lincoln reappointed him ambassador to the Papal States in January 1864. He held this post until late 1867. He returned to New York in 1868 and spent the next two years as comptroller of the Port of New York. He retired for reasons of health in 1870 and lived in quiet retirement until his death, which occurred in New York on October 13, 1876. He was sixty-two years old. He is buried in Grace Churchyard, Jamaica, New York.

Rufus King was a true gentleman who was well liked by his men and pretty much everyone else. His performance as a soldier, however, left much to be desired. He had two children, both sons. Brevet Major Rufus King, Jr., earned the Congressional Medal of Honor commanding artillery on the Eastern Front. The other, Charles King, was a brigadier general of volunteers in the Spanish-American War and a major general in the Wisconsin Militia.

EDMUND KIRBY, JR., was born in Brownsville, New York, on March 11, 1840. His grandfather was Major General Jacob Brown, the general-in-chief of the U.S.

Army from 1815 to 1828. His father was Colonel Edmund Kirby, a hero of the War of 1812 who married Brown's daughter. Colonel Kirby fought in the Black Hawk, Creek, and Seminole wars and died of a disease he contracted during the Mexican War. Edmund, Jr., entered West Point in 1856 and graduated in May 1861 (10/45). He was commissioned second lieutenant in the 1st Artillery Regiment and was promoted to first lieutenant ten days later.

Lieutenant Kirby commanded a section of artillery in Battery I, 1st Artillery. He fought in the First Battle of Bull Run (July 21) and the Battle of Ball's Bluff (October 21). He served in the Washington defenses until December, when he assumed command of Battery I and led it in the Peninsula Campaign, including the Siege of Yorktown and the Battle of Seven Pines (Fair Oaks). He fought in the Seven Days battles, the Maryland Campaign, and the Battle of Fredericksburg. He was sick on September 17, 1862, and missed the Battle of Antietam. Meanwhile, he was offered a transfer to the Corps of Topographical Engineers in July but declined it.

During the Battle of Chancellorsville, Kirby commanded his own battery and the 5th Maine Light Artillery Battery after all of its officers were killed or wounded. His battery was also decimated. As he was withdrawing his guns on May 3, a Confederate shot struck him in the leg. He was medically evacuated to Washington, D.C., where physicians amputated his leg. His wound became infected, and he died on May 28. Meanwhile, Abraham Lincoln learned of his injury and promoted him to brigadier general of volunteers on May 28, the day of his death. He was twenty-three years old. He was buried in Brownsville Cemetery in the town of his birth.

EDWARD NEEDLES KIRK was born on February 19, 1828, in Jefferson County, Ohio. Educated at the Friends' Academy in nearby Mount Pleasant, he taught school and studied law at Cadiz, which is also in southeastern Ohio. He passed the bar exam in 1853, briefly lived in Baltimore, and settled in Sterling, Illinois, a small town just south of Chicago. He was a highly successful attorney and was quite wealthy when the war began.

Kirk helped recruit the 34th Illinois Infantry (the "Rock River Regiment") and was elected its first colonel on August 15, 1861. It was mustered into Federal service on September 7, 1861. Because his regiment was so well disciplined and proficient at drill, he was given command of a brigade in the Army of the Ohio on Christmas Eve and led it at Shiloh, where he was wounded in the shoulder on April 7, 1862. It took him months to recover. He returned to his command in August and took part in the Kentucky Campaign but was not present at Richmond or Perryville.

Kirk was promoted to brigadier general on December 3. He was near the far-right flank of the Army of the Cumberland at Stones River on December 31, when the Confederates attacked at dawn in overwhelming force. Kirk and his men were ready, but his neighboring brigade under August Willich was not. Its men were eating breakfast, and their arms were stacked. This enabled the Rebels under General Cleburne to rout one brigade, then the other. In the process, Kirk was shot. A minié ball lodged in the side of his spine. He lingered for seven months and was ultimately taken to the Trenton House in Chicago. He died there on July 21, 1863, according to his wife and attending physician. He was thirty-five years old. General Kirk is buried in Rosehill Cemetery, Chicago.

JOSEPH FARMER KNIPE, the son of a blacksmith of German ancestry, was born in Mount Joy, Pennsylvania, on March 30, 1823. Joseph was a short man, standing only 5'1". He was a cobbler's apprentice in 1842, when he enlisted in the 2nd U.S. Artillery Regiment, fought in the Mexican War, and was discharged as a sergeant in 1847. He then established a cobbler's shop in Harrisburg, Pennsylvania. He worked in the railroad industry, joined the state militia, and was a major by 1861.

Knipe was involved in training new recruits from April to August 1, when the governor named him commander of the 46th Pennsylvania Infantry. Now a colonel, Knipe served under General Banks in the Shenandoah Valley in 1862. On May 25, during the First Battle of Winchester, he was wounded in the shoulder and right knee. He remained with Banks for the

Second Bull Run Campaign. On August 9, during the Battle of Cedar Mountain, he was wounded in the right hand and a projectile grazed his scalp.

On September 17, during the Battle of Antietam, General Mansfield, the commander of the XII Corps, was killed in action. He was succeeded by Alpheus Williams, and Knipe's brigade commander, Samuel W. Crawford, took charge of Williams's division. Knipe succeeded Crawford as brigade commander. He was promoted to brigadier general on April 15, 1863.

Knipe's command was in reserve at Fredericksburg but was heavily engaged at Chancellorsville. After that, Knipe, who was suffering from malaria and his Cedar Mountain wound, took a medical furlough. He was in Harrisburg when General Meade won the Battle of Gettysburg. Knipe assumed command of a brigade of inexperienced New York and Pennsylvania troops during the pursuit of Lee's army. He rejoined the XII Corps in September.

Transferred to the Western Front, General Knipe fought at Chickamauga, the Siege of Chattanooga, and the Atlanta Campaign. He was wounded in the left shoulder at Resaca (May 15, 1864) and commanded a division in the Army of the Cumberland (July 28 to August 27). As the Union Army closed in on Atlanta, General Thomas sent Knipe to Memphis to organize a new cavalry division, largely from deserters. He was remarkably successful and joined Thomas at Nashville, where he played a major role in the virtual destruction of the Confederate Army of Tennessee. He took six thousand prisoners as the remnants of the Southern army retreated.

Joseph Knipe's command was kept in reserve for most of the rest of the war. For some unknown reason, he did not receive a brevet promotion to major general at the end of the conflict. He was, however, named postmaster of Harrisburg by President Johnson. President Grant later dismissed him. Because of political patronage, General Knipe held a number of minor state and Federal jobs, including a term as postmaster for the United States House of Representatives. He died of cancer in Harrisburg on August 18, 1901, at age seventy-seven. He is buried in the Harrisburg Cemetery.

WLODZIMIERZ (WLADIMIR) BONAWENTURA "KRIZ" KRZYZANOWSKI was born on July 8, 1824, in Roznow. Formerly part of Poland, it was part of the Prussian province of Poznan in 1824. His father was a wealthy landowner, veteran of the Napoleonic Wars, and a Polish noble. Kriz was the first cousin of the famous composer and pianist, Frederic (Fryderyk) Chopin. Financial problems forced his father to sell the family estate in 1827, and following his death, Krzyzanowski's mother moved to the Russian area of the partition. Kriz, however, remained in Poznan and was adopted by members of his father's family. He was educated at the St. Mary Magdalen Gymnasium (high school) in Poznan.

Kriz took part in the Revolution of 1848, which was crushed by the Prussian Army. He managed to escape and reach the Free City of Hamburg, from which he sailed to the United States. He worked as a laborer in New York City while he learned English and continued his education, eventually becoming a civil engineer. He also became a Republican, an abolitionist, and a strong supporter of Abraham Lincoln. When the Civil War began, he was in Washington, D.C. Here, he recruited a militia company of Polish immigrants, of which he was a captain. Its enlistments expired after ninety days, so Kriz returned to New York and helped form the 58th New York Infantry (known as "the Polish Legion") with himself as colonel, effective October 1, 1861.

Krzyzanowski's regiment first saw action in the Battle of Cross Keys (June 8, 1862), where Union forces under General Fremont were defeated by Stonewall Jackson. Kriz was promoted to brigade commander eighteen days later. Lincoln appointed him brigadier general on November 29. The Senate, however, failed to act on his nomination, his appointment expired on March 4, 1863, and he reverted to the rank of colonel. He was renominated and confirmed on March 9, but for some reason, his confirmation was revoked on March 12, and Krzyzanowski became a colonel again. According to General Schurz, the nomination failed because some of the senators could not pronounce his name.

Kriz's brigade was not present at Antietam or Fredericksburg but was crushed at Chancellorsville in Stonewall Jackson's famous flanking attack of May 2. Krzyzanowski fought in the Battle of Gettysburg, where, on July 2, his horse was killed by an artillery shell and landed on the colonel, severely injuring him. He nevertheless remained on the field and launched a successful counterattack on Cemetery Hill, and distinguished himself in heavy fighting. He was transferred to the Western Front after Gettysburg and fought at Chattanooga (including Missionary Ridge) in November. At this point, the XI Corps was dissolved and Kriz was named commandant of the post of Stevenson, Alabama, where he was when the war ended. He was brevetted brigadier general by Abraham Lincoln on March 2, 1865, and was mustered out on October 1, 1865.

Postbellum, Krzyzanowski served in a series of minor Federal posts in Alabama, Georgia, California, Alaska Territory, South America, and San Francisco. He was named special agent of the Treasury Department in the New York City Custom House in 1883. He held this job until his death, which occurred on January 31, 1887. He was sixty-two years old. The causes of death were asthma and a lung disease. Kriz was buried in Green-Wood Cemetery, Brooklyn, but was reinterred in Arlington National Cemetery in 1937.

L

LANDER – LYTLE

FREDERICK WEST LANDER was born on December 17, 1821, in Salem, Massachusetts, into a prominent family. He was well educated at the Governor Dummer Academy, Byfield, Massachusetts; the Phillips Academy in Andover; and the Norwich Military Academy in Vermont. Trained as a civil engineer, he specialized in surveying and worked for a number of eastern railroads. In the 1850s, he worked on four transcontinental railroad surveys and one overland wagon survey, despite hostile Indians. The wagon survey was dubbed "the Lander Road" and was popular with leaders of wagon trains headed for Oregon Territory.

Lander was a tall, handsome, energetic man known for his temper. He would also prove to be an excellent tactician. As the Civil War approached, Lander volunteered for service and, at the request of Abraham Lincoln, went on a secret mission to Texas to meet with Sam Houston and to assess public sentiment there. He then joined the staff of General McClellan and fought at Philippi and Rich Mountain. Promoted to brigadier general on August 6, he assumed command of a brigade in General Stone's division the following month and took part in the debacle at Ball's Bluff (October 21). The next day, he was badly wounded in the leg during a skirmish at Edward's Ferry. Lander—who was also a prolific writer and poet—wrote a poem about Ball's Bluff, as well as several other patriotic pieces.

Lander returned to field duty in December and briefly commanded the Department of Harpers Ferry and Cumberland. He was given command of a division in McClellan's Army of the Potomac on January 5, 1862, and held the town of Hancock, Maryland, against a probe by Stonewall Jackson. He led a successful attack on the Rebel camp at Bloomery Gap on February 14. Shortly after, he developed pneumonia and died in Paw Paw, Virginia (now West Virginia), on March 2, 1862, after his requests for medical leave were ignored. He was forty-two years old. He was buried in the Broad Street Cemetery, Salem.

General Lander's sister was Louisa Lander, a famous sculptor. His brother Edward was the first chief justice of the Washington Territory. His wife was English actress Jean Davenport, the Shirley Temple of her day.

Lander – Lytle

After her husband's death, she spent two years as a supervising nurse in Union Army hospitals in South Carolina. The U.S. Supreme Court is now located where her house once stood. She and General Lander had no children.

JAMES HENRY LANE was born on June 22, 1814, in Lawrenceburg, Indiana. His father, Amos Lane, was an Indiana politician who served in Congress from 1833 to 1837. Thanks to his father, James became postmaster of Lawrenceburg in 1835. Later he read law and was admitted to the bar in 1840. During the Mexican War, he was elected colonel of the 3rd and later the 5th Indiana Infantry Regiments and played a minor role in the American victory at Buena Vista. He earned no brevets. He also exhibited a violent, unstable, and insubordinate temperament, to the point of striking his brigade commander in front of his troops. A duel was narrowly averted.

When he returned home, Lane failed to secure the gubernatorial nomination, but the successful candidate did give the charismatic Lane the number two spot. He was elected lieutenant governor as a Jacksonian Democrat, serving from 1849 to 1853. He was in Congress from 1853 to 1855. Lane was a brilliant orator and an entirely unscrupulous political chameleon. In one debate, for example, he attacked the intellectual inferiority of the entire black race. He supported the Kansas–Nebraska Act, which—too late—he realized would link him with the pro-slavery faction. With his political reputation shattered, he did not seek re-election in 1854 and moved to Kansas Territory in 1855.

Although he joined the Republican Party in 1855, Lane's conversion to Radical Republicanism was gradual. He opposed slavery but supported a proposed provision to the Kansas Constitution that barred the entrance of all blacks into the state forever. Gradually, however, he drifted toward the extreme abolitionist position, and his rhetoric became more and more violent. Eventually, he advocated genocide for every white man in South Carolina. Meanwhile, he was charged with the murder of one of his neighbors and was indicted but not convicted.

ENCYCLOPEDIA OF UNION GENERALS

When Congress finally admitted Kansas to the Union on January 29, 1861, the legislature selected Lane as one of the state's first U.S. senators. As soon as he arrived in Washington, he organized a company, the Frontier Guard, to protect Abraham Lincoln. For a few days, it actually occupied the White House. After the capitol was secure, Lane returned home and recruited a brigade of "Jayhawkers," which was also known as "the Kansas Brigade" or "Lane's Brigade." He invaded Missouri, where he was met by Confederate General Sterling Price and was thoroughly defeated in the Battle of Dry Wood Creek on September 2, 1861. He lost all his supplies, wagons, and mules. As they retreated, Lane and his men looted private homes and committed several murders, most notably during the sacking and burning of Osceola. His department commander, General Halleck, commented that Lane's conduct "has turned against us many thousands who were formerly Union men. A few more such raids will make this State unanimously against us." Lincoln nevertheless appointed Lane brigadier general of volunteers on December 18, 1861. His appointment was cancelled on March 21, 1862, over the issue of whether a sitting U.S. senator could simultaneously be a general. His commission was reinstated on April 11, and he was confirmed by the Senate. His new commander, however, was General David Hunter, who succeeded in curtailing Lane's military activities. Meanwhile, Lane fell out with President Lincoln after protracted arguments over the command structure in Kansas. He was named commissioner of recruiting for the state, where he formed the 1st Kansas Colored Infantry Regiment, which would perform well until April 18, 1864, when it was slaughtered by Confederate cavalry in the Battle of Poison Springs, Arkansas.

Lane was the main target of Quantrill's raiders when they attacked Lane's hometown of Lawrence, Kansas, on August 21, 1863. The pro-Southern cavalrymen roared into town shouting "Remember Osceola!" and gunned down more than 150 civilians and African American Union troops. Lane, however, escaped by running away and hiding in a cornfield.

Senator Lane served as a volunteer aide to General Samuel Curtis during the last campaign in Missouri in the fall of 1864.

James Lane was a man of highly questionable morals. A leech, he had mistresses and frequent liaisons with prostitutes. He also attempted to seduce various married women in Lawrence, but seems to have had little success with women he did not pay. His wife had enough of his infidelities and divorced him in 1856. (Divorce was very rare in those days.) They eventually reconciled and remarried in 1857. Strangely enough, Lane did not drink, although he was noted for his constant use of "dog leg" chewing tobacco.

A ruthless murderer, an adulterer, and a corrupt political thug, Lane is one of the few Civil War generals upon whom the label "scoundrel" can appropriately be applied. Under investigation for corruption and financial fraud, he shot himself in the head near Fort Leavenworth on July 1, 1866, while jumping from a wagon. It took him ten days to die. He was fifty-two years old. He is buried in the Oak Hill Cemetery, Lawrence.

JACOB GARTNER LAUMAN was born in Taneytown, Maryland, on January 20, 1813, but his parents moved to York County, Pennsylvania, as a child. He was educated at the York Academy and moved to Burlington, Iowa, in 1844. He was a successful businessman when the Civil War began.

In April and May 1861, Lauman engaged in recruiting infantry companies. Governor Samuel J. Kirkwood appointed him colonel of the 7th Iowa Infantry on July 11, 1861. He first saw action under Ulysses S. Grant at the Battle of Belmont, Missouri, on November 7, where he was severely wounded in the left thigh. His regiment lost more than four hundred men—the highest of any regiment in that battle. He suffered from his wound for the rest of his life.

When Lauman returned to duty on January 31, 1862, it was as a brigade commander. He performed well at the Battle of Fort Donelson and was promoted to brigadier general on March 22, 1862. His brigade formed part of Hurlburt's division at the Battle of Shiloh (April 6–7), where it suffered 458 casualties.

Lauman later took part in the Battle of Hatchie's Bridge, Mississippi (October 5), where it unsuccessfully attempted to cut off Confederate General Van Dorn's retreat after his defeat in the Second Battle of Corinth.

General Lauman was given command of Hurlbut's old division in late November. After a short period of garrison duty in Memphis, he was part of Sherman's XV Corps and later Edward O. C. Ord's XIII Corps in the Siege of Vicksburg.

On July 12, 1863, Lauman attacked entrenched Confederate forces near Jackson, Mississippi, where his division was slaughtered. One of his brigades lost 465 out of its 880 men engaged. General Ord charged Lauman with attacking without orders and in violation of his instructions and relieved him of his command. Sherman, the overall Union commander at Jackson, backed Ord, so General Grant ordered Lauman to return to Iowa and await orders, which never came. Lauman was unemployed for the rest of the war. He was nevertheless brevetted major general in 1866.

General Lauman blamed his failure at Jackson on a misunderstanding but was never able to clear his name. He had his first stroke in the spring of 1863, but it was mild. More serious strokes followed in early 1864, and he eventually was completely paralyzed on his right side. He died in Burlington, Iowa, on February 9, 1867, at age fifty-four. He is buried in the Aspen Grove Cemetery, Burlington.

MICHAEL KELLY LAWLER first saw the light of day at Monasterevin, County Kildare, Ireland, on November 16, 1814. He came to America with his parents in 1816. After living in Frederick County, Maryland, they settled in Gallatin County, Illinois, in 1819. He grew up on the family farm, married Elizabeth Crenshaw, the daughter of a wealthy slave-holding landowner, and engaged in large-scale agriculture by the standards of that time. He joined the "Gallatin Guards," a militia company, and became its captain in 1842. He was so efficient that the governor promoted him to brigadier general in 1844. He studied law and was admitted to the bar that same year.

When the Mexican War began, Lawler was commissioned captain in the 3rd Illinois Infantry. He commanded a company at Vera Cruz, and Cerro Gordo. When the enlistments of his twelve-month unit expired, Lawler returned to Illinois and organized a company of Mounted Troops called the Mameluke Legion (114 men). He took part in the campaign to capture Matamoros, engaged in some more skirmishing, and guarded the American supply line.

After Mexico surrendered, Lawler returned to agriculture. He also established a successful mercantile and hardware business and a general store in Shawneetown. In his spare time, he used his legal expertise to help Mexican War veterans.

When the Civil War began, Lawler organized the 18th Illinois Infantry, which elected him colonel on May 20, 1861. He enforced discipline on the regiment by knocking down unruly men with his fists. He sent the drunks to the guardhouse and had them fed a drug which induced vomiting. His actions led to a court-martial, with General Halleck presiding. He was found guilty and sentenced to dismissal from the service. Halleck, however, overturned the verdict, and he returned to his command. On August 17, he defeated a Confederate force at Charleston, Missouri, and captured fifty Rebels and killed thirteen. Lawler lost one man killed and seven wounded.

Lawler's regiment performed well at Fort Donelson (February 12–16), where the colonel was shot through the left forearm, and he permanently lost the use of his thumb and forefinger. (This was especially difficult for him because he was left-handed.) He also suffered a head injury during the bombardment which caused partial deafness. After he partially recovered, he served in western Tennessee and northern Mississippi, became a brigade commander on May 7, was promoted to brigadier general on April 15, 1863, and advanced to divisional command. He was with the XIII Corps during Grant's last Vicksburg Campaign, fighting at Port Gibson, Champion's Hill, and the Big Black River, where he led a charge and distinguished himself, capturing 1,120 prisoners when the Southern line collapsed. During the unsuccessful May 22 assault on the Vicksburg defenses, Lawler's men were the only ones to penetrate the Rebel defenses at the Railroad Redoubt, but they were not reinforced and could not hold it. The brigade lost 575 men killed, wounded, and missing.

After Vicksburg fell, Lawler's brigade fought in the Second Battle of Jackson. He was sent to Louisiana in August and became commander of the 1st Division of the XIII Corps on October 31. He gave up command on December 14 and went home on medical furlough. When he returned to active duty in February 1864, he was given command of a brigade in Indianola, Texas. He was transferred to Memphis and on November 23 was given command of a division. Transferred to the XVI Corps, he fought in the disastrous Red River Campaign of 1864. After that, Lawler held a number of positions in Louisiana, including commander of the District of East Louisiana, which headquartered in Morganza, about twenty miles northwest of Baton Rouge. Here he commanded as many as 18,691 men and tried to suppress guerrilla bands, with limited success. He was brevetted major general on April 27, 1865, and was mustered out in August.

After the fall of the Confederacy, Lawler remained in Louisiana for a year, buying and selling horses. He also purchased the Arlington Plantation near Baton Rouge at a sheriff's sale for $6,000. It was formerly valued at $200,000. He and his son also spent two years in Texas. Lawler eventually returned home and resumed his previous occupations. General Lawler died in Shawneetown, Illinois, on July 22, 1882, at age sixty-seven. He is buried in Hickory Hill Cemetery, Gallatin County, Illinois.

JAMES HEWETT LEDLIE was born on April 14, 1832, in Utica, New York. He attended Union College in Schenectady, New York, and became a civil engineer. He worked on the Erie Canal and in railroad construction. In May 1861, shortly after the Civil War began, he was named major of the 19th New York Infantry, which was organized at Elmira. It was reorganized in December 1861 as the 3rd New York Artillery Regiment. Ledlie was promoted to lieutenant colonel and to colonel in December.

The 19th/3rd was part of General Patterson's unsuccessful attempt to keep Confederate General Joseph Johnston's forces in the Shenandoah Valley in July 1861. It was then sent to the Carolinas and later served in the Army of the James. Ledlie, meanwhile, was given command of the Artillery Brigade of the Department of North Carolina in December 1862. He was promoted to brigadier general on December 24, but the Senate never acted on his promotion, and it lapsed on March 4, 1863. He was reappointed on October 7 and this time was confirmed. He spent his time in North

Carolina in garrison assignments and in coastal artillery emplacements. He was transferred to the Army of the Potomac in May 1864 and fought in Grant's Overland Campaign. He advanced to divisional command on June 9, after General Thomas Stevenson was killed. His conduct at the Battle of Cold Harbor, where he was seen running to the rear, smacked of cowardice.

Ledlie took part in the Siege of Petersburg. On July 30, Union engineers blew a huge crater, about 170 feet long, 60 feet wide, and 30 feet deep, in Confederate lines. Originally, the plan called for General Ferraro's division of African Americans to exploit the breakthrough, but only hours before the attack, General Meade ordered that white troops (i.e., Ledlie's division) be used instead. Ledlie did not brief his troops before the attack and did not provide them with ladders. Ferraro's troops were trained to advance along the rim of "the Crater," but Ledlie's untrained men went into the Crater itself, where they were unable to maneuver and, because of the steep walls of the Crater, were unable to climb out. They were slaughtered by the Rebels. Meanwhile, Ledlie and Ferraro were in a bunker at the rear, drinking rum.

In all, the North suffered 3,798 casualties in the Battle of the Crater out of 16,500 engaged. The Confederates lost about 1,500 of the 9,500 men who fought here. Even more importantly, the Union Army lost a golden opportunity to capture Petersburg and Richmond, and perhaps end the war. Grant called this battle "the saddest affair I have witnessed in the war," and telegraphed Halleck that he did not expect to have another such opportunity. He was right. A court of inquiry convened in September, and Ledlie was censured by both Grant and Meade, and virtually expelled from the service. He formally resigned his commission on January 23, 1865.

Leslie returned to the railroad construction business after the war and worked for the Union Pacific and the Nevada Center Railroads. He died on August 15, 1882, in New Brighton, Staten Island, New York. He was fifty years old. He was interred in Forest Hill Cemetery in the city of his birth.

ALBERT LINDLEY LEE was born on January 16, 1834, in Fulton, New York. He graduated from Union College in Schenectady in 1853 and then read law. After being admitted to the bar, he practiced in New York City until 1858, when he moved to Kansas Territory. He was elected a district

judge in 1859, was one of the founders of the *Elwood Free Press*, and was an associate justice of the Kansas Supreme Court when the Civil War began.

Lee joined the Union Army as a major in the 7th Kansas Cavalry in late October 1861. He took part in a few minor military operations in Kansas and western Missouri before he was promoted to colonel and regimental commander on May 17, 1862. Transferred east of the Mississippi, he took part in Halleck's advance on Corinth, Grant's drives on Vicksburg, and the Second Battle of Corinth under Rosecrans. He assumed command of a cavalry brigade in the Army of Tennessee in November 1862 and was promoted to brigadier general on April 4, 1863.

Lee was named chief of staff of McClelland's XIII Corps in May 1863 and fought in the battles of Port Gibson, Champion Hill, and Big Black River. He took command of an infantry brigade in the XIII Corps on May 18. The next day, during Grant's first assault on Vicksburg, a Confederate musket ball struck Lee's right cheek and exited via the back of his neck. He did not return to duty until July 26, when he assumed command of a division of the XIII Corps. In September, he was named commander of the Cavalry Division of the Army of the Gulf. He led it in the Red River Campaign of 1864.

Many of Lee's cavalrymen in Louisiana were recently converted infantrymen, and they were no match for the experienced Texas cavalry they had to face. Lee, however, did as well as could be expected under the circumstances, and he prevented Nathaniel Banks, his army commander, from blundering into a potentially disastrous ambush at Mansfield on April 8. Even so, Banks relieved him of his command on April 18, 1864. Later, Banks admitted he made a mistake in sacking Lee, who was briefly restored to his command in August. Shortly after, he was demoted to the command of a cavalry depot in New Orleans.

In April 1865, Lee led a raid against weak Confederate forces at Clinton, Louisiana, in East Feliciana Parish, east of Baton Rouge, and was defeated. Afterward, Banks's successor, Edward R. S. Canby, issued orders that Lee was not allowed to leave New Orleans. Lee resigned from the army on May 4, 1865, and was not brevetted major general in the omnibus promotions at the end of the war. Postwar, he was a newspaper editor in New Orleans, a banker in New Orleans and New York City, and a leader in the New York Republican Party. He died in New York City on December 13, 1907, at age seventy-three. His son, Albert Lee, Jr., became editor of *Harper's Weekly* and the author of several novels.

MORTIMER DORMER LEGGETT was born on April 19, 1821, on a farm near Ithaca, New York, but moved with his parents to a farm near Montville, Ohio, when he was fifteen. Leggett attended Western Reserve College, studied at Willoughby Medical College, and then read law while practicing medicine. He was admitted to the bar in 1844 and set up a practice in Akron. He became interested in setting up grade schools in Ohio and successively served as school superintendent in Akron, Warren, and Zanesville, while simultaneously practicing law. He also worked as the editor of *The Free School Clarion* and later the *Zanesville Courier*. He was a professor at the Poland Law College, the forerunner of the State and Law College in Poland, Ohio, from 1855 to 1857.

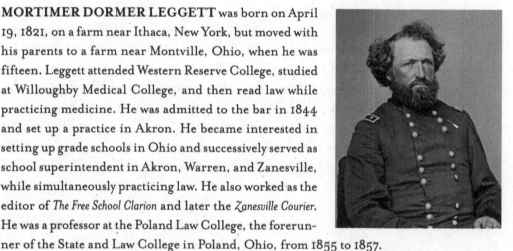

Leggett became a volunteer civilian aide to his friend, George B. McClellan, in the early months of the war and served in the Western Virginia Campaign. He joined the Union Army as lieutenant colonel of the 78th Ohio Infantry (which he helped raise) in December 1861 and became its colonel the following month. His regiment was lightly engaged at Fort Donelson and Shiloh, where Colonel Leggett was wounded. He was also wounded during the Siege of Corinth on May 16, 1862, and in a skirmish at Bolivar, Tennessee, on August 30. Meanwhile, he was given a brigade in August and promoted to brigadier general on April 15, 1863. He fought in the various Vicksburg campaigns and, near Fort Hill on the Vicksburg perimeter, he was severely wounded on June 25, when a shell struck a piece of wood near him and threw fragments of wood and dirt into his abdomen, shoulder, and right hip. Carried unconscious to the rear, he woke up to find doctors removing pebbles and gravel from his body. The wound resulted in a hernia, and he vomited blood for the several days. Although he did not drink, he did take some alcohol when a physician recommended it.

General Leggett suffered from his hernia for the rest of his life, but it did not prevent him from returning to the field. He was given command of a division in the XVII Corps in November 1863 and fought in the Atlanta Campaign, the March to the Sea, and the Carolinas Campaign. He particularly distinguished himself in the storming of Bald Hill near Atlanta on July 21, 1864. The hill was later named in his honor. He was brevetted major general in January 1864 and promoted to full rank on August 21, 1865. He was mustered out the following month.

Postwar, Leggett resumed his law practice in Zanesville. He was U.S. Commissioner of Patents from 1871 to 1875, when he resigned to go into private business. In 1880, he was the founder of the Brush Electric Company, a precursor of the General Electric Corporation. General Leggett died in Cleveland, Ohio, on January 6, 1896, at age seventy-four. He is buried in Lake View Cemetery, Cleveland.

L.

JOSEPH ANDREW JACKSON LIGHTBURN was born in Webster, Pennsylvania, south of Pittsburgh, on September 21, 1824, but his family moved to Lewis County, Virginia (later West Virginia), when he was a teenager. His father was a successful farmer, and Lightburn spent his youth working on the family farm. He was good and lifelong friends with a neighbor boy who later became famous as Stonewall Jackson, who frequently borrowed books from Joseph's father's library. The two competed for an appointment to West Point, which ultimately went to Jackson.

Lightburn enlisted in the army when the Mexican War began in 1846. He served until December 1851 and was discharged as a sergeant. He was very religious his entire life and became an ordained Baptist preacher in 1859. Lightburn rejoined the army in August 1861 as colonel of the 4th (West) Virginia Infantry. Two of his half-brothers joined his regiment; a third joined the Confederate Army. Joseph served in McClellan's Western Virginia Campaign of 1861. In March 1862, he was promoted to commander of a brigade (five thousand men), which he led in the Kanawha Valley Campaign of 1862, during which the Confederate attempts to recapture western Virginia failed.

Lightburn was transferred to the Army of the Tennessee in December 1862 and, after briefly returning to West Virginia to help check Rebel raiders, took part in Grant's attempts to capture Vicksburg. He was promoted to brigadier general on March 16, 1863. He fought in the Siege of Vicksburg, the Second Battle of Jackson, Mississippi, the Siege of Chattanooga (including the Battle of Missionary Ridge), and in the Atlanta Campaign, where he distinguished himself in the Battle of Kennesaw Mountain. He also fought in the battles of Resaca, Dallas, and Atlanta, after which he temporarily commanded a division. On August 19, 1864, during the Siege of Atlanta, he was shot in the head. It took him months to recover, and his wound caused him blurred vision and headaches the rest of his life. He was sent home to recover, after which he held a couple of minor commands in West Virginia (January–March 1865). He resigned his commission on June 22, 1865. He briefly returned to agriculture and served a term in the state legislature. He became a full-time minister in 1867. He spent the rest of his life in this profession.

General Lightburn was a preacher in Broad Run, West Virginia, when he died of asthma and heart problems on May 17, 1901, at age seventy-six. He is buried there in the Baptist Church Cemetery.

HENRY HAYES LOCKWOOD was born in Kent County, Delaware, on August 17, 1814. His father was a farmer who owned six slaves and lived with a free woman of color. Lockwood entered West Point in 1832, graduated in 1836 (22/49), and was commissioned brevet second lieutenant in the artillery. He served in Florida against the Seminoles but resigned his commission in 1837, engaged in agriculture for four years, and became a professor of mathematics at the United States Naval Academy in 1841. Except for a period in the Mexican War, he remained there until the Civil War began in 1861; meanwhile, he labored as a professor of natural philosophy and astronomy

(1847–51) and as professor of astronomy and gunnery (1851–61). In the war against Santa Anna, Lockwood served aboard a frigate and took part in the successful Battle of Monterey, California.

On May 25, 1861, Lockwood became colonel of the 1st Delaware Infantry Regiment. He was promoted to brigadier general on August 8 and guarded the lower Potomac after the disaster at Bull Run. He directed a couple of minor operations on the Eastern Shore of Virginia, during which he launched a successful pacification program and captured the region without a major battle. He spent most of the war protecting the Hampton Roads-Delmarva Peninsula sector, although he did command an ad hoc brigade in the XII Corps (Culp's Hill sector) during the Battle of Gettysburg.

After Gettysburg, Lockwood briefly commanded the Department of the Susquehanna and Harper's Ferry garrison before being given command of the Middle Department, headquartered in Baltimore. He was demoted to brigade commander in late March 1864, but was given command of a division on May 29, during the Overland Campaign. On June 1, he became confused by the labyrinth of a road network and did not get his division into action at Cold Harbor that day. General Warren, his corps commander, became furious, concluded that Lockwood was not competent enough to direct an important command, and demanded Lockwood be relieved. Generals Meade concurred and General Grant sent him back to Maryland on June 2. He was replaced by Samuel W. Crawford.

Lockwood directed a provisional brigade in the defense of Baltimore against Jubal Early in July 1864. He commanded a brigade in that city for the rest of the war. Mustered out in August 1865, he returned to the Naval Academy as a professor of natural and experimental philosophy. In 1870, he was assigned to the Naval Observatory, where he remained until he retired in 1876.

General Lockwood settled in Georgetown, District of Columbia, where he died on December 7, 1899. He was eighty-five. He is buried in the U.S. Naval Academy Cemetery, Annapolis, Maryland. He is the only army general so honored. One of his sons, James Booth Lockwood, was a famous explorer who died on an expedition to the North Pole in 1884. He is buried beside his father.

JOHN ALEXANDER "BLACK JACK" LOGAN was born on February 9, 1826, in Murphysboro, southern Illinois, the son of a medical doctor. He was homeschooled with his father as his private tutor and then attended Shiloh College for three years. Here, he excelled in oratory. In 1847, he enlisted in the 1st Illinois Infantry Regiment. He was sent to Santa Fe but did not see combat. Logan was a second lieutenant and regimental quartermaster when he was discharged in October 1848. He returned home, studied law under an uncle and at the University of Louisville, and graduated in 1851.

Logan was a pro-slavery Democrat and a supporter of Stephen A. Douglas. He was elected county clerk in 1849 and served in the Illinois House of Representatives (1853–1857), where he was successful in getting a law passed which prohibited African Americans (including freedmen) from settling in the state. He was elected to Congress in 1860.

In 1861, Logan attached himself to a Michigan unit and (wearing a top hat) fought at Bull Run as a civilian volunteer, picking up a rifle from a wounded soldier and fighting as if he were a private. Although pro-Southern antebellum, he strongly believed that the Union must be preserved. In August, he asked Lincoln to allow him to raise a regiment in his home district. Permission was granted and he became colonel of the 31st Illinois Infantry. He was an effective recruiter and champion of the Union cause, and it was later reported that all but twenty of his men were Democrats. General Grant later credited him with saving southern Illinois for the Union. He fought in the Battle of Belmont, where his horse was killed.

On February 15, 1862, Logan was wounded twice at Fort Donelson, when a Confederate minié ball struck his left shoulder. After he was bandaged, he returned to the battle, where another Confederate bullet struck his pistol, which was on his belt, and almost broke his ribs. He tried to remain on the field, although he was so weak from loss of blood that he could barely stay in the saddle but was finally taken to Grant's headquarters and eventually returned to Illinois to recover. He was promoted to brigadier general on March 22 and resigned from Congress on April 2. (There was a Colonel John Logan who was wounded at Shiloh, but this was a different officer.) General John A. Logan returned to duty on April 19 and assumed command of a brigade in the Army of the Tennessee.

John Logan was one of the best "political generals" to fight in the Civil War. He served in the Siege of Corinth, was given command of a division in June 1862, and served under Grant in the various Vicksburg campaigns and the subsequent siege. He was wounded in the thigh in June 1863 but not seriously. His health failed him, and he was on medical furlough from July to December.

Logan was promoted to major general on March 13, 1863. He was military governor of Vicksburg from July to November 1863, when he succeeded William T. Sherman as commander of the XV Corps. During the Atlanta Campaign, he was wounded in the left arm at Dallas, Georgia, on May 30. He briefly commanded the Army of the Tennessee after General McPherson was killed in action on July 22, 1864. Much to his disgust, he was superseded by Oliver O. Howard (a West Pointer) on July 27. He had a fierce hatred for West Point from then on. Shortly after, Logan (now a Republican) returned to Illinois for the elections and to campaign for Lincoln.

In December 1864, Ulysses S. Grant became impatient with General Thomas's failure to launch an offensive against the Confederate Army of Tennessee near Nashville. Thomas, however, refused to strike before the weather improved. Grant sent Logan to Tennessee with orders to relieve Thomas as commander of the Army of the Cumberland, but not to do so if Thomas launched the offensive before he arrived. Thomas did so and virtually destroyed the Army of Tennessee in the Battle of Nashville (December 15–16). Logan then rejoined Sherman's army, resumed command of the XV Corps, and took part in the Carolinas Campaign. He saved Raleigh, North Carolina, from being burned by Sherman's "bummers." General Logan resigned his commission on August 17, 1865, and resumed his political career.

John Logan was re-elected to Congress in 1866 and served from 1867 to 1871. He was elected to the Senate in 1870 and served in that body from 1871 to 1877 and from 1879 until his death, which occurred in Washington, D.C. on December 26, 1886, at age sixty.

In Congress, Logan was a radical Republican and was a house manager during the impeachment trial of Andrew Johnson. He was James G. Blaine's vice-presidential running mate in 1884, but they were defeated by Grover Cleveland and Thomas A. Hendricks. Logan also served as commander-in-chief of the Grand Army of the Republic veterans' organization (1868 to 1871) and was a major force behind the establishment of Memorial Day as a national holiday. He authored two books postwar (see bibliography).

General Logan was interred in the United States Soldiers' Home National Cemetery in Washington. His son, Major John A. Logan, Jr., fought in the Philippines, where he was killed in action in 1899 and was posthumously awarded the Congressional Medal of Honor.

ELI LONG was born in Woodford County, Kentucky, on June 16, 1837. He was educated in local public schools and graduated from the Kentucky Military Institute in 1855. The following year, he managed to acquire a direct commission as a second lieutenant in the 1st Cavalry. He served on the Western frontier, where he fought Indians. He was promoted to first lieutenant in March 1861 and to captain on May 24. Transferred to the 4th Cavalry, he served on the Western Front as a company commander and was severely wounded at Stones River on December 31, 1862.

In February 1863, Long was named colonel of the 4th Ohio Cavalry. This regiment was recently captured by the Confederate raider John Hunt Morgan and was exchanged, but its morale was shattered. Long showed great leadership, restored the confidence and pride of the unit, and converted it into one of the better Union cavalry formations. Long led it with success in the Tullahoma Campaign, which led to his promotion to brigade commander. He commanded infantry at the Battle of Chickamauga and was wounded in the left side during the Battle of Farmington, Tennessee (October 7, 1863). He also participated in the Battle of Fort Sanders near Knoxville in November.

Colonel Long fought in the Atlanta Campaign and was promoted to brigadier general on August 18, 1864. He was wounded in the head near Jonesboro on August 20 and in the right arm and thigh at Lovejoy's Station on August 21. He did not return to duty until November 16, when he assumed command of a cavalry division in the Military Department of the Mississippi, which was commanded by James Wilson. He served in the Franklin-Nashville Campaign and, on April 2, 1865, fought in the Battle of Selma, Alabama. Here he was shot in the head. This ended his field service in the Civil War. For the rest of his life, he suffered from partial paralysis of his tongue, his right arm, and the right side of his face. He was wounded five times during the war and cited for gallantry five times. He was mustered out of volunteer service in January 1866. He was brevetted major general in 1867.

Long's wounds prevented him from returning to field duty after the war. In 1867, after briefly commanding the Military Department of New Jersey, he was granted the rank of major general, Regular Army—on the retired list. A parsimonious government reduced his rank to brigadier general in 1875. In the meantime, Eli Long settled in Plainfield, New Jersey, studied law, was admitted to the bar, and became borough recorder. In 1903, he underwent an operation at the Presbyterian Hospital in New York City. It was not successful, and he died there on January 5, at age sixty-five. He is buried in Hillside Cemetery, Plainfield.

L.

WILLIAM WARREN LOWE was born on October 12, 1831, in Greencastle, Indiana, the son of a physician. He was admitted to West Point in 1849 and graduated four years later (30/52) as a brevet second lieutenant of dragoons. Sent to the Cavalry School for Practice at Carlisle Barracks, Pennsylvania, he was promoted to second lieutenant in 1854 and sent to Jefferson Barracks, Missouri. He was sent to the Texas frontier in 1855 and served as a scout. He was transferred back to Carlisle Barracks in 1860. Meanwhile, he was promoted to first lieutenant in the 1st Cavalry in 1856 and to captain, 2nd Cavalry, on August 3, 1861.

Lowe fought in the First Bull Run Campaign and served in the Washington defenses. He was transferred to Iowa in December, where he organized the 5th Iowa Cavalry Regiment (which included companies from Minnesota, Nebraska, and Missouri) and became its colonel on January 1, 1862. He then joined Grant's army and fought at Fort Donelson (February 13–16, 1862). After commanding Forts Donelson, Henry, and Heiman in West Tennessee while Grant moved on to Shiloh, Lowe directed some minor operations in Middle Tennessee, where he commanded a brigade and operated ineffectively against Nathan Bedford Forrest. He was promoted to brigadier general on November 29, 1862, but his promotion was withdrawn on February 13, 1863, for reasons not made clear by the records. He commanded Fort Donelson in February 1863 and led a cavalry brigade at Chickamauga. He was stationed in Huntsville, Alabama, during the winter of 1863/64 and briefly commanded a cavalry division in the spring of 1864.

Colonel Lowe was in charge of remounting cavalry for the Army of the Cumberland from July 1864 to January 1865, with headquarters at Nashville. He was mustered out of volunteer service on January 24, 1865, and was transferred to Fort Leavenworth, Kansas, as an acting assistant provost marshal general and a chief mustering and disbursing officer for Kansas, Nebraska, Dakota, and Colorado. He reverted to the rank of major, Regular Army, and was definitely put on the professional shelf. He was, however, brevetted brigadier general on March 13, 1865.

Post-war, William W. Lowe did garrison duty in Nashville and New Orleans between long periods when he was on leaves of absence. He resigned from the service in 1869. He became superintendent of the Smelting and Repair Works in Omaha, Nebraska, after he left the army, and engaged in business pursuits. He died in Omaha on May 18, 1898, at age sixty-nine. He was buried in Prospect Hill Cemetery, Omaha.

CHARLES RUSSELL LOWELL, III, was born in Boston, Massachusetts, on January 2, 1835, into a distinguished literary family. His mother wrote books on education, and his uncle was James Russell Lowell, a famous poet in his day. Charles was valedictorian of the Class of 1854 at Harvard. He then worked in an iron mill in Trenton, New Jersey, for several months and spent several years traveling abroad. He was brilliant and dynamic, but also noted for being demanding and using harsh words. He was treasurer of the Burlington & Missouri River Railroad from 1858 to 1860 and was manager of an iron foundry in Cumberland, Maryland, when the Civil War broke out.

Lowell accepted a captain's commission in the 3rd U.S. Cavalry on May 14, 1861. The 3rd was redesignated 6th Cavalry on August 10. Lowell, meanwhile, transferred to the staff of General George B. McClellan and served as his aide-de-camp until November 1862. He particularly distinguished himself as a dispatch runner in the Battle of Antietam, during which he rallied several broken units. As a result, he was selected to recruit a new regiment, the 2nd Massachusetts Cavalry. In the process, on April 9, he put down a mutiny of new recruits and Irish draftees in Boston. During the melee, he shot and killed one of the mutineers. An inquest cleared him of wrongdoing. He was promoted to colonel on May 10, 1863.

The 2nd took part in a few minor actions during the Gettysburg Campaign, after which it served in the Washington, D.C. defenses. Lowell was promoted to cavalry brigade commander in late December 1863 and played a major role in checking Jubal Early's raid on Washington in July 1864. Assigned to Sheridan's command, he fought in the Battle of Winchester (September 19, 1864), where he distinguished himself. On October 19, he was wounded in the arm at Cedar Creek but refused to leave the field. Subsequently, he led a charge against the Confederate lines. So far, he had led a charmed life and had not been seriously wounded, although at least seven horses had been shot from underneath him. Now his luck ran out. He was shot through the lungs and one bullet penetrated his body from shoulder to shoulder. He died the next day at Middletown, Virginia. At General Sheridan's insistence, he was promoted to brigadier general of volunteers, to rank from October 19.

General Lowell was twenty-nine years old when he died. He is buried in the Mount Auburn Cemetery, Cambridge, Massachusetts. His only child, a daughter, was born a month before, but he apparently never saw her. His younger brother, Lieutenant James Jackson Lowell, was shot in the abdomen during the Battle of Frayser's Farm in June 1862. He died in a Confederate hospital four days later.

THOMAS JOHN LUCAS was born on September 9, 1826, in Lawrenceburg, Indiana, an Ohio River town. He followed in his father's footsteps and became a watchmaker. During the Mexican War, he enlisted in the 4th Indiana Infantry Regiment as a drummer and rose to the rank of second lieutenant. He was mustered out in July 1848 and resumed his former profession.

On May 20, 1861, he returned to the colors as lieutenant colonel of the 16th Indiana Infantry (later Mounted Infantry) Regiment. He fought in the Ball's Bluff disaster in October. Transferred to the Western Front, he became colonel of his regiment when Pleasant A. Hackleman was promoted to brigade commander in May 1862.

Colonel Lucas participated in the Battle of Richmond, Kentucky, on August 30, 1862, where his regiment was smashed, losing two hundred killed or wounded and six hundred captured. Lucas managed to escape the debacle and rebuilt his regiment. He was then assigned to U.S. Grant's Army of the Tennessee and fought in the Vicksburg campaigns. He was wounded in the left leg on April 18, 1863, but continued in command until May 22, when Grant launched his second major assault on the fortress of Vicksburg. Here Lucas was shot in the leg, jaw, and face, and the division of his nose was destroyed. Sent home to recover, he returned to light duty in August. He was given command of a cavalry brigade in the Army of the Gulf in November.

Lucas fought in the unsuccessful Red River Campaign in Louisiana and was promoted to brigadier general on November 10, 1864. He took part in the drive on Mobile and briefly commanded a cavalry division (March 29–April 16, 1865). He was commanding a cavalry brigade at Vicksburg when the war ended.

Brevetted major general and mustered out in early 1866, Lucas returned to Lawrenceburg, where he worked for the [Internal] Revenue Service. Eventually he became postmaster of his hometown (1881–1885). He ran for Congress as a Republican in 1886 but was defeated.

General Lucas died of senility and chronic bronchitis in Lawrenceburg on November 16, 1908, at age eighty-two. He was buried in Greendale Cemetery, just outside Lawrenceburg.

NATHANIEL LYON, the son of a farmer, was born in Ashford, Connecticut (which is now part of Eastford), on July 14, 1818. He was educated in local public schools, at an academy in Brooklyn, Connecticut, and at West Point, where he graduated with the Class of 1841 (11/52). Here, he had an unfortunate romance and decided never to marry. He was also considered overly serious from his childhood and had grave doubts about religion. Commissioned second lieutenant in the 2nd U.S. Infantry, he was sent to Florida, where he fought in the Second Seminole War. Lyon had a fierce temper and was suspended for five months for beating, binding, and gagging an insolent private. Promoted to first lieutenant in 1847, he fought in the Mexican War, where he was brevetted captain for his "conspicuous bravery" at Contreras and Churubusco. He was wounded at Chapultepec on September 13. After the war, he was transferred to the 1st Dragoons in California, where his command was responsible for the Bloody Island Massacre, a.k.a. the Clear Lake Massacre, on May 15, 1850. They slaughtered at least sixty Pomo Indians. One source put the number at eight hundred. The truth is probably somewhere in between. Women and children were among the dead. This incident had no negative effect on Lyon's career. He was promoted to captain in 1851.

In 1854, Lyon was transferred to Fort Riley, Kansas, during the "Bleeding Kansas" period. He was not a staunch abolitionist as he has occasionally been portrayed. He opposed allowing slavery into the territories but did not want to disturb it where it already existed; he was, however, fiercely opposed to secession. A company commander in March 1861, he was sent with his men to St. Louis, where he assumed command of the vital St. Louis Arsenal. Missouri was neutral at this time, but Governor Claiborne F. Jackson was clearly pro-Southern.

Lyon realized that the pro-Confederates had enough strength to seize the arsenal if he did not act, so he secretly armed the pro-Union "Wide Awakes," a paramilitary organization. Meanwhile, Jackson's Missouri State Guard forces concentrated at Camp Jackson, south of St. Louis. Using the element of surprise, Lyon surrounded the camp on May 10 and forced it to surrender. Afterward, he faced civilian riots in St. Louis. Lyon fired on the rioters, killing twenty-eight and wounding between seventy-five and 100. Lincoln backed Lyon, named him commander of the Department of the West, and promoted himself to brigadier general on May 17. The ranks of major, lieutenant colonel, and colonel he skipped altogether. He became commander of the Army of the West on July 2, and a pro-Union Missouri State Convention declared the office of governor "vacant" on July 22.

Lyon, meanwhile, pursued Jackson and his allies. He occupied the capital, Jefferson City, on June 13 and defeated the State Guard at Boonville on June 17. He encamped at Springfield with six thousand men on July 13. Meanwhile, state and regular Confederate units under Generals Ben McCulloch and Sterling Price entered Missouri and advanced on Springfield. They had about twelve thousand men when they clashed with Lyon's forces at Wilson's Creek, southwest of Springfield, on August 10.

Badly outnumbered, Lyon fought bravely. He was shot in the leg, his head was grazed by a bullet, and his horse was shot from under him. Finally, about 9:30 a.m., he led a desperate counterattack, during which he was shot through the heart. His army collapsed and was routed. McCulloch, however, failed to pursue. The Confederates returned Lyon's body to his kinspeople, and it was eventually buried in the family plot at Eastford Cemetery. Fifteen thousand people attended his funeral. He was forty-three years old.

Lyon captured most of Missouri for the Union but clearly overplayed his hand when he advanced so far to the southwest.

WILLIAM HAINES LYTLE was born on November 2, 1826, in Cincinnati, Ohio, into a well-to-do and politically well-connected family. His father was a U.S. Congressman and close friend of Andrew Jackson. Both William's father and grandfather were militia generals. He attended Cincinnati College, graduated in 1842, studied law, and practiced in that city when the Mexican War began. He enrolled in the 2nd Ohio Infantry, served in Mexico, and was mustered out in 1848 as a captain. He returned home, was elected to the legislature twice, and narrowly lost a race for lieutenant governor. Governor Salmon P. Chase appointed him major general in the militia in 1857. Meanwhile, he became a nationally famous poet. He also ran for Congress but could not capture the Democratic nomination.

On May 3, 1861, Lytle became colonel of the 10th Ohio Infantry. He led it in the Western Virginia Campaign, where he was badly wounded when a bullet passed through his left leg at Carnifex Ferry on September 10. It also killed his horse. When he returned from convalescence leave in December, he was named commander of the recruit depot at Bardstown, Kentucky. He was subsequently given command of an infantry brigade, which he led at Perryville. Here he was wounded in the head, left for dead, and captured by the Confederates. He was quickly exchanged and promoted to brigadier general on November 29, 1862. He subsequently fought in the Stones River and Tullahoma campaigns.

Lytle was beloved in the 10th Ohio, whose officers presented him with a jeweled Maltese Cross on September 9. Eleven days later, during the Battle of Chickamauga, the Confederates broke through Sheridan's division and smashed it. General Lytle attempted to restore the situation by leading a counterattack on horseback. He was shot three times. One of the bullets struck him in the left corner of his mouth and exited out his right temple. He died minutes later, and his body was left behind. When they found out who he was, the Confederates gave him an honor guard. Many of their men recited his poetry over their campfires that night. He was thirty-six.

William Haines Lytle's body was taken back to Cincinnati, where it was buried in Spring Grove Cemetery.

M

· MACKENZIE – MOWER ·

RANALD SLIDELL "BAD HAND" MACKENZIE was born in Westchester County, New York, on July 27, 1840. His father was born with the last name "Slidell," but changed it to Mackenzie after an uncle he admired. His father, Alexander, was a commodore in the U.S. Navy, his older brother became a rear admiral, and his uncle was U.S. senator and Confederate diplomat John Slidell. Born into a wealthy and politically influential family, Mackenzie attended Williams College in Massachusetts before entering West Point in 1858. He graduated at the top of his class (1/28) on June 17, 1862, as a second lieutenant of engineers. Two months later, on August 29, he was wounded in both shoulders during the Second Battle of Bull Run.

Mackenzie recovered quickly and was named engineer in the Right Grand Division. He fought in the Battle of Fredericksburg and was promoted to first lieutenant in March 1863. He was brevetted captain for his performance in the Battle of Chancellorsville and was wounded at Gettysburg, for which he was brevetted major. He took part in the Overland Campaign, was brevetted lieutenant colonel, and on June 18, 1864, was severely wounded on the Jerusalem Plank Road during the Siege of Petersburg—hence his nickname. He lost the first two fingers on his right hand.

Mackenzie was not sidelined for long. On July 10, he was promoted to colonel and named commander of the 2nd Connecticut Heavy Artillery. Part of the VI Corps, he took part in the defense of Washington, D.C. against Jubal Early. He fought in the Shenandoah Valley Campaign, where he was wounded in the Third Battle of Winchester on September 19. A month later, he was given command of a brigade. He distinguished himself in the Battle of Cedar Creek (October 19), where he was wounded again, this time in the leg and chest. On November 30, President Lincoln appointed him brigadier general of volunteers.

On March 13, 1865, Mackenzie assumed command of the cavalry division of the Army of the James, and took part in the Appomattox Campaign. Grant praised him as the most promising young officer in the army. His men thought less of him and called him "the Perpetual Punisher" because he was such a harsh disciplinarian. He was brevetted major general on January 13, 1866, and mustered out of the volunteer service on January 15. He reverted to his Regular Army rank of captain.

Mackenzie was promoted to colonel of the 41st (later 24th) Infantry—a Buffalo Soldiers' regiment—in May 1867. In 1871, he assumed command of the 4th U.S. Cavalry Regiment, which he led in the Battles of Blanco Canyon and North Folk in western Texas. He led a highly successful raid into Coahuila and (in gross violation of Mexican sovereignty) destroyed several Apache and Lipan villages. He also fought in the Battle of Palo Duro Canyon in the Red River War (1874), where he brilliantly led 480 cavalrymen and routed a combined Comanche, Cheyenne, Arapaho, and Kiowa forces of about 1,500 braves, killing about 75 of them. Mackenzie's total casualties was one man wounded. He later captured the Indians' winter supplies and captured and slaughtered about two thousand horses and ponies. Without food or sufficient animals, the Indians agreed to return to the reservations in early 1875. Mackenzie experienced similar success in the Black Hawk Wars and subdued the Indians who massacred the 7th Cavalry at Little Big Horn. He was one of the greatest Indian fighters in American history.

Meanwhile, in 1871, Mackenzie took the seventh wound of his career in a battle with Indians on the Staked Plains. This caused him severe pain the rest of his life. Tragically, Mackenzie was severely injured in an accident at Fort Sill, Oklahoma, when he fell from a wagon and landed on his head. This affected his mental health and forced him to retire from the army in 1884 for reasons of insanity. He died at his sister's home on Staten Island, New York, on January 19, 1889, at age forty-eight. He is buried in the West Point Cemetery.

JASPER ADALMORN MALTBY was born November 3, 1826, in Kingsville, Ohio, and was educated in local public schools. He fought in the Mexican War as a private in the 15th U.S. Infantry and was wounded in the Battle of Chapultepec. Discharged in 1848, he moved to Chicago and eventually settled in Galena, Illinois, where he became a master gunsmith. He lived above his shop with his wife and son. Here he invented one of the first telescopic sights.

On December 15, 1861, Maltby returned to the colors as a private in the 45th Illinois (the "Lead Mine Regiment") but was elected its lieutenant colonel eleven days later. He fought at Fort Donelson, where on February 15, 1862, he was wounded in the elbow and both thighs. After a long recovery, he rejoined the army on March 5, 1863, as colonel and commander of the 45th. He took part in the Vicksburg Campaign and the subsequent siege. Attacking the formidable 3rd Louisiana Redan on June 25, he rushed into a crater created when Union engineers detonated 2,200 pounds of gunpowder under Rebel lines. The Confederates rallied more quickly than the Federals thought possible, however, and he and his men were pinned down in the crater. The Rebels rolled artillery shells with short fuses into the crater, smashing the 45th Illinois. Their commander was wounded in the head and right side—wounds from which he never fully recovered.

Maltby was promoted to brigadier general on August 4, 1863. He returned to duty in September and spent the rest of his life on garrison duty in Vicksburg, when he wasn't on medical leave. His brother, William H. Maltby, was a captain in the Confederate artillery. When he was captured, Jasper arranged for him to be sent to Vicksburg, where he remained until he was exchanged.

One author suggested that, despite his personal friendship with Ulysses S. Grant, Maltby was shelved because of a lack of effectiveness. It appears to this author, however, that he was given light duty because of his physical infirmities, caused by his wounds. But the reader can draw his or her own conclusions.

Maltby remained in the Regular Army after the war and was commander of the Western District of Mississippi, which headquartered in Vicksburg. It is unclear if he died of yellow fever or cardiac arrest; in any case, he passed away in Vicksburg on December 12, 1867, at age forty-one. He was buried in Greenwood Cemetery, Galena, Illinois.

JOSEPH KING FENNO MANSFIELD was born in New Haven, Connecticut, on December 22, 1803, but his family settled in Middleton. One of his cousins was Joseph G. Totten, a future Union general and the chief of engineers from 1838 to 1864. Mansfield entered the U.S. Military Academy in 1817, shortly before his 14th birthday, and graduated second in the Class of 1822 (2/40) at age eighteen. Commissioned second lieutenant in the engineers, he was promoted to first lieutenant in 1832 and captain in 1838. He spent most of his pre-Mexico career working on construction projects in the South.

Mansfield distinguished himself in the Mexican War, winning a brevet to major at Fort Brown, to lieutenant colonel at Monterrey, and to colonel at Buena Vista. He was wounded in the leg at Monterrey. His performance was so impressive that he was promoted to colonel and inspector general of the army on May 28, 1853, largely due to the influence of Secretary of War Jefferson Davis.

When the Civil War began, Winfield Scott recommended Robert E. Lee be named commander of the army being raised in Washington, D.C. When he declined the appointment, Scott recommended Mansfield, but Lincoln chose Irvin McDowell instead, because Mansfield was skeptical of the readiness of the volunteer troops, and Lincoln wanted to drive on Richmond as soon as possible. Mansfield's age and lack of political pull were also factors. He was nevertheless appointed brigadier general on May 18, 1861.

After the disaster in the First Battle of Bull Run, Mansfield again hoped to command the Eastern army, but the administration selected George B. McClellan instead. Perhaps for political reasons, McClellan did not offer Mansfield a command. He was posted to Hatteras Inlet, North Carolina, where he remained until the fall of 1862, rising to the command of a division in the VII Corps near Suffolk in July.

Joseph Mansfield was named commander of the XII Corps of the Army of the Potomac on September 15, 1862. Two days later, his corps clashed with the Confederate left flank in the East Woods at Antietam. Controversially, he kept his men in column formation, which was better suited to marching than fighting. It also made the men more exposed to Confederate artillery fire. The fact that half of his 7,200 men were raw recruits did not help. (Mansfield was afraid his green troops would break and run if he spread them out in battle formation.) Shortly after 7 a.m., he mistakenly thought a body of Confederates was Union troops. (Mansfield suffered from poor vision.) He rode into the 10th Maine and shouted at them to stop firing—they were shooting at their own men. A minute or so later, the bluecoats convinced the general he was mistaken—they were Stonewall Jackson's men. At that moment, his horse was shot from under him, and a Rebel bullet slammed into the right side of his chest and came out his back. Bleeding profusely, he was carried to a farmhouse, which had become a field hospital. He died there the next day. He was fifty-eight years old. Alpheus Williams replaced Mansfield as corps commander.

Mansfield was posthumously promoted to major general on March 12, 1863. He was buried in Mortimer Cemetery but was reinterred in Indian Hill Cemetery in Middletown, Connecticut, in 1867. One of his sons, Samuel M. Mansfield, served on his father's staff and emerged from the war as a brevet lieutenant colonel. He remained in the army and retired as a brigadier general.

MAHLON DICKERSON MANSON was born in Piqua, Ohio, on February 20, 1820. His father died when he was three and his family moved to Crawfordsville, Indiana, when he was a child. He became a druggist's clerk at an early age, to help support his family. He studied medicine at the Ohio Medical College in Cincinnati when he could and taught public school for a year in Montgomery County, Indiana. He served as a captain and company commander in the 5th Indiana Infantry Regiment and was with General Scott's army from Vera Cruz to Mexico City. He was mustered out in 1848 and returned to Crawfordsville, where he became a druggist and was elected to the legislature as a Democrat in 1851. He was a strong supporter of Stephen A. Douglas in 1860.

Four days after Fort Sumter surrendered, Manson joined the 10th Indiana Infantry Regiment as a captain. On April 25, 1861, he was promoted to major and then to colonel on September 18. Three days later, at New Albany, Indiana, his horse threw him, and he was severely injured.

When he returned to duty on November 30, he was given command of a brigade, which he led in the Battle of Mill Springs, Kentucky (January 19, 1862) with considerable success. He was promoted to brigadier general on March 26.

General Manson was less fortunate in the Battle of Richmond, Kentucky (August 29–30), where he was wounded in the thigh and captured by Kirby Smith's Confederates. Exchanged two months later, he took command of a division in the Army of Kentucky and played a role in the capture of General John Hunt Morgan in Ohio in July 1863. Advanced to the command of the XXIII Corps, he took part in the defense of Knoxville in the fall of 1863.

Manson was demoted to the command of a brigade in April 1864, which he led during Sherman's drive on Atlanta. On May 14, 1864, during the Battle of Resaca, he received a serious concussion when a shell exploded near him. A piece of the shell tore into his right shoulder and arm, disabling him for life. Unable to resume command, he resigned his commission on December 21. He did not receive a brevet to major general after the war.

Antebellum, Mahlon Manson (who was a Democrat) ran for political office several times—not always successfully. He was elected U.S. Congressman in 1870, state auditor in 1876, lieutenant governor in 1885, and collector of internal revenue. He defeated General Lew Wallace for Congress in 1870 but lost his re-election bid in 1872. He also lost elections for lieutenant governor, secretary of state, and Congress between 1864 to 1868. He died in Frankfort, Indiana, on February 4, 1895, at age seventy-four. He is buried in the Oak Hill Cemetery, Crawfordsville.

RANDOLPH BARNES MARCY was born on April 9, 1812, in Greenwich, Massachusetts, a village abandoned and inundated by the Quabbin Reservoir in 1938. He graduated from West Point in 1832 (29/45) and was commissioned brevet second lieutenant in the 5th U.S. Infantry. He was promoted to second lieutenant (1835), first lieutenant (1837), and captain (1846). He first saw action in the Black Hawk War in Illinois and western

Michigan Territory (now Wisconsin) (1832). Later, he served under Zachary Taylor in northern Mexico in 1846 and fought at Palo Alto and Resaca de la Palma but was then transferred to recruiting duty. He received no brevets.

After the Mexican surrender, Marcy served in Oklahoma and Texas, exploring, mapping, and escorting wagon trains. On one expedition, he found the headwaters of the Red River. He was part of Albert Sidney Johnston's Utah Expedition in 1857 and did a forced march through the Rocky Mountains in winter. His reports attracted the attention of the War Department, which transferred him to Washington, D.C., where he wrote *The Prairie Traveler: A Handbook for Overland Expeditions*. It was published by the U.S. government in 1859 and for decades was considered the indispensable guide to settlers heading for California, the Pacific Northwest, and points on route. In short, he was one of the great explorers of the American West.

After completing his handbook, Marcy was promoted to major in 1859 and transferred to the Paymaster Department. He was serving in the Pacific Northwest when the Civil War began. Marcy returned to the East, was promoted to colonel on August 9, 1861, and was named senior inspector general of the U.S. Army that same day. In the meantime, Marcy's daughter Mary Ellen (called "Nelly") accepted the marriage proposal of future Confederate General A. P. Hill, but her family (i.e., Randolph) objected, so Hill withdrew. Nine different men proposed to her, but she married George B. McClellan in 1860. He became commander of the Army of the Potomac on August 1, 1861, and appointed his father-in-law chief of staff on September 4. Marcy was promoted to brigadier general on September 23.

With Marcy's help, McClellan built a fine army but was defeated by General Lee in the Seven Days Campaign (June 25–July 1, 1862). The Senate allowed Marcy's promotion to expire on July 17, and he reverted to the rank of colonel. McClellan reappointed him on September 13, but Lincoln fired McClellan on November 5. His promotion expired again without Senate action on March 4, 1863, and he again reverted to the rank of colonel. He remained inspector general of the army until he retired in 1881. In 1878, he was promoted to brigadier general for the third time, and this time he was confirmed. Meanwhile, he was brevetted brigadier general and major general in 1868.

General Marcy died at home in West Orange, New Jersey, on November 22, 1887, at age seventy-five. He was more famous for his *Prairie Traveler* than his Civil War career and, through this work, was responsible for saving the lives of thousands of emigrants crossing the American West. He was buried in Riverview Cemetery, Trenton, New Jersey.

GILMAN MARSTON was born on August 20, 1811, in Oxford, New Hampshire, the son of a farmer. He worked his way through college as a schoolteacher and graduated from Kimball Vance Academy (1833), Dartmouth (1837), and from the Harvard Law Department (1840). He set up practice in Exeter, New Hampshire and was elected to the state House of Representatives in 1844—the first of thirteen terms he served in the New Hampshire legislature. He was known for his sharp tongue. Marston joined the Republican Party in 1854 and was elected to Congress in 1858, serving from March 4, 1859, to March 3, 1863. He was a stronger supporter of Abraham Lincoln. He lost his re-election bid in November 1862.

Meanwhile, when the Civil War began, Marston recruited the 2nd New Hampshire Infantry and became its colonel. As part of Burnside's brigade, he fought in the First Battle of Bull Run, where his right arm was shattered by a musket ball. After his wound was dressed, Marston returned to the battle, with an aide leading his horse. He never regained full use of his arm and, although surgeons told him his life depended on it, he refused to let them amputate it. He ordered his aide to shoot the doctors if they tried. He returned to Exeter to recuperate and went back to field duty in September, but was wounded again in December, when the servant of an officer accidentally discharged a pistol and the bullet struck Marston, but it was not a serious injury.

Marston led his regiment in the Peninsula, Seven Days, and Fredericksburg campaigns. He was promoted to brigadier general to date from November 29, 1862, and was given a district command in eastern Maryland, near Washington. He later commanded the infamous Point Lookout prison camp.

In the spring of 1864, Marston was named brigade commander in "Baldy" Smith's XVIII Corps. His command suffered heavy casualties in Grant's disastrous attack on Cold Harbor on June 3. He took command of a division in the Army of the James on June 18 and led it until August 27. He then commanded Union troops on the north side of the James until November 1864, when he was re-elected to Congress. He resigned his commission effective April 20, 1865.

Marston resumed his political and legal career after the war, but without his previous financial success. He was an oddity in the 1860s—an honest politician whose integrity was never questioned. He served in Congress until 1867 (he was defeated for re-election in 1866). He was re-elected to Congress in 1868 and served until 1877 but was defeated for re-election in 1876. President Grant offered him the governorship of Idaho Territory in 1870, but he declined it. In 1889, he was appointed to fill a vacancy in the U.S. Senate, but only served four months until a successor could be elected. He died at home in Exeter on July 3, 1890, at age seventy-eight. He is buried there in Exeter Cemetery.

Although he never married, General Marston loved children. He gave a home to an orphan girl and financed her education. He liked to dump bags of flour with nickels in them on the town square and watch the children scrabble through the pile, looking for the money.

JOHN HENRY MARTINDALE was born in Sandy Hill (now Hudson Falls), New York, on March 20, 1815, the son of a Whig Congressman. He entered the U.S. Military Academy in 1831 and graduated four years later (3/56). In spite of his high class standing, he was not selected for the Corps of Engineers but instead was appointed brevet second lieutenant in the 1st Dragoons. Disappointed, he resigned his commission in 1836 and studied law. He was admitted to the bar in 1838 and set up a practice in Batavia, New York. He was district attorney of Genesee County from 1842 to 1846 and from 1848 to 1851, when he moved to Rochester, New York. He was most famous for his advocacy for the

Tonawanda tribe of western New York. For a time, he was also construction engineer for the Saratoga & Washington Railroad.

When the Civil War began, Martindale advocated using Regular Army officers as drill instructors and letting the first and second classes (i.e., seniors and juniors) at West Point graduate early. Both of his recommendations were adopted. On August 9, 1861, just two weeks after the disaster at Bull Run, Martindale was commissioned brigadier general. He spent the winter of 1861–62 working on improving the defenses of Washington, D.C. The following spring, he was a brigade commander in the Army of the Potomac, fighting in the Peninsular Campaign and the Seven Days battles in General Porter's division. Here, after the Battle of Malvern Hill, he refused Porter's orders to retreat, stating that he would rather surrender than abandon his wounded men. Porter had him court-martialed for insubordination, but he was acquitted and restored to duty as military governor of Washington in November 1862.

Martindale did not receive another field command until May 20, 1864, when he was given a division in the XVIII Corps. He fought in the Battle of Cold Harbor, the Bermuda Hundred Campaign, and the Siege of Petersburg, and briefly commanded the XVIII Corps in July 1864. He contacted tuberculous, however, and he resigned his commission on September 13. In 1866, he was brevetted major general for his gallantry at Malvern Hill.

General Martindale was known for his integrity and character, which was above reproach. After the war, he returned to Rochester and the practice of law. He specialized in handling personal injury cases against the New York Central Railroad. He also served as attorney general of New York (1866–1869). In 1881, he went to Europe on an extended vacation, in hopes of improving his health, but he died in Nice, France, on December 13, at the age of sixty-six. He is buried in Batavia Cemetery, Batavia, New York.

JOHN SANFORD MASON was born in Steubenville, Ohio, on August 21, 1824. The son of a prominent physician and veteran of the War of 1812, he attended local schools and became a cadet at West Point in 1843. Mason graduated in 1847 (9/38) and was commissioned second lieutenant in the 3rd Artillery. He was sent to Mexico as part of the garrison at Tampico, where he contracted yellow fever. After returning to Ohio and recovering, he returned to Mexico and was a commissary officer at Puebla. Here, he experienced a second bout of yellow fever and was sent to New Orleans, where he again recovered.

Young Mason was promoted to first lieutenant in 1850. Antebellum, he served on garrison duty in a variety of posts, including Fort Adams, Rhode Island; Fort Yuma, Arizona Territory; and several garrisons in California. He was at Fort Vancouver, Washington Territory, when the Civil War began. He was promoted to captain in the 11th U.S. Infantry in May.

Mason was named colonel of the 4th Ohio Infantry on October 3, 1861. He served in the Western Virginia Campaign and in the Shenandoah and was transferred to the Army of the Potomac in the spring of 1862. He fought in the Peninsula Campaign and the Seven Days battles, as well as the Battle of Antietam, after which he was promoted to brigadier general on November 29. A hard fighter, he was commended for his bravery at Fredericksburg, where he was wounded.

John Mason's health was never robust after his yellow fever episodes, and it took him several months to recover from his Fredericksburg wounds. Even when he returned to active duty in April 1863, he was not physically ready for active campaigning. He commanded Camp Thomas, a training facility in north Columbus, Ohio, for more than a year. On March 7, 1865, he was named commander of the District of Arizona, which was part of the Department of the Pacific. He was there when the war ended. Mustered out of volunteer service in April 1866, he remained in the army as a major in the infantry. During the next twenty years, he served in a variety of posts, mainly in the West, and was promoted to lieutenant colonel (Regular Army) in 1873. He became a colonel and commander of the 9th U.S. Infantry at Fort Whipple, Arizona, in 1883. He left the army in 1888, after forty years' service, when he reached the mandatory retirement age of sixty-four, and settled in Washington, D.C.

As the result of a stroke which caused general paralysis, General Mason died at home on November 29, 1897. He was buried in Arlington National Cemetery. One of his two sons, Charles W. Mason, became a colonel of infantry. The other, a first lieutenant in the 9th Cavalry, died from exposure during the Sioux War in South Dakota in 1891.

CHARLES LEOPOLD MATTHIES was born **KARL LEOPOLD MATTHIES** on May 31, 1824, in Bromberg, Prussia (now Bydgoszcz, Poland). He attended the University of Halle and worked on his father's farm until 1848, when he joined the Prussian Army and helped suppress revolutionaries. The following year, he immigrated to the United States and settled in Burlington, Iowa, where he established a successful liquor business.

On May 14, 1861, Matthies was commissioned captain in the 1st Iowa Infantry. He became its lieutenant colonel on July 23 and was promoted to colonel of the 5th Iowa on May 23, 1862. He led the regiment in Missouri in 1861, including Island No. 10. Later, he fought in the Siege of Corinth and the Battle of Iuka, where the 1st Iowa lost 217 men killed, wounded, or captured, out of 482 engaged. He was given command of a brigade in the XVI Corps in December.

Colonel Matthies was a good brigade commander. He took part in Grant's various Vicksburg Campaigns and was promoted to brigadier general on April 4, 1863. He led a brigade in Sherman's XV Corps from Port Gibson to Jackson, Mississippi, to Vicksburg, which surrendered on July 4. Transferred to the Western Front after the Chickamauga disaster, he fought in the Siege of Chattanooga, including the celebrated attack on Missionary Ridge (November 25), where he was severely wounded when a Confederate bullet struck him in the head. Although he attempted to return to field duty in 1864 and did briefly command a division in the early stages of the Atlanta Campaign, he was forced to resign on May 16. He returned home to Burlington, where he was elected to the Iowa Senate. He passed away at age forty-four in Burlington on October 16, 1868, and was buried there in Aspen Grove Cemetery.

JOHN MCARTHUR was born in Erskine, Renfrewshire, Scotland, on November 17, 1826. His father was a blacksmith, a trade adopted by his son.

He emigrated to the United States when he was twenty-three and settled in Chicago, where he became the owner of the Excelsior Iron Works. He was quite successful and also joined the Chicago Highland Guards, a militia unit. He was captain of the company when the Civil War began.

McArthur was named colonel of the 12th Illinois Infantry on May 3, 1861, a ninety-day unit which garrisoned in Cairo and never left the state. McArthur missed some time because his right shoulder was dislocated when his horse threw him. The 12th was re-mustered as a three-year regiment in August.

After a somewhat poor start, McArthur distinguished himself on virtually all the major battlefields on the Western Front. He was elevated to brigade commander on January 31, 1862. His command was dubbed "the Highland Brigade" and wore Scottish caps. At Fort Donelson, it suffered heavy losses in the Confederate breakout attack of February 15, but McArthur withdrew it in good order. He was promoted to brigadier general on March 22, 1862. He succeeded General W. H. L. Wallace as acting division commander when he was mortally wounded at Shiloh on April 6, although McArthur had to leave the field before the day was out after a Confederate musket ball slammed into his right foot. He returned on April 9, but some weeks later was superseded as divisional commander by Thomas J. McKean and was briefly without a command. He was given another brigade, which he directed in the Siege of Corinth. He led a division in Ord's corps at Iuka and the Second Battle of Corinth. He participated in Grant's various unsuccessful attempts to take Vicksburg and the final, successful campaign, and the subsequent siege. He served as commandant of the city after it surrendered until August 1864, when his division was transferred to Missouri.

As part of the XVI Corps, General McArthur took part in the pursuit of Sterling Price during his disastrous Missouri Campaign of 1864. His division was then transferred to Tennessee, where it played a major role in the virtual destruction of the Confederate Army of Tennessee at Nashville on December 16, 1864. He was brevetted major general after this battle.

McArthur's last campaign was focused on Mobile, Alabama, which fell on April 12, 1865. He led his men in the Battle of Fort Blakeley (April 2–9), which surrendered after heavy fighting. He was stationed at Selma, Alabama, after the Confederate armies surrendered. He was mustered out of the service on August 24.

Highly esteemed in Chicago, McArthur held a number of jobs in the Windy City after the war, including commissioner of public works, city postmaster, and general manager of the Chicago and Vert Island Stone Company. He was by no means universally successful in civilian life as he was in the Union Army. His iron works failed, he was in charge of the fire department during the Great Chicago Fire of 1871, and was involved with a bank that failed and cost the Federal Government a severe financial loss. By judicial decree, McArthur was held personally responsible.

General John McArthur died in Chicago on May 15, 1906, at age seventy-nine. He was buried in Rosehill Cemetery, north Chicago.

GEORGE ARCHIBALD MCCALL was born in Philadelphia on March 16, 1802, a descendent of the famous Schuyler family. He entered West Point in 1818 and graduated in 1822 (26/40). Commissioned second lieutenant in the 1st Infantry, he served thirty-one years in the Regular Army before the Civil War began. He spent much of his time in Florida and particularly loved Pensacola. He fought in the Second Seminole War and distinguished himself in northern Mexico, earning a brevet majority for gallantry at Palo Alto and to lieutenant colonel at Resaca de la Palma. He also fought at Vera Cruz. Meanwhile, he was promoted to first lieutenant and captain, Regular Army, in 1829 and 1836, respectively. McCall also served on the Western frontier, including the Indian Territory and New Mexico. He  became a major (substantive rank) in 1847 and was appointed to the staff of the inspector general of the army with the rank of colonel in 1850.

George McCall retired from the army in 1853 and became a farmer but returned to the colors in May 1861. He was commissioned major general in the Pennsylvania Militia and was commissioned brigadier general of volunteers on August 7. He helped organize the famous Pennsylvania Reserve Division, which later became the 2nd Division, I Corps, Army of the Potomac. Later it was redesignated 2nd Division, V Corps.

General McCall was a conspicuous officer but was too old for this war. He fought in the Peninsular Campaign and the Seven Days battles, where he was heavily engaged north of the Chickahominy River. He saw particularly heavy fighting at Frayser's Farm on June 30, 1862, where his division held its line against several Confederate attacks but lost 3,180 men killed, wounded, or captured out of seven thousand engaged. Wounded (possibly by Union fire), McCall refused to leave the field. He was captured as night was falling when he accidentally rode into the lines of the 47th Virginia. He was incarcerated at Libby Prison in Richmond, where he suffered a relapse of a severe illness. He was exchanged for Confederate General Simon Bolivar Buckner in August 1862.

George McCall never regained his health. He found it impossible to return to active duty or even stay in the saddle. Suffering from congestion of the brain and other maladies, he resigned for health reasons on August 15, 1863. He retired to his estate, "Belair," in West Chester, Pennsylvania, where he died on February 25, 1868, at age sixty-five. He is buried in Christ Church Cemetery, Philadelphia.

GEORGE BRINTON "LITTLE MAC" MCCLELLAN was born in Philadelphia on December 3, 1826, the son of a prominent surgeon who founded Jefferson Medical College, which is now part of Thomas Jefferson University in Philadelphia. George entered the University of Pennsylvania as a medical student in 1840 at age fourteen. He dropped out in 1842 to enter West Point, from which he graduated in 1846 (2/59). He was commissioned brevet second lieutenant in the engineers.

After a brief tour of duty at West Point, McClellan was sent to northern Mexico, where he came down with dysentery and malaria. Considered an "up and coming" young officer, he was transferred to Winfield Scott's staff. He took part in the Siege of Vera Cruz, was brevetted first lieutenant for Contreras and Churubusco, and to captain for Chapultepec.

After Mexico fell, McClellan returned to West Point as commander of an engineer company. Later, he performed routine garrison duties at Fort Delaware; Fort Smith, Arkansas; and points in Texas. He also translated a manual on bayonet tactics from the original French. In 1853, he took part in the Pacific Railroad surveys and in scouting passes in the Cascade Mountains. He also went on a secret mission to scout the defenses of the Dominican Republic for Secretary of War Jefferson Davis, who became a friend.

In 1856, McClellan went to Europe as an official observer to the Crimean War. Here he was severely bruised when he was struck by a piece of spent shrapnel. When he returned home, he invented "the McClellan saddle," which was adapted from a Hungarian saddle. It was used by the U.S. cavalry for several decades.

McClellan resigned his commission in January 1857 and became vice president and chief engineer of the Illinois Central Railroad. He became president of the Ohio and Mississippi Railroad in 1860. That same year, he married Mary Ellen "Nelly" Marcy, a former fiancée of his good friend, A. P. Hill.

McClellan was frustrated and bored with civilian life. When the Civil War began, he quickly volunteered and was commissioned major general in the Ohio Militia on April 23, 1861. On the recommendation of Winfield Scott, Lincoln (who had not yet met him) promoted him to major general, Regular Army, on May 14.

McClellan's first campaign was in the western counties of Virginia (now West Virginia), where he won a brilliant victory at Philippi (June 3), completely routed the Confederates he did not capture, won another major victory at Rich Mountain on July 11, and did much to secure West Virginia for the Union. On July 25—four days after the Union disaster at the First Bull Run—he was placed in charge of the Military Division of the Potomac. This became the Army of the Potomac on August 17. He was named general-in-chief of the armies of the United States on November 1, 1861.

General McClellan was intellectually brilliant, possessed personal charisma, and was a highly competent administrator and an organizational genius. He created, organized, and trained the Army of the Potomac and turned it into arguably the most formidable army in American history, and increased its size from 50,000 to 168,000 by November 1862. He did not, however, know how to use it to anything like its maximum potential. McClellan experienced considerable success against Joseph E. Johnston, forced him out of the Peninsula, severely defeated him in the Battle of Seven Pines (May 31–June 1, 1862), and pushed to within six miles of Richmond. Against Robert E. Lee, he was less successful. He was defeated in the Seven Days battles, in which his army barely escaped from an army half its size. Later, in Maryland, a Confederate security blunder handed the Federals a golden opportunity to destroy Lee's Army of Northern Virginia, but McClellan was unable to take advantage of it. After a somewhat indecisive Union victory at Antietam (September 17), Lee's army was able to escape.

George McClellan's relationship with Abraham Lincoln was always tenuous. Lincoln relieved him as general-in-chief on March 11, 1862, and after he failed to destroy Lee's army after Antietam, the president relieved him of his command on November 7, 1862. He resigned his commission the next day.

The Democratic Party nominated McClellan for president in 1864 and it appeared for a time that he would win the election. (Abraham Lincoln thought so.) But after the fall of Atlanta (September 2), the Northern people saw "the light at the end of the tunnel" and handily re-elected the president, 55 to 45 percent. McClellan only carried three states against twenty-two for Lincoln.

After the war, McClellan and his family traveled in Europe. He returned to the states in 1868 and worked on engineering projects in New York City. He became chief engineer of the New York City Department of Docks in 1870 and president of the Atlantic & Great Western Railroad. To McClellan's surprise, the New Jersey Democratic Party nominated him for governor in 1877. He defeated the Republican candidate 97,837 to 85,094 and served from January 15, 1878, to January 18, 1881. A highly competent governor, his term was characterized by cautious, conservative spending, the creation of an experimental station to improve agriculture, and improvements in education and the New Jersey National Guard. He also cut state taxes in half and then abolished them entirely.

McClellan sought the post of secretary of war in Grover Cleveland's cabinet in 1884 but was blocked by a U.S. senator whom he defeated in the gubernatorial election of 1877. He spent his last years traveling and writing. He died unexpectedly of a heart attack in Orange, New Jersey, on October 29, 1885, at age fifty-eight. He was buried in Riverview Cemetery, Trenton, New Jersey.

JOHN ALEXANDER MCCLERNAND was born on May 30, 1812, in rural Breckinridge County, Kentucky, but his family moved to Shawneetown, Illinois, when he was a young child. Mostly self-educated, he was admitted to the bar in 1832, the same year he served in the Black Hawk War as a private.

After the war, he returned home, established a law practice, and became founder and editor of the *Shawneetown Democrat* in 1835. He was elected to the legislature, serving in 1836 and from 1840 to 1843. Noted for his bombastic oratory and his dislike of abolitionists, he was a Jacksonian Democrat and strong political ally of Stephen A. Douglas. He was also a friend of fellow Illinois lawyer Abraham Lincoln, with whom he served in the Black Hawk War, the legislature, and in Congress. Mrs. Lincoln and Mrs. McClernand were also personal friends.

McClelland served in the U.S. House of Representatives from 1843 to 1851 but declined to run for re-election in 1850. Back in Illinois, he developed a lucrative law practice and successfully engaged in land speculation. When Congressman Thomas L. Harris died in 1859, McClelland was chosen to succeed him. As the nation plunged toward Civil War, he was a strong advocate of remaining in the Union.

When the war began, McClernand raised an infantry brigade, and his friend Lincoln commissioned him brigadier general on August 6, 1861. (Southern Illinois was an area of mixed feelings about the war and the idea of preserving the Union, and Lincoln correctly believed that McClernand might be an effective recruiter there.) He was eventually assigned to the Department of the Missouri, which was commanded by Ulysses S. Grant. He played a credible role in the marginal Union defeat in the Battle of Belmont on November 7, during which his head was grazed by a Confederate bullet.

McClernand was less successful at Fort Donelson, where his division was essentially routed, although (according to his own reports), he was the hero of the battle. He was promoted to major general on March 22, 1862.

John McClernand often took credit for the achievements of other generals and conspired to replace Grant as commander of the Army of the Tennessee. He took advantage of his friendship with Lincoln to communicate directly with the commander-in-chief and criticize his superiors, including Grant. Meanwhile, he assumed command of the XIII Corps in December 1862 and, on January 4, 1863, took charge of the Army of the Mississippi. He led it well in the Battle of Arkansas Post, where he directed thirty thousand Federals against five thousand Confederates (January 9–11). Although his tactical direction of the battle was hardly perfect, he captured the entire garrison, as well as seventeen cannons.

In the meantime, General Sherman and Admiral David Porter convinced Grant that McClernand was incompetent. With the concurrence of Henry Halleck, the general-in-chief of Union forces, the Army of the Mississippi was dissolved on or about January 19, and McClernand reverted to the command of the XIII Corps. His leadership was poor in Grant's last, successful Vicksburg Campaign, and it was especially bad during the Battle of Champion Hill (May 16) and in the May 22 assault on Vicksburg. Grant sacked him for insubordination on June 19, and he was succeeded by Edward O. C. Ord.

Lincoln restored McClernand to the command of the XIII Corps on February 20, 1864. It was now part of the Department of the Gulf. General McClernand was stricken with malaria and General Thomas E. G. Ransom led the two divisions of the XIII that participated in the Red River Campaign, although McClernand was in command from April 27 to May 1. He resigned his commission on November 30, 1864.

After the war, General McClernand lived in Springfield, Illinois. He was elected district judge in 1870. He was unable to duplicate his antebellum financial success and was forced to apply for an Army pension, which was granted in 1896. He received $80 per month, and $100 per month in 1900.

After a lengthy illness, General McClernand died in Springfield, on September 20, 1900, at age eighty-eight. He is buried there in the Oak

Ridge Cemetery. His son, Edward John McClernand, (1848–1926) graduated from West Point in 1870, fought in the Indian Wars and in the Philippines, and earned the Congressional Medal of Honor. He retired as a brigadier general in 1901.

ALEXANDER MCDOWELL MCCOOK was born in Columbiana County, Ohio, on April 22, 1831. Of Scottish-Irish ancestry, his grandfather fought in the Irish Rebellion of 1798 and fled to America after it was defeated. One of the 14 "Fighting McCooks," his brothers included Union Generals Daniel McCook, Jr., and Robert Latimer McCook. His brother Edwin Stanton McCook and his cousins, Edward M. McCook and Anson G. McCook also became Union generals, but by brevet only. Alexander was the highest-ranking member of the family.

McCook entered West Point in 1847 and graduated in 1852 (30/43). He was commissioned brevet second lieutenant in the 3rd U.S. Infantry and was sent to New Mexico, where he fought Apache and Utes. Transferred back to West Point, he was an assistant instructor of infantry tactics when the Civil War broke out. Meanwhile, he was promoted to second lieutenant (1854), first lieutenant (1858), and captain, Regular Army (May 14, 1861). He was named commander of the 1st Ohio Infantry and was promoted to colonel of volunteers on April 16.

McCook was openly sympathetic to his colleagues in the Regular Army who "went South," saying he would have left the U.S. Army and joined Ohio if she had seceded. He nevertheless adhered to the Union and fought in the First Battle of Bull Run in July 1861, where his younger brother, Charles M. McCook, was killed in action. Two of his other brothers were later killed, as was his father, who fell at Buffington Island, Ohio, fighting John Hunt Morgan in July 1863. Meanwhile, Alexander McCook was stationed in the Washington defenses after the Manassas disaster. He was promoted to brigadier general effective September 3 and given command of a brigade in Buell's Army of the Ohio. Advanced to divisional command in October, he helped capture Nashville (February 1862), fought at Shiloh on the second day (April 7) and in the subsequent Siege of Corinth (April-May). He was promoted to major general on July 19 and assumed command of the I Corps, Army of the Ohio, on September 29.

General McCook took part in the Battle of Perryville, where his corps was pushed back a mile by the outnumbered Confederates and performed rather poorly. Transferred to the command of the Right Wing of the XIV Corps, his command suffered heavy casualties at Stones River. Named commander of the XX Corps in the newly formed Army of the Cumberland in January 1863, he was held partially responsible for the debacle at Chickamauga on September 20, where his corps was routed. A pro-slavery Democrat, he also aroused the hatred of Secretary of War Edwin Stanton. He was relieved of his command and court-martialed—at least partially for political reasons—but was acquitted. He was unemployed for almost a year, but when Confederate General Early threatened Washington in July 1864, he was rescued from professional obscurity because the Lincoln administration needed every veteran combat commander it could get. He successfully defended Fort Stevens and was largely responsible for saving the capital. Then he was put back on the shelf. In March 1865, after months of unemployment and near the end of the war, he was given command of the District of Eastern Arkansas.

Alexander McCook resigned his volunteer commission in October 1865 and once again became a captain in the Regular Army. In 1867, he was promoted to lieutenant colonel of the 25th U.S. Infantry. He spent most of the Reconstruction era in Texas. From 1875 to 1880, he was aide-de-camp to the general-in-chief, William T. Sherman. Promoted to colonel in 1880, he was named commander of the 6th U.S. Infantry Regiment (1880–1886). Later, he commanded Fort Leavenworth (1886–1890), the Department of Arizona (1890–1893) and the Department of Colorado (1893–1895). He was promoted to brigadier general in 1890 and to major general in 1894. He retired in 1895 but was recalled to active duty in 1898, to lead an investigation of the War Department's performance in the Spanish-American War. He retired again in 1899.

General McCook suffered a stroke and died in the home of his daughter in Dayton, Ohio, on June 12, 1903. He was seventy-two years old. He was interred in the Spring Grove Cemetery in Cincinnati, Ohio.

DANIEL MCCOOK, JR., was the brother of Generals Alexander and Robert McCook and the cousin of General Edward McCook. He was born in Carrollton, Ohio, on July 22, 1834. He graduated from LaGrange College in Alabama and then returned to Ohio in 1858, where he studied law in Steubenville. Afterward, McCook moved to Kansas, where he helped form a law firm, along with William T. Sherman, Hugh B. Ewing, and Thomas Ewing, Jr. All four would become Union generals. Meanwhile, McCook joined the Kansas Militia.

When the Civil War began, Daniel McCook accepted a captaincy in the 1st Kansas Infantry. He distinguished himself in the Battle of Wilson's Creek, where his regiment suffered 50 percent casualties. In November, he became assistant adjutant general (and de facto chief of staff) of the 2nd Division of the Army of the Ohio, which was commanded by his brother, Alexander. He fought at Shiloh on the second day (April 7, 1862). That summer, he returned to Ohio and, at Camp Dennison near Cincinnati, helped form the 52nd Ohio Infantry. He was promoted to colonel on July 15. Mustered into Federal service in August, McCook's regiment fought in the Battle of Richmond, Kentucky. McCook advanced to brigade command in September and fought at Perryville, where he performed well. Detached to guard wagon trains, he missed the Battle of Stones River but took part in the Battles of Chickamauga and Missionary Ridge, as well as the Siege of Chattanooga and the relief of Burnside at Knoxville.

On June 27, 1864, during the Atlanta Campaign, McCook's former law partner, General Sherman, chose his brigade to lead the assault on the Dead Angle of Kennesaw Mountain. Recognizing that the odds against him were horrible, McCook recited Thomas Macaulay's poem "Horatius" to his men before the attack. Just as he reached the top of the enemy's works, a Confederate shot him through the right lung.

The desperately wounded officer was taken to his brother George's home in Steubenville, where he received his promotion to brigadier general on July 16, 1864. He died the next day. Had he lived five more days, he would have been thirty years old. General McCook was buried in Spring Grove Cemetery, Cincinnati, Ohio.

EDWARD MOODY MCCOOK was born in Steubenville, Ohio, on June 15, 1833. One of the "Fighting McCooks," he was the brother of Brevet Brigadier General Anson C. McCook and the first cousin of Generals Alexander, Daniel, and Robert McCook, and Brevet Brigadier General Edwin S. McCook.

As a young man, Edward moved to Kansas Territory and became a lawyer. He took part in the Pike's Peak Gold Rush in 1859 and was elected to the Kansas Territorial legislature that same year. He was a successful attorney until May 1861, when he joined the 1st U.S. Cavalry as a second lieutenant in the Regular Army. In late September, he became a major in the 2nd Indiana Cavalry and served on the Western Front. He was promoted to lieutenant colonel in February 1862 and to colonel after Shiloh. He led a cavalry brigade in the Heartland Campaign and fought in the Battle of Perryville. He was wounded in the head in December but recovered quickly. He directed a mounted division at Chickamauga. McCook treated Southern civilians harshly and delighted in destroying civilian property.

He was promoted to brigadier general on April 30, 1864, and in late July, during the Atlanta Campaign, he tried to destroy the Macon & Western Railroad. One of his objectives was to free the Union prisoners held at Andersonville. He was thoroughly defeated by Confederate General Joseph Wheeler at the Battle of Brown's Mill on July 30. McCook (who had 3,600 troops) lost 950 men, two guns, and 1,200 horses. He fared better in the Tennessee Campaign of 1864, where Hood's Confederate Army of Tennessee was virtually destroyed.

In March and April 1865, McCook led a division in Wilson's Cavalry Corps. He fought in the Battle of Selma, where Nathan Bedford Forrest was finally crushed. Confederate Colonel George W. Scott surrendered the last Southern troops in Florida to McCook on May 13, 1865.

Edward McCook was mustered out of the service on January 15, 1866, two days after he was brevetted major general. He served as U.S. Minister to the Kingdom of Hawaii (1866–68) and, in 1869, was appointed governor of Colorado Territory by President Grant. Here, he was unpopular and was removed by a citizens' petition in 1873. Grant reappointed him in 1874 but he was removed again in 1875. He then retired from public life. He was, however, highly successful in business, land speculation, mining, and European telephone investments. He died in Chicago on September 9, 1909, at age seventy-six. He is buried in Union Cemetery-Beatty Park, Steubenville.

ROBERT LATIMER MCCOOK—another of the Fighting McCooks—was born in New Lisbon (then Lisbon), Ohio, on December 28, 1827. He attended local public schools, studied law, and set up a successful practice at Steubenville and Cincinnati. When the Civil War began, McCook organized the 9th Ohio Infantry. It was largely a German unit, leading McCook to remark that he was nothing more than a clerk "for a thousand Dutchmen!" He became the regiment's colonel on May 8 and led it in the West Virginia Campaign of 1861. He led a brigade in the Union victory at Carnifix Ferry on September 10.

Transferred to the Army of the Ohio that November, McCook distinguished himself in the Battle of Mill Springs in January 1862, where he led the bayonet charge which routed the Confederates. McCook, however, was shot in the right leg below the knee. This action led to his promotion to brigadier general on March 22, 1862. He was still in Cincinnati, recovering from his wound, at the time.

McCook returned to duty too soon. He found that he could still not ride a horse, so he rode in a wagon. On August 5, near Huntsville, Alabama, he allowed himself to become separated from the main body of his brigade. Here, he was ambushed by Confederate partisan rangers, led by Captain Frank B. Gurley. The captain called upon McCook to surrender, but he grabbed the reins of the wagon and tried to escape, so Gurley shot him through the abdomen. In intense pain, General McCook died on August 6, 1862, at age thirty-four. He never expressed any bitterness or animosity toward Gurley, who was later captured, treated harshly, tried for murder, and found guilty. He was never executed, despite the wishes of Judge Advocate General Holt. President Lincoln confirmed the sentence but would not authorize the execution, probably because General Grant wanted the matter dropped, which is eventually what happened. Gurley became a county sheriff and lived until 1920. Meanwhile, the 9th Ohio desolated the surrounding area in retaliation for McCook's death. McCook's body was interred in the Spring Grove Cemetery, Cincinnati.

IRVIN MCDOWELL was born in Columbus, Ohio, on October 15, 1818. He attended the College de Troyes in France before being admitted to the United States Military Academy in 1834. He graduated in 1838 (23/45) and was commissioned brevet second lieutenant of artillery. He was promoted to second lieutenant a week later and became a first lieutenant in 1842. He taught tactics at West Point from 1841 to 1845, was an aide-de-camp to General Wood in the Mexican War, and was brevetted captain for his actions in the Battle of Buena Vista. He spent the interwar years as a staff officer in the adjutant general's office in Washington, D.C., and mostly dealt with logistics and supplies.

He was a close friend of the general-in-chief, Winfield Scott, but his patron was Salmon P. Chase, former governor of Ohio and Lincoln's secretary of the treasury. Thanks to Chase, he was promoted to brigadier general, Regular Army, on May 14, 1861, and commander of the Army of Northeast Virginia shortly after. He was charged with the task of invading the Confederacy and capturing Richmond, although he had absolutely no command experience and, with his sizable stomach, he certainly did not look the part of a great commander. He also was sometimes consumed by nervous energy, which caused his face to flush and his speech to thicken. Although he did not drink, strangers sometimes thought he was intoxicated. In addition, he sometimes spoke unnecessarily sharply or harshly to subordinates. In short, he did not inspire his troops or his subordinates.

McDowell spent two months preparing the Army of Northeast Virginia for the invasion of Virginia. Although he knew his green troops were not ready to assume the offensive, he gave in to demands by politicians, editors, and General Scott that he advance, and he was thoroughly defeated in the

First Battle of Bull Run on July 21. He faced harsh criticism, rumor mongers asserted that he was a Southern spy, and he feared that he might be discharged, but President Lincoln would not do this. The following month, he was quietly demoted to the command of a division in the Army of the Potomac. When the I Corps was formed on March 14, 1862, McDowell became its commander and was promoted to major general on March 16. He defended Washington while McClellan fought the Peninsula Campaign and the Seven Days battles. McClellan (a Democrat) and McDowell (a Republican sympathizer) did not get along. In the subsequent Second Bull Run Campaign, McDowell directed the III Corps of John Pope's Army of Virginia. He performed well at Cedar Mountain but poorly at the Second Bull Run, where he was indecisive, disposed his troops poorly, did not communicate with his adjacent and subordinate commanders, and was generally inept. It was his last battle.

General McDowell agreed to testify against Fitz John Porter, a McClellan supporter who was the scapegoat for the disaster. He testified for four days in January 1863, deliberately misled the court, and may have perjured himself. This may have been part of the deal to let McDowell off the hook. (He and Pope were exonerated for any wrongdoing in February.) In any case, he was not court-martialed, but he was on the shelf for two years. He was named commander of the Department of the Pacific in 1864 and the Department of California in 1865. Later, he commanded the Department of the East (1868–1872), the Military Division of the South (1872–1876), and the Division of the Pacific (1876–1882). In 1882, Congress passed a law making sixty-four the mandatory retirement age for military officers. McDowell retired later that year after forty-eight years of continuous service.

General McDowell fell in love with San Francisco and spent the rest of his life there, engaging in landscaping and gardening. He succumbed to a heart attack on May 4, 1885, at age sixty-six. He is buried in San Francisco National Cemetery.

GEORGE FRANCIS MCGINNIS was born on March 19, 1826, in Boston, Massachusetts. His mother died when he was an infant, and he lived with an aunt in Hampden, Maine, until he was eleven; then his father (a hatter) took him to Chillicothe, Ohio. When the Mexican War broke out in 1846, he

joined in the 2nd Ohio Infantry as a first lieutenant and was part of Scott's Army of Mexico when Mexico City fell. The regiment suffered seventy-four dead to guerillas and disease. McGinnis was discharged as a captain in 1848. He settled in Indianapolis in 1850 and pursued the trade of hatter until 1861, when the Civil War commenced.

McGinnis joined the 11th Indiana Infantry as a private two days after Fort Sumter surrendered. He was promoted to captain the next day (April 16), to lieutenant colonel on August 31, and to colonel on September 3, when the original regimental commander, Lew Wallace, was promoted. Meanwhile, he took part in the early operations in western Virginia. Transferred to the Western Front, McGinnis distinguished himself at Fort Donelson and Shiloh, where he temporarily commanded a brigade. He also led his regiment in the Siege of Corinth and the various Vicksburg campaigns. He also commanded a brigade in eastern Arkansas (November 1862–January 1863) and was promoted to brigadier general on April 4, 1863. He led a brigade in Grant's last Vicksburg Campaign and earned special praise for his leadership at Champion Hill (May 16). During the Siege of Vicksburg, he commanded a sector near Fort Garrott.

McGinnis's association with Lew Wallace and John McClernand seems to have sidetracked his career. He was assigned to the Department of the Gulf, where he held a number of unimportant territorial commands. At the end of the war, he was in charge of the "Forces on the White River," a brigade-sized formation guarding the mouth of the White River. He was mustered out of the service at Camden, Arkansas, on August 24, 1865.

George McGinnis established a fiduciary business (managing other people's money) after the war. He also served a term as auditor of Marion County, Indiana. In 1900, he became postmaster of Indianapolis. He retired in 1905 and died in Indianapolis on May 29, 1910, at age eight-four, and is buried there in the Crown Hill Cemetery.

JOHN BAILLIE MCINTOSH was born on June 5, 1829, at Fort Brooke (now Tampa), Florida Territory. His father, James S. McIntosh, was a

Regular Army officer who was a colonel and brigade commander when he was mortally wounded at Molino del Rey during the Mexican War in 1847. John, meanwhile, sought an appointment to West Point but was unsuccessful because of a War Department policy which stipulated that only one family member could attend the Military Academy at one time, and John's brother James was already there. John McIntosh served as a midshipman aboard the *USS Saratoga* during the war with Mexico. He resigned at the end of the war and settled in New Brunswick, New Jersey, where he engaged in business with his father-in-law.

McIntosh joined the Union Army on June 8, 1861, as a second lieutenant (Regular Army) in the 2nd U.S. Cavalry. He was not promoted to first lieutenant for over a year. He served on the Eastern Front and fought in the Seven Days battles, after which he was brevetted major. He also fought in the Battle of Antietam, after which he was promoted to colonel and named commander of the 3rd Pennsylvania Cavalry (November 15, 1862). He was severely wounded near Hartwood Church on Christmas Day, 1862; he was sent home to recuperate.

After he partially recovered, McIntosh returned to the Army of the Potomac, where he was given command of a cavalry brigade in March 1863. Despite being ill, he performed well and was officially praised for his leadership in the Chancellorsville and Gettysburg campaigns. In September, he was injured when his horse fell on him. As a result, he was placed on light duty, commanding a cavalry depot near Washington, D.C.

John McIntosh rejoined the Army of the Potomac on May 2, 1864, and fought in the Overland Campaign. He was promoted to brigadier general on July 21. A tough warrior, his luck ran out during the Third Battle of Winchester on September 19. While he was leading dismounted skirmishers forward, he took a bullet in the right leg. Surgeons were forced to amputate the limb six inches below the knee that night. Although he never let his wounds affect his cheerful nature, McIntosh was finished as a field commander. When he returned to duty in February 1865, he was placed on a court-martial board. He was brevetted major general in 1866.

John McIntosh was discharged from volunteer service on April 30, 1866, but was offered a lieutenant colonelcy in the 42nd Infantry Regiment, which he accepted. Later, he was governor of the Soldiers' Home in Washington, D.C. He never really got over the loss of his leg, however, and suffered chronic pain. In March 1869, he applied for retirement, which was granted in July 1870, and he was discharged as a brigadier general. Meanwhile, in June 1869, he became superintendent of Indian Affairs in California. After he was granted his retirement, he returned to New Brunswick, where he died on June 29, 1888, at age fifty-nine. He was buried there in Elmwood Cemetery.

McIntosh's brother, James McIntosh, was a brigadier general in the Confederate Army, a fact John considered a blot on the family name. James was killed in action at Pea Ridge in March 1862.

THOMAS JEFFERSON MCKEAN was born in Burlington, Pennsylvania, on August 21, 1810. He became a cadet at the U.S. Military Academy in 1827 and graduated in 1831 (19/33). Commissioned brevet second lieutenant in the 4th U.S. Infantry, he was promoted to second lieutenant later that year and served three years of garrison duty in Baton Rouge, New Orleans, and Bay St. Louis, Mississippi, but resigned in 1834, and became a civil engineer.

McKean served in the Second Seminole War as adjutant of the 1st Pennsylvania Volunteers (1837–38). He moved to Iowa Territory in 1840 and was a member of the Constitutional Convention of 1844. During the Mexican War, he enlisted in the 15th U.S. Infantry as a private in April 1847 but was quickly promoted to sergeant major in May. He was offered a commission in the 2nd Dragoons the following month but turned it down and spent the entire war as an enlisted man. He took part in Winfield Scott's drive on Mexico City and was wounded in the Battle of Churubusco. He was back on duty in time to take part in the capture of Mexico City (September 13–14, 1847). He was discharged in August 1848 and returned to Iowa and civil engineering. He became chief engineer of the Dubuque and Keokuk Railroad, commissioner to locate the Seat of Government of Iowa (1855) and was elected sheriff of Linn County in 1859. He also engaged in agriculture.

In June 1861, after the Civil War began, McKean joined the Union Army as a paymaster. He was transferred to the cavalry in the Department of the Gulf in September and was placed in charge of Prisoner of War camps in Missouri in November. He was promoted to brigadier general of volunteers on November 21. He was commandant of Jefferson City from December 1861 to March 1862.

General McKean was given command of a division in the Army of the Tennessee in April 1862, just after the Battle of Shiloh. He took part in the Siege of Corinth and the Second Battle of Corinth (October 3–4) but was relieved as a division commander in December. Apparently, he was physically not up to an active field command. From 1863 to 1865, he directed numerous territorial commands in Missouri, Nebraska Territory, southern Kansas, western Florida, southern Alabama, and south Louisiana. He was discharged on July 30, 1865, and brevetted major general in 1866.

McKean returned to Marion, Iowa, where he became a farmer. He served as mayor of Marion from 1865 to 1869 and was a Ulysses S. Grant delegate to the Republican National Convention in 1868. As a reward, he was offered the job of pension agent for eastern Iowa but declined it for health reasons. His last months were characterized by general paralysis, and he was completely helpless. He died in Marion on April 19, 1870, at age fifty-nine, and is buried there in Oak Shade Cemetery.

JUSTUS MCKINSTRY was born on July 6, 1814, in Hudson, Columbia County, New York. His family moved to Detroit when he was a child, and his father was quite successful. Justus was admitted to West Point in 1832 but resigned in early 1833 due to difficulties with mathematics. With his influential father's help, he was readmitted in 1833 and, after being set back a year, graduated near the bottom of his class in 1838 (40/45).

Commissioned second lieutenant in the 2nd Infantry, McKinstry was promoted to first lieutenant in 1841 and to captain in 1847. Meanwhile, he fought in Mexico and was brevetted major for his actions at Contreras and Churubusco. He transferred to the quartermaster's branch in 1847. He was subsequently stationed in southern California and in St. Louis, where he became chief quartermaster of the Department of the West when the Civil War began. He moved up rapidly after John C. Fremont assumed command of the department on July 3, 1861. On August 3, McKinstry became a major, and on August 14 he was named provost marshal of St. Louis. He was promoted to brigadier general on September 2, and led a division in General Fremont's army during his drive on Springfield. Fremont illegally promoted him to major general on September 21, but Lincoln quickly revoked it.

Warner later wrote that McKinstry was "one of the most thoroughgoing rogues ever to wear a United States uniform." Fremont gave him virtually unlimited power to award government contracts, and he used it to line his own pockets. He was also supported by the powerful Blair politically family, although General Lyon thought he was untrustworthy. In one case, McKinstry paid $315,000 for some fortifications, when another contractor built similar fortifications for $60,000. Another contractor who wanted to do business with the U.S. Army "gifted" a $3,000 silver tea set ($91,422 in 2023 money) for Mrs. McKinstry.

He was under investigation for corruption on November 2, 1861, when Fremont (who did not realize what McKinstry was doing) was relieved of his command and replaced by David Hunter, who had McKinstry arrested on November 11. He was held in close confinement on the St. Louis Arsenal until February 22, 1862, when he was released from prison but not allowed to leave St. Louis. His appointment to brigadier general expired without Senate confirmation on July 17, 1862, and he reverted to the rank of major.

In October 1862, a court-martial presided over by Philip St. George Cooke convicted McKinstry of twenty-six counts of malpractice, forging vouchers, neglect of duty, and receiving kickbacks and payoffs from contractors. Justus McKinstry was cashiered on January 28, 1863—one of only three Union generals to suffer this fate. He was the only Union general cashiered for violation of his duty. After that, he became a stockbroker in New York City and a land speculator in St. Louis. He gradually descended into poverty, and his wife left him with their three sons and moved to

Ypsilanti, Michigan, around 1864, although they apparently remained in touch. She died in poverty in 1892, and he remarried in 1895.

Former General McKinstry died on December 11, 1897, in St. Louis, Missouri. He was eighty-three. He was buried in Highland Cemetery, Ypsilanti, Michigan. One of his older brothers was Commodore James P. McKinstry, who commanded the *USS Monongahela* during the Civil War.

NATHANIEL COLLINS MCLEAN was born in Ridgeville, Ohio, near Cincinnati, on February 2, 1815. His father was a congressman, postmaster general, Supreme Court justice, and presidential candidate in 1856 and 1860. Nathaniel was educated at Augusta College, Kentucky, from which he graduated in 1834, and at Harvard, where he received his law degree in 1838. He set up a law practice in Cincinnati and traveled extensively in Europe antebellum.

McLean joined the Union Army in May 1861 and organized the 75th Ohio Infantry, which was mustered into the service in September. It was sent to western Virginia as part of Fremont's Mountain Department and distinguished himself in the Battle of McDowell (May 8, 1862), where Union General Milroy was defeated by Stonewall Jackson. McLean later fought at Cross Keys (June 8), and was given command of an infantry brigade in the I Corps when the Army of Virginia was created on June 26.

McLean and his four Ohio regiments were on the extreme left flank of the Army of Virginia during the Second Battle of Bull Run. Here his brigade suffered heavy casualties at Chinn Ridge but held off the Confederates long enough for General Pope to establish a line north of the ridge. In doing so, McLean may have saved the army; certainly, the disaster would have been greater than it was, had it not been for McLean. As a result, Lincoln promoted him to brigadier general on November 29.

Placed in the Washington defenses during the Battle of Antietam, the I Corps became part of Franz Sigel's XI Corps of the Army of the Potomac. It was held in reserve during the Battle of Fredericksburg. Afterward, McLean was given command of a division, but the new corps commander,

O. O. Howard, replaced him with Charles Devens, whom he liked better, although McLean was certainly more popular with the men. Relegated to brigade command, McLean was on the Union right flank during the battle of Chancellorsville, where his command was overwhelmed by Stonewall Jackson's famous flanking attack of May 2, 1863. McLean succeeded to division command when Devens was shot in the foot. (He earlier begged Devens to let him reposition his brigade but—possibly under the influence of brandy—Devens refused. It would have been in the best possible position for the Union soldiers had McLean's request been granted.) After the Union defeat, for which Howard accepted no personal responsibility, McLean was transferred to the Department of the Ohio, where he was made provost marshal. He was not given another field command until the Atlanta Campaign, where he commanded a brigade in the Army of the Ohio. Here, he again came into conflict with Howard, who blamed him for his own failure at the Battle of Pickett's Mill on May 27. After the Battle of Kennesaw Mountain, he was sent back to Kentucky in July, he commanded a division in the Bluegrass State and fought in the Battle of Saltville in Southwest Virginia. In late December, he was given a brigade with Sherman's main army and fought in the Carolinas Campaign in 1865. McLean resigned his commission on April 20, 1865, just six days before the surrender of the Army of Tennessee, the main Confederate force on the Western Front.

Postwar, McLean returned to the practice of law, at first in Cincinnati. Later, he relocated to Minnesota, where he farmed and built an Episcopal church. In 1885, he re-located again, this time to Bellport, New York, where he lived in semi-retirement and set up another church. He died in Bellport on January 4, 1905. He was eighty-nine. General McLean was interred in Woodland Cemetery, Bellport. He fathered eleven children.

JAMES WINNING MCMILLAN was born in Clark County, Kentucky, on April 28, 1825, but he was a wanderer and moved frequently throughout his life. In 1846, when the Mexican War broke out, he was in Illinois, so he enlisted in the 4th Illinois Infantry, where he became a sergeant. He was discharged in October 1846 and became a private in the 3rd Louisiana Infantry Battalion. After being honorably mustered out, he traveled to Indiana, where he was involved in business at various locations.

In July 1861, McMillan joined the Union Army as a colonel, commanding the 21st Indiana Infantry. He took part in the capture of New Orleans in April 1862 and fought in the Battle of Baton Rouge on August 5. His unit suffered 126 casualties, and McMillan was wounded in the left arm and chest. His regiment was then sent to Berwick Bay, on the Atchafalaya River near the Gulf of Mexico, where it was converted to the 1st Indiana Heavy Artillery in February 1863.

Meanwhile, McMillan was given an infantry brigade in the XIX Corps and was promoted to brigadier general on March 4, 1863. He fought in the Red River Campaign of 1864, including the decisive Union defeat at Mansfield on April 8, 1864. Here, he was credited with helping stem the panic which gripped most of the Army of the Gulf during this disaster. He also fought at Pleasant Hill, Monett's Ferry, and the Siege of Alexandria, among other actions.

The XIX Corps was transferred to the Shenandoah Valley in July, and McMillan was given command of a division. He was wounded in the head by a piece of Confederate shrapnel during the Third Battle of Winchester on September 19. He distinguished himself at Cedar Creek on October 19, when he again stabilized panicking Federal troops. After this, he was sent to Grafton, West Virginia, where he commanded a temporary (provisional) division until the end of the war. He was brevetted major general on March 7, 1865. He resigned from the army on May 15.

Postbellum, McMillan lived in Kansas and engaged in business until 1875, when he was given a post in the Pension Bureau. He held this job until his death, which occurred in Washington on March 9, 1903. He was seventy-seven. He was buried in Arlington National Cemetery.

JOHN MCNEIL was born on February 14, 1813, in Nova Scotia, Canada. He was descended from Tories who fled the United States during the American Revolution. After receiving a local school education, he moved to Boston and trained as a hatter. After failing at business in New York City,

he moved to St. Louis, where he was more successful. He became president of the Pacific Insurance Company in 1855. He also served a term in the Missouri state legislature (1844–45).

McNeil's company was wiped out financially when the South seceded. He was a captain in the Missouri Militia when the Civil War began. A Democrat, it was thought he would join the South, but he adhered to the old flag and became commander of the 3rd Missouri Infantry, a 90-day unit. He led it in surrounding and capturing Camp Jackson, securing St. Louis for the Union. He also won a minor battle against pro-Southern state forces at Fulton on July 17. He became colonel of the 19th Missouri in August 1861 and took charge of a district on the Kansas border in December. He spent the winter protecting pro-Union citizens and became colonel of the 2nd Missouri Militia Cavalry Regiment on June 3, 1862.

John McNeil spent his entire Civil War career in Missouri, mostly fighting guerrillas. Most notably, he defeated Colonel Joseph C. Porter in the Battle of Kirksville (August 6, 1862), where McNeill was slightly wounded. He also played a discreditable role in the Palmyra Massacre, where ten Confederate prisoners and Southern sympathizers were executed without trial. Even many Union sympathizers in America and Europe denounced this action as murder. It also earned McNeil the sobriquet "the Butcher of Palmyra." Even so, Lincoln backed McNeil and promoted him to brigadier general on April 4, 1863.

In 1863, McNeil was relegated to district commands at Cape Girardeau and Rolla. During Confederate General Sterling Price's Missouri Raid of 1864, McNeil commanded a brigade in Pleasonton's cavalry division, until General Pleasonton relieved him of command for cowardice during the Battle of Westport. Pleasonton intended to court-martial him, but the proceedings were quashed. He was given command of the District of Central Missouri, which he held until April 22, 1865, when he resigned. He received a brevet to major general in 1866.

Postwar, John McNeil held a number of positions in Missouri, including clerk of the criminal court in St. Louis and county sheriff. He was also an inspector in the Bureau of Indian Affairs. He was superintendent of the St. Louis branch of the U.S. Post Office at the time of his death, which occurred in the Gateway City on June 8, 1891, at age seventy-eight. He was buried in Bellefontaine Cemetery, St. Louis. McNeil's sister was married to President Franklin Pierce.

JAMES BIRDSEYE MCPHERSON—whose names were pronounced James Birds' See Mack-Fur'-Son—was born in Clyde, Ohio, on November 14, 1828, the son of an unsuccessful, mentally unstable blacksmith. Forced to leave home at the age of thirteen, he worked in a rural store to help his mother support the family. His employer helped McPherson get a decent education, which included two years at the Norwalk Academy, Ohio, and to obtain an appointment to the U.S. Military Academy. He graduated at the head of his class (1/52) in 1853 and was commissioned brevet second lieutenant in the engineers. He was promoted to second lieutenant in 1854, first lieutenant in 1858, and captain on August 5, 1861. Meanwhile, he was an assistant instructor of practical engineering at West Point (1853–54), assistant engineer for the defenses of New York Harbor and for the improvement of the Hudson River (1854–57), and for constructing the defenses of Alcatraz Island in San Francisco (1858–61). While in the city by the bay, he fell in love with the daughter of a prominent family, but his wedding plans were derailed by the outbreak of the Civil War. Ultimately, it never happened.

No officer in the Union Army rose any faster than did McPherson. A first lieutenant in the summer of 1861, he was named aide-de-camp (ADC) to General Halleck and promoted to lieutenant colonel in November. He became chief engineer of the Army of the Tennessee under Grant in December, and in May 1862 was promoted to colonel and chief ADC to Grant. Two weeks later, on May 15, he was named military superintendent of the railroads of western Tennessee. He was promoted to brigadier general, Regular Army, on August 4, and to major general of volunteers on October 8, 1862. He was named commander of the Right Wing of the XIII

Corps in November. Meanwhile, he participated in the Battles of Fort Henry, Fort Donelson, Shiloh, the Siege of Corinth (a.k.a. First Battle of Corinth), and the Second Battle of Corinth. Although he never commanded a division or even a regiment, he had powerful friends in Halleck and Grant, who declared that he (McPherson) would be general-in-chief of the army one day. Grant appointed him commander of the XVII Corps. He assumed command on December 22, 1862.

McPherson lived large in enemy territory. He attempted to bypass Vicksburg via Lake Providence, Louisiana, and nearby streams. He appropriated Arlington, the home of a wealthy plantation owner who had a fine wine cellar. He and his staff used the bottom floor as a stable and the upper rooms as living quarters and party central, and they had a party every night. They also acquired a steam tugboat, which they used to tool around Lake Providence every night, while consuming alcoholic beverages and being serenaded by a regimental band. McPherson also confiscated slaves from nearby plantations and subjected them to hard manual labor, trying to dig a water route past Vicksburg. Although undoubtedly innovative, the effort ultimately failed, and a great many African Americans died.

During Grant's last Vicksburg Campaign, McPherson personally took part in the looting of the Ashwood Plantation, leading Mrs. Ingraham, the "Ole Miss" of the plantation, a native of Philadelphia, and the sister of Union General George G. Meade, to recall that General McClernand (who headquartered at Ashwood after McPherson left), was "much more considerate and decent than McPherson."

McPherson's performance in the Vicksburg Campaign was solid. He held the center of the Union line during the siege, but all his attempts to break the Confederate line failed. The Rebels were finally starved into submission. McPherson was briefly in charge of the city after it fell, and he showed compassion for the starving civilians. Meanwhile, Grant and Sherman showered praise on McPherson. Both were highly satisfied with his performance during the campaign.

James McPherson succeeded William T. Sherman as commander of the Army of the Tennessee on March 26, 1864. His request for a furlough to marry his fiancée was granted but quickly revoked by General Sherman, who declared he was needed to prepare for the upcoming Atlanta Campaign.

It began on May 7. Sherman planned to trap Confederate General Joseph E. Johnston in Dalton, Georgia. McPherson commanded the Union right wing and was charged with cutting off Johnston's retreat, but he failed to do so. Sherman charged him with being "too slow." He constantly looked over McPherson's shoulder from then on. Some historians, however, blame Sherman for Johnston's escape. The debate continues to this day.

On July 22, during the Battle of Atlanta, accompanied by a single orderly, General McPherson blundered into Confederate lines. Ordered to halt by a sentry, he raised one hand over his head and then pivoted his horse and fled. The Rebel's bullet went into McPherson's back, through his heart, and out his left breast. He died immediately. A squad of Confederates approached the orderly and asked who that man was. "Sir, it is General McPherson," he replied. "You have killed the best man in our army." Sherman wept openly when he learned of McPherson's death. He was also mourned by John Bell Hood, who recently replaced Johnston as commander of the Army of Tennessee. They were classmates at West Point and close personal friends.

McPherson was the second highest ranking Union officer killed in action, behind John Sedgwick, who was senior to him. He was taken back to the McPherson Family Cemetery in Clyde, Ohio, where his remains were interred. His fiancée lived until 1891. She never married.

GEORGE GORDON MEADE was born on December 31, 1815, in Cadiz, Spain, the son of a wealthy merchant who was ruined financially during the Napoleonic Wars. He nevertheless managed to finance an excellent education for George at the American Classical and Military Lyceum, a prestigious private school in Philadelphia. After his father died in 1828, Meade attended Mount Hope Institute in Baltimore. Although he wanted to go to law school, he entered West Point for financial reasons in 1831 and graduated in 1835 (19/56). Commissioned brevet second lieutenant in the 3rd Artillery, he served in Florida in the Second Seminole War in 1835 and 1836. Meade had no interest in making the military his career and resigned his commission in October 1836.

Hired by his brother-in-law as a civilian employee in the U.S. Army's Corps of Topographical Engineers, Meade returned to Florida as an assistant surveyor. Later, he worked on the Louisiana–Texas border, the Mississippi Delta, and the northeast border of Maine and Canada. In 1842, Congress passed a law making it illegal for the Corps to employ civilians, so Meade rejoined the army. A second lieutenant as of December 1835, he fought in northern Mexico and was brevetted first lieutenant for leading an attack on a fortified position at Monterrey. After the war, he returned to work for the topographical engineers and was involved in projects from the east coast to the Great Lakes to the Florida Keys. He was promoted to captain in 1856.

After the Civil War began, Meade was appointed brigadier general of volunteers on August 31, 1861, and was given command of a brigade in the Pennsylvania Reserves. He was initially involved in constructing defenses around the capital. He fought in the Peninsula Campaign, where his brigade lost 1,400 men in heavy fighting at Frayser's Farm (Glendale), and he was severely wounded in the right arm and in the back. He returned home to Philadelphia to recuperate and was back in time to fight at the Second Bull Run, where he made a desperate and heroic stand at Henry House Hill and covered the retreat of the fleeing Union army. He led a division at South Mountain, where he distinguished himself in the capture of Turner's Gap. After General Hooker was wounded at Antietam, Meade assumed temporary command of the I Corps, despite being wounded in the thigh. He reverted to divisional command on September 29, 1862. He was promoted to major general on November 29.

During the Battle of Fredericksburg, Meade was the only Union general to break Lee's lines. He was not reinforced, however, and Stonewall Jackson counterattacked and sealed off the breakthrough, and inflicted heavy losses on Meade's division. Meade never forgave the army commander, Ambrose Burnside, for not sending him reinforcements. General Meade was nevertheless named commander of the V Corps on December 22.

Meade's corps was held in reserve during most of the Battle of Chancellorsville. On June 28, 1863, as Lee invaded Pennsylvania, Lincoln named Meade commander of the Army of the Potomac. He was not Lincoln's first choice, for he was not a dynamic personality, but General Reynolds turned down the president's suggestion that he replace Hooker, and Generals Sedgwick, Slocum, and Couch—corps commanders all—recommended Meade. On the evening of July 1, he made the fateful decision to stand at Gettysburg. On July 2 and 3, he won what was arguably the most important victory of the Civil War.

General Meade was competent, rather than spectacular, and he depended heavily on his subordinates, with happy results for the Union. He did not pursue Lee aggressively after Gettysburg, which led to Lincoln and General Halleck expressing their dissatisfaction at his performance. Infuriated at being second guessed, Meade immediately offered to resign, which compelled Lincoln to hastily reverse himself, but the president nevertheless suspected Meade was too cautious and was disappointed that Lee's army was not destroyed after Gettysburg. Whether Meade could have accomplished this had he performed perfectly has been the subject of debate among historians for decades. I doubt it. Lee's army was badly damaged, it is true, but it was hardly at the point of collapse, and Meade's army (having lost more than twenty thousand men at Gettysburg) was not in particularly good shape either. It also had to divert several of its freshest regiments to New York City, to suppress the Draft Riots. But history is truly an argument without end, and I will leave it to the readers to draw their own conclusions.

During the second half of 1863, Meade directed the Army of the Potomac in two inconclusive campaigns: Bristoe and Mine Run. Afterward, Lincoln named Ulysses S. Grant general-in-chief of the Union Army, and he chose to travel with Meade's army during the campaigns of 1864 and 1865. As the war progressed, Grant was frustrated with Meade's cautiousness, and Meade was annoyed at his lack of autonomy and that Sherman and Sheridan were promoted to major general, Regular Army, before him. (Meade's promotion was confirmed by the Senate on February 1, 1865—two weeks after Sherman and Sheridan.)

Although Grant often interfered in the tactical dispositions of the Army of the Potomac, Meade remained its commander until the end of the war. Meade's greatest blunder occurred before to the Battle of the Crater, when he ordered General Burnside (now commanding IX Corps) to replace an African American division earmarked to lead the attack with a white division, despite the fact that the black unit was well-trained for the operation and the white unit had received virtually no training. The result was a debacle of the first order, a clear Confederate victory, and the loss of a major opportunity for the North.

Meade was not present when Lee surrendered. The Army of the Potomac was disbanded on June 28, 1865, and Meade spent the rest of his career commanding the Military Division of the Atlantic, the Department of the South, and the Third Military District, which headquarters in his home town of Philadelphia. At least partially because he was a Democrat, he was passed over as general-in-chief for Sherman in 1869. Unlike Sherman and Sheridan, he was never promoted to lieutenant general, and some of the Radical Republicans unsuccessfully sought to have him sacked. A competent officer, he was amiable except in times of stress, when he tended to lash out at whomever was available. He became known throughout the army for his short temper and earned the nickname "Old Snapping Turtle." He was respected and, to a degree, admired by his men, but not loved. The father of seven, George G. Meade died of pneumonia at his home in Philadelphia on November 6, 1872, at age fifty-six. He was buried in Laurel Hill Cemetery, Philadelphia.

THOMAS FRANCIS MEAGHER (pronounced MAW'-HER) was born on August 3, 1823, in Waterford, Ireland, the son of a wealthy merchant and member of Parliament. Educated in Catholic schools, including Clongowes Wood College (a Jesuit school in Dublin) and Stonyhurst College in Lancaster, England, from which he graduated in 1843. He then returned to Ireland. He and other supporters of an independent Ireland went to France to study the French Revolution. While there, he and some friends designed the flag of modern-day Ireland, a tricolor flag similar to that of France.

Meagher was a fervent advocate of Irish independence, an excellent and passionate orator, and a bit of a rabblerouser. This combination led to his being arrested and sentenced to hang for sedition in 1848, but the British banished him to Van Diemen's Land, a colony in Tasmania, instead. He escaped in 1851, leaving behind his pregnant wife. Meagher's first son died in Tasmania at age four months. Meagher never saw him.

Tom Meagher made his way to New York City, where his wife joined him briefly. Pregnant again, she returned to Ireland, where she was greeted as a hero by crowds of thousands. She gave birth to a second son in 1854, but she died shortly thereafter. Meagher's son and only surviving child was raised by in-laws; the general never saw him either.

In New York, Meagher became a lawyer, a journalist, a famous speaker, an American citizen, and a captain in the New York Militia. Despite pro-Southern sympathies, he joined the Union Army on April 29, 1861. (Meagher liked the South and Southerners and had an Irish rebel's sympathy for opponents of an overbearing government; however, he abhorred slavery, so he joined the North.) Meagher actively recruited Irish immigrants and became a company commander in Colonel Michael Corcoran's 69th New York Infantry, a Zouaves unit, on April 29, 1861. He fought at the First Bull Run, where Corcoran was captured, and Meagher (who was wounded) succeeded him as colonel. He returned to New York City, where in December 1861 Lincoln authorized him to recruit Irishmen from any state and from Ireland itself. He raised the Irish Brigade (four thousand men) and was promoted to brigadier general effective February 6, 1862.

Meagher first led his brigade in Union victory at Seven Pines, where he distinguished himself. He also fought in the Seven Days battles, where he again distinguished himself at Gaines' Mill (June 27, 1862). Afterward, Meagher and his men were looked upon as heroes. On September 17, he led his brigade in an attack on the Sunken Road, where it suffered 540 casualties, and Meagher was injured when his horse was shot from under him, although it was rumored that he was drunk and fell off the horse. These rumors, coupled with earlier whispers that he was intoxicated at Bull Run, cast doubt on his command abilities.

Meagher sent his 1,200-man brigade forward at Fredericksburg on December 13, where they suffered astronomical losses, and only 280 answered the rolls the next day. Meagher himself remained in the rear because of an ulcerated knee. He went on a medical furlough and returned to duty just before the Battle of Chancellorsville, where his brigade was lightly engaged.

Meanwhile, Michael Corcoran (who was exchanged) was promoted to brigadier general, so Meagher resigned on May 14, 1863. Corcoran, however, was killed by a Union sentry on December 22, so the War Department revoked Meagher's resignation on December 23 and restored him to rank. He was never given another brigade, however, and spent most of the rest of the war commanding the District of Etowah, Tennessee (headquartered in Chattanooga), although he directed a division in the Army of the Ohio for two weeks in February 1865. He resigned his commission on May 15. Hie was not brevetted major general in the omnibus promotions at the end of the war.

After the war, General Meagher was named secretary of the newly formed Territory of Montana. In the absence of the governor, he served as acting governor for more than a year. Suffering from dysentery, he nevertheless took a steamboat to Fort Benton, the terminus of navigation for steamboats on the Missouri River in June 1867. On the evening of July 1, under mysterious circumstances, he fell, jumped, or was pushed overboard, and his body was never recovered. It was suggested by various sources that he was drunk and fell off the boat, or committed suicide, or was murdered by political enemies. Confederates, Indians, and vigilantes have also been nominated as Meagher's killers. The truth will probably never be known.

MONTGOMERY CUNNINGHAM MEIGS (pronounced MEGGS) was born in Augusta, Georgia, on May 3, 1816, a son of a nationally known obstetrician who settled in Philadelphia. His grandfather was the president of the University of Georgia. Montgomery attended the University of Pennsylvania and (using family connections) was admitted to the United States Military Academy at West Point in 1832. He graduated in 1836 (5/49) and was commissioned second lieutenant of artillery, although he spent most of his pre-war career with the Corps of Engineers. He was involved in the construction of forts on the Delaware River, in making navigational improvements on the Mississippi River (where his commander was Robert E. Lee), and in constructing Fort Montgomery, New York. He later worked on the

Washington Aqueduct and supervised the construction of both wings and the dome of the U.S. Capitol (1853–60). In 1860, because of a falling out with Secretary of War John B. Floyd, he was banished to Dry Tortugas, a collection of coral islands which form the most isolated part of the Florida Keys. He returned to Washington in early 1861, after Floyd left office. On the orders of President Lincoln, he and Erasmus D. Keyes secretly devised plans to reinforce Fort Pickens, Florida, without the knowledge of the secretary of war or the secretary of the navy. Their plans were executed without a hitch.

Captain of Engineers Meigs was promoted to colonel of the 11th U.S. Infantry on May 14, 1861. The next day, he became quartermaster general of the U.S. Army, replacing Joseph E. Johnston, who had "gone South." Meigs was promoted to brigadier general, Regular Army, on June 12. He understood the importance and complexities of logistics, and according to Secretary of State Seward, the war might have been lost without him. His office handled everything from uniform design and procurement to the purchase and feeding of draft animals and wagons, to the handling of prisoners, burial and grave registration, to refitting entire armies, and many other aspects of logistics. By all accounts, he was an organizational genius and did an outstanding job as quartermaster general, a position he held for almost twenty-one years. He was also a confidant, advisor, and friend of Abraham Lincoln.

A staunch Unionist who hated the Confederacy, especially after his son (a lieutenant) was killed in action, Meigs established Arlington National Cemetery on the property of Robert E. Lee, at least in part out of revenge for Lee's joining the Rebels. Somewhat irrationally, Meigs believed that his son was murdered after he surrendered, despite conclusive evidence to the contrary.

Meigs was not a congenial person but was an efficient one. More than 3,400 government contracts passed through his office in 1864 alone. He kept politics out of the award of contracts—at least as far as possible. Contracts were awarded via public bidding, rather than by patronage, as had previously been the case.

Montgomery Meigs was brevetted major general on July 5, 1864. He retired in 1882 and died of pneumonia on January 2, 1892, at his home in Washington, D.C. at age seventy-five. He is buried in Arlington National Cemetery.

SOLOMON "LONG SOL" MEREDITH was born on May 29, 1810, in Guilford County, North Carolina, the youngest of twelve children. He received his nickname as a young man because he stood 6'7" tall. He moved to Wayne County, Indiana, when he was nineteen and became a farm laborer and a clerk at a general store in Centerville. He eventually opened his own store in Cambridge City and built an impressive farm, "Oakland," near the city. A natural leader and a fervent Whig, he was elected county sheriff in 1834 (at age twenty-four) and served two terms. He represented his county in the legislature from 1846 to 1849, when President Taylor named him U.S. marshal for Indiana. After serving four years, he returned home and was re-elected to the legislature as a Republican. He would eventually serve four terms. He also worked as director of the Indiana Central Railroad and the Cincinnati and Chicago Railroad and served as Wayne County Clerk of Court from 1859 to 1861.

Early in the Civil War, Meredith recruited the 19th Indiana Infantry and was appointed its colonel by Governor Oliver P. Morton on July 29, 1861. It was sent to Washington, where it was brigaded with three Wisconsin regiments, two Indiana regiments, and his own 19th Indiana, to form the Iron Brigade. Meredith's first action was a skirmish at Brawner's Farm on August 28, 1862, during the Second Bull Run Campaign. His horse was shot and fell on him, breaking several ribs. He fought at South Mountain, after which he reported himself unfit for duty due to his Brawner's Farm injuries. He thus missed the Battle of Antietam (September 17), where his replacement was killed. His brigade commander, John Gibbon, thought Meredith should have been sacked for taking medical leave. When Gibbon was promoted to divisional commander that autumn, he nominated two other men for brigade commander, but Governor Morton used his political influence with General Hooker to secure the appointment for Meredith. He was promoted to brigadier general on October 6.

Meredith first led a brigade at Fredericksburg, where he performed poorly and his divisional commander, Abner Doubleday, suspended him from command and replaced him with Colonel Lysander Cutler. Meredith managed to resume his position shortly after and led the brigade at Chancellorsville, where it was lightly engaged. Sol Meredith distinguished himself at Gettysburg on July 1, 1863, when he launched a successful counterattack, smashed Confederate General Archer's brigade, and captured Archer. That afternoon, however, the brigade was crushed by Pettigrew's attack, during which Rebel shrapnel struck him in the head, fractured his skull, and killed his horse, which fell on him, injuring his right leg and breaking his ribs. He never fully recovered from his wounds and was unfit for further field duty. After he partially recuperated, he was relegated to district command, mainly at Cairo, Illinois, and Paducah, Kentucky.

While still in the army, he ran unsuccessfully for Congress. During the campaign, he beat his opponent unconscious with a whip. Again, however, he was rescued by his political influence, and charges against him were dropped.

After the war, Meredith was mustered out in May 1865 and brevetted major general in 1866. He resumed farming, was active in the field of livestock improvement, and became the local tax assessor. In 1867, he was named surveyor general of Montana Territory, a post which he held until 1869. Returning again to his farm, he died there on October 2, 1875, at age sixty-five. He is buried in Riverside Cemetery, Cambridge City, Indiana.

SULLIVAN AMONY MEREDITH was born in Philadelphia on July 4, 1816, into a prominent Pennsylvania family. His ancestors included Lewis Morris, a governor of New Jersey and signer of the Declaration of Independence. Sources differ as to where he was educated, at the University of Pennsylvania or William and Mary. Independently wealthy, he spent years traveling the world and made two trips to China. He joined the Union cause on April 26, 1861, as colonel of the 10th Pennsylvania Infantry, part of General Patterson's command. He took part in Patterson's unsuccessful attempt to prevent General Joseph E. Johnston from leaving the Shenandoah Valley and joining Beauregard at Bull Run.

The enlistments of Meredith's regiments expired after ninety days, and he was mustered out on August 1. Shortly after, he was placed in charge of Camp Curtin, near Harrisburg, Pennsylvania, where he was responsible for training and equipping more than twenty thousand recruits for the Northern armies. On March 6, 1862, he was given command of the 56th Pennsylvania Infantry, which was part of Irwin McDowell's III Corps.

On August 28, near Gainesville, Virginia, during the Second Bull Run Campaign, a minié ball smashed through his right breast and right arm, which kept him on medical furlough until July 1863. Meanwhile, he was promoted to brigadier general on November 29, 1862.

Apparently unfit for field duty, Meredith was sent to Fort Monroe, where he was named commissioner for the exchange of prisoners. After Grant halted the prisoner exchanges in early 1864, Meredith served on court-martial boards. He was also transferred to St. Louis and appears to have been unemployed at the end of the war. He was mustered out on August 21, 1865.

After the war, Meredith was involved in the commercial drug business. He died suddenly, probably of a heart attack, in Buffalo, New York, on December 26, 1874, at age fifty-eight. Considered a gentleman and a devoted family man, he was a vestryman of the St. Luke's Episcopal Church. He was buried in Forest Lawn Cemetery, Buffalo.

WESLEY MERRITT was born in New York City on June 16, 1834, although one source listed his birthday as June 16, 1836. His family moved to St. Clair County, Illinois in 1840, and he was admitted to the United States Military Academy in 1855. Merritt graduated in 1860 (22/41) and was commissioned brevet second lieutenant in the 2nd Dragoons on July 1, 1860. He became regimental adjutant when it was reorganized as the 2nd Cavalry in 1861. He was promoted to second lieutenant in January 1861 and to first lieutenant on May 13, 1861.

Initially posted to Utah, his regiment was recalled to the East when the Civil War began. In 1862, Merritt was promoted to captain and was successively aide-de-camp to

Generals Philip St. George Cooke and George Stoneman. He distinguished himself in the Battle of Brandy Station (June 9, 1863), where he was wounded in the scalp and the left leg. On June 29, he, George Armstrong Custer, and Elon J. Farnsworth were promoted from captain to brigadier general and each was given command of a brigade of cavalry. Merritt—who was twenty-seven years old at that time—went on to become perhaps the most successful of the "boy generals" of the Civil War.

His brigade was held mostly in reserve or guarding supply trains during the Gettysburg Campaign, but on July 3, his division commander, Judson Kilpatrick, foolishly ordered an attack against Confederate infantry, which resulted in heavy losses. Later transferred to John Buford's command, Merritt assumed command of the division after Buford died of typhoid fever in December 1863. He was superseded by Brigadier General Alfred Torbert, but that officer was ill for most of the Overland Campaign, and Merritt commanded in his place. Wesley Merritt particularly distinguished himself in the Third Battle of Winchester (September 19, 1864), where he played a critical part in routing the Confederate Army of the Valley. He was brevetted major general of volunteers for his performance here.

Merritt spent the rest of the war with Sheridan and was particularly noted for destroying anything of value in the Valley. In just one day (October 5), near Port Republic, his division destroyed forty-seven mills, 410,000 bushels of wheat, hundreds of acres of corn, and numerous private dwellings. He later fought at Five Forks and was present at Appomattox. He was promoted to major general of volunteers (permanent rank) on April 1, 1865, but was never confirmed.

After the war, Merritt was transferred to San Antonio for a possible war with the French in Mexico. When this did not materialize, he was mustered out of volunteer service on January 28, 1866, and reverted to his Regular Army rank of lieutenant colonel. Part of the 9th Cavalry, and later as colonel of the 5th Cavalry (1876–1882), he spent most of the next seventeen years on the frontier. He was superintendent of West Point from 1882 to 1887, when he was promoted to brigadier general, Regular Army. He became a major general in 1895. During the Spanish-American War (1898), he commanded the VIII Corps, led the American forces that captured Manila, and served as the first military governor of the Philippines.

General Merritt retired in 1900 and had homes in Washington, D.C. and Natural Bridge, Virginia. He died of complications of arteriosclerosis in Natural Bridge on December 3, 1910. He was seventy-four. He was interred in the West Point Cemetery.

NELSON APPLETON MILES was born on August 8, 1839, in Westminster, Massachusetts. His father was a farmer. After acquiring a rudimentary education in local schools, Miles left home to work in a crockery store in Boston. Determined to improve himself and advance in life, he attended night school, read military history, and studied military science under the tutelage of a former French colonel. He later attended Fort Wayne College in Indiana.

Miles joined the Union Army as a first lieutenant in the 22nd Massachusetts Infantry on September 9, 1861, and would amass arguably the best record of any volunteer officer in the war. Initially posted to the Washington, D.C. area, he became an officer on the staff of Oliver O. Howard, and on May 31, 1862, was appointed lieutenant colonel in the 61st New York Infantry. Miles fought at Seven Pines, where he distinguished himself on June 1 while temporarily leading part of the 81st Pennsylvania. He was also wounded in the foot. He later fought in the Seven Days battles and the Battle of Antietam. He was promoted to colonel on September 30, but was shot in the mouth at Fredericksburg on December 13. Back in action at Chancellorsville, he fought so bravely that he was brevetted brigadier general and was awarded the Congressional Medal of Honor in 1892. He was also shot in the neck and abdomen. He was still recovering when the Battle of Gettysburg was fought, and the regiment (part of Hancock's II Corps) was commanded by its lieutenant colonel. He apparently arrived on the field the day after the battle and was given command of a brigade on July 4.

Miles took part in the Overland Campaign and fought in the Wilderness, Spotsylvania, and Cold Harbor, among others. In June 1864, during the Siege of Petersburg, he was wounded again, this time in the neck and shoulder. He was promoted to brigadier general on June 9. Given command of a division on July 29, he was brevetted major general for his actions at the Battle of Ream's Station on August 25. He led his division for the rest of the war, including the pursuit to Appomattox. He was promoted to major general of volunteers (full rank) on October 21, 1865. He was twenty-six years old.

Nelson Miles was commandant of Fort Monroe after the war. His most famous prisoner was Jefferson Davis, whom he was charged with mistreating. Miles obeyed orders and put the defenseless man in irons, without protest on his part.

In July 1866, Miles was appointed colonel, Regular Army. He continued to distinguish himself, commanding the 5th U.S. Infantry from 1869 to 1880. He directed campaigns against the American Indians and subdued the Kiowa, Comanche, and Southern Cheyenne along the Red River. He also married Mary Hoyt Sherman, the niece of the famous general. Their son, Sherman Miles (1882–1966), became a major general in the U.S. Army.

Miles was promoted to brigadier general (1880), major general (1890), brevet lieutenant general (1900), and lieutenant general (1901). He was the last general-in-chief of the U.S. Army (1895–1903), commanded the army during the Spanish-American War (1898), and personally directed the forces that captured Cuba and Puerto Rico. He stepped down in 1903 at the mandatory retirement age of sixty-four.

Miles remained physically active and is said to have never missed a circus. He was attending a Ringling Brothers and Barnum & Bailey Circus with his grandchildren in Washington, D.C. on May 15, 1925, when he succumbed to a heart attack at age eighty-five. He is buried in Arlington National Cemetery. One of the last of the Union generals, only John R. Brooke and Adelbert Ames survived him.

JOHN FRANKLIN MILLER was born on November 21, 1831, in South Bend, Indiana. He received his law degree from Ballston Spa, New York, at age twenty-one and began his law practice in South Bend. He moved to the Napa Valley of California in 1853 but returned to South Bend two years later. He was elected to the Indiana State Senate as a Republican in 1861.

Governor Morton appointed Miller colonel of the 29th Indiana Infantry on August 27, 1861. It became part of Buell's Army of the Ohio and fought on the second day of the Battle of Shiloh (April 7, 1862). After taking part in the Siege of Corinth and the invasion of northern Alabama, Miller and his regiment were sent to Kentucky but were not present at the Battle of Perryville. Sent back to Tennessee after Bragg retreated, Miller fought at Stones River, where he distinguished himself on January 2, 1863, leading a counterattack against General Breckinridge's advance. In the process, he was shot in the neck but was not disabled for long. He was given command of a brigade in the Army of the Cumberland on January 9.

Colonel Miller led his brigade in the Tullahoma Campaign until June 27, 1863, when he was severely wounded and lost his left eye in a skirmish at Liberty Gap. It took him a year to recuperate. In the meantime, he was promoted to brigadier general on April 10, 1864. He returned to duty as commander of the District of Nashville in June 1864. The garrison here was quite large, and he led twelve infantry regiments and fourteen artillery batteries in the Battle of Nashville (December 15–16). For his services here, he was brevetted major general in 1866.

Offered a colonelcy in the Regular Army after the fall of the Confederacy, Miller declined and resigned from the service on September 29, 1865. He moved back to California and was collector of customs at the Port of San Francisco until 1869, when he became president of the Alaska Commercial Company, which controlled the fur industry in the Pribilof Islands. The California legislature elected him U.S. senator in 1880.

General Miller enthusiastically supported the Chinese Exclusion Act of 1882 and was strongly anti-immigrant, believing that one white man was worth a hundred Chinese "barbarians." He also considered whites vastly superior to Native Americans. Senator Miller died in office in Washington, D.C. on March 8, 1886, at age fifty-four. Initially buried in Laurel Hill Cemetery, San Francisco, he was reinterred in Arlington National Cemetery in 1913.

STEPHEN MILLER, the fourth governor of Minnesota, was born on January 7, 1816, in Carroll, a rural township in Clinton County, Pennsylvania. He was of Pennsylvania Dutch heritage. Miller was a successful entrepreneur and became wealthy in the mercantile business. He was also editor of the *Telegraph*, a Whig newspaper in Harrisburg. Because of health issues, he emigrated to St. Cloud, Minnesota, in 1858, at age forty-two, because it was believed the climate there would be better for him. He quickly became prominent in the state Republican Party.

As soon as word arrived that the Rebels had fired on Fort Sumter, Miller enlisted as a private in the 1st Minnesota Infantry. He was promoted to lieutenant colonel on April 29 (despite a total lack of military experience) and fought in the First Battle of Bull Run, where the regiment suffered 20 percent casualties. Miller also fought in the Battle of Seven Pines and in the Seven Days Campaign, after which he was summoned back home.

On August 24, 1862, Miller was named commander of the 7th Minnesota Infantry and Camp Lincoln at Mankato, Minnesota. He took charge in November. Here, 303 Dakota Sioux were awaiting execution for their part in the Dakota War of 1862. Lincoln cut this number to thirty-eight and ordered them hanged. Miller supervised their hangings on December 26. It was the largest mass execution in U.S. history. The rest were sent to Iowa, where more than half of them died. Meanwhile, Stephen Miller was promoted to brigadier general on October 26, 1862.

In late 1863, Miller was elected governor of Minnesota and served from January 11, 1864 to January 8, 1866. He strongly supported and financed education in the state and unsuccessfully tried to add a black suffrage amendment to the state constitution. He did not run for re-election. Later, he became a railroad company field agent and member of the state legislature (1873–74). He suffered financial reverses in the 1870s and died alone and in poverty in Worthington, Minnesota, on August 18, 1881, at age sixty-five. He was buried in Worthington Cemetery.

ROBERT HUSTON MILROY was born on a farm near Canton, Indiana (a hamlet five miles from Salem), on June 11, 1816. His father was a major general in the Indiana Militia and fought in the War of 1812. Robert attended Norwich Academy, Vermont, from which he graduated in 1843. He finished at the head of his class but, to his frustration, was unable to

obtain a commission in the U.S. Army, feeding his distrust and hatred for West Point graduates. He then attended law school at the University of Indiana at Bloomington. He moved to Texas in 1845 but returned to Indiana in 1847, where he joined the 1st Indiana Infantry during the Mexican War. He became a captain but did not see combat.

After Mexico, Milroy resumed his legal studies, graduated in 1850, and set up his practice at Rensselaer, Indiana. He briefly served as a judge. In early 1861, he recruited a militia company and, on April 23, 1861, was formally appointed captain. Four days later, he entered Federal service as colonel of the 9th Indiana Infantry. He took part in the Western Virginia Campaign of 1861 and was promoted to brigadier general on September 3. In December, he assumed command of the Cheat Mountain District of the Mountain Department.

In 1862, Milroy advanced toward the Shenandoah Valley and threatened the Confederate rear. Stonewall Jackson marched quickly to meet the threat and, on May 8 and 9, defeated Milroy in the Battle of McDowell, although Milroy performed credibly. He led a brigade in the Battle of Cross Keys (June 8), where John C. Fremont was defeated by the Confederate General Ewell. Milroy also commanded a brigade during the Second Battle of Bull Run, another Rebel victory. He was nevertheless promoted to major general on March 10, 1863. After Antietam, he was placed in charge of the garrison at Winchester.

A strong, unbending Presbyterian and a fanatical abolitionist, Milroy believed God ordained the Union to abolish slavery and bring Old Testament-style punishment on those who supported the South—even to the point of executing people without trial for being pro-Confederate. His harsh treatment of their neighbors alienated even pro-Unionists in the Shenandoah.

In the summer of 1863, Milroy was commander of the 2nd Division of the VIII Corps (6,900 men). He was ordered to evacuate Winchester but did not do so, convincing General Schenck (his immediate superior) that he could hold the place. Milroy did not properly post scouts to observe the advancing Rebels, and those he did post were too close to the town. He had no idea Ewell was advancing on him with the entire II Corps—about 19,000 men. They fell on Milroy in the Second Battle of Winchester (June 13–15) and killed, wounded, or captured 4,443 of his men as well as all 28 of his field pieces and 300 loaded wagons. Milroy was thrown from his horse and injured his hip and in later life suffered pain and limited mobility because of it. He nevertheless escaped with his staff and his cavalry. He was later subjected to a court of inquiry, which exonerated him. Even so, Henry Halleck, the general-in-chief, decreed that he be given no more commands.

Milroy was engaged in recruiting militia regiments for General Thomas and commanding subdistricts in Tennessee in 1864 and 1865. He did take part in the Third Battle of Murfreesboro (December 1864), where he temporarily commanded two infantry brigades and did well. He resigned from the army on July 26, 1865.

Postbellum, Milroy was a trustee of the Wabash and Erie Canal Company and superintendent of Indian affairs for Washington Territory with headquarters at Olympia. He died of heart failure in Olympia on March 29, 1890, at age seventy-three. He is buried in Masonic Memorial Park, Tumwater, Washington.

ORMSBY MACKNIGHT "OLD STARS" MITCHEL was born in Union County, Kentucky, on August 28, 1810. The town of Morganfield is now located on the former site of his family's log cabin. His father died when he was an infant, and his mother moved the family to Lebanon, Ohio. He received a local public school education, clerked in a store in Xenia, and secured an appointment to West Point strictly on his own merits—i.e., without the aid of any political influence. A plebe in 1825, he graduated in 1829 (15/46) and was commissioned brevet second lieutenant in the artillery. The Military Academy retained him as an assistant professor of mathematics until 1832, when he resigned from the army, became a lawyer, and from 1834 to 1849 was a professor of mathematics and astronomy at the University of Cincinnati. He became nationally famous as an astronomer, and his inspired lectures attracted crowds of up to two thousand people. His work on the development of telegraphic determination of longitude was considered groundbreaking. Undoubtedly brilliant, he was also largely responsible for establishing the U.S. Naval Observatory, the Harvard Observatory, the Cincinnati Observatory, and the Dudley Observatory at Albany, New York. Later, he was a civil engineer for the Ohio & Mississippi Railroad. He was also a major general in the Ohio Militia from 1841 to 1848. Mitchel was director of the Dudley Observatory when the war began.

On August 9, 1861, Abraham Lincoln appointed him brigadier general of volunteers and commander of the Department of the Ohio. The department was absorbed by Buell's Army of the Ohio in December, and Mitchel became commander of its 2nd Division. He devised the plan which resulted in the Great Locomotive Chase of 1862, in which James J. Andrews, an espionage agent, tried to destroy the Confederate railroad to Chattanooga, while Mitchel attacked and captured the vital city. Both phases of the plan failed, and Andrews was captured and hanged.

Mitchel was more successful when he seized Decatur, Alabama, on April 12, 1862. He was promoted to major general on April 14. Unfortunately, he fell out with Buell, who proclaimed that his division sadly lacked discipline. Mitchel submitted his resignation, but the War Department refused to accept it. Instead, it promoted Mitchel to the command of the X Corps and the Department of the South, which headquartered at Hilton Head, South Carolina. He assumed command on September 17, but soon came down with yellow fever and died on October 31, 1862. He was fifty-two years old. General Mitchel was buried in Green-Wood Cemetery, Brooklyn, New York.

JOHN GRANT MITCHELL was born on November 6, 1838, in Piqua, Ohio. He graduated from Kenyon College in 1859 and then read law in Columbus, Ohio. In June 1861, he enlisted in the 3rd Ohio Infantry as a private but was promoted to first lieutenant and regimental adjutant on July 27. After serving under Rosecrans in the Western Virginia Campaign, he advanced to the rank of captain and company commander in December and participated in Ormsby Mitchel's raid into Tennessee and Alabama in the spring of 1862.

In the summer of 1862, he returned to Ohio and helped recruit the 113th Ohio Infantry. He was promoted to lieutenant colonel of that regiment on September 2 and to colonel on May 6, 1863. He took part in the Tullahoma Campaign and on September 9 assumed command of a brigade in the XIV Corps.

During the Battle of Chickamauga, Mitchell's brigade arrived on the field during the second day and played a major part in General Thomas's holding of Horseshoe Ridge and perhaps saving the routed Army of the Cumberland. He later took part in the Siege of Chattanooga, Sherman's attack on Missionary Ridge, and in relieving General Burnside at Knoxville. He was also heavily engaged at Rocky Face Ridge, Resaca, and New Hope Church during the Atlanta Campaign as well as the March to the Sea. On General Sherman's recommendation, he was promoted to brigadier general on January 12, 1865. He was twenty-six years old.

Mitchell fought in the Carolinas Campaign and distinguished himself at Averasborough and Bentonville, for which he was brevetted major general on March 18, 1865. He was present when the Confederate Army of Tennessee surrendered on April 26, 1865.

John Mitchell resigned from the army on July 3, 1865, and returned home to Columbus, where he resumed his legal career. He married the niece of his close friend, future President Rutherford B. Hayes, in 1862. They had four children. His only son, Grant Mitchell, became a leading character actor in Hollywood in the early twentieth century. Meanwhile, General Mitchell served as a Register in Bankruptcy, President of the Columbus City Council, and Ohio Pension Commissioner. He died in Columbus on November 7, 1894, the day after he turned fifty-six. He was interred in Green Lawn Cemetery, Columbus.

ROBERT BYINGTON "FIGHTING BOB" MITCHELL was born in Mansfield, Ohio, on April 4, 1823. He studied law in Mount Vernon and set up a

practice in Mansfield. During the Mexican War, he served in the 2nd Ohio Infantry Regiment as a first lieutenant in southern Mexico. Discharged in mid-1848, he returned to Ohio and was elected mayor of Mount Gilead in 1855. The following year, he moved to Kansas, where he was elected to the territorial legislature as a Democrat. He was territorial treasurer from 1859 to 1861.

When the Civil War began, Mitchell was adjutant general of Kansas from May 2 to June 30, 1861. Simultaneously, he was colonel of the 2nd Kansas Infantry from May 23. He led his regiment at Wilson's Creek, where he was shot off his horse and badly wounded in the hip and groin. It took him months to recover. He was promoted to brigadier general on April 14, 1862, and ten days later returned to duty as commander of a mixed brigade at Fort Riley. Transferred to the Western Front, he was given a division in Gilbert's III Corps and fought in the Battle of Perryville. After the Confederates abandoned Kentucky, he was stationed in Nashville for several months.

In March 1863, Mitchell was named commander of a cavalry division in the Army of the Cumberland and served as General Thomas's chief of cavalry during the Chickamauga Campaign. Apparently, his performance left something to be desired. He was relieved of his command on November 9, 1863, and sent to Washington on court-martial duty. He never received another significant command. He successively directed the District of Nebraska, the District of Northern Kansas, and the District of Kansas. Unemployed for several months after the war, he was mustered out on January 16, 1866. That same day, the Senate confirmed his nomination as governor of New Mexico Territory. He did not receive a brevet promotion to major general at the end of the war.

Robert Mitchell was sworn in as governor on June 16, 1866. He did not take his duties seriously and was often absent from Santa Fe for months at a time. The legislature was forced to send bills directly to Congress for approval, bypassing the governor. He finally resigned in 1869 and returned to Kansas, where he ran unsuccessfully for Congress in 1872. He then moved to the nation's capital, where he died on January 26, 1882, at age fifty-eight. He was buried in Arlington National Cemetery.

WILLIAM READING MONTGOMERY was born on July 10, 1801, in Monmouth County, New Jersey, and graduated from West Point in 1825 (28/37). He was commissioned second lieutenant in the 3rd U.S. Infantry. At various times, he was stationed on the Vermont–Canada border; in Florida during the Seminole War (1840–42); at Fort Jesup, Louisiana; at Jefferson Barracks; and in the occupation of Texas. He was promoted to first lieutenant in 1833 and to captain in 1838. Montgomery fought with the 8th Infantry in Mexico and was wounded at Resaca de la Palma and Molino del Rey. He was brevetted major and lieutenant colonel and was promoted to major, Regular Army, in 1852.

Major Montgomery was involved in unauthorized real estate transactions and was dismissed from the service in late 1855. He apparently used government funds to create a town on land he owned. Some sources, however, aver that he was railroaded out of the army because of his Free State convictions. He rejoined the army on May 21, 1861, as colonel of the 1st New Jersey Infantry. He helped cover the army's retreat after the Bull Run debacle and was promoted to brigadier general on August 9. This was the high point of his war.

After Bull Run, Montgomery served as military governor of Alexandria, Virginia (September–December 1861); commandant of Annapolis (January–March 1862); and commandant of Philadelphia (April 1862–March 1863). He was unemployed until October 1863, when he was named to a military commission in Memphis. He submitted his resignation (presumably due to poor health). It was accepted on April 4, 1864. He was too old for this war.

General Montgomery briefly worked as a merchant dealing with wood moldings but soon retired to his home in Bristol, Pennsylvania. He died there about midnight on May 31–June 1, 1871, at the age of sixty-nine. He was interred in Church of St. James the Greater Cemetery in Bristol.

GEORGE WEBB MORELL was born in Cooperstown, New York, on January 8, 1815. His maternal grandfather was a general in the Revolutionary

War, and his father was a major general in the New York Militia and later chief justice of the Michigan Supreme Court. George entered West Point in 1831 and graduated at the head of his class (1/56) in 1835. He was commissioned brevet second lieutenant in the engineers and was promoted to second lieutenant in 1836 but left the army in 1837 to become a civil engineer. After working for the Charleston & Cincinnati Railroad and the Michigan Central Railroad, he moved to New York City in 1840, studied law, and was admitted to the bar in 1842. He became a colonel in the New York Militia in 1852 and was a commissioner for the circuit court of the Southern District of New York from 1854 until the outbreak of the Civil War.

Morell re-entered active duty as a colonel in the quartermaster branch of the Department (later Army) of Northeast Virginia on May 16, 1861. On August 9, following the Bull Run disaster, he was promoted to brigadier general of volunteers and given a brigade in Fitz John Porter's division of the Army of the Potomac. He fought in the Peninsula Campaign, and when Porter moved up to command the V Corps, Morell succeeded him as division commander. He showed a considerable amount of skill in the Seven Days battles and was appointed to major general on July 4. He also fought in the Bull Run and Antietam Campaigns.

Following the disaster at the Second Bull Run, the "powers that be" in the Lincoln administration needed a scapegoat. Fitz John Porter was selected. Morell testified on Porter's behalf, which effectively ruined his military career. He was relieved of his command. The following March 4, his promotion to major general expired without Senate action. He never held another important command. Politics cost the Union Army a fine general.

Morell commanded the defenses of the upper Potomac for six weeks and then was placed in charge of the Draft Depot at Indianapolis. He resigned his commission and was mustered out of the service on December 15, 1864.

General Morell was a farmer the rest of his life. He died in Scarborough, New York, on February 11, 1883, at age sixty-eight. He is buried under the chancel of St. Mary's Episcopal Church in Scarborough, where he conducted services for five years when the church had no rector.

CHARLES HALE MORGAN was born in Manlius, New York, on November 6, 1834. He enrolled in West Point in 1853, graduated in 1857 (12/38) and was commissioned brevet second lieutenant in the 4th Artillery. After garrison duty at the Artillery School for Practice in Fort Monroe, Virginia, he was promoted to second lieutenant in September 1857 and sent to Utah. He was promoted to first lieutenant on April 1, 1861.

Recalled to the East, Morgan arrived in December 1861 and served in the Peninsula Campaign. He was on sick leave during the Maryland Campaign but returned to duty on October 1, 1862, as chief of artillery of the II Corps. He was promoted to lieutenant colonel, staff, and became chief of staff of Hancock's II Corps on January 1, 1863, a post he held until February 27, 1865. He fought in all the major campaigns of the Army of the Potomac and particularly distinguished himself at the Wilderness and Spotsylvania and was repeatedly brevetted. He was Hancock's chief of staff when he commanded the Middle Military District (February 27–June 22, 1865). Morgan was brevetted brigadier general in December 1864 and promoted to full rank on May 21, 1865. He reverted back to the Regular Army rank of captain on January 15, 1866, although he was promoted to major the following year.

Morgan was especially famous within the army for his profanity. It was said he could out-cuss anybody in the service except for his chief, Hancock. Postwar, he had a number of garrison assignments, including Fort Monroe and Alcatraz Island, California, where he died on December 20, 1875. He was buried in the military cemetery on Angel Island but was reinterred at Golden Gate National Cemetery at San Bruno, California, in 1947.

EDWIN DENISON MORGAN was born in Washington, Massachusetts, on February 8, 1811. His father was a farmer. His family moved to Windsor, Connecticut, when he was eleven, and he was educated at the Bacon Academy in Colchester. His was a true rags-to-riches story. As a teenager,

Morgan clerked for an uncle, who was a grocer in Hartford, Connecticut, which elected him to the city council at age twenty-one. He moved to New York City four years later, and by the time he was thirty, he was one of the leading merchants in the city. He was astute, possessed good judgment, and was not afraid to take a chance. Untouched by scandal, and with an undeniable talent for making money, he was soon a successful wholesale grocer, banker, and stockbroker as well. Among other activities, his E. D. Morgan & Company was the principal agent for issuing bonds for the State of Missouri, to the tune of $30,000,000 (more than $600,000,000 in today's money) between 1835 and 1860.

Morgan was also interested in public affairs. He rose to public prominence as chairman of the New York Sanitary Committee during the cholera epidemic of 1848. Tall, handsome, and physically impressive, he was elected to the state senate in 1850 and became State Commissioner of Immigration. He was the first chairman of the Republican National Committee (1856–1864) and held the post again from 1872 to 1876.

Meanwhile, Thurlow "Boss" Weed picked Morgan to be his candidate for governor. He was elected to this position twice by huge majorities, serving from January 1, 1859 to December 31, 1862, even though Morgan separated himself from Weed politically. In the meantime, the Civil War began. Lincoln appointed him major general of volunteers on September 28, 1861. He was both governor and commander of the Department of New York and did a commendable job in the latter position, raising and equipping 223,000 men for the Union cause. (Morgan was a poor orator but a brilliant organizer.) He did not run for re-election in 1862 and resigned his commission on January 3, 1863.

Morgan ran for the U.S. Senate in February 1863 and served until 1869. He was offered the job of secretary of the treasury by President Johnson but refused it. He was denied the Republican nomination for the Senate in 1868. He ran for governor again in 1876 but was defeated. He was again offered the post of secretary of the treasury by President Chester A. Arthur in 1881, and was even confirmed by the Senate, but he declined the position.

Edwin Morgan was famous for his philanthropy and his generous contributions to educational, medical, and religious institutions. He died in New York City on February 14, 1883, at age seventy-two. He was buried in the Cedar Hill Cemetery in Hartford.

GEORGE WASHINGTON MORGAN was born in Washington County, Pennsylvania, on September 20, 1820, the grandson of a U.S. Army colonel. He was educated in local public schools and attended Washington College but dropped out in order to go west and fight in the War for Texas Independence. Sam Houston granted him a regular army commission as a lieutenant, and he rose to captain, commanding the port of Galveston. He also served with the 1st Texas Rangers but resigned in 1839 and returned to Pennsylvania.

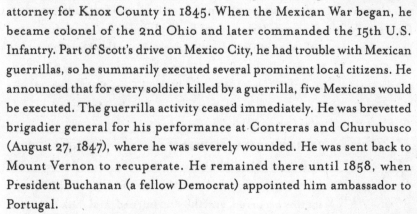

Morgan was admitted to West Point in 1841 but resigned in 1843 due to academic difficulties. He then settled in Ohio, studied law, and became prosecuting attorney for Knox County in 1845. When the Mexican War began, he became colonel of the 2nd Ohio and later commanded the 15th U.S. Infantry. Part of Scott's drive on Mexico City, he had trouble with Mexican guerrillas, so he summarily executed several prominent local citizens. He announced that for every soldier killed by a guerrilla, five Mexicans would be executed. The guerrilla activity ceased immediately. He was brevetted brigadier general for his performance at Contreras and Churubusco (August 27, 1847), where he was severely wounded. He was sent back to Mount Vernon to recuperate. He remained there until 1858, when President Buchanan (a fellow Democrat) appointed him ambassador to Portugal.

When the Civil War began, Morgan returned to America and was commissioned brigadier general on November 21, 1861. Part of Buell's Army of the Ohio, he was given command of a division in March 1862 and ordered to take the strategic Cumberland Gap. Operating against Confederate General Carter L. Stevenson, he captured the gap on June 18. He was, however, forced to hastily abandon the position in August, as

Braxton Bragg invaded Kentucky. His retreat was a masterpiece; he moved eight thousand men more than two hundred miles in sixteen days.

After briefly fighting in West Virginia, he was placed under Sherman (XV Corps), whom he perhaps hated worse than the enemy. After the Battle of Chickasaw Bluff (late December 1862), Sherman attempted to make him the scapegoat for the debacle. His performance, however, was superior to Sherman's. In any case, he played a prominent role in the capture of Arkansas Post, one of the most lopsided Union victories of the war. He briefly commanded the XIII Corps in January 1863.

Although Morgan believed the Union must be preserved at all costs, he was certainly not an abolitionist; believed that the government had no right to abolish slavery; and contended that African Americans were inferior to white people. President Lincoln consulted with General Morgan about the advisability of using black troops. He left the meeting thinking Lincoln had accepted his advice. When he found that his counsel had been rejected, he resigned his commission on June 8, 1863, and returned to Ohio.

A Democrat, Morgan supported George McClellan for president in 1864 and ran unsuccessfully for governor in 1865. The following year he was elected to Congress, serving from 1867 to 1868 and from 1869 to 1873, for a total of three terms. He opposed Radical Reconstruction and voted against the impeachment of President Johnson. He retired in 1873.

George W. Morgan died in Fort Monroe, Virginia, on July 26, 1893, at age seventy-three. He is buried in the Mound View Cemetery, Mount Vernon, Ohio. He was the last surviving general of the Mexican War.

JAMES DADA MORGAN was born on August 1, 1810, in Boston, Massachusetts, the son of a sailor. He became a merchant sailor and was aboard the USS *Berkley* when a mutiny occurred, and the ship burned, and sank. He spent two weeks at sea on an open lifeboat before reaching the coast of South America, from which he worked his way home. At age twenty-four he moved to Quincy, Illinois, which became his home for the rest of his life. Employed in the pork packing business, he was active in the "Quincy Grays," a militia unit, and was its captain when the

Mexican War began. The Grays became Company G, 1st Illinois Infantry, and Morgan was captain and company commander during the war with Mexico. He fought at Buena Vista, where he was brevetted major. Mustered out in June 1847, he returned home and became a successful merchant.

On April 29, 1861, he was named lieutenant colonel of the 10th Illinois and was promoted to colonel on May 20. He commanded a brigade in the Battle of Island No. 10, a major Union victory. He fought in the Siege of Corinth (April–May 1862) and, on the recommendation of U.S. Senator Orville H. Browning, was promoted to brigadier general on July 19. After briefly commanding a division in the Army of the Mississippi, he assumed command of a brigade in the Army of the Cumberland. His command was left to guard Nashville during the Stone River Campaign. He commanded a brigade in Granger's corps during the Battle of Chickamauga and later fought in the Battle of Missionary Ridge. During the Atlanta Campaign, he was advanced to divisional command, and took part in the Battle of Jonesboro, the March to the Sea, and the Carolinas Campaign. He distinguished himself in the Battle of Bentonville, for which he was brevetted major general in 1866. A fine commander who was idolized by his men, Morgan was mustered out on August 24, 1865.

Postbellum, Morgan returned to Quincy, where he was president of the First National Bank of Quincy, as well as a successful businessman. He was highly interested in Union veterans' affairs and reunions for the rest of his life. He died in Quincy on September 12, 1896, at age eighty-six. He was interred in Woodland Cemetery, Quincy.

WILLIAM HOPKINS MORRIS was born on April 22, 1827, in New York City, the son of a popular poet and songwriter. Educated in public schools, he was appointed to the U.S. Military Academy in 1846 and graduated in 1851 (27/42) as a brevet second lieutenant. He was assigned to the 2nd U.S. Infantry and posted to Fort Yuma, California. Promoted to second lieutenant in 1852, he resigned his commission in 1854. Returning to New York, he helped his father edit the *New York Home Journal* and, along

with Charles L. Brown, developed a carbine with an 8-shot conical cylinder. They patented it in 1860.

Morris rejoined the U.S. Army as a captain of volunteers on August 20, 1861. He was assistant adjutant general to Brigadier General John J. Peck and served in the Peninsula Campaign. When Peck moved up to divisional command, he took Morris with him. He was promoted to colonel and named commander of the 135th New York Infantry on September 2, 1862, and remained in command of the regiment when it was converted to the 6th New York Heavy Artillery the following month. He was stationed in Baltimore.

William Morris was given command of a brigade on March 16, 1863, and was promoted to brigadier general on that date. His brigade was stationed on Maryland Heights near Harpers Ferry until General Lee invaded the North in 1863, but was held in reserve during the Battle of Gettysburg. It was assigned to the III Corps during the pursuit after this battle and fought in the Bristoe and Mine Run Campaigns.

Undoubtedly a capable commander, Morris's active military career effectively ended on May 9, 1864, when, during the Battle of the Wilderness, he rode forward to inspect his command and was shot in the right knee by a Confederate rifleman. He did sit on courts martial boards from June to August 1864, and wrote a training manual, *Field Tactics for the Infantry*. Still suffering from his wound, he was mustered out of the service on August 24, 1865. In 1866, he was a delegate to the New York State Constitutional Convention. He was brevetted major general in 1867.

General Morris continued to be active in military affairs, serving in the New York National Guard (formerly Militia) as a brigadier general after the war and was its chief of ordnance. In 1877, he invented an automatic ejecting revolver. He also wrote a book on tactics for infantry armed with breech-loading or magazine rifles. It was published in 1879. His co-inventor of the 8-shot carbine, Charles L. Brown, was killed in action at Malvern Hill. When Morris modified their 1860 patent and it was reissued in 1871, he made sure Brown's name was included on the patent.

Morris died of chronic heart disease while on vacation in Long Branch, New Jersey, on August 26, 1900. He was seventy-three. His remains were interred in the Mountain Avenue Cemetery, Cold Spring, New York.

JAMES ST. CLAIR MORTON was born in Philadelphia on September 24, 1829, the eldest of eight children. He entered the University of Pennsylvania at age fourteen and enrolled in West Point four years later (1847). He graduated second in the Class of 1851 (2/42) and was commissioned brevet second lieutenant in the engineers. He was promoted to second lieutenant in 1854 and to first lieutenant in 1856. In 1851 and 1852, he was assistant engineer in the construction of the defenses of South Carolina (including Fort Sumter), but he spent most of the antebellum years constructing lighthouses and fortifications to defend New York City and as an assistant professor of mathematics and military engineering at West Point. He also served as chief engineer of the Washington Monument and of the water works for the District of Columbia. In 1860, he was charged with the task of determining if the construction of a railroad across the Isthmus of Panama was possible. He determined that it was but contracted malaria in the process. After spending time recuperating in Washington, he was posted to Dry Tortugas, Florida, in early 1861, with orders to put the defenses in fighting shape. He was promoted to captain on August 6, 1861. Meanwhile, his malaria incapacitated him again, and he did not enter an active theater of operations until June 1862, when he became chief engineer of Buell's Army of the Ohio.

While Buell marched to Kentucky to check Braxton Bragg's invasion of that state, he ordered Morton to remain behind and complete the fortifications of Nashville. Under Morton's direction, it became the most heavily fortified city in the United States, save for Washington, D.C. Much of his labor force was conscripted slaves or free men of color, who were also draftees. He employed 2,768 blacks from a nearby contraband camp when he built Fort Negley, the largest inland masonry fort in the United States at the time. Between six hundred and eight hundred of the "contrabands" died during the construction.

After Buell was sacked, Morris became chief engineer of William Rosecrans's Army of the Cumberland. Rosecrans felt he needed a pioneer (i.e., engineer) brigade, and Morton was the logical man to command it. He was promoted to brigadier general of volunteers on April 4, 1863.

Morton led his brigade (2,600 men) at Stones River (where he was reprimanded for delaying the advance of the XX Corps), the Tullahoma Campaign, Chickamauga (where he was slightly wounded), and the early stages of the Siege of Chattanooga. In the wholesale demotions and transfers after Chickamauga, Morton was relieved of his command on October 10 and replaced by William F. Smith. His request for a transfer was turned down, so on November 7, 1863, at his own request, he was mustered out of volunteer service and reverted to his Regular Army rank of major.

After briefly working on the Nashville fortifications, Morton was named chief engineer of Burnside's IX Corps. On June 17, 1864, during the Second Battle of Petersburg, he went forward on a reconnaissance, during which he was shot in the chest and killed. He was thirty-five years old. General Morton was buried in Laurel Hill Cemetery in the city of his birth.

GERSHOM MOTT was born on April 7, 1822, in Lamberton (now part of Trenton), New Jersey. His grandfather was a captain who guided George Washington and his army down the Delaware River during its advance on Trenton. Gershom, who had a strict Quaker upbringing, was educated at Trenton Academy and became a dry goods clerk in New York City at age fourteen. He was a second lieutenant in the 10th U.S. Infantry during the Mexican War but saw no foreign service. Discharged in 1848, he held a variety of jobs in the interwar years, including bank teller and collector of the port of Lamberton.

Mott joined the Union Army as lieutenant colonel of the 5th New Jersey Infantry on August 17, 1861. Part of the Army of the Potomac, Mott served in the Peninsula Campaign and was promoted to colonel on May 7. He distinguished himself at Williamsburg and the Battle of Seven Pines and took part in the Seven Days battles, where his regiment was lightly engaged.

Gershom Mott was severely wounded in the arm during the Second Battle of Bull Run and was promoted to brigadier general on September 7, 1862, while still recuperating. He missed the Maryland Campaign and did not return to duty until just after the Battle of Fredericksburg. He was part of the III Corps during the Battle of Chancellorsville, where he was wounded in the left hand on May 3, 1863. He missed the Gettysburg Campaign but led his brigade in the Bristoe and Mine Run campaigns.

When the III Corps was disbanded in March 1864, Mott's brigade was transferred to the II Corps. Mott assumed command of the 4th Division of the II Corps on May 2. His former III Corps troops were demoralized by their transfer and performed poorly in the Wilderness. On May 10, at Spotsylvania, the division was routed by a Confederate artillery barrage and fled the field in panic. Obviously no longer a fit fighting force, the division was disbanded, and its men scattered to other units. Mott was demoted to brigade commander. He was wounded in the side on May 19. When he returned to duty on June 18, he was given another division.

Mott led his new command (the 3rd Division of the II Corps) with great skill and gallantry and was one of the few Union commanders who earned praise for his part in the Battle of the Crater (July 30). He was brevetted major general and fought in the Siege of Petersburg. His war ended on April 6, 1865, when he was wounded in the leg at Amelia Springs. Lee surrendered three days later. Mott was promoted to major general of volunteers (full rank) on December 1, 1865. He resigned on February 20, 1866.

Gershom Mott was highly thought of by his superiors and was offered a colonelcy in the Regular Army but turned it down. He worked for a railroad and as a banker, and held several state jobs, including warden of the state prison, New Jersey state treasurer, and major general and commander of the New Jersey National Guard. He held this office from 1873 until his death, which occurred when he suddenly collapsed on a street in New York City on November 29, 1884, at age sixty-two. He suffered from heart disease and apparently had a heart attack. He was buried in Riverview Cemetery, Trenton.

JOSEPH ANTHONY "FIGHTING JOE" MOWER was born in Woodstock, Vermont, on August 22, 1827. His family moved to Lowell, Massachusetts, when he was six, and he was educated in local public schools and at the Norwich Academy. He always wanted to be a soldier. He worked as a carpenter until March 1847, when he enlisted in the army as a private and served in the Mexican War. Discharged in 1848, he managed to secure an appointment as second lieutenant in the 1st U.S. Infantry in 1855. He was promoted to first lieutenant in 1857.

Mower was with the 1st Infantry in the Battle of Wilson's Creek, Missouri, on August 10, 1861. Following this debacle, he was promoted to captain on September 9. He became colonel of the 11th Missouri Infantry on May 2, 1862, and distinguished himself in the Battle of Farmington, Mississippi, a week later. This was the start of one of the most distinguished combat careers in the Civil War. Mower would prove an extremely capable regimental, brigade, division, and corps commander. He fought in the Siege of Corinth and was given command of a brigade in the Army of the Mississippi. He led it at Iuka and in the Second Battle of Corinth (October 4), where he was wounded in the neck and captured by the Confederates. He soon escaped but was recaptured and eventually exchanged. He was promoted to brigadier general on March 16, 1863.

Mower led his brigade in Grant's final Vicksburg Campaign and in the subsequent siege of the city. He impressed his corps commander, General Sherman, who earmarked him for greater things. He was given a division in General Banks's Army of the Gulf and brilliantly spearheaded the attack on "the Confederate Gibraltar," Fort De Russy, Louisiana, on March 14, 1864. He also launched a brilliant surprise attack on Henderson Hill and captured most of the 2nd Louisiana Cavalry on the night of March 21/22. He fought in the Red River Campaign but was not present during the Battle of Mansfield, where Banks was decisively defeated. He commanded the rearguard at the end of the campaign.

Sherman called Mower "the boldest young soldier we have." He had Mower transferred to his command after the Red River, and he led a division in the Atlanta Campaign, the March to the Sea, and the Carolinas Campaign, during which he commanded the XX Corps. He was promoted to major general on August 12, 1864, and was sent to Texas in June 1865, when he occupied Galveston.

Mower was a Radical Republican who was loved by his men, respected by his superiors, and hated by the Southerners in the areas he controlled because of his support for civil and political rights for African Americans.

Mustered out of volunteer service on February 1, 1866, he reverted to his Regular Army rank of colonel and was given command of the District of Louisiana, where he organized and trained the 39th U.S. Infantry, an African American unit. (Later, it merged with the 40th Infantry to form the 25th U.S. Infantry.)

In late 1869, General Mower came down with pneumonia and died in New Orleans on January 6, 1870, at age forty-two. He is buried in Arlington National Cemetery.

N
NAGLE – NICKERSON

JAMES NAGLE was born in Reading, Pennsylvania, on April 5, 1822, the oldest of eight children. His family moved several times in his youth and finally settled in Pottsville, Pennsylvania, in 1835. Initially, he followed in his father's footsteps and became a painter and paperhanger. He also formed a militia company which became part of the 1st Pennsylvania Infantry. Captain Nagle and his men fought in several battles in Mexico, including the Siege of Vera Cruz and the fall of Mexico City. They were mustered out in September 1848.

Nagle returned to the painting and paperhanging business after the war. He married and fathered nine children. In 1852, he was elected sheriff of Schuylkill County, a position he held until the outbreak of the Civil War. On April 22, 1861, he was commissioned colonel of the 6th Pennsylvania Infantry, a three-month regiment. Mustered out in July, Nagle returned to the colors in October as colonel of the 48th Pennsylvania Infantry. It was sent to Fort Monroe, Virginia, and then North Carolina. Nagle was given command of a brigade in April 1862. Sent to the Eastern Front after the Army of the Potomac was defeated in the Seven Days battles, he fought in the Second Battle of Bull Run, where his brigade suffered heavy casualties. He was appointed brigadier general on September 10.

Nagle distinguished himself at Antietam, where he played a key role in capturing Burnside's Bridge. For some reason, his appointment was allowed to expire, and he reverted to the rank of colonel on March 4, 1863, but he was reappointed brigadier general on March 23. Sent to Kentucky with his brigade, he was diagnosed with heart disease and resigned his commission for reasons of health on May 9. Nevertheless, when General Lee invaded Pennsylvania, General Nagle organized the 39th Pennsylvania Militia Regiment, and the governor appointed him colonel. He was mustered out on August 2, after the Confederate tide receded. In 1864, when the Rebels threatened Washington, D.C., he organized the 149th Pennsylvania Infantry for a hundred days' service. It guarded the approaches to Baltimore until its term of enlistment expired. Nagle was mustered out for the last time on November 5, 1864.

General Nagle died of heart disease in Pottsville, Pennsylvania, on August 22, 1866. He was forty-four. He was buried in the Presbyterian Cemetery, Pottsville.

HENRY MORRIS NAGLEE was born in Philadelphia on January 15, 1815. He was admitted to West Point in 1831, graduated in 1835 (23/56), and was commissioned brevet second lieutenant in the 5th U.S. Infantry. After six months' service as a recruiter, he resigned his commission in December and became a civil engineer. He pursued this profession until the outbreak of the Mexican War (1846), during which he led a company in the 1st New York Infantry in California and Baja California, where he ordered two prisoners shot after they surrendered. For this crime, he was arrested by the U.S. military governor, but escaped punishment because of a general pardon issued by President Polk.

Mustered out in October 1848, Naglee remained in the Golden State and became a banker. He settled in San Francisco, joined the militia, and commanded the 1st California Guards. He also went to Europe, studied viticulture, built an estate (including vineyards) in San Jose, and became known as the father of the California brandy industry. When the Civil War began, he was commissioned lieutenant colonel, Regular Army, in the 16th U.S. Infantry (May 14, 1861) and was given command of a brigade in the Army of the Potomac on October 12. He was promoted to brigadier general of volunteers on February 12, 1862.

Naglee distinguished himself in the Battle of Seven Pines (May 31–June 1, 1862), where he was wounded four times (in the chest, right shoulder, and right leg) and had a horse shot out from under him. His subsequent report hugely inflated his role in the battle, which caused great criticism. After the Seven Days battles, he was transferred to North Carolina and in July 1863 was named commander of the District of Virginia, with headquarters in Norfolk. He quickly fell out with Francis H. Pierpont, the Union governor of Virginia ("the Restored Government of Virgina"), who demanded that all property owned by citizens who refused to take an oath of allegiance to the Restored Government should be confiscated by the Union Army. General Naglee refused to cooperate with this extreme measure. That he was a supporter of General McClellan did not help him. He was sacked on September 23, 1863, and ordered to Cincinnati, to await orders, which never came. He resigned and was mustered out on April 4, 1864.

Henry Naglee returned to California, where he became involved in two very public scandals. Mary L. Schell, one of his mistresses, tried to blackmail him. When he refused to pay, she published his love letters to her in 1867 (see Bibliography) and, in 1877, his nanny filed a lawsuit against him, alleging that he falsely proposed marriage to her, to seduce her. She became pregnant and, when Naglee would not marry her, she filed a breach of promise lawsuit. The nanny won the first trial and was awarded $27,500 ($805,805 in 2023 dollars), but this judgment was overturned on appeal.

Naglee's wife of twenty-four years died in 1869. He never remarried and devoted himself to his two daughters and his business interests. He died in the Occidental Hotel in San Francisco on March 5, 1886, at age seventy-one. He was buried in Laurel Hill Cemetery, Philadelphia.

JAMES SCOTT NEGLEY was born in East Liberty near Pittsburgh, Pennsylvania, on December 22, 1826, into an affluent family. He was educated in local public schools and at the Western University of Pennsylvania (now the University of Pittsburgh). He graduated in 1846 and, when the Mexican War broke out, joined the 1st Pennsylvania Infantry as a private, and fought at Cerro Gordo, La Porta, and Puebla, where he was wounded and commended for his bravery. He was mustered out as a sergeant in 1848. After the war, he became a farmer and an accomplished horticulturist. He also remained active in the militia and rose to the rank of brigadier general. Five days after Fort Sumter surrendered, he was appointed brigade commander in the Army of the Department of Pennsylvania.

Negley organized and saw to the equipping of the Union volunteers in the Pittsburgh area. He served under General Robert Patterson that summer and fought in the indecisive Battle of Falling Waters on July 2. Patterson was unable to prevent Confederate General Joseph Johnston from reinforcing Beauregard at Manassas, and thus contributed to the disaster at Bull Run. Negley's appointment expired on July 20, but he was reappointed brigade commander by the U.S. secretary of war on August 28. He became a brigadier general in the U.S. Army on February 12, 1862. Sent to the Western Front, he commanded a brigade in the Army of the Ohio and threatened Chattanooga during Bragg's invasion of Kentucky. He also successfully defended Nashville against Confederate raids and probes. He distinguished himself during the Battle of Stones River, and he was promoted to major general of volunteers on March 16, 1863.

Negley also performed well in the Tullahoma Campaign and proved himself a master of terrain analysis. His actions at Chickamauga on September 20, 1863, however, are controversial. After the Rebels broke the Union line, he withdrew fifty pieces of artillery from Snodgrass Hill to Rossville and established a second line of defense for the army. In *This Terrible Sound*, historian Peter Cozzens argues that Negley had lost his will to fight, withdrew the guns prematurely, and jeopardized the entire army. Union Generals Wood and Brannan held the same opinion. In his excellent Command and General Staff College thesis on Negley at Chickamauga, however, Major Keith Barclay disagrees, and holds that Negley acted in the best interests of the Army of the Cumberland, although he does point out that Negley was so ill on September 20 that he should have relinquished his command. In any case, Negley was brought up on charges of cowardice and desertion. Although cleared by a court of inquiry consisting of Generals Hunter, Cadwalader, and Wadsworth (January 29–February 23, 1864), his military career was ruined and effectively over. Later that year, General Grant did consider restoring him to command but elected not to. Negley served on a few administrative boards but finally resigned on January 19, 1865. For the rest of his life, he averred that he was the victim of West Point discrimination against civilian officers.

After the war, General Negley ran for Congress as a Republican in 1868 and served from 1869 to 1875. He later ran for Congress again in 1884 and held office from 1885 to 1887. He then retired from politics and worked in the railroad industry. The town of Negley, Ohio, was named after him.

James S. Negley died in Plainfield, New Jersey, on August 7, 1901. He was buried in Allegheny Cemetery, Pittsburgh.

THOMAS HEWSON NEILL was born on April 9, 1826, in Philadelphia, Pennsylvania. He attended local public schools and the University of Pennsylvania for two years before transferring to West Point in 1843. He graduated in 1847 (27/38) and was commissioned brevet second lieutenant in the 4th U.S. Infantry. He was promoted to second lieutenant later that year, to first lieutenant in 1850, and to captain in 1857. Meanwhile, he served in Mexico, on the frontier in west Texas and Indian Territory, in Utah, and as an instructor at West Point. He also fought the Navajo in New Mexico in 1860.

In April 1861, Neill was named assistant adjutant general to General Cadwallader, who oversaw operations on the Upper Potomac. Neill replaced David B. Birney as colonel and commander of the 23rd Pennsylvania Infantry on February 17, 1862.

Neill led the 23rd in the Peninsula Campaign, including the battles of Williamsburg and Seven Pines, where it suffered heavy casualties. It was less heavily engaged in the Seven Days battles, but Colonel Neill distinguished himself at Malvern Hill on July 1, 1862, where he was slightly wounded in the ankle. He led a brigade in the Battle of Fredericksburg and, on April 15, 1863, was promoted to brigadier general. He fought at Marye's Heights south of Fredericksburg during the Chancellorsville Campaign, where his horse was shot from under him. He served on the far-right flank of the army during the Battle of Gettysburg, as well as in the victory at Rappahannock Station (November 7) and the Mine Run Campaign (November 26–December 3).

In May 1864, Neill started the Overland Campaign as a brigade commander but assumed command of his division when General Getty was wounded during the Battle of the Wilderness on May 7. He directed the division until Getty returned on June 22 (including the Battle of Cold Harbor); Neill then joined the staff of the XVIII Corps and in October 1864 became an assistant inspector general on the staff of Phil Sheridan's

Middle Department. He was commander of Fort Independence, Massachusetts, from December 1864 to March 20, 1865. He was on leave for the next fifteen months. He was brevetted major general in 1866.

Following the war, Neill reverted to his Regular Army rank of major. After staff jobs in Washington, D.C. and Louisiana, he was promoted to lieutenant colonel of the 1st U.S. Infantry in 1869 and commandant of cadets at West Point (1875–79). He became commander of the 6th U.S. Cavalry as a colonel in 1879 and fought Apache in the New Mexico Territory. Thomas Neill retired in 1883 and returned to Philadelphia, where he died on March 12, 1885. He was fifty-eight. He was buried in the U.S. Military Academy Cemetery at West Point.

WILLIAM "BULL" NELSON was born in Maysville, Kentucky, on September 27, 1824, into an old Kentucky family. He attended the Maysville Academy and enrolled in the Norwich Academy (now University) in Vermont when he was thirteen. He attended the academy from 1837 to 1839 but left when his congressman secured for him an appointment as midshipman in the U.S. Navy. He sailed aboard the *USS Delaware* in 1840 and spent five years in the South Pacific. He then attended the U.S. Naval Academy at Annapolis as a member of its first class. In 1847, he served in a naval artillery battery during the Siege of Vera Cruz, where he distinguished himself and was awarded a sword for heroism. He joined the Mediterranean Squadron in 1849 and became acting lieutenant aboard the *USS Mississippi* in 1851. He continued to sail in the Mediterranean, as well as in African and American waters, until 1860, when he became an ordnance officer in the Washington Naval Yard. He was promoted to lieutenant in 1855.

Nelson was an articulate man of imposing presence, standing 6'2" and weighing more than thee hundred pounds. He was also blessed with a phenomenal memory. He was, however, dogmatic and argumentative when opposed. Despite his Southern manner, he visited President Lincoln two days after his inauguration and worked with him to secure Kentucky's adherence to the Union, which included smuggling arms to Unionists in

ENCYCLOPEDIA OF UNION GENERALS

the state during the state's neutrality phase. He also set up Camp Robinson, where he organized thousands of Kentucky Unionists into military units. Secretary of the Treasury Salmon Chase believed Nelson was primarily responsible for keeping the Bluegrass State in the Union. He saw to it that Nelson was detailed for service with the army with the rank of brigadier general on September 16, 1861.

Bull Nelson assumed command of a brigade in November and a division in December. His men respected "Big Buster," but did not care for his bluntness. Attached to Don Carlos Buell's Army of the Ohio, he fought at Shiloh on April 7, 1862, where his performance was excellent. He also distinguished himself in the Siege of Corinth and was reported the first man to enter the abandoned town. He was part of Buell's aborted drive on Chattanooga, after which he was sent to Kentucky, to oppose Confederate General Edmund Kirby Smith's drive into the state. He was promoted to major general on July 19. On August 29, with 6,850 mostly inexperienced men, Nelson met Kirby Smith (who had 6,500 men) in the two-day Battle of Richmond. The Federals were routed and lost 5,353 men (mostly captured), as opposed to 450 Rebel casualties. Nelson was wounded in the neck. He retreated to Louisville.

Meanwhile, Nelson clashed with Brigadier General Jefferson C. Davis, who was charged with preparing Louisville for defense. Nelson reprimanded Davis in front of other officers, said Davis "disappointed" him, and relieved him of his command. On September 29, they had another altercation in the Galt House in Louisville, which ended with Davis tossing a wadded-up piece of paper in Nelson's face, whereupon the former naval officer slapped him. Nelson then returned to his office. Davis, on the other hand, fetched a pistol. At 8 a.m., he shot Nelson in the chest, and the bullet penetrated his heart. Knowing he was dying, Nelson asked for a clergyman to baptize him. He passed away by 8:30 a.m.

Bull Nelson was thirty-eight years old when he died. He is buried in Maysville Cemetery, Maysville, Kentucky. He was the only naval officer on either side to reach the rank of major general.

Although General Buell had Davis arrested, and General William Terrill wanted to see him hanged, Jefferson C. Davis escaped earthly justice for what was the downright murder of an unarmed man.

JOHN NEWTON was born in Norfolk, Virginia, on August 24, 1822, the son of Thomas Newton, who was a U.S. Congressman for more than thirty years (1801 to 1833). John easily secured an appointment to the U.S. Military Academy in 1838 and graduated in 1842 (2/56). Commissioned second lieutenant in the engineers, he remained at the Academy for three years as an instructor of engineering. He was promoted to first lieutenant in 1852 and to captain in 1856. He spent the antebellum years constructing fortifications along the Atlantic and Great Lakes. He was also superintending engineer for Forts Pulaski, Georgia, and Jackson, Louisiana, and chief engineer of the Utah Expedition (1858).

When the Civil War began, Newton was initially appointed engineer for the Department of Pennsylvania and subsequently the Department of the Susquehanna. He was promoted to major on August 6, 1861, and was given command of a brigade on August 28. His promotion to brigadier general was dated September 23.

Newton was a fine brigade commander. He fought in the Peninsula Campaign and in Maryland, where he led a successful bayonet charge during the Battle of South Mountain. After fighting at Antietam, he was advanced to division commander in the VI Corps and was acting commander of that corps for ten days in January and February 1863. He was promoted to major general on March 30. Meanwhile, following the disastrous Union defeat at Fredericksburg in December 1862, he and six other officers conspired against Burnside. Newton and John Cochrane visited Abraham Lincoln at the White House on December 30 and informed him that the Army of the Potomac had no confidence in its commander, General Burnside. Burnside met alone with Lincoln at the White House after midnight on January 24, 1863. He carried with him General Order No. 8, which he intended to issue, subject to Lincoln's approval. It called for Newton, Joseph Hooker, and W. T. H. Brooks, a division commander, to be dismissed from the service; and the transfer of Generals William B. Franklin, William F. "Baldy" Smith, John Cochrane, Samuel D. Sturgis, and Lieutenant Colonel J. H. Taylor from the Army of the Potomac. He also submitted his resignation. He told Lincoln he should accept one or the other. Lincoln replaced Burnside with Hooker on January 26. This incident damaged Newton's career, because it earned him powerful enemies in Congress.

Newton was slightly wounded in the Battle of Salem Church during the Chancellorsville Campaign. After General Reynolds was killed at Gettysburg on July 1, 1863, Abner Doubleday succeeded him as commander of the I Corps, but General Meade had little confidence in him, so he replaced him with Newton. He led I Corps until March 24, 1864, when it was dissolved; simultaneously, Newton's promotion to major general expired because Congress did not act upon it. He reverted back to the rank of brigadier general and was transferred to the Western Front, where General Sherman (who thought highly of him) gave him command of a division in the IV Corps in Thomas' Army of the Cumberland.

Newton continued to distinguish himself in Georgia and played a major role in the Union victory at Peachtree Creek (July 20, 1864). He was, nevertheless, sent into professional exile in October, when he became commander of the District of Key West and the Tortugas. He was allowed to command an expedition to Tallahassee in 1865 but was defeated in the Battle of Natural Bridge (near Tallahassee) on March 6. He was, however, brevetted major general in 1866.

John Newton returned to the engineers after the conflict, reverted to the rank of lieutenant colonel, and oversaw improvements to waterways in New York and Vermont. A brilliant engineer, he was promoted to colonel in 1879 and to chief engineer of the U.S. Army and brigadier general in 1884. After forty-four years of service, he retired in 1886. He was New York City's commissioner of public works (1886–88) and president of the Panama Railroad Company (1888–95). General Newton suffered from rheumatism and heart disease in his last years. After a month-long illness, he died of pneumonia in New York City on May 1, 1895, at age seventy-two. He was interred in the West Point Cemetery.

FRANKLIN STILLMAN "FRANK" NICKERSON was born in Swanville, Maine, on August 27, 1826. He was educated at the East Corinth Academy, Maine, after which he read law. He was an official in the U.S.

Customs Service before the war. On June 15, 1861, he was elected major in the 4th Maine Infantry and performed well in the First Battle of Bull Run. He was promoted to lieutenant colonel of the 14th Maine on September 9 and to colonel on November 25.

Sent to Louisiana in 1862, he fought in the Battle of Baton Rouge (August 5) and was promoted to brigadier general on March 16, 1863. Part of Thomas W. Sherman's division of the Army of the Gulf, General Nickerson fought in the Siege of Port Hudson and briefly commanded the division after Sherman was wounded on May 27. He was replaced by General William Dwight and reverted to brigade commander on May 30. He continued to lead his brigade until Port Hudson fell.

Apparently, Nickerson was not highly thought of by his superiors. His brigade was part of General Franklin's XIX Corps during the Red River Campaign of 1864 but, because two of his regiments were on veterans' furlough, it didn't amount to much. It was stationed in Alexandria for most of the campaign. In July 1864, General Canby (who had replaced Banks as commander of the Department of the Gulf) relieved Nicholson of duty and sent him to Washington. He spent the rest of the war awaiting orders which did not come. He resigned his commission on May 13, 1865. He was not brevetted major general in the omnibus promotions after the war.

Post-war, General Nickerson moved to Boston and resumed his law practice. He died there in the residence of his son on January 23, 1917, at age ninety. He was buried in Forest Hills Cemetery, Jamaica Plain, Massachusetts.

OGLESBY – OWEN

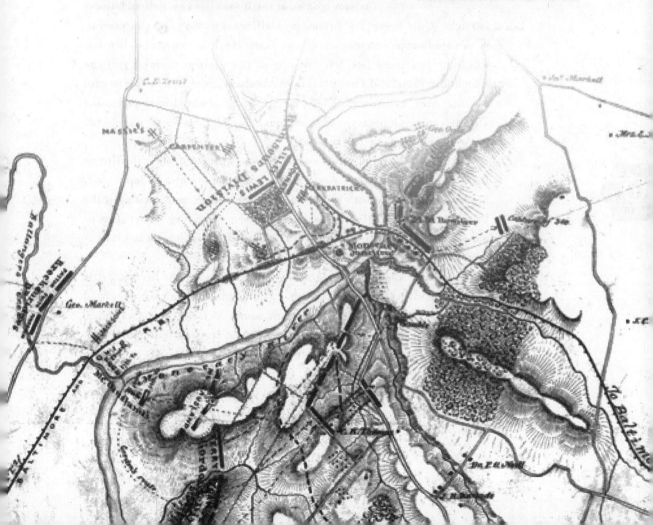

RICHARD JAMES "UNCLE DICK" OGLESBY was born in Floydsburg, Kentucky, on July 24, 1824. Both his parents died of cholera when he was nine, and he was raised by relatives. He later stated that the sale of the family slaves at this time turned him into an abolitionist. Meanwhile, he was sent to Decatur, Illinois, to live with an uncle. Poorly educated, he worked as a farmhand, a rope-maker, and a carpenter until 1846 and the outbreak of the Mexican War, when he became a first lieutenant in the 4th Illinois Infantry. He fought at Vera Cruz and Cerro Gordo before his regiment's enlistments expired, and he was mustered out in May 1847.

Oglesby studied at the Louisville Law School but was bitten by "Gold Fever" and headed for California in 1849. Very successful, he went to Europe and traveled for two years. He then returned to Illinois, where he practiced law, became one of the earliest members of the Republican Party, and a political ally of Abraham Lincoln, to whom he gave the nickname "rail-spitter." (They met in 1840 and were lifelong friends.) Oglesby ran for Congress in 1858 and was defeated; however, he was elected to the Illinois State Senate in 1860.

Dick Oglesby joined the Federal army as colonel of the 8th Illinois Infantry on April 25, 1861. Appointed brigade commander in September, he was quite popular with his men and was one of the most capable of the Union Army's political generals. He was present when Fort Henry surrendered and distinguished himself at Fort Donelson, which led to his promotion to brigadier general to date from March 22, 1862.

"Uncle Dick" took part in the Siege of Corinth and the Second Battle of Corinth on October 3, 1862. Here, a Confederate musket ball penetrated both his lungs, and his physicians unanimously declared that he was going to die. This he did not do, but he suffered a great deal and could not return to duty until April 1863. Meanwhile, he was promoted to major general on March 10, 1863.

Oglesby led the Left Wing of the XVI Corps of General Grant's Army of the Tennessee during the last Vicksburg Campaign and in the subsequent siege. At Lincoln's request, he then returned to Illinois, where he ran for governor and was elected. He resigned his commission on May 26, 1864.

Governor Oglesby spent the afternoon of April 14, 1865, with Abraham Lincoln, but declined his invitation to accompany him to Ford's Theater that night. He thus was not present when Lincoln was assassinated but was present in the Petersen House the following morning, when the president died.

Oglesby's subsequent political career was quite successful. He was three times governor of Illinois (1865–1869, 1873, and 1885–1889). He also served in the U.S. Senate (1873–1879). He attempted to return to the Senate after his third gubernatorial term but was defeated. He retired to his estate in Elkhart, Illinois, where he died on April 24, 1899. He was seventy-four. He was buried in Elkhart Cemetery. His son, John G. Oglesby, served two terms as lieutenant governor of Illinois.

JOHN MORRISON OLIVER was born in Penn Yan, New York, on September 6, 1828. He graduated from St. John's College on Long Island, New York, after which he moved to Monroe, Michigan, and became a druggist (now called a pharmacist). Five days after the Rebels fired on Fort Sumter, he enlisted in the 4th Michigan Infantry Regiment as a private. He was promoted to first lieutenant on June 20, 1861, and to captain on September 25. He was appointed colonel of the 15th Michigan on March 13, 1862.

Oliver fought in the Battle of Shiloh (April 6–7) and commanded a brigade in the Siege (First Battle) and Second Battle of Corinth, as well as the campaigns and Siege of Vicksburg, although he occasionally reverted back to regimental commander. Transferred to Chattanooga, he took part in the Atlanta Campaign and Sherman's subsequent March to the Sea. He distinguished himself in the attack on Fort McAllister, Georgia, in December 1864, for which he was somewhat belatedly promoted to brigadier general on January 12, 1865. He was given command of a division at the end of the war. He was posted to Louisville, Kentucky, and Little Rock, Arkansas, in the months immediately after the Confederate surrender.

John Oliver was mustered out on August 24 and was brevetted major general in 1866. Postwar, he practiced law in Arkansas and was an assessor of internal revenues. President Grant made him superintendent of the Little Rock Post Office in 1869, but he resigned because of ill health in 1871. He was offered an associate justiceship in the District of Columbia supreme court but declined it because of his health. He died in Washington, D.C. on March 30, 1872, at age forty-three and is buried in the Lakeview Cemetery in the town of his birth.

(SAMUEL) EMERSON OPDYCKE was born on the family farm in Trumbull County, Ohio, on January 7, 1830. He later dropped his first name and went by Emerson Opdycke. His grandfather fought in the American Revolution as a captain in the New Jersey Militia.

Educated in local public schools, Emerson was a gold prospector and a merchant in California but returned to Ohio in 1857. A fervent abolitionist, he joined the Union Army as a first lieutenant in the 41st Ohio on August 26, 1861. He was promoted to captain in January 1862. Sent to the Western Front, he fought in the Battle of Shiloh on April 6, 1862, where he grabbed the colors and rallied his regiment. He received two flesh wounds in the process. He took part in the subsequent advance to Corinth. He resigned his commission in September 1862 and returned to Ohio, where he recruited the 125th Ohio Infantry. He became its lieutenant colonel on October 1 and its colonel on January 14, 1863.

Colonel Opdycke distinguished himself in the Battle of Chickamauga, where his regiment held Horseshoe Ridge against repeated Confederate attacks. He further enhanced his reputation in the storming of Lookout Mountain during the fighting around Chattanooga. He took part in the Atlanta Campaign until May 14, 1864, when he was severely wounded in the left elbow during the Battle of Resaca. He fainted from loss of blood and was carried from the field. Opdycke returned in time to lead an attack on Kennesaw Mountain on June 27. On August 4, he was given command of a brigade in Thomas's Army of the Cumberland.

Opdycke most important battle occurred at Franklin, Tennessee, on November 30. The initial Rebel attack routed the forward Federal troops and threatened to cause the entire Union front to buckle. Opdycke reacted quickly, threw his brigade into action at the decisive moment, and stabilized the entire Union front. For this heroic action, he was brevetted brigadier general on February 7, 1865. Meanwhile, he fought in the Battle of Nashville and the subsequent pursuit in December 1864. He was one of the last men promoted to brigadier general of volunteers on July 26, 1865. He resigned from the army on January 1, 1866.

After the war, General Opdycke moved to New York City and was a banker and a dry goods dealer. On April 22, 1884, he accidentally shot himself in the stomach while he was cleaning his weapon. He died three days later at age fifty-four. His remains lie in Oakwood Cemetery, Warren, Ohio.

EDWARD OTHO CRESAP ORD was born on October 18, 1818, in Cumberland, Maryland, but his family moved to Washington, D.C. when he was an infant. Ord family tradition has it that he was the illegitimate grandson of King George IV of England. Julia Grant, wife of Ulysses Grant, later wrote that Ord "was brave and noble enough to be a king himself." Young Edward was considered a mathematical genius. He attended West Point, where his roommate was William T. Sherman. He graduated in 1839 (17/31) and was commissioned second lieutenant in the 3rd U.S. Artillery. He fought in the Second Seminole War and, as a battery commander, was stationed in Monterey, California, during the Mexican War. He also conducted the survey upon which the street grid of Sacramento was based. He was promoted to first lieutenant in 1841, to captain in 1850, and fought Indians in the Pacific Northwest. He was commanding Fort Vancouver, Washington Territory, and a battery of the 3rd U.S. Artillery when the Civil War began. He returned to the East and was promoted to

brigadier general of volunteers on September 14, 1861. He fought in the Union victory at Dranesville, Virginia in December.

Ord was successful at every level he commanded in the Civil War, including brigade, division, corps, and army. He was promoted to major general on May 3, 1862, and, after briefly commanding a division in the Department of the Rappahannock, was transferred to the Western Front as part of Grant's Army of the Tennessee. On October 5, 1862, while pursuing Confederate General Earl Van Dorn, who was defeated at Corinth the day before, he tried to cross the Hatchie River. He was wounded in the ankle by a bullet from the Rebel rear guard. By November, he could walk with the aid of crutches, so he reported for light duty. He did not return to field command until June 19, 1863, when he took charge of the XIII Corps during the Siege of Vicksburg, replacing John A. McClernand. After the city fell, he was transferred to the Department of the Gulf and worked in a secondary theater of operations.

Ord returned to the Eastern Front in July 1864, as commander of the XVIII Corps, Army of the James. On September 29, he led a successful attack on Fort Harrison, but his troops became disorganized after the fortification fell. Ord tried to rally his men, when he was seriously wounded in the thigh. He could not return to active command until December, when he was appointed commander of the XXIV Corps of the Army of the James. He became commander of the Army of the James on January 8, 1865, and led it until it was disbanded in August 1865. In the process, he played a major role in forcing General Lee to surrender at Appomattox.

Ord was mustered out of volunteer service and reverted to brigadier general, Regular Army, on September 1, 1866. He held a series of territorial commands, most notably in Arkansas and California, before he retired as a major general in December 1880. Afterward, he worked as a construction engineer on Mexican railroads. While on a ship bound from New York to Vera Cruz, General Ord contracted yellow fever. Taken ashore in Havana, Cuba, he died there on July 22, 1883, at age sixty-four. He was buried in Arlington National Cemetery. Fort Ord, California, is named after him.

One of his thirteen children, J. Garesche "Gary" Ord, was named after a colonel killed by General Ord's side at Stones River. Gary was with Teddy Roosevelt in his charge up San Juan Hill in 1898 and was killed there.

General Ord's grandson, James G. Ord, commanded the U.S. 28th Infantry Division in World War II.

WILLIAM WARD ORME was born in Washington, D.C. on February 17, 1832. His parents died when he was thirteen and he lived with his grandfather, who taught him to be a cabinetmaker. He attended Mount St. Mary's College in Emmittsburg, Maryland, and briefly moved to Chicago at age seventeen, where he worked as a bank messenger before settling in Bloomington, Illinois, in 1850. He passed the bar at age twenty and in 1853, became a partner in Leonard Swett's law firm. Orme was a friend of fellow Illinois lawyer Abraham Lincoln, who called him the most promising attorney in the state. He was one of the earliest members of the G.O.P.

Orme joined the U.S. Army in August 1862 as colonel of the newly formed 94th Illinois Infantry Regiment. He led a brigade in the Battle of Prairie Grove (December 7, 1862) and did well, but it was his lobbying with his friend Lincoln that led to his promotion to brigadier general on March 13, 1863. He took part in the Vicksburg Campaign of 1863 and the subsequent siege.

Orme contracted tuberculosis while campaigning in Mississippi. His brigade was transferred to the Department of the Gulf in August, but Orme was physically unable to perform field duty. In December 1863, he was transferred to Chicago, where he became commandant of Camp Douglas, the infamous prison camp. His health continued to deteriorate and, no longer able to work efficiently at even this rear-area assignment, he resigned his commission on April 26, 1864. He briefly became a supervising agent for the U.S. Treasury Department but finally retired in 1865.

General Orme died in Bloomington, Illinois, on September 13, 1866, at age thirty-four. He is buried in Evergreen Memorial Cemetery, Bloomington.

THOMAS OGDEN OSBORN was born on August 11, 1832, near the village of Jersey in Licking County, central Ohio. He graduated from Ohio

University in Athens in 1854, studied law under future Union General Lew Wallace in Crawfordsville, Indiana, and practiced law in Chicago from 1858 to 1861.

Osborn began recruiting the 39th Illinois Infantry in Chicago as soon as the news of Fort Sumter hit the streets. He had a difficult time getting it accepted into Federal service because Illinois had already filled its quota. Governor Yates used considerable political muscle to achieve its acceptance, but it was mustered into Federal service on October 11, 1861, with Osborn as its lieutenant colonel. He became its colonel on January 1, 1862. The regiment was nicknamed "Yates' Phalanx" in the governor's honor.

The 39th was initially sent to Missouri but at the end of October 1861 was transferred to Maryland, where it was fully armed and equipped. Its first mission was to guard the B & O Railroad. Its first major battle was at Kernstown, Virginia (January 1862), where Stonewall Jackson suffered his only significant defeat. It was later sent to Fredericksburg and then back to the Valley, where it took part in the defeat at Port Republic on June 9. It was hurriedly sent to the Virginia Peninsula but arrived too late to participate in the Seven Days battles.

Osborn and his men spent three months at Suffolk, Virginia, and were then transferred to the Department of the South and fought in North and South Carolina. Osborn was promoted to brigade commander on January 2, 1863, and took part in operations against Charleston, South Carolina, including the Morris Island fighting and the Battle of Fort Wagner. Here, he was wounded in the right arm in September 1863.

Transferred to the Army of the James in 1864, Colonel Osborn and his men fought in the Battle of Drewry's Bluff where, on May 14, a musket ball shattered Osborn's right elbow. He was in the hospital until September and could not return to duty until December. He suffered stiffness and pain from this wound the rest of his life.

Thomas Osborn was given command of a brigade in the XXIV Corps and distinguished himself in the last stages of the Siege of Petersburg. He was brevetted brigadier general on March 10, 1865, and helped storm Fort Gregg on April 2. After taking part in the Appomattox Campaign, he was promoted to brigadier general of volunteers on May 1, 1865. He briefly commanded a division in the XXIV Corps in the summer of 1865, resigned from the army on September 26, and returned to Chicago. He was brevetted major general in 1866.

Postwar, Osborn practiced law, was involved in several business ventures, and held a number of public offices. He was elected treasurer of Cook County and served from 1867 to 1869. He was U.S. minister to Argentina from 1874 to 1885. He returned to Illinois in 1890.

On March 27, 1904, in Washington, D.C., General Osborn suffered a massive cerebral hemorrhage that paralyzed him. Mercifully, he died ten hours later. He was seventy-one. They buried him in Arlington National Cemetery.

PETER JOSEPH OSTERHAUS was born in Koblenz, Rhenish Prussia, on January 4, 1823. He was educated at the Berlin Military Academy and became an officer in the Prussian Army. In 1848, however, he supported the Revolutionaries in Baden. They were defeated in June 1849, and Osterhaus fled to France and eventually Illinois, where he became a bookkeeper, a clerk, and a merchant. Financially ruined by the Panic of 1857, he settled in St. Louis, which had a large German-speaking population. Meanwhile, he became strongly pro-Union and joined the Republican Party

On April 27, 1861, Osterhaus joined the 2nd Missouri Infantry Battalion, a ninety-day unit, as a major. He distinguished himself in the Battle of Wilson's Creek (August 10) but was mustered out twelve days later, when the enlistments of the 2nd Missouri expired. Osterhaus rejoined the army a month later and commanded the 12th Missouri Infantry. He became a brigade commander in the Army of the Southwest on January 31, 1862, and helped save the Union left in the Battle of Pea Ridge (March 7–8). He was given command of a division on May 13 and was promoted to brigadier general on June 12. After serving in eastern Arkansas, he joined John McClernand's short-lived Army of the Mississippi in early 1863. He contracted malaria while in Arkansas and suffered from it for the rest of his life. Later that year, he was part of Grant's Army of the Tennessee and fought at Port Gibson, Champion Hill, Big Black River (where he was slightly wounded in the thigh), and the Siege of Vicksburg. He took part in Sherman's advance on Jackson, Mississippi, in July 1863.

Osterhaus was a solid leader at every command level. He took part in the capture of Lookout Mountain and the Atlanta Campaign, where he played a major role in the Battle of Jonesboro (Jonesborough), which doomed the city. He was promoted to major general on July 23, 1864, despite Sherman's opposition, and directed the XV Corps from September 23, 1864, to January 8, 1865, during Sherman's March to the Sea.

In March 1865, he was appointed chief of staff of the Military Division of West Mississippi (General Canby) and was involved in the reduction and capture of Mobile. He later represented the Union Army when the Confederate Trans-Mississippi Department surrendered. He commanded the Northern District of the Department of Mississippi and later the department itself in the second half of 1865. He was mustered out of volunteer service on January 15, 1866.

General Osterhaus was appointed U.S. Consul at Lyons, France, in 1866 and subsequently lived in Mannheim and later Duisburg, Germany, where he directed a wholesale hardware manufacturing association. He was granted a retirement pension as a U.S. brigadier general in 1905 and was reportedly the oldest pensioner on the U.S. Army's roster in 1915, when he was promoted to major general on the retired list. He died in Duisburg on January 2, 1917, just two days before his ninety-fourth birthday. Four months later, the U.S. joined the war against the Second German Reich. Meanwhile, Peter Osterhaus was interred in the family crypt in der Hauptfriedhof Koblenz (the Main City Cemetery, Koblenz), which has since been abandoned.

General Osterhaus was easily the best of the foreign-born leaders to serve in the Union Army. His son Hugo served in the U.S. Navy during World War I and became a rear admiral. Another son, Karl, was a major in the Imperial German Army when he died in Namibia, Africa, in 1904.

JOSHUA THOMAS "PADDY" OWEN was born in Carmarthen, Wales, on March 29, 1821. His family emigrated from the United Kingdom to the

European mainland when he was nine, and Owen later settled in the United States. He was a teacher at Jefferson College (Pennsylvania) in 1845 and later at the all-male Chestnut Hill Academy in Philadelphia. He served in the Pennsylvania legislature as a Democrat from 1857 to 1859.

When the Civil War began, Owen enlisted as a private in the Pennsylvania Militia but was named colonel of the 25th Pennsylvania Infantry, a nine-month regiment, on October 24, 1861. When that formation was mustered out, he became colonel of the 69th Pennsylvania, a predominantly Irish regiment which was part of the Philadelphia Brigade. As part of the II Corps, he took part in the Peninsula Campaign, the Seven Days battles, and the Battle of Antietam. He was promoted to brigadier general on November 29, 1862, but his appointment was allowed to expire, and he reverted to the rank of colonel on March 4, 1863. Owen was reappointed brigadier general on April 2, and this time, the Senate confirmed him. Meanwhile, he commanded the Philadelphia Brigade in the Battle of Fredericksburg and at Chancellorsville, where the brigade's performance was substandard. Three days before the Battle of Gettysburg, General John Gibbon arrested Owen and gave command of the brigade to Colonel (later Brigadier General) Alexander S. Webb, who defended "the Copse of Trees." Under Webb's leadership, the brigade's performance was exemplary. Owen, however, was restored to command shortly after.

Joshua Owen commanded his brigade at the Wilderness, Spotsylvania, and Cold Harbor (June 1864), where he failed to support another brigade, as he was ordered to do. General Gibbon (his division commander) arrested him for disobedience of orders in the face of the enemy. He was court-martialed and convicted, and President Lincoln ordered him expelled from the army on July 16. He was honorably discharged two days later.

Owen held several jobs after his discharge, including recorder of deeds, Philadelphia, County (1867–70). In 1871, he founded *The New York Daily Register*, a law journal that became the official publication of the New York court system. He died in Chestnut Hill, Pennsylvania, on November 7, 1887, at age sixty-six. He is buried in Laurel Hill Cemetery, Philadelphia.

P

PAINE – PRINCE

CHARLES JACKSON PAINE was born on August 26, 1833, in Boston, Massachusetts, the great-grandson of Robert T. Paine, a signer of the Declaration of Independence. The son of a wealthy family, he was educated at the Boston Latin School, graduated from Harvard in 1853, studied law, was admitted to the bar, and traveled abroad extensively. He was subsequently involved in several railroad endeavors, during which he made a fortune. He practiced law in Boston from 1858 to September 1861, when he raised a company of the 22nd Massachusetts Infantry.

Paine spent the winter of 1861–62 in the Washington defenses. He was promoted to major in the 30th Massachusetts in January 1862, but it was mustered out in March. Paine spent the next two years in the Department of the Gulf and was commissioned colonel of the 2nd (U.S.) Louisiana Infantry in October. This unit consisted mainly of African Americans recruited in New Orleans. Paine and his men performed well during the Siege of Port Hudson (May 24–July 9, 1863), although Paine move up to brigade command after Colonel Edward P. Chapin was killed in action on May 27. In November, he assumed command of a cavalry brigade in the Cavalry Corps of the Army of the Gulf.

Paine resigned his commission on March 8, 1864, but re-entered the service as a brigadier general on the staff of General Benjamin Butler on July 4. He led a division of black troops in the unsuccessful attacks on Drewry's Bluff in May and attacks on New Market Heights on September 29. General Paine was part of Butler's failed attacks on Fort Fisher, North Carolina, in December 1864 and in General Terry's successful operations against Fort Fisher and Wilmington in January and February 1865. He was brevetted major general on February 18, 1865.

After the war, Paine was commander of the District of New Bern. He managed to acquire Colonel Robert Gould Shaw's captured sword, which he returned to his family. He was mustered out in January 1866.

Postwar, General Paine was an executive for various railroads, but his main interest was yachting. Three of his yachts won the America's Cup against British challengers. He was a charter member of The Country Club

Paine – Prince

(Brookline, Massachusetts), which set the pattern for country clubs everywhere.

General Paine died on August 12, 1916, in his summer home in Weston, Massachusetts. He was eighty-two years old. He was buried in the Mount Auburn Cemetery in Cambridge, Massachusetts. His brother, Sumner E. J. Paine, was a lieutenant in the 20th Massachusetts. He was killed during Pickett's Charge on July 3, 1863. General Paine's son, who was also named Sumner, won an Olympic Gold Medal in the thirty-meter freestyle pistol event in 1896. His brother John finished second.

ELEAZER ARTHUR PAINE was born in the hamlet of Parkman, Geauga County, Ohio, on September 15, 1815. He was educated in local public schools and at West Point, from which he graduated in 1839 (24/31). He was commissioned second lieutenant in the 1st Infantry and sent to fight Seminoles in Florida, which provoked his resignation in 1840. He studied law, was admitted to the bar in 1843, and served as U.S. Deputy Marshal for Ohio (1842–45). He remained interested in military affairs, however. He wrote a training manual for volunteers, was active in the Ohio Militia, and was a lieutenant colonel by 1845, when he was promoted to brigadier general of militia. Meanwhile, he dabbled in Whig (and later Republican) politics. He practiced law in Painesville, Ohio, from 1843 to 1848, when he moved to Monmouth, Illinois. Meanwhile, he became personal friends with fellow lawyer Abraham Lincoln.

On April 26, 1861, Paine was mustered in to Federal service as colonel of the 9th Illinois Infantry, but the regiment was mustered out on July 26 without seeing combat. On September 3, he was promoted to brigadier general and given command of a brigade in Paducah, Kentucky. In early 1862, he commanded a division in John Pope's army in its operations against New Madrid and Island No. 10 and took part in the Siege of Corinth. His performance was considered unsatisfactory, and after Corinth, he was confined to rear area territorial commands in western Tennessee and western Kentucky only. From November 24, 1862, to May

4, 1864, he was in charge of the Gallatin, Tennessee, area, and guarding the railroad from Mitchellville to Nashville. Here, he developed a reputation for cruelty. He ordered that all guerrillas caught in his area of operations be executed. People were shot or hanged without trial and without evidence. He was not interested in facts; the accusations were enough for Paine. Any civilian who sympathized with the South was enough to classify him as a guerrilla. Unarmed civilians were often put on old horses and ordered to flee; they were then chased down by Paine's myrmidons and murdered. More than one hundred innocent civilians were hanged on trumped-up charges in the public square of Gallatin alone. "All General Paine wanted to see was a dead body," author Meg Groeling recorded. On one occasion, a private named Dalton deserted from the Confederate Army and took the Oath of Allegiance. The next day, Paine personally shot the unarmed man six times and murdered him. Paine was also personally corrupt and was famous for stealing and fencing furniture by the wagon-load. In short, he was a moral coward, a bully, a murderer, and a disgrace to his cause and his uniform. A special military commission investigated him and found him guilty of corruption, extortion, fencing stolen goods, unjust taxation, and immoral behavior. He was, however, protected by his friends in Washington. On July 18, 1864, he was transferred to the command of the District of Western Kentucky.

Finally, the Union high command had enough of his brutality. On September 11, General Sherman removed him from command and placed him in charge of guarding a bridge at Tullahoma, Tennessee, and he was formally reprimanded for his brutality toward civilians. He was sent home to await orders that never came. He resigned his commission on April 5, 1865. He did not receive the customary brevet to major general at the end of the war.

Paine resumed his law practice in Illinois postbellum. He died in Jersey City, New Jersey, on December 16, 1882, at age sixty-seven. He was buried in Oakland Cemetery, St. Paul, Minnesota.

HALBERT ELEAZER PAINE was born on February 4, 1826, in Chardon, Ohio. He was the first cousin of Union General Eleazar Paine. Halbert could trace his New England roots back to 1638. He attended public schools and graduated from Western Reserve College in 1845. He taught school in Mississippi for a year and returned to Cleveland, read law, and was admitted to the bar in 1848. He moved to Milwaukee in 1857, where he became law partners with German revolutionary Carl Schurz, another future Union general.

Paine joined the Union Army as colonel of the 4th Wisconsin Cavalry on July 2, 1861. He was involved in the capture of Fort St. Philip, the city of New Orleans (April 1862), the early, unsuccessful Vicksburg campaigns, the Battle of Baton Rouge (August 5), and the Bayou Teche Campaign. He was also involved in the suppression of guerrilla activities in south Louisiana and Mississippi. He was promoted to brigadier general on April 9, 1863. Given command of an infantry division in the XIX Corps on May 2, he fought in the Port Hudson Campaign until the general assault of June 14, where he was wounded in the left side, left leg, and left shoulder. He lay in an open field all day under the hot Louisiana sun. A wounded soldier tossed him a canteen taken from a dead man. General Paine later said this saved his life. Finally rescued, he was taken to New Orleans, where surgeons amputated his leg three or four inches below the knee. He was sent to Milwaukee in July and was in Washington, D.C. when Confederate General Early attacked the capital city. Paine commanded the Union line between Forts Totten and Stevens during the successful defense. Meanwhile, he was brevetted major general for Port Hudson.

Now fit only for emergency defensive commands or rear area duties, Halbert Paine assumed command of the District of Illinois in August 1864. He resigned from the army on May 15, 1865.

General Paine was a good commander and an independent thinker. In Baton Rouge, he was arrested by his commander, Brigadier General Thomas Williams, for refusing to return slaves to their masters, as Williams ordered him to do. When General Butler ordered him to burn Baton Rouge in August 1862, however, he refused to do so.

Paine entered the political arena after the war and served three terms in the U.S. House of Representatives (1865–1871). Although a Radical

Republican, he supported President Andrew Johnson. He declined renomination in 1870 and practiced law in Washington for several years. His writings on contested elections were considered definitive.

In 1878, Carl Schurz, his former law partner and now secretary of the interior, appointed him commissioner of patents. He used this office to introduce typewriters to the Federal bureaucracy. He held this office until 1880.

General Paine died in Washington, D.C. on April 14, 1905, at age seventy-nine. His remains lie in Arlington National Cemetery.

INNIS NEWTON PALMER was born in Buffalo, New York, on March 30, 1824. He attended local schools, entered West Point in 1842, and graduated in 1846 (38/59). Commissioned brevet second lieutenant in the 2nd Mounted Rifles, he was promoted to second lieutenant in 1847, fought in the Mexican War, and was brevetted first lieutenant "gallantry and meritorious conduct" at Contreras and Churubusco. He was brevetted captain for Chapultepec and fought in every major battle from Vera Cruz to Mexico City. He served on the Western frontier after Mexico, was promoted to first lieutenant in 1853, to captain (substantive rank) in 1855, and to major on April 25, 1861, just after the Civil War began.

Palmer led a cavalry battalion in the First Battle of Bull Run and was commended for his gallantry. He was promoted to brigadier general of volunteers on September 28, 1861. He commanded an infantry brigade in the IV Corps and performed well during the Peninsula Campaign and the Seven Days battles. That fall, he was busy organizing recruits in New Jersey and Delaware and directing the draft depot in Philadelphia. Sent to North Carolina at the end of 1862, he spent the rest of the war on this secondary front, commanding a brigade, a division, the Department of North Carolina, and the XVIII Corps. Most significantly, he successfully defended New Bern against a Confederate offensive led by George Pickett (his former classmate) in January and February 1864. He linked up with Sherman in March 1865 and helped complete the conquest of the state. He was mustered out of volunteer service on January 15, 1866, and was brevetted major general two days before.

Palmer reverted to lieutenant colonel of the 2nd Cavalry in 1866 and assumed command of the regiment as a colonel in 1868. He spent most of the rest of his career in what is now Wyoming and Nebraska. He went on sick leave from 1876 and retired in 1879. He settled in the Washington, D.C. area and died of kidney failure in Chevy Chase, Maryland, on September 10, 1900, at age seventy-six. He was buried in Arlington National Cemetery. His grandson, Innis Palmer Swift, commanded the 1st Cavalry Division and I Corps in the South Pacific during World War II.

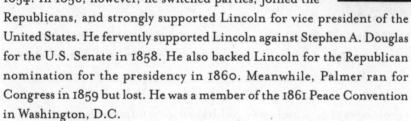

JOHN MCAULEY PALMER was born on September 13, 1817, in Eagle Creek, Kentucky, into an anti-slavery family, which moved to Alton, Illinois when he was fourteen. He attended Shurtleff College in Alton from 1834 to 1836, read law while working at odd jobs, was admitted to the bar in 1839, and opened a practice in Carlinville. He became probate judge of Macoupin County (1845), delegate to the Constitutional Convention (1847), state senator (1852), and county judge, all as a Free Soil Democrat. He played a major role in defeating Abraham Lincoln when he ran for the U.S. Senate nomination in 1854. In 1856, however, he switched parties, joined the Republicans, and strongly supported Lincoln for vice president of the United States. He fervently supported Lincoln against Stephen A. Douglas for the U.S. Senate in 1858. He also backed Lincoln for the Republican nomination for the presidency in 1860. Meanwhile, Palmer ran for Congress in 1859 but lost. He was a member of the 1861 Peace Convention in Washington, D.C.

Judge Palmer became colonel of the 14th Illinois Infantry on May 25, 1861, brigadier general on December 21, and major general on March 16, 1863. He led a division in John Pope's Army of the Mississippi in the Battles of New Madrid and Island No. 10 and commanded a brigade in the Siege of Corinth. He was back in divisional command at Stone's River (December 31, 1862–January 2, 1863).

One of the best political generals on either side, he took part in the Tullahoma Campaign of 1863 and commanded a division in Thomas Crittenden's XXI Corps at Chickamauga. He received a flesh wound at Redan (near Chattanooga) on September 26. It became inflamed, and he had to be hospitalized. He returned to duty on October 10 and seventeen days later assumed command of the XIV Corps of the Army of the Cumberland, which he led during the Atlanta Campaign.

General Palmer disliked West Pointers. He refused to subordinate himself to John Schofield, and a dispute with William T. Sherman ended with Palmer requesting to be relieved. (General McPherson had been killed in action and Sherman appointed O. O. Howard, a West Pointer, to the command of the Army of the Tennessee over Palmer, even though Palmer was senior.) Palmer's request was granted on August 6, 1864. The Union thus lost the services of another fine combat commander.

On February 10, 1865, Lincoln appointed Palmer commander of the Department of Kentucky, where his primary goals were suppressing guerrillas and destroying slavery in a state to which the Emancipation Proclamation did not apply. The situation was delicate, but Palmer handled it skillfully and was quite successful on both fronts. Palmer resigned his commission on September 1, 1866.

Postbellum, John Palmer had a highly successful political career, serving as governor of Illinois (1869–1873) and U.S. senator (1891–1897). He was a serious candidate for president in 1892 but withdrew to support Grover Cleveland. At age seventy-nine, he ran for president in 1896 as a Gold Democrat (a splinter party) but was defeated. His vice-presidential running mate was former Confederate General Simon Boliver Buckner.

In 1899, Palmer announced that he was suffering from cataracts, was blind in one eye and going blind in the other. He nevertheless wrote an autobiography, which was published posthumously in 1901 (see Bibliography). General Palmer suffered a heart attack and died in his sleep on September 25, 1900, in Springfield, Illinois. He was eighty-three. He was buried in the Carlinville City Cemetery, Carlinville, Illinois.

JOHN GRUBB PARKE was born on September 22, 1827, in Coatesville, Pennsylvania, but his family moved to Philadelphia when he was eight. He was educated in a private academy and at West Point, from which he graduated in 1849 (2/43). Commissioned brevet second lieutenant in the topographical engineers, he surveyed a railroad route from the Mississippi River to the Pacific Ocean and did survey work along the U.S.–Canadian northwest border. He was promoted to second lieutenant in 1854 and first lieutenant in 1856. He was in Washington Territory when the Civil War began. He then returned to the East, a trip which took months.

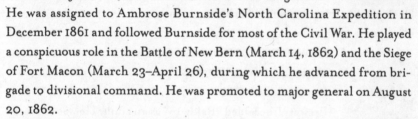

Parke was promoted to captain on September 9, 1861, and to brigadier general on November 23, skipping the ranks of major, lieutenant colonel, and colonel altogether. He was assigned to Ambrose Burnside's North Carolina Expedition in December 1861 and followed Burnside for most of the Civil War. He played a conspicuous role in the Battle of New Bern (March 14, 1862) and the Siege of Fort Macon (March 23–April 26), during which he advanced from brigade to divisional command. He was promoted to major general on August 20, 1862.

Meanwhile, Burnside's IX Corps was sent to Maryland with Parke as its chief of staff. It fought at Antietam, where Parke assumed command of its 3rd Division when Isaac Rodman was mortally wounded. When Burnside was named commander of the Army of the Potomac, Parke became its chief of staff of that army. After the debacle at Fredericksburg, Burnside was relieved of his command on January 26, 1863. General Parke commanded the IX Corps from March 19 to August 25. In mid-June 1863, it joined Grant's Army of the Tennessee and fought in the Siege of Vicksburg and Parke commanded Sherman's Left Wing in the Second Battle of Jackson (July 16). Parke became its chief of staff of Burnside's Army of the Ohio in September. He served in the Siege of Knoxville and, when the IX Corps was transferred to the East, in the Siege of Petersburg.

Burnside mishandled the Battle of the Crater and was relieved of his command on August 14, 1864. Parke was chosen to replace him and led the IX Corps for the rest of war, except when Meade was absent, and Parke was acting commander of the Army of the Potomac. He was in this position when Lee launched his final attack on Fort Stedman on March 25, 1865, which Parke repulsed. He also took part in the Appomattox Campaign. He commanded the XXII Corps after the South surrendered and was mustered out of the volunteer service on January 15, 1866.

Parke was one of the best officers to ever serve in the U.S. Army and performed exceptionally well at every level—brigade, division, corps, and army. He was also an excellent corps and army chief of staff.

Except for his Civil War service, Parke spent his entire career in the engineers. He reverted to the rank of major in 1866 and was promoted to lieutenant colonel in 1879 and to colonel in 1884. He was superintendent of the U.S. Military Academy from 1887 to 1889, when he retired. General Parke died in Washington, D.C. on December 16, 1900, at age seventy-three. He was interred in Saint James the Less Episcopal Churchyard, Philadelphia. He was married but had no children.

LEWIS BALDWIN PARSONS was born in Perry, New York, on April 5, 1818. He was the grandson of a Revolutionary War officer. Originally named "Lewis Parsons," he added "Baldwin" as an adult. He was educated in rural public schools and graduated from Yale in 1840. He taught at a classical school in Noxubee County, Mississippi, and liked the people but could not tolerate slavery. He returned to the North and graduated from Harvard Law School in 1844. He practiced law in Alton, Illinois, and in St. Louis, where he settled in 1854 and became president of the Ohio & Mississippi Railroad.

Parsons joined the Union Army as a captain and assistant quartermaster on October 31, 1861. He served as an aide to Francis P. Blair, Jr., and he briefly served as aide-de-camp to Henry Halleck. Antebellum, Parsons had worked in the railroad business with George McClellan, who recognized his abilities. He appointed Parsons director of transportation in the Department of Mississippi in March 1862. He held the same post for the Army of the Tennessee from September 1862 to December 1863. He was in charge of rail and river transport for the Military Division of the Mississippi from December 1863 to August 1864 and, after a tour of duty with the Quartermaster Branch, directed all rail and river transportation for the U.S. Army from September until the end of the war.

Logistics matter in war. Parsons was a highly efficient logistician and played a significant if unsung role in the Union victory in the West, especially in the field of railroad transportation. In a single year ending June 30, 1863, he transported 245,000 tons of supplies, 329,000 troops, 82,000 horses and mules, and 25,000 cattle out of his St. Louis headquarters alone. His assistants had similar statistics out of his Pittsburgh, Cincinnati, Louisville, Cairo, Memphis, and New Orleans branches. President Andrew Johnson recognized his contribution and appointed him brigadier general on May 11, 1865. He was mustered out on April 30, 1866, and was brevetted major general on May 14, 1866.

After the war, Parsons spent two years touring Europe and more than twenty years as director of several railroads and corporations and was president of a St. Louis bank. He was an unsuccessful Democratic candidate for lieutenant governor in 1880. He was also a member of the Presbyterian Church in Flora, Illinois, and often conducted services when the preacher was absent.

General Parsons died in Flora on March 16, 1907, at age eighty-eight. He was buried in the Bellefontaine Cemetery, St. Louis.

MARSENA RUDOLPH PATRICK was born near Watertown, New York, on March 11, 1811. He ran away from home as a youth and became a canal boat driver, schoolteacher, medical student, and a friend of General Stephen van Renssalaer, who secured for him an appointment to the U.S. Military Academy in 1831. He graduated in 1835 (48/56) and was commissioned brevet second lieutenant in the 2nd U.S. Infantry. He was promoted to second lieutenant in 1836, first lieutenant in 1839, and captain in 1847. Meanwhile, he fought in the Second Seminole War. He was brevetted major for meritorious service in Mexico. In 1850, he resigned from the army and returned to New York, where he was a farmer near Sackett's Harbor. He also served as president of a small local

railroad (1853–54). He was president of the New York State Agricultural College (a forerunner of Cornell University) from 1859 until the start of the Civil War in 1861.

Patrick's first service was as a brigadier general and inspector general of the New York Militia. He was named an assistant inspector general on the staff of the Army of the Potomac in November. He was given command of a brigade in General McDowell's Corps on March 12, 1862, and was appointed brigadier general of volunteers eight days later. He served briefly as military governor of Fredericksburg and in the Washington defenses, but did not see heavy combat until the Maryland Campaign, when he fought at South Mountain (September 14) and Antietam (September 17).

When the Army of the Potomac reorganized on October 6, 1862, Patrick was named provost marshal of the army. He tried unsuccessfully to stop vandals from sacking Fredericksburg in December but generally did a fine job as provost. He also created the Bureau of Military Information, a network designed to provide military intelligence about the Confederate Army. In addition, he also organized the transport of prisoners-of-war to prison camps, an especially difficult task after Gettysburg. Although harassed by Secretary of War Stanton, who disliked him, General Grant recognized Patrick's ability and named him provost marshal for the combined forces operating in Virginia.

Patrick had trouble with Radical Republicans, especially Stanton. Despite a stern demeanor and an intimidating voice, he had a kind heart. He hated to see innocent Southern women and children suffer, and he did what he could to mitigate their situations. This provoked the ire of some of the Radicals, who wanted them to suffer. Their wishes did not sway Patrick in the slightest.

After Lee surrendered, Patrick was named commander of the District of Henrico in northern Virginia. His compassionate behavior toward destitute civilians led to his being relieved at the behest of the Radical Republicans. He returned to civilian life on June 12, 1865, but was nevertheless brevetted major general in 1866.

As a Democrat, General Patrick ran unsuccessfully for New York State Treasurer in 1865. He moved to Manlius, New York, in 1867 and served as president of the New York State Agricultural Society. He became widely known as an authority and public speaker on agricultural issues. Later, he moved to Dayton, Ohio, where he was governor of the Central Branch of the National Home for Disabled Volunteer Soldiers. He died in Dayton on July 27, 1888, at age seventy-seven. He was buried in the Dayton National Cemetery.

FRANCIS ENGLE PATTERSON was born in Philadelphia on March 7, 1821. His father was Robert Patterson, a major general in the Pennsylvania Militia who famously failed to stop Confederate General Joseph E. Johnston from joining General Beauregard's army at Manassas during the First Bull Run Campaign. Young Francis attended the University of Pennsylvania but in 1846 joined the U.S. Army as a second lieutenant in the 1st U.S. Artillery. He fought in the Mexican War, where he was attached to the Texas Rangers. He remained in the service after the Mexican surrender, was promoted to first lieutenant in the 9th U.S. Infantry in October 1847 and to captain in 1855 but resigned his commission in 1857.

Patterson rejoined the army as colonel of the 17th Pennsylvania Infantry on April 25, 1861. He was mustered out on August 2 but rejoined the army as a brigadier general of volunteers on April 15, 1862. He was given command of a brigade in the III Corps of the Army of the Potomac. He took part in the Peninsula Campaign and fought at Williamsburg but relinquished command during the Battle of Seven Pines because he came down with typhoid fever. He thus missed the Seven Days battles. He resumed command of his old brigade that fall.

During the skirmishing around Catlett's Station, Patterson withdrew his brigade because of unconfirmed reports that Confederate troops were in the area. His corps commander, General Sickles, accused him of retreating without orders, relieved him of his command, and made plans to court-martial him. At Occoquan, Virginia, near Fairfax Court House, General Patterson shot himself on November 22, 1862. He was forty-one. At first it was not clear whether his death was an accident or suicide, but Captain Vreeland of the 8th New Jersey, who was present at the time, said the general took his own life in a moment of temporary insanity. Even so, his death was listed as an accident in the army records. He was buried in Laurel Hill Cemetery, Philadelphia, next to his father and brother, Robert Emmet Patterson, a brevet brigadier general in the Union Army.

GABRIEL RENE PAUL was born on March 22, 1813, in St. Louis, Missouri, the son of a colonel of engineers in Napoleon's army who was severely wounded at Trafalgar. Gabriel's grandfather built the first house in St. Louis. He entered West Point in 1829 and graduated in 1834 (18/36). Commissioned brevet second lieutenant in the 7th U.S. Infantry, he was promoted to second lieutenant in December 1834, to first lieutenant in 1836, and to captain in 1846. Between garrison assignments in Indian Territory, Louisiana, and Mississippi, he fought in the Second Seminole War in 1842 and in Mexico, where he was brevetted major for gallantry at Cerro Gordo, where he was wounded. He recovered in time to lead an assault party at Chapultepec.

Between the wars, Paul patrolled on the Rio Grande in Texas, where he captured the desperado Caravajal and his gang. He also fought Indians in Utah in 1858. He was with the 8th U.S. Infantry in Albuquerque, New Mexico Territory, when the Civil War began. He was promoted to major (substantive rank) on April 22, and became acting inspector general of the Department of New Mexico. He was named colonel of the 4th New Mexico Infantry on December 9. Summoned to the East the following spring, he was promoted to brigadier general on September 5, 1862, and assumed command of a brigade in the I Corps on October 14. He took part in the Fredericksburg Campaign and briefly served as acting commander of the 1st Division of that corps. His appointment expired on March 4, 1863, without Senate action, and he reverted to the rank of colonel. He was reappointed on April 18 and led his brigade in the Chancellorsville Campaign.

On July 1, 1863, during the Battle of Gettysburg, General Paul repulsed attacks by the Confederate III Corps of A. P. Hill. In the process, a Rebel bullet passed through his right temple, destroyed his right eye, and came out his left eye, permanently blinding him. It also damaged his senses of smell and hearing. He was erroneously reported as killed in action.

Gabriel Paul was unemployed until February 1865, when he retired as a brigadier general, Regular Army. He was in charge of the Military Asylum at Harrodsburg, Kentucky, from June 1865 to December 1866. His two slaves were freed in 1865, and he was officially mustered out of the service on July 28, 1866, as a major general, Regular Army. General Paul died in Washington, D.C. at age seventy-three on May 5, 1886. He was buried in Arlington National Cemetery.

JOHN JAMES PECK was born in Manlius, New York, on January 4, 1821. He entered the U.S. Military Academy in 1839 and graduated in 1843 (8/39). Commissioned brevet second lieutenant in the 2nd Artillery, he was promoted to second lieutenant in 1846 and first lieutenant in 1847. He fought at Palo Alto and Resaca de la Palma in northern Mexico before being transferred to General Scott's army. He took part in the Siege of Vera Cruz and was brevetted captain for Contreras and Churubusco and major for gallantry at Molino del Rey. Postwar, he was stationed in the New Mexico Territory. He resigned his commission in 1853 and settled in Syracuse, where he became a prominent businessman, banker, and railroad executive. He also served as president of the school board and was a delegate to the Democratic National Convention of 1860, where he supported Stephen A. Douglas.

Peck joined the Union Army after the Bull Run disaster and was appointed brigadier general on August 9, 1861. He was given command of a brigade in the Army of the Potomac and fought in the Peninsula Campaign, including the Siege of Yorktown, the Battle of Williamsburg, and the Battle of Seven Pines (Fair Oaks). He led a division in the IV Corps during the Seven Days battles and was promoted to major general on July 25.

Instead of being sent to northern Virginia or Maryland, as was most of McClellan's army, Peck's division was posted at Suffolk, south of the James River. Confederate General Longstreet attempted to retake the area in the spring of 1863 but was repulsed by Peck, who was seriously injured in the process, suffering a fall which injured his spine and appears to have troubled him for the rest of his life. After a three-month convalescence, he was named commander of the District of North Carolina, a.k.a. the Army of North Carolina (August 12, 1863 to April 25, 1864). After a medical furlough, he commanded the Canadian border sector of the Department of the East from July 1864 until he was mustered out of Federal service on August 24, 1865.

General Peck returned to Syracuse, and, in 1867, organized the New York State Life Insurance Company, with himself as president. He held this position until his death, which occurred in Syracuse on April 21, 1878, at age seventy-eight. He was buried in Oakwood Cemetery, Syracuse.

GALUSHA PENNYPACKER was born on June 1, 1844, near Valley Forge, Pennsylvania. His mother died when he was an infant, and he was raised by relatives. He was well educated in local private schools and, at age sixteen, enlisted in the 9th Pennsylvania Infantry as a quartermaster sergeant on April 22, 1861. He was commissioned captain in the 97th Pennsylvania in August and served as a company commander. Initially stationed at Fort Monroe, he fought in the Battle of Fort Pulaski, Georgia (February 7, 1862), and in the fighting around Charleston, South Carolina, including the battles of Secessionville, Morris Island, and Fort Wagner, and briefly served in Florida. He and his regiment were transferred to Virginia, on the south side of the James River, in the spring of 1864.

During the Battle of Ware Bottom Church (May 20) in the Bermuda Hundred Campaign, Pennypacker led three hundred men in a gallant counterattack and restored the broken Union line. In the process, he was severely wounded in the right arm, left leg, and right side. He was sent to Fort Monroe to recover. The date of his promotion to major is unclear. He became a lieutenant colonel on April 3, 1864, and a colonel on August 15. On September 14, he took charge of a brigade in the Army of the James. He participated in the battles of Cold Harbor and New Market Heights, where he was painfully wounded by a shell splinter in the ankle near Fort Gilmer on September 29.

Galusha Pennypacker distinguished himself in the Second Battle of Fort Fisher on January 15, 1865, when (as part of Newton Curtis's brigade) he personally led the decisive attack and planted the flag on the fort's traverse. The expedition's commander, General Alfred H. Terry, later called him "the real hero of Fort Fisher" and remarked that, had it not been for Pennypacker, the fort would never have been taken. He paid a heavy price for his bravery. Standing only a few feet away, a Confederate soldier shot him through the right hip. The bullet damaged his pelvic bone and exited through the genital area. He was in excruciating pain and, at first, his doctors unanimously declared that he would not live and even ordered him a coffin. He did not die but spent ten months in the hospital at Fort Monroe.

Pennypacker was brevetted brigadier general soon after Fort Fisher fell and was commissioned brigadier general of volunteers on April 28. He was twenty years old. He was brevetted major general in 1866. In 1891, he was awarded the Congressional Medal of Honor for his courage at Fort Fisher.

He stayed in the army after the war and was named colonel of the 34th U.S. Infantry in the reorganization of late 1866. It merged with the 11th Infantry in 1869 to become the 16th Infantry Regiment, with Pennypacker as colonel. Pennypacker served in the South during Reconstruction, after which he did garrison duty at Fort Leavenworth, Kansas. He retired in July 1883 at age thirty-nine. He died more than thirty years later in Philadelphia on October 1, 1916, at age seventy-two. He was buried in the Philadelphia National Cemetery. The youngest general in U.S. history, he was the only general in American history too young to vote for or against the president who appointed him.

WILLIAM HENRY PENROSE was born in Madison Barracks, Sackett's Harbor, New York, on March 10, 1832. His father, a career army officer, retired as a major and died in 1849. William attended Dickinson College in Carlisle, Pennsylvania, but dropped out after his junior year and moved to Michigan, where he became a merchant, and a civil and mechanical engineer.

On April 13, 1861, the day Fort Sumter surrendered, he joined the 3rd U.S. Infantry as a second lieutenant. (He secured a Regular Army commission because of his father's connections.) He was promoted to first lieutenant on May 14. He fought in the Peninsula, the Seven Days battles, the Second Bull Run, and Fredericksburg. On April 18, 1863, he was promoted to colonel of the 15th New Jersey Infantry. He distinguished himself at Marye's Heights in the Chancellorsville Campaign and, on May 3, 1863, assumed command of a New Jersey brigade in the VI Corps after its commander and senior regimental commander were wounded.

William Penrose was a brigade commander at Gettysburg. He was frequently commended and often received Regular Army brevets throughout his Civil War career. He fought in the battles of the Wilderness, Spotsylvania, Cold Harbor, and the early stages of the Siege of Petersburg before he and the entire VI Corps hurried to Washington, where they checked the Confederate drive on the nation's capital. Sent to the Shenandoah Valley, he fought at the Third Winchester and Cedar Creek, where he was wounded in the right arm. He was brevetted brigadier general after Cedar Creek.

Penrose and his brigade were sent back to the Petersburg front that winter. He was wounded in the hip on April 2, 1865, at Fort Welch (near Petersburg) but continued on duty and was present at Sayler's Creek and Appomattox. He was promoted to brigadier general of volunteers on June 27, 1865, after the fighting ended.

General Penrose was mustered out of volunteer service on January 15, 1866, and reverted to the Regular Army rank of captain. After seventeen years in that grade, he became a major (1883), lieutenant colonel (1888), and colonel of the 20th U.S. Infantry in 1893. He served mainly on the Western frontier until he retired in 1896 at age sixty-four. He settled in Salt Lake City, Utah, where he died of typhoid fever on August 29, 1903. He was seventy-one. His remains lie in Arlington National Cemetery. Two of his sons, Charles W. Penrose (1858–1920) and George H. Penrose (1861–1938) retired as colonels.

JOHN SMITH PHELPS was born in Simsbury, Connecticut, on December 22, 1814. He was educated in local public schools and attended Trinity College in Hartford, from which he graduated in 1832. He then read the law and was admitted to the bar in 1835. He moved to Springfield, Missouri, in 1837, and quickly became one of the state's top lawyers.

A Democrat, Phelps was elected to the Missouri legislature in 1840 and to the U.S. House of Representatives in 1844. He served from 1845 to 1863 and rose to the chairmanship of the powerful Ways and Means Committee. He was a firm supporter of the Union, cheap postage, and subsidies for railroads. He did not run for re-election in 1862.

When the Civil War began, Phelps enlisted in the Union militia as a private. He fought in the Battle of Wilson's Creek (August 10, 1861), where General Nathaniel Lyon was killed. After this Union defeat, Phelps's wife cared for the general's body while Phelps joined the retreat to Rolla. Afterward, he organized "Phelps Missouri Regiment," a six-month unit, and was mustered in as its lieutenant colonel on October 2, 1861. He became its colonel on December 19. By special arrangement with President Lincoln, the regiment was not numbered but retained Phelps's name. The Phelps Regiment spent the winter of 1861–62 garrisoning Fort Wyman at Rolla.

John Phelps fought in the Battle of Pea Ridge, where he suffered a severe concussion from a Rebel shell on March 7, 1862. He and his men were mustered out on May 13, but Lincoln appointed him Military Governor of Arkansas on July 19. On November 29, he named Phelps brigadier general of volunteers, to rank from July 19. The Senate, however, would not confirm his appointment, which expired on March 4, 1863.

Union control of Arkansas was limited in 1862 and consisted of little more than the area around Helena, across the river from Memphis. His forces were too small to launch a campaign but too large for the area they controlled. He was unable to control cotton speculation, which was rampant throughout the Mississippi Valley. He also clashed with Union General Curtis, who was issuing "Freedom Papers" to African Americans who fled to Union lines. A legalist and a slave owner, Phelps did not believe Curtis had a right to do this. Phelps's poor health also limited his effectiveness. His office was abolished on July 9, 1863.

Phelps returned to Missouri as colonel of the 72nd Missouri Militia Regiment and took part in operations in southwest Missouri, most notably against Sterling Price's 1864 invasion of the state. He ran for governor in 1868, but because many Missouri Democrats had served the Confederacy and thus lost their franchise, he was defeated. In 1876, after the Radical Republicans lost most of their power and voting rights to ex-Confederates were restored, he ran again. Seen as a unifier of the Northern and Southern factions in Missouri, he was overwhelmingly elected and is now regarded as one of Missouri's best governors. He served from 1877 to 1881, when he retired.

Governor Phelps died on in St. Louis on January 10, 1886. He was seventy-one. He was buried in Hazelwood Cemetery, Springfield, Missouri. His son, John Elisha Phelps, led a Union cavalry brigade during the war and was brevetted brigadier general. John Phelp's wife, Mary Whitney Phelps, was also a strong Unionist and an early and prominent advocate of women's suffrage. After the war, Congress appropriated $20,000 to her for her services to the Union cause. She used it to establish an orphanage.

JOHN WOLCOTT PHELPS was born on November 13, 1813, in Guilford, Vermont, the son of a judge. Educated in local public schools, he attended West Point and was commissioned brevet second lieutenant in the 4th U.S. Artillery on July 1, 1836 (24/49). He fought in the Seminole War in 1838 and helped direct U.S. forces in the Trail of Tears that same year. Later, he performed frontier duty in Michigan.

Phelps was promoted to first lieutenant in 1838 and took part in the Mexican War. He fought at Monterrey, Vera Cruz, Cerro Gordo, Contreras, Churubusco, Molina del Rey, and Mexico City. He declined a brevet to captain—possibly a unique occurrence. After serving for years on the Western frontier and taking part in the Mormon Expedition (1857–59), he resigned his commission in November 1859.

John Phelps hated Mormons, slavery, and the Masonic Order. For two years, he spent much of his time writing forceful articles attacking slavery and the slave states. On May 2, 1861, he was appointed colonel of the 1st Vermont Infantry. He was promoted to brigadier general on August 9. In November, he was transferred to the Department of the Gulf, and his brigade occupied Ship Island off the Mississippi coast. It took part in the battles of Forts St. Philip and Jackson and the occupation of New Orleans. U.S. Navy Captain David Dixon Porter, who was also involved in these operations, called him "crazy," and General Butler declared him "as mad as a March hare."

Certainly, General Phelps was uncompromising on the questions of abolition and emancipation. He set up a base camp (Camp Parapet) at Carrollton, seven miles from New Orleans, and welcomed fugitive slaves. He organized the men who were of military age into companies and asked Butler to provide them with weapons. Instead, Butler sent them axes with instructions for them to cut down trees. Phelps thought that using African Americans as mere laborers reduced them to the status of slaves and himself to the role of slave master. He demanded their immediate emancipation. When General Butler refused to concur, Phelps resigned on August 21, 1862, and returned home. Ironically, Confederate President Davis declared him an outlaw the same day he resigned.

After Lincoln issued the Emancipation Proclamation, he offered Phelps a major generalcy. Phelps refused to accept it unless his date of rank was backdated to the date of his resignation, an implied rebuke of Butler. Lincoln refused to do this. He withdrew his offer to Phelps.

Phelps lived in Brattleboro, Vermont, until he married in 1883 and returned to Guilford. He was active in the Vermont Historical Society, traveled throughout Europe, wrote numerous articles and several books on various subjects, and acquired a reputation as a scholar. He also wrote and translated several books on different subjects and became president of the Vermont Teachers' Association (1865–85). Continuing to operate on the fringes of American politics, he was the American Party and Anti-Masonic Party's presidential candidate in 1880. Among other things, he demanded that the Bible be required reading in all public schools, all secret lodges be abolished, and prohibition be initiated.

Although perhaps not crazy, as Admiral Porter declared, General Phelps was certainly an oddball for his time and place. He died on February

2, 1885, in the town of his birth. He is buried there in the Christ Church Cemetery.

ABRAM SANDERS PIATT was born in Cincinnati, Ohio, on May 2, 1821, the son of a federal circuit judge and entrepreneur. (Sometimes, his first name was listed as "Abraham"). He married in 1840 and fathered eight children. He received a classical education in local academies and attended Xavier University before settling the Macacheek (Mac-a-cheek) Valley of Logan County, Ohio. He became a prosperous farmer and published the local newspaper.

Piatt's wife died on April 10, 1861. Two days later, the Confederates fired on Fort Sumter. Her grief-stricken husband threw himself into the Union war effort, left the care of his children to family members and servants, and recruited the 13th Ohio Infantry, a three-month unit which never left the state. That summer, he recruited a three-year regiment, the 34th Ohio Infantry, a zouaves unit. He also recruited the 54th Ohio Infantry—both of which he helped feed and equip with his own money. He was commissioned colonel of the 13th on April 20, 1861, and colonel of the 34th on September 2.

The 34th Ohio was sent to western Virginia in September and spent the winter there, mostly on picket and scouting duty. It also had an occasional skirmish with guerrillas. Despite a lack of experience, Piatt was promoted to brigadier general on April 30, 1862. His brigade fought in the Second Battle of Bull Run, where he was one of the few officers praised by General Pope in his after-action report. He held a sector of the Washington defenses during the Maryland campaign, thus missing the Battle of Antietam.

General Piatt's back was severely injured on December 12, during the Battle of Fredericksburg, when his horse fell. This injury led to his resignation on February 17, 1863. He returned home, remarried, and resumed farming. He was so successful he built a castle. A prominent member of the Granger movement, he was co-editor or editor-in-chief of *The Capital* newspaper from 1871 to 1880. President Grant ordered him arrested in 1876 for inciting a riot. He ran for governor of Ohio as the Greenback candidate and was narrowly defeated. He returned to his farm in 1880 and retired in 1908.

General Piatt died of cancer at his home in Macacheek on March 23, 1908, at the age of eighty-six. He is buried in the Piatt Family Cemetery. His brother Donn (1819–1891) was a brevetted brigadier general and a noted writer and journalist.

BYRON ROOT PIERCE was born in East Bloomfield, New York, on September 20, 1829. He was educated in an academy in Rochester, New York, and went into the milling business. He also studied dentistry and moved to Grand Rapids, Michigan, in 1856, to practice that profession.

Pierce came from a long line of volunteer soldiers. Before the Civil War, he was captain and commander of the Valley City Light Guards, a militia company that became a company in the 3rd Michigan Infantry in June 1861. He fought at the First Battle of Bull Run, the Peninsula Campaign, the Seven Days battles, Groveton, Chantilly, and Fredericksburg, where he first commanded his regiment. Pierce was successively promoted to major in October 1861, lieutenant colonel on July 25, 1862, and colonel on January 1, 1863. He was wounded five times during the war. He was slightly wounded in the left hand and right arm at Chancellorsville (May 3), where he was commended for his gallantry.

On July 2, he fought in the Peach Orchard at Gettysburg, where he was wounded below his left knee. Although some sources state that his leg had to be amputated, Jack D. Welch, MD, in his book *Medical Histories of the Union Generals*, reported that "he was not hospitalized, and his wound was dressed by the regimental surgeon."

Pierce was elevated to brigade commander in the II Corps on December 30, 1863. He commanded it throughout the Overland Campaign and sometimes was acting division commander. He was promoted to brigadier general on June 7, 1864, and was wounded again near Petersburg on June 18. Pierce contracted dysentery during the siege and returned to Grand Rapids, but returned to duty in time for the Appomattox Campaign. In 1866, he was brevetted major general for his actions at Sayler's Creek (April 6, 1865). He was mustered out on August 24, 1865.

After the war, Byron Pierce worked for the postal service. He later operated a hotel and served as superintendent of the U.S. Soldiers Home at Grand Rapids from 1887 to 1891. He then operated a hotel but retired in 1899. He died in East Grand Rapids on July 10, 1924, at age ninety-four. He was reportedly Michigan's last surviving Civil War officer. He was buried in the Fulton Street Cemetery, Grand Rapids, Michigan.

WILLIAM ANDERSON PILE was born near Indianapolis, Indiana, on February 11, 1829. His family moved to Missouri when he was small. He studied theology and became a Methodist Episcopal Church minister. He joined the Union forces on June 12, 1861, as chaplain of the 1st Missouri Artillery. He transferred to the line on March 1, 1862, when he became a captain and battery commander in the 1st Missouri Light Artillery. He became lieutenant colonel of the 33rd Missouri Infantry in September and regimental commander on December 23.

Pile took part in the Fort Donelson Campaign and apparently fought Shiloh. He was certainly involved in the Siege of Corinth and the Yazoo River Expedition, one of the unsuccessful Vicksburg campaigns. Most of the time, however, his regiment was on garrison duty. He was nevertheless promoted to brigadier general on December 26, 1863, and was transferred to recruiting duty at Benton Barracks in St. Louis, where his job was to enlist former slaves (called USCT or United States Colored Troops) into the Union Army. This caused some friction because Pile did not care if the master of a particular slave was pro-Confederate or pro-Federal. (There were quite a few pro-Union slave holders in Missouri and Kentucky in those days, and the Emancipation Proclamation did not apply to their slaves.)

Pile was stationed at Port Hudson, Louisiana, in late 1864 and led a brigade of USCT troops in the Siege of Mobile, including the April 9, 1865, attack that captured Fort Blakely. He was brevetted major general effective April 9 and was mustered out on August 24, 1865.

Postbellum, Pile returned to Missouri and ran for Congress as a fanatically Radical Republican, advocating death for all supporters of the South, past or present. He was elected in 1866 and served from 1867 to 1869 but was defeated for re-election in 1868. President Grant appointed him territorial governor of New Mexico in 1869. He was unable to control the violence and lawlessness in that territory, although it grew worse under his successors. He was replaced in 1871 and named resident minister to Venezuela, serving until 1874. Afterward, he lived in Philadelphia, where he operated as an agent for the Venezuelan government and became quite well-to-do.

William Pile moved to Monrovia, California, near Los Angeles, in 1886, and built a fine home. He grew grapes on his estate and served a year as mayor. He died of pneumonia in Monrovia on July 7, 1889. He was sixty. He was interred in Live Oak Memorial Park, Monrovia.

THOMAS GAMBLE PITCHER was born on October 23, 1824, in Rockport, Indiana. His father, Judge John Pitcher, reportedly loaned law books to young Abraham Lincoln. Thomas, meanwhile, was appointed to the U.S. Military Academy in 1841 and graduated in 1845 (40/41). He was commissioned brevet second lieutenant in the 5th U.S. Infantry and was promoted to second lieutenant in 1846. Pitcher was involved in the military occupation of Texas and fought in northern Mexico, including the Battles of Palo Alto, Resaca de la Palma, and Monterrey. Transferred to Winfield Scott's army, he took part in the 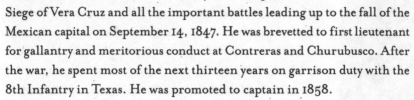 Siege of Vera Cruz and all the important battles leading up to the fall of the Mexican capital on September 14, 1847. He was brevetted to first lieutenant for gallantry and meritorious conduct at Contreras and Churubusco. After the war, he spent most of the next thirteen years on garrison duty with the 8th Infantry in Texas. He was promoted to captain in 1858.

Pitcher was on duty at Fort Bliss near El Paso when the Civil War began. He apparently spent most of 1861 in New Mexico but was recalled to the

East in 1862 and was part of the Harper's Ferry defense force in June. He commanded a battalion of skirmishers in the Battle of Cedar Mountain (August 9), where he was severely wounded in the right knee and captured. He was exchanged in January 1863 and appointed brigadier general on March 20.

Thomas Pitcher achieved a high reputation as a commissary officer during his years of service with the 8th Infantry. Now unable to serve in the field, he served as a commissary officer in New York, as an assistant provost marshal in Vermont, and as the provost marshal general in Indiana. He never fully recovered from his wound and was still using crutches in May 1864. He was mustered out of the volunteer service on April 30, 1866, and reverted to his Regular Army rank of major. He was appointed colonel of the 44th U.S. Infantry in July 1866, but he held the post for only a month. He was superintendent of the U.S. Military Academy at West Point from 1866 to 1870, when he became governor of the Soldiers' Home in Washington. He held this post until he was retired for disabilities incurred in the line of duty in 1878.

General Pitcher died, reportedly from tuberculosis, at Fort Bayard, New Mexico, on October 21, 1895. He is buried in Arlington National Cemetery. One of his sons, William Pitcher (1852–1930), retired as a colonel in the U.S. Army. Another, John Pitcher (1854–1926), retired as a lieutenant colonel. Both are buried in Arlington National Cemetery.

ALFRED PLEASONTON was born on June 7, 1824, in Washington, D.C. His father, Stephen, saved the original Declaration of Independence and Constitution when the British captured Washington in 1814. Educated in local schools and at West Point (7/25), Alfred graduated with the Class of 1844 and was commissioned brevet second lieutenant in the 1st Dragoons. He was stationed at Fort Atkinson, Iowa, and later in Florida (where he fought the Seminoles), Minnesota, and Texas. He was promoted to second lieutenant in 1845, fought in Mexico, and was brevetted first lieutenant for gallantry at Palo Alto and Resaca de la Palma. He was promoted to first lieutenant (substantive rank) in 1849 and to captain in 1855.

Pleasonton was with the 2nd Dragoons at Fort Crittenden, Utah Territory, when the Civil War began. He traveled with his regiment to Washington, where he attempted to use political influence to advance rapidly. He was initially unsuccessful and did not reach the rank of major until February 1862. He served with the 2nd Cavalry in the Peninsula Campaign without particular distinction; nevertheless, on May 1, President Lincoln promoted him to brigadier general. He commanded a brigade of cavalry in the Seven Days Campaign. He was given command of a cavalry division on September 2.

Now one of the leading cavalry commanders for the Army of the Potomac, Pleasonton provided intelligence to General McClellan during the Maryland Campaign. He was a good administrator and capable organizer but a mediocre field commander. He was also considered overbearing by his subordinates. He grossly overestimated the Confederate strength— estimates McClellan was far too eager to accept. He was wounded in the right ear by a Confederate artillery shell at Antietam (September 17) and, in his official report, badly overstated his contribution to the Union victory.

After the Battle of Chancellorsville, Pleasonton claimed to have temporarily checked Stonewall Jackson's famous flanking attack on May 2, 1863, and thus saved the U.S. XI Corps from total destruction. This was a gross exaggeration, but he convinced General Hooker and Abraham Lincoln it was true. He was promoted to major general to rank from June 22. Meanwhile, the performance of the Cavalry Corps during the Chancellorsville Campaign was poor, so Hooker sacked its commander, General Stoneman, and replaced him with Pleasonton.

On June 9, Pleasonton attacked Jeb Stuart's Confederate cavalry at Brandy Station. Although he was defeated, it was the first time the Union cavalry fought the Rebel horse soldiers on anything like equal terms. His reconnaissance efforts during the Gettysburg Campaign were not good. General Early's Confederate division marched undetected to Winchester, where they gobbled up the garrison. In the Battle of Gettysburg, General Meade kept Pleasonton at his (the Army of the Potomac's) headquarters and over supervised the Cavalry Corps, to its detriment.

When Ulysses S. Grant became general-in-chief, he sacked Pleasonton on March 25, 1864, and replaced him with Phil Sheridan. Pleasonton was transferred to the Trans-Mississippi Department, where his performance was vastly superior to what it was in the East. Most notably, he defeated General Sterling Price in the Battles of Westport, Byram's Ford, Mine Creek, and Marais des Cygnes (a.k.a. the Battle of the Trading Post) in October 1864. These battles decisively defeated Price's army and ended the last Confederate threat to Missouri. Alfred Pleasonton was mustered out of volunteer service on January 15, 1866.

Postwar, Pleasonton reverted to the rank of major of cavalry. He lobbied for higher rank but was not successful, although he was offered a lieutenant colonelcy in the infantry, which he turned down because he wanted to remain in the cavalry. Resentful at being subordinate to officers he once outranked, he resigned in 1868. President Grant appointed him commissioner of the Bureau of Internal Revenue (now the Internal Revenue Service), but later asked him to resign because he lobbied Congress to repeal the income tax and because he quarreled with Treasury Department officials. When he refused to resign, Grant fired him.

Pleasonton served for a time as president of the Terre Haute & Cincinnati Railroad. He attempted to secure a pension as a major general but failed. He finally received a pension as a retired major in 1888. General Pleasonton died in Washington on February 17, 1897. He was seventy-two. He is interred in the Congressional Cemetery, Washington. Still angry that he was not granted his due, he directed that he be buried with absolutely no military honors. He even decreed that he not be buried in his uniform.

His younger brother, Augustus James Pleasonton, was a brigadier general in the Pennsylvania Militia and fought at Gettysburg.

JOSEPH BENNETT PLUMMER was born in Barre, Massachusetts, allegedly on November 15, 1816. (He may have shaved a year or two off of his age to boost his chances of gaining admission to West Point.) Educated locally, he taught school for a few years. He managed to secure an appointment to the U.S. Military Academy in 1837, graduated in 1841 (22/52), and was commissioned second lieutenant in the 1st U.S. Infantry Regiment. He served in Mexico but was ill for a year and apparently missed the fighting. He spent most of the pre-war years on garrison duty in what is now called the Midwest and on the Texas frontier. He was promoted to first lieutenant in 1848 and to captain in 1852. He spent four years as regimental quartermaster.

Sent to Missouri after the war started, he led a battalion of Regulars at Wilson's Creek (August 10, 1861), where he was shot in the right hip. The bullet could not be removed. After commanding the post of Cape Girardeau, Missouri, for several months, he became colonel of the 11th Missouri Infantry on September 25. That same month, he was named commander of the 5th Brigade, District of Southeast Missouri, and simultaneously served as commandant of Cape Girardeau, Missouri. He was appointed brigadier general on March 11, 1862.

Plummer led the 5th Division of John Pope's Army of the Mississippi in the Union victories at New Madrid and Island No. 10. He also took part in the Siege of Corinth. Suffering from his Wilson's Creek wound, exhaustion, and prolonged exposure, he died in camp at Corinth on August 9, 1862. He was eventually buried in Arlington National Cemetery.

ORLANDO METCALFE POE was born on March 7, 1832, in Navarre, Ohio. He graduated from West Point in 1856 (6/49) and was commissioned brevet second lieutenant in the Topographical Engineers, the most coveted branch. He spent the antebellum years as an assistant topographical engineer on the survey of the northern Great Lakes. He was promoted to second lieutenant in October 1856 and to first lieutenant in 1860.

When the Civil War began, Poe was initially a topographical engineer with the Department of the Ohio and served with McClellan in the western Virginia Campaign. He followed "Little Mac" to the Army of the Potomac in the same capacity. He became colonel of the 2nd Michigan Infantry on September 16, 1861. He led his regiment with good success in the Peninsula Campaign and the Seven Days battles. He directed a brigade in the Second Battle of Bull Run, the Battle of Chantilly, and in the Fredericksburg Campaign, where it was lightly involved. He was appointed brigadier general effective November 29, 1862.

On March 4, 1863, Poe's promotion expired without action by the Senate and he reverted to his Regular Army rank of captain on March 4, 1863. Transferred to the Western Front, he was chief engineer of the XXIII Corps and played a key role in organizing the defense of Knoxville, Tennessee, and Longstreet's defeat at Fort Sanders on November 29. Because of this impressive victory, Sherman appointed Poe his chief engineer in December. He became a brigadier general again on December 26, 1863.

As chief engineer of the Military Division of the West, Poe was charged with burning Atlanta. He planned to destroy only buildings and facilities of military value and was furious when undisciplined soldiers committed arson and burned many civilian homes. During the March to the Sea, he kept the Union forces moving forward by improving roads and river crossings and erecting pontoon bridges while simultaneously destroying the Confederate infrastructure. He remained Sherman's chief engineer through the Carolinas Campaign.

Poe reverted to the rank of captain after the South surrendered. Postwar, he was involved in the construction of many of the early lighthouses on the Great Lakes and the design of the Poe Lock between Lakes Superior and Huron. He was promoted to major in 1867. Sherman (now general-in-chief) promoted Poe to colonel in 1873, and he served as Sherman's aide-de-camp from then until 1884.

On September 18, 1895, while inspecting the locks at Sault St. Marie, Michigan, Poe slipped, fell, and injured his left leg. Infection set in, and he died in Detroit on October 2, at age sixty-three. He was buried in Arlington National Cemetery.

An outstanding military engineer, it is hard not to conclude that the Senate made a mistake in not confirming Orlando Poe to the rank of brigadier general.

JOHN POPE was born on March 16, 1822, in Louisville, Kentucky, the son of a federal judge. His family was prominent and had many connections. Pope's friends included Abraham Lincoln, who married his second cousin, Mary Todd. He attended West Point, graduated in 1842 (17/56), and was commissioned brevet second lieutenant in the Corps of Topographical Engineers. The fact that he was assigned to this branch with such a low-class ranking suggests political influence. In any case, he served against the Seminoles in Florida and then helped survey the northeastern boundary between the U.S. and Canada. He was part of Zachary Taylor's Army of Occupation in northern Mexico, where he earned a brevet to first lieutenant at Monterrey and a brevet captaincy for Buena Vista, where he served on Zachary Taylor's staff. Post-war, Pope served on engineering projects in Minnesota, on the Red River, and in New Mexico. He also spent three years surveying a route for the Pacific Railroad. He was promoted to first lieutenant, Regular Army, in 1855 and to captain in 1856. He married the daughter of a Republican Congressman in 1859.

Pope was on lighthouse duty when Abraham Lincoln was elected president in 1860. He was one of four officers selected to escort the president-elect from Illinois to Washington, D.C. He offered to work as one of Lincoln's aides, but instead was appointed brigadier general of volunteers on June 14, 1861. He was given command of the District of Northern Missouri under General Fremont, whom he openly schemed to replace.

General Pope won some early victories. He defeated Sterling Price at Blackwater, Missouri, on December 18 and took 1,200 prisoners. General Halleck, the commander of the Western Department, gave Pope command of the Army of the Mississippi (25,000 men), which he used to capture Madrid, Missouri (March 14), and (supported by strong naval forces) to force the surrender of the Confederate garrison on Island No. 10 on April 7. Pope's performance here was excellent. He thus gained a false reputation as a military genius and a well-deserved reputation as a pompous braggart.

Pope was promoted to major general on March 22, 1862. He commanded the left wing of Halleck's army in the Siege of Corinth, which the Confederates evacuated on May 30.

The decline of Pope's professional career began on June 26, 1862, when he was named commander of the Army of Virginia. He immediately alienated his own command by issuing a general order, stating that, in the West he had only seen the backs of his enemies, suggesting that their performance was inadequate, but, under Pope, that would improve. He also hated two of his three corps commanders (McDowell and Sigel) and was indifferent to the third (Banks). He pompously issued orders from "Headquarters in the Saddle," allowing Stonewall Jackson to make him look foolish by stating that his headquarters was where his hindquarters should be. His orders toward the citizens of northern Virginia were severe, but he proved indecisive when facing Lee, Jackson, and Longstreet, who had fifty-five thousand men. Reinforced by McClellan's army to more than seventy thousand men, he was almost trapped south of the Rappahannock, whipped at Cedar Mountain, routed at the Second Bull Run (August 29–30), and defeated again at Chantilly (September 1). Forced to seek safety behind the Washington fortifications, he refused to accept responsibility for his own failures, cast blame on others, looked for scapegoats, and arranged to court-martial Fitz John Porter for cowardice and disobedience. Porter was cashiered, and the North lost another highly capable general. Brigadier General Alpheus Williams spoke for most of the army when he wrote that Pope was guilty of "insolence, superciliousness, and pretentiousness" and that "All hate him." He was relieved of his command on September 6.

Lincoln sent the disgraced general to Minnesota, where he commanded the Department of the Northwest until 1865. Here he brutally put down an Indian insurrection and earmarked three hundred Lakota Sioux for execution. President Lincoln personally reviewed their cases and commuted the sentence of most of them but personally selected thirty-eight for execution. They were hanged on December 26, 1862, in Mankato, Minnesota. It was the largest mass execution in a single day in American history.

After the war, Pope briefly commanded the Third Military District in Atlanta (1867), where his reign was characterized by high-handed arrogance. President Johnson relieved him on December 28 and replaced him with George G. Meade. He then commanded the Department of the Lakes with headquarters in Detroit, as later other districts. His prestige took another blow in 1879, when a Board of Inquiry overturned General Porter's conviction and described Pope's command of the Army of Virginia as reckless and dangerous.

In the post-war Federal military bureaucracy, seniority often triumphed above all else. John Pope retired in 1886 as a major general in the Regular Army. He died in his sleep on September 23, 1892, in the Ohio Soldiers and Sailors Home near Sandusky. He was buried in Bellefontaine Cemetery, St. Louis, Missouri. One of his sons, Francis Horton Pope, graduated from West Point, served in the Spanish-American War, the Philippines, and in France in World War I. He retired as a brigadier general.

ANDREW PORTER was born in Lancaster, Pennsylvania, on July 10, 1820. His father was George B. Porter, the governor of Michigan Territory from 1831 until his death in 1834. Andrew's grandfather, also named Andrew Porter, was a general in the American Revolution. The second Andrew was also a second cousin of Mary Todd Lincoln and first cousin of Horace Porter, who was an aide to General Grant and a brevet brigadier general in the Civil War.

Andrew entered West Point in 1836 but resigned six months later, presumably for academic deficiencies. Upon the outbreak of the Mexican War, he was commissioned directly into the 1st Mounted Rifles Regiment as a first lieutenant. He was promoted to captain the following year and brevetted major for his gallantry at Contreras and Churubusco, and to lieutenant colonel for Chapultepec. He spent the next fourteen years at various posts and garrisons on the American frontier. Meanwhile, he fought a duel with future Confederate General James J. Archer, whom he wounded. Archer's second was Stonewall Jackson.

Porter was stationed at Fort Craig, New Mexico, when the Civil War began. He returned to the East and was named commander of the newly formed 16th U.S. Infantry on May 14, 1861. Shortly after, he was given command of a brigade in David Hunter's division of McDowell's Army of Northeastern Virginia. His brigade suffered 464 killed, wounded, and captured at the First Battle of Bull Run (i.e., heavy casualties). He assumed command of the division after Hunter was wounded. He was promoted to brigadier general on August 6. Following the Federal retreat to the Washington defenses, he was named Provost Marshal of what became the Army of the Potomac. He surrendered this position after McClellan was fired in November 1862, when Porter became Provost Marshal of the State of Pennsylvania. He held this position until April 4, 1864, when he resigned due to reasons of health. He left the service on April 20.

General Porter suffered from malaria and chronic dysentery before the war. It came back in July 1861 and confined him to a hotel room in Philadelphia from July to December. His health continually deteriorated in 1863 and finally forced him to resign. He later traveled extensively in Europe to take advantage of the cooler summers and to perhaps find a physician who could cure him. This he could not do. He died in Paris, France, on January 3, 1872. His remains were shipped back to the United States, and he was interred in Elmwood Cemetery, Detroit, Michigan, near his father's grave.

FITZ JOHN PORTER was born in Portsmouth, New Hampshire, on August 21, 1822. He was the descendant of a famous naval family, and his cousins included Union Admirals David G. Farragut and David D. Porter. His father was a naval captain assigned to shore duty because of his alcoholism. Perhaps because of his chaotic childhood, Fitz decided to pursue an army career. He attended the Phillips Exeter Academy and West Point, from which he graduated in 1845 (8/41). He was commissioned a brevet second lieutenant in the 4th U.S. Artillery, a unit noted for transferring its officers frequently.

Porter was promoted to second lieutenant in 1846 and to first lieutenant in 1847. He fought in Mexico, commanded a battery at Vera Cruz, was brevetted captain for Molino del Rey, and major for Chapultepec on September 13. Here he was struck in the head by a spent musket ball, which gave him a concussion. Mexico City fell the next day.

Captain Porter was a cavalry and artillery instructor at West Point from 1849 to 1855. He also served a year as adjutant to the superintendent,

Colonel Robert E. Lee (1853–54). He spent the next years in Kansas and points west, fighting Indians and Mormons. He was stationed in Charleston Harbor, South Carolina, from 1859 until late 1860, when he was sent to Texas, to assist in the evacuation of U.S. soldiers from the Lone Star State after it seceded.

Porter was named chief of staff and assistant adjutant general of the Department of Pennsylvania in late April 1861. He was appointed colonel of the 15th U.S. Infantry on May 14 and was chief of staff to General Robert Patterson, the Pennsylvania militia commander, when he allowed Confederate General Joseph E. Johnston to successfully send his troops from the Shenandoah to Manassas, enabling the South to win the First Battle of Bull Run. General Logan later accused Porter of persuading Patterson to commit this blunder.

After briefly serving as chief of staff to General Banks, Fitz John Porter was promoted to brigadier general on August 7. He was given command of a division in the Army of the Potomac on August 28 and assumed command of the III Corps on March 13, 1862. He transferred to the command of the V Corps on May 18. He was very friendly with his army commander, George B. McClellan, who listened to Porter's advice.

Porter fought in the Peninsula Campaign and distinguished himself in the Seven Days battles. A brilliant defensive commander, Porter saved much of the Army of the Potomac by checking or slowing Lee north of the Chickahominy. He repulsed several major Confederate attacks during these battles and was promoted to major general on July 16. He was sent to northern Virginia in August, to reinforce John Pope (whom he called "an ass") and his Army of Virginia.

General Pope mishandled the Second Battle of Bull Run (August 29–30), which climaxed with Pope ordering Porter to attack Stonewall Jackson's main position with five thousand men. Porter reluctantly did so. Pope was unaware that Longstreet was waiting just south of Porter's position with thirty thousand men, and the V Corps was advancing into a trap. Longstreet took Porter in the flank and routed the entire Union army. Pope blamed Porter for his defeat and relieved him of his command on September 5.

McClellan restored Porter to the command of his corps, which he led at Antietam. At a critical point in this battle, Porter advised McClellan not to commit the V Corps because it was the last of the army's reserves. Historians generally agree that this was a serious mistake. It was also Porter's last battle. Shortly after Lincoln relieved McClellan of command of the Army of the Potomac, Porter was arrested on November 25.

Porter's court-martial was rigged. All the officers on the military commission which judged him were obligated to Secretary of War Stanton, who wanted to hurt McClellan (a Democrat) by convicting Porter. He was found guilty of insubordination and dismissed from the army on January 21, 1863. He spent most of the rest of life trying to restore his reputation. President Grant tended to believe Porter was guilty and ignored his appeals. President Hayes, however, established a board, which included Generals John M. Schofield (president), Alfred H. Terry, and George W. Getty. It completely and unanimously exonerated Porter in March 1879, and recommended he be restored to his former rank. (Ironically, when he was at West Point, Porter voted to expel Cadet Schofield for a disciplinary infraction.) The whole matter was now a political issue and it was not until 1886 when President Grover Cleveland, another Democrat, placed Porter's name on the army's rolls as a colonel of infantry, to date from May 14, 1861, but without back pay. Porter retired from the army two days later.

Meanwhile, Fitz John Porter was involved in various commercial enterprises. At various times, he served as New York City Commissioner of Public Works, Chief of Police, and NYC Fire Commissioner. General Porter died in Morristown, New Jersey, on May 21, 1901, at age seventy-eight. He was buried in Green-Wood Cemetery, Brooklyn.

EDWARD ELMER POTTER was born in New York City on June 21, 1823. He was educated in local schools and attended Columbia University, from which he graduated in 1842. He then studied law and, after a short stay in California during the Gold Rush, returned to New York and became a farmer.

Potter joined the Union Army as a captain in the commissary department on February 3, 1862. He took part in Burnside's North Carolina Expedition. Here, he received permission to recruit a regiment from pro-Union elements around Washington, North Carolina. The result was the 1st (Union) North Carolina Infantry Regiment. Potter became its lieutenant colonel on October 1. He was promoted to brigadier general on November 29. He became chief of staff of the XVIII Corps on January 12, 1863.

When Longstreet attempted to overrun eastern North Carolina, Potter distinguished himself in the Siege of Washington (March 30–April 19, 1863). He later commanded the posts of Norfolk and Portsmouth. Meanwhile, General Foster, the former commander of the XVIII Corps, became commander of the Army of the Ohio. He selected Potter as his chief of staff, a position he held from December 1863 to March 1864, when he returned to the Atlantic coast. He commanded the District of Hilton Head, South Carolina and, in November 1864, commanded a brigade in the Battle of Honey Hill, in which five thousand Northerners were defeated by 1,400 Georgia militiamen.

From January 1865 until the end of the war, Potter commanded the District of Beaufort. He led several raids into Confederate territory. He resigned from the army on July 24, 1865. He was brevetted major general in 1866. Potter returned to New York City, where he died of pneumonia and heart failure on June 1, 1889. He was sixty-five. He is buried in the New York City Marble Cemetery. He never married.

JOSEPH HAYDN POTTER was born on October 12, 1822, in Concord, New Hampshire. He entered West Point in 1839 and graduated in 1843 (22/39), one rank below Cadet Ulysses S. Grant. Commissioned brevet second lieutenant in the 1st U.S. Infantry, he became a full second lieutenant in 1845. He spent two years on garrison duty in Des Moines, Iowa, and Jefferson Barracks, Missouri; he then took part in the occupation of Texas and the subsequent war with Mexico. He was wounded in the leg at Monterrey, for which he was brevetted first lieutenant. He was promoted to first lieutenant (substantive rank) in 1847 and returned to Jefferson Barracks, where he again performed garrison duty. From 1851 to 1861, he served on the frontier and in Indian Territory; Fort Smith, Arkansas;

and New Mexico. He was promoted to captain in 1856 and took part in the Utah Expedition (1858–60).

Potter was stationed in Texas when the Civil War began. He tried to make his way back north but was captured by Confederate forces at St. Augustine Pass, New Mexico, on July 27, 1861, and was a prisoner of war until August 7, 1862, when he was finally exchanged. The following month, he was appointed colonel and commander of the 12th New Hampshire Infantry. He fought in the Maryland Campaign and at Fredericksburg, where he distinguished himself. A promotion to brigade commander followed on January 12, 1863.

On May 3, during the Battle of Chancellorsville, Joseph Potter was severely wounded in the leg and captured. He was exchanged in October of that same year and was given a rear area assignment as assistant provost marshal general of Ohio. In September 1864, he was given another combat position as commander of a temporary division in the Army of the James. He later reverted to brigade commander. Part of the XVIII Corps, he fought in the Bermuda Hundred sector, in the Battle of Fort Harrison (September 29–30), and in the Siege of Petersburg. He was chief of staff of the XXIV Corps from January to July 1865, well after the Confederate surrender. Meanwhile, he was brevetted brigadier general and promoted to brigadier general of volunteers (full rank) on May 1, 1865. He was mustered out of volunteer service on January 15, 1866.

In the reorganization of 1866, Potter was lieutenant colonel (Regular Army) of the 30th Infantry Regiment. Assigned to Kentucky, Arkansas, and then the Western frontier (mainly in Wyoming), he was promoted to full colonel and commander of the 24th U.S. Infantry Regiment in late 1873. He was governor of the Soldiers' Home in Washington, D.C. from 1877 to 1881, after which he returned to the regiment, then in Indian Territory. He was promoted to brigadier general on April 1, 1886. His last assignment was commander of the Department of the Missouri. He retired on October 12, 1886.

General Potter settled in Columbus, Ohio, where he died on December 1, 1892, at age seventy. He was buried in Green Lawn Cemetery, Columbus. His son, Joseph D. Potter, commanded a company in the Spanish-American War and was a colonel in the Ohio National Guard.

ROBERT BROWN POTTER was born on July 16, 1829, in Schenectady, New York, the son of an Episcopal bishop. He had a sister and eight brothers, one of whom was a Democratic congressman. He attended Union College in Schenectady, where his maternal grandfather was president. He read law, was admitted to the bar, and practiced in New York City until the war began.

Potter enlisted in the New York Militia as a private but was promoted to major in the 51st New York Infantry on October 14, 1861, and became its lieutenant colonel on November 1. Sent to North Carolina, he was shot in the hip at New Bern on March 14, 1862, but remained on the field. He advanced to regimental commander and was promoted to colonel on September 10. Meanwhile, as part of Burnside's IX Corps, he was transferred to the Eastern Front and fought in the Battle of Antietam, where he was wounded twice during the fighting around Burnside's Bridge. He was promoted to brigadier general on March 23, 1863.

Sent to the Western Front, General Potter led a division in the Siege of Vicksburg and commanded the IX Corps during the Knoxville Campaign. He spent three months on recruiting duty in New York (February–April 1864), led a division in the IX Corps during the Overland Campaign and the Siege of Petersburg, and was involved in especially heavy fighting from the Wilderness to Petersburg. He was brevetted major general for these actions. During the Battle of the Crater, he alone of all Burnside's senior officers was with his men when they vainly attempted to break Lee's lines.

The Confederate line around Petersburg finally broke on April 2, 1865. During this fighting, Potter was desperately wounded by a Rebel musket ball. It took him several weeks to heal, so he missed the final campaign, which ended at Appomattox. General Potter was promoted to major general (full rank) on September 29, 1865, and was mustered out of the service on January 15, 1866.

Postwar, Potter resumed his law practice and was receiver for the Atlantic & Great Western Railroad from 1866 to 1869. He lived in England from 1869 to 1873, when he returned to the United States and settled in

Newport, Rhode Island. He died there on February 19, 1887, at age fifty-seven. He was buried in Woodlawn Cemetery, The Bronx, New York.

BENJAMIN FRANKLIN POTTS was born on the family farm in Fox Township, Carroll County, Ohio, on January 29, 1836. He was educated in local, common schools and, at age seventeen, began working as a clerk in a dry goods store in nearby Wattsville. He attended Westminster College in Pennsylvania in 1854 and 1855 but ran out of money and returned to Ohio. He simultaneously taught school and read law until he passed the bar exam in 1859, after which he set up a successful practice in Carrollton. Meanwhile, he became a strong supporter of President James Buchanan and joined the Democratic Party. He was a delegate to the Democratic National Convention in Charleston, South Carolina, where he voted for Stephen A. Douglas.

When the Civil War began, Potts recruited his own company, which was mustered into Federal service as part of the 32nd Ohio Infantry on August 20, 1861, with Potts as captain. He took part in the western Virginia Campaign of 1861, including the Battle of Cheat Mountain, and fought unsuccessfully against Stonewall Jackson at McDowell, Cross Keys, and Port Republic.

Potts was at the Battle of Harper's Ferry (September 12–15), after which the garrison was forced to surrender to General Jackson. He was paroled and sent to Camp Douglas, Illinois, where he remained until exchanged in November. He was promoted to lieutenant colonel on November 26 and assumed command of the badly depleted and demoralized 32nd Ohio. He reorganized the regiment, saw to its recruiting and re-equipping, and got it ready for field duty. He was promoted to colonel on December 28, 1862.

Pott's regiment was transferred to the Army of the Tennessee and took part in Grant's Vicksburg campaigns, including the Battle of Port Gibson, after which he received a special commendation. He was also officially praised for his part in the Battles of Raymond, Jackson, and Champion Hill, where he captured eight Confederate guns and numerous prisoners.

He took part in the Siege of Vicksburg. In August 1863, he was part of an expedition that captured Monroe, Louisiana.

Promoted to brigade commander in November, he was part of Sherman's Meridian Expedition, during which he routed W. W. Adams's cavalry brigade in January 1864. He directed a brigade in the XVII Corps during the Atlanta campaign, fought at Big Shanty, Kennesaw Mountain, Jonesboro, and Lovejoy's Station, among others, and especially distinguished himself in the Battle of Atlanta (July 22). After the city fell, he was part of the March to the Sea and the Carolinas Campaign of 1865. He was promoted to brigadier general on January 12, 1865, and participated in the Grand Review of the Armies in Washington, D.C., (May 23–24). He was brevetted major general after the war and tried but failed to obtain a colonel's commission in the Regular Army. He was mustered out of the service on January 15, 1866.

Potts returned to Ohio and resumed his legal career postbellum. A moderate Republican, he was elected to the Ohio State Senate in 1867. He was offered the governorship of Montana in 1870 but declined it because the XV Amendment to the U.S. Constitution was before the Ohio Senate. It needed Potts' vote to pass. After it was affirmed, President Grant offered the governorship to Potts again. This time he accepted.

Benjamin F. Potts served as governor of Montana from July 13, 1870 to January 14, 1883. His bipartisan approach unified the state, brought stability, and helped suppress lawlessness. Several new towns were chartered under his reign. After he was replaced as governor by President Arthur, who distrusted his ability to work with a Republican administration and a Democratic legislature, Potts was elected to the territorial legislature. He also operated his own cattle ranch near Helena.

Governor Potts suffered from rheumatism from 1885 forward. He died in Helena on June 17, 1887, and was buried there in Forestvale Cemetery. His brother Isaiah was a private in the 16th Wisconsin Infantry and was killed in action in 1865.

WILLIAM HENRY POWELL was born on May 10, 1825, in Pontypool, Wales, in the United Kingdom. Both of his parents were Welsh. His father immigrated to the United States when he was two, and the rest of the family

followed five years later. His father was an ironworker. He lived in New Jersey, Pennsylvania, Nashville, Tennessee, and finally Wheeling, West Virginia. William followed him into that profession and, when he was twenty-two, established the Benwood Nail Works. He lost his right eye in an accident at work in 1846. He married in 1847 and moved to Ironton, Ohio, southwest of Wheeling, in 1853. Here, he established the Bellfonte Nail Works. He was the superintendent and financial agent for the Lawrence Iron Works, a large firm, when the Civil War began.

Powell did not volunteer for the service until after the First Bull Run, when it became obvious that the war would not be a short one. He recruited his own cavalry company, which became part of the 2nd West Virginia Cavalry in November 1861. Most of his men were from Ohio. Powell, meanwhile, was elected captain on August 14.

Captain Powell first saw action under the command of James A. Garfield in a minor victory at Louisa, Kentucky, on January 7, 1862. He then fought bushwhackers in the mountains of western Virginia and in the Kanawha Valley, which the Union lost in August and recaptured in November. On November 26, with five hundred men, Powell launched a surprise attack on a Rebel camp at Sinking Creek and captured 114 men and two hundred weapons. All that Powell's men lost was two horses. For this brilliant little action, he was awarded the Congressional Medal of Honor in 1890. Powell, meanwhile, was promoted to major (June 25) and lieutenant colonel (October 25). He was at home recovering from a severe illness when General Eliakim Scammon sacked the commander of the 2nd West Virginia Cavalry. Powell was chosen to succeed him, and he was promoted to colonel on May 18, 1863.

William Powell was second-in-command of a raid on Wytheville, southwestern Virginia, on July 18. It was a failure, the commander was killed, and Powell was shot in the back by one of his own men, hopefully by accident, and was captured. The bullet could not be removed and never was. Physicians from both sides thought he would die, but he rallied and eventually ended up in Libby Prison, Richmond. He was charged with robbery and murder by the citizens of Wytheville, but was exchanged for Colonel

Richard H. Lee, a distant relative of Robert E. Lee, in February 1864. He went home to recuperate and did not return to the field until June. When he did, he was a cavalry brigade commander. He fought in the inconclusive Battle of Cove Mountain (May 10) in General Hunter's unsuccessful Lynchburg Campaign and in the Shenandoah Valley campaign of 1864–65. He performed well and was constantly praised by his superiors. When Sheridan relieved General Averell on September 23, he gave Powell command of his division. He was promoted to brigadier general on October 19.

Now in charge of seven thousand men, Powell continued to perform well as Sheridan's army overran the Shenandoah. He resigned his commission on January 5, 1865, allegedly for family reasons. He may have been forced to resign, however, because he was hanging Rebel prisoners in retaliation for the acts of bushwhackers, and he hanged the wrong man. One of those he hanged was related to former U.S. Senator John Crittenden and Union General Thomas L. Crittenden. He was nevertheless brevetted major general in the omnibus promotions of 1866.

Powell returned to the business world after the war and declined a Republican nomination to Congress. He was seriously injured in a horse-and-buggy accident in 1870 and was no longer able to work in the iron works. He sold his nail works, moved to Kansas City, Missouri, and worked for Standard Oil Company and American Central Insurance. He moved to Belleville, Illinois, in 1876. Now recovered enough to return to the nail business, he became manager of the Waugh Company Nail Works. In 1895, his old friend, President William McKinley, named him an Internal Revenue Collector.

General Powell was considered a gentleman and one of the most respected men in Belleville. In the last years of his life, he suffered from rheumatism and respiratory problems related to his wound. He died on December 26, 1904, at his home, at age seventy-nine. He was buried in Graceland Cemetery, Chicago.

CALVIN EDWARD PRATT was born in Princeton, Massachusetts, on January 23, 1828. He was educated in local schools and at the collegiate Academy of Wilbraham.

He began studying law in 1849 and became a clerk of the Criminal Court in 1850. He was admitted to the bar in 1852. He set up a practice in Worcester and joined the local militia that same year. He was elected justice of the peace in 1853 but moved to Brooklyn in 1859, where he was an active member of the Democratic Party.

When the war broke out, he and a friend recruited and organized the 31st New York Infantry at their own expense. The regiment was mustered into Federal service on August 14, 1861, with Pratt as their colonel, although it fought in the First Bull Run a month earlier. It arrived on the field late in the day and was lightly engaged on July 21 and helped cover the army's retreat. It was part of Slocum's division of the VI Corps and fought in the Seven Days battles. Pratt was shot in the face during the Battle of Gaines Mill on June 27, 1862. The bullet pierced his left cheekbone an inch below the eye, passed through his face and nose, and lodged so deeply in the bone that it could not be felt; it was not removed until twenty-nine years later. He was sent back to New York to recuperate. (Some sources state that Pratt was wounded the day before, at Mechanicsville.) He rejoined the army after the Battle of Antietam.

Pratt was promoted to brigadier general on September 13, 1862. He assumed command of a brigade in the VI Corps on September 25. On February 3, 1863, he was given command of the Light (4th) Division of the VI Corps. Apparently still suffering from his wound, he resigned from the army on April 25. He returned to Brooklyn, resumed his law practice, and

became a collector of Internal Revenue. He was elected to the New York Supreme Court in 1869 and served continually until his retirement as an associate justice of the Appellate Court in 1891.

General Pratt died of apoplexy on his farm in Rochester, Massachusetts (on Buzzard's Bay), on August 3, 1896. He was sixty-eight. He was interred in Center Cemetery, Rochester.

BENJAMIN MAYBERRY PRENTISS was born in Belleville, Virginia, on November 23, 1819. His family moved to Hannibal, Missouri, in 1836, and to Quincy,

Illinois, in 1841. He engaged in the rope-making business and was also an auctioneer. Prentiss became a first lieutenant in the Illinois Militia in 1844, served in the 1st Illinois Infantry during the Mexican War, fought at Buena Vista, and was mustered out as a captain in 1847. After the war, he continued to serve in the Illinois Militia, reached the rank of brigadier general, married, was widowed, and remarried. He fathered twelve children.

Prentiss became a lawyer and a Republican. He ran for Congress in 1860 but was unsuccessful. When the Civil War began, he was mustered in as the colonel of the 10th Illinois on April 29, 1861. He was promoted to brigadier general on August 29. His orders were to clear northern Missouri of Rebel forces, and he achieved a measure of success. He assumed command of the 5th Division in Grant's Army of the Tennessee on March 26, 1862. He had a little more than 7,200 men.

At dawn on April 6, the Confederate Army of Mississippi launched a surprise attack which temporarily routed much of Sherman's division and a good part of Prentiss's, and overran Prentiss's camp. He made a stand along the Sunken Road, at a position called the Hornet's Nest, where he repulsed at least eight Confederate attacks. By 4 p.m., the Rebels deployed ten thousand men and more than fifty guns against Prentiss's position—the largest artillery concentration in the history of the North American continent up until that point. Eventually surrounded, he surrendered his 2,200 remaining men around 5:30 p.m. Grant was later critical of Prentiss for not making a timely withdrawal, but many historians (including me) consider him a hero of the first order and the man who saved Grant's army. Taking advantage of the time bought by Prentiss and General W. H. L. Wallace (who was killed), Grant was able to rally his forces and defeat the enemy the next day.

Ben Prentiss spent several months in prison but was exchanged on August 15. Instead of being given another field command, he was assigned to the court-martial board, which tried Major General Fitz John Porter. Unlike the majority, he voted for acquittal.

Prentiss was promoted to major general on March 13, 1863. In February 1863, he was given command of the District of Eastern Arkansas, which headquartered at Helena. On July 4, he was attacked by Confederate General Holmes. Prentiss's skillful handling of his troops, coupled with

Holmes's ineptitude, led to a Union victory. He was nevertheless relieved of his command on August 3 and ordered to report to Washington.

General Prentiss felt he deserved another command and was being shelved for no legitimate reason. Some historians believe his dissenting vote in the Porter case led to his being sacked. They are probably right. In any case, Prentiss was unemployed until October 28, when he resigned his commission and returned to Illinois. The North lost another excellent general for all the wrong reasons.

Prentiss practiced law in Quincy, Illinois, and later Kirksville and Bethany, Missouri. He was a delegate to the Republican National Convention in 1880 and 1884, and was named postmaster of Bethany in 1888. He died there on February 8, 1901. He was eighty-one. He was buried in Miriam Cemetery, Bethany.

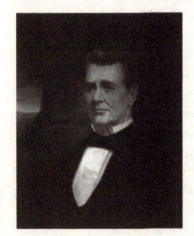

THOMAS LAWSON PRICE was born near Danville, Virginia, on January 19, 1809. Despite his father being a wealthy planter, he received only a very basic public school education. His father died when he was twenty, and Thomas inherited a large plantation and many slaves. The following year (1830), he married, and he moved to Missouri in 1831. Price intended to settle in St. Louis, but that city was experiencing an Asiatic Cholera epidemic when he arrived, so he continued upriver to Jefferson City, where he spent most of the rest of his life.

Price received a considerable influx of money from the sale of his inheritance, and he invested it wisely. By 1840, he owned a stage line, at least two hotels, and engaged in mercantile, manufacturing, and other business ventures. Later, he was an incorporator of the Capital City Bank and president of a land company. In 1838, he ran for state treasurer as a Democrat but was defeated. He became Jefferson City's first mayor in 1839 and served until 1843.

Thomas Price was also active in the Missouri Militia, where he became a major general and commander of a division. He was elected lieutenant governor in 1849. Politically, he was a fervent ally of Thomas Hart Benton, who was unpopular with many influential Missourians because of his opposition to the spread of slavery. He was also involved in the expansion of railroads from Missouri to Denver, Colorado, and Cheyenne, Wyoming. His term as lieutenant governor ended in 1853, but he was elected to the Missouri House of Representatives in 1860.

On September 21, 1861, shortly after the Civil War began, General Fremont appointed Price brigadier general of volunteers and placed him in command of the forces in and around Jefferson City. This appointment was illegal, and Abraham Lincoln revoked it on November 12. Meanwhile, Congressman John Reid joined the Confederacy and was expelled from the U.S. House of Representatives. Thomas Price ran for his vacant seat and, as a Democrat, was elected in late 1861. He served from January 21, 1862 to March 3, 1863. Lincoln, meanwhile, reappointed Price brigadier general on February 1, 1862, and his appointment was confirmed on March 27. Price, however, declined it and resigned his commission on April 21. He was a Union brigadier general for less than three months and did not see any action.

Price ran for re-election in late 1862 but was defeated by the Radical Republican candidate. He ran for governor in 1864 but was again defeated. He was a delegate to the Democratic National Convention in 1864 and 1868.

Thomas L. Price died in Jefferson City on July 15, 1870, at age sixty-one. He was buried in Riverview Cemetery, Jefferson City, Missouri.

HENRY PRINCE was born in Eastport, Maine, on June 19, 1811. He entered West Point in 1831, graduated in 1835 (30/56), and was commissioned brevet second lieutenant in the 4th U.S. Infantry. Sent to Florida, he was wounded twice in his first combat action, the Battle of Camp Izard (February 29, 1836) during the Seminole War. Both wounds were minor. Later he fought the Creeks (1838-39), served in Indian Territory (1839-41), again in Florida (1841-42), and on coastal survey and recruiting duty (1842-46). Meanwhile, Prince was promoted to second lieutenant (June 1836), first lieutenant (1838), and regimental adjutant (1846), and was brevetted captain for gallantry at Contreras and Churubusco during the

Mexican War. He was badly wounded in the Battle of Molino del Rey (September 8, 1847), for which he was brevetted major. It required him three years to recover, and he spent the rest of his life in pain. Later in 1847, he was promoted to captain (substantive rank). He was back on coastal survey duty from 1850 to 1855. He became a major, Regular Army, in 1855 and transferred to the paymaster branch, and served in Kansas, Nebraska, Dakota Territory, Utah, California, Minnesota, and Washington, D.C.

On April 30, 1862, Prince was transferred from the staff to the line and was promoted to brigadier general of volunteers. Given command of a brigade in Banks's II Corps of the Army of Virginia, he was captured a week later, at Cedar Mountain (August 9). He was walking his horse through a cornfield and suddenly found himself surrounded by the 23rd Virginia Infantry. He spent the next five months in Libby Prison. Exchanged in December, he briefly commanded a division in North Carolina, and succeeded Andrew Humphreys as commander of the 2nd Division, III Corps, shortly after the Battle of Gettysburg.

Prince developed a reputation for being too slow and cautious. He also got lost in the woods during the Mine Run Campaign, during which he showed a severe lack of speed and failed to make a scheduled rendezvous with the II Corps. The result was an indecisive check of a Union advance at Payne's Farm on November 27. His corps commander, General French, who himself was accused of being drunk during the battle, tried to saddle Prince with all of the blame. When the Army of the Potomac was downsized in March and April 1864, both French and Prince lost their positions.

General Prince was given rear-area, territorial commands or was on court-martial duty for the rest of the conflict. He did not receive the brevet to major general in the omnibus promotions at the end of the war. He was mustered out of volunteer service on April 30, 1866, and returned to the paymaster's branch as a major. He remained there for the rest of his career. Promoted to lieutenant colonel in 1877, he retired after forty-eight years' service on December 31, 1879.

Plagued by his Mexican War wound, General Prince traveled to Europe to seek medical help. While bathing in Baden, Germany, his wound reopened, requiring surgery the following month in Switzerland. He went to London, where he was diagnosed with Bright's Disease, a painful swelling of the kidneys. At Morley's Hotel in London, racked by pain and disease, Henry Prince shot himself in the head during the night of August 19–20, 1872. (His body was discovered by a chambermaid, so the exact time of his death could not be determined.) He was eighty-one years of age. He was buried in Hillside Cemetery in the town of his birth.

QUINBY

ISAAC FERDINAND QUINBY was born near Morristown, New Jersey, on January 29, 1821. He entered the U.S. Military Academy in 1839, graduated in 1843 (6/39), outranking his close friend, Ulysses S. Grant, who finished 21st. Quinby was commissioned brevet second lieutenant in the 2nd U.S. Artillery and served in various garrisons and as an assistant professor of natural philosophy at West Point. He served with the 3rd U.S. Artillery in Mexico but earned no brevets. Promoted to second lieutenant in 1845 and first lieutenant in 1847, he resigned his commission in 1852, and became a professor of mathematics and philosophy at the University of Rochester.

Quinby was appointed colonel of the 13th New York Infantry in April 1861. His regiment was mustered into Federal service in May and fought at Bull Run, where, as part of Sherman's brigade, it was routed by the Confederates. After a dispute with General Scott, Quinby resigned from the army in August and returned to academia, but (thanks to Grant) was re-mustered in as a brigadier general of volunteers on March 20, 1862. He was sent to the Western theater of operations, where he was given command of the District of Mississippi. His forces captured Fort Pillow on May 22. He held a number of territorial commands before September 24, when he assumed command of the 7th Division of McPherson's XVII Corps.

After the Yazoo Pass Expedition began in 1863, General Quinby's men were sent to reinforce Admiral Porter and General Ross in the assault on Fort Pemberton. When Quinby arrived, the Union forces were in retreat. Quinby persuaded Porter and Ross to try again. The result was two more checks, and the expedition was cancelled on April 5. Meanwhile, Quinby fell ill (apparently because of malaria) and was replaced by Marcellus M. Crocker. Quinby returned to Grant's army on the morning of May 16, during the Battle of Champion Hill. He did not resume command of the division that day, however, because Crocker was more familiar with the situation, because Quinby still felt feeble, and because Crocker was a better divisional commander than Quinby—or just about anyone else. Quinby did lead his command in the May 22 assault on Vicksburg, which was a total failure.

Isaac Quinby fell ill again during the siege (he suffered recurring bouts of malaria), and he went on sick leave on June 3. This time, he did not return to the field. He commanded the Draft Rendezvous Camp at Elmira, New York, until he resigned from the army on December 31, 1863. Not wanting to lose the services of his old friend completely, General Grant helped arrange for Quinby to be appointed provost marshal of the 28th Congressional District of New York, so he could return to academia and serve in the army simultaneously.

General Quinby was a professor at the University of Rochester from 1864 until 1869, when President Grant appointed him U.S. marshal for the northern district of New York. He held this post until 1877, when he returned to the university. He was surveyor of Rochester from 1885 to 1890. He died on September 18, 1891, at age seventy, at his home in Rochester, New York. He is buried in Mount Hope Cemetery, Rochester. John Gardner Quinby—one of his twelve children—became a captain in the U.S. Navy. Another, Henry Dean Quinby, Sr., became an internationally known investment banker.

R
· RAMSAY — RUTHERFORD ·

GEORGE DOUGLAS RAMSAY was born in Dumfries, Virginia (near Alexandria), on February 21, 1802, the son of a Scottish merchant. He entered the U.S. Military Academy in 1814 at age twelve, but did not graduate until 1820 (26/31). Commissioned second lieutenant in the artillery, he was assigned to the 1st U.S. Artillery in 1821, when that branch was organized into regiments. He was stationed in various garrisons in New England and at Fort Monroe, Virginia, which was the home of the Artillery School for Practice in those days. He also did a tour of duty with the Corps of Engineers.

Ramsay was promoted to first lieutenant in 1826, regimental adjutant in 1833, and captain in 1835. He was not promoted to major until April 22, 1861—twenty-six years later—although he was brevetted major for gallantry at Monterrey in the Mexican War. He served as chief of ordnance for Zachary Taylor's Army of Occupation in northern Mexico.

Ramsay found his niche in the Ordnance Branch. After serving as commandant of several arsenals, he sat on the Ordnance Board when the Civil War began. He received his second promotion of 1861 on August 1, when he was advanced to lieutenant colonel. He was promoted to colonel on June 1, 1863.

George Ramsay was a pleasant man who impressed Abraham Lincoln, and they became friends. The highly intolerant Secretary of War Edwin Stanton, however, hated him because he was too independent. Lincoln brevetted him brigadier general in 1862 and major general in early 1863, but neither appointment was confirmed by the Senate. In September 1863, Chief of Ordnance Brigadier General James Ripley was transferred out of his office. Lincoln wanted Ramsay to replace him, but Stanton backed Captain George T. Balch. Without Ramsay's knowledge, the two Republican politicians compromised. Ramsay was promoted to brigadier general and named chief of ordnance on September 26, but Balch received most of the power in the department. This unhappy situation continued for a year, during which it grew more contentious.

Ramsay was receptive to new ideas, but he refused to be a figurehead for Balch and constantly quarreled with Stanton. Given this factious, unhappy situation, it is amazing that the Union Ordnance Department functioned as well as it did, and the Union Army was abundantly supplied with munitions, arms, and equipment. The soap opera ended on September 12, 1864, when Ramsay retired, and Balch was transferred to West Point. Ramsay's retirement was largely theoretical; he continued on duty as commandant of the Washington Arsenal until February 1870, when he actually did retire. He was brevetted major general in 1866.

Ramsay was part of the honor guard at Abraham Lincoln's funeral. He remained in Washington, D.C., after his retirement and died there on May 23, 1882, at age eighty. He is buried in Oak Hill Cemetery, Washington. His son Francis retired as a rear admiral in 1897.

THOMAS EDWARD GREENFIELD RANSOM was born in Norwich, Vermont, on November 29, 1834. His father, Colonel Truman B. Ransom, was killed in action at Chapultepec during the Mexican War. Thomas entered Norwich University in 1848 and graduated with a degree in civil engineering in 1851. He moved to Illinois, where he worked as an engineer and engaged in land speculation. When the Civil War began, he worked for the Illinois Central Railroad. He recruited a company which became part of the 11th Illinois Infantry and joined the Union Army as a captain on April 24, 1861.

Promotions followed rapidly for Ransom: major (June 4, 1861); lieutenant colonel (July 30, 1861); colonel (February 15, 1862); and brigadier general (April 15, 1863). In the meantime, he amassed a superior combat record as a regimental, brigade, and divisional commander. He was wounded in the shoulder in a skirmish at Charleston, Missouri, during the night of August 19, but was out of action for only a week. Leading the 11th Illinois, he was hit in the shoulder again by a Confederate minié ball at Fort Donelson on February 15, 1862. After his wound was dressed, Ransom resumed his command. A brigade commander at the Battle of Shiloh (April 6, 1862), he was wounded in the head but kept going until his horse was killed. This time he was severely injured and confined to the hospital for a week.

Cited for his skill, gallantry, and courage, he was named assistant inspector general of Grant's Army of the Tennessee in May 1862. He was given command of a brigade in McPherson's XVII Corps in December 1862 and led it in the various Vicksburg campaigns and the subsequent siege. After Vicksburg surrendered, he was commandant of Natchez before he was transferred to the Department of the Gulf. In 1864, he took part in the Red River Campaign, in which he commanded the XIII Corps detachment (two infantry divisions).

He made his worst mistake in the Battle of Mansfield, Louisiana, on April 8, 1864. At a critical moment in the battle, with the Union line crumbling and Confederates in the Federal rear at several points, he sent his adjutant forward with instructions for the 48th Ohio and 130th Illinois to withdraw. Who shot and killed the adjutant is not known, but he never made it to the regiments. In critical and dangerous situations, Civil War generals frequently sent two dispatch riders with important messages via different routes to be sure the message arrived, but Ransom did not do this. As a result, both regiments were surrounded and overrun by the Rebels. As the Union front collapsed, General Ransom was wounded in the knee and had to be carried to the rear. He was sent back to Chicago to recover.

Thomas Ransom returned to duty during the Atlanta Campaign. He initially commanded a division in the XVI Corps. Both Ulysses S. Grant and William T. Sherman thought highly of Ransom, and he was brevetted

major general on September 1 and given command of the XVII Corps of the Army of the Tennessee on September 22. Unfortunately, he had still not recovered from his Louisiana wound when he contracted dysentery, He gave up command on October 10, when he was too weak to go on. On October 28, he was diagnosed with typhoid. The combination of his wound and two diseases caused his death in Rome, Georgia, on October 29, 1864. The North lost one of its best generals. He was twenty-nine years old. He was buried in Rosehill Cemetery, Chicago.

GREEN BERRY RAUM was born in Golconda, Illinois, on December 3, 1829. He was educated in local schools, studied law, and was admitted to the bar in 1853. He moved to Kansas in 1856 but returned to Illinois in 1858 and settled in Harrisburg, where he set up a law practice.

Raum joined the Union Army on September 28, 1861, as the major of the 56th Illinois Infantry. Sent to the Western Front after Shiloh, he took part in the Siege of Corinth (where he distinguished himself by leading a charge and capturing an enemy battery), Grant's unsuccessful Central Mississippi Campaign, the unsuccessful Yazoo Pass Expedition, the battles of Champion's Hill and Big Black River, and the Siege of Vicksburg. Meanwhile, Raum was promoted to lieutenant colonel on June 26, 1862, and colonel on August 31, 1862. He assumed command of a brigade during the siege and led it until November 25, 1863, during the Battle of Missionary Ridge, when a Confederate minié ball passed through his left thigh. This wound would cause him moderate pain, stiffness, and weakness in his left leg for the rest of his life. He was carried back to Illinois to recuperate.

Raum returned to duty in February 1864, when he assumed command of a brigade in the XV Corps of the Army of the Tennessee. His primary duty was to guard the rail line from Dalton to Acworth and from Kingston to Rome. That October, he reinforced the garrison at Resaca and held it against attacks from the Confederate Army of Tennessee.

Colonel Raum's brigade took part in the March to the Sea and the Carolinas Campaign. He was brevetted brigadier general on September 19 and promoted to brigadier general of volunteers (full rank) on February 28, 1865. He resigned from the army on May 6 and returned to Illinois.

Raum became the first president of the Cairo & Vincennes Railroad in 1866. That same year, he was elected to Congress as a Radical Republican but was defeated for re-election in 1868. He served as U.S. Commissioner of Internal Revenue from 1876 to 1883 and was U.S. Commissioner of Pensions from 1889 to 1893. He was acting chairman of the Republican National Convention in Chicago in 1880.

General Raum retired from politics in 1893 and spent the last sixteen years of his life practicing law. He died in Chicago on December 18, 1909, at age eighty. He was interred in Arlington National Cemetery.

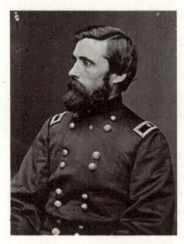

JOHN AARON RAWLINS was born in Galena, Illinois, on February 13, 1831. His father was an irresponsible heavy drinker who went to California to strike gold (which he never did), leaving John to take care of the farm, his mother, and six younger brothers. He was a teetotaler because he feared that, if he took even one drink, he would never stop.

Local schools were rather poor, so he devised his own program of self-study, read law under a local attorney, and was admitted to the bar in 1854. He ran for public office as a Douglas elector in 1860 but was defeated. When war came, he helped organize the 45th Illinois Infantry, which Colonel Ulysses S. Grant offered to help train. Grant was impressed with Rawlins and asked him to become his aide-de-camp. Rawlins accepted and was appointed captain, Regular Army, and assistant adjutant general (AAG) on August 30, 1861.

As AAG, Rawlins became Grant's *de facto* chief of staff. As Grant moved up, so did Rawlins, who was his most influential advisor and closest personal friend. He was an excellent chief of staff, despite his lack of military training. Rawlins was known for his efficiency, industriousness, intelligence, attention to detail, and adherence to protocol. He extracted a promise from Grant (who had a history of alcohol abuse) that he would not drink during this war—a promise Grant was unable or unwilling to keep. Rawlins frequently reprimanded Grant for drinking, and the general never reacted negatively, a fact which often astonished onlookers. He also strongly objected to Grant's offensive General Order No. 11, which expelled all Jews from Memphis, but to no avail.

John Rawlins played an often behind-the-scenes role in all of Grant's victories and was rewarded accordingly. He was promoted to major (May 14, 1862); chief of staff of the Army of the Tennessee (October 1862); lieutenant colonel (November 1, 1862); brigadier general of volunteers, (August 11, 1863); brigadier general, Regular Army (September 26, 1863); chief of staff, Military Division of the Mississippi (October 16, 1863); chief of staff of the General Headquarters of the United States Army (March 1864); brevet major general, Regular Army (February 24, 1865), and major general, Regular Army (May 9, 1865), although he was never confirmed at this rank by the Senate.

Rawlins's first wife died of tuberculosis, and he contracted the disease during the war. Grant wanted to appoint Rawlins military commander of the Southwest, with headquarters in Arizona, in hopes that the dry air would improve his health. Rawlins, however, declined the appointment, preferring to stay with Grant. Grant acquiesced and, when he became president, appointed Rawlins secretary of war. General Rawlins resigned from the army on March 12, 1869, to take this office. Perhaps his most significant act in office was to approve the construction of the Brooklyn Bridge. He also persuaded Grant to adopt a harsh policy toward Mormons in Utah. (Rawlins hated polygamy.) Additionally, he called upon President Grant to intervene in Cuba and support the revolutionaries against the Spanish, but Grant refused to do so.

John Rawlins died of tuberculosis in Washington, D.C., on September 6, 1869, at age thirty-eight. Grant mournfully declared that he could not be replaced. He was originally interred in a friend's vault in the Congressional Cemetery, but his remains were later buried in Arlington National Cemetery. He had six children.

HUGH THOMPSON REID was born on October 18, 1811, on a farm in Union County, Indiana Territory. He was educated in local schools. Sources differ as to where he received his higher education, it being variously reported that he graduated from Bloomington College (Indiana); Miami University (Ohio); and Indiana College (now Indiana University). He moved to Iowa Territory in 1839.

Reid was a ball of energy and noted for his tirelessness. He became a prominent lawyer at Fort Madison and Keokuk, Iowa, and was a prosecuting attorney for five counties from 1840 to 1842. He was known as "a terror" who rarely failed to convict. As a defense attorney, Mormon leader Joseph Smith was among his clients until he was assassinated in 1844.

Hugh Reid became famous as a builder of railroads and became president of the Des Moines Railroad Company, which headquartered in Keokuk. He joined the Union Army on February 22, 1862, at age fifty, as colonel of the 15th Iowa Infantry. He first saw action at Shiloh on April 6, when General Grant ordered him to prevent stragglers from leaving the battlefield. Here, a bullet passed through the right side of his neck. He fell from his horse, and onlookers thought he was dead. His body was taken to the rear, where he regained consciousness, mounted a horse, and (covered in blood) continued to rally the troops. No doubt about it—Hugh Reid was a hero of the highest order.

He was not able to return to duty until October, when he was given command of a brigade and fought in the Battle of Corinth. Later that month, he was given command of the post of Columbus, Kentucky, where he suppressed the Knights of the Golden Circle. Later he commanded posts in Cairo, Illinois; Bolivar, Tennessee; and Lake Providence, Louisiana, and was promoted to brigadier general on April 9, 1863. His command in Louisiana included USCT (United States Colored Troops) as well as white units. He was an early advocate of using African American troops in battle. "Remember that every colored soldier who stops a rebel bullet saves a White man's life," he told his white soldiers, many of whom objected to employing African Americans in a combat role.

General Reid resigned his commission on April 4, 1864, and returned to Iowa, where he resumed his railroad work. He died of Bright's Disease in Keokuk on August 21, 1874, at age sixty-two. He was buried there in Oakland Cemetery.

JAMES WILLIAM REILLY was born in Akron, Ohio, on May 20, 1828, the son of Irish immigrants. He was educated at Allegheny College, Meadville, Pennsylvania, and at Mount St. Mary's College in Emmitsburg, Maryland. He then studied law, passed the bar, and set up a successful practice in Wellsville, Ohio, beginning in 1848. It was common for him to walk fifteen miles to Lisbon, the country seat. He made it a rule to read twenty-five pages from a reputable author every day—a practice he continued for forty years. In 1858, he was elected to the Ohio legislature as a Republican.

Reilly joined the army as colonel of the 104th Ohio Infantry on August 30, 1862. After training at Camp Massillon (fifty miles south of Cleveland), the regiment was split up and garrisoned at various posts in Kentucky. It prepared to defend Cincinnati during Kirby Smith's invasion of Kentucky and was involved in a skirmish at Fort Mitchell in Kentucky.

Reilly and his men were assigned to Burnside's Army of the Ohio in the summer of 1863 and took part in his East Tennessee Campaign, including the capture of the Cumberland Gap and Knoxville. It also fought in the Siege of Knoxville, where Confederate General Longstreet unsuccessfully tried to take the city from Burnside. In 1864, he led his brigade in the Atlanta Campaign.

James Reilly was promoted to brigadier general on July 30, 1864. He assumed acting command of a division in the Army of the Ohio in September, but was back in command of his brigade on October 21 and distinguished himself in Hood's invasion of Tennessee. During the Battle of Franklin (November 30), his men initially broke in disarray under heavy enemy attack, but Reilly rallied them and checked the Confederate assault. He then counterattacked and took one thousand Rebel prisoners. He did not participate in the Battle of Nashville.

Considered highly competent, Reilly was given command of a division in North Carolina in late February 1865 and directed it in Sherman's Carolinas Campaign. He resigned from the army on April 20, 1865, shortly after General Lee surrendered but before Joseph E. Johnston capitulated. This may explain why he was never brevetted major general.

Reilly returned to Ohio and resumed his law practice. He served as president of the First National Bank of Wellsville for more than thirty years and was a delegate to the Ohio Constitutional Convention in 1873. He was known as a gruff man with a kind heart. A lifelong bachelor, he was involved in many local civic activities and local Republican politics. General Reilly died in bed at his home on November 6, 1905, at age seventy-seven. He was buried in St. Elizabeth Cemetery, Wellsville, Ohio.

JESSE LEE RENO was born on April 20, 1823, in Wheeling, Virginia (now West Virginia). His Huguenot ancestors were named "Renault" until

they Anglicized the name. His family moved to Venango County, Pennsylvania, around 1831, and he spent most of his childhood there.

Reno was admitted to West Point in 1842 and became close friends with Stonewall Jackson. He graduated in 1846 (8/59) and was commissioned brevet second lieutenant in the Ordnance branch. He nevertheless commanded an artillery battery during Winfield Scott's drive on Mexico City. He fought from Vera Cruz to Chapultepec (September 13, 1847), where he was seriously wounded. He was brevetted twice for gallant and meritorious conduct.

For the next fifteen years, Reno served in a variety of jobs and locations, mainly in ordnance positions. Among other things, he created a system of instruction for heavy artillery at West Point, designed a road in Minnesota, commanded Frankford Arsenal, northeast of Philadelphia, and was chief of ordnance on the staff of Albert Sidney Johnston during the Utah Expedition. He was promoted to second lieutenant in 1846, first lieutenant in 1853, and captain in 1860. He was commanding the Mount Vernon Arsenal in Mount Vernon, Alabama, when South Carolina seceded.

On January 4, 1861, Reno was forced to surrender the arsenal to Alabama state troops. He was then placed in command of Fort Leavenworth, Kansas, until November 12, 1861, when he was appointed brigadier general of volunteers. He was given command of a brigade in Burnside's North Carolina Expedition, which he led from December to April 2, 1862. Promoted to divisional commander in the IX Corps, he fought in the battles of the Second Bull Run and Chantilly against his old friend, Jackson. He was promoted to major general on August 20.

Reno was known as a soldier's soldier. He often went forward with his troops without a sword or badges of rank. He was with them on September 14, near Fox Gap during the Battle of South Mountain, when he was shot in the chest. Sources differ as to whether the shot came from Hood's Texans or an inexperienced soldier from the 35th Massachusetts. In any case, he was taken to the rear on a stretcher. He passed by Brigadier General Samuel D. Sturgis, a fellow alumnus of the Class of 1846, and told him he was dead. He sounded so natural that Sturgis thought he was joking. "Yes, yes, I'm dead—goodbye!" Reno replied. He passed away a few minutes later. He was thirty-nine years old.

General Reno was initially buried in a vault in Trinity Church, Boston. In 1867, his remains were reinterred in Oak Hill Cemetery, Washington, D.C. One of his five children, Jesse W. Reno, invented the escalator.

JOSEPH WARREN REVERE, the grandson of famous patriot Paul Revere, was born in Boston on May 17, 1812. He enrolled in the U.S. Naval School at age fourteen and, two years later, joined the navy as a midshipman. Over the next twenty-five years, he visited Europe, the Pacific, Singapore, the Baltic States, and Russia, where he met the Czar. In the meantime, he served in the Second Seminole War and did a tour on anti-piracy duty in the West Indies. He was on a ship that circumnavigated the globe in 1838. Promoted to lieutenant in 1841, he fought in the Mexican War and was involved in the conquest of California. In the process, he acquired almost nine thousand acres and established his own plantation, growing trees and potatoes.

In 1850, Revere (who was married) apparently had an affair with a married woman. This led to a court of inquiry and, to avoid a court-martial, Revere resigned his commission, although he later claimed that he quit because of slow promotions. The following year, he sold his property in California and joined the Mexican Army as a lieutenant colonel. He returned to the United States in 1852 and settled in Morristown, New Jersey, where he built a beautiful mansion. Later, he traveled throughout Europe and to India. He was present at the Battle of Solferino in Italy in 1859.

Revere joined the Union Army as colonel of the 7th New Jersey Infantry in September 1861. He fought in the Peninsula Campaign, the Seven Days battles, and the Second Battle of Bull Run, where he was wounded in the right leg by a minié ball. He was promoted to brigadier general on October 25. The following month, he assumed command of a brigade in the III Corps. His unit was lightly engaged at Fredericksburg but heavily engaged at Chancellorsville, where General Berry, his division commander, was mortally wounded. Command devolved on Revere. On May 3, instead of hurling his men at the enemy, as he probably should have done, he ordered a three-mile retreat to regroup. General Hooker, the commander of the Army of the Potomac, blamed him for the army's defeat, accused him of cowardice, and had him court-martialed. He was dismissed from the army on August 10. Near the end of the war, Abraham Lincoln overturned the conviction, restored him to rank, and accepted his resignation at the same time. Revere was brevetted major general in 1866. He received a pension of $20 a month as a partially disabled veteran.

Revere spent the rest of his life traveling the world, farming, and engaging in horse breeding. He also wrote a couple of novels and a great many pamphlets. He died in Hoboken, New Jersey, on April 20, 1880. He was sixty-seven years old. A convert to Catholicism during the war, General Revere was buried in Holy Rood Catholic Cemetery in Morristown, New Jersey. His brother, Colonel Paul Revere, was killed in action at Gettysburg, and was brevetted brigadier general posthumously.

JOHN FULTON REYNOLDS was born on September 21, 1820, in Lancaster, Pennsylvania. He was educated at the Lancaster County Academy and was appointed to West Point in 1837 by U.S. Senator James Buchanan, a family friend. He graduated in 1841 (26/52) and was commissioned brevet second lieutenant in the 3rd Artillery. He was stationed at Fort McHenry, Baltimore; St. Augustine, Florida; and Fort Moultrie, South Carolina, before joining Zachary Taylor's Army of Occupation in Texas. He fought in northern Mexico and was brevetted captain for gallantry at Monterrey and major for Buena Vista. Assignments in Maine, New Orleans, New York, and Oregon followed. He was promoted to captain (full rank) in 1855 and fought Indians in the Pacific Northwest and Mormons in Utah. In September 1860, he became commandant of cadets at West Point.

Reynolds was promoted to lieutenant colonel, Regular Army, on May 14, 1861, and was assigned to the 14th U.S. Infantry. He was advanced to brigadier general of volunteers on August 26 and was given command of a brigade of Pennsylvania Reserves. He briefly served as military governor of Fredericksburg, Virginia, in 1862 but was transferred to the Peninsula and fought in the Seven Days battles, where he distinguished himself at Mechanicsville. After two days of almost constant combat without sleep, an exhausted Reynolds lay down to rest near Boatswain's Swamp and woke up a prisoner of war. He was greatly embarrassed that he was captured in this manner. Sent to Libby Prison, he was exchanged for Confederate General Lloyd Tilghman on August 15.

When he returned, Reynolds was given command of a division in the III Corps. He fought at the Second Bull Run, where he launched a desperate counterattack which may have saved the disintegrating U.S. Army of Virginia from complete destruction. At the request of the governor, he commanded the Pennsylvania Militia during the Maryland Campaign of 1862 and missed the Battle of Antietam. He assumed command of the I Corps on September 29 and was promoted to major general to date from November 29, 1862.

The I Corps fought at Fredericksburg and was lightly engaged at Chancellorsville. On June 2, at the president's request, Reynolds met privately with Abraham Lincoln, who asked him if he would consider commanding the Army of the Potomac. Reynolds said he would do so only if he would be free of the political influences that plagued Union army commanders throughout the war. Lincoln did not feel able to meet this demand and promoted George G. Meade—an officer junior to Reynolds—instead.

On July 1, 1863, the first day of the Battle of Gettysburg, he exercised operational command of the I, III, and XI Corps and Buford's cavalry division. Here, at about 10:40 a.m., a rifle ball from a Rebel sharpshooter struck him behind the right ear and passed through his head. He was dead within a minute or two.

John Reynolds was loved by his men and highly respected by other generals on both sides of the line. Many considered him to be the best general in the army, and he was a very nice man to boot. He was forty-two when he died. General Reynolds was buried in Lancaster Cemetery, in the town of his birth, three days after his death. Reynolds was a Protestant but was engaged to Katherine May Hewitt, a Catholic. Because of their different religions, their engagement was kept secret until after his death.

Brokenhearted, Hewitt joined a convent. Reynolds's brother James was quartermaster general of Pennsylvania. Another brother, William, became a rear admiral in the U.S. Navy and is buried beside General Reynolds. A third brother, Samuel, was a paymaster and brevet lieutenant colonel during the war.

JOSEPH JONES REYNOLDS was born in Flemingsburg, Kentucky, on January 4, 1822. His family moved to Lafayette, Indiana, when he was fifteen. He attended Wabash College in Crawfordville for a year before going to West Point, from which he graduated in 1843 (10/39). He did garrison duty and was transferred back to West Point as an artillery instructor just before the Mexican War, which he missed. He was promoted to second lieutenant in 1846 but resigned his commission in 1857, to become a professor of engineering at Washington University in St. Louis. In 1860, he returned to Indiana and went into the wholesale grocery business with one of his brothers.

Reynolds returned to the colors as colonel of the 10th Indiana Militia within two weeks of Fort Sumter and served as commandant of Camp Morton. He was promoted to brigadier general on June 14, 1861, and took command of a brigade in the Department (later Army) of the Ohio. He fought in western Virginia that fall and was wounded in the left testicle. He resigned his commission on January 23, 1862, and returned home to settle his brother's estate.

Joseph Reynolds returned to duty in 1862 and was recommissioned brigadier general on September 17. He built a supply depot and fortifications at Carthage, Tennessee, before being appointed major general on November 29, 1862. He led a division of the XIV Corps at Chickamauga and was chief of staff of the Army of the Cumberland from October 1863 to January 1864. Transferred to the Army of the Gulf, he became commander of the XIX Corps on July 7, 1864, and led it in the capture of Mobile. He directed the Department of Arkansas at the end of the war.

Reynolds reverted to the rank of colonel and commander of the 27th U.S. Infantry in 1866. He was transferred to Texas in 1867 and immediately seized control of the state for the Republican Party. He sought a U.S. Senate seat in 1870 but withdrew because of opposition throughout the state and across party lines. Generally disliked in Texas, he returned to duty on the frontier in 1871 as commander of the 5th U.S. Cavalry and fought against the Sioux and Northern Cheyenne in Montana. Here he was wounded in the right testicle. Later, in the Battle of Powder River (March 17, 1876), he was defeated by a collection of Northern Cheyenne and Oglala Lakota Sioux, during which he ordered a premature retreat, leaving a wounded private to be captured. The Indians tortured the man to death, which led to Reynolds being court-martialed in 1876. Found guilty, he was sentenced to suspension of rank and pay for one year. The court suspended his sentence, giving him the opportunity to retire in disgrace, which he did in 1877.

General Reynolds settled in Washington, D.C., where he died on February 25, 1899, at age seventy-seven. He was buried in Arlington National Cemetery. His son Alfred (1853–1936) became an admiral in the U.S. Navy.

AMERICUS VESPUCIUS RICE was born in Perryville, Ohio, on November 18, 1835. He majored in classical studies at Antioch College in Yellow Springs, Ohio, and graduated from Union College in Schenectady, New York, in 1860. He was studying law when the Civil War began. Two weeks later, he was mustered into the Federal army as a captain in the 21st Ohio. When this 90-day regiment mustered out, Rice joined the 57th Ohio as a captain.

The 57th Ohio served on the Western Front, and Rice fought at Shiloh, the Siege of Corinth, the battles of Chickasaw Bluffs, Arkansas Post, Champion Hill, and the Siege of Vicksburg. Meanwhile, Rice was promoted to lieutenant colonel on February 8, 1862. On May 22, 1863, during Grant's second major assault on Vicksburg, Rice had a musket ball pass through his leg below the knee and ricocheted upward, lodging near his abdomen. He was sent to Memphis and then home to recover. He did not rejoin the army until February 1864. Meanwhile, his promotion to colonel was promulgated on May 24, 1863.

Colonel Rice led the 57th Ohio in the Atlanta Campaign, fighting at Resaca, Dallas, New Hope Church, and Kennesaw Mountain on June 27, 1864. Here he was shot three times, almost simultaneously. One of the bullets destroyed his leg just above his left ankle, which had to be amputated. He did not return to duty until June 23, 1865, when he was given command of a brigade in the XV Corps. Meanwhile, President Andrew Johnson appointed him brigadier general of volunteers on May 31, 1865. He was mustered out in January 1866.

After the war, Rice managed a private bank home in Ottawa, Ohio. He was elected to Congress as a Democrat in 1874 and served from 1875 to 1879. He did not seek re-election in 1878. Afterward, he returned to the banking business. He was a U.S. pension agent for Ohio from 1894 to 1898. He moved to Washington, D.C., in 1899 and became a purchasing agent for the U.S. Census Bureau. He died in Washington on April 4, 1904, at age sixty-eight. He was buried in Arlington National Cemetery.

ELLIOTT WARREN RICE, the brother of Samuel A. Rice, was born on November 16, 1825, in Allegheny, Pennsylvania, but his family moved to Belmont, Ohio, the following year. He was educated in Wheeling, Virginia (now West Virginia). He moved to Oskaloosa, Iowa, in 1855, studied law under the supervision of his brother, Samuel, and attended the University of Albany Law School in New York, from which he graduated in 1858. He was practicing law with his brother in Oskaloosa when the war began.

Rice enlisted in the 7th Iowa Infantry as a private on July 24, 1861. He was rapidly promoted to corporal and sergeant and on August 30 became a major. He fought at Belmont, where he commanded the regiment after his colonel was wounded and his lieutenant colonel killed. Rice himself was severely wounded in the leg and command devolved onto the senior captain. They were the first wounds he received during the war. The bullet in his leg could not be removed, and he carried it for the rest of his life. Still on crutches, Rice took part in the battles of Fort Henry, Fort Donelson, and Shiloh, where he again succeeded to regimental command after his colonel was incapacitated. Promoted to colonel effective April 7, 1862, he took part in the Siege of Corinth, in occupation duty at Bethel and La Grange, Tennessee, and in Grant's operations in northern Mississippi, including the Second Battle of Corinth (October 3–4). He became a brigade commander in July 1863 and was promoted to brigadier general on June 22, 1864.

As part of Sherman's army group, Rice fought in the Atlanta Campaign, the subsequent March to the Sea, and the Carolinas Campaign. His last battle was at Bentonville, North Carolina. He was discharged from the army on August 24, 1865, and brevetted major general in 1866.

After the war, General Rice lived in Washington, D.C., where he practiced law until 1885. Then, in declining health, he returned to Iowa and lived at his sister's home in Sioux City until his death, which occurred on June 22, 1887. He was fifty-one. He was interred in Floyd Cemetery, Sioux City.

JAMES CLAY RICE was born in Worthington, Massachusetts, on December 27, 1828. He was homeschooled before being admitted to Yale University, from which he graduated in 1854. He taught school in Natchez, Mississippi, for a year, worked at a newspaper, studied law, and was admitted to the bar. He was practicing in New York City when the war began.

Rice joined the Union Army as a first lieutenant in the 39th New York Infantry on May 10, 1861. He was a captain when he fought in the First Battle of Bull Run. His regiment was mustered out on September 12. The next day, Rice became lieutenant colonel of the 44th New York Infantry. He fought in the Peninsula Campaign and the Seven Days battles and became colonel of his regiment on July 4, 1862. Sent to northern Virginia, Rice fought in the Second Battle of Bull Run, where he became a brigade commander in Porter's V Corps after Colonel Henry A. Weeks was wounded. He came down with typhoid in early September and was sent home; thus, he missed the Maryland Campaign and the Battle of Antietam. He was married on December 10 and returned to duty almost immediately. He commanded his regiment at Fredericksburg on December 13 and at Chancellorsville, where it was lightly engaged.

James Rice made his greatest contribution to the Union cause during the Battle of Gettysburg on July 2, 1863. Here, in the struggle for Little Round Top, he assumed command of his brigade after Colonel Strong Vincent was mortally wounded. Ezra Warner later wrote: "It is not too much to say that this little band of four regiments, numbering scarcely a thousand muskets, saved the Union cause from disaster . . ." (*Generals in Blue*, p. 401). They checked the attacks of Law's (formerly Hood's) Division and prevented the Rebels from rolling up the Union's left flank. For his truly heroic performance, Rice was made a permanent brigade commander and was promoted to brigadier general on August 11.

General Rice led his brigade (part of the V Corps) in the Battle of the Wilderness and at Spotsylvania Court House, where a ball from a Confederate rifle shattered his thigh. Taken to the rear, he lost a great deal of blood before a tourniquet could be applied. Doctors were forced to amputate his leg, but it was too late. He regained consciousness, asked if he was dying, and was told that he was. When a surgeon asked which side he would prefer to lie on, Rice replied: "Turn me over and let me die with my face to the foe." These words are engraved on his gravestone. A hero of the first order, General Rice passed a few minutes later at age thirty-five. He was buried in Albany Rural Cemetery, Menands, New York. He had no children, and his wife never remarried.

SAMUEL ALLEN RICE, the older brother of General Elliott W. Rice, was born in Cattaraugus County, New York, on January 27, 1828, but moved with his family to western Pennsylvania and Belmont County, Ohio, where he grew up. He was educated at home, at Franklin College in Athens, Ohio, and Union College in Schenectady, New York, from which he graduated in 1849. He remained at Union another year, studied law, and moved to Oskaloosa, Iowa, in 1851, and set up a law practice. He was elected county attorney in 1853 and attorney general for the state of Iowa in 1856 and 1858. He lost a bid for Congress in 1862.

Rice was a highly partisan Republican and Unionist. In August 1861, he organized the 33rd Iowa Militia

Regiment, with himself as colonel. It was mustered into Federal service as the 33rd Iowa Infantry on October 1, 1862. Initially sent to St. Louis, Missouri, it was later posted to Columbus, Kentucky, and Union City, Tennessee. It saw its first significant action in northern Mississippi, where it took part in the unsuccessful Yazoo Pass Expedition (including the Battle of Fort Pemberton) and the skirmishes around Greenwood. The regiment was sent to Helena, Arkansas, in May 1863, where Rice was given command of a brigade in the XIII Corps. He was part of the defense of the town against Confederate Lieutenant Holmes's attacks of July 4. For this success, he was promoted to brigadier general on August 4. He was acting commander of a division in the Army of Arkansas during General Steele's drive on Little Rock in September but reverted to brigade commander in October.

Samuel Rice fought in the Camden Expedition of 1864. He was wounded in the head by shrapnel at Elkins' Ferry on the Little Missouri River on April 4, 1864, but remained with his soldiers. As the U.S. VII Corps retreated toward Little Rock, he fought in the Battle of Jenkins' Ferry on the Saline River on April 30. Here a Confederate bullet shattered his ankle and carried part of his spur into his ankle with it. He remained in a hospital in Little Rock for some weeks, but his wound would not heal and became infected. He was finally sent home to recuperate but developed blood poisoning. He endured a painful operation to remove bone fragments on June 15, but his condition did not improve, and he finally succumbed on July 6, at age thirty-six. He was buried in Forest Cemetery, Oskaloosa. General Rice left behind a wife and four children.

ISRAEL BUSH "FIGHTING DICK" RICHARDSON, who was also known as "Greasy Dick," was born in Fairfax, Vermont, on December 26, 1815. He was descendent of Revolutionary War General Israel Putnam. He was admitted to the U.S. Military Academy in 1836, graduated in 1841 (38/52), and was commissioned brevet second lieutenant in the 3rd U.S. Infantry. He was promoted to second lieutenant later that year and to first lieutenant in 1846. Meanwhile, he served in the Second Seminole War in Florida. He fought in Mexico, winning a brevet to captain for Contreras and Churubusco and major for Chapultepec. He served on the frontier, in Texas and New Mexico Territory, and was promoted to captain (substantive rank) in 1851, but heartbroken by the death of his wife and son, resigned his commission in 1855, moved to Pontiac, Michigan, and became a farmer. He remarried in 1861.

Richardson rejoined the army on May 25, 1861, as colonel of the 2nd Michigan Infantry—a regiment he helped organize—and was promoted to brigade commander in June. He fought in the First Battle of Bull Run and was promoted to brigadier general on August 9. In March 1862, he assumed command of a division in the II Corps. He fought in the Peninsula Campaign, including the Siege of Yorktown, the Battle of Seven Pines, and in the Seven Days battles. He was promoted to major general on July 25.

Known for being a tough, no-nonsense commander, General Richardson was nevertheless quite popular with his men because of his tactical ability and unflinching courage. He took part in the Second Bull Run Campaign and in the Maryland Campaign, including the Battle of South Mountain. On September 17, during the Battle of Antietam, he drove D. H. Hill's men from the Sunken Road (also known as the Bloody Lane) in the Confederate center. While organizing a follow-up attack and directing Union artillery fire, he was struck by enemy shrapnel, fired by guns under the command of his personal friend, James Longstreet. He was carried to the Pry House, the headquarters of General George McClellan. The physicians discovered that shrapnel was lodged in both of his lungs and feared that it would kill him. On October 4, he was visited by Abraham Lincoln, who reportedly suggested that he (Richardson) would replace McClellan as commander of the Army of the Potomac if he survived his wounds. (I rather doubt that this story is true, but stranger things have happened.) After seeming to be getting better, Richardson developed pneumonia, and his condition rapidly deteriorated. His wife visited him and was present during his last moments. He died in Sharpsburg, Maryland, on November 3, 1862, at age forty-six. He is buried in Oak Hill Cemetery, Pontiac, Michigan.

JAMES BREWERTON RICKETTS was born in New York City on June 21, 1817. He entered West Point in 1835, graduated in 1839 (16/31), and was commissioned second lieutenant in the 1st U.S. Artillery Regiment. He served on the northern frontier (in the vicinity of Plattsburg, New York and in Maine) during the Canadian border dispute before being sent to Louisiana in 1845. He took part in the occupation of Texas and Taylor's invasion of northern Mexico, where he fought at Monterrey and the Battle of Buena Vista. Remarkably, he was not brevetted. He was, however, promoted to first lieutenant in 1846 and captain in 1852. Routine garrison duty followed in Fort Columbus, New York; various locations in Texas; Baton Rouge, Louisiana; and Fort Monroe, Virginia.

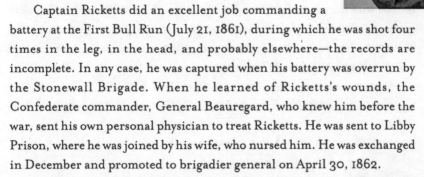

Captain Ricketts did an excellent job commanding a battery at the First Bull Run (July 21, 1861), during which he was shot four times in the leg, in the head, and probably elsewhere—the records are incomplete. In any case, he was captured when his battery was overrun by the Stonewall Brigade. When he learned of Ricketts's wounds, the Confederate commander, General Beauregard, who knew him before the war, sent his own personal physician to treat Ricketts. He was sent to Libby Prison, where he was joined by his wife, who nursed him. He was exchanged in December and promoted to brigadier general on April 30, 1862.

Ricketts returned to duty in May 1862 and assumed command of a brigade in McDowell's Corps. He fought at Cedar Mountain, Thoroughfare Gap (August 28), the Second Battle of Bull Run, and the battles of Chantilly, South Mountain, and Antietam, where he had two horses shot from under him. The second landed on him and injured him so badly that he did not return to combat duty until 1864. Meanwhile, he sat on courts-martials, including that of Fitz John Porter. His reputation suffered because he voted to convict.

Given a division in Sedgwick's VI Corps in March 1864, Ricketts served in the Overland Campaign. Many of his men were from Milroy's former command. They performed badly under Milroy and continued to perform poorly during the Battle of the Wilderness. Their performance at Spotsylvania was better, although they did not distinguish themselves. Even so, Ricketts and his men were rushed to Washington in July, to help check Early's drive on the capital. He returned to the Eastern Front and took part in the Battle of Cold Harbor and Siege of Petersburg, during which his command performed well. On October 16, he assumed command of the VI Corps in the Shenandoah Valley. Three days later, during the Battle of Cedar Creek, he was shot through the chest and disabled for life. Still, he rejoined his division on April 7, 1865, and was present when Lee surrendered at Appomattox two days later. Meanwhile, he was brevetted major general in December 1864.

After the war, Ricketts commanded a district in Virginia until he was mustered out of volunteer service on April 30, 1866. He declined a promotion to lieutenant colonel, Regular Army, in July 1866 and applied for retirement due to wounds. This was granted on January 28, 1867, when he retired with the rank of major general, although he did occasionally sit on court-martial boards after that date. He lived in Washington until his death, which occurred on September 22, 1887, at age seventy. He was buried in Arlington National Cemetery.

Ricketts was a nephew-in-law of President Franklin Pierce and the brother-in-law of Brevet Brigadier General William H. Lawrence.

JAMES WOLFE RIPLEY was born on December 10, 1794, in Windham County, Connecticut. He entered West Point in 1813—early in its history, when it was not yet a four-year institution—and graduated in 1814. He was commissioned second lieutenant in the artillery and served in the War of 1812.

Ripley was part of Andrew Jackson's invasion of Florida and fought in the First Seminole War. Promoted to first lieutenant in 1818 and to captain in 1825, he transferred to the Ordnance branch in 1832 and commanded U.S. forces at Fort Moultrie, South Carolina, in Charleston Harbor during the Nullification Crisis of 1832–1833. He prepared his positions for defense while simultaneously handling the South Carolinians with such tact and diplomacy that it earned the admiration of both sides. He was promoted to major of ordnance in 1833 and commanded the Kennebec Arsenal in Augusta, Maine, from 1833 to 1842. He directed the Springfield Armory from its opening in 1842 until 1854, during which time he was instrumental in developing the 1855 .58

caliber Springfield rifled musket, which became the principal weapon of Union infantrymen during the Civil War. He was promoted to major in 1838 and lieutenant colonel in 1854. That same year, he became commandant of the Watertown Arsenal in Massachusetts. He also did brief tours of duty as chief of ordnance for the Department of the Pacific and as inspector of arsenals.

When the Civil War began, Ripley was summoned to Washington, where he was promoted to colonel and was appointed chief of ordnance on April 23. He was brevetted brigadier general on July 2 and given full rank (Regular Army) on September 10. Called "Rip Van Winkle" behind his back, he was a stickler for regulations and often opposed progressive ideas, such as the adoption of breech-loading repeating rifles, on the grounds that they encouraged poor fire discipline and resulted in wasted ammunition. President Lincoln, however, favored this more modern weapon. Ripley's continued opposition led to his being forced into retirement as a brigadier general, Regular Army, on September 10, 1863.

Ripley also opposed the development of the Gatling gun, a rapid-firing multiple-barrel, crank-operated early machine gun. In Ripley's defense, the early Gatling guns were much more effective in modern Hollywood movies than in the field in the 1860s and 1870s. They required a high platform for the gunner, who was vulnerable to snipers and artillery fire; they were impossible to conceal in the days of black powder ammunition; they tended to foul quickly; and it required manual reloading. On the other hand, historians almost unanimously agree that his attempts to block the repeating rifle was a serious mistake. Many aver that it significantly lengthened the war.

Despite his retirement, Ripley remained on active duty as inspector of forts and fortifications on the New England coast (1863 to 1870). He was brevetted major general in 1866. He died in Hartford, Connecticut, on March 16, 1870, at age seventy-five. He was buried in the Springfield Cemetery, Springfield, Massachusetts. His nephew was Roswell Sabine Ripley, a brigadier general in the Confederate Army.

BENJAMIN STONE ROBERTS was born into an old New England family on November 18, 1810, in Manchester, Vermont. He graduated from

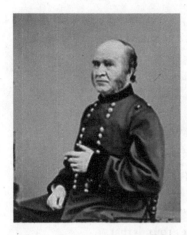

West Point in 1835 (53/56) and was commissioned brevet second lieutenant in the 1st Dragoons. He was stationed on the frontier in Iowa and Kansas. Roberts was promoted to second lieutenant in 1836 and first lieutenant in 1837 but resigned in 1839, to pursue a career as a civil engineer. He became New York State Geologist in 1841. In 1842, he relocated to Russia, where he was involved in constructing a railroad from Moscow to St. Petersburg. He returned to the United States and settled in Iowa, where he studied law and set up a practice in Des Moines.

When the Mexican War began in 1846, Roberts accepted a Regular Army commission as a first lieutenant in the Mounted Rifles Regiment. He was promoted to captain in 1847 and fought from Vera Cruz to the capture of Mexico City. He was brevetted major for leading a storming party at Churubusco and lieutenant colonel for general gallantry throughout the war.

Roberts remained in the army after the Mexican surrender and served mainly in Texas and New Mexico Territory on the southwestern frontier. He was at Fort Stanton in New Mexico Territory when the Civil War began. He became commander of the Southern District of New Mexico and was promoted to major on August 3, 1861. He was promoted to colonel of the 5th New Mexico Infantry on December 9. He distinguished himself in defeating the Confederate invasion of New Mexico in 1861 and 1862, especially in the Battle of Valverde. He was summoned to the Eastern Front shortly after and was named inspector general and chief of cavalry of Pope's Army of Virginia. He was promoted to brigadier general on July 19. He was wounded in the arm and the chest at Cedar Mountain on August 9 but not seriously. After the debacle of the Second Bull Run, he preferred charges against Fitz John Porter, which led to the ruin of his (Porter's) career.

Roberts was sent to Minnesota and into professional exile with John Pope. He was recalled to Washington, D.C., in early 1863, where he commanded the upper defenses of the capital. He commanded the District of Iowa later that year but was sent home to await orders and was unemployed for some months. He also held a minor command in south Louisiana in 1864 until October 26, when he became chief of cavalry of the Department of the Gulf. In early 1865, he was named commander of the District of West Tennessee. He was brevetted major general in the omnibus promotions of January 13, 1866, and was mustered out on January 15.

Reverting to his Regular Army rank of lieutenant colonel, Roberts was on recruiting service until 1867, when he returned to frontier duty in New Mexico. He was professor of military science at Yale from 1868 to 1870, when he retired after thirty years of continuous service. He died on January 29, 1875, in Washington, D.C., at age sixty-four. He is buried in Dellwood Cemetery in the town of his birth.

JAMES SIDNEY ROBINSON was born on October 14, 1827, in Mansfield, Ohio. Educated in local schools, he learned the printer's trade and moved to Kenton, Ohio, in 1845. He became editor and publisher of the Kenton *Republican* in 1847 and was chief clerk of the Ohio House of Representatives from 1856 to 1858.

Robinson enlisted in the 4th Ohio Infantry as a private on April 17, 1861—five days after the Rebels fired on Fort Sumter. He was elected first lieutenant the next day and captain on May 4. He commanded a company at Rich Mountain (July 11) during McClellan's western Virginia campaign.

The 4th Ohio's enlistments expired on July 24, and Robinson was mustered out of the service. He returned to Kenton, helped organize the 82nd Ohio Infantry, and returned to the colors as its major on December 31. He was promoted to lieutenant colonel on April 9, 1862, and to colonel on August 29. Meanwhile, he fought in the Valley Campaign of 1862, including the defeats at McDowell and Cross Keys. He was also involved in the battles of Cedar Mountain, First Rappahannock Station, and Second Bull Run—all Union defeats. The regiment was heavily engaged at Chancellorsville and emerged from that battle with only 134 men.

On July 1, 1863, as his regiment retreated into Gettysburg, Robinson was shot through the chest. He could not return to duty until December. He went to Tennessee with Hooker's XX Corps (the consolidated XI and XII Corps). Robinson fought in the Atlanta Campaign and the subsequent March to the

Sea and Carolinas Campaign. He was brevetted brigadier general in December and was promoted to brigadier general (full rank) on January 12, 1865. He was mustered out on August 15 and brevetted major general in 1866.

After the war, Robinson was elected to Congress as a Republican, serving from 1881 to 1885. He resigned on January 12, 1885, to take office as Ohio's secretary of state. He served in this position until 1889, when he retired from politics.

General Robinson died in Kenton of heart failure on January 14, 1892, at age sixty-four. He was buried in the Grove Cemetery, Kenton.

JOHN CLEVELAND ROBINSON was born in Binghamton, New York, on April 10, 1817. He entered West Point in 1835 but was court-martialed and expelled for insubordination in 1838. He studied law until the fall of 1839, when he was commissioned second lieutenant in the 5th U.S. Infantry. He became regimental quartermaster and was a brigade quartermaster in northern Mexico, where he fought at Palo Alto (May 8, 1846), Resaca de la Palma (May 9), and Monterrey. He was promoted to first lieutenant in 1846 and captain in 1850.

After Mexico, Robinson served in various garrisons and fought Indians in Texas and Florida during the Third Seminole War. He commanded Fort Bridger in Utah Territory from 1857 to 1859, after which he commanded Fort McHenry and its sixty-man garrison in Baltimore.

After the Civil War began, he was sent to Detroit to help recruit the 1st Michigan Infantry. It was mustered in on September 1, 1861, with Robinson as its colonel. He was given command of a brigade at Newport News, Virginia, in the spring of 1862, in preparation for the Peninsula Campaign, He was promoted to brigadier general on April 30. He led a brigade in the III Corps in the Peninsula and the Seven Days battles, where he distinguished himself. He took part in the Second Bull Run Campaign until August 27, when he was wounded by a shell fragment at Broad Run. He was unable to participate in the Maryland Campaign.

Robinson took part in the Battle of Fredericksburg and was promoted to divisional command on December 30. He was with the I Corps at Chancellorsville (where he was lightly engaged) and Gettysburg, where he was again commended for his valor. Here, his command lost 1,685 out of 2,500 men engaged. He led his division in the Mine Run campaign and was part of the V Corps in the Battle of the Wilderness. He fought his last battle at Laurel Hill (aka Alsop's Farm), Virginia, on May 8, 1864. As the Army of the Potomac pushed toward Spotsylvania Court House, Robinson placed himself at the head of his division and charged a Confederate field fortification. A Rebel minié ball slammed into his left knee joint. Taken to the rear, physicians had to amputate his leg.

Robinson was brevetted major general for Spotsylvania (in December 1864) and was later awarded the Congressional Medal of Honor for his courage. He returned to light duty in mid-September and commanded a district in northern New York. Later, he was transferred to western New York. Mustered out of volunteer service in September 1866, he remained in the army and commanded the Freedman's Bureau in North Carolina. In 1867, he directed the Military Department of the South and, in 1868, took charge of the Department of the Lakes. He retired from the army on May 6, 1869, and was promoted to major general, Regular Army, that same day.

John Robinson was popular in New York and the fact that he was a high-ranking Freemason did not hurt him. He was elected lieutenant governor of New York as a Republican in 1872. He also served two terms as commander-in-chief of the Grand Army of the Republic from 1877 to 1879. Tragically, his vision deteriorated, and he spent his last years totally blind. He died in Binghamton on February 18, 1897. He was seventy-nine. They buried him in Spring Forest Cemetery, Binghamton.

ISAAC PEACE RODMAN was born in South Kingstown, Rhode Island, on August 18, 1822. His wife was the daughter of Rhode Island Governor Lemuel H. Arnold, and his brother-in-law was future Union General Richard Arnold. He went into business with his brother and father and became a successful merchant and mill owner. Active in civic affairs, he was president of the town council for many years and served in both houses of the Rhode Island legislature. He was also a solid Christian, teaching Bible classes and directing a Sunday school.

Although he had moral reservations about killing, he organized a company of local residents when the Civil War began. It became part of the 2nd Rhode Island Infantry Regiment on June 6, 1861, with Rodman as captain. Part of Ambrose Burnside's brigade, the 2nd fought at the First Bull Run, where it suffered heavy losses and its commander, Colonel John S. Slocum, was killed. On October 3, the governor of Rhode Island appointed Rodman colonel of the 4th Rhode Island Infantry. Part of Burnside's North Carolina Expedition, he took part in the Battle of Roanoke Island and distinguished himself in the Battle of New Bern (March 14, 1862), which led to his promotion to brigadier general on April 30—despite the fact that he had no brigade to command. He commanded the 4th Rhode Island during the bombardment and capture of Fort Macon (April 25-26), which guarded the harbor of Beaumont. Afterward, part of the regiment returned to New Bern and part remained at Beaumont. Meanwhile, Isaac Rodman contracted typhoid fever and returned home to recuperate.

The IX Corps was recalled from North Carolina and sent to the Eastern Front in August 1862. General Burnside wrote a personal appeal to Rodman to return to the corps because he needed good officers to oppose Lee's invasion of Maryland. Even though he was still sick, Rodman responded at once. He rejoined the corps on September 3. Meanwhile, Burnside took charge of the Left Wing of the Army of the Potomac, and Jesse Reno became acting commander of the IX Corps. Rodman succeeded him as acting division commander, a position which became permanent after Reno was killed in action on September 14. Rodman, meanwhile, took part in the storming of Turner's Gap during the Battle of South Mountain.

Rodman's last battle was Antietam. After Burnside's Bridge was stormed, he found himself on the far-left flank of the army. At 4 p.m., just as it appeared that Lee's army might be destroyed, A. P. Hill's Light Division appeared on the scene to save the day for the Rebels. The fury of the

Confederate counterattack caused the Union line to buckle, the inexperienced 16th Connecticut fled the field in panic, and even the 4th Rhode Island wavered. Rodman realized that the entire Union line was in danger of collapse, so he ordered a desperate bayonet charge to stabilize the situation. It worked, but as he galloped across a cornfield, a minié ball from a South Carolina sharpshooter struck him in the chest, went through his left lung, and passed completely through his body. He was taken to a field hospital, where he suffered for days. He calmly placed his fate into the hands of the God he loved. He never complained, although at one point he did mutter: "This is rather tough." He died from internal bleeding on September 30, 1862, at age forty. He was buried in the family cemetery at Peace Dale, Rhode Island.

Isaac Rodman was a good man and a fine soldier. He rose from captain to brigadier general commanding a division in a single year due to skill and merit alone, without the aid of political influence. Deeply religious, he did not thirst for military glory and only sought to preserve the Union and defend his country. Beloved by all, he represented the American citizen soldier at his best and was the personification of all that was pure and noble in the Union Army.

The Rodman family was financially ruined by the war. It is ironic that Rodman Mills, the family's principal business, manufactured cloth, which was used primarily to clothe Southern slaves. Cut off from its market and its raw material (cotton), the business floundered. Its assets were sold at auction in May 1863.

WILLIAM STARKE "ROSY" ROSECRANS was born on a farm in Delaware County, Ohio, on September 6, 1819. His father served as adjutant to General (later President) William Henry Harrison during the War of 1812 and later operated a tavern and store, as well as the farm. He left home at age thirteen to clerk at a store in Utica and later Mansfield, Ohio. Rosy had little formal education but was a voracious reader and largely educated himself. Unable to afford college, he successfully competed for an appointment to West Point, where he excelled (5/56). He was commissioned brevet second lieutenant in the prestigious engineer branch in 1842.

After a year spent constructing sea walls at Fort Monroe, Virginia, Rosecrans became an instructor at West Point; he thus missed the Mexican War. Engineering projects in New England and the Washington Naval Yard followed. Meanwhile, Rosecrans married. His wife eventually bore him eight children. To support his growing family, Rosy resigned from the army in 1854 to take a job directing a mining business in western Virginia. He was very successful and also became an inventor, taking out several patents, including a more efficient method of manufacturing soap. Unfortunately, in 1859, one of his experiments with an oil lamp exploded, severely burning him. He had only just recovered when the Civil War began.

Rosecrans rejoined the army as a volunteer aide to George B. McClellan. He was appointed colonel of engineers in the Ohio Militia on April 23 and brigadier general, Regular Army, on June 14. He briefly commanded the 23rd Ohio Infantry Regiment in June and a brigade in July. When McClellan was summoned to Washington after the Bull Run disaster, General-in-Chief Scott recommended Rosecrans as his replacement and McClellan concurred. He became commander of the Department of Western Virginia on July 23. His forces won a significant victory at Cheat Mountain (September 12–15), but his department was used primarily as a reservoir for other commands to draw from for reinforcements. In March 1862, John C. Fremont, a political general, replaced him.

Outspoken and often brusque, Rosecrans quarreled with Secretary of War Stanton, who became his most vocal critic. He also quarreled with U.S. Grant and General-in-Chief Halleck. Although unquestionably brilliant, Rosecrans was gregarious by nature and was frequently charged with talking too much. Frozen out of command in the East, he was transferred to the Western Front and "kicked upstairs," to use a twentieth-century expression. He was given command of the Right Wing of John Pope's Army of the Mississippi and took part in the Siege of Corinth. He assumed command of the entire army after Pope was transferred to Virginia. Working under Grant's overall command, he defeated Sterling Price at Iuka on September 19 and Earl Van Dorn in the Second Battle of Corinth on October 3 and 4. Although he pursued the Confederates too slowly, Rosecrans became a hero in the Northern press. He also clashed with Grant, who felt he (Rosecrans) received credit that should have gone to Grant. Even so, Rosecrans was promoted to major general on October 25.

William Rosecrans assumed command of the Army of the Cumberland on October 24, 1862. He defeated Braxton Bragg in the Battle of Stones River, a somewhat indecisive action near Murfreesboro, Tennessee, from December 31, 1862 to January 2, 1863. Abraham Lincoln praised him, however, after the debacle at Fredericksburg, the North badly needed a victory, even an underwhelming one. He spent the next six months training his troops and building up supplies, despite urgings from Lincoln, Stanton, and Halleck that he advance. He finally moved on June 24, beginning the Tullahoma Campaign, which was his masterpiece and as brilliant as any in U.S. military history. He outflanked Bragg and captured agriculturally rich middle Tennessee without a major battle, eventually maneuvering Bragg out of Chattanooga. Confederate morale plummeted. Unfortunately, Rosecrans thought it would never recover—but it did.

Rosecrans made the mistake of his life during the second day of the Battle of Chickamauga, September 20, 1863. He moved Thomas J. Wood's division to cover a gap which did not exist. In doing so, he opened a very real gap in his line. Meanwhile, the Confederates scored the military equivalent of winning the lottery. They moved James Longstreet's corps of the Army of Northern Virginia 923 miles, over some very questionable railroads, and struck the gap just after Rosecrans created it. Most of the Union army was routed. Rosecrans was besieged in Chattanooga until October 19, when Ulysses S. Grant replaced him.

Chickamauga ruined Rosecrans's military career. He assumed command of the Department of Missouri in January 1864 and played a role in defeating Price's invasion of the state that fall, but he was unemployed from December 1864 to January 15, 1866, when he was mustered out of volunteer service. He was appointed major general, Regular Army, in 1866, but resigned from the service in 1867.

Rosecrans served as minister to Mexico from 1868 to 1869, but was replaced when U.S. Grant became president. He established a sixteen thousand-acre ranch in the Los Angeles area. He also invested heavily in mining and railroads—with generally negative results. He was elected to

Congress as a Democrat in 1880 and served from 1881–1885, where he was a passionate advocate of national reconciliation. He did not seek re-election in 1884. He was Register of the Treasury from 1885 to 1893. He died of pneumonia at Redondo Beach, California, on March 11, 1898, at age seventy-eight. He is buried in Arlington National Cemetery.

Raised a Methodist, Rosy converted to Catholicism while he was an instructor at West Point. He inspired his brother Sylvester to convert as well. Sylvester went on to become the first bishop of the Roman Catholic Diocese of Columbus, Ohio.

LEONARD FULTON ROSS was born on July 18, 1823, in Lewistown, Illinois. His family moved to Havana, Illinois, when he was young. He worked as a clerk in his father's store and in his father's ferry service and received little formal education. After his father's death, his mother moved the family to Canton, Illinois, where he attended a college preparatory school. He attended Jacksonville College, read law, and was admitted to the bar in late 1844. He set up a law office in Vermont, Illinois, but closed it in 1846 to enlist in the 4th Illinois Infantry as a private. He fought at Vera Cruz and Cerro Gordo in the Mexican War. At this point, the enlistments of the 4th Illinois expired, and Ross was discharged as a first lieutenant.

Leonard Ross returned home and eventually became probate judge and then county clerk of Fulton County. He was also a noted stockbreeder. A Democrat, he was a strong supporter of Stephen A. Douglas. He also married and fathered seven children.

Ross joined the Union Army as colonel of the 17th Illinois on May 25, 1861. He took part in several small skirmishes in Missouri and Kentucky in 1861 and early 1862. His brigade commander, Colonel William R. Morrison, was wounded at Fort Donelson, and Ross replaced him. He missed the Battle of Shiloh because his first wife died, and he briefly returned home. He was appointed brigadier general on April 26, 1862. He participated in the Siege of Corinth, after which he was elevated to divisional command. General Grant picked him to direct the Yazoo Pass

Expedition, one of his efforts to take Vicksburg, but he was checked at Fort Pemberton. Afterward he was sent to Helena, Arkansas, but was home on leave when the battle of July 4 took place. He commanded the District of Eastern Arkansas from July 6 to 22. He resigned his commission on July 22, 1863, to return home and take care of family matters.

General Ross remarried in 1865 and fathered four more children. He joined the Republican Party and ran for Congress twice (once as an Independent) but lost both elections. He also bred prize-winning cattle, traveled extensively, was a collector of Internal Revenue and, for a time, was manager of the Lewiston National Bank. He died at Galesburg, Illinois, on January 17, 1901, at age seventy-seven. He was buried in Oak Hill Cemetery, Lewistown. He had sixteen grandchildren when he passed. One of his sons, Frank F. Ross, earned the Congressional Medal of Honor in the Philippine-American War of 1899–1902.

LOVELL HARRISON ROUSSEAU was born on August 4, 1818, near Stanford, Kentucky, the descendant of Huguenots. His father died in a cholera epidemic when he was fifteen, and Rousseau was forced to abandon his formal education and sell his father's slaves to cover the family's debts. He worked as a common laborer on the construction of a turnpike for a time, but determined to rise, he studied on his own, eventually read law, and was admitted to the Indiana bar in 1841. He settled in Bloomfield, Indiana, which elected him to the legislature as a Whig in 1844.

When the Mexican War began, Rousseau raised a company of volunteers, which became part of the 2nd Indiana Infantry. He distinguished himself at Buena Vista, where he rallied wavering Indiana troops. After the war, he was elected to the Indiana Senate before he moved to Louisville, Kentucky, in 1849. Here, he was also elected to the state senate in 1860 but resigned in June 1861, to recruit soldiers for the Union. (He was an ardent foe of secession.)

Despite the opposition of many prominent Kentuckians who wanted to maintain neutrality, Rousseau raised two regiments and trained them at Camp Joe Holt, just across the Ohio River from Louisville. They kept

Louisville from falling into Rebel hands in September 1861 when Kentucky neutrality collapsed. Rousseau became colonel of the 3rd Kentucky (Union) Infantry on September 9 and commander of a brigade in Buell's Department (later Army) of the Cumberland. He was promoted to brigadier general on October 1. He fought at Shiloh on April 7, 1862, and took command of a division during the Kentucky Campaign. He distinguished himself at Perryville (October 8), after which he was promoted to major general on October 22.

Rousseau was a solid commander and an important one, although he is practically unknown today. He fought at Stones River, the Tullahoma Campaign, and the Siege of Chattanooga, and commanded the District of Tennessee (later the District of Middle Tennessee) from November 1863 until the end of the war. This included the fortified city of Nashville. He resigned from the service on November 30, 1865. Meanwhile, as a member of the Unconditional Union Party, he was elected to Congress from Kentucky. Although pro-Republican, he became a moderate and supported President Andrew Johnson. After being censured for beating Radical Republican Representative Josiah B. Grinnell with his cane, Rousseau resigned his seat, ran for re-election, and filled his own vacancy. He served until March 3, 1867. A few days later, President Johnson appointed him brigadier general, Regular Army, and brevet major general. He sent Rousseau to Alaska, where he managed the transfer of the territory from

Russia to the United States. In 1868, he was appointed commander of the Department of Louisiana. He died in New Orleans of natural causes on January 7, 1869, at age fifty. He was buried in Cave Hill National Cemetery in Louisville, but his wife had his remains reinterred in Arlington National Cemetery in 1892.

THOMAS ALGEO ROWLEY was born in Pittsburgh, Pennsylvania, on October 1, 1808. He became a cabinet maker and was elected justice of the peace. He joined the 1st Pennsylvania Infantry in 1846 and rose to captain in the Maryland and District of Columbia Volunteers during the Mexican War. He was mustered out in 1848. Returning to Pittsburgh, he became street commissioner in 1850 and clerk of court for Alleghany County in 1857.

When the Civil War began, he was appointed major and commander of a battalion at Camp Curtin near Harrisburg. He was named colonel of the 13th Pennsylvania Infantry, a 90-day unit, on April 25, 1861. This unit was mustered out on August 6, but Rowley became colonel of the 102nd Pennsylvania that same day. Most of the men from the 13th joined the 102nd. The regiment was on garrison duty in the Washington defenses until March 28, 1862, when it moved to the Peninsula. It served in the Siege of Yorktown, the Battle of Williamsburg, and the Battle of Seven Pines (Fair Oaks), where Rowley was wounded in the head by a spent minié ball. He was back in time to fight in the Seven Days battles, where he did well, especially at Malvern Hill. The 102nd was transferred to northern Virginia in time to help cover General Pope's retreat and to fight at Chantilly (September 1). It was in reserve during the Battle of Antietam.

Rowley was promoted to brigadier general on November 29, 1862. He briefly commanded a brigade in the Fredericksburg Campaign, but Frank Wheaton replaced him on December 15. Apparently unemployed until March 1863, he assumed command of a brigade in the I Corps, which he led at Chancellorsville. At Gettysburg on July 1, General Reynolds, the corps commander, was killed and Abner Doubleday replaced him. Rowley temporarily replaced Doubleday until July 3, when he was wounded by shell fragments and spent minié balls. His behavior at Gettysburg was erratic; he was sometimes hysterical, screamed at other officers, and claimed that he was in charge of the entire I Corps. He would never be given another field command.

On July 10, he assumed command of the Camp for Draftees at Portland, Maine. Charged with drunkenness and insubordination at Gettysburg, he was court-martialed and convicted on April 23, 1864. Rowley was cashiered (i.e., dishonorably discharged), but Secretary of War Stanton threw out his conviction and gave him command of the District of Monongahela in Pittsburgh (i.e., a rear area territorial command). He resigned his commission on December 29, 1864.

After the war, Rowley practiced law and was a U.S. marshal from 1866 to 1870. He died in Pittsburgh on May 14, 1892, at age eighty-three. He is buried there in the Allegheny Cemetery.

DANIEL HENRY RUCKER was born in Belleville, New Jersey, on April 28, 1812. As a child, his family moved to Grosse Ile, Michigan, a village near Detroit. His uncle was Alexander Macomb, the commanding general of the U.S. Army, who gave Rucker a direct commission as a second lieutenant in the 1st Dragoons in October 1837. Initially sent to Fort Leavenworth, Kansas, he fought against the Utes on the frontier and served in a variety of posts in the Northwest (now the Midwest) and the Southwest. He was promoted to first lieutenant in 1844 and captain in 1847. He was brevetted major for gallantry at Buena Vista.

Rucker transferred to the Quartermaster Corps in 1849 and served in the southwest, mainly in New Mexico Territory. He was called to Washington in 1861. Although it was not glamorous, his service during the Civil War was Herculean and included the procurement and distribution to the front-line units of every conceivable supply from ammunition to bandages, food to wagons to medicine, and thousands of other items in between. Most of the war, he was deputy to Montgomery C. Meigs, the quartermaster general. The Quartermaster Corps was the best run of all the Union Army's departments. Meanwhile, Rucker was promoted to major (substantive rank) on August 3, 1861, to colonel on September 28, and to brigadier general on May 23, 1863. He was brevetted major general in 1866.

When the army was reorganized in 1866, Rucker reverted to the rank of colonel. He remained Meigs's assistant until that officer retired in 1882. Rucker then became quartermaster general and was promoted to brigadier general on February 13. He retired ten days later. He remained in Washington, D.C., until his death on January 6, 1910, at age ninety-seven. Only one Union general (full rank) lived longer than Rucker. General Rucker was buried in Arlington National Cemetery. He was the father-in-law of General Philip Sheridan, and his brother, William Alexander Rucker, retired as a colonel in the Paymaster Department.

THOMAS HOWARD RUGER was born in Lima, New York, on April 2, 1833. He moved to Janesville, Wisconsin, in 1846, was admitted to the U.S.

Military Academy in 1850, and graduated in 1854 (3/46). Commissioned brevet second lieutenant in the engineers, he resigned his commission in 1855, returned to Wisconsin, and became a lawyer.

Ruger returned to the service as lieutenant colonel of the 3rd Wisconsin Infantry on June 29, 1861. He became its colonel on August 20. Sent to Frederick, Maryland, he suppressed the legislature, which might have seceded. He served under Banks in the Shenandoah Valley and at Cedar Mountain. He fought at Antietam, where he temporarily commanded George H. Gordon's brigade and where he was slightly wounded in the head. He was promoted to brigadier general on April 4, 1863. He led a brigade in the XII Corps at Chancellorsville and Gettysburg and temporarily commanded Alpheus Williams's division at Culp's Hill while Williams temporarily commanded the corps. After Gettysburg, he was sent to New York City, where he helped suppress the Draft Riots. After the XI and XII Corps were consolidated to form the XX Corps, Ruger led a brigade in the XX. He took part in the Atlanta Campaign and directed a division in the XXIII Corps during the Battle of Franklin in the Tennessee Campaign. He was brevetted major general for his service at Franklin. He later took part in the Carolinas Campaign. He was mustered out of the volunteer service in June 1866.

Ruger accepted a commission as colonel, Regular Army, in 1866 and commanded the 33rd U.S. Infantry Regiment. His subsequent appointments included head of the Freedman's Bureau in Alabama, military governor of Georgia during Reconstruction, and superintendent of West Point from 1871 to 1876. Other commands included the Department of the South, the Department of Dakota, the Military Division of the Pacific, the Department of California, the Military Division of the Missouri, and the Department of the East. He was promoted to brigadier general in 1886 and major general in 1895. He retired in 1897.

General Ruger spent his last years in Stamford, Connecticut, where he died on June 3, 1907, at age seventy-four. He was buried in the West Point Cemetery.

DAVID ALLEN RUSSELL was born in Salem, New York, on December 10, 1820. His father was a Congressman (1835–1841) who appointed his son to the United States Military Academy in 1841. He graduated in 1845 (38/41) and was commissioned brevet second lieutenant in the 1st U.S. Infantry Regiment. Initially stationed at Fort Scott, Kansas, he served with the 4th U.S. Infantry in Mexico and was brevetted first lieutenant for his bravery at the Ovejas Pass, Ovejas National Bridge, and Cerro Gordo. He was promoted to first lieutenant, Regular Army, in 1848 and to captain in 1854. Post-Mexican War, he served in various garrisons in Michigan, New York, Oregon, Washington Territory, and California, fought in the Rogue River and Yakima Wars in the Pacific Northwest, and was stationed at Fort Yamhill, Oregon, when the Civil War began.

The 4th U.S. Infantry was recalled to the East and was part of the Washington defenses in the winter of 1861–62. Russell was named colonel of the 7th Massachusetts Infantry, which he led in the Peninsula Campaign, the Seven Days battles, and Antietam. He performed well in all these actions. He was promoted to brigadier general on November 29, 1862, and was given command of a brigade in the Army of the Potomac on December 10, 1862.

Russell fought at Fredericksburg, Chancellorsville, and Gettysburg, where his brigade was in reserve for most of the battle. He distinguished himself in the Battle of Rappahannock Station on November 7, 1863, where he temporarily commanded a division. He personally led the decisive surprise attack against the northern part of the Confederate bridgehead, which collapsed. He captured four guns and more than one thousand Rebel prisoners. He was shot in the foot in the process.

The following month, Russell was given permanent command of a division in the VI Corps. He took part in the Overland Campaign from the Wilderness to Spotsylvania and was wounded in the arm at Cold Harbor on June 1.

In July 1864, Russell's division was rushed north, where it defended Washington, D.C., against Jubal Early's attack on the city. Subsequently,

Russell and his men were sent to the Shenandoah. During the Third Battle of Winchester on September 19, 1864, he was struck by a Confederate bullet. A physician tried to get him to dismount, but he replied: "That is not necessary, Doctor, the wound is a settler, but I will not dismount so long as I can sit on my horse and direct operations." A few minutes later, a shell fragment ripped through his heart, killing him instantly. "No more striking or heroic conduct in the fierce contests for the public weal is recorded in the annals of war," General Newton Curtis recalled. General Russell was forty-three. He was buried in Evergreen Cemetery, in the town of his birth. He was posthumously brevetted major general in 1867.

FRIEND SMITH RUTHERFORD was born in Schenectady, New York, on September 25, 1820. He was great-grandson of Dr. Daniel Rutherford, a Scottish physician and chemist who is credited with discovering the element nitrogen at the University of Edinburgh in 1772. Friend studied law in Troy, New York, moved to Edwardsville, Illinois, as a young adult, and relocated to Alton, Illinois, around 1857. Here he set up a law practice. He married Letitia Sloss of Florence, Alabama, in 1849, and fathered six children.

Rutherford and his fellow Illinois attorney Abraham Lincoln were friends before the war. At the final Lincoln-Douglas debate, which was held in Alton, Friend introduced Lincoln to the audience. He was a Lincoln delegate to the Republican National Convention in 1860.

Rutherford joined the Union Army as a commissary captain on June 30, 1862. He returned to Illinois in August to help raise the 97th Illinois Infantry. He resigned from the army on September 2 but was re-mustered into the service as colonel of the 97th on September 16. After briefly serving in central Kentucky, the regiment was transferred to Memphis, where it became part of Sherman's wing of the XIII Corps, which was later designated XV Corps. Its first major battle was Chickasaw Bayou, where it suffered heavy losses in Sherman's abortive attempt to take Vicksburg in late December 1862.

Rutherford distinguished himself in the successful assault on Arkansas Post (Fort Hindman) in January 1863 and in the Battle of Port Gibson (May 1). He also fought at Champion Hill (May 16) and the Battle of the Big Black River (May 17), another Union success. On May 19 and 22, he took part in Grant's attempts to take Vicksburg by direct assault. Although he earned official praise from Sherman, both attacks were failures. Rutherford and his men then took part in the Siege of Vicksburg, which fell on July 4. Suffering from dysentery, he left on sick leave the following day and returned to Alton.

Still ill, Rutherford did not get his medical leave properly extended, was charged with being absent without leave (AWOL) and was dismissed from the service on October 15, 1863. Rutherford appealed to Abraham Lincoln, who revoked his dismissal on November 11 and restored him to the command of his regiment, which was now in New Orleans. He was on provost duty until May 1864, when the 97th was transferred to Morganza. Still in poor health, he resigned his commission on June 15 and returned home.

Colonel Rutherford died of chronic diarrhea in Alton, Illinois, on June 20, 1864, at age forty-three. Meanwhile, President Lincoln nominated him for brigadier general on June 18, even though he had never commanded a brigade for even a single day. The Senate—unaware of his passing—ratified his appointment on June 28. He was buried in what is now the Alton National Cemetery.

Friend S. Rutherford was the older brother of George V. Rutherford and Reuben C. Rutherford, both of the Quartermaster Department, who were brevetted brigadier general in 1865.

S

SALOMON – SYKES

FRIEDRICH CHARLES SALOMON (who was also called Frederick) was born into a Jewish family on April 7, 1826, in Ströbeck, near Halberstadt, Saxony, in the Kingdom of Prussia. Educated in a *gymnasium* (i.e., a secondary school), he worked as a government surveyor before becoming a lieutenant in the artillery. He was a student at the Berlin School of Architecture when the Revolution of 1848 broke out. Salomon joined the revolutionaries and fled to the United States when they were defeated. He lived in Manitowoc, Wisconsin, worked as a surveyor, and was chief (civil) engineer of the Manitowoc & Wisconsin Railroad (1857–1859).

Salomon joined the 5th Missouri Infantry as a captain on May 19, 1861, as part of Franz Sigel's command, and fought at Carthage, Dug Springs, and Wilson's Creek (August 10). He helped organize the 26th Wisconsin, which consisted largely of German immigrants. It was mustered into Federal service in November with Salomon as colonel and took part in the "Indian Expedition" into what is now Oklahoma. Here, he arrested his commander, Colonel William Weer, for drunkenness, forcibly removed him from command, and retreated to Fort Scott, Kansas. He later returned to Missouri, where he was promoted to brigadier general on July 18, 1862. He led a brigade of about 4,500 men and unsuccessfully attacked Confederate Generals Douglas Cooper and Joseph Shelby in the First Battle of Newtonia (September 30, 1862). He led a small division in the Union victory at Helena on July 4, 1863. He also participated in the Camden Expedition of 1864, including the Battles of Elkin's Ferry and Jenkins' Ferry. He remained in Arkansas for the rest of the war, was mustered out in August 1865, and was brevetted major general in 1866.

General Salomon returned to the surveying profession after the war. From 1877 to 1885, he was U.S. Surveyor for the Utah Territory. He settled in Salt Lake City, where he died on March 8, 1897, at age seventy. He was interred in Mount Olivet Cemetery, Salt Lake City. His brother Charles was a brevet brigadier general; another brother, Edward, was the war-time governor of Wisconsin (1862–64). His cousin, Edward S. Salomon, was a brevet brigadier general and governor of Washington Territory (1870–72).

JOHN BENJAMIN SANBORN was born on December 5, 1826, in Epsom, New Hampshire. He was educated at Thetford Academy, the Pembroke Academy, and Dartmouth (1851–1852). He dropped out of college to study law and passed the bar exam in 1854. He moved to St. Paul, Minnesota, that same year and settled there. He served a term in the Minnesota House of Representatives and was elected to the state senate in 1860.

On April 24, 1861, Sanborn was appointed adjutant general of Minnesota. He organized and equipped three infantry regiments; then, in December, he became colonel of the 4th Minnesota Infantry. It was posted at Fort Snelling, Minnesota, and St. Louis. Sanborn was promoted to brigade commander in June 1862, joined Rosecrans's Army of the Mississippi, and fought in the Siege of Corinth, the Battle of Iuka (September 19), and the Second Battle of Corinth (October 3–4). Transferred to Grant's Army of Tennessee, he took part in his Central Mississippi Campaign and the battles of Port Gibson (May 1, 1863), Raymond (May 12), Jackson (May 14), Champion's Hill (May 16), and Big Black River (May 17). He fought in the Siege of Vicksburg (May 18–July 4) and briefly commanded a division in the XVII Corps. He was part of the Vicksburg garrison until October. He was appointed brigadier general on November 29, 1862. The Senate did not confirm his appointment, and he reverted to the rank of colonel in March 1863. Lincoln reappointed him on August 4, 1863, and this time he was confirmed.

Sanborn was named commander of the District of Southwest Missouri in October, where he helped suppress guerillas and played a major role in defeating Sterling Price's Missouri Raid in 1864. He was brevetted major general in February 1865. After the Southern capitulation, he directed the District of Upper Arkansas. He was mustered out on April 30, 1866.

John Sanborn returned to Minnesota and was a member of the Indian Peace Commission from February 1867 to 1869. He was reelected to the legislature in 1872. In 1874, he made a shady agreement with Grant's Secretary of the Treasury, William A. Richardson, to collect $427,000 in unpaid taxes. Sanborn made some questionable moves that amounted to extortion, but he collected $213,000, mainly from liquor companies and railroad corporations. After paying expenses and subordinates, he made a $57,000 profit ($1,514,573 in 2022 money). After news of the scandal hit the newspapers, Congress outlawed the practice.

Sanborn was active in veteran organizations and was elected president of the Minnesota Historical Society in 1903. He died in St. Paul on May 6, 1904, at age seventy-seven. He was buried in Oakland Cemetery, St. Paul. One of his sons, John B. Sanborn, Jr., became a Federal Circuit Court of Appeals judge.

WILLIAM PRICE "DOC" SANDERS, a cousin of Confederate President Jefferson Davis, was born near Frankfort, Kentucky, on August 12, 1833. His father was a wealthy attorney. Despite his nickname, Sanders was not a physician and did not hold a terminal degree.

Sanders was admitted to West Point in 1852 and graduated four years later (41/49). A poor student, Superintendent Robert E. Lee wrote a letter dismissing him from the Academy because he failed to apply himself, for deficiency in languages, and for his high number of demerits, but Secretary of War Jefferson Davis interceded on his behalf, and he was allowed to remain. Commissioned brevet second lieutenant in the 1st Dragoons, he spent the antebellum years in the West, including a tour in Utah. Sanders was promoted to second lieutenant in 1857, to first lieutenant on May 10, 1861, and to captain four days later.

Although his sympathies were solidly with the South, Sanders adhered to the Union. He served with the 6th Cavalry in the Peninsula Campaign, the Seven Days, and at Antietam. A charismatic leader, he impressed General Burnside, who promoted him to colonel and gave him command of the 5th Kentucky Cavalry in his own Department of the Ohio on March 4, 1863. Sanders was named chief of cavalry of the District of Central Kentucky in April. He led a raid into East Tennessee, and, when Confederate General John Morgan launched his disastrous Ohio raid in July 1863, Sanders helped destroy his command. He took part in Burnside's drive on Knoxville, Tennessee, which he reached on September 3. He was appointed brigadier general on October 18.

Sanders was more than six feet tall. Known for being brave, he was also handsome, kind, and considerate.

General Sanders briefly commanded a brigade in the XXIII Corps and then assumed command of a cavalry division in the cavalry corps of the Army of the Ohio. On November 18, while conducting a delaying action along Kingston Pike, as Burnside retreated into the Knoxville fortifications, a Rebel infantryman shot Sanders in the abdomen. Allegedly the shooter was under the command of E. Porter Alexander, Sanders's former roommate at West Point, who was commanding a mixed infantry and artillery battle group that day. Sanders was carried to the bridal suite of the Lamar House in Knoxville, where he died the following day, November 19, 1863. He was thirty years old. General Burnside was at his bedside. He was buried in the yard of the Second Presbyterian Church in Knoxville. His funeral was held at night, so that his fellow officers could attend. He was later reinterred in the National Cemetery in Chattanooga.

Because of his premature death, the Senate never confirmed Sanders's appointment, and some sources do not list him among the Union generals. A bachelor, Sanders was seeing Sue Boyd, a nineteen-year-old locally famous singer, at the time of his death. Sue was the cousin of Confederate spy Belle Boyd. She was informed of his death by General Burnside, who reportedly introduced them.

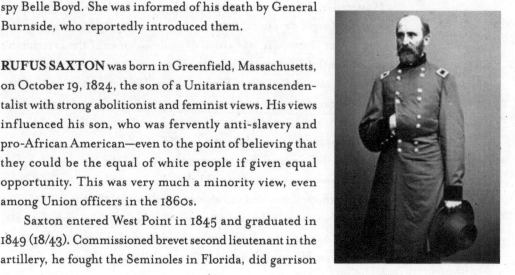

RUFUS SAXTON was born in Greenfield, Massachusetts, on October 19, 1824, the son of a Unitarian transcendentalist with strong abolitionist and feminist views. His views influenced his son, who was fervently anti-slavery and pro-African American—even to the point of believing that they could be the equal of white people if given equal opportunity. This was very much a minority view, even among Union officers in the 1860s.

Saxton entered West Point in 1845 and graduated in 1849 (18/43). Commissioned brevet second lieutenant in the artillery, he fought the Seminoles in Florida, did garrison duty at Fort Brown, Texas, surveyed the Rocky Mountains in support of the Northern Pacific Railroad, was stationed at Forts Niagara and Ontario, New York, taught artillery tactics at West Point, and went to Europe on "professional duty." He was promoted to second lieutenant in 1850 and first lieutenant in 1855. Meanwhile, he transferred to the Quartermaster Corps.

When the Civil War began, Saxton was in command of an artillery detachment in the St. Louis Arsenal. He served under Nathaniel Lyon in suppressing the pro-Southern Missouri State Guard and became his chief quartermaster. He worked under McClellan in western Virginia and in the Port Royal Expedition in South Carolina (September 1861–March 1862). Promoted to brigadier general on April 16, 1862, he was sent to Harpers Ferry in Shenandoah Valley. He commanded the defenses there against Stonewall Jackson in May and June, for which he was awarded the Congressional Medal of Honor in 1893.

Sent back to South Carolina, he was Military Governor of the Department of the South from July 1862 to January 16, 1865. Headquartered at Beaumont, his main job was to recruit and organize former slaves into military units. His 1st South Carolina Volunteer Infantry was the first African American regiment mustered into the Union Army. Despite his success, Saxton was demoted to assistant inspector general of the department in 1865.

Mustered out of volunteer service on January 15, 1866, and brevetted major general eight days later, Saxton reverted to the rank of major in the Quartermaster Corps. He was assistant commissioner of the Freedmen's Bureau of South Carolina, where his policy was to confiscate land from white landowners and give it to former slaves. He also opposed efforts to confiscate firearms owned by African Americans, which he deemed a violation of the Second Amendment. His views were unpopular, and he was sacked by President Andrew Johnson in 1866.

After South Carolina, Saxton served mainly on the northern frontier and in the Department of the [Great] Lakes. He was stationed in California from 1879 to 1883. Promoted to lieutenant colonel in 1872 and colonel in 1882, he reached the mandatory retirement age of sixty-four later that year. He settled in Washington, D.C., where he died on February 23, 1908, at age eighty-three. He was buried in Arlington National Cemetery.

ELIAKIM PARKER SCAMMON, who went by his middle name, was born on December 27, 1816, in Whitefield, Maine. He entered the U.S. Military Academy in 1833 (at age sixteen) and graduated in 1837 (9/50). He remained at West Point as an assistant professor of mathematics until September 1838, when he transferred from the artillery to the Corps of Topographical Engineers. He fought in the Seminole Wars and in the Mexican War, where he served on General Scott's staff. He then spent eight years in survey work on the Great Lakes. Commissioned as a second lieutenant, he was promoted to first lieutenant in 1846 and captain in 1855. His promising career was short-circuited in 1856 when, while constructing military roads in the New Mexico Territory, he was court-martialed and dismissed from the service for insubordination and conduct unbecoming of an officer.

Following his dismissal, Scammon moved to Ohio as a professor of mathematics at Mount Saint Mary's College. He became president and professor of mathematics at the Polytechnic College of the Catholic Institute in Cincinnati. After Fort Sumter, he returned to the colors on June 27, 1861, as colonel of the 23rd Ohio Infantry—a regiment which included future Presidents Rutherford B. Hayes (with whom he often clashed) and William McKinley, a mess sergeant. He saw action with McClellan in western Virginia.

Scammon became a brigade commander in the Kanawha Division in September and spent most of the war in what became West Virginia. He did see action at South Mountain and Antietam in the Maryland Campaign of 1862, where he was temporarily in charge of a division in Burnside's IX Corps. He was promoted to brigadier general on October 15, 1862. He became a permanent division commander in the Middle Department in March 1863 and later commanded the Department of West Virginia.

On February 3, 1864, General Scammon was aboard the *S.S. Levi*, a steamboat on the Kanawha River, when he was captured by partisans from the 16th Virginia Cavalry. He was exchanged in August and sent to South Carolina, where he was captured again on October 26, but was exchanged again six days later. He was given a brigade in the District of Florida, where he remained for the rest of the war. He was mustered out on August 24, 1865.

Postwar, Scammon served as U.S. Consul to Prince Edward Island from 1866 to 1870. After working as a civil engineer for a few years, he became a professor of mathematics at Seton Hall College in New Jersey from 1875 to 1885. He then moved to New York City, where he died of cancer on December 7, 1894, ten days before his seventy-eighth birthday. His remains lie in Calvary Cemetery, Queens, New York.

ROBERT CUMMING SCHENCK was born in Franklin, Ohio, on October 4, 1809, into a prominent Dutch family. His father was a successful land speculator, veteran of the War of 1812, and militia general. Robert's father died when Robert was twelve, and he was placed under the guardianship of General James Findlay, a mayor of Cincinnati. Robert was educated at the University of Miami in Oxford, Ohio, from which he graduated in 1827. He remained there until 1830, when he received his master's degree. Then he studied law, was admitted to the bar in 1831, and practiced in Dayton.

Schenck entered the political world in 1838, when he was defeated in an election for the state legislature. He was more successful in 1840, when he was elected to the Ohio House of Representatives, serving from 1841 to 1843. He was elected to the U.S. House of Representatives as a Whig in 1842 and served from 1843 to 1851. Here, he established a reputation as a brilliant speaker. In Congress, he was a strong abolitionist and was opposed to the Mexican War because he felt it would lead to the expansion of slavery. He declined to run for re-election in 1850, so President Fillmore named him U.S. Minister to Brazil in 1851. He was also accredited in Uruguay, Argentina, and Paraguay. A fine diplomat, he negotiated several treaties favorable to the United States.

Schenck returned to Ohio in 1854. His party, meanwhile, collapsed. Schenck's views coincided with the Republican Party, but because of his personal hatred for its 1856 nominee, John C. Fremont, he did not take part in that campaign. Meanwhile, his law practice flourished, and he became president of the Fort Wayne Western Railroad Company. He strongly supported Abraham Lincoln for president in 1860. He also became a brigadier general in the Ohio Militia.

When the Civil War began, Lincoln appointed Schenck brigadier general on June 5, 1861, and gave him command of a brigade in Tyler's division. His brigade was lightly engaged in the First Battle of Manassas, but it retired in relatively good order. After a period in the Washington defenses, Schenck and his men were assigned to General Rosecrans's command in western Virginia. He opposed Stonewall Jackson in the Shenandoah Valley Campaign of 1862 and—under Fremont—fought in the Battle of Cross Keys (June 8, 1862). He became a division commander on June 26.

Schenck briefly commanded the I Corps during Sigel's absence in July but was back in divisional command by August. He was with Pope's Army of Virginia in the Second Battle of Bull Run, where he was wounded in the right hand, wrist, and arm. His injuries were permanent, and he was unfit for further field command. Although he was not a successful military commander, Lincoln promoted him to major general on September 17, 1862, and gave him command of the Middle Department and the VIII Corps in December. It was a territorial command consisting mainly of Maryland. Schenck was unpopular with the generally pro-Southern citizenry. He resigned his commission on December 5, 1863. Meanwhile, he was again elected to Congress. (The incumbent, Clement Vallandigham, was unable to campaign because Lincoln expelled him from the United States.) Schenck became chairman of the Military Affairs Committee, where he strongly advocated conscription.

General Schenck served in Congress from 1863 to 1871 and was chairman of the House Republican Conference, 1869 to 1871. He lost the election of 1870 by 53 votes. As a consolation prize, President Grant named him U.S. Minister to Great Britain. He allowed his name to be used by the Emma Silver Mine in Utah. Influenced by Ambassador Schenck, British citizens invested heavily, but the mine was quickly exhausted, and a lot of money was lost. Schenck was forced to resign in 1875. A Congressional investigation determined that he did nothing wrong in the legal sense but had exercised very bad judgment. His political career was ruined.

General Schenck returned to the New World and settled in Washington, D.C., where he resumed his career as a successful lawyer. He also published a small book on draw poker, a game of which he was an internationally recognized authority. He died in Washington, D.C., on March 23, 1890, at age ninety. He is buried in the Woodland Cemetery, Dayton, Ohio. His older brother, James F. Schenck, was a career naval officer who retired as a rear admiral in 1868.

ALEXANDER FERDINAND SCHIMMELPFENNIG VON DER OYE, who shortened his name to **ALEXANDER SCHIMMELFENNIG** and dropped the aristocratic "von der Oye" after he arrived in America, was born on July 20, 1824, in Bromberg, East Prussia (now Bydgoszcz, Poland). Educated in the cadet schools, he joined the Prussian Army at age sixteen as a *Fahnenjunker* (officer-cadet or ensign) and was a lieutenant by 1842. He distinguished himself when the Prussian Army put down a revolt in the Schleswig and Holstein provinces of Denmark and was promoted to captain in 1848.

Meanwhile, Schimmelfennig fell in with some of the more radical German political groups and took part in the 1849 Palatine revolt on the side of the revolutionaries. The revolts were crushed by the Prussian Army. Schimmelfennig was wounded twice in the fighting but managed to escape to Switzerland. He was tried *in absentia* by the Palatine government and sentenced to death. As an exile, Schimmelfennig studied engineering and drafting. Meanwhile, he met Carl Schurz in Switzerland. They fled to London, where Schimmelfennig became part of the Communist movement. His faction, however, was led by Karl Schapper and August Willich (a future Union general), in opposition to the main body, which was led by Karl Marx and Friedrich Engels.

Alexander Schimmelfennig emigrated to the United States in 1853, where he secured employment in the War Department as a military engineer and wrote a book on the Crimean War. When the Civil War began, he raised an all-German regiment in Philadelphia. Unofficially known as the 1st

German Regiment of Pennsylvania, it was later redesignated 35th (later 74th) Pennsylvania Infantry. It was mustered in on September 1, 1861, with Schimmelfennig as its colonel. It was in the capital defenses until the spring of 1862. Its first major action was the Battle of Cross Keys (June 8, 1862), where it was defeated by Stonewall Jackson's men. Schimmelfennig, however, missed the war up until this point. In September 1861, his ankle was injured when his horse fell on him. It took him months to recover. His first Civil War action was at Freeman's Ford, a.k.a. the First Battle of Rappahannock, a minor Union defeat on August 22. Here, Schimmelfennig showed courage and tactical skill, and his brigade commander, Brigadier General Henry Bohlen, was killed. He was replaced by Schimmelfennig, whom Lincoln promoted to brigadier general on November 29 for political reasons. His first major battle was the Second Manassas, where he performed well. He was in reserve at Fredericksburg and led his brigade at Chancellorsville, where he foresaw Jackson's famous flanking attack but could not get anyone to listen to him. Joseph Hooker, the army commander, and O. O. Howard, his corps commander, were convinced that Lee was in full retreat. Schimmelfennig's unsupported brigade was routed, along with most of the XI Corps.

The German general did not look like a military commander. He was small and slender in stature, dressed in old uniforms, and had no interest in his personal appearance. He was also cross and somewhat anti-social, probably due to his chronic dyspepsia.

On July 1, during the Battle of Gettysburg, Schimmelpfennig briefly commanded a division, where he was wounded in his arm. As the XI Corps fled through the streets of Gettysburg, hundreds of his Germans were captured. Schimmelfennig himself was cut off and hid in a culvert. As he tried to get over a fence during his break for freedom, a Southern infantryman struck him in the head with the butt of his rifle. Schimmelfennig fell over the fence and played dead. Fortunately for him, he was not wearing his insignia of rank and the rebels left him where he lay. He then took the only shelter available: a pigsty. He lay there for two and a half days, surrounded by Rebels, without water, and the only food he had was that left behind by the pigs. He was not freed until the Confederates retreated. His troops—who thought he was dead—were delighted when he reappeared.

After Gettysburg, Schimmelfennig asked to be transferred out of General Howard's command. He was sent to South Carolina in August and took part in the Siege of Charleston, which fell on February 18, 1865. Schimmelfennig had the honor of accepting the city's surrender. He commanded the District of Charleston during Sherman's Carolinas Campaign.

During the siege, many of the Union forces were forced to occupy positions in the unhealthy Carolina swamps. Schimmelfennig contracted malaria and then a virulent form of tuberculosis. He went to a mineral spring near Wernersville, Pennsylvania, and "took the waters," in a vain attempt to arrest his decline. On September 7, 1865, he was in a cheerful mood, talking with his wife. He took a drink of water, returned the glass to the table, and slumped over dead. He was forty-one years old. General Schimmelfennig was buried in the Charles Evans Cemetery in Reading, Pennsylvania, not far from the grave of Union General David M. Gregg. He left behind three children.

ALBIN FRANCISZEK SCHOEPF was born on March 1, 1822, on the Vistula River town of Podgorze, Poland, which is now part of the city of Krakow, on March 1, 1822. He later Anglicized his name to **ALBIN FRANCISCO SCHOEPF**. Podgorze was part of the Austrian Empire in those days. Schoepf entered the Vienna Military Academy in 1837, earning his commission as a second lieutenant in 1841. He was a captain in 1848, when he resigned his commission and joined the Hungarian Revolutionary Army as a private. He was quickly promoted to major, but the revolt failed in 1849, and Schoepf was exiled to the Ottoman Empire (modern Turkey) and then Syria. He finally made his way to the United States in 1851 and obtained employment as a hotel porter. Later, he was successively a clerk at the U.S. Coastal Survey, the Patent Office, and the War Department, where he made influential friends.

Schoepf was appointed brigadier general of volunteers on September 30, 1861, and was given a brigade of seven thousand men in Kentucky. He performed well in his first Civil War action, the Battle of Camp Wildcat

(October 21, 1861), in which he defeated Confederate General Zollicoffer, who attacked him with 5,400 men. After the disaster at Bull Run, this was a welcome victory for the North. A few weeks later, the Confederates advanced again, he ordered a hasty retreat, and his men fled the field. The Confederates called it "the Wild-Cat stampede." On January 19, 1862, Schoepf did well in the Battle of Mill Springs, a Union victory in which General Zollicoffer was killed.

General Schoepf generally performed well and was a capable infantry commander. He did not get along well with his army commander, Don Carlos Buell, but he was nevertheless promoted to divisional commander in late September 1862. Near the end of the Battle of Perryville (October 8), the aggressive Schoepf wanted to launch an attack, but Buell refused to allow it. After that, their friction reached the point of no return, and Schoepf resigned his commission—allegedly because of deafness—later that month. The War Department refused to accept his resignation, so he asked for a transfer. General Halleck assigned him to the command of Fort Delaware, a most unpleasant prisoner-of-war camp. Schoepf remained there until after the end of the war. He was mustered out on January 15, 1866. He did not receive the customary brevet to major general.

After the war, Schoepf returned to the U.S. Patent Office. He died in Washington, D.C., after a long illness (probably stomach cancer) on May 10, 1886. He was sixty-four. He was interred in the Congressional Cemetery, Washington.

JOHN MCALLISTER SCHOFIELD was born in Gerry, New York, on September 29, 1831, the son of a Baptist minister who later moved to Bristol, Illinois, and then to Freeport, Illinois, when John was twelve. He worked on the family farm, was educated in public schools, worked as a surveyor in northern Wisconsin, and for a year taught public school in Oneco, Illinois. He received an appointment to the U.S. Military Academy in 1849, but as a teaching assistant in his senior year, he was expelled for allowing other cadets to tell offensive jokes and draw offensive sketches on the blackboard. Stephen A. Douglas used his

ENCYCLOPEDIA OF UNION GENERALS

influence to have a board of inquiry consider the matter, and it readmitted Schofield, but Lieutenant George H. Thomas was one of two instructors who voted against it. Their relationship was never right thereafter. Thomas later became Schofield's commander in the Civil War. In any case, Schofield graduated in 1853 (7/52), was commissioned brevet second lieutenant in the artillery, and was stationed at Fort Moultrie, South Carolina, and then Florida, where he contracted dysentery. He recovered in Culpeper, Virginia, and (after he regained his health) was an assistant professor of natural and experimental philosophy at West Point. He was promoted to second lieutenant in 1853 and to first lieutenant in 1855. In 1860, he went on extended leave to work as a professor of physics at Washington University in St. Louis. He was there when the Civil War erupted. He immediately became an aide to Nathaniel Lyon and was promoted to major of volunteers in the 1st Missouri (Union) Infantry on April 26, 1861. He served as Lyon's chief of staff until August 10, when that officer was killed in action at Wilson's Creek. More than thirty years later, Schofield would receive the Congressional Medal of Honor for his courage that day. He was promoted to brigadier general on November 21, 1861.

From 1861 to 1863, Schofield held a number of commands in the Trans-Mississippi, most notably the Army of the Frontier. His subordinate, General Blunt, won the Battle of Old Fort Wayne on October 22, 1862, and took possession of the Indian Territory north of the Arkansas River. Schofield was promoted to major general on November 29, 1862, but the Senate allowed his nomination to expire, and he reverted to brigadier general on March 4, 1863. He was promoted to major general again on May 12, 1863, to rank from November 29, 1862, and this time his appointment was confirmed.

On April 17, 1863, he took command of a division in the Army of the Cumberland. He was sent back west of the Mississippi as commander of the Department of the Missouri (May 1863–January 1864). He led the Army of the Ohio under Sherman during the Atlanta Campaign, where his performance was mediocre. When Sherman left on his March to the Sea, he placed Schofield under Thomas's Army of the Cumberland. Schofield won his major battle of the war when Confederate General Hood launched rash and suicidal attacks on his entrenched positions at Franklin. Meanwhile,

Schofield funneled false information to Ulysses S. Grant, the general-in-chief, to get Thomas fired and replaced by himself. His plot failed, however, and Thomas crushed the Confederate Army of Tennessee at Nashville on December 15–16. Schofield's troops played a significant role in this victory.

In 1865, Schofield was demoted to the command of the XXIII Corps. He operated with Sherman in North Carolina, moving his corps by rail and water, capturing Wilmington in February 1865. He was with Sherman's army at the end of the war.

During Reconstruction, Schofield served as military governor of Virginia. He opposed disenfranchising former Confederates and publicly expressed concern over the corruption of Congress and General Grant. After President Johnson fired Secretary of War Stanton, Grant declined the position. Schofield accepted it and served from June 1868 to March 1869. He was promoted to major general, Regular Army, on March 4, 1869.

Postwar, Schofield was commander of the Department of Missouri (1869–1870), the Military Division of the Pacific (1870–1876), superintendent of West Point (1876–1881), commander of the Department of the Gulf, the Military Division of the Pacific again, the Military Division of the Missouri, the Military Division of the Atlantic, and general-in-chief of the army (1888–1895). He was promoted to lieutenant general on February 5, 1895, and retired on September 29 of that same year. He wrote an autobiography, which was published in 1897.

General Schofield died on March 4, 1906, in St. Augustine, Florida. He was seventy-four. His remains lie in Arlington National Cemetery.

CARL CHRISTIAN SCHURZ (pronounced "Shirts") was born at Liblar-am-Rhein, Prussia, on March 2, 1829. Liblar, which is about twelve miles southwest of Cologne, is now part of Erftstadt. He was the son of a schoolteacher and a journalist. He later dropped his middle name. Schurz was educated at the Jesuit Gymnasium in Cologne and the University of Bonn. Here, he joined the revolutionaries in 1848 and fought the Prussian Army in the

ENCYCLOPEDIA OF UNION GENERALS

Palatinate and Baden, serving as adjutant to Fritz Anneke, who later became a colonel in the Union Army and commanded the 34th Wisconsin Infantry.

When the revolutionaries were crushed at the fortress of Rastatt, Schurz managed to escape to Zurich, Switzerland. He then secretly returned to Germany in 1850 and helped rescue his friend, former professor, and fellow Communist, Gottfried Kinkel, from the Spandau prison. They made their way to Edinburgh, Scotland. Schurz relocated to Paris, but the police forced him to leave in 1851. He moved to London, where he made a living teaching German. He migrated to the United States in 1852 and resided in Watertown, Wisconsin, where Schurz found a new cause: abolition. He joined the Republican Party, campaigned for John C. Fremont, and unsuccessfully ran for lieutenant governor of Illinois in 1857. Meanwhile, he studied law and passed the bar exam.

Schurz was a brilliant public speaker and worked tirelessly for Abraham Lincoln in the senatorial election of 1858 and the presidential race of 1860. Mostly, he addressed German immigrants, who were a major factor in getting Lincoln elected president in 1860. After he was elected, President Lincoln appointed Schurz minister to Spain.

On April 16, 1862, at Schurz's instigation, Lincoln named him brigadier general of volunteers. Despite his lack of qualifications, he became a division commander in June and took part in the Second Battle of Bull Run, where his troops were thrashed. They were in reserve at Fredericksburg but heavily engaged at Chancellorsville and Gettysburg, where they broke and ran on both occasions. Schurz blamed his corps commander, O. O. Howard, for this disaster, while Howard blamed Schurz. The German was heartily criticized in the press and appears to have been one of the poorer Northern political generals.

Carl Schurz led his division at Chattanooga, where he fell out with his new corps commander, Joseph Hooker. As a result, he was sent to Nashville, Tennessee, where he commanded a corps of instruction. In early 1865, he was on recruiting duty. Schurz returned to the front in early April 1865 as chief of staff to Slocum's Army of Georgia. He resigned from the army on May 6, 1865.

Postwar, Schurz moved to Detroit and became a newspaper editor. During Reconstruction, he became U.S. senator from Missouri (1869–1875) but was defeated for reelection by former Confederate General Francis Cockrell. He was secretary of the interior under President Rutherford Hayes (1877–1881). He remained active in public affairs and politics until his death, which occurred in New York City on May 14, 1906. He was seventy-seven. He was buried in Sleepy Hollow Cemetery, Westchester County, New York.

ROBERT KINGSTON SCOTT, who Ezra Warner described as a "unique a mixture of hero and rogue as ever were a United States uniform," was born on July 8, 1826, in Armstrong County, Pennsylvania. He studied medicine as a young man, became a member of the anti-slavery Liberty Party, and a captain in the 1st Pennsylvania Infantry (Militia) Regiment. During the Mexican War, he served with General Scott's army at Vera Cruz and in the conquest of Mexico.

Scott was a 49er during the California gold rush but moved to Henry County, Ohio, in 1851, where he set up a medical practice and a real estate business. Quite prosperous, his fortune was estimated at $300,000 in the mid-1860s. Rather than stay at home and enjoy his wealth, he joined the Union Army as a major in the 68th Ohio Infantry in October 1861 and was promoted to lieutenant colonel on November 30. Attached to Grant's army, the 68th fought at Fort Donelson, Shiloh, and the Siege of Corinth. Scott became its colonel in July 1862. After a period of occupation duty in west Tennessee, the regiment was part of Grant's unsuccessful Central Mississippi Campaign and the unsuccessful Lake Providence Expedition. Scott was with Grant when he landed at Bruinsburg and took part in the victories at Port Gibson, Raymond, Jackson (first battle of), Champion Hill, and the Siege of Vicksburg. He participated in Sherman's Meridian Campaign of early 1864.

Sent to Georgia, Scott became a brigade commander in March 1864. He fought in the Atlanta Campaign until July 22, during the Battle of Atlanta, when a Confederate shell exploded near him, and he was wounded in the neck and stunned. When he regained his senses, he was a prisoner of war. Three nights later, near Macon, Georgia, he jumped from a moving

ENCYCLOPEDIA OF UNION GENERALS

train and injured his back, chest, right knee, and right leg. He recovered in prison and was exchanged in October 1864.

Scott resumed his brigade command and was promoted to brigadier general on April 21, 1865, to rank from January 12. Meanwhile, he took part in the March to the Sea and the Carolinas Campaign and was brevetted major general in December 1865. He was assistant commissioner of the South Carolina Freedmen's Bureau from 1865 to July 1868, when he resigned his commission and entered the world of Reconstruction politics.

Seduced by alcohol and loose women, Scott was one of the worst governors in American history. Under his corrupt regime, Ku Klux Klan violence reached an all-time high, fraud abounded, and Carpetbaggers purchased state bonds for as low as one cent per dollar. South Carolina could not repay its Reconstruction debts until 1955. The legislature, which was 80 percent illiterate, voted itself a full-time saloon and restaurant at taxpayers' expense. Burlesque queen Pauline Markham seduced Scott, in exchange for a fraudulent issue of state bonds. He also allegedly accepted bribes involving the sale of railroad bonds. Additionally, he was charged with issuing three warrants for $48,645 to non-existent payees in 1871 alone. He avoided impeachment by bribing legislators.

Scott was re-elected in 1870 because former Confederates could not vote. Term-limited, he remained in South Carolina until 1877, when Southern whites led by former Confederate General Wade Hampton regained control of the government. Scott fled the state to avoid prosecution for fraud and corruption.

General Scott returned to Napoleon, Ohio, where he built himself a luxurious mansion. On Christmas Day, 1880, his fifteen-year-old son went missing. The boy had a history of drinking, and Scott suspected he was hiding in the apartment of twenty-three-year-old Warren Drury. Scott knocked on Drury's door and demanded admittance. When Drury refused, Scott shot him. Drury died the next day. Scott was tried for murder but claimed the gun accidentally discharged. To the outrage of the public, he was acquitted under suspicious circumstances. This is reportedly where the expression "getting off scot free" originated. He was cornered by a lynch mob from Toledo, but (protected by his own hastily formed militia), he convinced them to disperse, with the assistance of two free barrels of whiskey.

A better general than he was a man, Robert K. Scott died August 12, 1900, in Napoleon at age seventy-four. He was buried in Glenwood Cemetery, Napoleon.

WINFIELD SCOTT, old "Fuss and Feathers," was born on June 13, 1786, at Laurel Branch, a plantation in Dinwiddie County, Virginia, not far from Petersburg. His father was a militia officer and a veteran of the Revolutionary War. He grew into an imposing figure of 6' 5" and 230 pounds in his prime; the average Union soldier stood just over 5' 7" and weighed 143 pounds.

Scott was educated in private schools and briefly attended William and Mary, but he left the college to study law. He was admitted to the bar in 1806 but was not happy in that profession. On May 3, 1808, with the help of his family's political influence, Winfield Scott became a captain in the light artillery. The entire regular army at that time totaled only 2,700 officers and men, and Captain Scott was deeply concerned about its corruption, lack of professionalism, and widespread alcoholism. His denunciation of the army's commander, James Wilkinson, for his lack of integrity led to his court-martial in 1810, and Scott was suspended for a year. During that time, Wilkinson was sacked for insubordination and replaced by General Wade Hampton. Scott spent his year off studying strategy and tactics. When he returned, he was greeted with cheers from his colleagues.

Scott distinguished himself as a genuine hero during the War of 1812 and was one of the greatest soldiers in American history. He became a brigadier general on March 9, 1814, and was one of six generals retained by the U.S. Army after the War of 1812. He led the American forces in the Black Hawk War (1832), in the Nullification Crisis (1832–33), in border disputes with the English, and in the Indian removals of the 1830s. He was promoted to major general on June 25, 1841, and general-in-chief of the U.S. Army on July 5.

Scott personally commanded the American forces during the invasion of Mexico. In one of the most brilliant campaigns in U.S. military history, he landed at Vera Cruz—perhaps the largest amphibious landing in modern history until that point—and drove on Mexico City, which he captured on September 14. He was less successful in the political sphere and was defeated in the presidential election of 1852.

By the time the Civil War began, Scott's age began to tell on him, and, at more than three hundred pounds, he was not even able to mount a horse or walk more than a short distance without resting. He also suffered from rheumatism, gout, and vertigo. His influence with President Lincoln was mixed. At Scott's recommendation, the president offered command of the main Union army to Robert E. Lee, but he opted to "go South" with his native state, Virginia. Scott advised Lincoln not to try to reinforce Fort Sumter because successful resupply was impossible and the effort would lead to war, but Lincoln ignored him. Scott did, however, develop the strategy which ultimately led to Union victory. Dubbed the Anaconda Plan by dismissive Northern newspapers, it called for the capture of the Mississippi River and the blockade of Southern ports, and gradually squeezing the Confederacy into submission. In 1861, however, Lincoln and the Northern public favored a direct assault against the South's main army. Lincoln selected Irvin McDowell to lead it. Scott thought McDowell too unimaginative and inexperienced for his post (he was a major in the supply department in 1860—clearly a poor qualification for an army commander). Scott advised against the attack because the new volunteer army was too inadequately trained and was not ready for the offensive, but, again, Lincoln ignored his advice and (along with other politicians and newspaper editors) pressured him into ordering General McDowell to advance. The result was a disastrous Union defeat in the First Bull Run.

Lincoln replaced McDowell with John B. McClellan and began to elbow Scott aside, so he submitted his resignation in October 1861. General Scott retired to West Point where, two weeks before his eightieth birthday, he died on May 29, 1866. He was buried there in the post cemetery.

Clearly, Winfield Scott was the most dominant figure in American military history between the War of 1812 and the Civil War. If one considers the totality of his career—not just the seven months he served during the War Between the States—he was perhaps the most illustrious general to serve in the Civil War. But he was too old for this war.

JOHN SEDGWICK was born on September 13, 1813, in Cornwall, Connecticut. His grandfather was a lieutenant colonel in the Revolutionary War. Young Sedgwick was educated in private academies and taught school for two years before obtaining an appointment to the U.S. Military Academy in 1833. He graduated in 1837 (24/50). Commissioned second lieutenant in the 2nd U.S. Artillery, he served in the Seminole War and fought in Mexico, where he was brevetted captain for Contreras and Churubusco. He was promoted to first lieutenant (1839), captain (full rank) (1849), major (1855) and lieutenant colonel (March 16, 1861). He transferred to the cavalry in 1855 and fought against the Cheyenne in 1857. Sedgwick was stationed at Fort Wise, Colorado Territory, when the Civil War began.

Sedgwick was promoted to colonel and commander of the 1st U.S. Cavalry, but missed the First Battle of Bull Run because he contracted cholera. He was nevertheless promoted to brigadier general on September 5, 1861. He proceeded to amass a sterling record as one of the best combat commanders in the Civil War. Given command of a division in the Army of the Potomac in February 1862, he fought at Yorktown, Seven Pines, the Seven Days battles, including Frayser's Farm (June 30), where he was wounded twice by Rebel bullets—once in the arm and once in the leg. Neither injury was serious. He was promoted to major general on July 25.

Antietam brought more serious wounds for General Sedgwick. General Sumner, his corps commander, impulsively ordered an advance without proper reconnaissance, and Stonewall Jackson was waiting for him. Sedgwick's division marched into an ambush. Surrounded on three sides, the bluecoat infantry broke and fled. Mounted, Sedgwick tried to rally his men, and made a prominent target. First, a bullet went through his leg. Moments later, a second bullet fractured his wrist. He refused to dismount while a surgeon treated his injury and recommended he go to the rear. Instead, Sedgwick headed for the enemy, where he was shot through the shoulder. This time, he was carried to the rear. Half his division was lost.

It took John Sedgwick months to recover, and he could not return to duty until late December 1862. He briefly commanded the II Corps

(December 1862–January 1863) and the IX Corps (January–February 1863) before assuming command of the VI Corps on February 4. He fought at Chancellorsville, where he captured Fredericksburg and Marye's Heights but was eventually forced to retreat across the Rappahannock. At Gettysburg, his corps was dispersed to various points to plug holes in the Union line. He was sent to New York City in July, to help suppress the Draft Riots. His performance in the Battle of Rappahannock Station on November 7 was exceptional, and he captured 1,800 Rebels.

Sedgwick almost lost his job during the reorganization of the Army of the Potomac in the spring of 1864. He was an outspoken admirer of General John B. McClellan, which earned him the hatred of Secretary of War Stanton. The Radical Republicans disliked him in general because he criticized General Benjamin Butler (one of their favorites), and he showed insufficient enthusiasm for abolition. He was, however, considered too good a general to be dismissed for political reasons.

The VI Corps was on the Union right during the Battle of the Wilderness, where he checked attacks from Ewell's II Corps. On May 9, 1864, during the Battle of Spotsylvania Court House, Sedgwick approached members of his staff who were ducking from bullets fired by Confederate snipers. "Why are you dodging like this?" Sedgwick snapped. "They couldn't hit an elephant at this distance." He was not aware that one of the Rebels had a Whitworth rifle, the best sniper weapon of its day. His bullet struck Sedgwick in the cheek, just below the left eye, and he never regained consciousness. He was fifty years old.

General Sedgwick was the highest-ranking general of Union volunteers killed in the Civil War, although General McPherson held higher Regular Army rank. Sedgwick was buried in the Cornwall Hollow Cemetery in the town of his birth.

WILLIAM HENRY SEWARD, JR., was born on June 18, 1839, in Auburn, New York. His father was the governor of New York when he was born. Later, he was U.S. senator and Lincoln's secretary of state. Junior was private secretary to his father until 1860, when he organized a private bank in Auburn. He joined the Union Army as lieutenant colonel of the 138th New York Infantry in August 1862. This unit was redesignated 9th New York Heavy Artillery the following month. He became its commander on May 21, 1863, and was promoted to colonel on June 10, 1864.

The 9th was on garrison duty in the Washington, D.C., defenses from December 1862 to May 1864, when it was reorganized as an infantry unit and sent to the Eastern Front. It fought in the Battle of Cold Harbor (June 1–12), the first attack on Petersburg (June 18–19), and in the early days of the subsequent siege. It was hurriedly sent back to the defense of the capital to check Confederate General Early's thrust on the capital. On July 9, during the Battle of Monocacy, Seward was wounded in the arm, and his leg was broken when his horse was shot and fell on him. He was promoted to brigadier general on September 13.

Seward returned to duty in January 1865 as a brigade commander in West Virginia. He commanded a division for six days after General Crook was captured by enemy partisan rangers in February 1865. After the Confederacy fell, he resigned from the army on June 1, 1865.

William Seward returned to banking after the war. Highly prominent in western New York, he also directed several corporations and helped build the Auburn City Hospital. Additionally, he was known for his charitable work. He died in Auburn, New York, on April 29, 1920, at age eighty. Only six Union generals survived him (excluding brevets). He was buried in Fort Hill Cemetery, Auburn.

TRUMAN SEYMOUR was born in Burlington, Vermont, on September 24, 1824, the son of a Methodist minister. He spent two years at Norwich University before becoming a West Point cadet in 1842. He graduated in 1846 (19/59), was commissioned brevet second lieutenant in the artillery, and was promoted to second lieutenant in 1847. Initially stationed at Fort Pickens, Florida, he fought in the Mexican War, where he was brevetted captain for his gallantry at Contreras and Churubusco on August 20, 1847. He was promoted to first lieutenant six days later.

After returning to the United States, Seymour was stationed at Forts Hamilton and Columbus, New York; West Point (as an assistant professor of drawing); Fort Moultrie, South Carolina; and in Florida, fighting the Seminoles. After a year in Europe, he was sent back to Fort Moultrie. He was present during the bombardment of Fort Sumter (April 12–13, 1861) and was brevetted major for his conduct in that battle. After a brief tour at Fort Hamilton, he commanded the Camp of Instruction at Harrisburg, Pennsylvania until December, when he became part of the Washington defenses. He was named artillery commander of McCall's Division in March 1862 and was given command of a brigade in the Department of the Rappahannock on April 28. He was promoted to brigadier general on April 30.

As part of the V Corps, Seymour fought in the Peninsula Campaign and in the Seven Days battles. He assumed temporary command of the division after McCall was captured at Frayer's Farm on June 30. Reverting to brigade commander, he did well in the Second Bull Run Campaign, South Mountain, and Antietam. Transferred to South Carolina in late 1862, he became chief of staff of the Department of the South. Advanced to divisional command in April 1863, Seymour fought at Folly Island and directed the failed attack on Fort Wagner on July 18, when the famous 54th Massachusetts Infantry was slaughtered. Seymour was severely wounded by grapeshot that day and did not return to duty until October.

In February 1864, Seymour commanded an operation aimed at capturing Tallahassee, Florida. With 5,500 men, he clashed with 5,000 Rebels under General Joseph Finegan at Olustee. The fighting was fierce. The Northerners lost 2,000 men; the South lost about half that. Defeated, Seymour returned to Jacksonville. Shortly after, Seymour was given a staff job in the Army of the Potomac. He assumed command of a brigade on May 5, 1864, during the Battle of the Wilderness. He was captured the next day. He was exchanged in August and was given a division in the VI Corps after General Ricketts was wounded. He led it in the last battles in the Shenandoah and at the end of the Siege of Petersburg. He was present when Lee surrendered at Appomattox and was brevetted major general in 1866.

Mustered out of the volunteer service in August 1865, Seymour reverted to the rank of major in the 5th U.S. Artillery. He was stationed at Key West,

Florida; with the Artillery Board in Washington; and successively commanded Fort Warren, Massachusetts; Fort Preble, Maine; and Fort Barrancas, Florida. He retired in 1876 after thirty years' service.

General Seymour loved art and was a noted watercolor painter. He retired to Florence, Italy, where he died on October 30, 1891, at age sixty-seven. He is buried in the Cimitero Evangelico aggli Allori, Florence.

JAMES MURRELL SHACKELFORD was born on July 7, 1827, in Lincoln County, Kentucky. He became a lieutenant in the 4th Kentucky Infantry Regiment during the Mexican War, but the fighting was essentially over by the time he reached Mexico. He returned to the Blue Grass State, studied law, and was admitted to the bar in 1851. He practiced law until January 1, 1862, when he joined the Union Army as colonel of the 25th Kentucky Infantry. He fought at Fort Donelson, but his health faltered, and he was forced to resign on March 24. After he recovered, he organized the 8th Kentucky Cavalry and was re-mustered into Federal service on September 23. He was promoted to brigadier general on March 17, 1863, and commanded a brigade in the XXIII Corps.

The high point of General Shackelford's Civil War occurred in July 1863, when he directed the pursuit against Confederate General John Hunt Morgan across three states. Morgan surrendered the last of his command at Wellsville, Ohio, on July 20.

Shackelford's command was part of Burnside's IX Corps during the Knoxville Campaign. He was wounded in the left foot during a skirmish with Stovepipe Johnson's men at Geiger's Lake, Kentucky, but returned in time to be present at the surrender of the Cumberland Gap. He commanded a division in the XXIII Corps (September–November 1863) and directed the Cavalry Corps of the Army of the Ohio during the Siege of Knoxville from November 3 to December 15, 1863, when he resigned his commission. His wife died and he returned home to take care of his children. He was mustered out on January 18, 1864.

General Shackelford was known for his amiability and his legal expertise. A staunch Republican, he practiced law in Evansville, Indiana, but moved to Indian Territory in 1883 when he was appointed to the Federal bench. He remained there until his retirement.

James M. Shackelford died at his summer home in Port Huron, Michigan, on September 7, 1909. He was eighty-two years old. He was buried in Cave Hill Cemetery in Louisville, Kentucky.

ALEXANDER SHALER was born in Haddam, Connecticut, on March 19, 1827, but his family moved to New York City in 1834. He became a building supplies dealer and a major in the New York Militia. Part of the Washington, D.C., garrison in late April 1861, Shaler returned home in June and helped organized the 65th New York (also known as the 1st U.S. *Chasseurs* [light infantry]), with himself as lieutenant colonel. John Cochrane was his colonel.

Shaler returned to Virginia and took part in the Peninsula Campaign. He was promoted to colonel on June 17, 1862, and fought in the Seven Days battles. He took part in the Maryland Campaign of 1862 but was not engaged at Antietam. He fought in the Battle of Fredericksburg (where his brigade was lightly engaged) and was advanced to brigade commander in March 1863. On May 3, during the Chancellorsville Campaign, he personally grabbed a Union flag and led his men in the storming of Marye's Heights at a critical point in the battle. Thirty years later, he was awarded the Congressional Medal of Honor for his courage that day. Meanwhile, he was promoted to brigadier general on May 26, 1863.

During the Battle of Gettysburg, Shaler's brigade was attached to the XII Corps and helped it hold Culp's Hill, but was shifted to the center in time to face Pickett's Charge. That winter, Shaler was commandant of the Johnson's Island POW camp, but returned to the Army of the Potomac on April 18, 1864, as a brigade commander. He was wounded and captured during Confederate General Ewell's attack of May 6, during the Battle of the Wilderness. He was held in Libby Prison and in Macon, Georgia, before being sent to Charleston, South Carolina, which was being bombarded by Union guns. He thus came under "friendly fire." He was exchanged on September 12.

After a medical furlough, Shaler was transferred to the Department of the Gulf, where he briefly commanded a brigade in Louisiana before taking charge of a division in eastern Arkansas at the end of 1864. He took part in a few minor skirmishes before the war ended. Mustered out in August 1865, he was brevetted major general in 1866. After the war, Shaler was commissioner of the New York City Fire Department (1867–1873) and a major general in the state militia. He was arrested for corruption in 1885 in regard to the location of armories. He was tried twice but both times the jury could not reach a verdict. He was, however, forced out of the militia. Afterward, he became president of the Automatic Signal Telegraph Company and a founder of the National Rifle Association.

Shaler eventually moved to Ridgefield, New Jersey, where he became a realtor and served as mayor of the city from 1899 to 1901. He retained a home in New York City, where he died on December 28, 1911, at age eighty-four. His only son built the first subway in Manhattan.

ISAAC FITZGERALD SHEPARD was born on July 7, 1816, in Natick, Massachusetts. He was educated at Harvard, from which he graduated in 1842. He was principal of a grammar school in Boston from 1844 to 1857 and simultaneously was editor of the Boston *Daily Bee* from 1846 to 1848. He also served in the Massachusetts legislature in 1859 and 1860.

A strong abolitionist and a fervent advocate of the cause of the African American, he went to Missouri in 1861 and joined the staff of General Nathaniel Lyon with the rank of major. He became Lyon's assistant adjutant general and was with him when the general was killed at Wilson's Creek on August 10. Shepard was also wounded but not seriously.

After Lyon's death, Shepard became lieutenant colonel of the 19th Missouri Infantry and then colonel of the 3rd Missouri in January 1862.

He played a prominent role in the Battle of Arkansas Post in January 1863 and was warmly praised by Generals William T. Sherman and Alvin P. Hovey. On May 9, he was named commander of the 51st U.S. Colored Infantry and shortly thereafter became commander of the African Brigade of the XVII Corps (three regiments), which he led during the Siege of Vicksburg. After the fall of the Confederate Gibraltar, Shepard's men were used mainly as construction and security troops in West Tennessee, so he saw little combat. He was, however, promoted to brigadier general on November 17, 1863.

Without Senate action, Shepard's appointment expired on July 4, 1864, so he left the army and returned to Missouri, where at different times he was adjutant general of the state, U.S. consul to Swatow and Hankow, China, and editor of the Missouri *Democrat*. He retired to Bellingham, Massachusetts in 1886, and died there on August 25, 1889, at age seventy-three. He was interred in the Ashland Cemetery in Middlesex County, Massachusetts.

GEORGE FOSTER SHEPLEY was born on New Year's Day, 1819, in Saco, Maine, the son of a U.S. senator. He attended Harvard, graduated from Dartmouth in 1837 (at age eighteen), studied law, and was admitted to the bar in 1839 at age twenty. He was in private practice in Bangor from 1839 to 1844, when he moved to Portland. In 1848, he became the Federal district attorney for Maine but was fired by President Taylor (a Whig) in 1849. He was reappointed by President Pierce (a fellow Democrat) in 1853 and held the office until 1861.

Shepley was commissioned colonel of the 12th Maine Infantry on November 16, 1861. He was given a brigade in the Department of the Gulf in March 1862 and took part in the occupation of New Orleans. He was promoted to brigadier general on July 26. Thanks to General Benjamin Butler, he was military governor of New Orleans from May to July 2, 1862, when he was named governor of Louisiana. Highly corrupt, he lost most his power when General Banks replaced Butler as commander of the Department of the Gulf. He resigned on January 24, 1864, after Michael Hahn, a civilian, was elected governor.

Sent to Virginia with his old friend, Butler, he was placed in charge of the District of Eastern Virginia, with headquarters in Norfolk, in May 1864. He was chief of staff of Major General Godrey Weitzel's XXV Corps from February 1865 to April 3, when Weitzel named him military governor of Richmond. His tenure was short, however, because General E. O. C. Ord, the commander of the Army of the James, sacked him. (Ord was investigating his corruption in Norfolk.) He resigned his commission on July 1, 1865, probably to avoid prosecution. He was not brevetted major general in the omnibus promotions of 1865 and 1866.

Shepley returned home and made a political comeback. He was a member of the Maine legislature from 1866 to 1867. In 1869, President Grant appointed him U.S. Judge for the First Judicial Court of Maine. He held this position until his death, caused by Asiatic cholera, on July 20, 1878, in Portland, Maine. He was fifty-nine. He is buried there in the Evergreen Cemetery.

PHILIP "LITTLE PHIL" SHERIDAN was born on March 6, 1831, in Albany, New York, the son of Irish Catholic immigrants. He grew up in Somerset, Ohio. He worked as a clerk in a general store before he obtained a last-minute appointment to West Point in 1848, after the original nominee from his Congressional district failed the entrance exam. He was set back a year because of a fist fight he had with William R. Terrill, another future Union general. He graduated in 1853 (34/52) and was commissioned brevet second lieutenant in the 1st U.S. Infantry. He was ordered to frontier duty in Texas, followed by duty in the Pacific Northwest. He fought the Yakima and Cayuse  tribes and was wounded in a skirmish with Indians in 1857 when a bullet grazed his nose. Meanwhile, he had several Indian mistresses, lived with a Native American Indian woman when he was stationed in the Rogue River area of Oregon, and had a daughter with her in 1857. He was promoted to second lieutenant in 1853 and to first lieutenant on March 1, 1861.

When the Civil War began, he was promoted to captain in the 13th Infantry (May 14, 1861). He traveled from Fort Yamhill, Oregon, to Jefferson Barracks, Missouri, where he was initially posted to the staff of

Henry Halleck, whom he impressed. (Halleck had him audit the accounts of his predecessor, John C. Fremont, and Sheridan was able to straighten out his financial mess.) He was promoted to assistant quartermaster of the Army of the Southwest in December. He served under General Curtis at Pea Ridge but landed in trouble when some of Curtis's officers stole horses from Southern civilians and tried to sell them to the army. Sheridan sharply refused to pay for stolen property. Curtis then had him arrested, but Halleck quashed the proceedings. He served under Halleck again during the Siege of Corinth. He was appointed colonel of the 2nd Michigan Cavalry on May 27, 1862, despite having no experience in the cavalry. After winning a small battle at Booneville, Mississippi, he was given a brigade and was promoted to brigadier general on September 13.

Sheridan was given command of an infantry division in the Army of the Ohio in September and performed well during the Battle of Perryville. At Stones River on December 31, he held his line despite repeated Confederate attacks until his men ran out of ammunition. This led to his promotion to major general on April 10, 1863. He thus rose from captain to major general in two years.

Sheridan continued to perform well during the Tullahoma Campaign, but his division was routed at Chickamauga. He redeemed himself at Chattanooga, where he led a breakthrough at Missionary Ridge and was lavishly praised by General Grant.

When Grant became general-in-chief, he summoned Sheridan to Virginia, and named him commander of the Cavalry Corps of the Army of the Potomac on April 4, 1864. In May, he tried to capture Richmond via a cavalry raid, which succeeded in killing Confederate General Jeb Stuart. The rest of the raid was unsuccessful. His command was also smashed by Wade Hampton at Trevilian Station on June 11 and 12. Despite these failures, Grant promoted Sheridan to commander of the Army of the Shenandoah on August 7. Placed in charge of the VI and XIX Corps as well as three divisions of cavalry (forty-three thousand effectives), he defeated Confederate General Jubal Early at the Third Winchester, Fisher's Hill, and Cedar Creek, and lay waste the Shenandoah Valley. So effective was his scorched earth campaign against Southern civilians that four hundred square miles of the Shenandoah were basically made uninhabitable. Lincoln approved of his actions and promoted him to major general, Regular Army, on November 14.

During the winter of 1864–65, General Lee stripped Early of most of his forces, which were needed to hold Richmond and Petersburg. Sheridan finished off Early's rump army at Waynesboro on March 2, 1865, smashed Lee's reserves at Five Forks on April 1, and cut off Lee's retreat in the Appomattox Campaign, leading to his surrender on April 9.

After the war, Sheridan commanded the Fifth Military District, where he supported the oppressive Reconstruction policies of the Radical Republicans. He dismissed the mayor of New Orleans, the attorney general of Louisiana, a district judge, and the governors of both Louisiana and Texas. He especially hated Texas, declaring, "If I owned Texas and Hell, I would rent Texas and live in hell." So severe and high-handed were his measures that President Johnson relieved him of his command after six months. The Radicals issued only a mild protest. After Grant became president and Sherman rose to general-in-chief, Sheridan was promoted to lieutenant general in 1869. He held several posts until 1883, when he succeeded Sherman as general-in-chief. He treated the Indians as harshly as he treated the Southerners, famously remarking that the only good Indian was a dead Indian—although certain historians now aver that he never said this.

Sheridan was mentioned as a possible candidate for president of the United States, but he disdained politics. He was promoted to full (four star) general in June 1888. He died a few weeks later in Nonquitt, Massachusetts, on August 5, 1888. He was fifty-seven. Sheridan is buried in Arlington National Cemetery.

Sheridan was arrogant, self-important, high-handed, and full of hatred for anyone who opposed him. He was, however, a competent tactician, although by no means a brilliant one. His tactics in the Shenandoah Valley have been compared to those Hitler used in Russia in 1941 and remain controversial to this day.

FRANCIS TROWBRIDGE SHERMAN was born on New Year's Eve, 1825, in Newton, Connecticut. His family moved to Illinois when he was nine, and his father became mayor of Chicago, which had a population of 350 in those days. Young Francis became a postal clerk and brickmaker before coming down with Gold Fever and traveling to California during the gold rush. He did not strike it rich, returned to Chicago, and pursued various occupations. On October 31, 1861, he joined the Union Army as lieutenant colonel of the 56th Illinois Infantry. Mustered out in February 1862, he rejoined the army the following month as major of the 12th Illinois Cavalry.

Sherman did not see any significant action in the cavalry. On September 4, 1862, however, he was appointed colonel of the 88th Illinois Infantry (also known as the 2nd Board of Trade Regiment), which he led at Perryville and Stones River, where his regiment suffered heavy casualties. He became commander of a brigade in the Army of the Cumberland in February 1863.

Colonel Sherman was not present at Chickamauga but did fight in the Siege of Chattanooga, where he led one of the charges up Missionary Ridge. He fought in the Atlanta Campaign and on May 22, 1864, became chief of staff of O. O. Howard's IV Corps. He was captured near Atlanta on July 7. Exchanged on October 7, he was appointed assistant inspector general of the Cavalry Corps of the Army of the Potomac. He was brevetted brigadier general in 1865 and was transferred to the Department of the Gulf. On July 21, 1865, he was promoted to brigadier general of volunteers (full rank).

He was mustered out of the service on January 15, 1866.

Postbellum, Francis Sherman engaged in various businesses. He ran a sugar plantation in Louisiana for a year, where he suffered heavy financial losses, and spent two years as postmaster of Chicago. His stone and sand company was ruined by the Great Chicago Fire of 1871. He served a term in the Illinois legislature in the 1870s and eventually settled in Waukegan, Illinois, where he died on November 9, 1905, at age seventy-nine. He was buried in Graceland Cemetery, Chicago.

THOMAS WEST "TIM" SHERMAN was born in Newport, Rhode Island, on March 26, 1813. When he was 18, he walked from Newport to Washington, D.C., to secure an appointment to West Point from President Andrew Jackson. He entered the Academy in 1832, graduated in 1836 (18/49), and was commissioned second lieutenant in the 3rd U.S. Artillery. He was immediately sent to Florida, where he fought the Seminoles. He took part in the transfer of the Cherokees from Georgia to Indian Territory, followed by another assignment in Florida, garrison duty at Fort Moultrie, South Carolina, and a tour of recruiting duty. He was promoted to first lieutenant in 1838 and captain in 1846.

Sherman was sent to northern Mexico in 1846 and distinguished himself at Buena Vista (February 22–23, 1847), after which he was brevetted major. During the interwar period, he was on garrison duty in California and Rhode Island; Fort Snelling, Minnesota; in Bleeding Kansas, suppressing border disturbances; and commanding an expedition to Kettle Lake, Dakota Territory. He was promoted to major on April 27, 1861, and to lieutenant colonel of the 5th U.S. Artillery on May 17.

Abraham Lincoln appointed Sherman brigadier general of volunteers on August 6, 1861. He commanded the ground forces in the Port Royal Expedition on the South Carolina coast. He led a division in the Siege of Corinth and in Louisiana (1862–1863) and commanded the New Orleans defenses in 1863. He was given command of a division in Nathaniel Banks's Army of the Gulf in January 1863.

On May 27, Banks ordered an all-out assault on the Confederate fortress of Port Hudson. Sherman, who knew the fortress could be starved into submission, did not approve of Banks's plan and did not want to attack at all. While three of Banks's divisions launched uncoordinated attacks, Sherman did not advance. Furious, Banks rode to Sherman's headquarters and demanded he attack. When Sherman protested that this would be suicidal, Banks relieved him of his command. When his replacement, General George Andrews, arrived, he found Sherman drunk, at the head of his division, ready to strike. Andrews decided to let Sherman lead the charge—which turned out to be a wise decision on the part of Andrews. Sherman ran into a wall of fire. He was hit by a large grapeshot, which killed his horse and shattered the bones in his right leg. Carried to the rear, he was not expected to live, but he did. He lost his leg, however. He spent the rest of the war in administrative and territorial posts in Louisiana. He was brevetted major general in March 1866 and mustered out on April 30, 1866.

Postbellum, Sherman reverted to his Regular Army rank of colonel and commanded the 3rd U.S. Artillery Regiment at Fort Adams, Rhode Island. Later it was transferred to Fort Taylor in the Florida Keys. He retired on December 31, 1870, as a major general because of disabilities caused in the line of duty. He returned to his home, "Twin Beeches," in Newport, where he died on December 31, 1879. He was sixty-six. General Sherman is buried in Island Cemetery, Newport.

WILLIAM TECUMSEH "CUMP" SHERMAN was born on February 8, 1820, at Lancaster, Ohio. His father, a justice on the Ohio Supreme Court, died of typhoid fever when Sherman was nine, leaving his mother with eleven children and no inheritance to speak of. Sherman was raised by his neighbor and family friend, Thomas Ewing, a prominent Whig and later U.S. senator and secretary of the interior. Two of his foster brothers became Union generals and his younger brother, John, became a U.S. senator and secretary of state. "Cump" Sherman eventually married his stepsister, Ellen Ewing, although he became a noted *bon vivant*.

Although his stepmother and his wife were fervent Catholics, Sherman was more a deist or agnostic. He was greatly distressed when his son Thomas decided to abandon his career as an attorney and become a Jesuit priest. Cump Sherman did not take communion after 1865 and probably not before then.

Senator Ewing obtained Sherman an appointment to the U.S. Military Academy when he was 16. He graduated in 1840 (6/42) and was commissioned second lieutenant in the 3rd Artillery. He spent most of the next six years stationed in the South, where he fought the Seminoles. Ironically, as a member of a prominent Whig family, he was popular in South Carolina society. Sent to California in 1847, he earned a brevet for meritorious service during the Mexican War. He resigned his commission in 1853 to go into the banking business, where he was a failure. He then became a lawyer in Leavenworth, Kansas, but failed at that also. In 1859, he became superintendent of the Louisiana State Seminary of Learning and Military

Academy at Pineville, which was later moved to Baton Rouge and became Louisiana State University. He resigned when the state seceded and moved to St. Louis, where he was briefly president of a streetcar company. He was appointed colonel of the 13th U.S. Infantry on May 14, 1861. Politically well-connected, he was given a brigade three days later and led it in the First Bull Run, where he was grazed by bullets in the knee and shoulder.

Sherman made it clear that he had no problem with slavery (and indeed owned slaves when he was in Pineville), but he had absolutely no tolerance for secession. He was promoted to brigadier general on August 7. Named commander of the Department of the Cumberland in October, Sherman foresaw some of the horrors of the upcoming war and the stress—at this stage—proved too much for him. He asked to be relieved of his command in early November and was transferred to Missouri, where General Halleck found him unfit for duty and sent him home. Here, he had a nervous breakdown and even admitted that he contemplated suicide.

Sherman was recalled to duty in early 1862. Initially in rear area positions, he provided logistical support for Grant's attack on Fort Donelson. Grant gave him command of a division on March 1. Posted to Shiloh, he thought a major Confederate offensive was impossible, so he refused to entrench, build abatises, or even send out reconnaissance patrols. He was taken by surprise on April 6, but fought well and eventually rallied his troops. In the process, he had three horses shot from under him and was wounded twice, in the hand and in the shoulder. He performed better on April 7, when he helped push the Rebel army off the field. He was promoted to major general on May 2.

Sherman's performance as a military commander was mixed. Sometimes it was excellent (such as at Shiloh on April 7), other times mediocre, and occasionally even poor. At Chickasaw Bluffs in December 1862, for example, he caught the Confederates flat-footed. Less than ten miles from Vicksburg, he could have taken the city, but, instead, he wasted a day burning a town and destroying a railroad on the Louisiana side of the river. By the time he did attack, the Rebels had recovered and were waiting for him. He lost 1,900 men as opposed to two hundred for the Southerners, and the entire operation was a failure. His piecemeal attacks on Kennesaw Mountain in 1864 were also failures. On the other hand, his maneuvering in northern Georgia was brilliant, and he pushed Confederate General Joe Johnston out of the most defensible part of that state and brought him to the edge of Atlanta. At the same time in Virginia, Grant pushed to the gates of Richmond but suffered four times as many casualties as Sherman and was unable to capture the city. Sherman took Atlanta on September 2, 1864, and ended the Confederacy's last real chance to survive the war. Sherman, meanwhile, advanced steadily, commanding the XV Corps (1863), the Army of the Tennessee (1863–1864), and the Military Division of the Mississippi (1864–1866), which was for all practical purposes an army group. After Atlanta fell, he launched his famous March to the Sea, cutting a 40-mile swarth of desolation through the heart of Georgia. Some historians call this the first modern war. He made no provision for the civilian population and at least 130,000 people starved to death. Eighty thousand of them were African Americans.

In his last Civil War campaign, Sherman overran South Carolina and most of North Carolina. General Johnston surrendered to him on April 26, 1865. In 1866, Cump Sherman was promoted to lieutenant general. He became a full general and general-in-chief of the army after Ulysses S. Grant became president of the United States.

General Sherman waged a harsh war against the Indians and even called for the extermination of the Sioux in 1866. He encouraged the eradication of the buffalo, on which the Indians depended, and strongly backed the expansion of the railroads into the American West. He waged a number of successful wars against the Native Americans and forced them onto reservations.

William T. Sherman despised politicians of all stripes and moved the headquarters of the army from Washington to St. Louis in 1874 to be away from them. He refused to seek political office himself and stepped down as commanding general in 1883. He retired in 1884. He died of pneumonia in New York City on February 14, 1891, at age seventy-one. He was buried in Calvary Cemetery, St. Louis.

JAMES SHIELDS was born in Altmore, Ireland, on May 10, 1806. His father died when he was six, and he was raised by an uncle, who was a professor of Greek and Latin. He saw to it that James received an excellent classical education. The future Union general attempted to emigrate to the United States in 1822, but his ship ran aground off the coast of Scotland; he was one of only three or four survivors. Shields eventually made it to Quebec before relocating to Kaskaskia, Illinois, where he studied law, taught French, and was admitted to the bar. He was elected to the Illinois House of Representatives in 1836 and became state auditor in 1841. A Democrat, he clashed with Abraham Lincoln (a Whig) over monetary policy. Lincoln was a "low road" politician in those days and wrote a scathing letter to the editor, denouncing Shields in harsh and slanderous terms. The auditor then confronted Lincoln, telling him that another letter would result in a duel. Lincoln had already started a second letter but decided not  to finish it. Mary Todd, the future first lady, and a friend of hers finished the letter and sent it to the editor without Lincoln's knowledge. This led to a challenge and the two met on the field of honor in September 1842; however, the seconds convinced the principals not to fight. Shields and Lincoln eventually became close friends, but Abe did not write any more nasty letters.

Meanwhile, Shields had an impressive political career. He replaced Stephen A. Douglas as an Illinois Supreme Court justice in 1845 and was commissioner of the U.S. Land Office under President Polk (1845–47). In 1846, he was commissioned brigadier general of volunteers and led a brigade at Vera Cruz, Cerro Gordo (where he was severely wounded), Contreras, Churubusco, and Chapultepec, where he was again wounded, and his arm fractured. He was brevetted major general for Cerro Gordo, returned to the United States, and was mustered out in 1848.

Shields was offered the governorship of Oregon Territory but decided to run for U.S. senator from Illinois. He served from 1849 to 1855 but was defeated for re-election. He then moved to Minnesota, where he served as U.S. senator in 1858 and 1859, but was again defeated for re-election. After that, he migrated to California and directed a mine in Mexico. He was there when he was commissioned brigadier general of volunteers on August 19, 1861. He took charge of a division in Virginia and, on March 22, 1862, in the Battle of Kernstown, he inflicted on Stonewall Jackson the only significant tactical defeat he suffered in the Civil War. Shields finished the battle in a field hospital. He was too close to an exploding shell, which fractured his arm and threw shrapnel into his shoulder. It took him five weeks to recover. Lincoln promoted him to major general on March 23.

Shields and Jackson had a rematch at Port Republic on June 9. This time the Confederate won. This effectively ended Shields's Civil War career. The Senate rejected his promotion to major general on June 12, and Shields submitted his resignation, which was accepted on March 28, 1863. The president reportedly informally offered Shields the command of the Army of the Potomac after the Maryland Campaign, but Shields declined it because he intensely disliked Secretary of War Stanton.

Shields returned to California but neither he nor his wife liked living there. They moved to Missouri in 1866, where Shields bought a farm near Carrollton. He re-entered the political world in 1868 when he lost a close and contested election to Congress. He later served in the Missouri legislature and as state railroad commissioner. Although he lacked money in his later years, he still worked *pro bono* on charitable causes. When the yellow fever epidemic struck the Atlanta area, he raised a considerable amount of money for the sufferers. In 1879, the Missouri legislature elected him to fill a vacant seat in the U.S. Senate. He only served three months and declined to run for re-election, but he still made history as the only man to serve as a senator from three different states.

While on a lecture tour, James Shields died unexpectedly on June 1, 1879, in Ottumwa, Iowa. He was seventy-three. His body was interred in St. Mary's Cemetery, Carrollton, Missouri.

HENRY HASTINGS SIBLEY was born in Detroit, Michigan, on February 20, 1811. Michigan was part of the frontier at that time, but he was well educated at the Academy of Detroit and by a private tutor. He was just a baby when the British surrounded Fort Detroit during the War of 1812. His mother was holding him in her arms when a British cannonball slammed into the adjacent room, killing four officers, one of whom was her cousin.

Henry became a clerk in a sutler's store in 1828 and a clerk for the American Fur Company in 1829. He became a fur trader himself around 1833. In 1836, he built a private residence made of stone in what became Minnesota at Fort Snelling at the confluence of the Minnesota and Mississippi Rivers. He eventually took up with Red Blanket Woman, the daughter of a Dakota chief, whom he refused to marry but who bore him a daughter, with whom he maintained a close relationship until her death from scarlet fever in 1860. He married a white woman in 1843.

Sibley negotiated treaties between the Indians and the fur company. He was elected a Wisconsin Territory delegate to the U.S. Congress in 1848 and was instrumental in the establishment of the Minnesota Territory in 1849. He was its territorial delegate to Congress from 1849 to 1853. Thereafter, he sat in the state legislature. He was the first governor of the state of Minnesota from May 24, 1858 to January 2, 1860. Meanwhile, he invested in sawmills, the timber business, steamboats, and a general merchandise store, and helped relegate the Indians to reservations.

On August 19, 1862, the governor appointed Sibley colonel of volunteers and ordered him to suppress a revolt by the Dakota Sioux. He crushed them and set up a military commission, which tried them. It was a kangaroo court, and 307 men were sentenced to hang. Lincoln approved 39 of the death sentences, and 38 men were hanged at Mankato on December 26, 1862, under the supervision of General John Pope. The rest of them were confined to a makeshift prison along with 1,600 other Indians. Hundreds of them died in a measles epidemic which swept the camp that winter. Sibley, meanwhile, was appointed brigadier general of volunteers on September 29, 1862. His first appointment was allowed to expire on March 4, 1863, but Lincoln reappointed him on March 12, and he was confirmed by the Senate this time. He spent the next two years conducting brutal military campaigns against the Indians. He never saw an armed Confederate. He was brevetted major general in November 1865 and mustered out in April 1866.

A wealthy man, Henry H. Sibley spent the rest of his life conducting business operations and contributing to the development of Minnesota, including many charitable projects. Among other things, he served as president of the board of regents of the University of Minnesota. He died in St. Paul on February 18, 1891, at age seventy-nine. He was buried in

Oakland Cemetery, St. Paul. His cousin, Henry Hopkins Sibley, was a brigadier general in the Confederate Army.

DANIEL SICKLES was a rogue. He was born on October 20, 1819, into a wealthy New York City family. He was educated at the University of the City of New York (now New York University), studied law in Benjamin Butler's office, and was admitted to the bar in 1843. As a prominent member of the Tammany Hall political machine, he was elected to the New York legislature in 1847. He was censured for bringing Fanny White, a known prostitute, into the legislative chambers.

In 1852, he married the beautiful Teresa Da Ponte Bagioli against her parents' wishes. She was fifteen; he was thirty-two. The following year, he was appointed secretary of the U.S. legation to London. A notorious womanizer and whoremonger, Sickles left his pregnant wife behind and carried a prostitute with him. He later introduced her to Queen Victoria, calling her by the name of one of his political opponents. Later, he caused an international incident by snubbing the queen at an Independence Day celebration. Even so, he was elected to Congress in 1856.

Meanwhile, Teresa Sickles decided that two could play at the adultery game. She had an affair with Philip Barton Key II, the U.S. attorney for the District of Columbia and the son of Francis Scott Key, the author of "The Star-Spangled Banner." At Lafayette Square on February 27, 1859, just across the street from the White House, a jealous Sickles shot Key to death. During a sensational trial, Sickles was acquitted for reasons of temporary insanity. This was the first time in U.S. history this defense was successfully used. Sickles's attorney was Edwin Stanton, the future secretary of war.

After the trial, Sickles publicly forgave his wife and temporarily withdrew from public life, although he did not resign from Congress. The public seems to have been more outraged by the forgiveness than the murder. In any case, Sickles received a commission as major in the 12th New York Militia Regiment in the 1850s.

When the Civil War began, Sickles sought to redeem himself in the public eyes by raising units for the Union Army. He played a major role in forming four infantry regiments. He was named colonel of the 70th New York Infantry on June 29, 1861. Because of his political influence, he was given command of the Excelsior Brigade appointed brigadier general on September 3. The Senate, however, refused to confirm his appointment in March 1862. Lincoln renominated him, and he (Sickles) went to Capitol Hill to lobby for the promotion. He was successful and was confirmed on May 12.

Whatever else may be said about Sickles, no one can criticize his energy or his courage. He took part in the latter stages of the Peninsula Campaign (missing the Battle of Williamsburg because he was in Washington, lobbying for promotion), the Battle of Seven Pines, and the Seven Days battles. He assumed command of a division in the III Corps on September 5. His division was in the Washington defenses on September 17, so he missed the Battle of Antietam. His men were in reserve at Fredericksburg.

The war did not improve Sickles's private conduct. He continued to be a hard drinker and his headquarters resembled a brothel. He was, however, a close ally of Joseph Hooker, his former division commander and now the commander of the Army of the Potomac, whose HQ has been compared to a bordello. Even so, President Lincoln appointed Sickles major general on March 11. Hooker gave Sickles command of the III Corps on February 5, 1863. He was the only corps commander without a West Point education.

As a corps commander, Dan Sickles was a train wreck. He was aware of Stonewall Jackson's flanking movement on May 2, but he did not know what it meant and thought Jackson was retreating. At Gettysburg on July 2, General Meade (Hooker's replacement) ordered him to defend the southern end of Cemetery Hill. Thinking he knew better, Sickles disobeyed orders and marched his corps to the Peach Orchard, a mile in front of the rest of the Union Army. By the time Meade learned of his mistake, it was too late. The Rebels under James Longstreet attacked from three sides and virtually destroyed the III Corps, which suffered so many casualties that it had to be disbanded. Ironically, Sickles was awarded the Congressional Medal of Honor for this battle thirty-four years later. His war ended that afternoon when a piece of solid shot shattered his right leg, which had to be amputated at the hip. The bones of his leg are displayed at the National Museum of Health and Medicine, along with a photograph of Sickles, on crutches, observing them.

Remarkably, Sickles remained in the army and claimed credit for the Union victory at Gettysburg (!), falsely claiming that Meade wanted to retreat from the battlefield. He also applied for another combat command. Ulysses S. Grant, however, was wise enough to reject this request. Unemployed until after the South surrendered, he was given command of the Department of the South in 1865, where he halted property foreclosures, outlawed discrimination against African Americans, and made wages of farm laborers the first lien on crops. He also outlawed the production of whiskey. He retired as a major general in 1869.

Sickles was U.S. ambassador to Spain from 1869 to 1874, where he apparently had an affair with deposed Queen Isabella II. He was chairman of the New York Monuments Commission, formed to honor New York soldiers and units at Gettysburg, but was forced out when it was determined that $27,000 was embezzled from the commission. It is significant that every senior Union commander at Gettysburg received a monument except Sickles. When asked why this was, Sickles replied: "The entire battlefield is a memorial to Sickles."

He was chairman of the New York Civil Service Commission in 1888 and sheriff of New York County in 1890. In 1892, he was re-elected to Congress, serving from 1893 to 1895, when he retired. General Sickles died of a cerebral hemorrhage in the city of his birth on May 3, 1914. He was ninety-four. He was interred in Arlington National Cemetery.

FRANZ SIGEL was born Sinsheim, in the Grand Duchy of Baden, in what is now southwest Germany, on November 18, 1824. He was educated at the Classical School at Bruchsal and the Karlsruhe War School and was commissioned second lieutenant of infantry in the Grand Duke's Army. In 1847, after killing a fellow officer in a duel (and being wounded himself), he was arrested and compelled to resign his commission. He enrolled in law school at the University of Heidelberg later that year. A charismatic leader, he joined the revolutionaries in 1848, organized a Freikorps in Mannheim, and (as a colonel) became their minister of war in Baden. He commanded more than four thousand men in the Battle at Freiburg on April 23, where he was defeated by numerically inferior but better led Prussian troops. He was wounded in a skirmish in the spring of 1849.

After the revolutionaries were defeated, Sigel led his remaining troops into exile in Switzerland that summer but, fearing arrest, fled to England, where he became a colleague of Karl Marx and Friedrich Engel. He emigrated to the United States in 1852. He taught school in New York City until 1857, when he moved to Missouri as a professor at the German-American Institute in St. Louis, teaching English, history, math, and military science. He became director of the public schools in St. Louis in 1860. An influential leader in the large German immigrant community, he became colonel and commander of the 3rd Missouri Infantry on May 4, 1861.

Sigel took part in the capture of Camp Jackson on May 10. He led a column to Carthage, where numerically superior Rebel forces defeated him on July 5. He was with General Lyon in the Battle of Wilson's Creek on August 10. Routed, he assumed command of the Union forces after Lyon was killed and directed the retreat to Rolla. On August 7, he became one of the several political generals Lincoln elevated to brigadier general of volunteers.

Sigel commanded a division in the Battle of Pea Ridge, Arkansas, on March 7–8, 1862. Despite having a severe case of the flu, it was his finest performance of the war, and he played a major role in defeating the Confederate Army of the West. He was promoted to major general on March 22 and was transferred to the Eastern Front. Here, he fought in the Shenandoah Valley, where his forces were defeated by Stonewall Jackson. He was nevertheless promoted to the command of the I Corps of the Army of Virginia, which he led in the U.S. disaster at the Second Bull Run, where he was wounded in the left hand. His slowness was a major factor in the Union defeat. His demoralized corps was left in the Washington defenses during the Maryland Campaign. It was redesignated XI Corps on September 12.

Sigel commanded the Reserve Grand Division (XI and XII Corps) at Fredericksburg. He reverted to corps commander after General Burnside was sacked in January 1863. By now, Sigel had a reputation as an inept general but a fine recruiter, especially of German immigrants, which made up much of his corps. He was replaced as corps commander by O. O. Howard in February. Unemployed for several months, he was given a minor territorial command in Pennsylvania. General Halleck, the general-in-chief, detested Sigel and tried to avoid giving him a major command. The German immigrants, however, continued to love the charismatic Sigel and looked upon him as one of their own. Abraham Lincoln yielded to political pressure in March 1864 and directed Secretary of War Stanton to appoint Sigel commander of the Department of West Virginia. In this capacity, he invaded the Shenandoah Valley on April 29, 1864.

This was one of Lincoln's more unfortunate appointments. At New Market on May 15, Sigel and his 6,200 men were routed by 4,000 Confederates, some of whom where V.M.I. cadets. Sigel was demoted to the command of the District of Harpers Ferry, where he failed to engage Confederate General Early as he drove on Washington. Sigel was sacked by General Halleck on July 8 and was unemployed for the rest of the war.

Franz Sigel resigned his commission on May 4, 1865. He worked in the newspaper business post-war, ran for New York secretary of state as a Republican in 1869 but lost, was a collector in internal revenue, was city register for New York, and labored in the advertising business for several years. He died in New York City on August 21, 1902, at age seventy-seven. He was buried in Woodlawn Cemetery, The Bronx, New York.

JOSHUA WOODROW SILL was born on December 6, 1831, in Chillicothe, Ohio. He was homeschooled by his father, who was an attorney. He was admitted to West Point in 1849, graduated in 1853 (3/52) and was commissioned brevet second lieutenant of ordnance. He was stationed at the Watervliet Arsenal in New York (1853–54); at West Point as an assistant professor of geography, history, and ethics (1854–57); at the Allegheny Arsenal in Pennsylvania (1857–58); commander of the Vancouver Ordnance Department in Washington state (1859–59); back to Watervliet (1859–60); Fort Monroe Arsenal, Virginia (1860); and commander of the Leavenworth Ordnance Department (1860). Promoted to second lieutenant in

1854 and first lieutenant in 1856, he resigned his commission in January 1861 to become a professor of mathematics and civil engineering in the Brooklyn Collegiate and Polytechnic Institute.

In April 1861, when the Civil War began, he returned to the flag as assistant adjutant general of the state of Ohio. He took part in the Western Virginia Campaign of 1861 and was promoted to colonel of the 33rd Ohio in August. He was given command of a brigade in Buell's Army of the Ohio on November 30.

Sill was a competent, kind, and humble officer and his men loved him. He was promoted to brigadier general on July 19, 1862. After seeing action in northern Alabama and in the Kentucky Campaign of 1862 (including the Battle of Perryville), he asked to be transferred to Sheridan's command in the Army of the Cumberland. (He and Sheridan were roommates at West Point and developed a lifelong friendship.) He fought in the Battle of Stones River on December 31, 1862, where a musket ball struck him squarely in the head, killing him instantly. He was thirty-one years old. General Sill was buried on the battlefield, but a citizens' delegation from his hometown went south and asked for his body, which was given to them. He was buried in Grandview Cemetery in the town of his birth. In 1869, General Sheridan named Fort Sill, Oklahoma, after him.

JAMES RICHARD SLACK was born on September 28, 1818, in Bucks County, Pennsylvania. He moved to Indiana in 1837, where he worked as a laborer on his father's farm. He also taught school, studied law, and was admitted to the bar in 1840. He relocated to Huntington, where he was elected county auditor in 1842, a job he held for nine years. He was then elected to the Indiana State Senate for the first of his seven terms. He ran for Congress in 1854 but was defeated.

Slack was commissioned colonel of the 47th Indiana Infantry on December 13, 1861. In February 1862, he was promoted to brigade commander in the Army of the Mississippi and led it in the Battle of Island Number 10 (February 28 to April 8). He briefly directed a district in

eastern Arkansas before taking charge of a brigade in Grant's army. He fought in the Vicksburg campaigns and the subsequent siege, before being transferred to the Department of the Gulf, where he spent the rest of the war. He served in the disastrous Red River Campaign, after which he directed the Thibodaux, Louisiana, district. He was promoted to brigadier general on November 10, 1864.

A good brigade commander, Slack's last campaign was aimed at capturing Mobile. He took part in the battles of the Spanish Fort, Fort Blakely, and the capture of the city itself (April 12, 1865). He was brevetted major general and mustered out in January 1866.

General Slack returned to Huntington, resumed his law practice, and was appointed judge of the state circuit court in 1872. He ran for Congress again in 1880 but was defeated. He held his judgeship until his death, which occurred from to a heart attack he suffered while on a visit to Chicago on July 28, 1881. He was sixty-two. He was buried in Mount Hope Cemetery, Huntington, Indiana.

ADAM JACOBY SLEMMER was born on January 24, 1828, in Montgomery County, Pennsylvania. Educated in local schools, he was admitted to West Point in 1846 and graduated in 1850 (12/44). Commissioned brevet second lieutenant of artillery, he was sent to Florida, where he fought the Seminoles. After he was promoted to second lieutenant in 1851, he was transferred to southern California, where he did four years frontier duty. He was promoted to first lieutenant in 1854. After briefly serving at Fort Moultrie, South Carolina (1855), he was an assistant professor at West Point, where he taught mathematics (1855–59). Following another brief tour at Fort Moultrie, he was sent to Florida, where he helped defend Fort Pickens, Florida, in Pensacola harbor, during the opening weeks of the Rebellion.

Slemmer was named major of the 16th U.S. Infantry, then forming in Chicago, on May 14, 1861. He was an acting inspector general on the staff of the Army of the Ohio by August, and took part in General Buell's campaigns of 1861 and 1862, including the Siege of Corinth and the Heartland (Kentucky) Campaign. He was severely wounded in the left leg just below the knee during the first day of the Battle of Stones River (December 31, 1862). The next day, while being transported to the rear, he was captured by Confederate cavalry. Deemed too badly injured to be moved via horseback, they paroled him. He was unable to return to duty until July 1863, and even then, he was on crutches. Meanwhile, on April 4, 1863, he was promoted to brigadier general. The ranks of lieutenant colonel and colonel he skipped altogether.

General Slemmer spent the rest of the war as president of the Board of Examination for sick and wounded officers at Columbus and Cincinnati, Ohio. He was mustered out in August 1865, reverted to the rank of lieutenant colonel, Regular Army, and was stationed at various garrisons, mainly in New York state. He was on frontier duty at Fort Laramie, Dakota Territory, from November 1867 to October 17, 1868, when he suddenly died. He was forty years old.

Adam J. Slemmer was buried in Montgomery Cemetery, Norristown, Pennsylvania.

HENRY WARNER SLOCUM, SR., was born in Delphi Falls, New York, on September 24, 1827. He was educated at the State Normal School in Albany and the Cazenovia Seminary in Madison County. He received a teachers' certificate at age sixteen and taught for five years before being admitted to West Point in 1848. He graduated in 1852 (7/43) and was commissioned second lieutenant in the 1st U.S. Artillery. He served in Florida against the Seminoles (1852–53) and was stationed at Fort Moultrie, South Carolina (1853–56). He was promoted to second lieutenant in 1852 and first lieutenant in 1855 but resigned his commission in October 1856.

As a civilian, Slocum became a lawyer in Syracuse (he was admitted to the bar in 1858) and was elected to the New York General Assembly in 1859. He was also an instructor of artillery to the New York Militia, where he reached the rank of colonel in 1859.

Slocum joined the Union Army as colonel of the 27th New York Infantry on May 21, 1861. He fought at Bull Run (July 21), where he was severely wounded in the right thigh by a musket ball. He was unable to return to duty until September. Meanwhile, he was promoted to brigadier general on August 9, 1861. Assigned a brigade in the Washington defenses, he was transported to the Virginia Peninsula in April 1862. As part of the Army of the Potomac, he fought in the Siege of Yorktown, the Seven Days battles (including Gaines Mill, Frayer's Farm, and Malvern Hill), the Second Bull Run, South Mountain, Antietam, Fredericksburg, Chancellorsville, and Gettysburg, where his successful defense of Culp's Hill was one of the keys to Union victory. Meanwhile, he was promoted to division commander (May 18, 1862), major general (July 25, 1862), and commander of the XII Corps (October 20, 1862).

When Joseph Hooker was fired as commander of the Army of the Potomac in June 1863, Slocum was senior corps commander, but he was passed over in favor of George G. Meade. Slocum graciously agreed to serve under Meade, who was his junior in rank—with happy results for the Union.

That fall, Slocum and the XII were sent to the Western Front. When it appeared that he would have to serve under Hooker, Slocum wrote to Lincoln directly and declared that he would rather resign. Abraham Lincoln personally intervened and saw to it that Slocum would not be under Hooker's command. The president did not want to lose the highly competent New Yorker.

In 1864, Lincoln was rewarded by another outstanding series of performances by Slocum. He commanded the District of Vicksburg with great efficiency and was named commander of the XX Corps (which was formed by consolidating the XI and XII Corps) during the Atlanta Campaign. When the city fell, Slocum and his men were the first to enter the city. As military commandant of Atlanta, he made the occupation as tolerable as possible for the Southern civilians. He commanded the Army of Georgia (Sherman's left wing) during the March to the Sea and the Carolinas Campaign. After the Confederacy fell, Slocum commanded the Army of the Mississippi. He was offered a colonelcy in the Regular Army but turned it down and resigned from the army on September 28, 1865.

Postwar, Slocum was the Democratic candidate for New York secretary of state but was defeated by General Francis C. Barlow. He settled in Brooklyn and was elected to Congress, serving from 1869 to 1873. He narrowly lost the Democratic nomination for governor in 1882. He returned to Congress from 1883 to 1885. Meanwhile, he was involved in several successful business ventures and was director of the People's Trust Company and the Williamsburg City Fire Insurance Company. He also worked for the exoneration of General Fitz John Porter and became commissioner of the Brooklyn Department of City Works. Active in veterans' affairs until the end, General Slocum died of liver disease on April 14, 1894, in Brooklyn, New York, at age sixty-six. He was buried in Green-Wood Cemetery, Brooklyn.

JOHN POTTS SLOUGH (pronounced "Slow") was born on February 1, 1829, in Cincinnati, Ohio, the son of a steamboat builder. He attended the University of Cincinnati Law School, was admitted to the bar, practiced in his hometown, and was elected to the Ohio legislature as a Democrat in 1850. Known for his explosive temper, he was expelled from the General Assembly for striking another legislator and for conduct unbecoming of a gentleman. He was re-elected to his own vacant seat and became secretary of the Central Democratic Committee in 1852. He moved to Leavenworth, Kansas, in 1857, during the Bleeding Kansas era, became a member of the Wyandotte Constitutional Convention (which made Kansas a free state), and again settled a dispute with his fists. Strongly anti-slavery, he moved to Colorado in 1860, where he helped organize the territory's judicial system.

When the Civil War began, Slough immediately began recruiting for the Union Army. He joined the service as a captain in the 1st Colorado Infantry Regiment on June 24, 1861, became its colonel on August 26, and fought in New Mexico Territory. He commanded U.S. forces at Glorieta Pass, which was a tactical defeat for the Union but—because Slough got into the Rebel rear and destroyed their wagon train—it was a strategic victory for the Federals. Meanwhile, he got into a dispute with General Canby, who charged Slough with disobeying orders. Slough submitted his resignation and headed for Washington, D.C.

Slough's wife was the daughter of a congressman and a relative of a Supreme Court justice. Using his political influence, Slough was appointed brigade commander in the Army of the Shenandoah. He was stationed at Harpers Ferry most of the time, however, and saw little action. He was promoted to brigadier general on August 25, 1862, and that same day, he was appointed military governor of Alexandria, Virginia. He retained this position for the rest of the war. He was mustered out in August 1865. He remained in Washington as an attorney until January 1866, when President Andrew Johnson appointed him chief justice of the New Mexico Supreme Court.

Slough found a great deal of corruption in Santa Fe, and he dealt with it in his usual high-handed manner. He also created an uproar when he ruled that Pueblo Indians were U.S. citizens and were equal to white people in the eyes of the law. (He considered the system of peonage he found in New Mexico similar to slavery, which Slough detested.) There was a resolution in front of the legislature to remove him from office on December 15, 1867, when he was shot by a member of the corrupt Santa Fe Ring, which was made up of politically prominent Republicans. He died two days later

at age thirty-eight. His assassin (a member of the territorial legislature) was tried and found not guilty for reasons of self-defense, even though Slough did not draw his derringer until after he was shot. He was too badly wounded to fire, however. He was buried in the Spring Grove Cemetery in Cincinnati.

ANDREW JACKSON "WHISKEY" SMITH was born on a farm in Bucks County, Pennsylvania, on April 26, 1815. He was admitted to West Point in 1834, graduated four years later (36/45), and was commissioned second lieutenant in the 1st Dragoons. He was promoted to first lieutenant in 1845 and captain in 1847. He served in Kansas, on the southwest frontier, in the Mexican War, and fought Indians in the Pacific Northwest. He was promoted to major on May 13, 1861.

Smith was at Fort Walla Walla, Washington Territory, when the Civil War began. He became colonel of the 2nd California Cavalry in October 1861 and was named chief of cavalry for the Department of Missouri in February 1862. He was given the same job in the Department of the Mississippi the following month. He was promoted to brigadier general on March 20.

Whiskey Smith took part in the Siege of Corinth and in Grant's various Vicksburg campaigns. He was given command of an infantry division in October and led it in Sherman's Chickasaw Bluff campaign, which was a disastrous failure. He also took part in the victory at Arkansas Post, Grant's successful Vicksburg campaign, and the Siege of Vicksburg.

Smith was a good division and corps commander—when he was sober. His capture of Fort DeRussy on the Red River left no room for criticism and led to the capture of Alexandria. His counterattack at Pleasant Hill on April 9, 1864, saved the Army of the Gulf from annihilation. His conduct that night, however, was abysmal. Smith had more than the average Regular Army officer's contempt for volunteer officers. When the army commander, General Banks, summoned his generals for an officers' call, Smith chose to ignore him. After the meeting, Smith learned that Banks had decided to retreat. He became completely unhinged. He met with Generals Franklin and Emory and, after a hate-filled tirade, asked Franklin to arrest Banks, take charge of the army, and continue the drive on Shreveport. This was too much for Emory, who stood up and declared, "Gentlemen, this is mutiny!" and walked out the door. Realizing that he had gone too far, Smith quickly dropped the subject.

Smith commanded the rear guard in the retreat to Alexandria. After the Union naval flotilla escaped, he burned the town and fell back across the Atchafalaya. Meanwhile, on May 14, Lincoln promoted him to major general. He was sent to Mississippi, where he defeated Stephen Dill Lee in the Battle of Tupelo, but then retreated to Memphis. General Grant was not entirely pleased with his performance, so he ordered Smith to try to capture northern Mississippi again. Smith took Oxford but was forced to retreat after Nathan Bedford Forrest entered Memphis. He burned the town as he left.

Unable to defeat Forrest, Smith and his ad hoc corps were sent to Missouri, where they played a major role in defeating Sterling Price's Missouri Raid. He was sent to Nashville in early December and helped crush the Confederate Army of Tennessee on December 15–16. He commanded the XVI Corps in the capture of Mobile, which fell on April 12, 1865. It was the last campaign of the war.

Smith was mustered out of volunteer service on January 15, 1866, and reverted to the rank of colonel. He commanded the 7th U.S. Cavalry in the West until 1869, when he resigned from the army. Postwar, he was postmaster of St. Louis and city auditor of St. Louis. He was reappointed colonel of cavalry in January 1889 and retired from the army that same day. He died at home of a brain seizure on January 30, 1897, and is buried in Bellefontaine Cemetery, St. Louis.

CHARLES FERGUSON SMITH was born in Philadelphia on April 24, 1807. The grandson of a Revolutionary War colonel, he entered West Point in 1820, graduated in 1825 (19/37), and was commissioned second lieutenant in the 2nd U.S. Artillery. After tours of duty at Fort Delaware and the Augusta Arsenal, he returned to the Military Academy in 1829 and remained there the next thirteen years, serving as an instructor of infantry tactics, adjutant, and commandant of cadets. Called tall, graceful, and handsome, he helped train Cadets Grant and Sherman (among others), who had high opinions of him. He was promoted to first lieutenant in 1832 and captain in 1838.

After further garrison duty in New York and Pennsylvania, he fought in Mexico under both Taylor and Scott, earning brevets to major, lieutenant colonel, and colonel for Palo Alto and Resaca de la Palma; Monterey; and Contreras and Churubusco, where he commanded the Light Infantry Battalion. Very few men earned three brevets in Mexico, and none earned four.

An exceptionally good officer, he performed more or less routine garrison duties in the interwar period, being stationed at Fort Marion, Florida;

Washington, D.C.; Carlisle Barracks, Pennsylvania; Fort Snelling, Minnesota; Fort Crawford, Wisconsin; and in the Utah Expedition. He was promoted to major (substantive rank) in 1854 and lieutenant colonel in 1855. He commanded the Department of Utah (1860–61) and was commander of the District of Washington, [DC] when the Civil War began. He was a soldier rather than a politician, however, and did not fit in well in the nation's capital; nevertheless, he did successfully prepare it for defense.

Colonel Smith was Superintendent of the General Recruiting Office at Fort Columbus, New York, from April to August 1861. He was promoted to brigadier general of volunteers on August 31 and was transferred to Paducah, Kentucky, where he commanded a number of minor operations, including the capture of Fort Heiman (February 6, 1862), which was across the river from Fort Henry. He was one of the heroes at Fort Donelson, where he commanded a division with his customary coolness and courage. General Halleck telegraphed McClellan, who was then General-in-Chief: "... make him [Smith] a major-general. You can't get a better one." McClellan agreed, and he was promoted on March 22.

Charles Smith directed the expedition to Savannah, Tennessee, in March 1862. During this operation, while jumping into a rowboat, he injured his shin. Soon, an infection developed, which, along with a case of dysentery, led to his death at Savannah on April 25. He was fifty-five. Grant later remarked that Smith was his *beau ideal* of a soldier, while Sherman remarked that, had Smith lived, neither he nor Grant would ever have been heard of. There is no question that he was one of the best of the Union generals, and his leadership and experience was sorely missed at Shiloh.

General Smith was buried in Laurel Hill Cemetery, Philadelphia. His son Allen (1849–1927) retired as a brigadier general.

GILES ALEXANDER SMITH was born on September 29, 1829, in Jefferson County, New York. His older brother was future Union General Morgan L. Smith. Giles moved to southwest Ohio when he was eighteen and later to Cincinnati, where he engaged in business. He settled in Bloomington, Illinois, where he operated a hotel. He entered the Union Army as a captain in the 8th Missouri Infantry in June 1861.

Smith fought at Fort Donelson, Shiloh, the Siege of Corinth, and the operations against Vicksburg. He was promoted to lieutenant colonel (June 12, 1862), colonel (June 30), and commander of a brigade in the XIII Corps in November. He fought at Chickasaw Bluffs and in Grant's final, successful drive on Vicksburg and in the subsequent siege. He was wounded by a minié ball in the right hip during the assault of May 19, 1863. He did not return to duty until after the city fell. He was promoted to brigadier general on August 4.

General Smith was sent to Chattanooga, where he fought in the siege and in the assault on Missionary Ridge on November 25. Here, he was wounded in the chest and arm and could not return to duty until February 1864. A fine commander, he participated in the Atlanta Campaign, the March to the Sea, and the Carolinas Campaign, most of the time as a division commander in the XVII Corps. On November 24, 1865, he was promoted to major general of volunteers—the last man from the Civil War to achieve that distinction.

Highly thought of within the army, Giles Smith was offered a colonelcy in the Regular Army but declined it. He was mustered out on February 1, 1866. President Grant named him second assistant postmaster general in 1869, but he resigned in 1872 because of declining health. He moved to California in 1874 to improve his condition but was not successful. He returned home to die in the fall of 1876. He succumbed to consumption in Bloomington, Illinois, on November 8, 1876, at age forty-seven. He was buried in Evergreen Memorial Cemetery, Bloomington.

GREEN CLAY SMITH was born on Independence Day, 1826, in Richmond, Kentucky. He was a member of the famous Clay family of Kentucky, which included slaveholders and abolitionists, the most famous of which was Cassius M. Clay, a Union major general during the war. Smith (who was called Clay) could have enjoyed a life of wealth and privilege, but when the Mexican War erupted, he joined the 1st Kentucky Infantry as a second lieutenant. After the war, he attended Transylvania University and graduated with a baccalaureate degree in 1849. He then studied law, was admitted to the bar in 1852, and set up a practice in Covington. He was elected to the Kentucky House of Representatives in 1861 and served until 1863.

Smith was a fervent Unionist. He joined the Union Army as a private but was soon promoted to major of the 3rd Kentucky Cavalry. He became colonel of the 4th Kentucky Cavalry on March 15, 1862, and was promoted to brigadier general on June 12, 1862. He operated mostly in his home state and in Tennessee against Confederate raider John Hunt Morgan. His performance as a cavalry brigade commander left something to be desired, and his superior, General Jeremiah Boyle, asked General Buell to take Smith off his hands. He was transferred to the staff in August 1863 as provost marshal of Kentucky but resigned on December 1. Meanwhile, he was elected to Congress in November 1862 as a member of the Constitutional Union Party, serving from 1863 to July 1866. He was brevetted major general in 1866.

Congressman Smith resigned his seat to accept President Johnson's appointment as governor of Montana. He was mainly occupied in trying to prevent or mitigate hostilities between settlers and Indians. He resigned on April 9, 1869, to become a pastor.

A better man than he was a general, Clay Smith was ordained in the Baptist church and pastored several congregations, mostly in Kentucky. Simultaneously, he became a leader in the temperance movement. In 1876, he was the National Prohibition Party's nominee for president of the United States, but only received about ten thousand votes.

In 1890, Smith became pastor of the Metropolitan Baptist Church (now the Capitol Hill Baptist Church) in Washington, D.C. He held this position until his death, which occurred in Washington on June 29, 1895, at age sixty-eight. He was buried in Arlington National Cemetery.

His wife was the sister of Confederate General Basil Duke, John Hunt Morgan's second-in-command.

GUSTAVUS ADOLPHUS "GUS" SMITH was born on December 26, 1820, in Philadelphia, Pennsylvania. He lived in Maryland and Ohio before

settling in Decatur, Illinois, where he became a carriage manufacturer. He joined the Union Army as the colonel of the 35th Illinois Infantry Regiment on September 1, 1861.

Sent to Missouri, he was in the Battle of Pea Ridge on March 7, 1862, where his horse was shot from under him. He was waiting for another horse and directing an artillery battery, when his sword was shot from his hand, his belt was shot from his waist, and he was struck in the right shoulder and on the right side of his head by Confederate shell fragments. At first it was thought his wounds were mortal, and he did not fully recover until 1868.

Gus Smith returned to limited (recruiting) duty in July 1862 and was promoted to brigadier general to rank from September 29, 1862. His appointment, however, was allowed to expire without Senate action on March 4, 1863, and he reverted to the rank of colonel. Because of fraudulent recruiting practices, he was dismissed from the service on September 22, 1863.

Smith was recalled to duty as colonel of the 155th Illinois Infantry Regiment and was engaged in defending the Nashville & Chattanooga Railroad until the end of the war. He was mustered out in December 1865. He was brevetted major general in 1866.

After the war, he lived in Alabama until 1870 when his friend, President Ulysses S. Grant, appointed him collector of internal revenue for the District of New Mexico. He lived there until his death on December 11, 1885, in Santa Fe. He was sixty-four. He is buried in the Santa Fe National Cemetery.

JOHN EUGENE SMITH was born on August 3, 1816, in Bern, Switzerland. His father served under Napoleon and emigrated to Philadelphia after the Emperor fell. Smith trained as a jeweler and a goldsmith and, in 1836, moved to Galena, Illinois. Three days after Fort Sumter was fired on, he became an aide-de-camp to Governor Richard Yates. It was Smith who suggested to the governor that a former Galena resident, Ulysses S. Grant, should know how to command a regiment. Meanwhile,

Smith organized the 45th Illinois Infantry and became its colonel on July 23, 1861. He served under Grant at Fort Henry, Fort Donelson, and Shiloh. He was promoted to brigadier general on November 29, 1862. He commanded an infantry division off and on until June 1863, when he was placed in permanent command of a division in the Army of the Tennessee.

Smith took part in all Grant's operations against Vicksburg, fighting at Port Gibson, Raymond, Champion Hill, the assaults on Vicksburg on May 19 and 22, 1863, and the subsequent siege. His division joined Sherman for the Siege of Chattanooga and fought in the Battle of Missionary Ridge. He led a division in the XV Corps in the Atlanta Campaign, the March to the Sea, and the Carolinas Campaign. He especially distinguished himself in the capture of Savannah, for which he was brevetted major general in 1867.

Mustered out of volunteer service on April 30, 1866, Smith accepted a colonelcy in the post-war army and commanded the 15th U.S. Infantry and later the 14th Infantry. He also commanded Fort Phil Kearny in northeast Wyoming. He was a favorite of Chief Red Cloud and helped bring peace between the Sioux and the Americans. He retired in 1881.

General Smith spent his retirement years in Chicago, where he died on January 29, 1897, at age eighty. He was interred in Greenwood Cemetery, Galena, Illinois. One of his sons, Alfred T. Smith, was a captain in the Regular Army during the war and earned brevets to major and lieutenant colonel. He eventually retired as a brigadier general.

MORGAN LEWIS SMITH was born in Mexico, New York, on March 8, 1822. His family moved to Jefferson County, New York, when he was a child. As a young man, he was a wanderer; he also spent five years in the Regular Army under an assumed name. He was a boatman on the Ohio and Mississippi Rivers when the war began. He was largely responsible for recruiting the 8th Missouri Infantry Regiment in the spring and summer of 1861. A Zouave unit, it consisted mostly of German and Irish immigrants and misfits from the St. Louis waterfront, with Minnesota and Illinois

elements attached to bring it up to strength. Smith (now going by the alias "Martin L. Sanford") became its colonel on July 4. Smith employed a firm hand and turned it into one of the best units on the Western Front. Initially engaged in fighting guerillas and protecting Union wagon trains in Missouri, it was attached to Grant's forces at Cairo that fall. Smith was advanced to brigade command on February 1, 1862, and fought at Fort Donelson and Shiloh, where Smith's performance rallying disorganized and demoralized troops was superb. He also distinguished himself in the Siege of Corinth and was promoted to brigadier general on July 16.

Smith was part of Sherman's Chickasaw Bluffs Expedition that winter. While on reconnaissance in the fog on the morning of December 28, 1862, he was struck in the hip by a Confederate bullet, which could not be removed. He could not return to duty until October 1863, and the wound bothered him for the rest of the war.

General Smith commanded a division in the Siege of Chattanooga and in the Atlanta Campaign, where he temporarily led the XV Corps. (The corps commander, John A. Logan, was acting commander of the Army of the Tennessee after General McPherson was killed.) After leading the XV in the Battle of Atlanta, he returned to divisional command and fought at Ezra Church (July 28) but was physically unable to continue because of his Chickasaw Bluffs wound. Given a rear area command, he directed Union forces at Vicksburg for the rest of the war.

Morgan Smith resigned from the army on July 12, 1865. He was offered a Regular Army commission but declined it. For some reason, he was never brevetted major general. He was U.S. consul in Honolulu, Hawaii, under President Johnson (1866–1869), but stepped down after President Grant was inaugurated. He then engaged in a variety of business operations in the Washington, D.C., area, including working for a building association. He died suddenly while on a business trip in Jersey City, New Jersey, on December 29, 1876, at age fifty-two. He is buried in Arlington National Cemetery. General Sherman called him "one of the bravest men in action I ever saw." He was the older brother of General Giles A. Smith.

THOMAS CHURCH HASKELL SMITH was born in Acushnet, Massachusetts, on March 24, 1819. He attended Harvard, where he finished second in his class, and then moved to Marietta, Ohio, where he studied law. He was admitted to the bar and set up a practice in Cincinnati. He was a co-founder of the Morse Telegraph System and, from 1848 to 1851, was involved in constructing telegraph lines connecting Pittsburgh, Cincinnati, and New Orleans. After that, he returned to his law practice and, in 1852, joined the Literary Club of Cincinnati, whose members included future Union generals John Pope and Rutherford B. Hayes.

A Douglas Democrat before the war, Smith fervently embraced the Union cause in 1861 and became lieutenant colonel of the 1st Ohio Cavalry in early September 1861. After serving in Kentucky, Smith was sent to the Western Front the following spring, where he took part in the Siege of Corinth, and earned a special commendation from General Buell for his courage in an action at Booneville, Mississippi, in June.

Thereafter, Smith was associated with John Pope for the rest of his military career. Transferred to the Eastern Front, he was one of Pope's aides at the Second Battle of Manassas. After this debacle, Smith testified against General Fitz John Porter, whom the Republicans made the scapegoat for the disaster. Smith's testimony was quite damaging to Porter and also highly imaginary. Perhaps as a reward, Smith was promoted to lieutenant colonel on September 1, skipped the rank of colonel altogether, and was promoted to brigadier general on March 16, 1863.

Smith was sent into professional exile with Pope, under whom he commanded the District of Wisconsin, which was part of the Department of the Northwest. He briefly commanded the District of Missouri in the summer of 1865, after Pope became commander of the Department of the Missouri. Smith was mustered out in January 1866. Significantly, he was never brevetted major general in the omnibus promotions at the end of the war.

After the war, Smith raised livestock in southwest Missouri. He was affluent until 1871, when the Great Chicago Fire destroyed his sources of independent wealth, and he had to return to the government for his livelihood. He worked for the Treasury Department and was chief of its Appointments Division under his old friend, President Hayes. He was appointment major in the U.S. Army's paymaster department in 1878. He was stationed in Santa Fe, New Mexico, from 1879 to 1882 and retired in 1883, at the mandatory age of sixty-four. He then moved to Nordhoff (now Ojai), California, where he died on April 8, 1897, at age seventy-eight. He was buried in the Santa Barbara Cemetery, Santa Barbara, California.

THOMAS KILBY SMITH was born in Boston, Massachusetts, on September 23, 1820. His family moved to Hamilton County, Ohio, when he was eight. Raised on the family farm, he was educated at a military school operated by Ormsby Mitchel, a noted astronomer and future Union major general. He graduated from Cincinnati College in 1837; was a civil engineer for a time, studied law in the offices of future Chief Justice Salmon P. Chase; and became a special agent for the Post Office Department in 1853. Later, he became U.S. marshal for the Southern District of Ohio and deputy clerk of court for Hamilton County.

Smith joined the Union Army as lieutenant colonel of the 54th Ohio Infantry on September 9, 1861. He became its colonel the following month and was initially stationed at Camp Dennison near Cincinnati. Transferred to Paducah, Kentucky, in February 1862, he served under William T. Sherman and distinguished himself at Shiloh, where he assumed command of a brigade on the second day (April 7, 1862).

Smith led his brigade in the Siege of the Corinth and the subsequent Vicksburg campaigns. He took part in the early phases of the Siege of Vicksburg but was replaced as brigade commander by General Joseph A. J. Lightburn on May 24. The records are unclear if he was wounded or fell ill, but he did not return to duty until September. In any case, he was promoted to brigadier general on August 11.

General Smith took part in the Meridian Expedition and was stationed in Mississippi until March 1864, when he was named commander of the

Provisional Division of the XVI Corps of the Army of the Gulf. He escorted Admiral David D. Porter's fleet during the Red River Expedition. After the Union disaster at Mansfield, Smith ordered the destruction of the Louisiana State University Library at Alexandria during the subsequent retreat, but it was spared at the request of General Sherman, who was the institution's first superintendent before the war. Smith continued in divisional command until January 17, 1865, when he was relieved of duty for reasons of health. Immediately after the war, he returned to duty as commander of the Department of Southern Alabama and Florida. He briefly commanded the District of Maine before he was mustered out on January 15, 1866. He was brevetted major general later that year.

Postwar, Smith was U.S. Consul to Panama under President Johnson. He moved to Torresdale, Pennsylvania, in 1869, and became a journalist. Later, he lived in New York City, where he died on December 14, 1887, at the age of sixty-seven. His body was interred in Saint Dominic Church Cemetery in Torresdale.

Thomas Kilby Smith was not a brilliant general, but he was a highly capable one. A devout Catholic, he left behind five sons and three daughters.

WILLIAM FARRAR "BALDY" SMITH was born St. Albans, Vermont, on February 17, 1824. He entered the U.S. Military Academy in 1841, graduated in 1845 (4/41), and was commissioned brevet second lieutenant in the topographical engineers. He was promoted to second lieutenant in 1849, first lieutenant in 1853, and captain in 1859. Meanwhile, he served in the topographical engineers in the northern Great Lakes, Texas, Florida, and on the Lighthouse Board. He was also an assistant professor of mathematics at West Point from 1855 to 1858.

When the war began, Smith initially did mustering in duty and briefly served on the staff of Benjamin Butler at Fort Monroe, Virginia, before being promoted to colonel and assuming command of the 3rd Vermont Infantry on July 16, 1861 and fought in the First Battle of Bull Run (July 21, 1861). He assumed command of a brigade in the Washington defenses the following month and was promoted to brigadier general on August 13.

General Smith commanded a division in the VI Corps during the Peninsula and Maryland campaigns, led the VI during the Battle of Fredericksburg, and was promoted to major general on July 25, 1862. After the Fredericksburg disaster, he and General William B. Franklin wrote a letter to Lincoln, severely criticizing General Burnside's new plans. That, coupled with his close friendship with George B. McClellan, explains why he was sent into professional exile and, after a few months' unemployment, held a couple of relatively minor assignments, commanded a division in the Department of the Susquehanna during the Gettysburg Campaign and in the Department of West Virginia. The Senate allowed his appointment to expire on March 4, 1863. He was reappointed on March 24, 1864, and this time was confirmed.

Meanwhile, Smith was named chief engineer of the Army of the Cumberland, where he played a major role in saving that army by establishing a tenuous supply line to Chattanooga after the Chickamauga disaster. He also played a significant role in the Battle of Missionary Ridge. Although he clashed with General Rosecrans, he was praised by Generals Thomas, Sherman, and Grant, who brought him east in the spring of 1864. Given command of the XVIII Corps, he denounced his army commander, General Butler, as "helpless as a child in the field and as visionary as an opium eater in council."

Undoubtedly an engineering genius, he ruined his career during the Battle of Petersburg. Ordered to take the town with a division of African American troops in June 1864, he hesitated at the decisive moment and allowed the Rebels time to recover. Many historians aver that he might have ended the war in 1864, had he attacked. He was relieved of his command on July 19. He was in New York City awaiting orders until late November, after which he was on special duty under the secretary of war. He resigned his volunteer commission on November 4, 1865. Reverting to the rank of major of engineers, he resigned from the Regular Army in 1867.

Postwar, Smith was president of the International Telegraph Company (1864–1873) and commissioner of police for New York City (1875–1881). He worked for the U.S. government as a civil engineer in the 1880s and was named major of engineers on the retired list in 1889. He continued to work on improvements to the harbor of Wilmington, Delaware, and made several contributions to Civil War literature. He retired in 1901 and died in Philadelphia on February 28, 1903, at age seventy-nine. He was buried in Arlington National Cemetery. His cousin was J. Gregory Smith, the governor of Vermont from 1863 to 1865. His son, Stuart Farrar Smith, was a captain in the U.S. Navy and earned the Navy Cross during World War I.

WILLIAM SOOY SMITH was born on July 22, 1830, in Tarlton, Ohio. He worked his way through Ohio University at Athens, from which he graduated in 1849, and gained admission to West Point that same year. He graduated in 1853 (6/52), was commissioned brevet second lieutenant in the artillery on July 1, and was promoted to second lieutenant eight days later. After serving a year on recruiting duty, he resigned in 1854 and began a distinguished career in railroad bridge construction.

When the Civil War began, he was stationed at Camp Dennison, Ohio, as an assistant adjutant general, and was commissioned colonel of the 13th Ohio Infantry on June 26, 1861. He fought in the western Virginia Campaign in 1861 and was transferred to the Western Front in early 1862. As part of General Buell's army, he fought at Shiloh on the second day (April 7) and, on April 16, was promoted to brigadier general. He took part in the Siege of Corinth in May and, after a few weeks guarding railroads, was ordered to Kentucky, where he commanded a division at the Battle of Perryville on October 8. After operating in the Cumberland Gap area, he was sent to Mississippi, where he commanded a division in Hurlbut's XVI Corps in the operations against northern Mississippi and Vicksburg.

Smith's military career was ruined during the Meridian Campaign. Given command of an elite, hand-picked Union cavalry force of seven thousand men, he attempted to take the grain-producing region of northern Mississippi from Nathan Bedford Forrest, who had 2,500 men—of which only 1,900 were armed. Smith was nevertheless routed at Okolona on February 22, 1864. Forrest chased him eleven miles, and Smith and the remnants of his command were back in Tennessee by February 26. He remained in command of the Union cavalry in northern Mississippi and western Tennessee (now distinctly secondary sectors) until July 15, 1864, when he resigned his commission due to rheumatoid arthritis.

After the war, Smith returned to civil engineering. Regaining his previous vigor, he made huge contributions to railroad bridge building. He constructed the first all-steel bridge in the world across the Missouri River at Glasgow, Missouri, and he built or helped construct virtually every tall building in Chicago before 1910.

Late in life, Sooy Smith moved to the village of Medford, Oregon, but remained active in his profession until the end. He died at Medford, Oregon, on March 4, 1916, at age eighty-five. He was buried at Forest Home Cemetery in Forest Park, Illinois.

THOMAS ALFRED SMYTH was born in Ballyhooly Parish, County Cork, Ireland, on December 25, 1832. He worked on his family farm until 1854, when he emigrated to the New World and Philadelphia. Heeding the call of adventure, he joined William Walker and his filibusters in Nicaragua. After the expedition failed, he settled in Wilmington, Delaware, in 1858, where he became a candlemaker.

In April 1861, almost at the very start of the war, Smyth joined the 24th Pennsylvania Infantry as a company commander. It was an all-Irish 90-day regiment which saw little action during Patterson's advance on Harper's Ferry. It was mustered out on August 10. Smyth promptly joined the 1st Delaware Infantry, a three-year formation. It took part in the occupation of Norfolk, Virginia, and in the battles of Antietam and Fredericksburg, after which Smyth was promoted to lieutenant colonel. He assumed command of the regiment on February 7, 1863, and led it at Chancellorsville. Smyth commanded a brigade in the II Corps at Gettysburg, where he distinguished himself. During Pickett's Charge, Colonel Smyth was wounded in the head by a shell, but he was able to return to duty the following day.

Thomas A. Smyth was an excellent combat commander who continued to render outstanding service on the Rappahannock, in the Overland Campaign, and in the Siege of Petersburg, including the battles of Deep Bottom and Hatcher's Run. He was promoted to brigadier general on October 1, 1864. He briefly commanded a division in August 1864, early 1865, and on April 6 and 7, 1865, after Brigadier General William Hays was assigned to command of the artillery reserve.

On April 7, 1865, during the Battle of Farmville, Smyth was leading his skirmish line forward when a Rebel sharpshooter shot him through the mouth. The bullet shattered a cervical vertebra. Taken to a nearby home (the residence of Colonel S. D. Burke), he died in Burkeville, Virginia, on April 9—the day General Lee surrendered. He was the last Union general killed during the war. He was age thirty-two. General Smyth was buried in the Wilmington and Brandywine Cemetery, Wilmington. He was brevetted major general posthumously.

JAMES GALLANT SPEARS was born on March 29, 1816, in Bledsoe County, east Tennessee. He grew up in poverty, but after receiving a basic education—mainly by his own efforts—he studied law, was admitted to the bar, and set up a practice in Pikeville, Tennessee. He was also a successful planter. Elected clerk of the circuit court in 1848, by the early 1850s, he was wealthy in both land and slaves. Politically, he was a strong Douglas Democrat and a fervent supporter of the Union. He became a leading and outspoken anti-secessionist and said so during the Knoxville and Greeneville conventions of May and June 1861, during which he advocated forming a separate East Tennessee state within the Union—by violence if necessary. (Spears was hot-headed.) After this, Spears learned that the Confederates planned to arrest him, so he fled to Kentucky. Here, he helped organize the 1st Tennessee (Union) Infantry and became its lieutenant colonel on September 1.

Spears successfully led his men at Wild Cat Mountain and Mill Springs and was promoted to brigadier general on March 6, 1862. Assigned to the Army of the Ohio, he took part in the capture of Cumberland Gap and the subsequent retreat to the Ohio. Given another brigade in the Army of the Cumberland, he was lightly engaged in the Stones River Campaign.

James Spears was a heavy-handed commander and, in mid-1863, was relieved and court-martialed for "tyrannical and ungentlemanly conduct," but was acquitted and restored to his command. He continued to ruthlessly assert his authority, and twenty-seven of his officers petitioned General Rosecrans to sack Spears. Nothing was done, however.

Spears's brigade was present during the Chickamauga Campaign (as part of Granger's reserve) and was forced off Lookout Mountain by Nathan Bedford Forrest. Later, he took part in the relief of Knoxville, near which he captured six guns in December.

Meanwhile, Spears fiercely denounced the Emancipation Proclamation, which he considered unconstitutional and illegal. His opposition was so violent that his words reached the ears of Abraham Lincoln, and he was arrested on February 6, 1864, and was court-martialed. Given the opportunity to resign, he refused, and was dismissed from the service on August 30, 1864.

Spears spent the rest of his life rebuilding his fortune. His health eroded during the war, and he died at home on his farm in Bledsoe County, on July 22, 1869, at age fifty-three. He was buried in Pikeville City Cemetery.

FRANCIS BARRETTO SPINOLA was born on March 19, 1821, in Old Field, New York, on the north shore of Long Island. (Some sources list his birthplace as nearby Stony Brook.) He attended Quaker Hill Academy in Dutchess County, read law, passed the bar in 1844, and established a practice in Brooklyn. He was elected alderman in 1846 and subsequently re-elected in 1849, serving a total of five years. This was followed by six years in the state assembly and three years in the state senate (1858–1861), succeeding future Union General Dan Sickles. He was a delegate to the Democratic National Convention in 1860 and was commissioner of New York Harbor when the war began.

Spinola organized a brigade of four regiments in 1862 and was commissioned brigadier general on October 2. During the winter of 1862–63, he took part in a number of minor operations in North Carolina and southeastern Virginia, commanding a brigade of Pennsylvania militia. Recalled after Chancellorsville, Spinola was given command of the "Excelsior Brigade" (part of the III Corps) on July 11, 1863. Spinola took part in the pursuit of the Army of Northern Virginia and was wounded in the right foot and abdomen near Manassas Gap on July 23.

In the fall of 1863, the I and III Corps of the Army of the Potomac—which had suffered heavy losses at Gettysburg—were disbanded, leaving numerous supernumerary officers. Spinola was one of these. He returned home on recruiting duty and was involved in colluding with bounty brokers to defraud recruits. He was court-martialed and sentenced to be dismissed from the service. The courtmartial, however, was never confirmed and he resigned on June 8, 1865.

After the war, Spinola was a banker and an insurance agent. Highly successful, he became wealthy, and he was worth more than $1,000,000 in 1897 (more than $37,150,000 in 2024 currency). Meanwhile, he was re-elected to the State Assembly in 1877, 1881, and 1883, and was a congressman from 1887 to 1891. He died in office from pneumonia in Washington, D.C., on April 14, 1891, shortly after his third term began. He was seventy. General Spinola was buried in the Green-Wood Cemetery, Brooklyn, New York.

JOHN WILSON SPRAGUE was born in the village of White Creek, New York, on the Vermont border, on April 4, 1817. He was educated in local schools and at Rensselaer Polytechnic Institute in Troy, New York, but dropped out to enter the grocery business. He moved to Milan, Ohio, where he worked in the commission sales and shipping. He later settled in Sandusky, Ohio, and served a term as treasurer of Erie County, Ohio. Highly successful, he organized and operated a fleet of sailboats and steamers on Lake Erie in the 1850s.

When the Civil War began, Sprague raised a company of infantry that became part of the 7th Ohio Infantry Regiment. Stationed at Camp Dennison near Cincinnati,

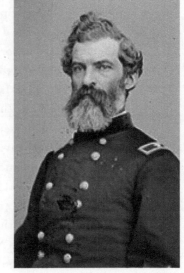

it was sent to western Virginia. On August 11, while returning home on leave, he was captured by Confederate raiders. Incarcerated in Richmond, Virginia, and Charleston, South Carolina, he was exchanged at Norfolk on January 9, 1862. He was promoted to colonel of the 63rd Ohio Infantry on January 23.

Colonel Sprague joined John Pope's Army of the Mississippi and fought in the battles of New Madrid and Island Number 10, where the Confederate forces were destroyed. He later took part in the Siege of Corinth, the Battle of Iuka (where he temporarily commanded a brigade), and the Second Battle of Corinth (October 3–4), where his regiment lost nine of its thirteen senior officers and suffered 45 percent casualties.

Sprague and his men spent 1863 on garrison duty in western Tennessee, northern Alabama, and Mississippi. They joined Sherman's army group in preparation for the Atlanta Campaign, and Sprague was named commander of a brigade in the XVI Corps in April 1864. On July 22, while the main army fought the Battle of Atlanta, Sprague brilliantly saved the entire ordnance and supply trains for the XV, XVI, XVII, and XX Corps (400 wagons), despite being heavily outnumbered, in the Battle of Decatur, Alabama. For this action, he was awarded the Congressional Medal of Honor in 1894—a few weeks after his death. More immediately, he was promoted to brigadier general on July 30, 1864.

General Sprague took part in the March to the Sea and the Carolinas Campaign and briefly commanded a division in October 1864. He was brevetted major general on April 26, 1866. For more than a year after the war, he directed the Freedman's Bureau for Missouri, Kansas, and Indian Territory and later in Arkansas. Here he tried to treat all parties fairly. He declined a Regular Army commission as a lieutenant colonel and was mustered out September 1, 1866.

After leaving the service, John Sprague managed a railroad in Minnesota and was general manager of the Western Division of the Northern Pacific Railroad. He was also a co-founder of Tacoma, Washington, and became its first mayor. Additionally, he served as the president of the National Bank, the Chamber of Commerce, and the Tacoma Steam Navigation Company. He died of heart disease on December 27, 1893, at age seventy-six. He is buried in the Tacoma Cemetery.

JULIUS STAHEL was born **JULIUS GYULA SZAMWALD** in Szeged, the Kingdom of Hungary, about 120 miles southeast of Budapest, on November 5, 1825. He was also known as **JULIUS STAHEL-SZAMWALD**. Educated in Szeged and Budapest, he joined the Austrian Army as a private and was commissioned lieutenant. During the Revolution of 1848, he cast his lot with the Rebels, who were defeated by the Prussian Army in 1849. Stahel fled to England where he worked as a teacher but migrated to New York City around 1856. Here, he was employed by the *Deutsche Illustrirte Familienblaetter*, a weekly German language newspaper. Meanwhile, he dropped the "Szamwald" part of his name.

When the Civil War began, he and Louis Blenker recruited the 8th New York Infantry (a.k.a. the 1st German Rifles) from the city's German immigrants. Blenker became its colonel and Stahel its lieutenant colonel. Blenker led a brigade covering the retreat of the Union Army after the First Bull Run disaster (July 21, 1861), while Stahel commanded the regiment. Both performed very well. Stahel was promoted to colonel on August 11 and to brigadier general on November 12.

Stahel commanded a brigade in Fremont's Mountain Department during the Shenandoah Valley Campaign of 1862 and took part in the defeat at Cross Keys, where his flank was turned by the Confederates. Transferred to Sigel's corps of Pope's Army of Virginia, Stahel assumed command of General Schenck's division after that officer was wounded on August 30. He helped cover the army's retreat after Pope was defeated. He remained in the Washington defenses for some time. In January 1863, he was acting commander of the XI Corps but only for nine days.

In March 1863, Stahel was given command of the cavalry division in the capital defenses. He was promoted to major general on March 17, 1863. When his unit was transferred to the Army of the Potomac in June 1863, General Pleasonton, the Cavalry Corps commander, immediately fired Stahel and replaced him with Judson Kilpatrick. Stahel took charge of the cavalry in the Department of the Susquehanna on July 2 and led it in the

Gettysburg Campaign. He was transferred to the Shenandoah Valley the following spring.

Stahel was with General Hunter when his army was routed at New Market on May 15, 1864. He made a fine professional "comeback" at Piedmont on June 5, when he played a major role in smashing Confederate General William E. "Grumble" Jones's cavalry—an action for which he was awarded the Congressional Medal of Honor in 1893. Meanwhile, he was seriously wounded in the shoulder but only allowed surgeons time to dress the wound before he returned to action. By the end of the day, Jones was dead, and the Rebels were on the run. Stahel continued in command until June 9, when he could finally go no longer. He spent the rest of his military career recovering or on light (court-martial) duty until February 8, 1865, when he resigned from the army. His overall military record was definitely positive but not universally so.

After the war, Julius Stahel joined the diplomatic service in Yokohama (1866–1869) and Osaka, Japan (1877–1884). He was Consul General in Shanghai, China, in 1884 and 1885. Between Yokohama and Osaka, he labored as a mining engineer. After 1885, he worked for the Equitable Life Insurance Company in New York City, where he died on December 4, 1912, at age eighty-seven. He is buried in Arlington National Cemetery.

DAVID SLOANE STANLEY was born on June 1, 1828, in Cedar Valley, Ohio. He graduated from West Point in 1852 (9/43) and was commissioned brevet second lieutenant in the 2nd Dragoons. Antebellum, he served on the west Texas and Dakota frontiers, and fought Comanches in the Indian Territory and the Cheyenne in Kansas. Stationed at Fort Washita, Indian Territory, when the Civil War began, he successfully led his men to Fort Leavenworth, Kansas. Meanwhile, he was promoted to second lieutenant (1853), first lieutenant (1855), and captain (March 16, 1861).

Stanley took part in the Missouri Campaign of 1861, including the Battle of Wilson's Creek (August 10), where his main duty was guarding the supply trains. He was nevertheless appointed brigadier general on September 28, 1861. He commanded cavalry under John Pope in the Battles of New Madrid and Island No. 10, before crossing the Mississippi and commanding a division of infantry in the Siege of Corinth, the Battle of Iuka, and the Second Battle of Corinth. He led the cavalry of the Army of the Cumberland during the Battle of Stones River. He was appointed major general on March 11, 1863.

General Stanley commanded the Union cavalry in the Tullahoma Campaign, but fell ill with dysentery and missed the Battle of Chickamauga. After leading an infantry division in the Siege of Chattanooga, he fought in the Atlanta Campaign, including the Battle of Kennesaw Mountain. When General James B. McPherson, the commander of the Army of the Tennessee, was killed in action on July 22, Oliver O. Howard replaced him. Stanley succeeded Howard as commander of the IV Corps and led it for the rest of the war. He was slightly but painfully wounded in the groin at Jonesboro on September 1 but was back on duty a week later.

Sherman sent Stanley to Tennessee to join General Thomas's Army of the Ohio against John Bell Hood's invasion. (Sherman privately held Stanley responsible for allowing Hardee's Confederate corps to escape at Jonesboro, which might have factored in the decision to send IV Corps to Tennessee instead of on the March to the Sea.) In any case, Stanley distinguished himself by leading a decisive counterattack in the Battle of Franklin on November 30. For this act, he was awarded the Congressional Medal of Honor in 1893. In the process, Stanley's horse was killed underneath him and he was severely wounded in the neck. He was not able to return to duty until after the Battle of Nashville.

Sent to Texas after the war, General Stanley was mustered out of volunteer service on February 1, 1866. Reverted to the rank of colonel, he was named commander of the 22nd U.S. Infantry, which was stationed in the Dakota Territory until 1873. Stanley successfully commanded the Yellowstone Expedition in northwest Wyoming and Montana Territory against the Northern Cheyenne and Lakota Sioux. He later commanded in Michigan, in north Texas, and in New Mexico. He was promoted to brigadier general, Regular Army, in 1884, and commanded the Department of Texas. He retired in 1892, although he continued as the governor of the National Soldiers' Home in Washington, D C, until 1898. General Stanley died on

March 13, 1902, at age seventy-three. He is buried in the U.S. Soldiers' and Airmen's Home National Cemetery in Washington, D.C. His son, David Sheridan Stanley (1873–1942), retired from the army as a colonel.

GEORGE JERRISON STANNARD was born in Georgia, Vermont, on October 20, 1820. He was educated in local public schools, attended private academies in Georgia and Bakersfield, worked as a farm hand, teacher, clerk, and was co-owner of a foundry in St. Albans by 1860. He also served as a sergeant of militia during troubles with Canada in 1838. He was named colonel of the 4th Vermont Militia Regiment in 1858.

Stannard was apparently the first Vermonter to answer the governor's call for troops in April 1861. He helped organize the 2nd Vermont Infantry Regiment and was appointed its lieutenant colonel on June 20. He fought in the First Battle of Bull Run and did well enough to be offered command of the 3rd Vermont Infantry. He turned it down, however, because he did not believe he had served long enough to command a regiment. He fought in the Peninsula and Seven Days campaigns and distinguished himself in the Battle of Williamsburg on May 5, 1862. He was promoted to colonel and named commander of the 9th Vermont on July 9.

During the Maryland Campaign, Stannard's new command was at Harpers Ferry, where it performed well in the defense of Bolivar Heights. It could not, however, prevent Stonewall Jackson from gobbling up the entire garrison on September 15. Stannard was exchanged in January 1863, and returned to Vermont. He was promoted to brigadier general on March 14, 1863, and was given command of the 2nd Vermont Brigade (four infantry regiments) the following month.

George Stannard distinguished himself at Gettysburg, where his brigade was one of the main units involved in the defeat of Pickett's Charge. Stannard was wounded in the right thigh by a shell fragment. Despite his pain, he would not leave the field until the battle was won. After the Rebels fell back, he was taken to the rear and was not able to return to limited duty until September. He briefly commanded the post of New York City in late 1863. He could not return to the Eastern Front until May 1864 as a brigade commander in the Army of the James. (He replaced General Heckman, who was captured on May 16.) Stannard fought at Cold Harbor, where he was slightly wounded twice, and in the Second Battle of Petersburg and the subsequent siege. In July, he was shot in the second finger of his left hand. He spent almost three months in hospitals or recovering in Vermont. He returned to the front on September 15, but, on September 30, during the Battle of Fort Harrison, a musket ball shattered his right arm above the elbow. It was amputated that night. He was brevetted major general after Fort Harrison but did not return to duty until January 1865, and even then, it was only light duty in Vermont. After briefly serving as assistant commander of the Freedmen's Bureau in Maryland, he resigned from the army in June 1866.

Postwar, General Stannard was a customs officer on the Vermont–Canada border. He was the doorman of the U.S. House of Representatives from 1881 until his death, which occurred on June 1, 1886. He was sixty-five. He was buried in Lakeview Cemetery, Burlington, Vermont.

JOHN CONVERSE STARKWEATHER was born in Cooperstown, New York, on February 23, 1829. He attended local schools and Union College in Schenectady, graduating in 1850. He studied law, was admitted to the bar, and moved to Milwaukee, Wisconsin, in 1851. He helped organize the Milwaukee Light Guard in 1855 and served as its captain from 1857 until the Civil War broke out.

The 1st Wisconsin Infantry was formed in Milwaukee on April 16, 1861, with Starkweather as colonel. It was mustered into Federal service on May 17, 1861, as a 90-day unit. It was sent East and fought its first engagement at Hoke's Run, Virginia, on July 2. It remained on the upper Potomac and was sent home when its enlistments expired in August but was quickly re-mustered as a three-year unit. Sent to Kentucky, it performed garrison and security duties until Bragg's invasion of the Blue Grass State.

As part of Buell's Army of the Ohio, it fought in the Battle of Perryville, where Starkweather commanded a brigade. He led his formation at Stones River, Chickamauga, and Chattanooga and was promoted to brigadier general on July 17, 1863. He was wounded in the left leg at Chickamauga on September 20.

Two years in the field was rough on General Starkweather. He developed lung disease and acute rheumatism and suffered from depression. He never returned to the field after Chickamauga but rather performed court-martial duty in Washington, D.C., and commanded rear area posts, mainly that of Pulaski, Tennessee. He resigned from the army on May 11, 1865.

After the war, John Starkweather was a farmer in Wisconsin for several years. He later moved to Washington, D.C., where he pursued cases against the government for damages, pensions, etc. He died in Washington on November 15, 1890, at age sixty-one. He was buried in Forest Home Cemetery, Milwaukee, Wisconsin. He and his wife had at least ten children, five of whom reached adulthood.

JAMES BLAIR "STEADY" STEEDMAN was born on July 29, 1817, in Northumberland County, Pennsylvania. His was a poor family, and he had no formal education. After his parents died when he was fifteen, Steedman went to work to support his siblings. He was a typesetter for newspapers in Lewisburg and Louisville until 1835, when he went to Texas, joined Sam Houston, and fought in the War of Texas Independence in 1836. Afterward, he settled in Ohio, bought a printing press, and began publishing the *Northwest Democrat* newspaper. Eventually, he became a contractor and built sections for the Wabash and Erie Canal and the Toledo, Wabash & Western Railroad.

Steedman went into politics in 1847 when he was elected to the Ohio legislature for the first of two terms. He also worked as a railroad conductor and went to California as a 49er. Unsuccessful, he returned to Ohio and was on the state's board of public works from 1852 to 1857. Simultaneously, he passed the bar and set up a practice in Toledo.

From 1857 to 1860, he was a printer for the U.S. Congress. He ran for Congress as a Democrat in 1860 but was defeated.

When the war began, he raised the 14th Ohio Infantry Regiment and was elected its colonel on April 27, 1861. This 90-day unit later re-enlisted for three years. It first saw action in the Union victory at Philippi, (West) Virginia, on June 3. Sent west, it fought in the Battle of Mill Springs in January 1862, which temporarily secured Kentucky for the Union. The regiment also fought in the Siege of Corinth, after which Steedman was promoted to brigadier general on July 19 and assumed command of a brigade in the Army of the Ohio.

Steedman fought in the Battle of Perryville on October 8 and received high marks from Don Carlos Buell, the army commander. He also participated in the Battle of Stones River and in the Tullahoma Campaign. He was given command of a division in Granger's Reserve Corps in August 1863. As the vanguard commander of this corps, his timely reinforcement of General Thomas saved the Army of the Cumberland on September 20. His horse was shot from under him, and he was severely injured in the fall. He later took part in the Siege of Chattanooga. He was promoted to major general on April 24, 1864, and took part in the Atlanta Campaign until June 15, when he assumed command of the District of Elowah.

Steedman formed an *ad hoc* division of eleven regiments (six thousand men) in George Thomas's army during the Battle of Nashville. He was the only division commander in the army who was not a West Point graduate. He was involved in heavy fighting before the Confederate Army finally collapsed on December 16. Steedman then returned to Elowah. He directed the Department of Georgia after the war and resigned his commission on August 18, 1866.

After the war, Steedman was collector of internal revenue in New Orleans until 1869, when he returned to Toledo, where he again became a newspaper editor. He was elected to the Ohio Senate in 1870 and became chief of police of Toledo in May 1883. He died of pneumonia in Toledo on October 18, 1883, at age sixty-six. He was buried in Woodlawn Cemetery, Toledo.

FREDERICK STEELE was born on January 14, 1819, in Delhi, New York. His family was prominent in the history of Hartford, Connecticut.

He entered West Point in 1839, graduated in 1843 (30/39), and was commissioned brevet second lieutenant in the infantry. After performing garrison duty at Buffalo Barracks, New York, and Fort Mackinac, Michigan, he served with Scott's army in Mexico, earned a brevet to first lieutenant for gallantry and meritorious conduct for Contreras and Churubusco and to captain for Chapultepec.

His antebellum career included tours of duty in California; Carlisle Barracks, Pennsylvania; and at forts in the Dakota Territory, Minnesota Territory, Nebraska, and Kansas Territory. Meanwhile, he was promoted to second lieutenant (1840), first lieutenant (1848), and captain in the 2nd U.S. Infantry (1859). He became a major in May 1861, shortly after the war broke out.

Steele was given command of a brigade in Missouri in July 1861 and fought in the Battle of Wilson's Creek (August 10). He became commander of the 8th Iowa Infantry in September 1861 but was quickly elevated to brigade commander. He was promoted to brigadier general on January 30, 1862.

Frederick Steele was a fine commander at every level. He led a division in Missouri and Arkansas and took part in the capture of Helena. He became commander of the District of Eastern Arkansas in November 1862 and led a division in Grant's army during the final Vicksburg Campaign, including the siege. Meanwhile, he was promoted to major general on March 17, 1863. Named commander of the Army of Arkansas in July 1863, he directed a brilliant campaign which culminated in the capture of Little Rock on September 10. His command was redesignated VII Corps in early 1864.

Steele disapproved of the Union's "total war" strategy and was called a Copperhead behind his back. In April 1864, he launched the Camden Expedition, very much against his will. He did not believe he could supply a corps in sparsely settled southwestern Arkansas. He also declared that the dirt roads there would never hold up under the wagons and artillery which would accompany the expedition. General Grant insisted that he make the effort, and General Steele was proven correct: the mission was a failure, and Steele did well to escape with the bulk of his command. He was nevertheless reduced to divisional commander of a predominately African

American unit. This did not bother Steele, as he was one of the few Union generals who believed black soldiers were as good in combat as white soldiers. He was proven right at Mobile, where his men stormed Fort Blakely on April 9, 1865.

General Steele was sent to Texas for a possible war with France over Mexico in June 1865. This did not materialize, and he was mustered out of volunteer service on March 1, 1867. He reverted to colonel and commanded the 20th Infantry Regiment and the Department of Columbia [Oregon]. He was on leave in San Mateo, California, when he fell from a buggy he was driving and died on January 12, 1868, two days before his forty-ninth birthday. Originally buried in San Francisco, he was re-interred in the Woodlawn Memorial Cemetery, Colma, California. His brother John, a Democrat, was a U.S. Congressman (1861–1865). Another sibling was a Republican and a California judge.

BARON ADOLPH WILHELM AUGUST FRIEDRICH VON STEINWEHR, commonly called **ADOLPH VON STEINWEHR**, was born on September 22, 1822, in Blankenburg, the Duchy of Brunswick, which later became part of Germany. His was a military family. His grandfather, Friedrich Wilhelm von Steinwehr, was a *Generalleutnant* (major general in U.S. terms) under Frederick the Great. After attending the Brunswick Cadet School, Adolph was commissioned *Leutnant* in the Brunswick Army in 1841. He resigned his commission in 1847 and emigrated to the United States. He joined an Alabama regiment and fought in the Mexican War, where he was struck in the face with a machete, swung by a drunk mestizo. It left a permanent scar, which is why he only allowed photographers to use his left profile. Unsuccessful in his efforts to obtain a Regular Army commission, Steinwehr worked for the U.S. Coastal Survey until 1852, when he returned to Brunswick. He emigrated to the United States again in 1854 and purchased a farm in Wallingford, Connecticut. He resided in Albany, New York, from 1858 to 1861, where he worked as an architect and civil engineer.

When the Civil War began, Steinwehr raised the 29th New York Infantry, a regiment consisting mainly of German immigrants from New York City. He was commissioned colonel on May 23, 1861. The 29th was in reserve during most of the Battle of Bull Run but did well covering the Union retreat. Steinwehr was given command of a brigade on October 12. He was stationed in the Mountain Department (West Virginia), although he was not present at Cross Keys. He was promoted to brigadier general on June 12, 1862.

On June 22, 1862, Steinwehr assumed command of a division in the I Corps of the Army of Virginia, which later became the XI Corps of the Army of the Potomac. He fought in the Second Battle of Bull Run, where his division suffered heavy casualties. He was acting commander of the XI Corps from February 22 to March 5, 1863. His division was routed at Chancellorsville and Gettysburg, although his personal performance was good. At Chancellorsville, for example, he erected earthworks and offered what little resistance to Jackson's flanking attack that was put up by the XI Corps. His units helped hold Cemetery Hill on July 1 and 2, and thus played a significant role in the Battle of Gettysburg.

Although German units were looked down upon during the war, General von Steinwehr was not. He was considered likeable, intelligent, and tactically skillful. Even so, when the XI and XII were consolidated to form the XX Corps in April 1864, he lost his division. He was offered command of a brigade but declined it and was unemployed after April 16. Disappointed at not being promoted to major general, he resigned his commission on July 3, 1865.

After the war, Steinwehr became a geographer and cartographer. He was a professor at Yale University, where he wrote three geography textbooks and produced and published several other important works. He died in Buffalo, New York, on February 25, 1877, at age fifty-four. He was buried in the Albany Rural Cemetery, Menands, New York. One of his brothers, Wilhelm Ludwig Bogislav von Steinwehr (1774–1854), earned the *Pour le Merite* fighting Napoleon in 1807, and rose to the rank of *Generalleutnant*.

ISAAC INGALLS STEVENS, the descendant of some of Massachusetts's earliest Puritans, was born in North Andover on March 25, 1818. He had a troubled childhood. His father was harsh, his mother died early, and he intensely disliked his stepmother. On one occasion, his father worked him so hard on the family farm that he almost died of a heat stroke. In addition, he was small and quite short, standing 5'1". Stevens later recalled that he almost had a nervous breakdown as a youth. He nevertheless attended Phillips-Andover Academy for more than a year, gained admission to West Point in 1835, and finished at the top of his class in 1839 (1/31). Commissioned second lieutenant of engineers, he spent seven years building fortifications on the New England coast. He advanced to first lieutenant in 1840—an unusually rapid promotion.

Stevens continued to distinguish himself in Mexico, serving as adjutant of General Scott's engineers at Vera Cruz, and earning brevets to captain and major for gallant and meritorious conduct at Contreras, Churubusco, and Chapultepec. On September 13, 1847, during the final assault on Mexico City, he was seriously wounded.

Lieutenant Stevens returned to engineering duties after he recovered but resigned his commission in 1853 to become territorial governor of Washington. On his way to his assignment, he simultaneously served as director for exploration for the Northern Pacific Railroad survey, and, in the process opened up one hundred thousand square miles to white settlement. He was a very effective governor, although he was sometimes heavy-handed and often arbitrary. He ruled by martial law, jailed judges, and once pardoned himself after he was held in contempt of court. He made every effort to settle the Indian problems peacefully, but when the Yakima War broke out in 1855, he crushed it fiercely and, with the aid of the army, put the surviving Indians on a reservation.

Stevens was governor of Washington Territory from 1853 to 1857 and the territorial delegate to the U.S. House of Representatives from March 4, 1857 to March 3, 1861. He was defeated for re-election because of his support for the pro-slavery John C. Breckinridge–Joseph Lane presidential ticket in 1860. (Joseph Lane was his close personal friend.) He volunteered to rejoin the army when the Civil War broke out. There was some reluctance to accept him but, after the Bull Run disaster, he was named colonel of the 79th New York Infantry, the "Highlanders." The regiment was demoralized and on the edge of mutiny after Manassas, where its colonel was killed, but Stevens quickly put things in order and won the respect of his men. After he was promoted to brigadier general on September 28, 1861, they petitioned to be transferred to his brigade.

Sent to South Carolina, Stevens fought at Port Royal and led a division at the Battle of Secessionville (June 16, 1862). Here he was forced to lead an attack against his will and suffered 25 percent casualties. Sent back to Virginia, he fought in the Second Battle of Bull Run and at Chantilly (September 1), where he grabbed the colors of his old regiment (the banner of Saint Andrew's Cross) after a standard bearer was wounded and rallied his troops. Advancing into heavy Confederate fire, he was shot in the temple and died before he hit the ground. He was forty-four. He was buried in Island Cemetery, Newport, Rhode Island.

Abraham Lincoln and Secretary of War Stanton were reportedly considering placing him in charge of the Army of Virginia at the time of his death. He was posthumously promoted to major general.

Stevens fathered five children. His only son, Hazard Stevens, was severely wounded near his father at Chantilly. As far as is known, Hazard and P. B. Van Trump were the first men to climb Mount Rainier in Washington State. Hazard earned the Congressional Medal of Honor later in the war and was brevetted brigadier general for his part in breaking General Lee's lines on April 2, 1865.

JOHN DUNLAP STEVENSON was born on June 8, 1821, in Staunton, Virginia. He attended the College of South Carolina before setting up a law practice in Franklin County, Missouri, in 1842. He was a company commander in the 1st Missouri Mounted Regiment during the Mexican War and took part in the New Mexico Campaign. Discharged in June 1847, he returned to Missouri and was elected to the state legislature. When the Civil War began, Stevenson adhered to the Union, despite his Southern birth and background. He became colonel of the 7th

Missouri Infantry on June 1, 1861. Known as the "Irish 7th," it served in Missouri before being transferred to Grant's Army of the Tennessee in the summer of 1862. It was used mainly on guard and security duty until 1863. Stevenson, meanwhile, was promoted to brigade commander in November 1862. He became a brigadier general on March 4, 1863.

Stevenson led "the Irish Brigade" of the XVII Corps in Grant's decisive Vicksburg Campaign and distinguished himself in the Battle of Champion Hill, where he broke the Confederate left flank. He took part in the Siege of Vicksburg, after which he commanded the Subdistrict of Corinth. He resigned his commission on April 22, 1864, but was recommissioned on August 7 and assigned to the Department of West Virginia, where he commanded a division. He was mustered out of volunteer service in January 1866 and brevetted major general the following month.

John Stevenson was commissioned colonel in the Regular Army on July 28, 1866, and assumed command of the 30th U.S. Infantry Regiment. Apparently unsuccessful in this role, he was without an assignment in early 1869 and was discharged at the end of 1870. He practiced law in St. Louis for the remainder of his life and died there on January 22, 1897. He was seventy-five. He was buried in Bellefontaine Cemetery, St. Louis.

THOMAS GREELY STEVENSON was born in Boston, Massachusetts, on February 3, 1836. Interested in military affairs from childhood, he enlisted in the Massachusetts Militia as soon as his age would permit and, by 1861, was a major in the 4th Massachusetts Militia Battalion. He was appointed colonel of the 24th Massachusetts Militia Regiment on December 3, 1861. His former battalion formed the core of this new regiment.

Stevenson commanded the 24th in Burnside's North Carolina Expedition and fought in the Union victories on Roanoke Island and at New Bern. When most of the U.S. Army was transferred back to Virginia, Stevenson (a brigade commander since April 1862) remained behind. He participated in the Goldsboro Expedition of December

1862, a minor Union victory, but mostly his was a quiet sector. Thomas Stevenson was appointed brigadier general on December 24, 1862, but his promotion expired on March 4, 1863. He was re-appointed on April 9, and this time was confirmed.

Stevenson participated in the Siege of Charleston in 1863, where he contracted malaria in the South Carolina swamps. His brigade was in reserve during the Battle of Fort Wagner. He became a division commander in April 1864. Sent back to Virginia, he was part of Burnside's IX Corps during the Overland Campaign and was considered one of Burnside's best generals. He was resting under a tree during the Battle of Spotsylvania on May 10, 1864, when a Confederate sharpshooter shot him in the back of the head, killing him instantly. He was twenty-eight. He is buried in Mount Auburn Cemetery, Cambridge, Massachusetts. His brother Robert (1838–1928) was brevetted brigadier general in 1865.

JAMES HUGHES STOKES was born on July 11, 1816, in Havre de Grace, Maryland, but later moved to Baltimore. Admitted to West Point in 1831, he graduated in 1835 (17/56) and was commissioned brevet second lieutenant in the artillery. He was stationed at Fort Hamilton, New York before fighting the Creeks (1836) and the Seminoles (1836–38). He was also involved in transporting the Cherokees to Indian Territory. Promoted to second lieutenant in 1836, first lieutenant in 1838, and captain in 1839, when he transferred to the quartermaster branch. He resigned his commission in 1843 and became the proprietor of a glass factory in New York. He later went into the railroad business and from 1858 to 1861 was an executive with Illinois Central.

In April 1861, when the war had just begun, Stokes removed twenty thousand stands of arms from the St. Louis armory to Springfield, Illinois. This deprived the Rebels of badly needed weapons and materially contributed to saving St. Louis for the Union, for which he received a vote of thanks from the Illinois legislature. He was then employed by the state of Illinois in securing arms for the state's volunteers. He also organized the Chicago Board of Trade Battery but did not formally join the Union Army until July

31, 1862, as captain and battery commander. He fought at Perryville, Stones River, Chickamauga, the Siege of Chattanooga, and the Battle of Missionary Ridge and briefly commanded the artillery for a cavalry division.

In early 1864, Stokes was promoted to lieutenant colonel in the quartermaster branch. He was quartermaster general of the Military Division of the Mississippi (February–August 1864) and assistant adjutant general and *de facto* chief of staff of the Washington defenses from August 1864 to August 1865. He was advanced to brigadier general of volunteers on July 22, 1865—one of the last men so appointed. He was mustered out on August 24.

Because of a disease he contracted in Florida, General Stokes went blind in 1868. He nevertheless worked in the real estate business in Chicago until 1880, when he moved to New York City. He died there on December 27, 1890, at age seventy-four. He is buried in Washington Street Cemetery, Geneva, New York.

CHARLES JOHN STOLBRAND was born near Kristianstad, Sweden, on May 11, 1821. He was one of nine illegitimate children of Adolf Fredrik Tornerhjelm and his chambermaid and mistress, Christina Möller. He entered the Royal Wendes Artillery Regiment as an officer-cadet in 1839, when he changed his name from Möller to Stahlbrand. He earned his commission and fought in the First Schleswig War against Prussia and on the side of Denmark. He resigned his Swedish commission and emigrated to the United States in 1850 with his wife and three-year-old son. Changing his name to Stolbrand, he settled in Chicago, Illinois. He worked as a land surveyor and a clerk in the Cook County Recorders' Office. Prominent in local Swedish affairs, he organized what became Battery G of the 2nd Illinois Light Artillery when the Civil War began. It was accepted into Federal service on October 5, 1861, with Stolbrand as captain. He was promoted to major on December 3.

Sent to Tennessee in 1862, he fought at Forts Henry and Donelson, Shiloh, the Siege of Corinth, and the Second Battle of Corinth. He then directed the artillery for Logan's division in the Vicksburg and Chattanooga. Still under Logan, he became chief of artillery of the XVII Corps and served until May 19, 1864, when (while out on a reconnaissance) he was captured by a Confederate patrol near Kingston, Georgia, and was sent to Andersonville. He eventually escaped and rejoined his command in October. During the March to the Sea, Stolbrand commanded an artillery brigade of ten batteries (forty-six guns) and almost one thousand men.

Annoyed and depressed because he had not been promoted, Stolbrand submitted his resignation at the end of January 1865. Sherman, who did not want to lose him, sent him to Washington, D.C., with dispatches to be delivered directly to Abraham Lincoln. One of them recommended Stolbrand for promotion. Lincoln promoted him to brigadier general on the spot. His appointment was dated March 11, 1865, with a date of rank of February 18. He was given command of an infantry brigade in the XVII Corps and led it in the last weeks of the war.

After being assigned to the District of Kansas for six months, General Stolbrand was mustered out in January 1866. He settled in Columbia, South Carolina, where he joined the Carpetbagger regime. He was a presidential elector for Ulysses S. Grant in 1868 and was warden of the state penitentiary. After home rule was re-established, Stolbrand was superintendent of the new Federal courthouse and post office in Charleston, South Carolina. He died in Charleston on February 3, 1894, at age sevventy-two. General Stolbrand was buried in Arlington National Cemetery.

CHARLES POMEROY STONE was born on September 30, 1824, in Greenfield, Massachusetts, into a family of Puritan descent. He entered West Point in 1841, graduated in 1845 (7/41), and was commissioned brevet second lieutenant of ordnance. He was retained at the Academy as an assistant professor of geography, history, and ethics (1845–46). Brief tours of duty at the Watervliet Arsenal in New York and Fort Monroe, Virginia, followed before being sent to Mexico. He fought in the Siege of Vera Cruz and all the way to Mexico City, earning a promotion to second lieutenant and brevets to first lieutenant and captain for Molino del Rey and Chapultepec, respectively. He was promoted to first lieutenant (substantive rank) in 1850.

Stone continued to advance in the peacetime army and was commander of the Fort Monroe Arsenal (1850–51) and was chief of ordnance of the Pacific Division (1851–55). He also spent two years in Europe (1848–50). He resigned his commission in 1856 and went to work as a banker in San Francisco. Later he worked for the Mexican government, surveying the states of Sonora and Lower California. He was acting U.S. consul at Guaymas, Mexico for a year, and was living in Washington, D.C., on January 1, 1861, when he rejoined the army as a colonel. Initially, he was in charge of the capital defenses. He commanded a brigade in Robert Patterson's army during the Bull Run Campaign. He was promoted to brigadier general on August 6, 1861, to rank from May 17, making him the eighth highest ranking man in the Union Army. This was the high point of his war.

Stone was given command of a division (called "the Corps of Observation") on the Upper Potomac. One of his brigade commanders, Edward D. Baker, rashly attacked Confederates at Ball's Bluff near Leesburg, Virginia, on October 21 and was slaughtered. Stone was made the scapegoat for this disaster. (Baker, who was killed in action, was a U.S. senator and loyal Republican, so he was not eligible for disgrace, but Stone was.) He already incurred the wrath of the Radical Republicans for ordering his subordinates not to encourage servile insurrection among the African Americans in his area of operations. On the orders of Secretary of War Stanton, he was arrested on January 28, 1862, and held in prison without trial until August. No charges were ever filed against him.

Stone was unemployed from August 1862 to May 1863, despite the fact that General McClellan asked for him and General Hooker requested that he be named chief of staff of the Army of the Potomac. Finally, he was appointed chief of staff of the Army of the Gulf under Nathaniel Banks, another political general. They did not get along well and Banks called Stone a "very weak" man. On April 4, 1864, Stanton stripped him of his volunteer commission, and he reverted to the rank of colonel, Regular Army. He was held partially responsible for the disastrous Red River Campaign of 1864 (as a scapegoat, Stone was always an easy target) and he was unemployed until

August 1864. After briefly commanding a brigade in the Army of the Potomac, he resigned his commission on September 13, 1864.

In the civilian economy, Stone worked as a mining engineer until 1870, when he became chief of staff to the Khedive of Egypt. (William T. Sherman was among those who recommended him.) He held this post for thirteen years and did a fine job, establishing an Egyptian General Staff, expanding the country's boundaries, and establishing schools for the soldiers and their families. He returned to the United States in 1883. After working for a canal company in Florida, he was chief engineer for the Statue of Liberty project in New York Harbor. He died in New York City of pneumonia on January 24, 1887, at age sixty-two. He was buried in the West Point Cemetery. His son John was a pioneer in the field of radio technology.

ROY STONE was born on October 16, 1836, in Plattsburgh, New York. Stone's father owned a large estate. He attended Union College in Schenectady, New York, from which he graduated in 1856. He became an engineer, a lumberman, and a major in the militia.

Stone was of average height but stood erect, was handsome, sported close-cropped hair and beard, and had a commanding appearance. He had no difficulty getting his orders obeyed. Within two weeks after the Rebels fired on Fort Sumter, Stone was energetically enlisting volunteers to fight for the Union. He formed the Raftsman Guards (101 men), mostly from tough lumbermen. They joined the Bucktail Regiment, which was redesignated 13th Pennsylvania Reserve Infantry Regiment. A three-year unit, it was mustered in to Federal service on June 21 with Stone as its major. It first saw action at Dranesville, Virginia, which was a Union victory. It fought well.

In May 1862, the regiment was divided. Stone was placed in charge of a battalion of six companies and joined the Army of the Potomac. It fought in the Seven Days battles, including Mechanicsville, where Stone and three companies were cut off by A. P. Hill's Light Division but eventually worked their way through the swamp and returned to Union lines. Stone then covered the retreat of McCall's Division, although portions of the battalion were overwhelmed. Stone lost more than half his men and returned to U.S. lines with only six officers and 125 men. He was highly praised by Generals George A. McCall, John F. Reynolds, and Truman Seymour.

After Gaines' Mill, Stone was ordered back to Pennsylvania, where he organized the 149th Pennsylvania (2nd Bucktail) Infantry, which was posted to the Washington defenses. Stone was promoted to brigadier general on November 29, 1862, and was given command of a brigade in the I Corps on February 16, 1863. Meanwhile, for political reasons, his nomination for brigadier general was withdrawn on February 12, and he reverted to the rank of colonel. Why he was not renominated is a mystery because he was obviously a fine commander. He led his brigade at Chancellorsville and on the first day of the Battle of Gettysburg (July 1). Here, while conducting a delaying action near the McPherson Barn west of the town, he again distinguished himself in heavy fighting, but the Rebels turned thirty-four guns on his men. His 149th Pennsylvania suffered 74.4 percent casualties and the 150th Pennsylvania lost 263 out of its 400 men, or 65.7 percent casualties. (Stone Avenue at Gettysburg was named in his honor). He was severely wounded by minié balls in the arm and hip and was carried to the McPherson barn, where he was captured when the army retreated. He was paroled on July 4 and returned to duty on October 31. After a period of light duty, he was given a brigade in the V Corps on March 23, 1864, which included his old 149th and 150th Pennsylvania Regiments. When he returned, his men cheered and threw their hats in the air. "We fairly worship him," one of his soldiers wrote. But the replacement troops he received from Pennsylvania did not measure up to the standards of his veterans. Also, when veteran officers are severely wounded and return to duty months later, they often do not possess their former *elan*. Such was the case with Roy Stone.

Stone's next (and last) battle was the Wilderness, which was his worst action of the war. During this battle, his brigade performed poorly, was routed by a Confederate surprise attack, and Stone was accused of being drunk. (The charges appear to be true.) On the second day of this battle (May 6), his horse fell on him, reinjured his hip wound from Gettysburg, and ended his combat career. He submitted his resignation on July 28, but it was not acted upon. On September 7, 1864, he was brevetted brigadier general and assumed command of Camp Curtin near Harrisburg,

Pennsylvania (a volunteer depot), and in December, became commandant of the prison at Alton, Illinois. Apparently, this duty did not suit him, so he resigned his commission effective January 27, 1865. This time it was accepted.

General Stone became an engineer in civilian life and was involved in several important projects. He blew up the "Hell Gate" rocks and removed the bars in New York City Harbor, invented a form of elevated railroad for Philadelphia, and invented a suction dredge for harbor work. Eventually, his interest turned to road work, and on October 3, 1893, Stone established the Office of Road Inquiry in the Department of Agriculture. This grew into the Federal Highway Administration.

Stone returned to the colors in 1898 as a brigadier general. He was chief engineer of U.S. forces in Puerto Rico during the Spanish-American War and briefly commanded an ad hoc battle group. It was here that, according to his family, he contracted the disease that eventually caused his death.

General Stone returned to the United States and left government service in 1899. His last employment was as chief engineer of the Union Terminal Company in New York City. He died in Mendham, New Jersey, on August 5, 1905, at age sixty-eight. He was buried in Arlington National Cemetery.

Stone had a son, and a daughter named Romaine, who married a British baron and became Lady Monson.

GEORGE STONEMAN was born on August 8, 1822, on his family's farm in Busti, New York, the oldest of ten children. He attended the Jamestown Academy, entered West Point in 1842 (where his roommate was Stonewall Jackson), graduated in 1846 (33/59), and was commissioned brevet second lieutenant in the Mormon Battalion, the only unit in American military history recruited solely from one religious body. He served in Mexico but, by the time his battalion arrived, the fighting was over. He spent most of the next fifteen years on frontier duty, where he fought Indians in California and Oregon as well as Cortina's marauders on the Rio Grande. He also took a leave of absence and spent a year in Europe. He was part of the garrison of the Cavalry School for Practice at Carlisle, Pennsylvania, when the Civil War began. Meanwhile, he was promoted to second lieutenant (1847), first lieutenant (1854), captain (1855), and major (May 9, 1861).

Stoneman served on General McClellan's staff during the western Virginia Campaign of 1861. He was promoted to brigadier general on August 13, and was named commander of the Cavalry Reserve for the Army of the Potomac. He led a cavalry division in the Peninsula Campaign. His relationship with McClellan, however, was not good; McClellan thought cavalry should be split up into small units and assigned to infantry brigades, while Stoneman wanted it employed in large formations. After the Union defeat in the Seven Days battles, Stoneman was transferred to the command of an infantry division in the II Corps. He took charge of Phil Kearny's division in the III Corps after that officer was killed at Chantilly. He assumed command of the entire corps on October 30 and led it in the Fredericksburg disaster.

When General Hooker assumed command of the Army of the Potomac, he united the cavalry into a single corps and named Stoneman commander. He was promoted to major general on March 16, 1863. Stoneman's performance during the Chancellorsville Campaign, however, left much to be desired. Sent on a raid into Lee's rear, he bogged down on the Rapidan and accomplished little. Hooker relieved Stoneman of his command and sent him back to Washington for medical treatment. (He suffered from chronic hemorrhoids.) Here, Stoneman was placed in charge of the U.S. Cavalry Bureau, a desk job.

In early 1864, Stoneman asked his old friend, General John Schofield, the commander of the Army of the Ohio, to give him another field command. He was named commander of the cavalry division of the Army of the Ohio, which he led in the Atlanta Campaign. He decided to launch a raid to free the Union prisoners at Andersonville. It was a disastrous failure, and Stoneman was captured at Clinton, Georgia, on July 31. It was stated that Stoneman was the highest-ranking Union officer captured during the war, but he was not (see the essay on William B. Franklin.) In any case, he was exchanged in only three months, thanks to the intercession of his friend, William T. Sherman. After briefly commanding the Department of the Ohio, Stoneman was placed in charge of the Department of the Tennessee, from which he led a successful raid into North Carolina near the end of the war. After the surrender, he commanded occupation forces in Memphis and Petersburg. He was mustered out of volunteer service on September 1, 1866, and reverted to the rank of colonel.

Stoneman was a Democrat who opposed the harsh Reconstruction policies of the Radical Republicans. As a result, he was transferred to Arizona. Here, his men massacred a group of Pinal and Aravaipa Apache (April 30, 1871), who had already surrendered. This led to a series of skirmishes, battles, and campaigns, which lasted until 1875. For his failures, Stoneman was relieved of his command and requested a disability retirement at the rank of major general. This was granted in August 1871. Three days later, however, President Grant revoked it, forcing Stoneman to retire as a colonel.

George Stoneman settled in California and established a four-hundred-acre ranch in the San Gabriel Valley. He was elected state railroad commissioner in 1879 and governor in 1882, serving from 1883 to 1887. Here he clashed with the Southern Pacific Railroad and tried unsuccessfully to limit its power, but it controlled the legislature. Stoneman was not renominated for a second term and retired from politics. He returned to New York for medical treatment around 1893 but had a stroke in April 1894 and never recovered. He died on September 5, 1894, in Buffalo, New York. He was seventy-two. His remains were interred in Bentley Cemetery, Lakewood, New York.

EDWIN HENRY STOUGHTON (pronounced "Stowton") was born on June 23, 1838, in Chester, Vermont. He enrolled in the United States Military Academy in 1854 and graduated in 1859 (17/22). Commissioned brevet second lieutenant in the 4th U.S. Infantry on July 1, he was promoted to second lieutenant on September 1 and was stationed at Fort Columbus, New York. He resigned his commission on March 4, 1861, but helped form the 4th Vermont Infantry Regiment when the war began. He was promoted to colonel when the regiment was mustered into Federal service on September 21, 1861. At age twenty-three, he was reportedly the youngest of the Union colonels.

Stoughton did a good job commanding the 4th Vermont in the Peninsula and Seven Days campaigns and at Antietam; as a result, he was given command of a brigade in the VI Corps in October 1862 and was promoted to brigadier general on November 5, when he was transferred to the command of a brigade in the Washington defenses. At age twenty-four, he was the youngest Union general at that time. His promotion, however, was not acted upon by the Senate and expired on March 4, 1863. Four days later, Confederate partisan ranger John Singleton Mosby led a daring raid on Stoughton's headquarters at Fairfax, Virginia and, in the middle of thousands of Union troops, captured the general and thirty-two of his men, as well as fifty-eight horses. President Lincoln declared that he could stand the loss of the general, but he hated to lose those horses.

Stoughton was asleep when Mosby woke him up and informed him, he was a prisoner. His career was ruined by the "bedroom raid." He was held in Libby Prison, Richmond, until May when he was exchanged. He was not offered another command and, realizing that his military career was finished, the disgraced general resigned that same month. He later became a lawyer and was practicing in New York City when he died on Christmas Day, December 25, 1868, at the age of thirty. He was buried in Immanuel Cemetery, Bellows Falls, Vermont. His brother, Charles Bradley Stoughton, was the colonel of the 4th Vermont Infantry. He lost an eye in the Gettysburg Campaign and left the service in 1864, but was brevetted brigadier general at the end of the war.

GEORGE CROCKETT STRONG was born in Stockbridge, Vermont, on October 16, 1832. He attended the Williston Seminary but dropped out in 1851. He was admitted to West Point in 1853, graduated in 1857 (5/38), and was commissioned brevet second lieutenant of ordnance. He was posted to various arsenals in Pennsylvania, Virginia, and Alabama, and was a first lieutenant and assistant commander of the Watervliet Arsenal in New York when the war began.

Strong was an ordnance officer on the staff of General McDowell during the First Bull Run Campaign. He was later on the staff of General McClellan (July–September 1861) and General Butler (September 1861–March 1862). He was promoted to major and assistant adjutant general on October 1, 1861.

Major Strong accompanied Butler to Louisiana and, as de facto chief of staff of the Department of the Gulf, commanded successful expeditions against Ship Island, Mississippi, and Ponchatoula, Louisiana, where he destroyed a large Confederate supply train. On March 23, 1863, he was promoted to brigadier general.

Strong was transferred to South Carolina that summer and commanded Union forces on St. Helena Island in June 1863. He was given command of a brigade in the X Corps (Department of the South) on July 5. On July 18, he led the famous assault on Battery Wagner (a.k.a. Fort Wagner) on Morris Island. Here he was struck in the thigh by a musket ball. Medically evacuated to New York City, he died of tetanus (lockjaw) on July 30, 1863. He was thirty years old. He was posthumously promoted to major general, to rank from the day of his wounding. General Strong was buried in Green-Wood Cemetery, Brooklyn, New York.

Strong was the author of the book, *Cadet Life at West Point*, which was anonymously published in 1862.

WILLIAM KERLEY STRONG was born in Duanesburg, New York, on April 30, 1805, the son of a Revolutionary War soldier who fought in the Battle of Trenton and lost a leg serving under George Washington at Germantown. William became a wool merchant and became quite wealthy. In 1839, for example, he built an 11,634-square-foot home overlooking Seneca Lake, which he called "Rose Hill Mansion." It is now a museum.

Strong was a Democrat who was known for his inspiring pro–Union speeches. He retired early to enjoy his wealth and was traveling in Egypt when the Civil War began. When he heard the news, Strong hurried to France, where he purchased arms for the Union cause. Despite his lack of military training, Abraham Lincoln appointed him brigadier general of volunteers on September 28, 1861.

General Strong initially commanded the Benton Barracks under General Fremont. In March 1862, he was placed in command of the District of Cairo, replacing General Eleazar Paine, who was sacked for disobeying orders. He was named commander of the District of St. Louis on June 16, 1863, under General Schofield. He resigned his commission on October 20. Still active, he met with Secretary of War Stanton in November, where he advocated enlisting African Americans to help fill New York's draft quota. Shortly thereafter, in Central Park, he was thrown from a carriage he was driving. Paralyzed for the remainder of his life, he died of apoplexy in New York City on March 16, 1867, at age sixty-one. He was buried in Green-Wood Cemetery, Brooklyn. General Strong was married twice and fathered nine children.

DAVID STUART was born on March 12, 1816, in Brooklyn, New York, but his family moved to Michigan when he was young and eventually settled in Detroit. His father was prominent in the fur trading business and served a term as state treasurer of Michigan. David was educated at Phillips Academy, Oberlin College, and Amherst College, from which he graduated in 1838. He then studied law, was admitted to the bar, and set up a practice in Detroit. He was elected to Congress as a Democrat in 1852 but was defeated for re-election in 1854. He served in the House of Representatives from 1853 to 1855. After that, he moved to Chicago and became a lawyer for the Illinois Central Railroad.

When the Civil War began, Stuart raised two thousand volunteers for the Union cause and equipped them at his own expense. He was named lieutenant colonel of the 42nd Illinois Infantry on July 22, 1861, and colonel of the 55th Illinois on October 31. He became a brigade commander on March 1, 1862, but (as part of Sherman's command) was badly wounded in the shoulder at Shiloh on April 6. He returned to duty in October as commander of a brigade in the XIII Corps at Memphis. He was promoted to brigadier general effective November 29, 1862.

General Stuart commanded his brigade at Chickasaw Bayou (aka Chickasaw Bluffs) in December 1862 and at Arkansas Post (January 9–11, 1863). His promotion to brigadier general was rejected by the Senate on March 11, and he resigned from the army on April 3. He returned home and resumed the practice of law. He died on September 11, 1868, in Detroit, Michigan. He is buried there in Elmwood Cemetery. His brother, Robert Stuart, Jr., was a lieutenant in the 2nd New York Cavalry when he drowned in Cedar Creek, Virginia, in 1863.

FREDERICK SHEARER STUMBAUGH was born near Shippensburg, Pennsylvania, on April 17, 1817. He was educated locally, read law, was admitted to the bar in 1854, and set up a practice in Chambersburg. Always interested in the militia, he helped form the 2nd Pennsylvania Infantry, a 90-day regiment, which was activated for Federal service with himself as colonel on April 20, 1861, only a week after Fort Sumter surrendered. It performed guard duty on the Potomac fords until its enlistments expired.

Stumbaugh was not formally employed again until October 26, 1861, when he became colonel of the 77th Pennsylvania Infantry. Part of Buell's Army of the Ohio, it fought at Shiloh on the second day (April 7, 1862) and in the Siege of Corinth. It served in the Kentucky (Heartland) Campaign of 1862 and took part in the Battle of Perryville. The regiment was stationed at Nashville during the winter of 1862/63.

Frederick S. Stumbaugh was a fine regimental commander but why he was appointed brigadier general effective November 29, 1862, is not known. He had never served more than one day at a time as an acting brigade commander. His promotion was revoked by the Senate on January 22, 1863. Meanwhile, his health deteriorated, and he suffered from diarrhea and rheumatism. This is apparently why he resigned his commission. He was discharged on May 15, 1863. He then returned to Pennsylvania and his law practice. A Republican, he was elected to the Pennsylvania House of Representatives in 1865 and 1866 but did not seek re-election in 1867.

General Stumbaugh eventually moved to Iowa and then to Topeka, Kansas, where he settled. He served a term in the Kansas legislature (1879–1880). He died in Topeka on February 25, 1897, at age seventy-nine, while playing chess and just after he was checkmated. He was buried in the Topeka Cemetery.

SAMUEL DAVIS STURGIS was born in Shippensburg, Pennsylvania, on June 11, 1822. He graduated from West Point in 1846 (32/42) and was commissioned brevet second lieutenant in the 2nd Dragoons. His first assignment was Mexico. While out on a reconnaissance near Buena Vista, he was captured by the Mexicans on February 20, 1847, but was freed eight days later, after Santa Anna was defeated. He was then sent to California, where he served until 1851.

He spent most of the rest of his antebellum career on the frontier, fighting Apache, Cheyenne, Cherokee, Kiowa, and Comanche in New Mexico, Kansas, and Indian Territory. He was promoted to second lieutenant (1847), first lieutenant (1853), captain (1855), and major (May 3, 1861).

Given a brigade in the Army of the West, Sturgis was posted to Missouri and served under Nathaniel Lyon. He assumed command of the defeated Union forces after General Lyon was killed at Wilson's Creek on August 10, 1861. He was brevetted lieutenant colonel, Regular Army, for his actions that day and, on March 7, 1862, was promoted to brigadier general of volunteers. After further assignments in Missouri and Kansas, he was placed in command of a brigade in the Washington defenses in August 1862. He fought in the Second Battle of Bull Run as a brigade commander and at South Mountain, Antietam, and Fredericksburg as commander of a division in the IX Corps.

Sam Sturgis was transferred to the West in late 1863 and commanded Union cavalry in Kentucky. He was chief of cavalry for the Department of the Ohio from July 1863 to April 1864, and organized Cincinnati for defense during John Hunt Morgan's famous Ohio raid. He was highly successful against Rebels in eastern Tennessee and western North Carolina. He was then transferred to western Tennessee to operate against General Forrest.

There can be no doubt that Sturgis vastly underestimated Nathan Bedford Forrest. He amused himself drinking and cavorting in Memphis and did not properly prepare his troops for action, either psychologically or logistically. He did not feel he had to. He invaded northern Mississippi with well over 10,000 men against 3,200 ill-equipped Rebels led by a first-grade dropout. On June 10, 1864, he marched straight into a Forrest trap at Brice's Cross Roads, and, by the end of the day the survivors of his command were fleeing for their lives. It took them ten days to travel from Memphis to Brice's Cross Roads. It only took them only sixty-four hours to get back, but they were unencumbered by artillery, caissons, wagons, or ambulances. All of them were lost to the Confederates, as well as more than 1,200 men killed and wounded, and 1,600 captured. It was one of the most embarrassing defeats in the history of the U.S. Army. General Sherman fired Sturgis on June 13. He was unemployed for the rest of the war. He was still awaiting orders on August 15, 1865, when he was mustered out of volunteer service. He was brevetted major general of volunteers in 1868.

Sturgis reverted to the rank of lieutenant colonel in 1865 and was given command of the 6th Cavalry in Austin, Texas. He was promoted to colonel of the 7th Cavalry on May 6, 1869. He was on detached duty as superintendent of the Mounted Recruiting Service and commander of the Cavalry Depot in St. Louis in 1876, while his second-in-command, Lieutenant Colonel George Armstrong Custer, led the regiment in the Great Sioux War. Much of the 7th Cavalry was destroyed in the Battle of Little Big Horn, Montana, on June 25, 1876. Sturgis returned to the command of the remnants of the 7th Cavalry and rebuilt it at Fort Lincoln, Dakota Territory. He was governor of the Soldiers' Home in Washington, D.C., from 1881 to 1885.

General Sturgis reached the mandatory retirement age of sixty-four in 1886. He died in Saint Paul, Minnesota, on September 28, 1889, at age sixty-seven. He was buried in Arlington National Cemetery. One of his sons, Lieutenant James G. "Jack" Sturgis, fell with Custer at Little Big Horn. Another son, Samuel Davis Sturgis, Jr. (1861–1933), graduated from

West Point in 1884 and rose to the rank of major general. The Union general's grandson, Lieutenant General Samuel D. Sturgis, III, became chief of engineers for the U.S. Army.

JEREMIAH CUTLER SULLIVAN was born in Madison, Indiana, on October 1, 1830, the son of a justice on the Indiana Supreme Court. He attended the U.S. Naval Academy at Annapolis, graduated in 1848, became a midshipman, and spent most of the next six years at sea. He resigned his commission in 1854 to study law. In 1861, he helped recruit the 6th Indiana Infantry (a 90-day regiment) and was mustered in as a captain on April 18. He fought in the Battle of Philippi in western Virginia on June 3. On June 19, he was named colonel of the 13th Indiana Infantry. He returned to western Virginia and fought at Rich Mountain and Cheat Mountain that summer and fall. He was given command of a brigade in January 1862. He took part in the Battle of Kernstown on March 23, 1862, which led to his being promoted to brigadier general on April 30.

Transferred to the Western Front, Sullivan fought at Iuka and the Second Battle of Corinth, where he was wounded by a shell splinter on October 3. He was given command of the District of Jackson, Tennessee, in November. He tried to defend the sector against Nathan Bedford Forrest but with limited success.

Sullivan was assigned to General Grant's staff as acting inspector general in the spring of 1863. After Vicksburg fell, he briefly served as General McPherson's chief of staff before being transferred to the Department of West Virginia. Given command of a division, he was tasked with guarding the B & O Railroad from Confederate raiders. He was wounded in the head and hand and his horse was killed during the Battle of Piedmont (June 5, 1864).

During the summer of 1864, David Hunter, the commander of the Army of the Shenandoah, became dissatisfied with Sullivan's lack of initiative. He replaced him with George Crook on July 16. He briefly commanded a brigade in the Kanawha District of West Virginia that fall but was unemployed for most of the rest of the war. Neither Sheridan nor Hancock had positions for him. He resigned his commission on May 11, 1865, and was not brevetted major general in the omnibus promotions just after the war.

General Sullivan lived in Oakland, Maryland, after the war but moved to California around 1878. He never resumed his law practice and subsisted by holding a series of minor clerical jobs. He died on October 21, 1890, in Oakland, California. He was sixty years old. He was buried in Mountain View Cemetery, Oakland.

ALFRED SULLY was born in Philadelphia, Pennsylvania, on May 22, 1820. His father was Thomas Sully, a famous painter. Alfred entered West Point in 1837, graduated in 1841 (34/52), and was commissioned second lieutenant in the 2nd U.S. Infantry. Between garrison and recruiting assignments, he fought the Seminoles in Florida (1841–42), the Mexicans at Vera Cruz (1847), and the Sioux and Cheyenne in Minnesota and Nebraska. He spent several years in California and a year in Europe. He was promoted to first lieutenant in 1847 and captain in 1850.

When the Civil War began, Sully was initially posted to northern Missouri and Kansas, and to the Washington, D.C., defenses. On February 22, 1862, he was named colonel of the 1st Minnesota Infantry. Sent to Virginia, he participated in the Peninsula Campaign, including the Siege of Yorktown and the Battle of West Point. He distinguished himself in the Battle of Seven Pines (Fair Oaks), where a bullet grazed his ear. He led a brigade in the II Corps during the Seven Days battles, South Mountain, and Antietam. He was commended for his performance at Malvern Hill (July 1) and was promoted to brigadier general on September 26, 1862. He also fought at Fredericksburg (where he was slightly wounded when a bullet grazed his leg) and at Chancellorsville, where General John Gibbon relieved him of his command for failing to quell a mutiny by the 34th New York. Gibbon attempted to have Sully court-martialed for dereliction of duty, but a court of inquiry cleared him of those charges. His Civil War career, however, was over.

In May 1863, Sully (who was now in professional exile) was transferred to the District of Dakota, where he served for the rest of the war. He gained fame for committing several reprisals (atrocities/massacres) against the Lakota Sioux. After his science officer and topographical engineer was killed, Sully ordered the Indians responsible be decapitated and that their heads be mounted on poles overlooking the Missouri River. He was brevetted major general of volunteers in March 1865.

Mustered out of volunteer service on April 30, 1866, Sully reverted to the rank of major but was promoted to lieutenant colonel two months later. He continued to serve in the Indian Wars in the Northwest and did a tour of duty in Louisiana (1871–74). His health was poor in the last years of his life, but he was nevertheless given command of the 21st U.S. Infantry in December 1873. He died at Fort Vancouver, Washington Territory, on April 27, 1879. He was fifty-eight. His commanding officer, General O. O. Howard, issued an Obituary Order, praising Sully for his "marked ability . . . unflinching courage" and his "generosity and honesty of spirit." Howard ordered his men to wear a badge of mourning for the next thirty days.

General Sully was interred in Laurel Hill Cemetery, Philadelphia.

EDWIN VOSE "BULL HEAD" SUMNER was born on January 30, 1797, in Boston, Massachusetts. He was a cousin of famous abolitionist and U.S. Senator Charles Sumner. He attended Milton Academy and became a merchant but, dissatisfied with that career, joined the U.S. Army as a second lieutenant in 1819. During his forty-three-year military career—most of which he spent in the cavalry or the dragoons (mounted infantry)—he fought in the Black Hawk War, the Mexican War, various Indian campaigns, "Bleeding Kansas," and the Civil War. He received his nickname because of his booming voice and because a spent musket ball once reportedly bounced off his head during the Battle of Cerro Gordo.

During the antebellum years, Sumner held increasingly responsible positions, including company commander in the 1st Dragoons, commander of the Cavalry School for Practice at Carlisle Barracks, Pennsylvania, commander of Fort Atkinson, Iowa Territory, military governor of New Mexico (1851–1855), commander of the 1st Cavalry Regiment (1855–57), commander of Fort Leavenworth (1856–57), commander of a punitive expedition against the Cheyenne (1858), and commander of the Department of the West (1858–61). General Scott selected him to escort Abraham Lincoln from Springfield to Washington, D.C., in early 1861. Meanwhile, he was promoted to first lieutenant (1825), captain (1833), major (1846), brevet lieutenant colonel for Cerro Gordo (1847), brevet colonel for Molino del Rey (1847), lieutenant colonel (1848), and colonel (1855). When General David Twiggs was dismissed from the army for treason, Lincoln promoted Sumner to brigadier general. Regular Army, on May 12, 1861.

Sumner initially commanded the Department of the Pacific and thus did not take part in the campaigns of 1861. In March 1862, when the Army of the Potomac was organized into corps, Sumner was given command of the II Corps. He commanded it in the Peninsula Campaign, where his performance was definitely mixed and General McClellan, the army commander, expressed a low opinion of him. He wrote to his wife and declared that Sumner was an even "greater fool than I had supposed." He was slow and hesitant in the Battle of Williamsburg (May 5), but his prompt actions in sending reinforcements across the dangerously flooded Chickahominy River during the Battle of Seven Pines prevented a major Union disaster. He also performed well in the Seven Days battles, where he was struck in the arm and hand by spent bullets during the Battle of Frayser's Farm. He was promoted to major general on July 5.

During the Battle of Antietam, Sumner ordered General John Sedgwick to launch an attack into the West Woods. Several historians later deemed this action as reckless. Sedgwick's division was slaughtered. Sumner personally accompanied Sedgwick's men and thus lost control of his other divisions. He was also greatly shaken by the disaster. Major General William B. Franklin, the commander of the VI Corps, wanted to attack with his corps, but Sumner (who was senior to him) refused to allow it. McClellan backed Sumner. This decision materially contributed to the survival of Lee's Army of Northern Virginia.

During the Battle of Fredericksburg, Sumner commanded the Right Grand Division, which included the II Corps, IX Corps, and the Cavalry Division. The battle was yet another disaster, although Sumner bears no blame for it. When Lincoln replaced Burnside as commander of the Army of the Potomac with Joseph Hooker, Sumner asked to be relieved of his command. He was appointed commander of the Department of Missouri but never reached his new post. The oldest corps commander on either side during the Civil War, he became ill and stopped at Syracuse. He died there on March 21, 1863, at age sixty-six. He was buried in Oakland Cemetery, Syracuse, New York.

One of his sons, Edwin V. Sumner, Jr., commanded the 1st New York Mounted Rifles and a cavalry division in the Army of the James. Brevetted brigadier general at the end of the war, he commanded the 7th U.S. Cavalry Regiment (1894–98) and retired as a brigadier general, Regular Army, in 1899. Another son, Samuel S., commanded a cavalry brigade in Cuba during the Spanish–American War and retired as a major general. His daughter Mary married future Confederate Brigadier General Armistead L. Long, who commanded the artillery of the II Corps of Lee's army.

WAGER SWAYNE was born in Columbus, Ohio, on November 10, 1834, the son of an associate justice of the U.S. Supreme Court. He graduated from Yale in 1856 and Cincinnati Law School in 1859. He was practicing law when the Civil War began.

Ohio Governor William Dennison appointed Swayne major of the 43rd Ohio Infantry on August 31, 1861. He was promoted to lieutenant colonel on December 14. He fought in the Battle of Island No. 10, the Siege of Corinth, the Battle of Iuka, and the Second Battle of Corinth (October 3–4, 1862). Here, his regimental commander, Joseph L. Kirby Smith, was mortally wounded and died on October 12. Swayne replaced him and led a decisive counterattack on October 4. For this action, he was awarded the

Congressional Medal of Honor in 1893. He was promoted to colonel on October 18, 1862.

Swayne and his men spent 1863 garrisoning various posts in northern Mississippi and western Tennessee. He continued to perform well in the Atlanta Campaign, Sherman's March to the Sea, and the Carolinas Campaign. On February 2, 1865, during the Battle of River's Bridge, South Carolina, on the Salkehatchie River, he was struck in the right knee by a shell fragment. In great pain, he was taken to an old barn, which was being used as a field hospital. Doctors were unable to save the leg.

Although he only served as an acting brigade commander for a few weeks in 1864, Abraham Lincoln promoted him to brigadier general of volunteers on March 13, 1865. He was brevetted major general in 1866 and mustered out of volunteer service in September 1867.

After the war, General Swayne headed the Freedmen's Bureau in Alabama from 1865 to 1868. He remained in the Regular Army as colonel of the 45th U.S. Infantry Regiment and, as military governor of Alabama, he effectively ran the state from March 2, 1867 to July 14, 1868. His regiment was dissolved in 1869, and he was unemployed until 1870, when he retired from the army.

General Swayne practiced law in Toledo from 1870 until 1881, when he moved to New York City, where he established another law practice, specializing in the representation of telegraph and railroad corporations. He died in New York City on December 18, 1902, at age sixty-eight. He was buried in Arlington National Cemetery.

THOMAS WILLIAM "FIGHTING TOM" SWEENY was born on Christmas Day, December 25, 1820, in Cork, Ireland. His family emigrated to the United States in 1833. When the Mexican War began, he joined the 2nd New York Infantry as a second lieutenant and served in Winfield Scott's Army of Mexico. He was severely wounded in the groin at Cerro Gordo, and his right arm was so badly shattered at Churubusco that it had to be amputated. "Fighting Tom," as his comrades called him, remained in the army after the war, serving with the 2nd U.S. Infantry. He fought in the Yuma River (1850–53) and was wounded in the neck by an arrow in Cocopah County, California, in May 1852.

Sweeny was promoted to first lieutenant in 1851 and to captain on January 19, 1861. When the Civil War began, he was commander of the St. Louis Arsenal, which he declared he would blow up rather than allow it to be captured by secessionists. He was second-in-command to Nathaniel Lyon on May 10, 1861, when his forces surrounded Camp Jackson and compelled it to surrender. Sweeny was named brigadier general in the [pro-Union] Missouri Militia on May 20.

Sweeny accompanied Lyon to Wilson's Creek, where Lyon was killed and Sweeny was wounded in the right leg on August 10. It took him months to recover. He became colonel of the 52nd Illinois Infantry in January 1862 and led it at Fort Donelson. He commanded a brigade in Grant's army at Shiloh, where he was shot in his left foot and twice in his only arm on April 6. He refused to leave the field until the end of the battle. He returned to the command of his regiment in August but again became a brigade commander when General Hackleman was killed at Corinth. Sweeny remained in northern Mississippi in 1863. He was promoted to brigadier general on March 16, 1863.

Tom Sweeny led a division in the XVI Corps during the Atlanta Campaign. During the Battle of Atlanta (July 22, 1864), he blocked John Bell Hood's flanking attack. His corps commander, General Dodge, personally directed one of Sweeny's brigades at a decisive moment. Furious at this breech of protocol, Sweeny castigated Dodge, and the incident ended in a fist fight, which General John Fuller joined on the side of the corps commander. Dodge had Sweeny court-martialed, but he was acquitted; he was not, however, restored to command. (No senior general wanted him.) He was mustered out of volunteer service in August 1865. He was dismissed from the Regular Army on December 29, 1865, for being AWOL; however, he was reinstated in November 1866.

Sweeny was a member of the Fenian Brotherhood, an Irish Republican organization based in the United States. He commanded the Fenian Invasion of Canada in 1866. It failed, and he was imprisoned for breaking the neutrality laws of both Britain and the United States. He was soon released, however, and restored to his post-war rank of major, Regular Army. He retired as a brigadier general in 1870.

General Sweeny's last years were uneventful. He died in Astoria, Long Island, New York, on April 10, 1892, at age seventy-one. He is buried in Green-Wood Cemetery, Brooklyn, New York.

GEORGE SYKES was born on October 9, 1822, in Dover, Delaware. He entered West Point in 1838, graduated in 1842 (39/56), and was commissioned brevet second lieutenant in the 3rd U.S. Infantry. He fought the Seminoles in Florida (1842–43), did garrison duty in Missouri and Louisiana, and took part in the occupation of Texas (1845–46). He fought in the Mexican War, including the Battle of Monterrey. He was with Scott's army all the way from Vera Cruz to Mexico City, earning a promotion to first lieutenant (full rank) and a brevet to captain for gallant and meritorious service at Cerro Gordo. Garrison and frontier duty followed, including skirmishes against the Apache and Navajo. He was promoted to captain (substantive rank) in 1855 and major on May 14, 1861.

Sykes was with the 14th U.S. Infantry at the First Bull Run and was given command of a brigade of regulars in the Washington defenses after that. He was promoted to brigadier general on September 28, 1861. He commanded the Infantry Reserve of the Army of the Potomac during the Peninsula Campaign and was given command of an infantry division in Porter's V Corps on May 18, 1862. Nine of his eleven regiments were Regular Army troops. His performance obviously left something to be desired, although he was brevetted colonel, Regular Army, for his actions at Gaines' Mill (June 27). In any case, his Old Army reputation followed him. There, he was known as "Tardy George" and "Slow Trot Sykes." He was considered tenacious in the defense but slow and ponderous when boldness and initiative were called for.

Sykes's division was involved in heavy fighting at the Second Bull Run but was lightly engaged at Antietam. It was heavily engaged on the northern end of the Union line at Fredericksburg, where it suffered two thousand casualties. It was lightly engaged at Chancellorsville. Meanwhile, Sykes was belatedly promoted to major general on November 29, 1862. After General Meade was named commander of the Army of the Potomac, Sykes succeeded him as commander of the V Corps on June 28, 1863.

George Sykes performed well in the Battle of Gettysburg. His troops supported the crippled III Corps, held the Little Round Top, held the Union left flank, and drove the Rebels across the "Valley of Death." He was less successful in the Mine Run and Bristoe campaigns, where General Meade found him too slow. He was relieved of his command in March 1864, when doctors diagnosed him with a severe case of sciatica, a nerve disfunction which causes pain in the lower back and the back of the leg(s). He returned to duty in September as commander of the District of South Kansas, a backwater post which he held for the rest of the war. He was mustered out of volunteer service in January 1866 and reverted to the rank of lieutenant colonel, Regular Army. He was lieutenant colonel of the 5th U.S. Infantry until 1868, when he became colonel of the 20th U.S. Infantry and was stationed in Baton Rouge, Louisiana. He was later commander of the District of Minnesota (1869–73), Fort Snelling (1873–77), and of the District of the Rio Grande (1877–80).

General Sykes died of cancer in Fort Brown, Texas, on February 8, 1880, at age fifty-seven. He is buried in the West Point Cemetery.

T

TAYLOR – TYNDALE

GEORGE WILLIAM TAYLOR was born in Hunterdon County, New Jersey, on November 22, 1808, the son of a prominent businessman. He graduated from Captain Partridge's Military Academy in Middleton, Connecticut, and was commissioned midshipman in 1827. After four years in the navy, he resigned his commission, returned to New Jersey, and became a farmer. When the Mexican War began, he became a captain in the 10th U.S. Infantry Regiment and served under Zachary Taylor (no relation) in northern Mexico. Discharged in 1848, he spent three years in California, searching for gold near San Francisco. He returned to New Jersey in 1852 and worked with his father in the mining and smelting of iron.

Taylor helped recruit the 3rd New Jersey Infantry when the Civil War began. The governor appointed him colonel on June 4, 1861, and he took part in the First Bull Run and Peninsula Campaigns. When his close friend and mentor, Phil Kearny became a divisional commander, Taylor succeeded him as commander of the 1st New Jersey Brigade. He was promoted to brigadier general on May 12, 1862. After fighting in the Seven Days battles, he was sent to northern Virginia.

On August 27, 1862, he led his brigade on a reconnaissance. Near the Bull Run bridge, he blundered into Stonewall Jackson's entire corps, which quickly routed it. Taylor was seriously wounded in the left leg by artillery shell fragments. He was carried to a hospital in Alexandria via a railroad handcar, and his leg was amputated twenty-six hours after he was wounded. He failed to rally from the operation and died at 4:00 a.m. on September 1, 1862. He was fifty-three. Sources differ as to whether he was buried in the Clinton Presbyterian Churchyard, Clinton, New Jersey, or the Rock Church Cemetery in Hunterdon County, New Jersey. His oldest son Archibald was his aide-de-camp and later served as an officer in the 1st New Jersey Infantry. He became a major in the Marine Corps after the war.

JOSEPH PANNELL TAYLOR was born on May 4, 1796, in Louisville, Kentucky. He was the brother of President Zachary Taylor, the uncle of Confederate Lieutenant General Richard Taylor, and his niece, Sara Knox, married Jefferson Davis. Joseph Taylor married Evelyn McLean, the daughter of a justice on the U.S. Supreme Court. During the War of 1812, he was commissioned third lieutenant in the 28th U.S. Infantry (1813). He was discharged as a first lieutenant in 1815 but rejoined the army as a second lieutenant the following year. He became a first lieutenant in 1817 and a captain in 1825. He was appointed Assistant Commissary General for Subsistence in 1829 and remained in the commissary department for the rest of his long career, with promotions to major (1838), lieutenant colonel (1841), and colonel (1848).

Taylor was appointed Commissary General for Subsistence for the U.S. Army on September 29, 1861, and did a fine job in this vital position. He was promoted to brigadier general, Regular Army, on February 21, 1863. General Taylor died of diarrhea and partial paralysis in Washington, D.C., on June 29, 1864, at age sixty-eight. He was buried in Oak Hill Cemetery, Washington. He was succeeded by Amos B. Eaton.

Joseph Taylor's son, John M. Taylor, was brevetted brigadier general at the end of the war. Another son, Joseph Hancock Taylor, became a lieutenant colonel.

NELSON TAYLOR was born on June 8, 1821, in South Norwalk, Connecticut. His early career was checkered. Educated in local public schools, he joined the army in 1846 as a captain in the 1st New York Infantry and was immediately sent to California. After the war ended in 1848, he chose to remain in the Golden State and was one of first members of the California Senate. He neglected his duties, however, and was expelled from that body due to excessive absences. (He was in New York City on business at the time.) He returned to California and was elected sheriff of San Joaquin County in 1855 but resigned the following year to become a student at Harvard Law School. He graduated in 1860, moved to New York City, and ran for Congress in 1860, but was defeated.

Taylor was commissioned colonel of the 72nd New York on July 23, 1861. He fought in the Peninsula Campaign, including the Battle of Williamsburg, where he was acting brigade commander. He also took part in the Seven Days battles and the Second Battle of Bull Run. He was promoted to brigadier general on September 7, 1862. He was given command of a brigade in the I Corps in November.

Nelson Taylor particularly distinguished himself in the Battle of Fredericksburg. On December 13, he attacked the center of the Confederate line and breached the Richmond, Fredericksburg & Potomac Railroad embankment, a critical position for both sides. He assumed command of his division when General Gibbon was wounded and even held the embankment for a time after he ran out of ammunition. When the Rebels advanced in strength, however, he was compelled to fall back, ending the only real chance the Union Army had to capture Fredericksburg. Taylor rightly received high praise from his troops, his superiors, and his enemies for his performance.

Apparently, Taylor grew frustrated by Burnside's "Mud March" and resigned his commission on January 19, 1863. He returned to New York City and resumed his law practice. He ran for Congress in 1864 and, as a War Democrat, narrowly defeated the Tammany Hall candidate with 51 percent of the vote. He supported the war but opposed the Freedmen's Bureau and any form of financial support for the defeated South. He was defeated for re-election by the Tammany Hall candidate in 1866 and left office on March 4, 1867.

After his defeat, General Taylor returned to South Norwalk, Connecticut, in 1869 and set up his law practice. He died there on January 16, 1894, at age seventy-two. He was buried in the Riverside Cemetery, Norwalk.

WILLIAM RUFUS TERRILL was born in Covington, Virginia, on April 21, 1834. His father was a lawyer and a member of the Virginia legislature before and during the war. Raised in Warm Springs, Virginia, his was a divided family, and his brother, James B. Terrill, was a brigadier general in the Confederate Army and was killed in action during the Battle of Cold Harbor in 1864. William was admitted to West Point in 1849, graduated in 1853 (16/52), and was commissioned brevet second lieutenant in the artillery. He was promoted to second lieutenant in November of that same year. He became a first lieutenant in the 4th U.S. Artillery in 1856 and a captain on May 14, 1861. In the pre-Civil War years, he did garrison duty in New York, was an assistant professor of mathematics at West Point, served on the frontier in Texas and Michigan, fought in the Third Seminole War (1856–57), and in "Bleeding Kansas."

As the nation teetered on the brink of Civil War, Terrill reportedly met with his father at their home in Warm Springs, Virginia, and decided he would adhere to the Union, as long as he did not have to serve in Virginia. Initially posted to Washington, D.C., he briefly commanded the 24th Pennsylvania and the Washington Arsenal but was soon sent to Kentucky, where he commanded the artillery at the Camp of Instruction at Louisville. For the first six months of 1862, he was chief of artillery of McCook's division in the Army of the Ohio, where he earned lavish praise for his performance in the Battle of Shiloh. He also took part in the Siege of Corinth and the Kentucky Campaign of 1862, where he fought at Richmond (August 30). He was given command of a brigade in September and was promoted to brigadier general on September 9.

At 4:00 p.m. on October 8, 1862, during the Battle of Perryville, he was struck in the side by a shell fragment, which carried away part of his left lung. He died in a field hospital that night at the age of twenty-eight. He was buried in the West Point Cemetery.

ALFRED HOWE TERRY was born in Hartford, Connecticut, on November 10, 1827. He attended Yale Law School in 1848 but quit after he passed the bar in 1849. He practiced in New Haven, Connecticut, where he was clerk of superior court from 1854 to 1860. Active in militia affairs, he raised the 2nd Connecticut Infantry Regiment and became its colonel on May 7, 1861. He fought in the First Bull Run and, after the enlistments of the 2nd Connecticut expired, became colonel of the 7th

Connecticut, a three-year regiment. Sent to South Carolina in September, he took part in the capture of Port Royal in November, and in the capture of Fort Pulaski in April 1862, where he remained until July. He took command of a brigade that spring.

Terry was promoted to brigadier general on April 26, 1862. He commanded Union forces at Hilton Head from October 1862 to May 1863 and was deeply involved in the Siege of Charleston from then until April 1864. As a division commander, he captured Fort Wagner in September 1863.

As part of the X Corps, General Terry was transferred to the Army of the James in the spring of 1864. He fought in the Bermuda Hundred Campaign and the Siege of Petersburg and was briefly commander of the X Corps on several occasions before it was temporarily dissolved.

Terry's most distinguished moment came commanding a provisional corps in North Carolina in the Second Battle of Fort Fisher (January 13–15, 1865). His command was then redesignated X Corps, and he was promoted to major general on January 16. In the last weeks of the war, he took part in the capture of Wilmington and the Carolinas Campaign.

Alfred Terry was mustered out in September 1866 but immediately accepted a Regular Army commission as a brigadier general—most unusual for a non-West Pointer volunteer officer. Highly capable, he distinguished himself fighting Indians on the Western Frontier in the 1870s and 1880s. He retired as a major general, Regular Army, in 1888.

General Terry died in New Haven, Connecticut, on December 16, 1890. He was sixty-three. He was interred in the Grove Street Cemetery, New Haven.

HENRY DWIGHT TERRY was born in Hartford, Connecticut, on March 16, 1812. He moved to Michigan as a young man, studied law, and practiced in Detroit. When the Civil War began, he recruited and organized the 5th Michigan Infantry and became its colonel on June 10, 1861. It was part of the Washington defenses during the winter of 1861-62.

Terry fought in the Peninsula Campaign, where he was slightly wounded in the Battle of Williamsburg. He also fought in the Battle of Seven Pines, where his regiment suffered heavy casualties. Terry was a good regimental commander, but he was not in good health for much of the war. He was nevertheless promoted to brigadier general on July 19, 1862.

Given a brigade with men from Michigan, Pennsylvania, and New York, he was sent to Suffolk, Virginia, where he was unsuccessfully besieged by Confederate General Longstreet in April and May 1863. His brigade was posted to Keyes's IV Corps at White House, Virginia, in June, where it threatened Richmond. It took part in a poorly conducted probe on the Confederate capital in July, where Terry and his commanders (Keyes and Dix) showed timidity. Transferred back to the Army of the Potomac that summer, he was given command of a division in the VI Corps, but he was unable to endure long marches in hot weather. He took part in the failed Mine Run Campaign, after which he and his division were sent to Sandusky, Ohio, and Johnson Island prison camp in January 1864.

Terry's division was sent back to Virginia in May 1864, but Terry was not. He was unemployed until February 7, 1865, when he resigned his commission. After leaving the army, he practiced law in Washington, D.C., where he died on June 22, 1869, at age fifty-seven. He is buried in Clinton Grove Cemetery, Macomb County, Michigan, near Detroit.

JOHN MILTON THAYER was born in Bellingham, Massachusetts, on January 24, 1820. He attended local schools in Norfolk County, taught in public schools, and attended Brown University, from which he graduated in 1841. He read law, was admitted to the bar, set up a practice in Worcester, Massachusetts, edited a local magazine and historical journal, and became a lieutenant in the local militia. He moved to Nebraska in 1854.

Thayer prospered in Nebraska and soon owned a large farm near Omaha. He was appointed brigadier general and later major general in the territorial militia, which he led successfully in the Pawnee War of 1859, and established a reputation as an Indian fighter. He also became a leader in the Republican Party and was elected to the territorial legislature in 1860.

He became colonel of the 1st Nebraska Infantry Regiment in June 1861 and spent the entire war on the Western or Trans–Mississippi fronts. He led a brigade at Fort Donelson, Shiloh, and the Siege of Corinth, and was promoted to brigadier general on October 4, 1862. His appointment, however, expired on March 4, 1863, without Senate action, and he reverted to the rank of colonel. He was reappointed to rank from March 13 and this time was confirmed. Meanwhile, he fought at Chickasaw Bluffs, Fort Hindman (Arkansas Post), and the final Vicksburg Campaign, including the siege.

In January 1864, Thayer assumed command of the District of the Frontier, which headquartered at Fort Smith, Arkansas, on the border of Indian Territory (now Oklahoma). His men treated the Indians harshly. They took part in the unsuccessful Camden Expedition, where his troops were defeated by Choctaw and Chickasaw regiments serving in the Confederate Army. A great many of them were scalped. He was more successful in the Battle of Jenkins Ferry, where he helped save the embattled VII U.S. Corps.

In February 1865, Thayer was named commander of the post of St. Charles, Arkansas, where he commanded a regiment of cavalry and a single battery of artillery—a definite demotion. He was nevertheless brevetted major general in 1866, even though he resigned from the army in July 1865.

After the war, Thayer resumed his political career. In 1867, when Nebraska was admitted to the Union, he was elected one of its first U.S. senators. A strong Radical Republican, he was defeated for re-election by another Republican in 1871. His former commander, President Grant, appointed him the second governor of Wyoming Territory in February 1875. Not re-appointed by President Hayes in 1878, he returned to Nebraska and resumed his law practice. He was elected governor in 1886 and re-elected in 1888. He contested the results of the 1890 election and remained in office until the U.S. Supreme Court ruled in favor of his opponent. He served from January 6, 1887 to February 8, 1892. After his ouster, Thayer retired from politics and enjoyed the quiet life. He died in Lincoln, Nebraska, on March 19, 1906, at age eighty-six. He was buried there in Wyuka Cemetery.

GEORGE HENRY "PAP" THOMAS, who was nicknamed "Slow Trot Thomas" and "the Rock of Chickamauga," was born on July 31, 1816, in Newsom's Depot, Virginia. Of Welsh and Huguenot descent, he grew up on a plantation and, ironically, at age fourteen, was almost killed in Nat Turner's Slave Revolt. He attended West Point, graduated in 1840 (12/42), and was commissioned second lieutenant in the 3rd Artillery. He did garrison duty in the South and fought the Seminoles in Florida (1840–42), where he was brevetted in 1841. Part of the military occupation of Texas, he fought at Fort Brown, Monterrey, and Buena Vista, earning brevets to captain and major for gallant and meritorious conduct.

During the antebellum years, he served in various garrisons and as an instructor of artillery and cavalry at West Point (1851–54). In 1855, he transferred to the 2nd U.S. Cavalry and became close friends with its second-in-command, Lieutenant Colonel Robert E. Lee. Thomas later fought the Kiowa and Comanche in Texas. He was wounded by a Comanche arrow in 1860 but not seriously. A train accident in Virginia later that year, however, damaged his back and caused him pain for the rest of his life. Meanwhile, Thomas was promoted to first lieutenant (1844), captain (1853), and major (1855).

Thomas was no opponent of slavery and indeed owned slaves most of his life. He was offered a Confederate commission in 1861 and agonized over his decision but decided not to accept it. When he chose to remain in the Union Army, his family ostracized him, turned his picture to the wall, and never spoke of him again. After the war, when the South was financially ruined and his sisters were destitute, he offered them money. They angrily refused to accept it and declared that they had no brother. Because he was a Southerner, he was also viewed with suspicion by certain Northerners. Apparently, these included Abraham Lincoln—at least early in the war. Thomas nevertheless advanced rapidly to lieutenant colonel in the 2nd Cavalry on April 25, 1861, replacing Robert E. Lee; and to colonel on May 12, replacing Albert Sidney Johnston. He was promoted to brigadier general of volunteers on August 17.

ENCYCLOPEDIA OF UNION GENERALS

Initially assigned to command a brigade in Pennsylvania and the Shenandoah, he was ordered west in August, to train recent recruits in Kentucky. Given command of a division in November, he drove the Confederates out of eastern Kentucky by winning a decisive victory at Mill Springs on January 18, 1862. As part of Buell's army, he arrived on the field at Shiloh just after the battle. He was nevertheless promoted to major general on April 26, 1862.

Thomas successfully led his division in the Siege of Corinth, in the Kentucky Campaign (where he was second-in-command of the Army of the Ohio), and at Stones River. He assumed command of the XIV Corps of the Army of the Cumberland in January 1863. His outstanding moment came at Chickamauga on September 20, 1863, where his determined stand saved the army and earned him the nickname "the Rock of Chickamauga." He was named commander of the Army of the Cumberland on October 17, 1863, and led it for the rest of the war. Victories at Lookout Mountain, Missionary Ridge, and in the Atlanta Campaign followed.

George Thomas successively defended Nashville against John Bell Hood (his former student) and practically destroyed the Confederate Army of Tennessee on December 16, 1864. General Grant tried to rush him into the attack, but Thomas refused to launch an offensive until the weather was good and the ground was frozen. Grant even dispatched General John A. Logan to replace him, but Logan was ordered not to assume command if Thomas had attacked when he arrived. History has proven that Thomas acted correctly. During the conflict, Thomas developed a reputation as a slow, deliberate, but highly competent commander who despised self-promotion. He was a modest man, especially for a general. General Thomas pursued Hood into northern Alabama and Mississippi in early 1865 and remained in command in Tennessee and Kentucky until after the war. He shunned politics and, when President Johnson offered him a promotion to lieutenant general, he refused to accept it. He asked to be given command of the Military Division of the Pacific in 1869, and his request was granted. He died of a stroke in San Francisco on March 28, 1870, at age fifty-three. He was buried in Oakwood Cemetery, Troy, New York.

Although often underappreciated then and now, George Henry Thomas was one of the best generals on either side during the Civil War.

General Edward S. Bragg, for example, declared he was the ablest officer on the Union side, but "he couldn't get anywhere because he was a Democrat and a Virginian."

HENRY GOODARD THOMAS was born in Portland, Maine, on April 5, 1837. He was educated in private schools in Portland, graduated from Amherst College in 1858, and was admitted to the bar in 1861. He enlisted in the 5th Maine Infantry (a 90-day regiment) in April 1861, when the war began.

Thomas was promoted to captain on June 24 and led a company in the First Battle of Bull Run, after which he was commended for his courage. He was recommended for a Regular Army commission by O. O. Howard and joined the 11th U.S. Infantry as a captain. He spent the rest of 1861 and all of 1862 on recruiting duty. On March 20, 1863, he was promoted to colonel, commanding the 7th Infantry Regiment, Corps d'Afrique (later redesignated the 79th U.S.C.T.), making him the first Regular Army officer to accept command of an African American unit. He was instrumental in forming several other U.S.C.T. units. He initially served in Louisiana, where he contracted malaria and typhoid fever. Transferred back to Virginia, he was with his parent regiment, the 11th U.S. Infantry, in the Rappahannock and Mine Run Campaigns.

Reappointed colonel, from January to May 1864 he led the 19th U.S.C.T. Infantry Regiment. On May 4, 1864, he assumed command of a brigade of African American troops and, as part of the IX Corps, participated in the Overland Campaign. Later involved in the Siege of Petersburg, he took part in the Battle of the Crater debacle. He was promoted to brigadier general of volunteers on November 30, 1864 (at age twenty-seven), and briefly commanded a division in the XXV Corps in early 1865.

Thomas led black troops until the end of the war. He was mustered out of volunteer service in January 1866 and brevetted major general in 1867. He remained in the service and reverted to his Regular Army rank of captain in the 20th U.S. Infantry. He was promoted to major in 1876.

Major Thomas transferred to the Paymaster Department in 1878. He spent much of postbellum service in the Dakota Territory and Colorado, where he suffered from serious dental decay and diabetes. He retired in 1891 and died on January 23, 1897, at age fifty-nine, in Oklahoma City, Indian Territory. He is buried in the Evergreen Cemetery in the town of his birth.

LORENZO THOMAS was born on October 26, 1804, in New Castle, Delaware. He entered West Point in 1819, graduated in 1823 (17/35), and was commissioned second lieutenant in the 4th U.S. Infantry. He served in Florida and Georgia (1824–31), on recruiting duty (1831–33), in the adjutant general's office in Washington (1833–36), in the war against the Seminoles (1836–37), in the Quartermaster General's Office in Washington (1837–38), as chief of staff of the army in Florida (1839–40), and again in the Adjutant General's Office (1840–46).

Brevetted major in 1840, he was a captain (substantive rank) when the Mexican War began. He was sent to Taylor's army, where he won a brevet to lieutenant colonel at Monterrey. Promoted to major in 1848, he was assistant adjutant general of the army from 1848 to 1853. Remaining in Washington, he was Winfield Scott's chief of staff from 1853 to 1861. He was promoted to colonel and adjutant general of the U.S. Army on March 7, 1861, and became a brigadier general on August 10.

Thomas was somewhat overwhelmed by the tremendous demands of his vastly expanded department and did not get along with the overbearing secretary of war, Edwin Stanton, who sent him on detached duty (i.e., professional exile) in the spring of 1863. He was tasked with recruiting black troops for the Military Division of the Mississippi, and he did an excellent job. He was brevetted major general in 1866.

Lorenzo Thomas returned to Washington after Appomattox and resumed his post. President Johnson named him secretary of war *ad interim* on February 21, 1868. Edwin M. Stanton, however, refused to let Thomas into his office, resulting in an impeachment crisis which Johnson barely survived. General John Schofield eventually succeeded Stanton as secretary of war.

General Thomas retired on February 22, 1869, less than two weeks before Johnson left office. He died in Washington, D.C., on March 2, 1875. He was seventy. He is buried in the Oak Hill Cemetery. His son, Evan Thomas, commanded a battery in the 4th U.S. Artillery during the war. Later promoted to major, Evan was killed by Modoc Indians in California in 1873.

STEPHEN THOMAS was born in Bethel, Vermont, on December 6, 1809. His grandfather fought in the American Revolution, and his father died in the War of 1812, when Stephen was four years old. He went to work early to help his widowed mother (who had five children) and received only a grammar school education. He grew up in poverty and later told a friend that he knew what it was to cry for a crust of bread. He eventually started his own business, which was destroyed by fire, but rebounded nicely and was a prosperous manufacturer by the 1840s. He also entered politics as a Democrat, serving as registrar of probate for the Bradford District (1842–46), probate judge (1847–49), a member of the Vermont House of Representatives (1838–40, 1845–47, and 1859–62), and a Vermont State Senator (1849–51). He was an unsuccessful candidate for lieutenant governor in 1860. He was also a captain in the Vermont militia.

Thomas joined the Union Army on February 8, 1862, as colonel of the 8th Vermont Infantry. He was part of Benjamin Butler's Army of the Gulf and took part in the occupation of New Orleans in April. He participated in the various campaigns in southern Louisiana in 1862 and 1863 and in the Siege of Port Hudson. Despite acute diarrhea and possible typhoid, he refused to go to the hospital during the siege, even though his weight fell from 160–165 pounds to 117. He was wounded on May 27 but remained in command. After the fortress fell, he was hospitalized in New Orleans for a time. He was on recruiting duty in Vermont from November 1863 to January 1864.

During 1864, Thomas suffered from rheumatism and deafness. He commanded a brigade in the Army of the Shenandoah from October 15 to

21 and from November 1 to December 9, 1864, and particularly distinguished himself at Cedar Creek (October 19), where he fought the enemy hand-to-hand. For his desperate courage in this battle, he was awarded the Congressional Medal of Honor in 1892.

Thomas's health finally sidelined him in late 1864 and he was mustered out of the service in January 1865. Oddly, he was re-mustered back into the volunteer service the following month, was promoted to brigadier general on April 21, 1865, and was mustered out again on August 24. He returned to Vermont and, now a Republican, refused to run for governor, although he did serve as lieutenant governor under John B. Page (1867–69). He was a Grant delegate in the Republican Convention of 1868, and President Grant appointed him a pension agent in 1870. He held this office for eight years. He was later president of the U.S. Clothespin Company in Montpelier and president of the North Haverhill Granite Company. In between jobs, he farmed. He suffered from senility during his last year and required constant care. General Thomas died in Montpelier, Vermont, on December 18, 1903, at age ninety-four.

CHARLES MYNN THRUSTON was born on February 22, 1798, in Lexington, Kentucky, the son of a U.S. senator. He entered West Point in 1813 and graduated in 1814, at age sixteen, before they had class rankings. (Academy standards were low before Sylvanus Thayer became superintendent in 1817.) Thruston was the 109th graduate in the history of the Academy and was commissioned second lieutenant in the artillery. He served in the War of 1812 and subsequently on garrison duty with the 3rd U.S. Artillery, mainly at Fort McHenry, Maryland; Fort Trumbull, Connecticut; and Fort Monroe, Virginia. He was promoted to first lieutenant (1813) then captain (1827) and fought the Seminoles in Florida in 1836 but resigned on August 31 of that year. He became a slaveholder, the president of the local bank, a farmer in Cumberland, Maryland, and was mayor of the town when the war broke out.

Cumberland was an important center of the Baltimore & Ohio (B & O) Railroad as well as the starting point of the National Road, where it joined the Chesapeake and Ohio Canal. On September 7, 1861, Thruston was commissioned brigadier general of volunteers and tasked with the mission of protecting the B & O. This was an impossible job. Confederate raiders routinely tore up the line and often sent annoying telegrams to Washington, announcing what they were about to do. Thruston was also handicapped by the fact that he was one of the oldest generals on active duty on either side. Cognizant of the need to appoint a younger and more energetic officer to this duty, he withdrew his nomination for brigadier general on February 27, 1862. He resigned from the service on April 17 and returned to farming in the Cumberland area. General Thruston died near Cumberland on February 18, 1872, and was interred there, in Rose Hill Cemetery.

WILLIAM BADGER TIBBITS was born on March 31, 1837, in Hoosick, New York, the son of a wealthy entrepreneur. He was educated in local schools and at Brown University, from which he graduated in 1859. He was engaged in the manufacturing business on the morning of April 15, 1861, when he learned that the Confederates had fired on Fort Sumter. He walked out of his business to obtain permission to recruit a company and never looked back. As a result, his business failed. Later, however, he received an enormous inheritance.

Tibbits was mustered in to the Federal Army as a captain and company commander in the 2nd New York Infantry. He fought in the Battle of Big Bethel, served in the Peninsula Campaign, the Seven Days battles, the Second Bull Run, Fredericksburg, and Chancellorsville, and was praised by his superiors for his courage and excellent judgment. He was promoted to major (October 13). He was mustered out with his regiment on May 23, 1863, but received authorization to form a cavalry regiment. He re-entered the service on February 5, 1864, as colonel of the 21st New York Cavalry, which was also known as the Griswold Light Cavalry Regiment after a local

Congressman. He was given command of a cavalry brigade in April and led it in the Battle of New Market and subsequent operations in West Virginia. He was brevetted brigadier general in October 1864 and was given command of a cavalry division in February 1865.

An excellent commander and a brave one according to every account, Tibbits served in the lower Shenandoah Valley from late 1864 until the end of the war, when he was transferred to Fort Leavenworth, Kansas. While here, he was promoted to brigadier general of volunteers on October 18, 1865—one of the last Union veterans to receive that rank. He was mustered out January 1866 and was brevetted major general on May 4, 1866.

William Tibbitts returned to Troy, where he died of pneumonia on February 10, 1880, at age forty-three. He left $100,000 for the erection and maintenance of a home for indigent Union soldiers—a huge amount in that day. He was interred in Oakwood Cemetery in Troy.

DAVIS TILLSON was born in Rockland, Maine, on April 14, 1830. He was admitted to West Point in July 1849, but his leg was punctured in an accident that same month. Although the records do not indicate exactly what happened, his condition failed to improve, and he was transferred to a hospital at Governors Island, where his leg was amputated on March 23, 1850. Unable to walk without crutches, he resigned from the Academy in September 1851. He returned home, became a civil engineer, was elected to the legislature as a Republican in 1857, became a customs collector, and, in 1858, adjutant general of the Maine Militia.

When the Civil War began, he organized the 2nd Maine Battery, and was mustered in as a captain on November 30, 1861. By now, Tillson had mastered his handicap to the point no one suspected he had an artificial limb. His battery was stationed on the Canadian frontier during the Trent affair, when it appeared that the United States and Great Britain might come to blows. He was promoted to major in May 1862 and was named chief of artillery of E. O. C. Ord's division in Virginia. He fought in the Battle of Cedar Mountain (August 9) and was promoted to chief of artillery of McDowell's III Corps the next day. He took part in the Second Battle of Bull Run, after which he took leave because his artificial limb was damaged. He returned to duty in October and was appointed an inspector of artillery on the staff of the Army of the Potomac. He was promoted to lieutenant colonel in December.

Sent west, Davis Tillson supervised construction on the defenses of Cincinnati and the repair of the Louisville & Nashville Railroad in 1863 and 1864. He was promoted to brigadier general on March 21, 1863. He assumed command of a brigade in the Army of the Cumberland in April 1864.

General Tillson was placed in charge of the Knoxville area, where he received permission from General Grant to form an African American artillery regiment. The result was the 1st U.S. Colored Troops Heavy Artillery Regiment, which remained with Tillson for the rest of the war. He was given command of the District of East Tennessee in January 1865 and was simultaneously commander of a division in the XXIII Corps.

After the war, Tillson was acting assistant commissioner for the Freedmen's Bureau in Georgia. Brevetted major general in February 1866, he was mustered out of the service in December and returned home, where he became a highly successful businessman. He organized the Hurricane Island Granite Company and employed 1,400 workers. He also developed a lime quarry and orange groves in Florida.

General Tillson died of heart disease on April 30, 1895. He was sixty-five. He was buried in Achorn Cemetery, Rockland, Maine.

JOHN BLAIR SMITH TODD was born on April 4, 1814, in Lexington, Kentucky. He entered the U.S. Military Academy in 1832, graduated in 1837 (39/50), and was commissioned second lieutenant in the 6th U.S. Infantry. He was promoted to first lieutenant in December and served in the Second Seminole War from 1837 to 1840 and 1841 to 1842. Posted to Indian Territory from 1842 to 1846, he was promoted to captain in 1843 and fought in the Mexican War, including the Siege of Vera Cruz and the Battle of Cerro Gordo. More frontier duty followed,

mainly in Minnesota and the Dakota Territory, where he fought the Sioux. He resigned his commission in 1856 to become a sutler at Fort Randall, Dakota. He also studied law and was admitted to the bar in 1861, setting up a practice at Yankton, (South) Dakota.

Todd's Civil War career was brief. He was mustered in as a brigadier general of volunteers on September 19, 1861, and was given command of the District of North Missouri (headquartered in St. Joseph) in October. He was named commander of a division in the Army of the Tennessee in June 1862, but his appointment expired on July 17. Meanwhile, in December 1861, the Territory of Dakota was officially formed with Yankton as its capital. Todd was named its delegate to the U.S. House of Representatives. He served until March 1863 when he was defeated for re-election. He successfully contested this election and served from June 1864 to March 1865, when he was again defeated. He returned to Yankton and served as speaker of the state legislature in 1865 and 1867. He ran for Congress again in 1868 but lost, after which he retired from public life.

General Todd died in Yankton County, Dakota Territory, on January 5, 1872, at age fifty-seven. He is buried in the Yankton Cemetery. John Todd was at Ford's Theater on April 14, 1865, and occupied the booth next to Abraham Lincoln when he was assassinated. He helped carry the president's body to the Petersen House and was present when Lincoln died the following morning.

ALFRED THOMAS ARCHIMEDES TORBERT was born on July 1, 1833, in Georgetown, Delaware. Educated locally, he secured an appointment to West Point in 1851 and graduated in 1855 (21/34). He was commissioned brevet second lieutenant in the infantry on July 1 but was promoted to second lieutenant nineteen days later. Sent to Texas, he skirmished against the Lipan Indians in 1856 before being transferred to Florida, where he fought the Seminoles (1856–57). He also took part in the Utah Expedition (1857–60) and in garrison duty in Missouri and New Mexico. He was promoted to first lieutenant on February 25, 1861.

Torbert was appointed first lieutenant in the Confederate Army on March 16, but rejected it. He was on recruiting duty in New Jersey until September 1, when he became colonel of the 1st New Jersey Infantry. Initially part of the Washington defenses, he fought in the Peninsula Campaign and the Seven Days battles. He became a brigade commander in the VI Corps of the Army of the Potomac during the Second Bull Run Campaign. He also fought in the Maryland Campaign. He was slightly wounded at South Mountain on September 14, 1862, but still led his brigade at Antietam on September 17. He was promoted to brigadier general on November 29.

Torbert fought in the Battle of Fredericksburg but was on medical furlough during the Battle of Chancellorsville. Back in command in June, he took part in the Battle of Gettysburg. When the Army of the Potomac was reorganized in the spring of 1864, Torbert was given command of a cavalry division in Sheridan's corps, which he led in the Overland Campaign and in the Shenandoah, including the Third Battle of Winchester and Cedar Creek. On October 9, he defeated Rebel cavalry under Tom Rosser and L. L. Lomax at Tom's Run, where he captured 11 pieces of artillery. He was brevetted major general on December 1. He was commander of the Army of the Shenandoah from April 22 to July 12, 1865, and commanded occupation forces in the Districts of Winchester and Southeastern Virginia after the war. Despite his many accomplishments, he reverted to his Regular Army rank of captain when he was mustered out of volunteer service in January 1866. He resigned from the army on October 31, 1866.

Postwar, General Torbert worked in the diplomatic service. He was U.S. Consul to El Salvador and Consul General to Havana. He was U.S. Consul General in Paris in 1873. In 1880, he boarded the steamship *Vera Cruz* and sailed for Mexico. On August 29, the ship ran into a hurricane off the coast of Cape Canaveral, Florida, and General Torbert drowned. He was forty-seven. His remains were recovered on a beach two days later and were interred in the Avenue Methodist Episcopal Cemetery, Milford, Delaware.

JOSEPH GILBERT TOTTEN was born on August 23, 1788, in New Haven, Connecticut. The U.S. Military

Academy at West Point opened on July 1, 1802, and Totten became a plebe on November 4. He was one of the three cadets to matriculate in 1805 and was the 10th graduate in the history of the Academy. Commissioned second lieutenant in the Corps of Engineers, his military career would span sixty-two years with only one break in service. From 1806 to 1808, he was secretary to the Surveyor-General of Northwestern Territory, who was his uncle. He was promoted to first lieutenant in 1810 and to captain in 1812 but truly distinguished himself during the War of 1812. He was brevetted major for meritorious service repulsing the British fleet on Lake Ontario in 1813 and to lieutenant colonel for gallant conduct at the Battle of Plattsburg, New York, later that year.

Postwar, he was supervising engineer in the construction of Fort Adams, Rhode Island (1825–38), and for harbor improvements in New York and Boston. He was promoted to major (full rank) (1818), lieutenant colonel (1828), and colonel and chief engineer of the U.S. Army (1838).

While keeping his position as chief engineer of the army, he acted as chief engineer of Winfield Scott's Army of Mexico, including the Siege of Vera Cruz, for which he was brevetted brigadier general. (Like most people who knew Totten, Scott had unbounded confidence in him.) He was present at the Mexican surrender. Totten was prominent in several scientific advancements, including the lighting of navigational hazards, harbor and river improvements, and coastal defenses.

Joseph Totten served as commander of the Corps of Engineers and chief of the Engineer Bureau in Washington, D.C., for most of the Civil War. He was promoted to brigadier general, Regular Army, on April 13, 1863. A legendary soldier and military engineer, General Totten died suddenly of pneumonia in Washington, D.C., on April 22, 1864, at age seventy-five. He was buried in the Congressional Cemetery.

ZEALOUS BATES TOWER was born on January 12, 1819, in Cohasset, Massachusetts. He graduated from West Point at the head of his class (1/52) in 1841 and was commissioned second lieutenant in the Corps of Engineers.

He was an assistant on the Board of Engineers (1841–42), an assistant professor at the Academy (1842–43), and was involved in constructing the defenses of Hampton Roads, Virginia (1843–46). Tower served in Mexico and earned three brevets (to first lieutenant, captain, and major), fighting from Vera Cruz to Mexico City. He led storming columns at Churubusco and Chapultepec, where he was wounded. He was promoted to first lieutenant (substantive rank) in 1847 and to captain in 1855. Meanwhile, he was involved in harbor defense projects at Portland, Maine; Portsmouth, New Hampshire; and on Alcatraz Island in San Francisco Bay.

Major Towers was chief engineer in the defense of Fort Pickens, Florida, from February 1861 to January 1862, took part in the Battle of Santa Rosa Island (October 9), was promoted to major in August 1861, and brevet lieutenant colonel in November. Transferred to Virginia, he was promoted to brigadier general on June 12, 1862.

Tower was given command of a brigade in the III Corps of General Pope's Army of Virginia in June 1862. He led it until August 1862, when he was severely wounded in the left knee during the Second Battle of Bull Run. It took him well over a year to recover and, even then, he was incapable of further field service. General Tower was superintendent of West Point from July to September 1864, when he became chief engineer for the defenses of Nashville. His efforts were a contributing factor to the defeat the Confederate Army of Tennessee suffered on December 15 and 16, 1864.

General Tower was brevetted major general on January 13, 1866, and was mustered out of volunteer service two days later. He reverted to the rank of lieutenant colonel. He was involved in several engineering and harbor improvement projects throughout the United States, was promoted to colonel of engineers in 1874, and retired after forty years' service in 1883. He returned to the town of his birth, where he died on March 20, 1900, at age eighty-one. He was buried there in the Central Cemetery.

IVAN VASILYEVICH TURCHANINOV, alias **JOHN BASIL TURCHIN**, was born in the Don Province of the Russian Empire on January 30, 1822, the son of a Russian

ENCYCLOPEDIA OF UNION GENERALS

major. He attended the cadet school at St. Petersburg, joined the Russian Army in 1843, received a commission in the horse artillery, and graduated from the Imperial Military School (the Russian equivalent of a General Staff college) in St. Petersburg in 1841. He took part in the suppression of the Hungarian Revolution of 1848, joined the staff of the Imperial Guards in St. Petersburg, and eventually became a colonel on the General Staff of the crown prince, who later became Czar Alexander II. He also served in the Crimean War (1854–56).

Turchaninov emigrated to the United States in 1856 and adopted the name "Turchin." He settled in Chicago and worked as a civil engineer for the Illinois Central Railroad until the Civil War began. He was named colonel of the 19th Illinois Infantry. He produced a well-trained and well-disciplined regiment which initially served in Missouri and Kentucky, where he adopted European methods in dealing with civilians, instead of the more humane American tradition. He was promoted to brigade commander in November.

In April 1862, while Buell headed west to Shiloh, Turchin's brigade was part of Ormsby Mitchel's division. Mitchel pushed from Nashville into northern Alabama, where one of Turchin's regiments captured Athens, Alabama. On May 2, Turchin told his men that he would shut his eyes for two hours, and they could do whatever they wanted to. They sacked the town, robbed everything and everybody, raped a fourteen-year-old African American and a pregnant white woman, who miscarried and died. When they heard about Turchin's actions, Mitchel and Buell were outraged. Turchin offered to resign, but Buell court-martialed him for neglect of duty, conduct unbecoming of an officer, and disobedience of orders. Convicted of all charges, Turchin's career was saved by his wife, who visited Washington, D.C., and convinced Abraham Lincoln to set aside his conviction and to promote him to brigadier general on July 19. He returned to Chicago, where he was hailed as a hero.

Turchin was assigned to the Army of the Cumberland, which he led at Chickamauga and Chattanooga, and he distinguished himself leading a successful assault on Missionary Ridge. He participated in the Atlanta Campaign but suffered a heat stroke in July 1864. Unemployed for several weeks, he resigned for reasons of health on October 4. He did not receive a brevet to major general in the omnibus promotions at the end of the war.

After he resigned, Turchin returned to Chicago, where he was a patent solicitor, a civil engineer, and a real estate agent. Turchin died in poverty in the Southern Illinois Hospital for the Insane in Anna, on June 18, 1901. He was seventy-nine. He is buried in Mound City National Cemetery, Mound City, Illinois.

JOHN WESLEY TURNER was born in Saratoga, New York, on July 19, 1833. He attended West Point, graduated in 1855 (14/34), and was commissioned brevet second lieutenant in the 3rd U.S. Artillery. He was promoted to second lieutenant in November of that year. He served on frontier duty at Fort Dalles, Oregon (1855–56) and saw action against the Seminoles in Florida (1856–58). Tours of duty at Fort Adams, Rhode Island, Fort Leavenworth, Kansas, and the Artillery School for Practice at Fort Monroe, Virginia, followed. He was promoted to first lieutenant a week after Fort Sumter surrendered.

Turner remained at Fort Monroe until November 1861, when he was transferred to Kansas/western Missouri as David Hunter's Chief of Commissariat for Subsistence. Promoted to captain in August, he was sent to the Department of the South in March 1862 and commanded a battery in the reduction of Fort Pulaski, Georgia (April 10–11). He was promoted to colonel on May 3, and was named chief of staff of Benjamin Butler's Department of the Gulf on May 22. He returned to the Department of the South in 1863, when General Hunter replaced Quincy A. Gillmore as department commander.

From July to September 1863, Turner commanded the Union artillery during the Siege of Fort Wagner and subsequent operations against Fort Sumter. He assumed command of a division in the X Corps in September 1863 and was promoted to brigadier general on September 21.

Turner and his division were transferred to the Army of the James in early May 1864. They fought in the Bermuda Hundred, in the unsuccessful battle for Drewry's Bluff, and in the Siege of Petersburg. He was brevetted major general on March 9, 1865, led the Independent Division of the XXIV Corps from March 20, 1865, and took part in the capture of Petersburg and the pursuit to Appomattox. Following the war, Turner commanded the District of Henrico, which included Richmond, from June 1865 to April 1866, after which he directed the Department of Virginia for six weeks. He was awaiting orders from May to September 1, 1866, when he was mustered out of volunteer service. He reverted to the rank of colonel, Regular Army, and was officer in charge of the commissary depot at St. Louis. He was temporarily attached to the Commissioner of Indian Affairs, but he preferred to remain in Missouri. He retired from the army in 1871.

As a civilian, Turner remained in St. Louis, where he was street commissioner for several years. Prominent in local civic affairs, he was on the board of directors of two banks. He died of pneumonia at his home on April 8, 1898, at age sixty-five. He was interred in Calvary Cemetery, St. Louis.

JAMES MADISON TUTTLE was born on September 24, 1823, in rural Monroe County, Ohio, in what is now Noble County. His family moved to Indiana when he was ten. He worked on the family farm, was educated in local schools, and moved to Farmington, Iowa, about 1846. Here he became a farmer and a merchant. He entered local politics as a Democrat and was elected sheriff of Van Buren County in 1855 and county treasurer and recorder in 1857.

Tuttle raised a volunteer company in April 1861 and was elected its captain. He was mustered into the Union Army on May 31, as lieutenant colonel of the 2nd Iowa Infantry. He became its colonel in September. Tuttle and his men were initially posted to northern Missouri but were sent to the Western Front in early 1862. On February 15, outside Fort Donelson, he was standing on a log when it was hit by a Rebel cannonball. He was wounded in the right arm and injured his back when he fell. He was back with the 2nd in time to fight at Shiloh, where he commanded a brigade in W. H. L. Wallace's division. When Wallace was mortally wounded on April 6, Tuttle assumed command of the division and fought at "the Hornet's Nest," where he narrowly avoided capture. In recognition of his skill and gallantry, he was promoted to brigadier general on June 12. Meanwhile, on April 14, Thomas A. Davis assumed command of the division, and Tuttle reverted to brigade commander.

Tuttle led his brigade during the Siege of Corinth, after which he commanded the major supply depot at Cairo, Illinois. He was given command of a division in Grant's army in April 1863. As part of Sherman's XV Corps, he distinguished himself during the first capture of Jackson, Mississippi. He was engaged in the subsequent Siege of Vicksburg and, after the city fell, commanded Union troops in Natchez.

Tuttle sought to take advantage of his growing military reputation by running for governor of Iowa as a Democrat in 1863 and 1864 but was defeated both times. He resigned his commission on June 14, 1864, and returned to his home state.

Postbellum, General Tuttle resided in Des Moines, where he engaged in various businesses, including farming, real estate, pork packing, and mining in the southwestern US. He ran for Congress in 1866 but was defeated by former General Grenville Dodge. He was twice elected to the Iowa House of Representatives, once as a Democrat (1871) and once as a Republican (1883).

General Tuttle died of a stroke while visiting the Jack Rabbit Mine at Casa Grande, Arizona, on October 24, 1892, at age sixty-nine. He was buried in Woodland Cemetery, Des Moines, Iowa.

DANIEL "UNCLE DAN" TYLER was born on January 7, 1799, in Brooklyn, Connecticut. He was the son of a veteran of the Battle of Bunker Hill and the uncle of General Robert O. Tyler. He entered West Point in 1816, graduated in 1819 (14/29), and was commissioned second lieutenant in the light artillery. He was stationed in various garrisons in New England and at the Artillery School for Practice in Fort Monroe, Virginia. From 1828 to 1830, he was on duty at the Artillery School for Practice in Metz, France, and translated "Manoeuvres of

ENCYCLOPEDIA OF UNION GENERALS

Artillery." On Ordnance duty from 1830 to 1834, he resigned his commission on May 31, 1834, because of internal army politics, and became a civil engineer, an iron manufacturer, and a developer of businesses. He erected the first coke, hot–blast furnace ever built in America. His specialty was taking over virtually bankrupt canal and railroad companies and making them profitable. He also built blast furnaces and rolling mills. He was president of the Schuylkill & Susquehanna Railroad when the Civil War began.

In April 1861, Tyler was a volunteer aide to General Robert Patterson of the Pennsylvania Militia. On April 23, he assumed command of the 1st Connecticut Infantry, but was promoted to brigadier general of Connecticut militia on May 10. He commanded a division in the advance on Manassas and clashed with Rebels under General Longstreet at Blackburn's Ford on July 18. On July 21, he showed a lack of aggression and failed to pin down Southern forces on the Confederate right flank; as a result, they were able to reinforce General Beauregard, Stonewall Jackson, et al, and were a major contributing factor to the Confederate victory.

Tyler was part of the Washington defenses until he was mustered out of the service on August 11, when his term of service expired. He was appointed brigadier of volunteers on March 16, 1862, and was sent to Mississippi, where he fought at Farmington (May 23) and in the Siege of Corinth. He went on sick leave on June 27. Tyler organized Connecticut volunteers for a month (August–September); briefly commanded Camp Douglas, Illinois; was an investigator into Buell's Kentucky Campaign; and was back in Virginia in 1863, where he served as commander of Harpers Ferry when Lee invaded Pennsylvania. He commanded the District of Delaware from July 3, 1863 to April 6, 1864, when he resigned his commission. He was well past the mandatory retirement age.

After the war, General Tyler was a founder of the town of Anniston, Alabama, which he named after his daughter-in-law. He developed it into an industrial complex which included the Woodstock Iron Company (which he owned), a cotton mill, a water works, and a railroad car factory. He was also president of the Mobile & Montgomery Railroad for several years. He died while on a trip to New York City on November 30, 1882, at age eighty-three. He was buried in Hillside Cemetery, Anniston. One of his sons,

Colonel Augustus Cleveland Tyler (USMA, 1873), commanded the 1st Connecticut Infantry in the Spanish-American War.

ERASTUS BERNARD TYLER was born on April 24, 1822, in West Bloomfield, New York, but his parents moved to Ohio when he was a child. He was educated in local schools and at Granville College (now Denison University), settled in Ravenna, Ohio, and was a successful fur merchant when the Civil War broke out.

Tyler was a brigadier general in the Ohio Militia in April 1861. He quickly recruited the 7th Ohio Infantry Regiment, was elected its colonel (defeating future President James Garfield) and was mustered into Federal service on April 25.

Erastus Tyler had no previous military training before the war. This was apparent in his first battle, which took place at Kessler's Cross Lanes in western Virginia on August 26. He was surprised by Confederate General John B. Floyd, and his command was routed. He was nevertheless given a brigade command in early 1862 and was appointed brigadier general on May 15, 1862. As part of James Shields's division, he was involved in several skirmishes and battles against Stonewall Jackson in the Valley Campaign of 1862, including the Battle of Port Republic, where he was involved in some of the heaviest fighting of the campaign, and where he was eventually defeated.

Tyler was present at Antietam, but his brigade was held in reserve. It was heavily engaged in the assaults on Marye's Heights during the Battle of Fredericksburg, where General Tyler was severely wounded in the head and the left side by an exploding shell. He returned to duty in late March 1863, and helped stabilize the Union right flank at Chancellorsville in early May but was forced to withdraw when his men ran low in ammunition.

In June, the enlistments of three of his four regiments expired. He went to the War Department in Washington, which placed him in command of the Baltimore defenses during the Gettysburg Campaign. General Tyler briefly commanded the VIII Corps from September 28 to October 10, 1863, but thereafter reverted to brigade command.

When Confederate General Early drove on Washington, Tyler successfully defended Jug Bridge with two regiments of inexperienced recruits during the Battle of Monocacy (July 9, 1864). President Lincoln later reportedly said that the Union was "more indebted to General Tyler than any other man for the salvation of Washington."

It seems clear to this author that Erastus Tyler was a much better commander in 1864 than he was in 1861, and that his ability increased with his experience. At this point, the reader might remark that the battlefield is no place for on-the-job training, and s/he would be absolutely right, but both sides were forced to resort to using untrained but willing officers when the war began. They simply had no choice. This is one reason casualties in the Civil War were so high.

Tyler remained in the Middle Department (the Washington-Baltimore area) for the rest of the war. He was mustered out of the service on August 24, 1865, and was brevetted major general April 1866. He settled in Baltimore after the war, became a prominent citizen, and was, for a time, the city's postmaster.

Erastus B. Tyler died in Baltimore, Maryland, on January 9, 1891, at age sixty-eight, from intestinal complications caused by his Fredericksburg wound. He is buried in Green Mount (Greenmount) Cemetery, Baltimore. His wife was granted a federal pension after his death.

ROBERT OGDEN TYLER was born on New Year's Eve, 1831, in Hunter, New York. General Daniel Tyler was his uncle. Robert's family moved to Hartford, Connecticut, when he was seven. He attended West Point, graduated in 1853 (22/52), and was commissioned brevet second lieutenant of artillery. He was promoted to second lieutenant on Christmas Eve, 1853.

Most of Tyler's antebellum career involved performing frontier duty and Indian fighting in California, the Pacific Northwest, and Minnesota. He was part of the garrison of the Fort Columbus, New York, Recruiting Depot when the sectional crisis reached its boiling point. He was on board the naval expedition sent to relieve Fort

Sumter, but a storm in the Atlantic dispersed the convoy. Tyler had to watch the bombardment without being able to help the garrison. The following month, he engaged in opening communications between Washington and Baltimore. He was promoted to captain in the quartermaster branch on May 17 and managed the supply depot at Alexandria, Virginia, until August 29, when he became colonel of the 4th Connecticut Infantry Regiment, which became the 1st Connecticut Heavy Artillery in January 1862. It was initially part of the Washington defenses but was part of the Army of the Potomac's siege artillery during the Peninsula and Seven Days battles. Despite the horrible roads, he only lost one gun in the entire campaign. He was promoted to brigadier general on November 29, 1862. During the Battle of Fredericksburg, he oversaw the artillery for Hooker's Center Grand Division, and at Chancellorsville and Gettysburg he was OIC (Officer in Charge) of the artillery reserve for the entire army. Many of his 130 guns played a role in defeating Pickett's Charge on July 3, 1863.

After Gettysburg, Tyler was placed in charge of the heavy artillery in the Alexandria defenses (i.e., the south side of the Washington defenses). Because Grant suffered so many casualties during his Overland Campaign, Tyler's units were converted to infantry and were sent to the front. He fought in the last phase of the Battle of Spotsylvania, the Battle of North Anna, and the Battle of Cold Harbor, where a Confederate bullet slammed into his ankle and rendered him unfit for further field service. He was brevetted major general on February 7, 1865.

After holding some minor staff positions, he was placed in charge of the District of Delaware and the Eastern Shore in December 1865. He was discharged from volunteer service in July 1866 and reverted to the rank of lieutenant colonel in the Quartermaster Service. He spent the rest of his life at various locations in the South and California, while simultaneously taking frequent leaves of absence due to his health. His condition, however, steadily deteriorated.

General Tyler finally succumbed in Boston on December 1, 1874, at the age of forty-two. His remains lie in Cedar Hill Cemetery, Hartford, Connecticut.

GEORGE HECTOR TYNDALE, who went by his middle name, was born in Philadelphia, Pennsylvania, on March 24, 1821. He later dropped the "George." His father was a prominent china and glassware importer. Hector followed in his footsteps and became an expert in porcelain and pottery. He also became a Republican and, although not an abolitionist, escorted Mrs. John Brown to Virginia to claim her husband's body after he was hanged in late 1859.

Tyndale was in Europe on a business trip when the Civil War began. He returned home and entered the Union Army as the major of the 28th Pennsylvania Infantry on June 28, 1861. He was promoted to lieutenant colonel on April 25, 1862. Stationed at Harpers Ferry, he first saw action against Stonewall Jackson at Front Royal in May 1862. He also fought in the Battle of Cedar Mountain, the Second Battle of Bull Run, and Antietam where, despite his relatively low rank, he found himself commanding a brigade and led the XII Corps attack on the Dunker Church. Early in the battle, he was struck in the hip, but ignored his wound. Near the church, however, he was hit in the back of the head by a musket ball, which fractured his skull. Knocked unconscious, one of his lieutenants dragged him fifty yards back to a haystack. Surgeons removed the ball, and he was ordered back home to recover. He did not return to duty until July 1863. Meanwhile, he was promoted to brigadier general on April 9, 1863. He skipped the rank of colonel altogether.

Tyndale was given command of a brigade in the XI Corps, which accompanied General Hooker to the Western Front. He distinguished himself in the Battle of Wauhatchie (October 28–29, 1863), where he led a bayonet charge that turned the Confederate right flank. His health failed him, however, and he gave up command of his brigade on May 2, 1864. He resigned from the army on August 26. He was nevertheless brevetted major general in 1868.

Hector Tyndale returned to his business in Philadelphia and unsuccessfully ran for mayor in 1868. He died in Philadelphia on March 19, 1880, at age fifty-eight. He was buried in Laurel Hill Cemetery, Philadelphia.

U

ULLMAN – UPTON

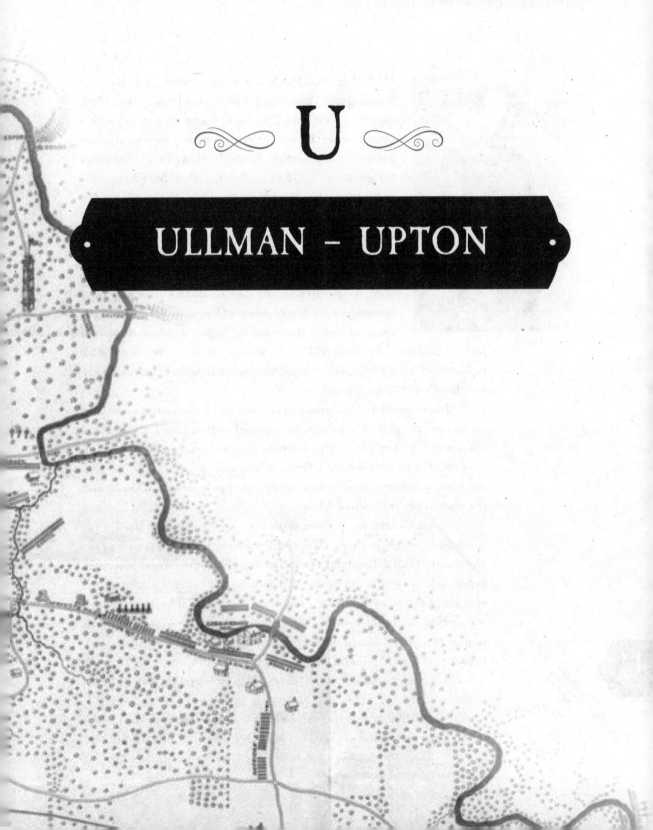

DANIEL ULLMAN was born on April 28, 1810, in Wilmington, Delaware. He graduated from Yale in 1829, moved to New York City, and became an attorney with a large practice. He was the Whig nominee for state attorney general in 1851 and the Know-Nothing Party's candidate for governor in 1854. After the Civil War began, he recruited the Highlanders (a.k.a. the Cameron Highlanders and the 78th New York Infantry Regiment) and was mustered into Federal service as its colonel on April 28, 1862. The 78th was initially part of the Washington defenses but was sent to Harper's Ferry in late May. It operated in the Shenandoah Valley and later became part of Pope's Army of Virginia. It fought in the Battle of Cedar Mountain on August 9, where it suffered only 22 casualties, but Colonel Ullman was one of them. He was sick with typhoid and, unable to join the retreat, was captured by the Rebels and taken to Libby Prison in Richmond.

Ullman was released on parole in October and subsequently exchanged on January 13, 1863. Meanwhile, he approached Abraham Lincoln about the possibility of enlisting African Americans as Union soldiers. Lincoln approved the idea, promoted Ullman to brigadier general on January 13, 1863, and sent him to New Orleans to organize five regiments. They formed the nucleus of the "Corps d'Afrique."

General Ullman was present at the Siege of Port Hudson but did not command any troops there. (General Banks was now commander of the Army of the Gulf. Ullman held Banks responsible for the Cedar Mountain defeat and the two did not work well together.) Banks kept Ullman in rear area assignments, as did Banks's successor, General Canby. He remained at Port Hudson until November 1864, when he was given command of the post of Morganza, Louisiana. He was transferred to Cairo, Illinois, in February 1865. He remained there, awaiting orders, until August 1865, when he was mustered out of the service. He was brevetted major general in 1866.

General Ullman returned to New York but retired from public life. He traveled extensively and engaged in scientific studies and literary pursuits.

He died in Nyack, New York, on September 20, 1892, at age eighty-two. He was buried in Oak Hill Cemetery, Nyack.

ADIN BALLOU UNDERWOOD was born in Milford, Massachusetts, on May 19, 1828, the descendent of an old colonial family and the son of a militia brigadier general. He graduated from Brown University in 1849, and subsequently attended Harvard Law School. He was admitted to the bar in 1853, after which he went to Prussia and studied at Heidelberg University and the University of Berlin. He returned to America and settled in Boston in 1855.

In 1861, Underwood actively recruited for the Union Army, which he joined as a captain in the 2nd Massachusetts Infantry on May 25, 1861. It was part of General Patterson's army in the Shenandoah Valley in July 1861 and subsequently performed picket duty on the Potomac and garrison duty at Harpers Ferry. That spring and summer, it fought Jackson as part of General Banks's Army of the Shenandoah. Underwood, meanwhile, returned to Massachusetts and became major of the 33rd Massachusetts in July 1862. It was mustered into Federal service in August, and Underwood became its lieutenant colonel on August 13. It marched to Fredericksburg but arrived too late to fight in the battle of December 13, but did participate in Burnside's "Mud March" of January 1863. Underwood was promoted to colonel and regimental commander on April 3 and led the 33rd at Chancellorsville, Brandy Station, Gettysburg, and Bristoe Station.

Colonel Underwood and his men were transferred to the Army of the Cumberland in September and October. They fought at Wauhatchie, Tennessee, at the foot of Lookout Mountain, on October 28 and 29. During the second day of this battle, Underwood's upper right leg was shattered by a ball which left him crippled for the rest of his life. He remained in a log cabin near the battlefield for two weeks, where he was joined by his wife. They moved to Nashville, where they lived in private quarters for five months, under the care of three physicians. It was here Underwood learned that he had been promoted to brigadier general on November 19, despite having never commanded a brigade for so much as a day.

Adin Underwood was brevetted major general in February 1866 and mustered out of the service in August 1865. He returned to Boston, where he practiced law and was surveyor of the port for almost twenty years. He died in Boston on January 24, 1888, at age fifty-nine. He was buried in Newton Cemetery, Newton, Massachusetts.

EMORY UPTON was born on his family's farm near Batavia, New York. He spent two years at Oberlin College before being admitted to West Point in 1856. When Cadet Wade Hampton Gibbes of South Carolina made remarks about Upton's relationships with African American women at Oberlin, Upton demanded an apology. When no apology came, Upton challenged him to a duel. They fought with swords in a darkened room in the cadet barracks and the larger Gibbes gave Upton a beating and cut his face, but he was not seriously wounded. Upton graduated in 1861 (8/45) and was commissioned second lieutenant in the 4th U.S. Artillery on May 6. (The traditional graduation day of July 1st was moved up seven weeks because of the war.) He was promoted to first lieutenant on May 14.

Upton was an aide-de-camp to General Daniel Tyler during the Bull Run Campaign and was wounded in the arm and left side during the skirmish at Blackburn's Ford (July 18), but he remained on the field. After the Battle of Bull Run (July 21), he took three weeks' medical leave due to his injuries. He spent the winter of 1861/62 in the Washington defenses and commanded a battery in the Peninsula Campaign and the Seven Days battles. He directed the artillery for the 1st Division of VI Corps in the Maryland Campaign, including the battles of Crampton's Gap (South Mountain) and Antietam. He became colonel of the 121st New York Infantry in October 1862. A fine regimental commander, he fought at Fredericksburg and in the Chancellorsville Campaign (May 1–6, 1863). At Salem Church (May 3–4), the regiment clashed with the 9th Alabama and was involved in some of the fiercest fighting of the war. Upton's horse was shot out from under him, and he continued to command on foot. The 121st New York suffered 62 percent casualties in a battle that lasted fifteen to twenty minutes.

Upton was the acting commander of an infantry brigade in the VI Corps at Gettysburg. He was given command of another brigade in October and distinguished himself at Rappahannock Station (November 7), where 1,600 rebels were captured. Total Federal losses were 419.

After the Mine Run Campaign, Upton fought in the Battle of the Wilderness and Spotsylvania Court House, where on May 10, 1864, he took twelve regiments and introduced a new infantry tactic by attacking in column and assaulting a small part of the enemy line while advancing rapidly and not bothering to halt and trade fire. Using these superior tactics, he penetrated the Mule Shoe Salient, but was not properly supported and eventually had to withdraw. He was slightly wounded in the process,

Emory Upton was promoted to brigadier general on May 30. Meanwhile, he fought in the Overland Campaign, at Cold Harbor, in the early stages of the Siege of Petersburg, and in the Valley Campaign of 1864. He commanded a division in the Third Battle of Winchester (September 19) after the original commander, Brigadier General David A. Russell, was mortally wounded. Upton himself was severely wounded in the thigh but refused to leave the field. He directed his command from a stretcher. He was brevetted major general for his actions in this battle.

Upton returned to duty in December 1864 and commanded the Cavalry Corps of General James Wilson's Military Division of the Mississippi. He fought in the Battle of Selma, Alabama (April 2, 1865), where Nathan Bedford Forrest was finally defeated. His last battle was at Columbus, Georgia (April 16), where he led a successful night attack and took 1,500 prisoners. It was the last major action of the war.

He was only twenty-five years old when the war ended. A remarkably brilliant and courageous officer at every level, he advanced from cadet to brevet major general and a corps commander in only four years and distinguished himself commanding units in all three branches—infantry, artillery, and cavalry. He was indeed one of the most remarkable officers in U.S. military history.

Upton was mustered out of volunteer service at the end of April 1866 and reverted to his Regular Army rank of captain. In July, however, he was appointed lieutenant colonel of the newly formed 25th U.S. Infantry. He was commandant of cadets at West Point from 1870 to 1875 and taught infantry, cavalry, and artillery tactics. He did a tour of world's armies (1875–77), including Germany, France, Britain, Russia, Persia, Italy, China, India, and Japan. He was most impressed by the Prussians. When he returned, he submitted fifty-four pages of recommendations to Congress, warning that the European armies were ahead of the U.S. Army because they (especially the Prussians) had institutionalized military professionalism. His recommendations included the establishment of military schools, a General Staff, a system of personnel evaluations, and promotion examinations. Many of his recommendations were enacted. He was considered one of the foremost military thinkers of his time and was promoted to colonel in July 1880.

Meanwhile, tragedy struck. In 1868, General Upton married twenty-one–year-old Emily Norwood Martin, the daughter of a prominent family, and was very much in love. Within a year, however, she developed tuberculosis. She went to the Bahamas, where it was hoped her condition would improve, but it only worsened. She died in March 1870. Devastated, the twenty-eight-year-old never remarried.

Upton became commandant of the 4th U.S. Artillery and the Presidio in San Francisco in December 1880. By this time, he suffered from excruciating headaches. It is not clear whether they were migraines, a brain tumor, or brain cancer. In any case, on March 15, 1881, he sat at his desk in the Presidio, wrote out a letter of resignation, and shot himself in the head. He was forty-one. He was buried in Fort Hill Cemetery, Auburn, New York.

V

VAN ALEN – VOGDES

JAMES HENRY VAN ALEN was born in Kinderhook, New York, on August 17, 1819. His father was a wealthy merchant, and James was educated by private tutors, although he never had to focus on a single profession, other than managing his great wealth. When the Civil War began, he recruited the 3rd New York Cavalry and equipped it entirely at his own expense. He was mustered in as the unit's colonel on August 28, 1861.

Initially part of the Washington defenses, the 3rd patrolled along the Potomac River and was lightly engaged in the Battle of Ball's Bluff (October 21). It was ordered to North Carolina on April 6. Van Alen, however, was sent to the Virginia Peninsula, as cavalry commander of the II Corps. He was promoted to brigadier general on April 16, 1862.

Apparently, the senior Union generals did not think highly of Van Alen as a cavalry commander. He was named military governor of Yorktown, Virginia, on May 4 and remained in this backwater post until October. He then served as one of the members of the court of inquiry investigating General McDowell's conduct at the Second Battle of Bull Run (November 1862–February 1863). He was an aide-de-camp to General Joseph Hooker in the Battle of Chancellorsville but on May 7, 1863, was placed in charge of the Union defenses along Aquia Creek, including the adjacent Richmond, Fredericksburg & Potomac Railroad. For reasons not revealed in the records, he resigned from the army on July 14 and returned to civilian life.

James H. Van Alen built a luxurious mansion in Newport, Rhode Island, and traveled extensively from 1863 on. General Van Alen was traveling with his grandchildren aboard the RMS *Umbria* from Liverpool to New York on the night of July 22, 1886, when he either jumped or fell overboard. He was sixty-six. His body was never recovered.

HORATIO PHILLIPS VAN CLEVE was born on November 23, 1809, in Princeton, New Jersey. He attended the College of New Jersey (now Princeton) for two years, entered West Point in 1827, graduated in 1831 (24/33), and was commissioned brevet second lieutenant in the 5th U.S. Infantry. He was stationed on the frontier at Forts Howard and Winnebago,

Wisconsin, until 1836, when he resigned his commission. He became a farmer near Monroe, Michigan; a schoolteacher in Cincinnati; a farmer near Ann Arbor, Michigan; a civil engineer; a surveyor in Minnesota; and a stockman in Minnesota.

Van Cleve was commissioned colonel of the 2nd Minnesota Infantry on July 22, 1861. He was sent to Kentucky, where he fought under General Thomas at Mill Springs on January 19, 1862. He was promoted to brigadier general on March 22, 1862. Given a brigade in the Army of the Ohio, he took part in the Siege of Corinth and the Kentucky Campaign, during which he rose to divisional command. At Stones River, he caught a musket ball in the right leg on December 31 and was medically evacuated back to Nashville. He returned to duty as a divisional commander in the XXI Corps in March 1863.

Van Cleve took part in the Tullahoma Campaign and the Battle of Chickamauga, where his division (part of the XXI Corps) was smashed. The corps was disbanded the following month, and the other two divisional commanders, Thomas Wood and John Palmer, were retained, but Van Cleve was given a rear area post at Murfreesboro, Tennessee, where he spent the rest of the war and where he remained until he was mustered out of volunteer service in August 1865. He was nevertheless brevetted major general in 1867.

Post-war, General Van Cleve was adjutant general of Minnesota from 1866 to 1870 and from 1876 to 1882. He was postmaster of St. Anthony, Minnesota, from 1871 to 1873. He retired to Minneapolis, where he died on April 24, 1891, at age eighty-one. He was buried in Lakewood Cemetery, Minneapolis. Oddly, Congress reinstated him to active duty as a second lieutenant on June 11, 1890, and when he turned eighty years old, he retired at that rank.

FERDINAND VAN DERVEER (sometimes spelled Vanderveer) was born on February 27, 1823, in Middletown, Ohio. He was educated in common schools and at Farmer's College. He studied law, passed the bar, and set up

a practice in Middletown. When the Mexican War broke out, he enlisted in the 1st Ohio Infantry as a private. He fought in northern Mexico and commanded an assault column at Monterrey. He emerged from the war as a captain. From 1850 to 1852, he searched for gold in California but was not successful. He returned home, resumed his law practice, and served as county sheriff for several years.

When the Civil War began, he organized the 35th Ohio Infantry. It was mustered into Federal service on September 24, 1861, with Van Derveer as colonel. He fought at Mill Springs, Perryville, Stones River, Chickamauga, the Siege of Chattanooga, and Missionary Ridge. In the process, almost half his 921 men were killed or wounded. Van Derveer was given command of a brigade in the Army of the Ohio in late November 1863. He was mustered out with his original regiment at Chattanooga on August 26, 1864, but returned to the colors on October 4, 1864, and was promoted to brigadier general the same day.

Van Derveer's new command operated in the Huntsville area of northern Alabama. His brigade was dissolved in June 1865, so he resigned. He was mustered out on June 15. He returned to Butler County, where he became a judge. He died in on November 5, 1892, at age sixty-nine. He was buried in Greenwood Cemetery, Hamilton, Butler County, Ohio.

WILLIAM VANDEVER was born on March 31, 1817, in Baltimore, Maryland. He was educated in local schools, moved to Illinois in 1839, and worked as a surveyor and newspaper editor. He moved to Iowa in 1852, where he studied law and was admitted to the bar that same year. He started a practice in Dubuque, ran for Congress as a Republican in 1858, was successful, and was re-elected in 1860. He was a member of the Peace Conference of 1861, which unsuccessfully tried to find a way to avoid the approaching war.

Vandever served in Congress until September 24, 1861, when he was mustered into the Union Army as colonel of the 9th Iowa Infantry. (He never officially resigned from Congress, however.) He was given command of a brigade in the Army of the Southwest on February 9, 1862, and fought in the

Battle of Pea Ridge (March 7–8). He was promoted to brigadier general on November 29, 1862. He took part in the capture of Arkansas Post in January 1863, after which he was given command of a division in the Army of the Frontier. On May 1–2, he fought Confederate General John Marmaduke in the Battle of Chalk Bluff, in extreme northeastern Arkansas. Marmaduke was attempting to cross the St. Francis River and, although Vandever had ten thousand men and outnumbered him five to one, he could not prevent the crossing. Marmaduke, however, realized that the odds against him were too great, so he called off his offensive.

Transferred to the Western Front, Vandever commanded a brigade in the XIII Corps during the Siege of Vicksburg. Short tours of duty in the Department of the Gulf and on recruiting duty in Iowa followed. In 1864, he was part of Sherman's army group during the Atlanta Campaign but was on court-martial duty during the March to the Sea. He was given another brigade at Savannah in late 1864 and took part in the Carolinas Campaign, where he commanded a division. He was brevetted major general in June and was mustered out on August 24, 1865.

Postwar, Vandever returned to his law practice in Dubuque. President Grant appointed him Indian inspector in 1873, a post he held until Grant left office in 1877. He moved to Ventura, California, in 1884, and again practiced law. He was again elected to Congress in 1886 and served from 1887 to 1891. He did not run for re-election in 1890.

General Vandever died in Ventura on July 24, 1893, at age seventy-six. He is buried in Ventura Cemetery.

STEWART VAN VLIET was born on July 21, 1815, in Ferrisburg, Vermont. He graduated from West Point in 1836 (9/42) and was commissioned second lieutenant in the 3rd U.S. Artillery. He fought in the Seminole War and served in various garrisons, mostly in the South, and took part in the Mexican War, fighting at Monterey and Vera Cruz. Promoted to first lieutenant (1843) and captain, staff (1847), he transferred from the artillery to the Quartermaster Department in 1847.

From 1847 to 1851, Van Vliet was engaged in building posts along the Oregon Trail. At various times, he was quartermaster at Fort Kearny, Nebraska; Fort Laramie, Dakota Territory; Fort Brown, Texas; and Fort Leavenworth, Kansas. He also participated in the Battle of Ash Hollow (a.k.a. Blue Water Creek), Nebraska, on September 3, 1855, where the army defeated the Lakota Sioux and killed dozens of women and children.

Van Vliet was at Leavenworth when the Civil War began. He was promoted to major in the Quartermaster Department on August 3, 1861, and on August 10, he became chief quartermaster of the Army of the Potomac. He was promoted to brigadier general on September 23, 1861. Relieved of his post with the Army of the Potomac on July 10, 1862, his volunteer commission expired on July 17, 1862, and he reverted to the rank of major. He then became quartermaster for the Department of the East, headquartered in New York City, where he remained until the end of the war, coordinating transportation and supplies for the field armies. He did an excellent job and was brevetted lieutenant colonel, colonel, and brigadier general. He was reappointed brigadier general of volunteers on November 23, 1865, and mustered out on September 1, 1866.

General Van Vliet reverted to the rank of staff lieutenant colonel after the war and was quartermaster in a variety of posts, mostly in the eastern United States. He was promoted to colonel, staff rank, in 1872. He retired in 1881 after forty-five years' service. He died in Washington, D.C., on March 28, 1901, at age eighty-five. He was interred in Arlington National Cemetery.

CHARLES HENRY VAN WYCK was born on May 10, 1824, in Poughkeepsie, New York, the descendent of an old Dutch family. He was educated in preparatory schools and at Rutgers College, from which he graduated at the head of his class in 1843. He later read law and was admitted to the bar in 1847. He was elected district atttorney of Sullivan County in 1850 as a Democrat. He later switched to the Republican Party and was elected to Congress, serving from 1859 to 1863.

As a Congressman, Van Wyck was a prominent investigator into fraud and considered "loyal" war profiteers more despicable than "traitors in arms." He was also fiercely anti-slavery, stating that the South was guilty of crimes against God and nature. One of his passionate speeches led to an assassination attempt in February 1861, and only a notebook in the breast pocket of his coat prevented the blade of a Bowie knife from going into his chest. His three attackers fled and were never identified.

Meanwhile, Van Wyck recruited the 56th New York Infantry, also called the "10th Legion," with himself as colonel. It was mustered into Federal service on September 1, 1861. After spending the winter of 1861–62 in the Washington defenses, the regiment fought in the Peninsula Campaign (including the Siege of Yorktown and the Battle of Williamsburg). Its colonel, however, spent much of his time in Washington, attending to his Congressional duties. He was present at Seven Pines (Fair Oaks), however, and was slightly wounded in the left knee.

The 10th Legion was left behind at Fort Monroe when the Army of the Potomac was transported to northern Virginia. In December, it was transferred to North Carolina, and in January 1863 was sent to Port Royal, South Carolina. In 1863, it was involved in the operations against Charleston including the Siege of Fort Wagner and the operations against Fort Sumter.

In late 1863, Van Wyck contracted miasmatic fever and spent weeks in the hospital. In March 1864, he was sent back to the North, both to recruit and in hopes the change of climate would improve his health. It did. He returned to South Carolina in January 1865 as a brigade commander in the Department of the South. He took part in the occupation of Charleston the following month and remained there until January 1866, when he was mustered out. He was brevetted brigadier general in 1865 and, on September 27, 1865, was promoted to brigadier general of volunteers, full rank.

Post-war, Van Wyck returned home and was re-elected to Congress in 1866, serving from 1867 to 1869. It initially appeared that he was defeated for re-election but contested the results and was eventually seated. He served until March 1871.

General Van Wyck moved to Nebraska in 1874 and engaged in farming. He was elected to the state senate in 1877, 1879, and 1881, and was a U.S. senator from 1881 to 1887. He was defeated for re-election. In 1892, he ran for governor of Nebraska on the Populist ticket and lost, after which he retired from public life. He died in Washington, D.C., on October 24, 1895, at age seventy-one. He was buried in Milford Cemetery, Milford, Pennsylvania.

JAMES CLIFFORD VEATCH was born on December 19, 1819, near Elizabeth, Indiana, but moved to Rockport on the Ohio River when he was a child. His family was locally prominent. His great-grandfather was mortally wounded in the Battle of Camden in the Revolutionary War, his grandfather was a lieutenant in the Tennessee Volunteers, and his father was a member of the state legislature. James was educated in public schools and by private tutors. He read law, was admitted to the bar in 1840, and set up a practice in Rockport. He was the Spencer County auditor from 1841 to 1855.

Veatch was a member of the legislature when the war began. He helped form the 25th Indiana Infantry, was mustered in as its colonel on August 19, 1861, and fought in the Battle of Fort Donelson. The day after the fort surrendered, he was advanced to brigade commander. He distinguished himself in the Battle of Shiloh, where he exhibited great courage. He was promoted to brigadier general on April 30.

After taking part in the Siege of Corinth and the Second Battle of Corinth, Veatch fought in the Battle of Hatchie's Bridge (October 5), where he was wounded in the side by Confederate grapeshot and was forced to leave the field. He did not return to duty until January 6, 1863, when he became commander of the District of Memphis. He was given command of a division in the XVI Corps in March but remained in the west Tennessee/northern Mississippi area until early 1864, when he took part in Sherman's Meridian Expedition. Veatch and his men accompanied Sherman to Georgia and, as part of the Army of the Tennessee, fought at Resaca, Dallas, and Kennesaw Mountain during the Atlanta Campaign.

General Veatch went on a 20-day sick leave on July 17, 1864. (He suffered from rheumatism and heart trouble.) While he was gone, his army commander, General McPherson, was killed in action. When Veatch returned to duty, Oliver O. Howard, the new army commander, relieved him and instructed him to return to Memphis and await orders. He was without a command for some time and held only minor commands in western Tennessee and the Department of the Gulf until February 1865, when he was given a division in Granger's XIII Corps. He led it in the Mobile Campaign and fought in the Battle of Fort Blakeley (April 2–9), which led to the fall of the city. He was mustered out August 24, 1865, and was brevetted major general in 1866.

Postwar, General Veatch practiced law, was adjutant general of Indiana (1869–70), and a collector of internal revenue (1870–83). He died on December 22, 1895, in Rockport, at age seventy-six. He was buried in Sunset Hill Cemetery, Rockport.

EGBERT LUDOVICUS VIELE was born on June 17, 1825, in Waterford, New York. His family could trace its American roots back to New Amsterdam in 1639. Egbert graduated from Albany Academy, entered West Point in 1842, graduated in 1847 (30/38), and was commissioned brevet second lieutenant in the 2nd U.S. Infantry. He was immediately sent to Mexico, where he was promoted to second lieutenant on September 8. Six years of frontier duty in Texas followed. He was promoted to first lieutenant in 1850 but resigned his commission in 1853 to become a civil engineer in New York and New Jersey. Among other projects, Viele was chief engineer of Central Park in New York City and Prospect Park in Brooklyn. He was also State Topographical Engineer for New Jersey from 1854 to 1857.

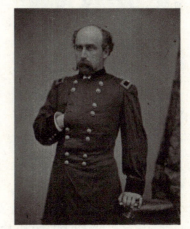

Viele rushed to the colors when the war began. Fort Sumter surrendered on April 13, 1861, and Viele was commissioned captain of engineers in the 7th New York Militia Regiment on April 19. Initially assigned to the Washington defenses, he was promoted to brigadier general on August 17, 1861. He commanded the Camp of Instruction near New York City. In April

1862, he directed the South Atlantic Expedition that captured Fort Pulaski, Georgia, which won him high praise. The following month he was transferred to the Department of Virginia and took part in the capture of Norfolk (May 10). He remained there as military governor until October 1863, when he was named superintendent of the draft in northern Ohio. Apparently, this position did not suit Viele, who resigned his commission on October 20.

General Viele continued his distinguished engineering career postwar, most notably in railroads, elevated railroads, and parks. His *Topographical Atlas of the City of New York* was published in 1876 and is still used by NYC engineers. He was Park Commissioner of New York City in 1883 and served as a Democratic Congressman from 1885 to 1887 but was defeated for re-election in 1886. He died in New York City on April 22, 1902, at age seventy-six.

STRONG VINCENT was born on June 17, 1837, in Waterford, Pennsylvania, the son of an iron foundry owner. He attended the Erie [Pennsylvania] Academy; Trinity College in Hartford, Connecticut; and Harvard, from which he graduated in 1859. He was admitted to the bar in 1860 and was practicing law in Erie when the war began.

Vincent was commissioned first lieutenant in the Erie Regiment of the Pennsylvania Militia on April 21, 1861. He married Elizabeth Carter that same day. Discharged with his unit when its 90-day enlistment expired, Vincent was mustered into the Union Army as lieutenant colonel of the 83rd Pennsylvania Infantry on September 14, 1861. He served in the Siege of Yorktown and the skirmish at Hanover Court House on May 27 during the Peninsula Campaign, but was then stricken with malaria ("Peninsula fever") and did not return to duty until late 1862. Meanwhile, during the Seven Days battles, his regimental commander was killed at Gaines' Mill. Vincent was promoted to colonel on June 27, 1862, although he could not assume command until just before the Battle of Fredericksburg, where his regiment suffered two hundred casualties.

The 83rd Pennsylvania was part of Meade's V Corps in the Battle of Chancellorsville, where it was lightly engaged. Vincent was given command of a brigade in the V Corps on May 20, 1863. It included his own 83rd Pennsylvania, Joshua Chamberlain's 20th Maine, the 16th Michigan, and the 44th New York.

If any brigade should be given more credit than any other for saving the Army of the Potomac at Gettysburg, it (arguably) should be Vincent's. At Little Round Top on July 2, while Chamberlain launched his famous bayonet attack, the 16th Michigan collapsed. Vincent rushed into the middle of the fighting and rallied his men, waving a riding crop and shouting "Don't give an inch!" At that moment, he was cut down. A minié ball passed through his left groin and lodged in his right groin. Placed on a stretcher, he was carried to a farmhouse four miles southeast of Gettysburg, where he died on July 7. Meanwhile, on the recommendation of General Meade, he was promoted to brigadier general on July 3, although it is doubtful if he ever knew it.

General Vincent was buried in Erie Cemetery, Erie, Pennsylvania. He was twenty-six years old. His wife was pregnant with their only child when he died. His daughter was born two months after his death, but died a year later. She is buried next to her father.

FRANCIS LAURENS VINTON was born on June 1, 1835, at Fort Preble, Maine. His father was a Regular Army officer who was killed in the Siege of Vera Cruz. Francis was admitted to West Point in 1851, graduated in 1856 (10/49), and was commissioned second lieutenant in the 1st Cavalry. He spent his graduation leave in France and resigned his commission on September 30. He remained in France to attend the Imperial School of Mines, from which he graduated in 1860. He was an instructor of mechanical drawing at Cooper Union when the Civil War started.

Vinton returned to the service as a captain, Regular Army, in the 16th U.S. Infantry on August 5, 1861. On October 31, he was named colonel of the 43rd New York Infantry. He participated in the Peninsula Campaign and the Seven Days battles but for unknown reasons was not present at the Battle of Antietam, where the regiment was commanded by its major. Nevertheless, Vinton was appointed brigadier general on September 19, 1862.

Vinton was back in action at Fredericksburg on December 13 and was badly wounded when a minié ball passed through his abdomen and exited near the spine. He had not returned to duty when his appointment expired on March 4, 1863, and he reverted to the rank of colonel. He was reappointed on April 9 and this time was confirmed. Vinton, however, resigned both his volunteer and Regular Army commissions on May 15 because of his poor health.

In 1864, Francis Vinton became the first professor of civil and mining engineering at the recently opened Columbia School of Mines in New York. He resigned his professorship in 1877 and moved to Denver, Colorado, where he was a consulting mining engineer. He died of erysipelas (a type of bacterial infection) on October 6, 1879, in Leadville, Colorado, at age forty-four. His remains lie in the Swan Point Cemetery, Providence, Rhode Island. His uncle, David H. Vinton, who was a colonel in the Quartermaster Department, was brevetted major general at the end of the war.

ISRAEL VOGDES was born on August 4, 1816, in Williston, Pennsylvania. He was educated in local schools, attended the U.S. Military Academy, graduated in 1837 (11/50), and was commissioned second lieutenant in the 1st U.S. Artillery. He immediately became an assistant professor of mathematics at the Academy (1837–49) before going to Florida to fight the Seminoles (1849–50). After serving on garrison duty at Key West, he again fought the Seminoles (1856). Garrison duty at Fort Moultrie, South Carolina, and Fort Monroe, Virginia, followed. He was at Fort Pickens, Florida, when the war began. Meanwhile, he was promoted to first lieutenant (1838), captain (1847), and major (May 14, 1861).

Vogdes was captured during the Confederate night attack on Santa Rosa Island in Pensacola, Florida, on October 9. He was exchanged in August 1862 and briefly served on the staff of General John F. Reynolds on the

Pennsylvania-Maryland border. He was then sent to South Carolina, where he constructed batteries for the reduction of Fort Sumter. Meanwhile, he was promoted to brigadier general on November 29, 1862. He commanded a brigade on Morris Island and Folly Island during the Siege of Charleston. From February to April 1864, he commanded a brigade in Florida, before directing the defenses of Portsmouth and Norfolk, Virginia, from then until the end of the war. He had a territorial command in Florida immediately after the war and was discharged from volunteer service in January 1866.

Postwar, Vogdes reverted to the rank of colonel and commander of the 1st U.S. Artillery Regiment. At various times, he headquartered at Fort Hamilton, New York; Charleston, South Carolina; and Fort Adams, Rhode Island. He retired after more than forty years' service in 1881. General Vogdes died in New York City on December 7, 1889, at age seventy-three. He was buried in the West Point Cemetery. One of his sons, Anthony Wayne Vogdes, was a brigadier general in World War I.

WADE – WRIGHT

MELANCTHON SMITH WADE was born on December 2, 1802, in Cincinnati, Ohio. His father was David E. Wade, a Revolutionary War officer and one of Ohio's first settlers. Melancthon was educated in local common schools and went into the dry goods business, where he was so successful that he was able to retire in 1840, when he was 38. He was active in the Ohio Militia and, from 1825 to 1849, rose from sergeant to brigadier general.

When the Civil War began, he devoted himself to recruiting and organizing Ohio volunteers. He was given command of the newly formed Camp Dennison, a piece of flat land seventeen miles from Cincinnati. He was the first commandant and assumed his post in April 1861. He was given a full regiment of infantry to guard the camp, maintain it, and assist in training and drilling new recruits. On the recommendation of General Ormsby Mitchel, he was mustered into Federal service on October 1, 1861, as a brigadier general of volunteers.

Wade was fifty-eight years old when the war began. His age and health prevented him from having much of a role in the war. On March 18, 1862, the Senate rejected his nomination for brigadier general. He resigned from the army the same day. He retired to his estate in Avondale, Ohio (now part of Cincinnati) and engaged in horticulture and fruit production.

General Wade died in Avondale on August 11, 1868, at age sixty-five. He was buried in Spring Grove Cemetery, Cincinnati. His service was so obscure that his name does not appear in the index of the *Official Records*.

JAMES SAMUEL WADSWORTH was born on October 30, 1807, in Geneseo, New York. His family was incredibly wealthy and owned a great deal of land. James attended both Harvard and Yale and studied law but never intended to practice; instead, he was groomed to manage his family's estate. He was a philanthropist and keenly interested in agriculture. He was president of the New York State Agricultural Society (1842–43).

Wadsworth was also interested in politics. A Democrat in the 1840s, he was anti-slavery and became an organizer of the short-lived Free Soil Party in 1848. He joined the Republican Party in 1856 and was a Lincoln presidential elector in 1860. He wanted peace and to avoid the breakup of the Union and was a member of the Washington Peace Conference of 1861, an unofficial attempt by Northern and Southern moderates to avoid the rapidly approaching war.

Despite having no military background or training, he was named major general in the New York Militia in May 1861. He became a civilian volunteer aide to General McDowell on June 8, 1861, and took part in the Battle of the First Bull Run. On McDowell's recommendation, he was commissioned brigadier general on August 9, 1861. He was the richest man in the Union Army. He was given command of a brigade in McDowell's division of the Army of the Potomac on October 9 and was made commander of the Military District of Washington on March 17, 1862.

Wadsworth opposed McClellan's plan to invade Virginia by the Peninsula because he felt it would leave him with insufficient forces to defend the capital. Lincoln (who was always sensitive when it came to defending Washington) sided with Wadsworth and withheld McDowell's entire corps, earning McClellan's permanent enmity. Meanwhile, Wadsworth ran for governor of New York, but refused to leave active duty, and thus did not campaign. He was defeated by Horatio Seymour.

After Lincoln fired McClellan in November 1862 and Burnside was crushed at Fredericksburg, Wadsworth was given command of a division in the I Corps on December 27. He twice briefly commanded the I Corps but first tasted serious action as a combat commander at Chancellorsville. Here, he was slow, and his performance left much to be desired. At Gettysburg, however, he did much better, but his division was finally overwhelmed, and his troops fled through the town. Wadsworth's forces suffered more than 50 percent casualties on July 1, mostly captured. On July 2, he played a significant role in holding Culp's Hill.

The I Corps was smashed at Gettysburg. Wadsworth spent most of the next eight months on detached duty, primarily inspecting U.S.C.T. in the Mississippi Valley. When the Army of the Potomac was reorganized in March 1864, I Corps was disbanded, and Wadsworth was given command of a division in the V Corps. On May 6, 1864, while leading his men in an attempt to repel a Confederate attack during the Battle of the Wilderness, General Wadsworth was shot in the back of the head. He fell from his horse and was captured by the Rebels but never knew it because he never regained consciousness. He died in a Confederate field hospital at Spotsylvania, Virginia, on May 8, 1864. He was fifty-six. He was buried in Temple Hill Cemetery in the town of his birth.

Wadsworth was nominated for promotion to major general the day before he was mortally wounded. The Senate returned his nomination to the president on July 2 without acting on it, because he was already dead. He was posthumously brevetted major general. His son, Craig Wadsworth, became a colonel during the war and a major general in the New York Militia in 1867. Another son, James, became a major in the Union Army and a four-term U.S. Congressman.

GEORGE DAY WAGNER was born on September 22, 1829, in Ross County, Ohio, but his family moved to Warren County, Indiana, when he was four. He was educated in local schools, became a prosperous farmer, and was elected to the state legislature, where he was a strong supporter of Abraham Lincoln. He was president of the Indiana State Agricultural Society when the war began.

Wagner was mustered into the Union Army on June 14, 1861, as colonel of the 15th Indiana Infantry and initially served in western Virginia. He was named commander of the 21st Brigade of the Army of the Ohio in February 1862. He fought at Shiloh, Perryville, and Stones River and was appointed brigadier general on April 4, 1863.

General Wagner was involved in the capture of Chattanooga in September 1863 and was still there when the Army of the Cumberland was mauled at Chickamauga. His brigade took part in the Siege of Chattanooga and suffered heavy losses in the Battle of Missionary Ridge (November 25, 1863). He led a brigade in the IV Corps during the Atlanta Campaign and suffered heavy casualties at Kennesaw Mountain. Wagner was given command of a division on September 30, 1864.

Wagner destroyed his own military career on November 30, 1864, during the Battle of Franklin. He occupied a position forward of the main Union line. His superior, General Cox, ordered him to fall back to the army's main defensive position, but he chose to ignore these instructions. As a result, the Confederates were able to crush his isolated units, and two of his brigades were routed. Because they did not want to kill their own comrades, the Union soldiers did not fire as Wagner's men ran through their lines. Unfortunately, the Rebels were right on their heels and were able to penetrate the Federal center. Union reinforcements managed to stabilize the position, but it was a near-run thing, and Wagner's actions almost cost the Yankees the battle. He was forced to give up command on December 2.

George Wagner was in Indiana awaiting orders until April 1865, when he was assigned to duty in St. Louis. He was mustered out in August 1865. He returned home, where he again became president of the Indiana Agricultural Society. He died suddenly on February 13, 1869, in Indianapolis. He was thirty-nine. He was buried in Armstrong Cemetery, Green Hill, Indiana. Despite his previously exemplary service, Wagner has gone down in history as the man whose conduct at Franklin almost led to a major disaster.

CHARLES CARROLL WALCUTT was born on February 12, 1838, in Columbus, Ohio. He was a maternal cousin of Davy Crockett. He was educated in local schools, graduated from the Kentucky Military Institute in 1858, and became a county surveyor. When the Civil War began, Walcutt organized a company of Ohio infantry. He was appointed its captain on April 17, 1861, but Ohio already reached its quota, and his new formation was rejected for Federal service. He was appointed major in the Ohio Militia in June and served in western Virginia as a staff officer. He returned to the Buckeye State and became the major of the 46th Ohio on October 1. He became its lieutenant colonel on January 30, 1862,

Walcutt's first major action was Shiloh on April 6, where he was shot in the left shoulder. The bullet could not be removed, and he carried it until the day he died. As part of the Army of the Tennessee, the 46th Ohio took part in the Siege of Corinth and subsequent operations in Mississippi, culminating in the Siege of Vicksburg. Walcutt, meanwhile, became its colonel on October 26, 1862.

Colonel Walcutt distinguished himself in the Battle of Missionary Ridge (November 23–25, 1863), where he took command of Brigadier General John Corse's brigade after that officer was seriously wounded, repulsed several counterattacks, and earned the official praise of General Sherman. General Howard reported that "there is not a braver or better officer" in the Union Army than Walcutt.

Walcutt fought in the Atlanta Campaign and again distinguished himself at Kennesaw Mountain (June 27, 1864) and the Battle of Atlanta (July 22). He was promoted to brigadier general on July 30. He took part in the March to the Sea, where he was severely wounded when a shell fragment ripped into the calf of his right leg during the Battle of Griswoldville on November 22. He could not return to duty until April 4, 1865, when he was given command of a division in the XIV Corps. He was mustered out on January 15, 1866, was brevetted major general three days later, and became warden of the Ohio Penitentiary in Columbus. In July, he accepted a Regular Army commission as lieutenant colonel in the 10th Cavalry at Fort Leavenworth but resigned in December, stating that he was "unwilling to endure army life in time of peace."

General Walcutt returned to Ohio and again became warden of the penitentiary. He was a presidential elector for Grant in 1868 and in 1869 became a collector of internal revenue, a job he held until 1883. He was also president of the local board of education for seven years and, in 1883, was elected mayor of Columbus. He served two terms and retired in 1887.

Walcutt's health failed him in 1897, and he went to Mexico to recover. This effect failed, and he attempted to return home to die, but he did not make it. He succumbed to kidney failure in Omaha, Nebraska, on May 2, 1898, at age sixty. He was buried in Green Lawn Cemetery, Columbus, Ohio.

LEWIS "LEW" WALLACE was born on April 10, 1827, at Brookville, Indiana. His father, David Wallace, graduated from the U.S. Military Academy in 1821 but left the army in 1822. He established a law practice and eventually became governor of Indiana (1837–40). Lew was educated in public schools in Covington and Indianapolis, Indiana; at a preparatory school associated with Wabash College; and a private academy in Centerville, Indiana. He was studying law under his father when the Mexican War broke out. He joined the 1st Indiana Infantry in 1846 and rose to the rank of first lieutenant but arrived in northern Mexico too late to see combat. He was discharged in 1847, returned to Indiana, and was admitted to the bar in 1849. He eventually set up a practice in Crawfordsville, Indiana, and was elected to the Indiana State Senate as a Democrat in 1856.

The Civil War began on April 12, 1861, and Wallace was appointed Indiana adjutant general on April 16. He accepted the post on the condition that he be made the commander of the regiment of his choice. Indiana's quota of six regiments was filled within a week, and Wallace became colonel and commander of the 11th Indiana Infantry on April 25. Sent to Virginia, he was part of the minor Union victory at Romney on June 5. He was promoted to brigadier general on September 3, 1861, and was given command of a brigade. On February 1, 1862, he became a division commander in Grant's army.

Wallace performed brilliantly in the Battle of Fort Donelson and was promoted to major general on March 22, 1862. At the time, he was thirty-four years old and the youngest major general in the Union Army. His performance at Shiloh, however, was poor. On April 6—the first day of the battle—he was stationed only five miles from Pittsburg Landing and Grant's base but took the wrong road and did not arrive on the battlefield in time to be of any help to the rest of the army. This almost led to the destruction of the Army of the Tennessee, and both Grant and Halleck placed the blame squarely on Wallace's shoulders. He was relieved of his command in June.

Wallace did not get another major field command for two years. He did direct an *ad hoc* force (eight thousand men) tasked with defending Cincinnati during the Heartland Campaign of 1862, but the decisive battle occurred at Perryville. He briefly commanded the POW Camp Chase, but he was largely without a command until March 1864, when he assumed command of the Middle Department and the VIII Corps in Baltimore.

It was intended that Wallace be relegated to a rear-area, territorial commands until Jubal Early's Confederate army threatened Washington, D.C. Wallace met him at Monocacy River on July 9. Outnumbered more than 2.5 to 1, Wallace was defeated, but he slowed the Rebels long enough to allow reinforcements from the Army of the Potomac to reach Washington, and thus he made a significant contribution to the salvation of the capital. He commanded the Middle Department until August 1865.

Post-war, Wallace was a member of the commissions investigating the Lincoln assassination and Andersonville. He resigned from the U.S. Army in November 1865. He accepted a major generalcy in the Mexican Army for $100,000 ($2,024,286 in 2023 currency) but apparently was never paid. He returned to the United States in 1867 deeply in debt.

Wallace began practicing law in Indiana in 1867 but preferred politics. He ran for Congress in 1868 and 1870 but was defeated. He supported Rutherford B. Hayes for president in 1876; as a result, President Hayes appointed him governor of the New Mexico Territory in 1878. He held this post until 1881, when he replaced former Confederate General James Longstreet as U.S. minister to the Ottoman Empire. Meanwhile, he wrote a novel, *Ben-Hur: A Tale of the Christ*, which was published in 1880 and is considered by some to be the most influential Christian book of the nineteenth century. His memoirs were published after his death.

Thanks to his royalties, Wallace retired quite wealthy. He died in Crawfordsville, Indiana, on February 15, 1905, at age seventy-seven. He is buried there in Oak Hill Cemetery.

His wife, Zerelda, became a prominent suffragist and temperance advocate.

WILLIAM HERVEY LAMME WALLACE, whose third name is cited as "Lamb" or "Lamm" in some sources. Was commonly known as **W. H. L. WALLACE**. He was born on July 8, 1821, in Urbana, Ohio, but the family moved to Mount Morris, Illinois, in 1840, so W. H. L. could be educated at Rock River Seminary. He studied law and was admitted to the bar in 1846. That same year, he enlisted in the 1st Illinois Infantry as a private, became regimental adjutant, fought at Buena Vista, and was discharged as a second lieutenant in 1847. He returned to Illinois and became a district attorney in 1853.

Wallace was elected colonel of the 11th Illinois Infantry on May 1, 1861. He rose to brigade commander in September and served in southeast Missouri and the District of Cairo. Attached to McClernand's division of Grant's Army of the Tennessee, he fought at Fort Donelson, where he distinguished himself for his tactical ability and his coolness in heavy fighting. He was promoted to brigadier general on March 22, 1862.

During the movement to Savannah, Tennessee, Major General Charles F. Smith injured his leg and was forced to turn command of his division over to Wallace. On April 6, during the Battle of Shiloh, he bravely withstood six hours of Confederate attacks in the Hornet's Nest/Sunken Road sector. Only when he was loosely surrounded did Wallace order his men to break out. Some escaped. Wallace did not. He was struck in the head by a shell fragment. Some of his men found him barely alive. They took him to General Grant's headquarters at the Cherry Mansion in Savannah, Tennessee. Coincidentally, his wife had just arrived there on a surprise visit. She nursed him for four days, but he died on April 10, 1862. He was forty years old. He was buried in the Wallace-Dickey Cemetery in Ottawa, Illinois.

His younger half-brother was Brevet Brigadier General Martin R. M. Wallace (1829–1902), who commanded the 4th Illinois Cavalry during the war.

JOHN HENRY HOBART WARD was born in New York City on June 17, 1823. He was educated at Trinity Collegiate School and enlisted in the 7th U.S. Infantry Regiment in 1842. By 1845, he had risen through the ranks to sergeant major. He was present at Fort Brown when the Mexican War began. He fought in the Siege of Fort Brown (May 1846) and later in the Battle of Monterrey, where he was wounded. He later took part in the Siege of Vera Cruz and the Battle of Cerro Gordo, where he was again wounded. Discharged in 1851, he joined the New York Militia, and became assistant commissary general in 1851 and state commissary general in 1855, a post he held until 1859.

On June 8, 1861, at the start of the Civil War, Ward became colonel of the 38th New York Infantry. He fought in the First Battle of Bull Run (July 21), where he led a charge on Henry House Hill. Together with the 69th New York, he established a foothold on the hill but was pushed off by the Confederates. He assumed command of Orlando Willcox's brigade after that officer was wounded and captured. Ward reverted to regimental command the following month.

Ward was part of the Peninsula Campaign and fought at Yorktown, Williamsburg, and Seven Pines, where he was highly praised, especially for his part in the Battle of Seven Pines, where he again assumed command of a brigade after its commander was wounded. Lightly engaged in the Seven Days battles, he also took part in the Second Battle of Bull Run and the Battle of Chantilly. Here, his division commander, Phil Kearny, was killed. He was succeeded by David Birney, and Ward replaced Birney as brigade commander. This time it was permanent. John Ward was promoted to brigadier general on October 4, 1862.

General Ward participated in the battles of Fredericksburg, Chancellorsville, and Gettysburg, where he was slightly wounded in the Devil's Den on July 2. By the start of the Overland Campaign, he had a solid reputation as a fine brigade commander. On May 6, 1864, however, during the Battle of the Wilderness, Ward panicked and fled to the rear, riding a caisson. On May 10, he was wounded when a shell fragment struck him in the head. Two days later, he again departed for the rear while his men were engaged in the Battle of Spotsylvania Court House. Generals Hancock and Birney both saw him and concluded that he was intoxicated. On May 9, Assistant Secretary of War Charles Dana reported that Ward ran away during the Battle of the Wilderness.

It appears to me that, after three years of war, General Ward finally snapped. He was relieved of his command on May 12 and, the following month, was arrested and sent to Fort Monroe. He was never brought to trial, no doubt because of his previously exemplary service, his many wounds, and his long military career. He was honorably discharged on July 18.

John Ward spent the next thirty-two years as a clerk with the Superior Court and Supreme Court of New York. On July 24, 1903, while vacationing in Monroe, New York, where one of his daughters lived, he was struck and killed by a train. He was eighty. He is buried in Community Cemetery, Monroe.

WILLIAM THOMAS "OLD PAP" WARD was born on August 9, 1808, in Amelia County, Virginia. His family emigrated to Kentucky when he was a child. He attended local schools and St. Mary's College near Lebanon, Kentucky, studied law, set up a practice in Greensburg, and became a major in the 4th Kentucky Infantry during the Mexican War. He was a state legislator in 1850 and was elected to Congress later that year, serving from 1851 to 1853. He did not seek re-election.

Kentucky declared its neutrality when the war began, but Ward adhered to the Union and, by August 1861, had twenty companies ready to serve under him. After Kentucky's neutrality collapsed in September, he had no trouble raising a brigade. Ward was commissioned brigadier general on September 18, 1861. He initially served in the Department of Kentucky under General Boyle, but his efforts to rein in Confederate raider John Hunt Morgan were not successful. He commanded a brigade in the Army of the Ohio in 1862 and was commandant of Gallatin, Tennessee from November 1862. He spent 1863 in reserve or in rear area assignments. Part of the time, his brigade was posted to Nashville. He was acting commander of a division in the XI Corps of the Army of the Cumberland from January to April 1864. Reverting to brigade commander, he was part of Sherman's command during the Atlanta Campaign. Ward was wounded twice (in the left arm and side) by a Rebel musket balls at Resaca, Georgia, on May 15, 1864, but remained with his unit. He was given command of a division on June 29 and led it for the rest of the war, taking part in the capture of Atlanta, the March to the Sea, and the Carolinas Campaign. He was brevetted major general on February 25, 1865, and was mustered out in August 1865.

After the war, Ward returned to Kentucky, where he set up a law partnership with his son in Louisville. He died in Louisville on October 12, 1878, at age seventy. He was buried in Cave Hill Cemetery, Louisville.

JAMES MEECH WARNER was born on January 29, 1836, in Middlebury, Vermont. His family could trace its roots back to Massachusetts Bay in 1630. He attended Middlebury College (1851–55) and West Point (1855–60) in the days of the five-year course. He graduated next to last (40/41) and was commissioned brevet second lieutenant in the infantry. He was stationed in Fort Wise, Colorado, and was promoted to second lieutenant in February 1861 and to first lieutenant on May 30. He commanded the fort for the first half of 1862.

Warner was recalled to the East in July 1862 and served with the heavy artillery in the Washington defenses until September 1, 1862, when he became commander of the 1st Vermont Infantry. It was converted into a heavy artillery unit and was redesignated 1st Vermont Heavy Artillery Regiment on December 10, 1862. It was effectively converted back to infantry in the spring of 1864 and joined the VI Corps of the Army of the Potomac on May 12 for the Battle of Spotsylvania Court House. Three days later, Warner was walking the earthworks when a Confederate bullet struck him in the neck, passed upward to the base of the skull, and out below his right ear. He was disabled for two months but returned just in time to help repulse Early's attack on Fort Stevens on July 11–12. He was brevetted brigadier general for Spotsylvania.

Warner assumed command of a brigade in the Washington defenses in July 1864. He returned to the combat zone in September as a brigade commander in Sheridan's army and took part in the Third Battle of Winchester, Fisher's Hill, and Cedar Creek, where he again distinguished himself. In 1865, he helped break Lee's lines at Petersburg (April 2), fought at Sayler's Creek (April 6), and was present at Appomattox (April 9). He was promoted to brigadier general of volunteers (full rank) on May 8.

Warner was with the VI Corps in the Washington, D.C., area until it was disbanded in July; then he was on leave, awaiting orders, until he was mustered out of volunteer service in January 1866. He resigned his Regular Army commission the following month.

Post-war, Warner settled in Albany and became a paper manufacturer. He was postmaster of the city during Benjamin Harrison's administration (1889–93) and ran for mayor of the Republican ticket but was defeated. He was attending a play in New York City on March 16, 1897, when he suddenly died of a stroke. He was sixty-one. He was buried in Middlebury Cemetery in the town of his birth. He was the great uncle of legendary Civil War historian Ezra J. Warner.

FITZ HENRY WARREN was born in Brimfield, Massachusetts, on July 11, 1816. He was educated locally and moved to the Iowa Territory in 1844, where he worked as a journalist. He became a Whig activist and an early supporter of Zachary Taylor for president of the United States. Taylor was elected in 1848, was inaugurated in 1849, and appointed Warren assistant postmaster general. Taylor died in 1850 and was succeeded by Millard Fillmore, who supported the Fugitive Slave Law. Warren resigned in protest. With the support of the anti-slave wing, Warren became secretary of the Whig Party's National Executive Committee. After the party collapsed in 1854, Warren went over to the Republican Party.

Warren joined the Union Army as colonel of the 1st Iowa Cavalry Regiment on June 13, 1861. It totaled more than 1,200 men and operated in central and western Missouri against the Confederate guerrilla, Bill Quantrill, and assorted bushwhackers. He was promoted to brigadier general on July 18, 1862. He continued to operate in Missouri until March 1863, when he ran for the Republican nomination for governor of Iowa. He was the leading candidate when the convention began, but other candidates united to defeat him, and William M. Stone was nominated. (He also won the General Election.)

Warren returned to duty in December 1863 and commanded a brigade in the XIII Corps, Department of the Gulf. He seems to have spent the rest of the war in rear area commands in Texas; Baton Rouge, Louisiana; and western Mississippi. He was mustered out in August 1865 and was brevetted major general in 1866.

General Warren was elected to the Iowa State Senate in 1866. After he attended a single session, President Johnson named him U.S. minister to Guatemala. He served from 1866 to 1869. Shortly before his death, he moved back to the town of his birth. He died in Brimfield, Massachusetts, on June 21, 1878, at age sixty-two. He was buried in the Brimfield Cemetery.

GOUVERNEUR KEMBLE WARREN was born on January 8, 1830, in Cold Spring, New York. He entered West Point, which was just across the Hudson River from his hometown, in 1846, when he was fifteen. He graduated in 1850 (2/44) and was commissioned brevet second lieutenant in the topographical engineers. He was promoted to second lieutenant in 1854 and first lieutenant in 1856. Meanwhile, he worked as a topographical engineer on the Mississippi River, in the Dakota Territory, and in the Nebraska Territory (where he fought the Sioux). He was also an assistant professor of mathematics at West Point, where he was when the Civil War began. He was sent to Virginia on April 27, 1861.

Warren was named lieutenant colonel of the 5th New York Infantry on May 14. He took part in the Battle of Big Bethel Church on June 10. He was temporarily detached to Baltimore, which he prepared for defense. He became colonel of the 5th New York on August 31 and participated in the Peninsular Campaign, during which he assumed command of a brigade in the V Corps. He fought in the Seven Days battles and was slightly wounded at Gaines' Mill, where he was struck in the knee by a spent bullet. He distinguished himself checking a Southern attack at Malvern Hill (July 1, 1862).

Colonel Warren and his men saw further action at the Second Bull Run but were in reserve at Antietam. Warren was promoted to brigadier general on September 26, 1862. After the Fredericksburg Campaign, in which his brigade was again in reserve, he was named chief topographical engineer for the Army of the Potomac. He was commended for his performance at Chancellorsville.

Warren had a fine eye for terrain. At Gettysburg on July 2, 1863, he realized the importance of Little Round Top before anyone else. He saw to it that the position was occupied by Strong Vincent's brigade only minutes before the Confederates attacked. He thus saved the Union left flank, and it is not going too far to say that, had it not been for Warren, the Yankees would have lost the Battle of Gettysburg. He was wounded in the neck during the fighting but not seriously. Recognized as a hero of the campaign, he was promoted to major general on August 8, 1863.

General Warren replaced a wounded General Hancock as commander of the II Corps on August 16 and held the post until March 1864. He then commanded the V Corps, which he led during the Overland Campaign and the Siege of Petersburg. Meanwhile, he annoyed General Sheridan, with whom he had clashed before. On April 1, 1865, during the Battle of Five Forks, Sheridan relieved him of his command for moving too slowly. (Sheridan was not famous for his fairness.) This ruined Warren's career. He resigned his volunteer commission on May 27 and reverted to his Regular Army rank of major. He spent the next seventeen years as an engineer, rising to the rank of lieutenant colonel in 1879.

Warren spent years trying to get a court of inquiry to investigate his actions, but President Grant covered for his friend Sheridan and would not convene one. President Hayes, however, ordered a court of inquiry, which exonerated Warren and criticized Sheridan's unjustified actions. Unfortunately, the results of the court were not published until after Warren's death from diabetic complications. He passed away on August 8, 1882, in Newport, Rhode Island. He was fifty-two. He was buried in Island Cemetery, Newport.

CADWALLADER COLDEN "C. C." WASHBURN was born on April 22, 1818, in Livermore, Massachusetts (now Livermore, Maine). He attended school in Wiscasset, Maine, and taught there from 1838 to 1839. He then moved to Davenport, Iowa Territory, where he again taught school and worked as a surveyor. He later moved to Mineral Point, Wisconsin Territory, read law, and was admitted to the bar in 1842.

Washburn was an entrepreneur and a highly successful one at that. He became a land speculator, established a bank, and founded the Minneapolis Mill Company. He moved to La Crosse, Wisconsin, in 1853 and established the La Crosse Lumber Company in 1871. It eventually sawed 20,000,000 board feet of lumber a year. He also owned the largest shingle mill in the upper Mississippi Valley. After the war, he established a flour corporation which eventually became General Mills.

C. C. Washburn was also interested in politics. He ran for Congress as a Republican in 1854 and served from 1855 to 1861. He declined to run for re-election in 1860. Strongly opposed to slavery, he nevertheless was a delegate to the 1861 Peace Convention, where he and other prominent leaders sought to avoid civil war. After war came, he became colonel of the 2nd Wisconsin Cavalry on February 6, 1862. It served mainly in Missouri and Arkansas. Meanwhile, on July 18, 1862, Washburn was promoted to brigadier general. He took part in some insignificant actions in Arkansas before crossing the Mississippi, where he commanded the cavalry of the XIII Corps in the Vicksburg Campaign. When the siege began, he directed a three-division detachment from the XVI Corps. U.S. Grant was impressed with him, declaring Washburn "one of the best administrative officers we have." Reverting to divisional command after Vicksburg surrendered, he took part in the Army of the Gulf's unsuccessful operations against the Texas coast.

In the meantime, President Lincoln appointed him for major general on February 13, 1863. The Senate returned his nomination to the president on February 14. Lincoln renominated him on March 5, and this time he was confirmed.

Stephen Hurlbut, the commander of the District of West Tennessee, was unsuccessful in his efforts to check Confederate General Nathan Bedford Forrest and his raids into the territory. On April 17, 1864, Grant replaced Hurlbut with Washburn, who was also unsuccessful. The low point of Washburn's war occurred on August 21, when Forrest's men rode their horses into the lobby of the Gayoso Hotel in Memphis, where Washburn had his headquarters. Washburn only escaped by fleeing through the streets of the river city in his nightshirt, while Forrest's brother made off with his best uniform. Hurlbut remarked that they fired him because he could not keep

Forrest out of western Tennessee, but Washburn could not keep Forrest out of his bedroom. Washburn, however, was more successful in Tennessee than Hurlbut and went down in history as one of the better "political generals" of the Civil War. Certainly, he was more highly respected than Hurlbut.

Washburn remained in Memphis until the end of the war. He resigned his commission on May 25, 1865, and returned to Wisconsin. He was re-elected to Congress in 1866 and served from 1867 to 1871. He was governor of Wisconsin from January 1, 1872 to January 5, 1874. In addition to his successful businesses and political career, C. C. Washburn was a generous philanthropist, endowing hospitals and educational institutions.

General Washburn went to Eureka Springs, Arkansas, in 1882, to "take the waters" and improve his health. He died there on May 14, 1882, at age sixty-four. He was buried in Oak Grove Cemetery, La Crosse, Wisconsin. His brothers were also successful. Israel Washburn, Jr., was governor of Maine (1861 to 1863). Elihu was a congressman for many years, as well as minister of France. He was also the principal sponsor and promoter of Ulysses S. Grant. William D. Washburn was a congressman and U.S. senator from Minnesota, and Charles A. Washburn was U.S. minister to Paraguay and the inventor of an early typewriter.

LOUIS DOUGLASS WATKINS was born near Tallahassee, Florida Territory, on November 29, 1833. His family moved to the District of Columbia, where Douglas was educated and where he was living on April 12, 1861, when the Civil War erupted. Three days later, Watkins enlisted in the 3rd District of Columbia Infantry Battalion as a private. He was commissioned first lieutenant, Regular Army, in the 14th U.S. Infantry Regiment on May 14 but transferred to the 5th U.S. Cavalry on August 3.

Watkins fought in the Peninsula Campaign and the Seven Days battles, where he was severely wounded at Gaines' Mill (June 27, 1862) near Woodbury's Bridge on the Chickahominy. He was also trampled by several horses. He recovered quickly, however, and was back on duty in July. He was promoted to captain on July 17.

Transferred to Kentucky, Watkins was an aide to General A. J. Smith during the Kentucky Campaign of 1862 and briefly became chief of cavalry of Gordon Granger's Army of Kentucky in December. He was promoted to colonel and named commander of the 6th Kentucky Cavalry on February 1, 1863. He skirmished with Confederate units and took part in sorties into East Tennessee. He distinguished himself at Thompson's Station (March 5) and was given command of an infantry brigade in the Army of the Cumberland in July. He took part in the Tullahoma, Chickamauga, and Chattanooga Campaigns. During Sherman's drive on Atlanta, Watkins guarded the railroad and defeated Rebel raiders in the Battle of Lafayette, for which he was brevetted brigadier general on June 23, 1864. He distinguished himself in the Battle of Resaca and served in the Franklin-Nashville Campaign and in the pursuit of General Hood's broken army.

Watkins's brigade was dissolved in January 1865. He spent the rest of the war as commandant of Louisville and was promoted to brigadier general of volunteers on September 25, 1865. He was mustered out in September 1866 and reverted to lieutenant colonel, Regular Army, and was stationed at Baton Rouge and New Orleans.

General Watkins died suddenly in New Orleans on March 29, 1868, after a short illness. He was thirty-four. Watkins was interred in New Orleans but ultimately was buried in Arlington National Cemetery. His wife was Mary Rousseau, the daughter of Union General Lovell Rousseau.

ALEXANDER STEWART WEBB was born in New York City on February 15, 1835. His father was a diplomat, newspaper owner, and former Regular Army officer. His paternal grandfather was wounded at Bunker Hill and served on George Washington's staff during the Revolution. Alexander was educated at Colonel Churchill's Military School in Sing Sing, New York, and at West Point, from which he graduated in 1855 (13/34). Commissioned brevet second lieutenant in the 4th U.S. Artillery in July, he was promoted to second lieutenant that same year. He fought the Seminoles in Florida, did garrison duty in Massachusetts, and frontier duty at Fort Snelling,

Minnesota. He was an assistant professor of mathematics at West Point from 1857 to early 1861, when he was sent to Fort Pickens, Florida. He was promoted to first lieutenant on April 20 and to captain on May 14.

Webb fought in the First Battle of Bull Run (July 21) and was named assistant to the chief of artillery of the Army of the Potomac later that month. He became major of the 1st Rhode Island Artillery in September and was in the Washington defenses during the winter of 1861/62. He served as a staff officer in the V Corps in the Peninsula Campaign and Seven Days battles and was chief of staff of the corps in the Maryland Campaign. Promoted to lieutenant colonel, staff, on August 20, 1862, he was assistant inspector general of the Camp of Instruction near Washington (November–December 1862), chief of staff of the Central Grand Division at Fredericksburg, and chief of staff of the V Corps during the Chancellorsville Campaign. He became a brigade commander in the II Corps on June 28. He was promoted to brigadier general on July 1, 1863.

Webb was an affable person and a meticulous dresser, but he was also a hard worker, strong on discipline and attention to detail. The men of his brigade responded positively to his leadership. On July 3, at the climax of the Battle of Gettysburg, Webb's brigade was in the center of the U.S. line and defended the "Copse of Trees," which was the focal point of Pickett's Charge. The fighting was fierce, and Webb's brigade suffered 451 casualties, including the general himself, who was shot in the thigh and groin, but he continued fighting. Twenty-eight years later, he was awarded the Congressional Medal of Honor for his actions that day. More immediately, he was made acting commander of Gibbon's division in August and brevetted major general in 1864.

Webb led his division during the Rappahannock (Rapidan) Campaign and distinguished himself in the Battle of Bristoe Station (October 14). When Gibbon returned to duty in the spring of 1864, Webb reverted to brigade commander. He fought in the Battles of the Wilderness and Spotsylvania Court House until May 12, 1864, when a bullet passed through the corner of his right eye and out his ear. He did not return to duty until January 11, 1865, when he became chief of staff of the Army of the Potomac, a post he held until the end of the war. He was mustered out of volunteer service in January 1866.

General Webb reverted to the rank of lieutenant colonel and was a professor of geography, history, and ethics at West Point from 1866 to 1868. He was president of the College of the City of New York for thirty-three years, from 1869 to 1902, when he retired. He died in Riverdale, The Bronx, New York, on February 12, 1911, at age seventy-five. He is buried in the Post Cemetery at West Point.

MAX WEBER, sometimes called **MAX VON WEBER**, was born on August 27, 1824, in the town of Achern, in the Grand Duchy of Baden. He attended the Karlsruhe War School, graduated in 1843, and became a *Leutnant* (second lieutenant) in the Grand Duke's army. He joined Franz Sigel's revolutionaries in 1848 and, after the revolt was crushed by the Prussian Army, became a political refugee, settling in New York City in 1849. He eventually became owner of the Konstanz Hotel in New York.

When the Civil War began, Weber organized the Turner Rifles, which was mustered into Federal service as part of the 20th New York Infantry on May 9, 1861, with Weber as colonel and regimental commander. He was stationed at Fort Monroe and took part in the capture of Fort Hatteras, North Carolina (August 28–29). He commanded Camp Hamilton, near Fort Monroe, from September 1861 to May 1862. He was promoted to brigadier general on April 30, 1862, to rank from April 28.

Weber took part in the capture of Norfolk, Virginia, in May 1862. After serving as commandant of Suffolk, he and his brigade were transferred to Maryland. As part of the II Corps, Weber distinguished himself in the fighting for the Sunken Road at Antietam. Here, his right arm was so badly shattered by a musket ball that he could not return to even light (court-martial) duty until the summer of 1863. He was given command of Harper's Ferry in April 1864, but his wound re-opened and he was again *hors d'combat*. He remained in rear area assignments until May 13, 1865, when he resigned. After the war, he was an assessor or collector of internal revenue from 1870 to 1883. He later served as U.S. consul in Nantes, France.

General Weber died in Brooklyn, New York, on June 15, 1901, at age seventy-six. He was buried in the Evergreens Cemetery, Brooklyn.

JOSEPH DANA WEBSTER was born in Hampton, New Hampshire, on August 25, 1811. He graduated from Dartmouth College in 1832, moved to Massachusetts, and became a civil engineer. He secured an army commission in 1838 as a second lieutenant in the topographical engineers. He served in the Mexican War and was promoted to first lieutenant in 1849, then captain in 1853, but resigned his commission in 1854. He settled in Chicago, Illinois, where he helped establish the sewage system and raised downtown to a higher level than nearby Lake Michigan.

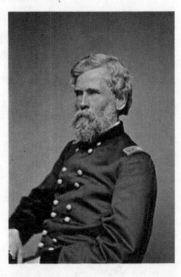

Webster returned to the colors on June 1, 1861, as a major in the Paymaster Department. He was sent to Cairo, Illinois, where he supervised the construction of the town's defenses. He was Grant's chief of staff during the Battle of Belmont in November and became commander of the 1st Illinois Light Artillery on February 1, 1862, with the rank of colonel. This appointment was largely theoretical, because none of the regiment's batteries served together, but it did give Webster the rank he needed to act as Grant's chief of staff at Fort Henry, Fort Donelson, and Shiloh. On April 6, 1862, during the Battle of Shiloh, when it appeared the Southerners might push the Army of the Tennessee into the river, Webster assembled more than fifty guns in a last-ditch defensive position overlooking Pittsburg Landing. Confederate General Beauregard opted not to attack these massed batteries. The Federals won the battle the following day.

Colonel Webster served as chief of transportation for the Army of the Tennessee during the Vicksburg campaigns and in the subsequent siege. He was promoted to brigadier general on April 4, 1863. After the city fell, he was chief of transportation for the Military Division of Mississippi. He became chief of staff to General Sherman—the commander of the Military Division of Mississippi—from March 1864 until the end of the war, and took part in the Atlanta Campaign, the March to the Sea, and the Carolinas

Campaign. Webster was a fine chief of staff. He resigned his commission in November 1865 and was brevetted major general in 1866.

After the war, he was Chicago city assessor for internal revenue and later was a district collector of internal revenue in Illinois. He died in Chicago on April 12, 1876, at age sixty-four. He was buried in Rosehill Cemetery, Chicago.

STEPHEN HINSDALE WEED was born in Potsdam, New York, on November 17, 1831. He entered West Point in 1850, graduated in 1854 (27/46), and was commissioned brevet second lieutenant in the artillery. He was promoted to second lieutenant at the end of the year and to first lieutenant in 1856. Meanwhile, he joined the 4th U.S. Artillery, served on the Texas frontier, fought the Seminoles in Florida, helped quell disturbances in bleeding Kansas, and took part in the Utah Expedition and subsequent occupation (1858–61), during which he fought Indians. He was promoted to captain in the 5th U.S. Artillery on May 14, 1861.

Weed returned to the East in 1861 and was engaged in recruiting in New York in late 1861. He spent the winter of 1861/62 at Camp Greble, near Harrisburg, Pennsylvania. In March 1862, he became a divisional artillery officer in the V Corps and took part in the Peninsula Campaign and the Seven Days battles, including Gaines' Mill (June 27, 1862), where he was slightly wounded when a shell fragment brushed his face. Sent to northern Virginia, he fought in the Second Battle of Bull Run, Antietam, and the Battle of Chancellorsville, where he commanded the Artillery Brigade on the V Corps. He was promoted to brigadier general on June 6, 1863, and was given command of an infantry brigade in the V Corps.

On July 2, 1863, at Little Round Top during the Battle of Gettysburg, while he was directing the fire of his guns, a Confederate bullet paralyzed him below the shoulders. He was carried behind some rocks and eventually moved to a field hospital, where he died a few hours later. He was thirty-one. He is buried in Moravian Cemetery, in New Dorp, Staten Island, New York.

According to esteemed historian Ezra Warner, Weed was as distinguished in the saving of the Union left flank at Gettysburg as Strong Vincent and Joshua Chamberlain.

GODFREY "DUTCH" WEITZEL was born in Winzeln, the Palatinate, Kingdom of Bavaria (now part of Germany) on November 1, 1835. His parents emigrated to the United States in 1837 and settled in Cincinnati, where his father operated a grocery store. Through hard work, he obtained an excellent preparatory education and was admitted to West Point in 1851 at age sixteen. He graduated in 1855 (2/34) and was commissioned brevet second lieutenant in the Corps of Engineers. Promotions to second lieutenant (1856) and first lieutenant (1860) followed. He was assistant engineer in the construction and repairs of the defenses of New Orleans from 1855 to 1859. He was assistant professor of engineering at West Point from 1859 until January 1861.

Weitzel had the reputation of being a fine military engineer and, in rapid succession, he worked on the defenses of Washington, D.C., Fort Pickens, Florida, and Cincinnati, Ohio. His company served as bodyguards for Abraham Lincoln during his first inauguration.

Godfrey Weitzel was named chief engineer of Benjamin Butler's Department of the Gulf in early 1862. After New Orleans fell in late April, Butler appointed Weitzel mayor of the city. He participated in the Lafourche Campaign and was promoted to brigadier general on August 29, 1862. He commanded the Lafourche District until April 1863, when he led a brigade in Banks's Port Hudson Campaign. He was given command of a division after the town fell on July 9.

General Weitzel was transferred to the Eastern Front in early 1864. He commanded a division in the XVIII Corps (May 2–20, 1864), was chief engineer of the Army of the James (June–September), and commander of the XVIII Corps (October–December 1864). Promoted to major general on November 17, 1864, he directed the XXV Corps from December 3, 1864, until the end of the war. His troops (mostly African Americans with white officers) were defeated in their attempt to capture Fort Fisher, North

Carolina (December 24–27), but were among the first to enter Richmond on April 3, 1865. At the urging of the mayor, Weitzel and his men helped put out fires set by the retreating Confederates.

After the South fell, Weitzel and his men were sent to Texas, to expel the French from Mexico. This proved unnecessary. Weitzel was mustered out of volunteer service in August 1866 and reverted to the rank of major of engineers, Regular Army. He spent the rest of his career working on various engineering and lighthouse projects throughout the United States. He was promoted to lieutenant colonel in 1882.

As his health failed, Weitzel was given a less arduous assignment in Philadelphia. Ironically, he contracted typhoid here and died on March 19, 1884. He was forty-eight. He was buried in Spring Grove Cemetery, Cincinnati, Ohio.

WILLIAM WELLS was born on December 14, 1837, in Waterbury, Vermont. He was one of ten children. He was educated in local schools and at Kimball Union Academy in Meriden, New Hampshire, and became a merchant in Burlington, Vermont.

Wells enlisted as a private in the 1st [and only] Vermont Cavalry Regiment on September 9, 1861. He was promoted to first lieutenant in October, captain in November, major on December 10, 1862, and colonel on July 2, 1864. Meanwhile, he fought in the Shenandoah Campaign of 1862, including the Battle of Winchester (May 25), Pope's Second Bull Run Campaign, and the Gettysburg Campaign, where (along with General Farnsworth) he led a charge near Big Round Top on July 3, 1863. This charge was ordered by General Kilpatrick and was ill-advised, to say the least, but Wells exhibited extreme bravery and was awarded the Congressional Medal of Honor for it in 1891. Farnsworth was killed in this attack.

Wells was wounded by a saber cut at Boonsboro, Maryland, on July 8 and by a shell burst at Culpeper Court House, Virginia, on September 13. He fought in the Bristoe Campaign (October 9–22) and the Mine Run campaign (November 26–December 2), and the ill-fated Dahlgren Raid on

Richmond (February 28–March 4, 1864). Colonel Wells took part in several battles around Richmond during the Overland Campaign and the Siege of Petersburg, and was with Sheridan in the Shenandoah Valley in 1864. During the Third Battle of Winchester, he assumed command of a cavalry brigade after Brigadier General George H. Chapman was wounded and led it for most of the rest of the war. He was brevetted brigadier general in February 1865.

General Sheridan remarked of Wells: "He is my ideal of a cavalry officer." After Lee surrendered, he and Custer recommended him for promotion to brigadier general (full rank). The promotion was granted on May 19, 1865. He was brevetted major general on January 13, 1866, and was mustered out two days later.

Postwar, William Wells returned to Burlington. He was a wholesale druggist, a member of the Vermont legislature, adjutant general of Vermont (1866–72), and a collector of customs for thirteen years. He then returned to the business world. He died suddenly of angina pectoris in New York City on April 29, 1892. A genial and highly respected man, and highly active in his church, the city of Burlington practically shut down for his funeral. He was buried in Lakeview Cemetery, Burlington.

THOMAS WELSH was born in Columbia, Pennsylvania, on May 5, 1824. He had a hard childhood. His father died when he was two, and he left home at age eight and went to work in a nail factory. Other jobs he held included factory work, farming, and the lumber business. In his early twenties, he was an itinerant carpenter in Cincinnati and Fort Smith, Arkansas. Welsh only had perhaps five years of formal schooling but educated himself between and during jobs.

When the Mexican War broke out, he enlisted as a sergeant in the 2nd Kentucky Infantry and served with Zachary Taylor's army in northern Mexico, fighting at Monterrey. He was promoted to first sergeant but then was busted down to private. At Buena Vista, a musket ball shattered his right leg just below the knee. Although he would limp the rest of his life, his surgeon saved the knee, and Welsh later named his first son after the doctor.

Welsh fought in the Siege of Vera Cruz in March 1847, and in December of that same year accepted a commission as second lieutenant in the 11th U.S. Infantry. His leg had not healed, however, so he was sent home (to Columbia, Pennsylvania) on medical leave. Here, he joined the Democratic Party and spoke against anti-slavery legislation. He favored the doctrine of popular sovereignty instead.

Thomas Welsh became a businessman in the late 1840s and opened a dry goods store in Columbia. He also sold insurance, operated several canal boats, and was involved in the lumber business. He was elected justice of the peace and president of the Borough Council.

When the Civil War began, Welsh joined the 2nd Pennsylvania Infantry as a captain and company commander on April 20, 1861. A 90-day regiment, it briefly served in the Shenandoah Valley in 1861 but was mustered out in July. Welsh remained on duty as commandant of Camp Curtin, a major processing center for Union recruits, where he improved sanitation and discipline. He was named colonel of the 45th Pennsylvania Infantry in October. Under Welsh, it became one of the best regiments in the Union Army.

After serving in the Washington defenses, the 45th was sent to South Carolina, where it was involved in the unsuccessful operations against Charleston. In July 1862, it was transferred north with the IX Corps, where it fought at South Mountain and Antietam. The regiment pushed further into Confederate territory than any other unit in the battle and actually advanced into the town of Sharpsburg before it was recalled. Highly praised by his superiors, Welsh was advanced to division commander on September 26 and was promoted to brigadier general on January 19, 1863. His appointment expired on March 4, without Senate action, even though it should have been confirmed.

Welsh briefly commanded a division of the IX Corps in Kentucky before he was transferred to the Western Front during the Siege of Vicksburg in June 1863. After Vicksburg fell, he was part of Sherman's corps in the Second Battle of Jackson, Mississippi. Unfortunately for the Union, he came down with congestive chills (probably malaria) on August 6. Sent to a hospital in Cincinnati, he died on August 14, 1863. He was 39. He was buried in Mount Bethel Cemetery in the town of his birth.

HENRY WALTON WESSELLS was born on February 20, 1809, in Litchfield, Connecticut. He attended West Point, graduated in 1833 (29/43), and was commissioned brevet second lieutenant in the infantry. He served in various garrisons in Maine, Massachusetts, Michigan, and Wisconsin from 1840 to 1842, when he fought the Seminoles in Florida. After a tour of duty in New York, he fought in Mexico, including the Siege of Vera Cruz, Cerro Gordo, and Contreras, where he was wounded. He also took part in the Battle of Churubusco and the assault and capture of Mexico City. Meanwhile, he was promoted to second lieutenant (1836), first lieutenant (1838), captain (1847), and brevet major for gallantry and meritorious conduct in Mexico.

After Mexico, Wessells served on the frontier and fought the Sioux. He was at Fort Riley, Kansas, when the Civil War began. As a member of the 6th U.S. Infantry, he was promoted to major on June 6, 1861. He was named colonel of the 8th Kansas Infantry on September 29 and served on the Missouri–Kansas frontier. He was transferred to the East in early 1862 and fought in the Peninsula Campaign, including the Siege of Yorktown. He was promoted to brigadier general on April 26, 1862, and assumed command of a brigade in the IV Corps on May 19. He was wounded in the shoulder at Seven Pines on May 31, 1862, but did not leave the field.

Wessells participated in the Seven Days battles but apparently his performance did not satisfy the "powers that be." He was sent to a secondary sector and was placed in charge of the defense of Suffolk, Virginia, until December 1862. He was involved in actions in North Carolina from December 1862 to April 1864, including the battles of Kinston, Goldsborough, and New Bern. He oversaw the defense of Plymouth, North Carolina (April 17–20, 1864), where he was attacked by Confederate General Hoke, who had 10,000 men. Wessells had 3,000 men and 25 guns but excellent fortifications. He was nevertheless forced to surrender. Hoke only lost 50 men. Wessells was exchanged on August 3.

General Wessells was in rear area assignments for the rest of the war. He commanded POW camps in the West from November 1864 to February 1865 and the Draft Rendezvous at Hart's Island, New York, from February 1865 to February 1866. Mustered out of volunteer service in January 1866, he reverted to the rank of lieutenant colonel in the 18th U.S. Infantry. He was not brevetted major general in the omnibus promotions after the war.

He directed forts in the Dakota and Nebraska Territories and the Depot of the General Recruiting Service in Newport, Kentucky. He retired in 1871 after thirty years' service and returned to his hometown in Connecticut. General Wessells died while on a visit to Dover, Delaware, on January 12, 1889, at age seventy-nine. He was buried in East Cemetery, Litchfield, Connecticut.

His son, Henry Walton Wessells, Jr., was a sergeant in the infantry at the end of the war. He later served in the 3rd Cavalry and retired in 1901 for disabilities incurred in the line of duty. He was promoted to brigadier general on the retired list in 1904.

JOSEPH RODMAN WEST, who went by the name **J. RODMAN WEST**, was born in New Orleans, Louisiana, on September 19, 1822. His family moved to Philadelphia in 1824, and he was educated in private schools. He also attended the University of Pennsylvania but did not graduate. He moved back to The Big Easy in 1841 but joined the Maryland and District of Columbia Volunteers during the Mexican War as a private and rose to the rank of captain. He went to California in 1849 and became a newspaper owner.

When the Civil War erupted, West was commissioned lieutenant colonel in the 1st California Infantry and was promoted to colonel on June 1, 1862. He was stationed in California until February 1862, and saw action in New Mexico and Arizona territories, where he fought Apache. He named commander of the District of Arizona (part of the Department of New Mexico) in September 1862 and was promoted to brigadier general on October 25.

On January 18, 1863, after the Apache Chief Mangas Coloradas entered his camp to discuss peace under a flag of truce, West ordered him tortured to death, and his body was mutilated.

General West was transferred to Arkansas in April 1864, where he commanded a division in the VII Corps. He was given command of a division in the Military Division of West Mississippi in April 1865. Mustered out in June 1865, he was brevetted major general in 1866.

West returned to Louisiana after the war and was a deputy U.S. marshal and a customs auditor from 1867 to 1871. He was elected to the U.S. Senate in 1871 as a Republican and a carpetbagger but did not seek re-election in 1876. When Reconstruction collapsed, he fled Louisiana for Washington, D.C., where he was a commissioner of the District of Columbia and was the equivalent of mayor of the city in 1882 and 1883. He died in Washington on October 31, 1898.

Parker West, one of his sons, served in the cavalry during the Indian Wars and in the Philippines. He retired as a lieutenant colonel.

FRANK WHEATON was born in Providence, Rhode Island, on May 8, 1833. He enrolled in Brown University, where he studied civil engineering. He dropped out in 1850 to take a job with the Mexican American Boundary Commission, where he worked until 1855, when he was commissioned first lieutenant in the 1st Cavalry Regiment. Antebellum, he fought Indians on the frontier and was stationed in Bleeding Kansas. He was promoted to captain on March 1, 1861.

Wheaton returned home when the war started and was commissioned lieutenant colonel of the 2nd Rhode Island Infantry, which was mustered into Federal service on July 10—although it was already at Camp Sprague in Washington, D.C. It fought at the First Bull Run (July 21), where its colonel was wounded, and Wheaton assumed command. He transferred to the 4th U.S. Cavalry in August and was promoted to colonel, to rank from July 21. Wheaton led his regiment in the Peninsula Campaign, the Seven Days battles, and the Battle of Antietam, where the 4th Cavalry was held in reserve. Wheaton was promoted to brigadier general on November 29, 1862. During the Battle of Fredericksburg, he was given command of an infantry brigade in the VI Corps, which he led in heavy fighting at Chancellorsville. At Gettysburg, he commanded John Newton's division after General Reynolds was killed and Newton assumed temporary command of the I Corps.

Back in brigade command that fall, he fought in the Overland Campaign of 1864, the defense of Washington, D.C., and Sheridan's operations in the Shenandoah Valley. On September 21, he assumed command of the 3rd Division of the VI Corps after its commander, David A. Russell, was killed in the Third Battle of Winchester (September 19). He led it with considerable distinction for the rest of the war. He was brevetted major general in December 1864 and was present at Appomattox. He was mustered out of volunteer service in April 1866.

Post-war, Wheaton remained in the Regular Army as a lieutenant colonel of the 39th U.S. Infantry and was stationed in Omaha. He held a variety of posts over the next thirty-one years. Most controversially, he directed American forces at the First Battle of the Stronghold in 1873. With 400 men, he was defeated by 50 Modoc Indians, who were defending a strong position in the northern California lava fields. At least 35 of his men were killed (one source said 42) and many were wounded. The Modoc suffered no casualties, and Wheaton was relieved of his command. He was nevertheless promoted to full colonel the following year.

Frank Wheaton was promoted to brigadier general in 1892 and major general on April 3, 1897. He reached the mandatory age of sixty-four the next month. He retired to Washington, D.C., where he died of a brain hemorrhage on June 18, 1903, at age seventy. He was buried in Arlington National Cemetery.

He was the son-in-law of Samuel Cooper, the highest-ranking Confederate general for most of the war.

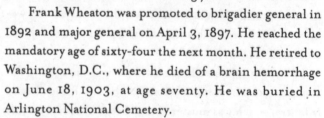

AMIEL WEEKS WHIPPLE was born in Greenwich, Massachusetts, on October 21, 1817. He graduated from the United States Military Academy in 1841 (5/52) and was commissioned second lieutenant in the artillery. He transferred to the topographical engineers three months later and was involved in a number of interesting projects including the Mexican Boundary Survey (1849–53). He was also assistant astronomer on the Northeastern Boundary Survey between the British provinces and the US, and engineer on several railroad surveys, including ones through California and Arizona Territory as well as the Pacific Railroad Survey. He was promoted to first lieutenant in 1851 and captain in 1855. He was considered one of the top military engineers in the U.S. Army.

When the war broke out, Whipple was chief topographical engineer for the defense of Washington south of the Potomac. He fought in the First Bull Run, after which he was brevetted lieutenant colonel for gallant and meritorious service. Later he was chief engineer of General McDowell's division and of the I Corps. He was promoted to brigadier general on April 18, 1862, and commanded a brigade in the Washington defenses. He was elevated to divisional command in the III Corps in October 1862 and fought at Fredericksburg.

On May 4, 1863, during the Battle of Chancellorsville, he was sitting on his horse, writing out an order to dislodge a particular Confederate sharpshooter, when the man shot him. The bullet when through his stomach and out his back near the spine. He received the last rights on the battlefield and was transported back to Washington, D.C., where he died on May 7, 1863. He was forty-four. Abraham Lincoln, when he found out about his personal friend Whipple's wound, was upset. He promoted him to major general on May 7, just before he died. The president rode in an open carriage in Whipple's funeral procession. He also gave both Whipple's sons appointments to the military academy of their choice. General Whipple was buried in Proprietors' Burying Ground, Portsmouth, New Hampshire.

WILLIAM DENISON WHIPPLE was born in Nelson, New York, on August 2, 1826. Appointed to West Point, he graduated in the Class of 1851 (31/42) and was commissioned brevet second lieutenant in the 3rd Infantry, beginning a military career which lasted thirty-nine years. In the 1850s, he fought Apache and Navajo in New Mexico Territory. He was promoted to second lieutenant (1851) and first lieutenant (1856). He became an assistant adjutant general (AAG) and was promoted to captain on May 11, 1861. He was AAG of Hunter's division at the First Bull Run.

Whipple served as a staff officer throughout the war. He was brevetted lieutenant colonel and was promoted to brigadier general of volunteers on July 17, 1863. He served as AAG (and de facto chief of staff) of the Army and Department of the Cumberland, taking part in the Siege of Chattanooga and the Battle of Missionary Ridge. His appointment expired on July 4, 1864, without Senate action, and he reverted to colonel.

Whipple served in the Atlanta Campaign and the Battle of Nashville, where he was Thomas's chief of staff. He was mustered out of volunteer service in January 1866 and was brevetted major general, Regular Army, later that year. He remained in the adjutant general's branch for the rest of his career, much of which he served as AAG to the general-in-chief. He retired as a colonel in 1890. General Whipple died in New York City on April 1, 1902, at age seventy-five. He was buried in Arlington National Cemetery.

WALTER CHILES WHITAKER was born on August 8, 1823, in Shelbyville, Kentucky. He attended Bethany College, Virginia (now West Virginia), and was an attorney in Shelbyville when he joined the 3rd Kentucky Infantry for the Mexican War in October 1847. The regiment reached Mexico City after the war ended, and he was discharged as a second lieutenant in 1848. Whitaker returned to his practice, established a large farm, and was elected to the General Assembly in 1861.

Whitaker called on the legislature to support the Union. When the state's tenuous neutrality collapsed, he assisted in organizing the 6th Kentucky Infantry, which was mustered into Federal service on December 14 with Whitaker as colonel. He fought with Buell at Shiloh and led a charge on the second day, stabbing a Louisiana gunner with a Bowie knife. He also took part in the Kentucky Campaign (including Perryville) and distinguished himself at Stones River on December 31, holding a critical position in the Round Forest against repeated Rebel attacks. Here, he was shot in the left arm just above the elbow, which left the limb permanently weakened. He was on medical leave for several weeks.

Walter Whitaker was promoted to brigadier general on June 25, 1863, and assumed command of a brigade in Granger's Reserve Corps in August. He played a significant role in holding Horseshoe Ridge at Chickamauga on September 20, but was shot in the abdomen in the process. He returned to duty on October 10.

It was reported that Whitaker was drunk at Chickamauga and was drinking at Lookout Mountain in November, although it was obviously not enough to impair his judgement. A Confederate shell burst over his head at Resaca, Georgia, on May 15, 1864, gave him a concussion, and made him deaf in one ear. When he returned to duty in September, he was given a division in the Army of the Cumberland and fought at Franklin and Nashville. He was mustered out in August 1865 and brevetted major general in 1866.

General Whitaker settled in Louisville and became a noted criminal attorney. He spent some years after the war in a mental institution but had recovered by the time of his passing. He died from chronic diarrhea (which he contracted in 1865) in Lyndon, Kentucky, on July 9, 1887, at age sixty-three. He was buried in Grove Hill Cemetery, Shelbyville.

JULIUS WHITE was born on September 23, 1816, in Cazenovia, New York. He moved to Chicago when he was twenty and went into various businesses. He later moved to Milwaukee as an insurance agent. In 1848, he was elected to the legislature as a Whig but left office after a year and returned to Chicago, where he became a prominent insurance agent and underwriter. Eventually, he was elected president of the Chicago Board of Underwriters. He also became a good friend of Abraham Lincoln, who appointed him customs collector of the Port of Chicago in 1861.

White was commissioned colonel of the 37th Illinois Infantry on July 18, 1861, and was sent to Missouri, where it was part of Fremont's Army of the Southwest. He performed well in the Union victory at Pea Ridge (March 7–8, 1862) until a Confederate bullet fractured his leg. Back on duty by the end of the month, he was promoted to brigadier general on June 12, 1862. Sent to the East, White was given a brigade in the VIII Corps. It was posted at Martinsburg, (West) Virginia, when Lee invaded Maryland. White retreated into Harper's Ferry and joined the garrison of Colonel Dixon S. Miles, an old Regular Army officer. Although White outranked Miles, he knew nothing of the local terrain and deemed it better to leave Miles in command of the garrison and waived his rank. This turned out to be a fatal mistake, because Miles was not able to conduct an effective defense. The battle was fought from September 12–15, and Miles was one of the last men killed. The onerous duty of formally surrendering the 12,500-man garrison fell to White. It was the largest mass surrender by the Union Army in the war.

Julius White was exchanged in January 1863 and was subsequently arrested and brought before a court of inquiry, but was cleared of all charges. He was assigned to command the District of Eastern Kentucky (February–August 1863), then a division in the XXIII Corps of Burnside's Department of the Ohio. He spent four months commanding the Springfield Draft Depot (February–June 1864) and was Burnside's chief of staff in the Battle of the Crater.

White directed a division of the IX Corps after the Crater, but he came down with typhoid fever, and his health collapsed. Bedridden for two months, and too feeble to return to the field, he resigned on November 19 after his division was disbanded. He was brevetted major general in 1866. He returned to the insurance business, went into real estate, and was elected chairman of the first Cook County Board of Commissioners in 1871. He was also one of the founding members of the First Congregational Church of Evanston.

General White served as U.S. minister of Argentina from late 1873 to March 1874. He died in Evanston, Illinois, on May 12, 1890, at age seventy-three.

EDWARD AUGUSTUS WILD was born in Brookline, Massachusetts, on November 25, 1825, the son of a homeopathic doctor. Edward earned his medical degrees at Harvard in 1844 and Jefferson Medical College in Philadelphia in 1846. He practiced in Brookline with his father until 1855, when he joined the Ottoman Army as a medical officer. He participated in the Crimean War and returned home to practice medicine.

Dr. Wild, who was a fervent abolitionist, joined the Union Army as a captain and a combat officer in the 1st Massachusetts Infantry. He fought in the First Bull Run and at Seven Pines (Fair Oaks), where he was wounded twice. One, to the knee, was slight. The second occurred when a bullet passed through his right hand between the first and second knuckles, causing permanent damage to two fingers.

Wild returned to duty in August 1862 as a colonel and commander of the 32nd Massachusetts Infantry. On September 14, during the Battle of South Mountain (with his right arm still in a sling), his left arm was shattered by an explosive bullet. He had to walk two to three miles for help. At the field hospital, surgeons had to amputate his arm, and it took him months to partially recover. He was nevertheless promoted to brigadier general on April 24, 1863.

In February 1863, Wild returned to limited active duty, recruiting African American infantrymen. He formed "Wild's African Brigade" and led it in the Charleston, South Carolina, area, but with little success. He also ordered that no guerillas be taken prisoner.

In December, he led an expedition to Camden, North Carolina. En route, he threatened to hang the wives of two Confederate officers if a missing Union solder was not returned. North Carolina Governor Zebulon Vance threatened to retaliate if he did, so Wild released the women and hung a Confederate soldier named Daniel Bright of the 62nd Georgia Infantry instead and made the women watch. Confederate General Pickett hung an Ohio soldier in retaliation. Wild, meanwhile, led expeditions into southeast Virginia and northeastern North Carolina, freed 2,500 slaves, and resettled them on Roanoke Island.

Wild and his black soldiers were transferred to Norfolk in January 1864. He was commandant of Norfolk for a time and fought in the Siege of Petersburg, and the capture of Richmond. His men performed well.

General Wild was sent back to Georgia after Appomattox and, in July 1865, while searching for missing Confederate gold, he tortured a civilian family and forced the women to completely disrobe.

Wild was mustered out of the service in January 1866 but received no brevet in the omnibus promotions at the end of the war, indicating what some of the Union high command might have thought about his behavior. Minus one arm and crippled in the other, he was unable to return to medicine, so he went into the mining business in Nevada and South America. He died of diarrhea on August 28, 1891, in Medellin, Colombia, and is buried there in the Cementerio de San Pedro.

ORLANDO BOLIVAR WILLCOX was born on April 16, 1823, in Detroit, Michigan. He graduated from West Point in 1847 (8/38) and was appointed second lieutenant in the 4th Artillery. Sent to Mexico, he arrived too late to see action, but he did garrison duty at Mexico City and Cuernavaca. Frontier and garrison duty followed, including a stint in conflict with the Seminoles (1856–57). He resigned his commission as a first lieutenant in 1857 to become a lawyer in Detroit. He was also a captain in the Michigan Militia.

Willcox became colonel of the 1st Michigan Infantry on May 1, 1861, and took part in the occupation of Alexandria, Virginia, 23 days later. He fought in the First Battle of Bull Run (July 21), where he took over Heintzelman's brigade after that officer was wounded. Despite being wounded, Willcox repeatedly led charges against Confederate positions until he was captured. (A piece of shell struck him in his right forearm, but he bound it and remained in the field.) In 1895, he was awarded the Congressional Medal of Honor for his bravery on this day.

Willcox was in prison for more than a year, part of it as a hostage. The Federals were threatening to hang some Confederate privateers and the Rebels threatened to execute Willcox if they did. Willcox was finally released on August 19, 1862, and promoted to brigadier general the same day. His date of rank was July 21, 1861.

Willcox was given a division in Burnside's IX Corps and led it at South Mountain, Antietam, Fredericksburg, Knoxville, the Overland Campaign, and the Crater. He was acting commander of the IX Corps on more than one occasion but was never a permanent choice, probably because he was a volunteer officer, not a regular army one. He probably should have been; he was certainly a fine officer. He was brevetted major general in 1867.

When the army was reorganized in 1866, Willcox was given command of the 29th Infantry Regiment, initially in Lynchburg, Virginia, and later on Alcatraz Island in San Francisco Bay. He remained in San Francisco until 1878, when he assumed command of the Department of Arizona, where he fought Apache. He was appointed brigadier general and named commander of the Department of the Missouri in 1886 and retired from active service the following year, having reached the mandatory age of sixty-four. He later did a two-year tour as governor of the Soldiers' Home in Washington, D.C.

General Willcox spent his last years in Cobourg, Ontario, Canada. He died there on May 11, 1907, at age eighty-four. He was buried in Arlington National Cemetery.

ALPHEUS STARKEY "POPS" OR "PAP" WILLIAMS

was born on September 20, 1810, in Deep River, Connecticut. When his father died, he used his large inheritance to travel extensively in the United States and Europe. When he returned, he settled in Detroit, Michigan, became a lawyer, and married into a prominent family.

In the antebellum era, Williams was a probate judge, bank president, newspaper owner, editor, and postmaster of Detroit (1849–53). He was also lieutenant colonel of the 1st Michigan Infantry Regiment during the Mexican War but arrived too late to experience any combat. He was a major in the militia in 1859.

Williams spent the early months of the war training troops in Michigan. He was commissioned brigadier general on August 9, 1861, and was given command of a brigade in Banks's Army of the

Shenandoah. In March 1862, he assumed command of a division and took part in Banks's unsuccessful operations against Stonewall Jackson. Subsequently transferred to Pope's Army of Virginia, Williams's division was posted to Bristoe and did not take part in the Second Battle of Bull Run.

General Williams fought at Antietam where the XII Corps suffered 25 percent casualties and, after General Mansfield was killed, temporarily replaced him as corps commander. Henry Slocum was chosen as permanent corps commander in October, and Williams returned to his division. In reserve at Fredericksburg, Williams's division suffered 1,500 casualties at Chancellorsville. At Gettysburg, it held Culp's Hill, on the extreme Union right, while its commander again temporarily directed the XII Corps, while Slocum directed the Union right wing.

Transferred to the Western Front, Williams's men were used to guard the railroads north of Chattanooga in the last quarter of 1863. They participated in the Atlanta Campaign (where Williams was slightly wounded at New Hope Church), the March to the Sea, and the Carolinas Campaign, where he temporarily commanded the XX Corps. Although he was never given his second star (substantive rank), Williams was brevetted major general on January 12, 1865. It appears the Union High Command only wanted Regular Army officers commanding corps, not volunteers. The fact that Williams was a Democrat, did nothing to promote himself in the newspapers, and not a West Point graduate, did not help him advance in rank or position. He was, however, the longest-serving divisional commander in the history of the Union Army and richly deserved the second star he never received, except by brevet.

Alpheus S. Williams was mustered out in January 1866. He returned to Michigan briefly but soon accepted the post of U.S. minister to El Salvador (1866–69). He ran for governor of Michigan in 1870 but was defeated. He ran for Congress four years later and was elected, serving from March 4, 1875, until his death. On December 21, 1878, in the U.S. Capitol Building, he suffered a stroke and died. He is buried in Elmwood Cemetery, Detroit. *From the Cannon's Mouth*, a biography of him featuring his letters, was edited by M. M. Quaife in 1959.

ROBERT WILLIAMS was born in Culpeper County, Virginia, on November 5, 1829. He was admitted to the United States Military Academy in 1847, graduated in 1851 (19/42), and was commissioned brevet second lieutenant in the 1st Dragoons. He was promoted to second lieutenant in 1853, first lieutenant in 1855, and captain, staff, on May 11, 1861.

Antebellum, Williams served on the frontier in Oregon and Washington territories between assignments as an instructor of Cavalry at West Point. He was an assistant adjutant general at Annapolis and in the Department of the Shenandoah before assuming command of the 1st Massachusetts Cavalry on October 7, 1861. He fought in South Carolina, including the Battle of Secessionville. He commanded a brigade in the Department of the South from April to July 1862 and was promoted to brigadier general on April 30, but his nomination was tabled on July 16, and he reverted to the rank of colonel. Transferred to Maryland, Williams fought in the Battle of Antietam. He resigned his volunteer commission on October 1 and returned to Washington, D.C., as a major, staff, and an assistant in the adjutant general's office. He remained in the adjutant general branch at various locations for the rest of his career.

Brevetted brigadier general at the end of the war, Williams was promoted to lieutenant colonel, staff, in 1869, colonel, staff, in 1881, and brigadier general and adjutant general of the U.S. Army in 1892. He retired in 1893.

General Williams died in Netherwood, New Jersey, on August 24, 1901, at age seventy-one. He was buried in Arlington National Cemetery.

Williams married the widow of Senator Stephen A. Douglas in 1866. Their oldest son, Robert C. Williams (1867–1921), fought in the Spanish-American War and World War I, and was a colonel at the time of his death.

SETH WILLIAMS was born on March 22, 1822, in Augusta, Maine. He graduated from West Point in 1842 (23/56), was commissioned second lieutenant in the 2nd Artillery, and did three years garrison duty in New York and New England before being sent to Texas. He fought in northern Mexico (including Palo Alto and Resaca de la Palma) and in Scott's drive on Mexico City from Vera Cruz to the enemy's capital, most of that time as

General Robert Patterson's aide. Meanwhile, he was promoted to first lieutenant (1847) and brevet captain for gallantry and meritorious conduct at Cerro Gordo. Further garrison duty in Pennsylvania and New York followed, including a stint as adjutant of the U.S. Military Academy. He was adjutant of the Department of the West when the war began.

Williams was transferred to the Department of the Ohio as assistant adjutant general (AAG) in June 1861, held the same position with the Army of the Potomac from August 1862 to March 1864, and was on the staff of General Grant after that as an inspector general. Meanwhile, he was promoted to major on August 3, 1861, and to brigadier general September 28, 1861. He was briefly AAG of the Military Division of the Atlantic in 1866 before falling sick. After a brief illness, General Williams died March 23, 1866, in Boston, Massachusetts, at age forty-four. He was buried in Forest Grove Cemetery, Augusta, Maine.

General Williams was a light-hearted man and genial officer who made friends easily. His quarters were the ones everyone went to when they wanted to relax or socialize. One person called him the friendliest officer in the army, and another mentioned his inexhaustible patience, his personal magnetism, and "inextinguishable cheerfulness."

THOMAS WILLIAMS was born on January 16, 1815, in Albany, New York. His grandfather, also named Thomas, settled in Detroit in 1765. His father, General John R. Williams, was the first mayor of the town.

Williams enlisted in the army as an infantry private in the Black Hawk War in 1832, serving under his father's command. He gained admission into West Point in 1833, graduated in 1837 (12/50), and was commissioned a brevet second lieutenant in the 1st Artillery. He was almost immediately sent to Florida, where he fought the Seminoles. He served in various garrisons, on the frontier in northern Michigan, as an aide to General Scott, and as an assistant professor of mathematics at West Point. He fought in Mexico from Vera Cruz to Mexico City, performed garrison duty in New York and Michigan, and back to Florida to fight Seminoles again (1856–57).

Following a tour in "Bleeding Kansas," he took part in the Utah Expedition in 1858 and did tours of duty in Nebraska and Dakota territories. He was stationed at the Artillery School for Practice at Fort Monroe, Virginia, when the Civil War began. Meanwhile, he was promoted to first lieutenant (1840), brevet captain for Contreras and Churubusco (1847), captain (1850), and major (May 14, 1861).

Williams was inspector general for the Department of Virginia in June 1861 and commanded his regiment (the 5th U.S. Artillery) at Harrisburg, Pennsylvania, from late June to October 2. He was promoted to brigadier general on September 28, 1861, and took part in the North Carolina Expedition of 1861. He commanded Fort Hatteras, North Carolina, from October 1861 to March 1862, when he was transferred to the Department of the Gulf. He directed the infantry in the first (unsuccessful) Siege of Vicksburg in 1862 and tried unsuccessfully to build a canal and bypass the fortress-city.

On August 5, 1862, he defended Baton Rouge against a Confederate counteroffensive. During the battle, in which the Union garrison managed to hold out, despite being badly outnumbered, General Williams was struck in the chest and killed by a rifle ball. He was forty-seven. He is buried in Elmwood Cemetery, Detroit.

Williams had two sons. One became the first bishop of the Episcopal Diocese of Marquette. The other was a physician. Williams's widow was a co-founder of the Marquette-Williams Sanitarium, a medical and surgical center in Denver, Colorado.

JAMES ALEXANDER WILLIAMSON was born in Adair County, Kentucky, on February 8, 1829. His family moved to Indiana when he was three and to Keokuk County, Iowa, when he was fifteen. James grew up working on the family farm before attending Knox College in Galesburg, Illinois, and becoming a lawyer. He moved to Des Moines around 1854, and was instrumental in getting the state capitol moved from Iowa City to Des Moines. He also became chairman of the Iowa State Democratic Committee.

Williamson entered the Union Army as a first lieutenant and adjutant of the 4th Iowa Infantry Regiment on August 8, 1861. He was promoted to lieutenant colonel on March 4, 1862, and was wounded in the Battle of Pea Ridge three days later. It was the first of five wounds he suffered during the war. After a stint of garrison duty at Helena, Arkansas, he joined Sherman's corps and fought in the Battle of Chickasaw Bluffs, where he was struck by three musket balls but was not seriously injured. His fearlessness in this battle would result in his being awarded the Congressional Medal of Honor in 1895.

Colonel Williamson took part in the capture of Arkansas Post, the Vicksburg Campaign, and the Siege of Vicksburg, after which he assumed command of a brigade in Sherman's corps. Following a medical furlough, he fought in the Battle of Lookout Mountain and the Atlanta Campaign, during which he was slightly wounded in the hand at Jonesboro (Jonesborough). He participated in the March to the Sea and was brevetted brigadier general in January 1865. Given full rank on April 1, 1865, he was sent back to Iowa and briefly commanded the District of St. Louis. He was mustered out on August 24, 1865, and was brevetted major general in 1868.

Williamson returned to Iowa as a member of the Republican Party. He resumed the practice of law and was commissioner of the General Land Office from 1876 to 1881. He later became president of the Atlantic & Pacific Railroad. He died in Jamestown, Rhode Island, on September 7, 1902, at age seventy-three. He was buried in Rock Creek Cemetery, Washington, D.C.

AUGUST WILLICH, who was born **JOHANN AUGUST ERNST VON WILLICH**, first saw the light of day on November 19, 1810, in Braunsberg, East Prussia (now Braniewo, Poland). He was educated in the cadet schools in Potsdam and Berlin. By age eighteen, he was a first lieutenant (*Oberleutnant*) in the 7th (1st Westphalian) Field Artillery Regiment. He was a captain at age twenty-one. He became a fervent Communist and resigned his commission in 1846. His letter of resignation was so harsh that, instead of being accepted, he was court-martialed but was acquitted. Only then was he permitted to resign. About this time, he renounced his noble title, "von."

Willich took part in the Revolutions of 1848–49 and was a leader of the Freikorps in Baden-Palatinate. He managed to escape to Switzerland after the collapse of the revolts and ended up in London, where he insulted Karl Marx for being too conservative (!) and even challenged him to a duel, but Marx refused to fight. Instead, Konrad Schramm, one of Marx's young associates, challenged Willich, who shot and wounded the young man.

Willich emigrated to the United States in 1853 and found employment as a carpenter in the Brooklyn Navy Yard. He later worked for the coastal survey and moved to Cincinnati in 1858, working as editor of a German-language newspaper. He was here when the Civil War began.

August Willich joined the Union Army as a first lieutenant and adjutant of the 9th Ohio Infantry on May 8, 1861, but was promoted to major on June 13. He became the colonel of the 32nd Indiana Infantry on August 24. An excellent recruiter of German Americans, he brought 1,500 young men to the colors. Although universally considered eccentric, he was a fine regimental commander and a strong disciplinarian who expected his men to perform evolutions in response to bugle calls, both on the drill field and the battlefield. Native-born Americans thought this was laughable and were astonished when it actually worked.

The 32nd Indiana was probably the best all-German regiment in the Union Army. It fought at Rich Mountain in western Virginia and at Rowlett's Station in Kentucky, where it repulsed an attack from Terry's Texas Rangers. Willich particularly distinguished himself during the second day of the Battle of Shiloh. His troops wavered, so he placed himself at the head of his regiment and, with his back to the enemy, put it through the manual of arms. This restored stability; he then led them in a bayonet charge.

Promoted to brigadier general on July 19, 1862, Willich was given a brigade in the Army of the Ohio, which he led at Perryville and Stones River. On December 31, the first day of the battle, his horse was killed and fell on him. He was unable to extract himself before the Confederates arrived. He was incarcerated at Libby Prison in Richmond until May 1863, when he was exchanged. Willich returned to the Western Front and served in the Tullahoma and Chickamauga campaigns, commanding a division in the XX Corps in the last-named battle.

During the Siege of Chattanooga, Willich's brigade captured Orchard Knob and, without orders, attacked Missionary Ridge, broke the Rebel line, and played a major role in routing the Southern army.

Willich took part in the Atlanta Campaign, but his luck ran out on May 14, 1864, during the Battle of Resaca, when he was shot through the shoulder. He could not return to light duty until August and never returned to field duty. He spent the rest of the war in territorial commands in Cincinnati and northern Kentucky. He was brevetted major general in October 1865 and was mustered out in January 1866.

Postwar, August Willich held several minor government positions in Cincinnati. He returned to Germany in 1870 and offered his services to the Kaiser, who declined them. He remained in the Fatherland, made amends with Marx, attended the University of Berlin, and received a degree in philosophy. He returned to the United States and died in St. Marys, Ohio, on January 22, 1878, at age sixty-seven. He was buried in Elm Grove Cemetery, St. Marys.

JAMES HARRISON WILSON was born on his family's farm in Shawneetown, Illinois, on September 2, 1837. He briefly attended McKendree College before entering West Point in 1855, which was then a five-year institution. He graduated in 1860 (6/41) and was commissioned brevet second lieutenant in the topographical engineers. His initial assignment was as assistant topographical engineer for the Department of Oregon. He was promoted to second lieutenant on June 10, 1861, and to first lieutenant on September 9.

Wilson was the chief topographical engineer of the Port Royal Expedition and of the Department of the South from October 1861 to August 1862 and took part in the Siege of Fort Pulaski, Georgia (February–April 11, 1862), where he earned a brevet to major. Transferred to the Eastern Front, he was an aide to General McClellan at South Mountain and Antietam.

James Wilson was recognized early as a brilliant young engineer. His next assignment was chief topographical engineer of the Army of the Tennessee, which led to his promotion to lieutenant colonel on November 8. He aided in Grant's successful effort to flank Oxford, and he breached the Mississippi River levee in a vain attempt to turn Vicksburg via Moon Lake and the Yazoo Pass. He continued on Grant's staff in the drive on Jackson—mainly bridging streams—and the subsequent Siege of Vicksburg. He was promoted to brigadier general on October 30, 1863.

Wilson served in the Siege of Chattanooga and was Sherman's chief engineer when he relieved Knoxville. He was transferred to the mounted branch as chief of the Cavalry Bureau in February 1864, where he proved to be a brilliant organizer and administrator. Grant promoted him to the command of a division under Sheridan.

General Wilson tried to implement Grant's strategy of destroying Lee's rail lines and thus compel him to evacuate Petersburg and Richmond. In a daring raid (beginning on June 22) he tore up sixty miles of track and severely damaged the Confederate infrastructure. He suffered the only real defeat of his career when he tried to capture the Staunton River Bridge on June 25. Wilson outnumbered the Rebels (local home guards) 5,000 to 1,000, but they were well entrenched, the situation offered no scope for maneuver, and Wilson's frontal assaults failed. Then he was caught in the rear by "Rooney" Lee's cavalry, and his men were routed.

Before Lee and Early could be decisively defeated, Wilson was transferred back to the west as chief of cavalry to Sherman's Military Division of the Mississippi. He fought at Franklin and Nashville, overwhelmed Nathan Bedford Forrest's little corps at Selma, Alabama (April 2, 1865), ending his brilliant combat career, and captured Columbus, Georgia (April 16), in the last major battle of the war. He capped a brilliant Civil War career by capturing Jefferson Davis on May 10. He was promoted to major general on June 21, 1865.

Wilson was easily the best and most distinguished of the "boy generals" of the Civil War. He was in command of the Department of Georgia after the surrender, and at least one Southern historian described his reign as enlightened. He distributed excess supplies and captured mules and horses to the poor and did what he could to alleviate the suffering of the people. He was mustered out of volunteer service in January 1866 and became lieutenant colonel of the 35th U.S. Infantry. He worked on engineering projects until the end of 1870, when he resigned.

Wilson worked as a railroad construction engineer after he left the service. He settled in Wilmington, Delaware, and engaged in business until 1898, when he returned to the colors for the Spanish-American War. He served as a major general in Cuba and Puerto Rico and, in 1901, was in China during the Boxer Rebellion. He represented the United States at the coronation of Edward VII in the United Kingdom.

General Wilson died in Wilmington on February 23, 1925, at age eighty-seven. He was buried in the Old Swedes Churchyard, Wilmington.

ISAAC JONES WISTAR was born in Philadelphia, Pennsylvania, on November 14, 1827. He was educated at Westtown Friends School, Haverford College, and the University of Pennsylvania, where he received his doctorate. He became a lawyer but left Philadelphia for California in 1849 to seek his fortune in the gold fields. Over the next twelve years, he was a miner, trapper, mountaineer, Indian fighter, farmer, and lawyer. On one occasion, he was severely wounded by an arrow. He passed the California bar in 1854 and started a practice in San Francisco but returned home in 1857. He was practicing law in Philadelphia when the Civil War began. Wistar raised a company of infantry, was elected its commander, and became a captain in the 71st Pennsylvania. He was promoted to lieutenant colonel on June 28.

The 71st was initially stationed at Fort Monroe, Virginia, but was quickly moved to Washington, D.C., following the disaster at the First Bull Run. It first saw action at Ball's Bluff on October 21, 1861. Here its commander, Brigadier General Edward D. Baker, was killed in action. Wistar replaced him and was involved in the heaviest fighting. A bullet (or small stone) struck him in the jaw, but he continued on. Another bullet went through his thigh and filled his boot with blood. The colonel cut a hole in the boot and continued in command until just before dark, when a ball shattered his right elbow. He had to be evacuated north of the Potomac via rowboat. Surgeons tied up his arm in the position it would remain in for the rest of his life.

Wistar was promoted to colonel on November 11 and recovered sufficiently to rejoin the army for the Siege of Yorktown. Here, he came down with typhoid and almost died. Sent home, he could not rejoin the army until August 1862. He fought at Antietam, where he was severely wounded in the left arm. His men affixed a tourniquet and left the colonel behind. Both Federals and Confederates passed by him, and, at one point, a Rebel (supposedly John Singleton Mosby) gave him a drink and adjusted his tourniquet. He was promoted to brigadier general on March 16, 1863, but did not return to duty until May 16, when he was given command of a brigade in the VII Corps.

General Wistar was commander of the District of Yorktown in July 1863. He briefly commanded a division in the XVIII Corps of the Army of the James in April 1864, but reverted to brigade commander on May 7. He fought in the Bermuda Hundred Campaign but his performance during the main battle on May 16 was deemed inadequate. He was relieved of his command on May 18. He was never reemployed and resigned from the army on September 15, 1864.

Isaac Wistar returned to Philadelphia and the practice of law. He also became a noted penologist—a person who studies the punishment of crime and prison management. Additionally, he was a vice president of the Pennsylvania Railroad Company, the founder of the Wistar Institute of Anatomy and Biology at the University of Pennsylvania, and inspector of the Pennsylvania State Penitentiary. He wrote an autobiography and several articles about war and penology. General Wistar died at his summer home in Claymont, Delaware, on September 18, 1905, at age seventy-seven. His ashes lie in the Wistar Institute, Philadelphia.

THOMAS JOHN "TOM" WOOD was born on September 25, 1823, in Munfordville, Kentucky. He was a second cousin of future Confederate General Benjamin H. Helm. Wood graduated from West Point in 1845

(5/41), was commissioned brevet second lieutenant in the topographical engineers, and was immediately sent to Texas. He transferred to the 2nd Dragoons in 1846 and was promoted to second lieutenant late that same year.

Wood served on Zachary Taylor's staff in northern Mexico, fought at Palo Alto and Monterrey, and earned a brevet to first lieutenant at Buena Vista. He was on garrison duty in New Orleans and then Mexico City after it surrendered. Except for two years on leave in Europe, he spent the next thirteen years on frontier duty in Texas, Kansas, Utah, and Indian Territory. He was promoted to first lieutenant (1851), captain (1855), major (March 16, 1861), and lieutenant colonel (May 9).

Thomas Wood was engaged in mustering volunteers in Indiana from April to October 1861. He was promoted to brigadier general of volunteers on October 11, 1861, and commander of a brigade at Camp Nevin, Kentucky. He briefly commanded a brigade in the Army of the Ohio but assumed command of a division in February 1862. He fought at Shiloh on the second day, in the Siege of Corinth, and the Heartland Campaign, including the Battle of Perryville. A minié ball struck his left foot at Stone River on December 31, and he was *hors d'combat* for six weeks. He participated in the Tullahoma Campaign in June and July 1863.

His most controversial moment came on September 20, during the Battle of Chickamauga, when he obeyed a questionable but emphatic order from his army commander, General Rosecrans, to reposition his division. Rosecrans had dressed Wood down in front of his entire staff only ninety minutes earlier for moving too slowly and now Wood moved at once. This opened a gap in Union lines only minutes before it was struck by James Longstreet's entire Confederate corps, resulting in a disaster and the rout of most of the Union army.

With the benefit of hindsight, certain historians have criticized Wood for obeying Rosecrans's order but to have not done so would have left him open to charges of insubordination—and Wood had no way of knowing Longstreet was even in the same state he was in. I think their charges are unfair, but the reader must—of course—draw his or her own conclusions.

Wood's division reformed in Chattanooga and later distinguished itself in the attack on Missionary Ridge (November 25), where it was the first division to drive the Confederates from their fortifications. Wood successfully led his men in the Atlanta Campaign until September 2, 1864, when his left foot was shattered at Lovejoy's Station. He refused to leave the field and, for six months, exercised command from an ambulance and walked on crutches. He was promoted to commander of the IV Corps on December 1.

Tom Wood was promoted to major general on February 22, 1865. He directed his corps in the Battle of Nashville and in the subsequent pursuit of Hood's shattered army. He was in Nashville when the South surrendered. After serving in central Arkansas, Mississippi, and Nebraska, he was mustered out of volunteer service in January 1868 and reverted to the rank of colonel. Frustrated with Reconstruction policies and the Freedmen's Bureau, he applied for retirement owing to disabilities from wounds received in battle. It was granted in June 1868. He retired as a major general, although his rank was reduced to brigadier general in 1875.

General Wood settled in Dayton, Ohio, where he died on February 26, 1906, at age eighty-two. He was the last surviving member of his West Point class. He is buried in the West Point Cemetery. His son George was a colonel during World War I and retired as a brigadier general in the Ohio National Guard.

DANIEL PHINEAS WOODBURY was born on December 16, 1812, in New London, New Hampshire. He was educated at Hopkinton Academy, Dartmouth College, and the U.S. Military Academy, from which he graduated in 1836 (6/49) and was commissioned second lieutenant in the 3rd U.S. Artillery. He was initially appointed assistant engineer in the construction of the Cumberland Road (1836–40) and transferred to the Corps of Engineers as a brevet second lieutenant in 1837. He was promoted to first lieutenant in 1837.

Woodbury spent the next quarter century working on many engineering projects, including the construction of

Fort Warren in Boston Harbor and fortifications in New Hampshire, North Carolina, Nebraska Territory, Dakota Territory, Florida, and on the Oregon Trail. He was promoted to captain in 1853 after fourteen years in grade.

Woodbury was in Florida when the South seceded. Jefferson Davis offered him major increases in rank if he joined the Confederacy, but he refused. Davis then granted him, his wife, and children a special pass through Rebel lines. He took part in the First Bull Run Campaign, during which he conducted important reconnaissance missions. These led to his promotions to major (August 6, 1861) and lieutenant colonel (September 28). In March 1862, he was given command of the Engineer Brigade of the Army of the Potomac and was promoted to brigadier general of volunteers (March 20, 1862). He again distinguished himself in the Peninsula Campaign. Woodbury and his command were in the Washington defenses and missed Antietam. At Fredericksburg, however, he was in charge of laying the army's pontoon bridges. He was criticized for going too slowly, which (it was said) gave General Lee time to complete his nearly impregnable defenses on Marye's Heights. This is apparently the reason he was sent into professional exile.

On March 16, 1863, Woodbury assumed command of the District of Key West and Tortugas, Florida. Here, he caught yellow fever and died in Key West on August 15, 1864. He was fifty-one. He is buried in the Barrancas National Cemetery, Pensacola, Florida. He was posthumously brevetted major general in 1867. His son Thomas was a colonel when he died of a stroke in 1911.

CHARLES ROBERT WOODS was born on February 19, 1827, in Newark, Ohio. He was the younger brother of General William B. Woods and the brother-in-law of Colonel and Brevet Major General Willard Warner. He was homeschooled on the family's farm until 1848, when he was admitted to West Point. He graduated in 1852 (20/43) and was commissioned brevet second lieutenant in the 1st U.S. Infantry. He was promoted to second lieutenant on July 31, 1852. After briefly serving in Fort Columbus, New York, he was sent to Texas, where he performed frontier duty until 1855. After a short tour at Fort Monroe, Virginia, he was transferred to Washington Territory (1856–60). He was on recruiting duty back east when the sectional crisis boiled over.

Lieutenant Woods was in charge of the reinforcements (200 men) aboard the *Star of the West*, which was sent to reinforce Fort Sumter in January 1861. It was turned back by South Carolina gunners on January 8, 1861; some historians cite these as the first shots fired in the Civil War. Woods, meanwhile, returned to New York and was promoted to captain on April 1. He was acting assistant quartermaster to General Patterson during the First Bull Run Campaign. Later, he held the same job on the Upper Potomac under General Banks. On October 13, he was named colonel of the 76th Ohio Infantry. After briefly serving in western Virginia, he was sent to the Western Front and fought at Fort Donelson and Shiloh. He led a brigade during the Siege of Corinth and was part of Sherman's XV Corps during the Battle of Chickasaw Bluffs. He was appointed brigadier general on November 29, but the Senate returned his nomination to the president on February 12, 1863, without acting upon it, and it was subsequently withdrawn.

Colonel Woods performed well in the capture of Arkansas Post, the final Vicksburg Campaign and the ensuing siege, and the Second Battle of Jackson. He was promoted to brigadier general again on August 4, and, this time, he was confirmed by the Senate.

Woods was transferred to Chattanooga after the disaster at Chickamauga. After helping break the siege, he guarded railroads in northern Alabama, until he was given command of a division in the XV Corps for the Atlanta Campaign. He took part in the March to the Sea and the Carolinas Campaign, and was brevetted major general in January 1865.

General Slocum called Woods "an experienced and seasoned soldier, disdainful of ease, inured to hardships . . . sound in judgment and cool and intrepid in the hour of danger or emergency . . . ."

After the war, General Woods was on occupation duty in Mobile, Alabama, and Macon, Georgia. He was mustered out of volunteer service in September 1866 and became lieutenant colonel of the 33rd U.S. Infantry Regiment, then on the Chattahoochee River and later at Newport Barracks, Kentucky. He was promoted to colonel commanding the 2nd U.S. Infantry

in 1874, but his health failed him, and he retired at the end of the year. He died in the town of his birth on February 26, 1885, at age fifty-eight. He is buried there in Cedar Hill Cemetery.

WILLIAM BURNHAM WOODS, the older brother of General Charles R. Woods, was born in Newark, Ohio, on August 3, 1824. He attended Western Reserve University (now Case Western Reserve University) before transferring to Yale, from which he graduated with honors in 1845. He then returned home, read law, and was admitted to the bar in 1847. A Democrat, he was elected mayor of Newark in 1856 and to the Ohio legislature in 1858. Here, he served as speaker of the house and later as minority leader. He was considered a fine orator.

Woods opposed slavery and the Civil War, but also the breakup of the Union. He joined the Union Army on February 6, 1862, as lieutenant colonel of the 76th Ohio Infantry. He served on the Western Front, fighting at Fort Donelson, Shiloh, the Siege of Corinth, Chickasaw Bluffs, Arkansas Post (aka Fort Hindman), Jackson, and Vicksburg. He was slightly wounded at Arkansas Post on January 11, 1863.

Woods was promoted to colonel on September 10, 1863. He fought in at least forty-four major battles during the war, including Lookout Mountain, Ringgold Gap, Resaca, Kennesaw Mountain, Atlanta, Ezra Church, and Jonesboro. He took part in the March to the Sea and was brevetted brigadier general for Atlanta and Savannah. Elevated to brigade commander on January 21, 1865, he was promoted to brigadier general of volunteers on May 21, 1865.

Postwar, General Woods performed occupation duty in Alabama. He was mustered out February 1866, brevetted major general three months later, and remained in Alabama, which he made his home. Now a Republican, he became a judge in the Chancery court in 1868 and a federal circuit judge in 1869. He moved to Atlanta in 1877.

Unlike many Reconstruction officials, Woods was highly respected throughout the South because he was honest, administered the law fairly, and worked tirelessly. In 1880, President Hayes appointed him to the

Supreme Court. He was the first Southerner appointed to the Court since 1853. Although there was some opposition because Hayes was a lame duck, Woods's sponsors ranged from General Sherman to John A. Campbell, who resigned his seat on the Supreme Court in 1861 and served the Confederacy as an assistant secretary of war. Woods was confirmed on January 5, 1881. His short tenure was basically free of controversy.

Justice Woods died in Washington, D.C., on May 14, 1887, at age sixty-two. He was buried in Cedar Hill Cemetery, Newark, Ohio.

JOHN ELLIS WOOL was born on February 29, 1784, at Newburgh, New York, only a year after the Revolutionary War ended. He was orphaned at an early age and raised by a grandfather. He was poorly educated, having dropped out of a public school at age twelve. He went to work in a variety of low-paying jobs but nevertheless managed to read law and was admitted to the bar. He was practicing law in Troy, New York, when the War of 1812 began. At age twenty-eight, he volunteered and was commissioned captain in the 13th U.S. Infantry Regiment.

Wool was wounded in the Battle of Queenston Heights, which led to his promotion to major in the 29th Infantry. He distinguished himself in the Battle of Plattsburgh in 1814 and was brevetted lieutenant colonel. He remained in the service after the war and was promoted to colonel and inspector general of the army in 1816. Highly intelligent, he was sent to Europe to observe foreign military organizations and participated in the removal of Indians from the southeast. He was promoted to brigadier general in 1841. During the Mexican War, he commanded a division and was brevetted major general for his actions during the Battle of Buena Vista. After commanding occupation forces in northern Mexico, Wool directed the Department of the Pacific and the Department of the East (1857–61).

Wool was seventy-seven years old when the Civil War erupted. He moved quickly and reinforced Fort Monroe, Virginia, which was never captured by the Confederates. Named commander of the Department of Virginia in August 1861, he captured Norfolk and the Gosport Naval Yard in May 1862, an operation personally witnessed by Abraham Lincoln. Wool was rewarded with an immediate promotion to major general. Lincoln also decided Wool should have a less demanding assignment, so he named him commander of the Middle Department on June 9, 1862. It became the VIII Corps a month later. He was responsible for Federal forces in New Jersey, Pennsylvania, Delaware, and part of eastern Maryland. He returned to the command of the Department of the East on January 3, 1863.

General Wool mishandled the New York Draft Riots in July 1863. On August 1, Lincoln sent an order retiring Wool after fifty-one years' service. He was outraged and sent letters of protest to the War Department, but without effect. He applied for a return to active duty with Presidents Johnson and Grant but to no avail.

John Wool was the oldest officer to exercise command in the Civil War. He retired to Troy, New York, where he passed away on November 10, 1869, at age eighty-five. He is buried there, in Oakwood Cemetery.

GEORGE WRIGHT was born on October 22, 1803, in Norwich, Vermont. He was educated at what is now Norwich University and at West Point, from which he graduated in 1822 (24/40). Commissioned second lieutenant in the 3rd U.S. Infantry, he served in various garrisons and on frontier and recruiting duty in Wisconsin; Fort Leavenworth, Kansas; and on the Canadian border, among other places. He fought the Seminoles in Florida (1840–43) and served in Mexico from Vera Cruz to Molino del Rey (September 8, 1847), where he was wounded leading a storming party. He was promoted to first lieutenant (1827), captain (1836), brevet major for "zeal, energy, and perseverance" against the Seminoles (1842), brevet lieutenant colonel for Contreras and Churubusco (1847) and brevet colonel for Molino del Rey.

Wright spent 1848 to 1852 in garrison duty at Fort Columbus, New York, before he was commander of the Northern District of California (1852–55). He fought Yakima Indians in Washington Territory in 1856, and commanded various forts in Oregon and Washington Territories from then until 1861. Meanwhile, he was promoted to major (1848), lieutenant colonel (February 1855), and colonel (March 1855).

When the Civil War broke out, Wright was commander of the Department of Oregon. He preferred service in the East; however, he was named commander of the Department of the Pacific (October 20, 1861 to July 1, 1864) and the District of California (July 1, 1864 to July 27, 1865). He directed 6,000 men. He had to keep an eye on secessionists, protect the coast, guard the frontier, guard against Indian raiders, and send whatever troops he could East. He did a fine job. He was promoted to brigadier general on September 28, 1861.

At the end of the war, Wright was named commander of the Department of the Columbia, probably so General Irwin McDowell could replace him in California. On July 28, 1865, he left San Francisco for his new command aboard the steamship *Brother Jonathan*. It was old, overloaded, and in need of repair. On July 30, the ship hit a reef during a storm near Crescent City, California, and sank. Most of the passengers perished, including General Wright and his wife. His body was found in October, 150 miles from the site of the wreck. He was sixty-one. He was buried in the Sacramento Historic City Cemetery, Sacramento.

His son, Brevet Brigadier General Thomas F. Wright, was killed in action against the Modoc Indians in the Battle of Lava Beds, Oregon/northern California, in 1873.

HORATIO GOUVERNEUR WRIGHT was born on March 6, 1820, in Clinton, Connecticut. He was educated at Alden Partridge's military academy (now Norwich University) and West Point, graduating with the Class of 1841 (2/52). Commissioned second lieutenant in the Corps of Engineers, he was an assistant on the Board of Engineers (1841–42 and 1844–46), on the faculty at West Point, teaching French and Engineering (1842–44), and superintending engineer on the construction of Fort Jefferson, Dry Tortugas, Florida (1846–56), as well as other engineering projects. He was promoted to first lieutenant (1848) and captain (1855) and was an assistant to the Chief Engineer

at Washington, D.C., (1856–61) when the war began. He was the engineer in charge of destroying the Gosport Naval Yard at Norfolk in April 1861.

Wright was involved in improving the defenses of Washington, D.C., until mid-July, when he became chief engineer of Heintzelman's division. He fought in the First Battle of Bull Run and in the Port Royal, South Carolina, Expedition as chief engineer. He was promoted to major of engineers on August 6 and to brigadier general of volunteers on September 14, 1861, and commanded a brigade in the capture of Hilton Head (November 7). He was involved in the Florida Expedition of 1861–62 and took part in the capture of Fernandina, Jacksonville, and St. Augustine. Given command of a division in the Department of the South, he took part in the Battle of Secessionville (June 16, 1862), which was a Union defeat.

General Wright was appointed commander of the Department of the Ohio on August 19. (The original department became the Army of the Ohio under Don Carlos Buell. The department and the army were different entities in August 1862.) Wright's territorial responsibilities included Ohio, Michigan, Indiana, Illinois, Wisconsin, and Kentucky east of the Tennessee River. Wright provided logistical support for Buell during the Kentucky Campaign of 1862. He was promoted to major general on August 20, 1862, but his promotion was negated by the Senate for political reasons on March 12, 1863. A brigadier general was not considered sufficient to command such a vast department, so Wright was superseded by Ambrose Burnside on March 17. Meanwhile, Wright's promotion was reconsidered on March 13 but rejected again on March 24.

Horatio Wright was transferred to the Army of the Potomac and assumed command of a division in the VI Corps on May 23. It was present at Gettysburg but held in reserve. It was involved in the Mine Run Campaign (November 1863), the Battle of the Wilderness (May 5–6, 1864), and the Battle of Spotsylvania Court House, where the VI Corps commander, General Sedgwick, was killed in action on May 9. Wright assumed command of the corps and was promoted to major general on May 14. This time he was confirmed by the Senate.

Wright led the VI Corps in the Overland Campaign, including Spotsylvania and Cold Harbor, in the defense of Washington, and in the Shenandoah Valley (1864–65). Sent back to Petersburg, the VI Corps was the first to break through Lee's lines on April 2, 1865. It fought at Sayler's Creek on April 6, and captured thousands of Confederate soldiers, including Lieutenant General Richard S. Ewell. It was present at Appomattox.

Sent west after the surrender, General Wright commanded the Army of Texas from July 1865 to August 1866. Mustered out of volunteer service in September 1866, he went from commanding an army to lieutenant colonel of engineers. Postwar, he was involved in a number of interesting projects, including the Brooklyn Bridge and the completion of the Washington Monument as well as several river and harbor improvement projects. He was promoted to colonel in March 1879 and brigadier general and chief of engineers, U.S. Army, on June 38, 1879. He left the army on March 6, 1884, having reached the mandatory retirement age of sixty-four.

General Horatio Wright settled in Washington, D.C., where he died on July 2, 1899, at age seventy-nine. He was buried in Arlington National Cemetery.

Z

ZOOK

SAMUEL KOSCIUSZKO ZOOK, who was born **SAMUEL KURTZ ZOOK**, was born in Tredyffrin Township, Chester County, Pennsylvania, the descendent of Mennonites. His father was a major during the American Revolution, and Samuel grew up at Valley Forge, which fueled a life-long interest in military affairs. He joined the Pennsylvania Militia at an early age and was a lieutenant at age nineteen.

Early on, Zook took an interest in telegraphy and became proficient as an operator and in every other aspect of his profession. He moved to New York City in 1846 or 1851 (depending on one's source), became superintendent of the Washington and New York Telegraph Company, and established a reputation as an authority in his field. He also rose to the lieutenant colonelcy of the 6th New York Militia by the time the Civil War began.

Zook was military governor of Annapolis in the early days of the war. The 6th New York was mustered out after ninety days, but Zook received authorization to recruit his own regiment, which he did. The 57th New York (aka the National Guard Rifles) was mustered in to Federal service on October 19, 1861, with Zook as its colonel. It fought during the Seven Days battles, during which Zook scouted behind Confederate lines, where he discovered that Confederate General Magruder was conducting an elaborate deception and did not have nearly as many men as the Federal high command was led to believe. He reported this fact to General McClellan, the commander of the Army of the Potomac, but was ignored.

Zook's regiment was not present at the Second Bull Run, and Zook was absent from the Battle of Antietam. (He was on medical leave, suffering from chronic severe rheumatism.) When he returned on October 6, he was given command of a brigade in the II Corps. He led an attack on Marye's Heights during the Battle of Fredericksburg, during which his horse was shot out from under him. He nevertheless led his brigade to within sixty yards of the Stone Wall, earning him the praise of General Hancock. His brigade suffered 527 casualties, and Zook was profoundly affected by the carnage. He was promoted to brigadier general on April 4, 1863.

Zook

Samuel Zook was a firm—sometimes severe—disciplinarian. He was nevertheless popular with his men because he was a good tactician, quick-witted, and totally without fear. His brigade was relatively lightly engaged at Chancellorsville, where it suffered 188 casualties. On July 2, 1863, during the Battle of Gettysburg, Zook joined the battle in the Wheatfield, where Longstreet's Confederates were crushing the III Corps. Zook, on horseback, reinforced the crumbling blue line but, in the process, attracted the attention of the South Carolina infantry. He was shot three times, in the shoulder, chest, and abdomen. Carried to the rear, he died shortly after midnight on July 3. He was forty-two. General Zook was buried in Montgomery Cemetery, Norristown, Pennsylvania.

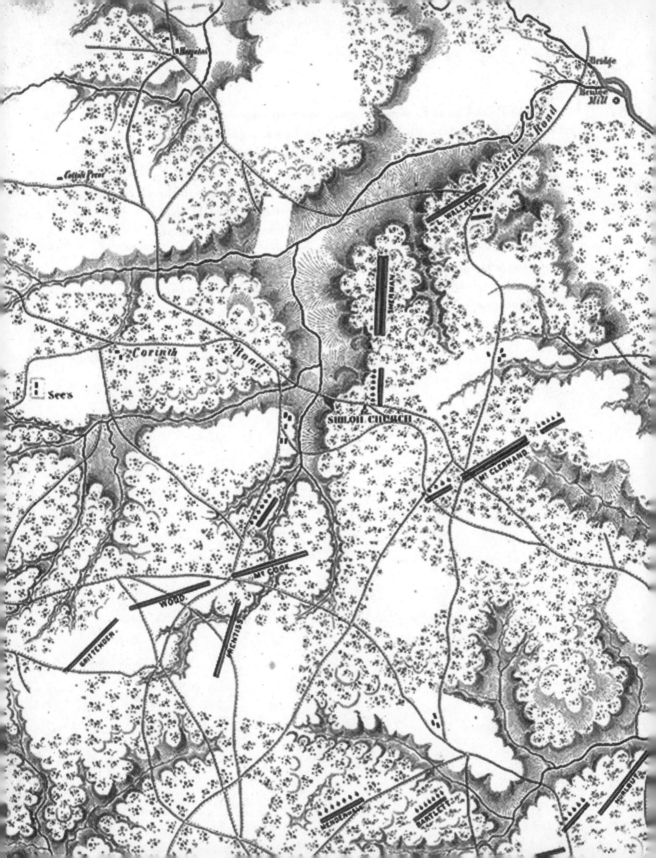

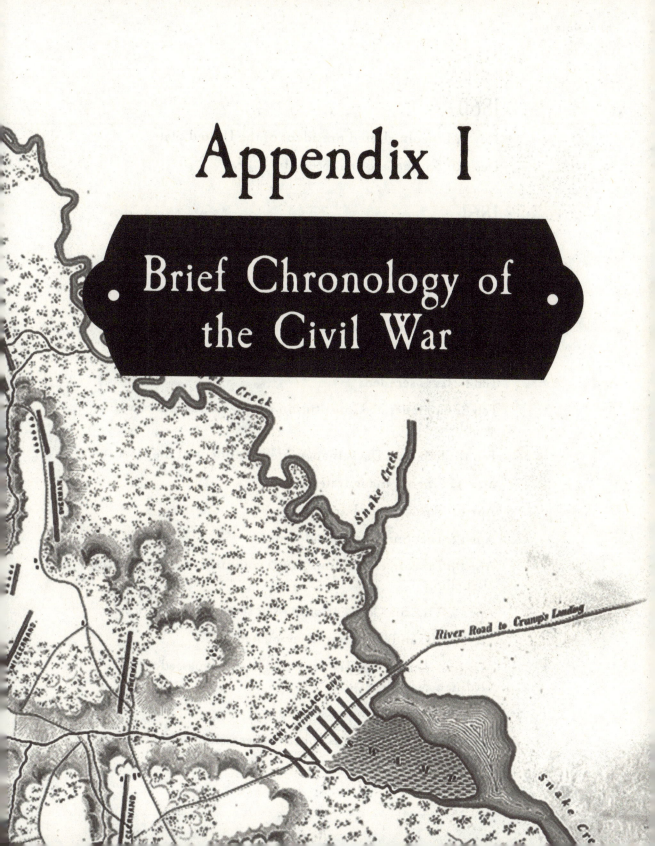

Appendix I

Brief Chronology of the Civil War

APPENDIX I

1860

Nov 6: Lincoln elected president of the United States.

Dec 20: South Carolina seceded

1861

Jan 9: Mississippi seceded

Jan 10: Florida seceded

Jan 11: Alabama secedes

Jan 19: Georgia Convention passed an ordinance of secession

Jan 26: Louisiana seceded

Feb 1: Texas seceded

Feb 8: Confederate Constitution adopted; Confederacy established

Feb 18: Jefferson Davis inaugurated president of the CSA.

Mar 4: Lincoln inaugurated

Apr 12: Fort Sumter bombarded

Apr 13: Fort Sumter surrendered

Apr 15: Lincoln called for 75,000 volunteers to suppress the "Rebellion"

Apr 17: Virginia Convention passed secession resolution

May 5: Alexandria, Virginia, evacuated

May 6: Arkansas and Tennessee legislatures passed Ordinances of Secession

May 20: North Carolina secedes

May 23: Virginia citizens approved secession, 96,750 to 32,134

APPENDIX I

Jun 3: Battle of Philippi, (West) Virginia

Jun 10: Battle of Big Bethel, Virginia

Jun 17: Battle of Boonville, Missouri

Jul 5: Battle of Carthage, Missouri

Jul 11: Battle of Rich Mountain, (West) Virginia

Jul 13: Battle of Corrick's Ford, western Virginia

Jul 18: Engagement at Blackburn's Ford, Virginia

Jul 21: First Battle of Manassas

Aug 10: Battle of Wilson's Creek, Missouri

Aug 19: The Confederate Congress admitted Missouri into the Confederacy

Sep 2: Confederate forces under General Polk entered Kentucky, occupied Columbus.

Sep 6: Union forces under Grant occupied Paducah. Kentucky neutrality ended.

Sep 10: Engagement at Carnifex Ferry, (West) Virginia

Sep 11–15: Cheat Mountain Campaign, (West) Virginia

Sep 15: Albert Sidney Johnston superseded Polk as Confederate commander in the West.

Sep 20: Union garrison at Lexington, Missouri, surrendered.

Oct 8–9: Battle of Santa Rosa Island, near Fort Pickens, Florida

Oct 21: Battle of Ball's Bluff or Leesburg, Virginia

Nov 1: Winfield Scott replaced as Union General-in-Chief by John B. McClellan.

Nov 3–7: Battle of Port Royal Sound, South Carolina; U.S.

APPENDIX I

established a foothold between Savannah and Charleston.

Nov 7: Battle of Belmont, Missouri

Nov 8: Robert E. Lee assumed command of the Department of South Carolina, Georgia, and East Florida.

Nov 9: U.S. captured Beaufort, South Carolina

Dec 20: Engagement at Dranesville, Virginia

1862

Jan 1–10: Stonewall Jackson's Romney Campaign

Jan 9–11: Battle of Arkansas Post

Jan 19: Battle of Mill Springs (a.k.a. Logan's Cross Roads), Kentucky

Feb 6: Fort Henry, Tennessee, surrendered

Feb 8: Battle of Roanoke Island, North Carolina

Feb 12–15: Battle of Fort Donelson

Feb 16: Fort Donelson surrendered.

Feb 21: Battle of Valverde, New Mexico

Feb 28: U.S. General Pope began an advance on New Madrid, Missouri

Feb 29–Mar 2: Polk evacuated Columbus, Kentucky

Mar 3: Siege of New Madrid began

Mar 4: General Sibley entered Santa Fe

Mar 7–8: Battle of Pea Ridge (Elkhorn Tavern)

Mar 9: Joseph Johnston evacuated the Centreville-Manassas sector.

Mar 9: Naval battle between the USS Monitor and CSS

APPENDIX 1

Merrimack (CSS Virginia)

Mar 9–11: Joseph Johnston evacuated Manassas area and retreated to the Rappahannock.

March 14: New Madrid fell. Rebels retreated to Island No. 10

March 14: New Bern, North Carolina, fell

March 18: Secretary of War Judah Benjamin replaced by R. M. T. Hunter.

March 23: Battle of Kernstown, Virginia

March 23–June 11: Stonewall Jackson's Valley Campaign

March 28: Battle of Glorieta Pass, New Mexico

April 4–June 24: Peninsula Campaign.

April 4–May 3: Siege of Yorktown, Virginia

April 6–7: Shiloh

April 7: Island No. 10 fell

April 11: Fort Pulaski, Georgia, fell, blocking the main channel to Savannah.

April 16: Battle of Lee's Mill, Virginia

April 18: Union fleet began its bombardment of Forts St. Philip and Jackson below New Orleans.

April 25: Union fleet reached New Orleans

April 28: Forts Jackson and St. Philip surrendered

April 28–May 30: Siege of Corinth (a.k.a. First Battle of Corinth)

May 1: Union army occupied New Orleans

May 3: Yorktown evacuated; Johnston retreated up the Virginia Peninsula

May 4: Yankees occupied Yorktown

APPENDIX I

May 5: Battle of Williamsburg, Virginia

May 8: Battle of McDowell, Virginia

May 9: Norfolk evacuated

May 11: U.S. occupied Natchez, Mississippi.

May 15: Battle of Drewry' Bluff, Virginia

May 18-July 27: First Siege of Vicksburg

May 23: Battle of Front Royal, Virginia

May 25: First Battle of Winchester, Virginia

May 29/30: Corinth evacuated

May 31-June 1: Seven Pines

June 25: The Battle of Oak Grove (in Huger's sector) began the Seven Days Battles

June 26: Battle of Mechanicsville (a.k.a. Beaver Dam Creek)

June 27: Battle of Gaines' Mill (also called the First Cold Harbor)

June 28: White House, McClellan's main supply base, was abandoned and burned.

June 29: Savage's Station

June 30: Battle of Frayser's Farm (a.k.a. White Oak Swamp)

July 1: Malvern Hill; end of the Seven Days Battles

July 13: First Battle of Murfreesboro

August 9: Battle of Cedar Mountain

Sept 12–15: Siege of Harpers Ferry

Sept 13: Battle of Charleston, (West) Virginia

Sept 14: Battle of South Mountain, including Crampton's Gap and Turner's Gap

APPENDIX I

Sept 14: Confederates occupied Charleston, (West) Virginia

Sept 14–17: Battle of Munfordville, Kentucky

Oct 28: Rebels evacuate Charleston, (West) Virginia

Nov 18: Battle of Cane Hill, Arkansas

Dec 7: Battle of Prairie Grove, Akansas

1863

Jan 11: Arkansas Post surrendered

Feb 3: Wheeler's unsuccessful attack on Fort Donelson

April 11-May 4: Siege of Suffolk, Virginia

May 18-July 4: Siege of Vicksburg

May 25-July 9: Siege of Port Hudson, Louisiana

June 11: Battle of Trevilian's Station

June 23-July 4: Tullahoma Campaign

July 9–16: Siege of Jackson, Mississippi

Aug 10-Sep 10: Little Rock Campaign

Aug 16: U.S. Army of the Cumberland began Chattanooga Campaign

Aug 25: (Second) Battle of Reams' Station

Sep 2: Knoxville abandoned

Sep 19–20: Battle of Chickamauga

Oct 13-Nov 7: the Bristoe Campaign

Nov 6: Battle of Droop Mountain ended Confederate resistance in West Virginia.

Nov 24: Battle of Lookout Mountain

APPENDIX I

Nov 25: Battle of Missionary Ridge; Siege of Chattanooga broken

Nov 26-Dec 2: Mine Run Campaign

Nov 27: Battle of Ringgold Gap, Georgia.

1864

Feb 3-Mar 6: Sherman's Meridian Expedition

Feb 14: Meridian fell

March 23-May 2: Camden Expedition in Arkansas

Apr 18: Battle of Poison Spings, Arkansas

Apr 23: Battle of Monett's Ferry, Louisiana

May 7-Sep 2: Atlanta Campaign

May 16: (Second) Battle of Drewry's Bluff

Jun 1-3: Battle of Cold Harbor

July 9: Battle of Monocacy, Maryland

Aug 21: Battle of Globe Tavern, Virginia (a.k.a. Second Battle of the Weldon Railroad)

Aug 31-Sept 1: Battle of Jonesboro, Georgia

Sept 2: Fall of Atlanta

Sept 19: Third Battle of Winchester

Sept 19-Oct 29: Price's Missouri Raid

Nov 4-5: Battle of Johnsonville

Nov 21-Dec 27: Hood's Middle Tennessee Campaign

Dec 20: Confederates evacuated Savannah

Dec 21: Savannah fell

APPENDIX I

1865

Jan 13–15: Battle of Ft. Fisher, N.C.

Mar 16: Battle of Averysboro

Mar 19–21: Battle of Bentonville

Mar 25: Battle of Fort Stedman

Apr 1: Battle of Five Folks

Apr 2/3 (night of): Richmond evacuated

Apr 3: Fall of Richmond

Apr 9: General Lee surrendered at Appomattox

Apr 26: Joseph Johnston surrendered the Army of Tennessee at Bennett Place, near Durham, N.C.

May 5: President Davis officially abolished the Confederate government.

May 10: President Davis captured.

May 26: The Confederate Trans-Mississippi Department surrendered.

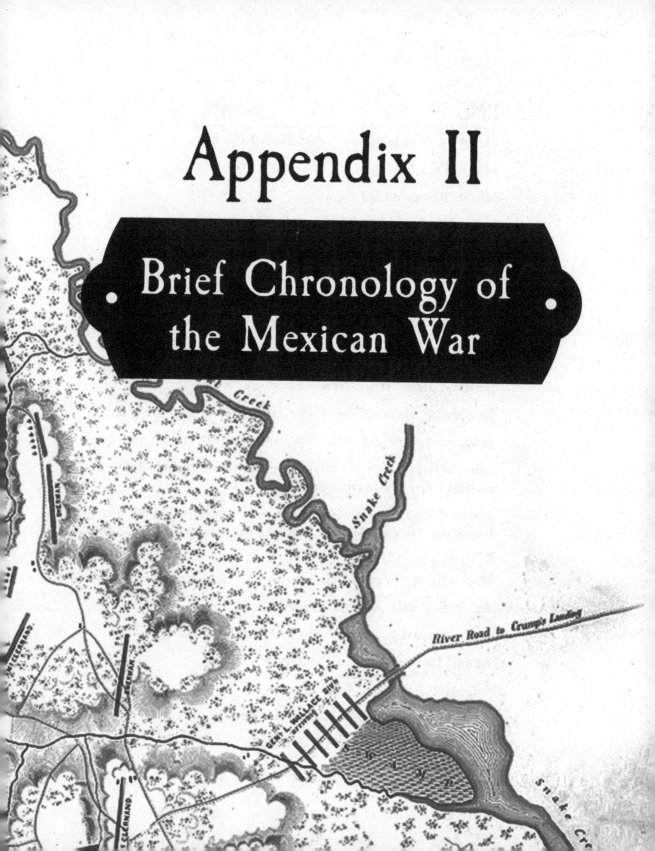

Appendix II

Brief Chronology of the Mexican War

APPENDIX II

1846

May 3–10: Battle of Fort Texas (Fort Brown)

May 8: Palo Alto

May 9: Resaca de la Palma

May 13: U.S. declared war on Mexico

August 13: U.S. forces occupied Los Angeles

August 15: U.S. forces captured Santa Fe, New Mexico

September 20–24: Battle of Monterrey

1847

January: Taos Revolt, New Mexico

January 12: Mexican forces in California surrendered

January 13: Mexican resistance in California ended

February 22: Battle of Buena Vista; effective end of Mexican resistance in northern Mexico

March 9–29: Scott landed on the coast of central Mexico and began the drive on Mexico City, the decisive campaign of the war.

March 9–29: Siege of Vera Cruz.

April 18: Battle of Cerro Gordo

May 1–August 7: Scott's Army of Mexico paused at Puebla

August 19–20: Battle of Contreras

August 20: Battle of Churubusco

September 8: Battle of Molino del Rey

September 13: Battle of Chapultepec

APPENDIX II

September 8–14: U.S. forces stormed the Gates of Mexico City and the city surrendered.

1848

February 2: Treaty of Guadalupe Hidalgo

BIBLIOGRAPHY

BIBLIOGRAPHY

Allen G. H. Forty-Six Months with the Fourth Rhode Island Volunteers. Providence, Rhode Island: 1887.

American Battlefield Trust. "Richard James Oglesby." https://www.battlefields.org/learn/biographies/richard-james-oglesby. Accessed 2023.

Andrews, Christopher Columbus. History of the Campaign of Mobile. 2nd ed. New York: 1889.

Anonymous. General Henry Goddard Thomas, 1837–1897: Memorial. Portland, Maine: 1898.

Asbury, Samuel E. "Extracts from the Reminiscences of General George W. Morgan." The Southwestern Historical Quarterly. Vol. 30, No. 3 (January 1927).

Asher, Brad. The Most Hated Man in Kentucky: The Lost Cause and the Legacy of Union General Stephen Burbridge. Lexington, Kentucky: 2021.

Baden, Adam. Military History of Ulysses S. Grant, from April 1861 to April 1865. New York: 1868. 3 volumes.

Baggett, James Alex. "Granger, Gordon (1821–1876)." Texas State Historical Association. Handbook of Texas. https://www.tshaonline.org/handbook/entries/granger-gordon. Accessed 2023.

Baker, Lafayette C. The History of the United States Secret Service. Philadelphia: 1867.

Balance, Jim. "Major General James Henry Carleton." Californians and the Military. Accessed 2023.

Barclay, Keith A. "Major General James Scott Negley and His Division at Chickamauga: A Historical Analysis." Unpublished Master's Thesis, United States Army Command and General Staff College. Fort Leavenworth, Kansas: 2001. Accessed online, 2023.

Bartlett, J. R. Memoirs of Rhode Island Officers. Providence: 1867.

Beatty, John. The Citizen Soldier, or Memoirs of a Volunteer. Cincinnati: 1879.

Biographical Encyclopedia of Maine of the 19th Century. Boston: 1885.

Blakeman, A. Noel, ed. Personal Recollections of the War of the Rebellion. New York: 1897.

BIBLIOGRAPHY

Blumberg, Arnold. "Alfred Duffie: A 'Napoleon' in the Civil War." Warfare History Network. August 2012. https://warfarehistory network.com/article/alfred-duffie-a-napoleon-in-the-civil -war/. Accessed 2023.

Bolden, Kenneth. Personal communication, 2023.

Bonekemper, Edward H., III. A Victor, Not a Butcher: Ulysses S. Grant's Overlooked Military Genius. Washington, D.C.: 2004.

Borders, Matthew. Faces of Union Soldiers at Fredericksburg. Arcadia Publishing: 2022.

Borders, Matthew. "Henry Baxter. Interview in Civil War Digital Digest, https://www.youtube.com/watch?v=sUP_BR8KI7I. N.d.

Bowen, James L. Massachusetts in the War, 1861–1865. Springfield, Massachusetts: 1889.

Brooke, John R. Final Report of Major-General John R. Brooke. Havana, Cuba: 1899.

Cadwallader, Sylvanus. Four Years with Grant. Philadelphia: 1896.

"Calvin E. Pratt." Historical Society of the New York Courts. https://history.nycourts.gov/biography/calvin-e-pratt/ Accessed 2023.

Castle, Henry A. "General James Shields: Soldier, Orator, Statesman." Minnesota Historical Society. Vol. XV (1915).

Catton, Bruce. The Centennial History of the Civil War. Volume I: Mr. Lincoln's Army. Volume II: Terrible Swift Sword. Volume III: Never Call Retreat. New York: 1965.

Catton, Bruce. The Army of the Potomac Trilogy. Volume I: Mr. Lincoln's Army; Volume II: Glory Road. Volume III: A Stillness at Appomattox. New York: 1952.

Central Arkansas Library System. Encyclopedia of Arkansas. https://encyclopediaofarkansas.net. Various articles. Accessed 2022.

Chernow, Ron. Grant. New York: 2017.

Chetlain, Augustus L. Recollections of Seventy Years. Galena, Illinois: 1899.

CivilWarTalk, civilwartalk.com. A forum, accessed 2023.

BIBLIOGRAPHY

Clay, Cassius Marcellus. The Life of Cassius Marcellus Clay. Cincinnati, Ohio: 1886.

Clendenen, Clarence C. "General James Henry Carleton." New Mexico Historical Review, Vol. 30, No. 1 (1955).

Condon, William H. Life of Major-General James Shields. Chicago: 1900.

Costigan, David. "Common Soldier's General: James Dada Morgan." Historical Society of Quincy & Adams County. August 19, 2012. https://www.hsqac.org/common-soldier-s-general-james-dada-morgan9dac8c73. Accessed 2023.

Cox, Jacob D. Military Reminiscences of the Civil War. New York: 1900. 2 volumes.

Cox, Jacob D. The March to the Sea: Franklin and Nashville. New York: 1882.

Cox, Jacob Dobson. Military Reminiscences of the Civil War. New York: 1900. 2 volumes.

Cozzens, Peter. No Better Place to Die: The Battle of Stones River. Urbana-Champaign, Illinois: 1989.

Cozzens, Peter. This Terrible Sound: The Battle of Chickamauga. Chicago: 1996.

Crawford, R. W. "Henry Washington Benham." Professional Memoirs, Corps of Engineers, United States Army and Engineer Department at Large, Vol. 7, No. 31 (January-February 1915).

Crawford, Samuel Wylie. The Genesis of the Civil War: The Story of Sumter, 1860–61. New York: 1887.

Croffut, W. A., ed. Fifty Years in Camp and Field: Diary of Major-General Ethan Allen Hitchcock. New York: 1909.

Cullum, George Washington. Biographical Register of the Officers and Graduates of the U.S. Military Academy at West Point, New York. Cambridge, Massachusetts: 1891–1901. 4 volumes.

Curtis, Newton M. From Bull Run to Chancellorsville. New York: 1906.

Cutrer, Thomas W. "Clark, William Thomas (1831–1905)." Texas State Historical Association (TSHA) (1976), accessed 2022.

Dana, Charles A. Recollections of the Civil War. New York: 1893.

BIBLIOGRAPHY

De Falaise, Louis. "Gen. Stephen Gano Burbridge's Command in Kentucky." The Register of the Kentucky Historical Society. Vol. 69, No. 2 (April 1971).

Dictionary of North Carolina Biography. Chapel Hill: 1988. Various articles.

Dix, Morgan, comp. Memoirs of John Adams Dix. New York: 1883. 2 volumes.

Dodge, Grenville M. Personal Recollections of President Abraham Lincoln, General Ulysses S. Grant, and General William T. Sherman. Council Bluffs, Iowa: 1914.

Dodge, Grenville M. The Battle of Atlanta and Other Campaigns, Addresses, Etc. Council Bluffs, Iowa: 1910.

Dorris, J. T. "Michael Kelly Lawler: Mexican and Civil War Officer." Journal of the Illinois State Historical Society. Vol. 48, No. 4 (Winter, 1955).

Doubleday, Abner. Gettysburg and Chancellorsville. New York: 1882.

Doubleday, Abner. Gettysburg Made Simple. New York: 1888.

Doubleday, Abner. Reminiscences of Forts Sumter and Moultrie in 1860–61. New York: 1876.

Dunkelman, Mark H. Patrick Henry Jones: Irish American, Civil War General, and Gilded Age Politician. Baton Rouge: 2015.

Dyer, Frederick H. A Compendium of the War of the Rebellion. Des Moines, Iowa: 1908. 3 volumes.

Eicher, John H. and David J. Eicher. Civil War High Commands. Stanford, California: 2001.

Emerging Civil War. emergingcivilwar.com. Various articles. Accessed 2022 and 2023.

Encyclopedia of Arkansas. Various articles. Accessed 2022 and 2023.

Encyclopedia of Indianapolis. Various articles. Accessed 2022 and 2023.

Find a Grave Memorials, various individuals. Accessed 2021–2023.

Fox, William F. Regimental Losses in the American Civil War, 1861–1865. Albany, New York: 1898.

Fry, James B. McDowell and Tyler: The Campaign of Bull Run. New York: 1884.

853

BIBLIOGRAPHY

Fry, James B. Operations of the Army Under Buell from June 10th to October 30, 1862. New York: 1884.

"General Gilman Marston—Class of 1833." Kimball Union Academy: April 12, 2012. https://www.kua.org/news-detail ?pk=639329. Accessed 2023.

"General Leonard F. Ross." Iowa Historical Record. Vol. IV, No. 4. October 1888.

Gibbon, John. Personal Recollections of the Civil War. New York: 1928.

Gillmore, Quincy A. Engineer and Artillery Operations Against the Defences of Charleston Harbor in 1863. New York: 1865.

Gilmor, Harry. Four Years in the Saddle. New York: 1866.

Goc, Michael J. Hero of the Red River Campaign: The Life and Times of Joseph Bailey. Friendship, Wisconsin: 2007.

Gordon, George H. "History of the Second Mass. Regiment of Infantry." Second Paper. Delivered at the Second Annual Meeting of the Second Mass. Regiment of Infantry, May 11, 1874. Boston: 1874.

Gordon, George H. A War Diary of Events in the War of the Great Rebellion, 1863–1865. Boston: 1882.

Gordon, George H. History of the Campaign of the Army of Virginia Under John Pope, Brigadier-General, U.S.A., Late Major General, U.S. Volunteers, From Cedar Mountain to Alexandria, 1862. Boston: 1882.

Gough, Robert E. South Kingstown's Own: A Biographical Sketch of Isaac Peace Rodman, Brigadier General. Unpublished Manuscript, 2011. Available online. Accessed 2023.

Gould, Edward K. Major-General Hiram G. Berry. Rockland, Maine: 1899.

"Governor John Frederick Hartranft." Pennsylvania Historical & Museum Commission. http://www.phmc.state.pa.us/portal /communities/governors/1790–1876/john-hartranft.html Accessed 2023.

Grant, Ulysses S. Memoirs and Selected Letters: Personal Memoirs of U.S. Grant. New York: 1886. 2 volumes.

Grant, Ulysses S. Personal Memoirs of U.S. Grant. New York: 1885–1886. 2 volumes.

BIBLIOGRAPHY

Groeling, Meg. "Commanding the Regiment: Galusha Pennypacker: The Civil War's Youngest General." The Emerging Civil War. https://emergingcivilwar.com/2023/06/25/commanding-the-regiment-galusha-pennypacker-the-civil-wars-youngest-general/ . Posted June 25, 2023. Accessed 2023.

Groeling, Meg. "Eleazer Paine—The Man, the Myth, the Hair." Emerging Civil War. Posted October 17, 2011. Accessed 2023.

Groom, Winston. Shrouds of Glory: From Atlanta to Nashville: The Last Great Campaign of the Civil War. New York: 1995.

Grose, William. The Story of Marches, Battles and Incidents of the 36th Regiment, Indiana Volunteer Infantry. New Castle, Indiana: 1891.

Hamblin, Deborah. Brevet Major-General Joseph Eldridge Hamblin. Boston: 1902.

Heitman, Francis B. Historical Register and Dictionary of the United States Army. Washington, D.C.: 1903. 2 volumes.

Henry, Robert S. The Story of the Confederacy. New York: 1931. Reprint ed., Old Saybrook, Connecticut: 1999.

Historycentral.com. Accessed 2023.

Hollandsworth, James G., Jr. Pretense of Glory: The Life of General Nathaniel P. Banks. Baton Rouge, Louisiana: 1998.

Holthof, Duane Edward. "The Impeachment and Trial of Secretary of War William Worth Belknap." Unpublished Masters Thesis, Western Michigan University. Kalamazoo, Michigan: 1985.

Hopkins, Alphonso A. The Life of Clinton Bowen Fisk. New York: 1890.

Howard, Oliver O. The Autobiography of Oliver Otis Howard. New York: 1908. 2 volumes.

http://penelope.uchicago.edu/Thayer/E/Gazetteer/Places/America/United_States/Army/USMA/Cullums_Register/home.html

Humphreys, Andrew A. From Gettysburg to the Rapidan. New York: 1883.

Humphreys, Andrew A. The Virginia Campaigns of '64 and '65. New York: 1883.

855

BIBLIOGRAPHY

Hunter, David. Report on the Military Services of Gen. David Hunter, U.S.A., During the War of the Rebellion. New York: 1873.

Hyde, Samuel C. A Wisconsin Yankee in the Confederate Bayou Country: The Civil War Reminiscences of a Union General [Halbert E. Paine]. Baton Rouge: 2009.

Jastrzembski, Frank. "'Down Fame's Ladder': Brigadier General Thomas W. Egan's Unending War. Emerging Civil War. https://emergingcivilwar.com/2019/07/29/down-fames-ladder-brigadier-general-thomas-w-egans-unending-war. 7/29/2019. Accessed 2023.

Jastrzembski, Frank. "Joshau Sill: The Hero and His Threatened Monument. Historynet.com. 4/27/2018. Accessed 2023.

Johnson, Brigham. Iowa: Its History and its Foremost Citizens. Des Moines, Iowa: 1918. 2 volumes.

JJohnson, Richard. A Soldier's Reminiscences in Peace and War. Philadelphia: 1886.

Johnson, Richard. Memoir of Maj.-Gen. George H. Thomas. Philadelphia: 1881.

Johnson, Rossiter, ed. The Biographical Dictionary of America. Boston: 1906. 10 volumes.

Kansas Historical Society. Kansapedia. Kshs.org. Various articles, accessed 2022.

Kennedy, John F. Profiles in Courage. New York: 1955.

Lahasky, Alex. The March of the Union Armies: James Henry Lane, the Union, and the Development of Total War on the Kansas-Missouri Border. Pittsburg State University, Pittsburg, Kansas: Electronic Thesis Collection, 2017.

Lehrman Institute, The. "Edwin D. Morgan (1811–1883)." Mr. Lincoln and New York. https://www.mrlincolnandnewyork.org/new-yorkers/edwin-d-morgan-1811–1883/. Accessed 2023.

Leonard, Elizabeth D. "Lincoln's Judge Advocate General: Joseph Holt of Kentucky." The Register of the Kentucky Historical Society. Vol. 110, No.s 3 and 4 2012.

Lewis, Adam J. "The Civil War Experiences of Quincy Adams Gillmore: The Challenges of Transitioning from the Tactical to the Operational Level of Command." School of Advanced Military Studies. United States Army Command and General Staff College. Fort Leavenworth, Kansas: 2011. Accessed online, 2023.

Longacre, Edward. "Irvin McDowell (1818–1885)" *Encyclopedia Virginia*. Virginia Humanities, (07 Dec. 2020). Accessed 2023.

Lyman, Theodore. Meade's Headquarters, 1863–1865. George R. Agassiz, ed. Boston: 1922.

Maine: An Encyclopedia. https://maineanencyclopedia.com. Various articles

Marten, James. "Hamilton, Andrew Jackson (1815–1875)." Texas State Historical Association. Austin, Texas: 1952. See tshaonline.org. Accessed 2023.

McClaughry, John. "John Wolcott Phelps: The Civil War General Who Became a Forgotten Presidential Candidate in 1880." Vermont History: The Proceedings of the Vermont Historical Society. Vol. XXXVIII No. 4 (Autumn 1970).

McClellan, George B. McClellan's Own Story. New York: 1886.

McKinney, Tim. "Benjamin F. Kelley." E-WV. The West Virginia Encyclopedia. 07 December 2015. Accessed 2023.

Miller, Rex. "John Thomas Croxton: Scholar, Lawyer, Soldier, Military Governor, Newspaperman, Diplomat and Mason." Register of the Kentucky Historical Society, Vol. 74, No. 4 (October 1976).

Mitcham, Samuel W., Jr. Confederate Patton: Richard Taylor and the Red River Campaign of 1864. Gretna, Louisiana: 2012. Second ed., Columbia, South Carolina: 2023.

Mitcham, Samuel W., Jr. Encyclopedia of Confederate Generals. Washington, D.C.: 2022.

Mitcham, Samuel W., Jr. "War, By the Numbers." Confederate Veteran. Vol. 80, No. 1 (January/February 2022).

Mitcham, Samuel W., Jr. Voices from the Confederacy. New York and Nashville: 2022.

Moore, Frank. The Portrait Gallery of the War, Civil, Military, and Naval: A Biographical Record. New York: 1865.

Mr. Lincoln's White House. https://www.mrlincolnswhitehouse.org /residents-visitors/the-generals-and-admirals/ Accessed 2023.

BIBLIOGRAPHY

Naglee, Henry M. The Love Life of Brig. Gen. Henry M. Naglee, Consisting of a Correspondence of Love, War and Politics. Mrs. Mary L. Schell, ed. New York: 1867.

Nash, Eugene Arus. A History of the Forty-fourth Regiment, New York Volunteer Infantry in the Civil War, 1861–1865. Chicago: 1911.

National Park Service. "Hooker Takes Command." Fredericksburg & Spotsylvania National Military Park. https://www.nps.gov/articles/000/hooker-takes-command.htm. Accessed 2023.

Newell, Clayton R. The Regular Army Before the Civil War. Washington, D.C.: 2014.

Nicolay, John G. The Outbreak of the Rebellion. New York: 1881.

Nicolson, John. "Hawley, Joseph Roswell." NCPedia. Dictionary of North Carolina Biography. Chapel Hill: 1988. https://www.ncpedia.org/biography/hawley-joseph-roswell. Accessed 2023.

Ogilvie, J. S. History of the Assassination of James A. Garfield. New York: 1881.

Owen, Thomas McA. History of Alabama and Dictionary of Alabama Biography. Chicago: 1921. 4 volumes

Palmer, John McAuley. Personal Recollections of John M. Palmer: The Story of an Earnest Life. Cincinnati: 1901.

Parrish, William E. Frank Blair: Lincoln's Conservative. Columbia, Missouri: 1998.

Perry, Oran. Indiana in the Mexican War. Indianapolis: 1908.

Poore, B. P. The Life and Public Service of Ambrose E. Burnside. Providence, Rhode Island: 1882.

Porter, Horace. Campaign with Grant. New York: 1897.

Pratt, Harry E. "Lewis B. Parsons, Mover of Armies and Railroad Builder." Journal of the Illinois State Historical Society. Vol. 44, No. 4 (Winter 1951).

Pruden, William. "William Burnham Woods." New Georgia Encyclopedia. Accessed 2023.

Raphelson, Alfred C. "Alexander Schimmelfennig: A German-American Campaigner in the Civil War." Pennsylvania Magazine of History and Biography. Vol. 87, No. 2 (April 1963).

BIBLIOGRAPHY

Robarts, William Hugh. Mexican War Veterans: A Complete Roster. Washington, D.C.: 1887.

"Robert H. Milroy." American Battlefield Trust. https://www.battlefields.org/learn/biographies/robert-h-milroy. Accessed 2023.

Roe, Alfred S. The Tenth Regiment, Massachusetts Volunteer Infantry, 1861–1864, a Western Massachusetts Regiment. Springfield, Massachusetts: 1909.

Rogers, J. P. "Edward Harland: A man of great executive ability and boundless energy." February 1, 2020. Oliver Cromwell Case. https://olivercromwellcase.wordpress.com/2020/02/01/edward-harland-a-man-of-great-executive-ability-and-boundless-energy-2/ Accessed 2023.

Ropes, John Codman. The Army in the Civil War. Vol. IV: The Army Under Pope. New York: 1881.

Rutherford B. Hayes Presidential Library & Museums. Gilded Age Collections. "Force, Manning Ferguson." https://www.rbhayes.org/collection-items/gilded-age-collections/force-manning-ferguson. Accessed 2023.

Schell, Mary L., ed. The Love Life of Brig. Gen. Henry M. Naglee. No city, 1867.

Schofield, John M. Forty-Six Years in the Army. New York: 1897.

Schouler, William. A History of Massachusetts in the Civil War. Boston: 1868.

Sesser, David. "Napoleon Bonaparte Buford (1807–1883). Encyclopedia of Arkansas. https://encyclopediaofarkansas.net/entries/napoleon-bonaparte-buford-17667/ Accessed 2023.

Sherman, William T. Memories of Gen. William T. Sherman, Written By Himself." New York: 1875. 2 volumes.

Shine, Gregory P. "William Selby Harney (1800–1889)." Oregon Encyclopedia. https://www.oregonencyclopedia.org/articles/harney_william_selby/ Accessed 2023.

Shoemaker, Raymond L. "Ebenezer Dumont." Encyclopedia of Indianapolis. 1994. Revised June 2021. Accessed online, 2022.

Sifakis, Stewart. Who Was Who in the Civil War. New York: 1988.

BIBLIOGRAPHY

Smith, Charles W. Life and Military Service of Brevet Major General Robert S. Foster. Indianapolis: 1915.

Sones, Bruce V. "Brigadier General Jefferson C. Davis, Civil War General." Unpublished Masters thesis, U.S. Army Command and General Staff College. Fort Leavenworth, Kansas: 2000.

Speed, Thomas, R. M. Kelly, and Alfred Pirtle. The Union Regiments of Kentucky. Louisville: 1897.

Strong, George Crockett. Cadet Life at West Point by an Officer of the United States Army. Boston: 1862.

Stumpf, David A. "Brigadier General Isham Nicholas Haynie," http://stumpf.org/Ill48Inf/haynie-ds.html. Accessed 2023.

Styple, William. "General Philip Kearny." C-Span, American History TV, February 5, 2023. https://www.c-span.org/video/?525794-1/general-philip-kearny. Accessed 2023.

Taylor, William A. Ohio Statesmen and Annals of Progress, from the Year 1877 to the Year 1900. Columbus, Ohio: 1899. 2 volumes.

Tennessee Department of Tourist Development. "James St. Clair Morton." Tennessee Civil War Trails. https://www.tnvacation.com/civil-war/person/2117/james-st-clair-morton/. Accessed 2023.

Thomas, Henry G. "Twenty-two Hours Prisoner in Dixie," War Papers Read Before the Commandery of the State of Maine, Military Order of the Loyal Legion of the United States. Read September 5, 1888.

Tidwell, William A. Come Retribution: The Confederate Secret Service and the Assassination of Abraham Lincoln. Oxford, Mississippi: 1988.

Trulock, James A. "Robert Sanford Foster." Encyclopedia of Indianapolis. https://indyencyclopedia.org/robert-sanford-foster. Accessed 2023.

Turchin, John Basil. Chickamauga. Chicago: 1888.

Union Army: A History of Military Affairs in the Loyal States, 1861–65. Volume VIII, Biographical. Madison, Wisconsin: 1908.

United States War Department, Military Secretary's Office. Memorandum Relative to the General Officers in the Armies of the United States During the Civil War—1861–1865. Washington, D.C.: 1906.

United States War Department, Office of the Chief of Staff. Bibliography of State Participation in the Civil War, 1861–1866. War Department Library, Subject Catalogue No. 6. 3rd Edition. Washington, D.C.: 1913.

Warner, Ezra J. Generals in Blue. Baton Rouge, Louisiana: 1964.

Webb, Alexander S. The Peninsula: McClellan's Campaign of 1862. New York: 1881.

Welch, Jack D. Medical Histories of Union Generals. Kent, Ohio: 1996.

Welles, Gideon. Diary of Gideon Welles. Boston: 1911. 3 volumes.

Williams, Alpheus S. From the Cannon's Mouth: The Civil War Letters of General Alpheus S. Williams. M. M. Quaife, ed. Detroit: 1959

Williams, Alpheus S. From the Cannon's Mouth: The Civil War letters of General Alpheus S. Williams. Whitefish, Montana: 2011.

Williams, Stephen D. "William Farquhar Barry: The Real Man Behind the Guns." Carlisle Barracks, Pennsylvania: 1991.

Wilson, James G. and John Fiske. Appleton's Cyclopedia of American Biography. New York: 1900. 6 volumes.

Wilson, James G., John Fiske and Stanley L. Klos, ed.s. Appleton's Cyclopedia of American Biography. New York: 1887–1891. 6 volumes.

Wolfe, Brendan. "Crater, Battle of the" *Encyclopedia Virginia*. Virginia Humanities, (07 Dec. 2020). Web accessed 22 Nov. 2023.

Wolfe, Brendan. "John Newton (1822–1895)" *Encyclopedia Virginia*. Virginia Humanities, (07 Dec. 2020, updated 22 Dec. 2021). Accessed 2023.

Wolmar, Christian. Engines of War. London: 2010.

Woodbury, Augustus. Ambrose E. Burnside and the Ninth Army Corps. Providence, Rhode Island, 1875.

BIBLIOGRAPHY

Woodward, Ashbel. Life of General Nathaniel Lyon. Hartford, Connecticut: 1862.

Wright, Marcus J. Memorandum relative to the General Officers in the Armes of the United States during the Civil War, 1861–1865. Washington, D.C.: 1906.

Zogbaum, Rufus F. "The Regulars in the Civil War." The North American Review. Vol. 167, No. 500 (July 1898).